MISSIONARIES, MADNESS & MIRACLES

VOLUME I

Schwarz, Schulze, Kempe (Lutheran Archives P02601 05001)

MISSIONARIES, MADNESS & MIRACLES

THE BEGINNINGS OF HERMANNSBURG-NTARIA, 1875–1894

VOLUME I

* * *

ROBERT J KEMPE

Translation by Victor C Pfitzner

Wakefield Press

Wakefield Press
16 Rose Street
Mile End
South Australia 5031
www.wakefieldpress.com.au

First published 2025

Copyright © Robert J Kempe, 2025
Translation copyright © Victor C Pfitzner, 2025

ALL RIGHTS RESERVED.
This book is copyright. Apart from any fair dealing for the purposes of private study, research, criticism or review, as permitted under the Copyright Act, no part may be reproduced without written permission. Enquiries should be addressed to the publisher.

Cover painting by Rae Kempe, adapted from an historical photograph
Designed and typeset by Duncan Blachford, Typography Studio

ISBN for the two volumes: 9781923388505
ISBN volume I: 9781923388468
ISBN volume II: 9781923388475

A catalogue record for this book is available
from the National Library of Australia

Wakefield Press thanks Coriole Vineyards
for their continued support

For Rae

Contents

Cultural Acknowledgement   xi
Acknowledgements   xiii
Preface   xv

            *   *   *

About this book   1
     Origins   1
     Translation and transcription   3
     Publication   5
About the translation   7
     On the word 'heathen'   8
What this book is about   10
     The Missionaries   11
     The Colonists/Settlers   15
     The Wives   17
     The Arrarnta People   19
     The Lutheran Church   24
     Hermannsburg Mission Society and Institute/Seminary   31
     Finke River Mission   36
     South Australia and Northern Territory   39
     The Currency   47
Source Material and Abbreviations   49

            *   *   *

1	Arrivals and Commissionings	53
2.	The Journey: Bethany to Hergott Springs	68
3.	Around the 'Old' Station	86
	The Mound Springs	99
4.	The Journey: To Dalhousie Springs	100
	Heidenreich's Account	101
	Kempe's Account	117
	Schwarz's Account	128
5.	Reconnaissance Trip	133
	Kempe's Account	133
	Heidenreich's Account: the *Missionsblatt* Version	139
	Heidenreich's Account: the *Kirchenbote* Version	145
	A Personal Reflection: Heidenreich I	152
6.	Waiting at Dalhousie	155
	Personal Reflection: Heidenreich II	183
7.	The Journey: Arriving at the Mission Site	185
	The Missionaries' Reports	186
	Heidenreich Travel Notes	188
	The Account of the Trip (cont.)	192
8.	Setting Up	198
	Water	198
9.	The Arrival of Schulze, the Fiancées, and Others	215
	The Case of a Missing Letter	219
10.	Settling In	241
11.	The Removal of Theodor Harms	262
12.	Language, Weather and Mumblings	271
	1879	271
	Research and Publication	283
13.	Mixed Blessings	286
	Land and work – Aboriginal Spirituality	286

14. The Flint Report and Afterwards 297
    1880 297
15. Kempe Major Report 308
16. Business Matters, More Arrivals, New Church
    and School, Christmas 343
    Financial Management 343
    More New Arrivals 353
    Pastoral Interlude 356
    Dedication of the Church and School 357
    Christmas in the new church 361
17. A Year in the Life of the Mission 367
    1881 367
    Inter-Church Relationships: Germany, Missourians 369
    Correspondence with Baron von Müller 402
18. Friction, Fighting and Fred 406
    1882 406
    A terse Jürgens Interlude 413
    The tragic story of Fred 418
19. The Cold, Colonists, Rabbits and Railways 425
    The Colonists – 1882 428
    The Coming of the Railway to South Australia/
    Northern Territory 448
20. Death of Dmataka. More on Language and Culture 452
    1883 452
21. Finances, Synods, and Routine 472
    Synods – and the Missionaries. A personal reflection. 475

* * *

Image Credits 492
Bibliography 493
Endnotes 498

Cultural Acknowledgement

We who are responsible for the material in this book are aware that it contains words, terms, names and graphics that, though the publishing of them may have been acceptable at the time of their original publication, are not acceptable today. Many of them will be offensive to numbers of our readers.

Rather than omit or alter any such material, we have chosen to retain it. We have done in the interests of authenticity and truth, and wish to stress that these views are not our own.

We also apologise to our Aboriginal brothers and sisters for any pain our actions may cause them, and are sorry for this. We trust that they will understand, if not agree, with our motives in publishing what we have. In engaging in the production of this book, and in our inter-actions with Aboriginal people, it has always been our desire and intention to grow closer to each other. That intention remains.

Bob Kempe. Emeritus pastor of the Lutheran Church of Australia and New Zealand, emeritus lecturer in pastoral theology at Australian Lutheran College, Adelaide. Education Consultant within Clinical Pastoral Education.

Vic Pfitzner. Emeritus pastor of the Lutheran Church of Australia and New Zealand (65 years). Lecturer in New Testament theology (38 years). Principal of Australian Lutheran College, Adelaide, for nine years.

Dorothea Prenzler. Daughter of German Lutheran missionaries in Papua New Guinea. Married to John, pastor of the LCANZ. They served together in PNG during the 1980s. Dorothea also served for a time as a teacher at Katherine Lehmann School, Wau. Now retired.

Acknowledgements

Until one actually embarks upon the writing of a book, it is not really possible to appreciate the number and depth of all those who contribute to such an undertaking. And in seeking to recall all such contributors to *Missionaries, Madness and Miracle*, there is a concern about those who might be missed out. Please forgive any such omissions.

First of all, thank you to Vic Pfitzner, without whose translation work this book would not have been. Over almost ten years of weekly get-togethers, I have learnt so much through you, and treasure the friendship that has grown between you and Rae and myself. I will never be able to thank you enough for your input to this book: it permeates every page.

To Dorothea Prenzler, who graciously allowed herself to be dobbed into this project by son, Michael, and whose transcription work opened up twice as much material as we started with, almost all of it brand new. What a gift that has been!

To Michael Bollen of Wakefield Press, who accepted the challenge of taking on this book at a time when Wakefield was not seeking new work, and who has been a tremendous source of critique, advice and encouragement.

To the staff at Australian Lutheran Archives: Rachel Kuchel, Jeanette Schirmer, Lois Zweck, Bethany Pietsch, Ben Hollister. You have provided most of the source material for this work, and have been invaluable in the gracious provision of your time, knowledge and practical help.

Also to the Friends of Lutheran Archives, for their interest in and promotion of this venture.

To the Historical Society in Alice Springs, and its resource centre, especially to Olga Radke for her enthusiastic interest.

To Hartwig Harms in Hermannsburg, Germany, great-grandson of Director Harms. I value the friendship that grew between us through this project, and the gift of supplying missing copies of the *Hermannsburger Missionsblatt*. It was sad to learn of Hartwig's death in Hermannsburg, Germany, on 12 August 2024.

To the staff at Australian Lutheran College library, especially Trevor Schaefer and Tim Oestmann, for their location of treasured materials for the book.

To staff at the Public Library of South Australia, for their assistance in digitizing the voluminous amounts of microfiche files.

To the South Australian History Trust, for a grant and their encouraging feedback.

To those innumerable people whose monetary donations, referral to and provision of books, articles, personal anecdotes and experiences added inestimable value in making the translation work and book possible. I have been amazed and overwhelmed by the way in which you all seem just to have 'appeared' in our work, and by your kindness and interest. For reasons of potential sensitivity you here remain anonymous, but you know who you are.

To the Finke River Mission field staff who, over many years, have mentored and taught me in the way of Aboriginal people in ways of which they are probably unaware. Paul Albrecht, Gary Stoll, Paul Eckert, Ken Hansen, David Moore, Basil Schild, David Roennfeldt, Paul Traeger, Norm Wurst.

To the many Aboriginal communities and pastors and people who make up the Finke River Mission. It was a privilege to visit and stay in your communities, so many of them isolated, and to experience, if only a little, what life is like for you. Engaging with your pastors, evangelists, and trainee-pastors in our training weeks has been a delight. You introduced me in a unique way to your heritage, language and culture, and helped me to realise that, for all I have learnt from you, there is ever so much yet to learn.

To Dean Zweck and Ev Leske as the first generously to wade through this vast chronicle, and to provide critique and other feedback. And for your contributions to the back cover 'blurb'.

To my family, and especially to our children: Karen, Sheryl and Josie and your families, and for your loving interest and support. I hope the book will play its small part in your appreciation of your great-great grandparents, and of your children's great-great-great grandparents, even great-great-great-great grandparents, and those with whom they lived and worked.

And, finally, to Rae, for her unflinching support and encouragement. You have given so much, often at the expense of your own pursuits, to this oft-times demanding project, that I know I could never thank or repay you enough. You have put yourself into it almost as much as I have, and I stand in awe of the feedback, criticism, insight and passion you have provided. Please know that I treasure you and your giftedness beyond what words are capable of expressing.

Preface

From the dictionaries:[1]

mission *n.* **1.** Body sent by religious community to propagate its faith. **2.** Person's vocation or divinely appointed work in life. **3.** A sending or being sent for some duty or purpose.

missionary *a & n.* **1.** Of, concerned with, characteristic of, religious or similar missions. **2.** A person sent to work for the propagation of their religious faith in a heathen land.

mad *a.* **1.** (Of person or conduct or idea) wildly foolish, infatuated. **2.** With disordered mind, insane.

madness *n.* **1.** Extremely foolish, dangerous, or reckless behaviour. **2.** A state of wild or chaotic activity.

miracle *n.* **1.** Marvellous event due to some supposed supernatural agency. **2.** An effect in the physical world which surpasses all known human or natural powers and is therefore ascribed to supernatural agency.

This work is not to be quickly read.

About this book

Origins

My great-grandfather, Adolf Hermann Kempe, was one of the first two missionaries to establish the Hermannsburg Mission on the Finke River in Central Australia. The other was Wilhelm Friedrich Schwarz. What these men and their colleagues achieved was quite remarkable, although I am aware there are those who will disagree with that sentiment.

When I was young, great-grandpa and Hermannsburg were never much talked about in our family. I suspect the reason for this was a sense of shame at how that first mission endeavour ended. Thus, it was only in my early forties that I first visited Hermannsburg, and I suspect this book was conceived on that visit.

My first impressions of Hermannsburg were far from favourable. It was the mid-1980s, and Hermannsburg was a mess and in a state of crisis, so much so that white people did not feel safe within the community. A barbed-wire compound had been erected within the township, and white staff and visitors were accommodated behind padlocked gates within that compound. At night, the shouting and yelling beyond those gates were quite frightening.

On a couple of afternoons I took a walk around the township, out along the dry Finke and beyond. During the day it felt safe to do so; in fact, it was quite a peaceful experience. The magnificent gums and Australian bush: it really is lovely in that place. The only thing that spoiled it was the mess of wine casks and beer bottles that littered the area way beyond the township itself.

And I wondered: 'Why did he do it? What on God's good earth would move any human being to come to the middle of this country, to these people, to this place, and spend his life working here? And why would any woman come with him? Were they mad? Naïve? Ignorant?' Probably.

On the Sunday, I attended worship in the Hermannsburg church. That, too, was something of a culture shock. It was the first time I had been a part of an all-Aboriginal congregation, the first time I was acutely aware of my whiteness and their blackness. I felt uncomfortable, yet fascinated. There was a casualness about the way people wandered in and out of the church. I was not used to little kids chasing each other all over the church. Nor was I used to dogs wandering in and out and plonking themselves down under the pews. But the singing—wow! Their devotion to the acts of worship chilled me, even if there was an occasional conversational outburst between one or the other of the congregation.

At the end of the service, the pastor, John Pfitzner, embarrassed me by inviting me out to the front of the congregation. 'This is Nkata (Pastor) Kempe', he told them, 'the great-grandson of Missionary Kempe.' And a little more. But what I most noticed as he did this was the way in which the faces of many in the congregation lit up in recognition of great-grandpa's name. Then, what really moved me almost to tears was how many of them afterwards came up to shake my hand, and almost without exception said something like, 'Thank you, thank you. Thank you for your great-grandfather, and for the way he brought us the good news of Jesus.'

It was on that trip that I also first learned that, because of great-grandpa, we Kempes have some kind of kin relationship with the Arrarnta people. I do not understand how that works, nor what it actually means. Even so, the notion intrigues me and engenders a sense of privilege and connection that I can only brush with the tips of my fingers.

Over the next 20 years great-grandpa and Hermannsburg floated around the edges of my life, until, in the year 2000, I accepted a position as lecturer at Australia Lutheran College, Adelaide (ALC). As part of that call, I was appointed co-ordinator of the Aboriginal Ministry program of the Lutheran Church of Australia. This program was primarily concerned with the oversight of the training and equipping of Aboriginal pastors within their own communities, and it necessitated visits to Yalata, Ceduna/Kooniba, Darwin, Cairns, Wujal-Wujal, Hope Vale and, of course, the Centre.

Over the next ten years or so, I travelled to the Centre around three times a year, spending a week to ten days there at a time, visiting one or the other of the communities that comprise the Finke River Mission. The focus of the work was face-to-face time with the Aboriginal pastors and the training staff, especially in the ALC 'Sem in the Bush' program. This program provided bi-annual, on-site teaching courses for the Aboriginal pastors, and the teaching activity was shared between the ALC teaching staff. Outside of the teaching activity, however, I enjoyed just being with the people, chatting, talking, learning as much as I could from them about their lives and themselves. Plus, there was lots of research as I prepared for those visits and sought to grasp an appreciation of this world so different from my own.

Somewhere within all this, the idea of a book was born. The spark for that book was discovering the wealth of primary resources on the Hermannsburg mission in the Lutheran Archives in Adelaide. There were hundreds of microfiche pages of the original reports sent by the missionaries to Hermannsburg, Germany. Alas, however, they were totally indecipherable to me, handwritten as they were in old German style, and often in rough form. Encouragingly, though, there were as many other reports published in the *Hermannsburger Missionsblatt* and in *Der Lutherische Kirchenbote für Australien*, but written in the German Gothic style, and easy for me to read. I decided I would like to translate all of these published reports. Parts of some of them had been translated and published elsewhere (especially in Scherer's *Venture of faith*), but I could find no copy of all of them having been translated. So, this became my goal: to translate and perhaps publish all of the reports of the first missionaries between the years 1875 and 1894.

Translation and transcription

I believe that the Spirit of God lives and moves in our world, and that when we are in touch with that Spirit-world, good things happen. What happened next was, I believe, one of those God-wondrous moments, and it arrived in the person of my friend, Vic Pfitzner. Vic is fluent in German, and he offered to take on the role of translator for the project. He said he was looking for something of a challenge at the time. Besides, he thought he might enjoy it.

So it came about that one evening in early October 2017, Vic and I sat in the family room of our home, a photocopied page of *Missionsblatt* earlier procured from the Archives in front of us, a glass of whiskey in hand, and Vic began speaking an off-the-cuff translation into a voice recorder. Rae was in our adjoining kitchen, listening to what we were doing, tossing in her own comment here and there, and preparing an evening meal for us.

That created the pattern for this work for the next five years. Friday night was shared translation work. It was my job then to type up what Vic had translated and tidy it along the way. Not too long after we had begun, Vic expressed a preference to actually have the original text at home, and hand-write his translation. I then typed that up, with any revisions I spotted. And we spent the Friday evenings reading through the translation again, checking, discussing, modifying.

We were well on our way with the 200 or so published reports we had when we experienced another God-wondrous moments, this time in the person of Dorothea Prenzler. Dorothea had been born in Germany. At the age of 11 her family moved to Papua New Guinea where Dorothea's father was a missionary. However, instead of going with her parents to PNG, Dorothea was sent to a boarding school in Brisbane for her education, and every week thereafter, her mother wrote her a letter in the old, handwritten German script, just like that in the reports. Thus, Dorothea was naturally adept at being able to read and transcribe the reports. We approached her wondering if she might be willing to help us by transcribing those reports. She was!

The microfiche resources doubled the number of reports and letters we had, to over 400. The most valuable features of those extra letters were that nearly all of them had never been published anywhere, and they contained a significant amount of personal material that was not always obvious in the more official, published reports. This meant that this material had the capacity to provide a different slant on aspects of the story of those first missionaries. Those microfiche materials were a gold-mine.

Thus did our project grow, way beyond anything originally envisaged. From the original two missionaries, the authors of the reports expanded to include the third missionary, Louis Schulze, as well as the Superintendent of the Australian Lutheran mission, G A Heidenreich. There were reports from the Harms family in Germany, plus from the occasional settler. Somewhere along the way, I was put in touch with the South Australian History Trust which provided grants for projects like ours. We applied for a grant for the transcription work and received it. The Finke River Mission Board was interested in what we were doing and provided another grant. Various individuals did the same, and some of those gifts were exceptionally generous. And I regularly received e-mails and calls from other family members of the first missionaries or from people who had 'just heard' of the project, or who were somehow else connected with the story. Some of those folk provided personal information connected with the story, while others referred me to books and articles they knew of that also related to the story. It was all pretty exciting stuff.

Publication

Ever in the back of Vic's and my minds was the question of whether or not we published our material and, if so, what? Our natural inclination was to publish. The encouragement from others was the same. We looked to self-publishing for a while, but that looked rather daunting. Then, one day, I took a punt and contacted Wakefield Press who were surprisingly encouraging, and engaging their services became our desired objective. However, from the outset Wakefield were clear that they were not interested in publishing only the translation, at least in book form. Consequently, the decision was made to take a selection of the letters and reports, to add a commentary to these, and to publish this as a book. And then to publish all of the reports as a separate e-publication available on-line.

So, we have finished up with two publications.

1. The Translation

This contains all of the letters and reports we translated from between 1875 and 1894, together with a brief, comprehensive Introduction, and Index. As stated above, this version is being made available as an electronic file, available through the Wakefield Press website.

For people who are interested, *The Translation* fills in all the gaps in the commentary. But it will also be of interest to those desiring simply to read the raw, unadorned story.

2. The Book

This comprises a selection of most of the original letters and reports, but with comprehensive introductory material and comments along the way. Two points to make about the commentary are these:

1. The notes and comments are intended to serve the primary purpose of this book: to allow the missionaries and others involved in the establishment of Hermannsburg on the Finke to tell the story of that venture in their own words. Mostly brief, the comments and notes help the voices of those people to be heard more clearly and with greater understanding.
2. The notes and comments do contain personal reflections. As stated at the beginning of this Introduction, this project has also been a personal journey for me, and I would like to intertwine something of that journey with the journey of those first missionaries to the Centre.

I am aware that the injection of the personal into a historical account is fraught with the danger of over-subjectivity, thus detracting from the important central activity of factually telling the story. However, the work is primarily a translation of other people's historical recollections, and engaging with a translation creates a special dynamic with the person whose words one is translating. In his book, *A history of reading*, Alberto Manguel says that 'translating is the ultimate act of comprehending'.[1] By this I understand Manguel to be referring to the comprehension not only of words and concepts with which a translator might be wrestling, but also of the person, soul and essence of the one who has enunciated those words. One of my colleagues once echoed this sentiment with the observation that translating is a very intimate process. It takes the translator beyond the mere activity of reading from one language into another, and invites them in an exceptionally personal way into the world, life and being of the other.

This has been my experience as we have worked on this project. And, rather than ignore or minimise that personal connection with the story and the people in the story, I have chosen to make it another thread that contributes to the tapestry of this work.

About the translation

The task of translating these German documents from the second half of the nineteenth century presents several problems. First, the diction is often old-fashioned, employing expressions no longer in common usage. There is the added factor that the texts reflect the German Lutheran piety (and evangelical piety in general) that tended to repeated standard wishes and prayers, as well as thanks and fulsome praise to God. To our modern ears much of this may sound like an excessive display of devotion and religiosity, apart from being rather ponderous, but it must be faithfully preserved in translation.

Throughout the translation we have resisted the temptation to edit, delete or modernise the style, for example using common English abbreviations such as 'can't', 'wouldn't' etc. Nor have errors been corrected in the main text. The first rule or principle followed is that of **accuracy**. That does not include incorrect spelling of names of places and of people, and to obvious errors that may have arisen in the process of transcribing old German script into Gothic texts. Where such errors occur or are suspected we have corrected them, often with a footnote.

No attempt has been made to soften the observations of the first missionaries. Their first judgements on the Indigenous people reflect the common view of European colonisers that the original inhabitants are lazy, sly, and so on, and their language poor. Yet there is no debating the missionaries' concern and eventual love for these people. Further, some views became moderated over time. Be that the case, all their attitudes must be faithfully rendered.

The second principle is **intelligibility.** As is often the case with German writing, sentences are often very lengthy, longer than with English. Since the main verb frequently comes at the end of a long period, sentences have often been broken up into two or more. This is a relatively easy process since the writers in question often use *syndeton,* that is, they simply connect parts of the sentence with *and.* We have adopted a more asyndetic style, purely for the sake of ease of understanding, using shorter sentences with one or two subordinate clauses. Further, to aid clarity, colloquialisms or aphorisms in the German have to be expressed with a similar expression in the target language. So, the German saying *ehrlich bleibt am längsten* (honesty lasts the longest) must appear as 'honesty is the best policy'. This follows the principle of dynamic equivalence rather than formal correspondence, giving the intended sense rather than a literal word-for-word rendition.

The third guiding principle has been that of **fluency** or fluidity. Logical connections and presuppositions must be clear, even if that requires the deletion or subtraction of a word in order to make the sequence of thought clear. The German texts in question use a great many connectors such as 'since', 'but', 'whereas', 'however', 'now', 'then', 'still', 'yet'. This use of 'pack-words' can lead to a somewhat ponderous style at times. The translation can often omit such connectors since the relevant sentence within the context is clear without them, and perhaps even easier to follow. In passing, it may be of interest to note that each of the four main writers has his own distinctive style. Kempe is easy to understand with his clear and direct style. Schulze can have a more literary flavour, as can Heidenreich who writes for publication and is polished but can be quite involved; Schwarz can sometimes be quite torturous! So can Heidenreich!

Fourthly and finally, the translation has followed the rule of **consistency**. Some German terms have been variously translated to avoid monotony and taking context into consideration. Thus, the German noun *Weg* can be rendered with 'way', 'road', 'track', 'path', 'trail', 'journey' etc. However, we have expressed date and numbers in a consistent form to avoid confusion. More importantly, key words and phrases have been consistently translated with one English expression. For *Heiden* we have always used 'heathen' rather than 'pagan', since the latter sounds more European to our ears.

Good translating requires skill and art; we claim a high level in neither. Hopefully, we have captured accurately what the writers long ago meant to say, and have done so faithfully. Fidelity is a key concept for these admirable pioneers, whether used of God or of the faithful.

V C Pfitzner

On the word 'heathen'

On numerous occasions the missionaries and others refer to the Aboriginal people as *die Heiden*, which as Vic has said above we have chosen to translate as 'the heathen'.

While that word and its corresponding expressions (e.g. 'poor heathen'; German, *arme Heiden*) may sound pejorative and condescending to our ears, in itself it is not. It is simply how the missionaries spoke of the Aboriginal people, and they were not the only ones to do so: other Europeans and other translations do the same thing. And in translating the word this way there is no intention to belittle the Aboriginal people or to offend them or others.

Perhaps the best way to appreciate how the word is to be understood is by recognising that in the German Bible (Martin Luther's translation) the word *Heiden* is used for the Greek τα ἔθνη, which is traditionally translated as 'the Gentiles'. It simply denotes someone who is other than Jewish, Within the Christian context we understand the word to refer to someone who is not a Christian—not in a derogatory way but in a descriptive way, as an objective statement of fact. In that sense, 'the heathen' are any who are not Christian, regardless of race, colour, nationality or geographical location.

One way to avoid using the word because of its potential for offence would be by choosing some other word. However, there is no other word that so neatly meets the translation requirements. There are, for example, words like 'native', 'indigenous', 'non-Christian', 'people'. However, each of those has its own special word in German or, as in the case of 'native', for example, our writers use the English.

Consequently, after much careful thought, we have decided to stand by the word 'heathen', trusting that readers will

- realise that the word is originally intended to be used in an emotionally neutral way;
- be open to the fact that any offence taken in the use of the word more than likely lies in the receptors of the text (i.e. the reader) not because of what the word originally meant, but because of what we have made it to mean;
- appreciate that, even though imperfectly, the missionaries cared very deeply about the Aboriginal people.

What this book is about

It is fashionable to be critically hostile toward missionaries and pastoralists (actually any Australians of European heritage), accusing them of harm done to aborigines and their land. They are easy targets who do not talk back. But after learning their stories, I find them all, in light of their own intentions, nothing short of heroic. I doubt that I would have wanted to be close personal friends with the Hermannsburg missionaries, or they with me, but they gave their lives selflessly to what they considered the greatest cause.[1]

This book tells the story of the establishment of the Hermannsburg Mission on the Finke River in Central Australia during the years 1875 to 1894. It is a story told through the eyes and voices of the four main characters involved in that work (Kempe, Schwarz, Schulze, Heidenreich), using their recorded words from the many reports they wrote during that period.

Like any good story, the story in *Missionaries, Madness and Miracles* is multi-faceted: several stories, inter-connected. The missionaries have their story, and so do the Arrarnta people. There are the stories behind those stories: the story of Lutherans in Germany joining in what was almost a frenetic international Christian endeavour 'to go into all the world and preach the gospel to all creation' (Mark 16:15). Intimately linked with that story is the account of German Lutherans establishing themselves as a Church within Australia, with special focus on Lutherans in South Australia. Running like a thread through all these stories is the vexed tale of White people establishing themselves in this land they call Australia.

Each of those stories requires its own introduction and commentary to enable readers the better to appreciate the letters and reports that constitute the bulk of this book. Space dictates that these complementary materials be brief, servants to the letters and reports themselves.

The Missionaries

First there were two: Kempe and Schwarz. They arrived in Adelaide from Germany in late 1875, took until June 1877 to travel to the proposed site of the Hermannsburg mission, and established the settlement. At the end of 1877, the third missionary, Schulze, arrived, bringing with him the fiancées of Kempe and Schwarz: Dorothea Queckenstedt and Dorothea Schulz.

Friedrich Adolph Hermann Kempe was born in the village of Deuben, Saxony, on 26 March 1844. His father, Adolf Kempe, was a coal miner, and while Friedrich Adolph Hermann was still a young lad the family moved to Gittersee/Freital, near Dresden. Kempe was baptised when he was two weeks old and confirmed at the age of 14. When he was 12 years old, his mother died and, in his words, 'of my childhood I have but a few recollections except that I still had a sister. All other children in the family had died.'[2]

After he completed high school, Kempe worked in the same coal mines as his father. During this time, he drifted away from the Church and the Faith, took up with some rather rough characters and 'headed by leaps and bounds towards my ruin, sinking deeper and deeper from one sin into another'.[3] After three years, he tired of that kind of lifestyle, and decided on an apprenticeship in Dresden as a blacksmith. Having completed this in 1862, at the age of 18, he took to travelling around various 'states' (Lauenburg, Mecklenburg, Holstein) as a journeyman, but continued to live the life of a wild young lad.

Then, through a series of fortuitous encounters, Kempe's life was changed. The blacksmith for whom he was working in the village of Oldenburg (a couple of hours from Hermannsburg) took him to task for his foul language. This man was not a Christian, and that such a person should so berate him pulled the young Kempe up short. Next, there was a family whom Kempe used to visit in the village, and one Saturday evening he unexpectedly called on them, only to discover that they were in the middle of an extended family devotion. Kempe found himself extremely moved by the experience. Finally, he came into contact with the Lutheran Church and Mission Society in Hermannsburg and was so impressed by the pastors, teachers, preaching and people he encountered there that, as he says, 'gradually I now acquired the inclination to become a missionary.'[4]

In 1869 Kempe's father was killed in a coal-mine disaster. 'That would truly have shattered me', he says, 'had I not been able to cling to the Lord.'[5] In 1870 he was admitted as a student into the Hermannsburg Mission House. His studies occupied him for five years, and of this time he says: 'My term of study in the Mission House was the loveliest time of my life.'[6]

Graduation and ordination took place in mid-1875. Kempe and one of his classmates, Schwarz, were designated for mission work in Central Australia.

At the time of graduation, both men were single, because during their course of studies they were forbidden 'to carry on a love affair or even to propose marriage to anyone'.[7] So, they 'quickly had to look around for a life-companion'[8] and, after a set-back or two, found one. Thus it was that, at the age of 31, Kempe became engaged to Dorothea Queckenstedt, aged 22, from Knesebeck, a town about 50 kilometres from Hermannsburg. A few weeks later they set out from Hermannsburg for the trip to Australia, but Dorothea and Kempe separated at Hamburg, he to travel on alone to their new country, and she to follow him later, once he had established their home in Australia.

Wilhelm Friedrich Schwarz [9] was born two years before Kempe, on 20 March 1842, in the village of Dürrmenz in the territory of Würtemberg. He was baptised a week later and confirmed at the age of 14. His father was a baker.

In a similar vein to Kempe, once he completed school, Schwarz followed in his father's footsteps and became an apprentice baker to his father. However, when his mother died he left home and travelled about as a journeyman baker. According to Vallee, he was an 'unsettled and unhappy young man ... a drinker and a gambler',[10] and yet within him was a yearning for peace with God. In his quest for that peace, he says he mistakenly 'sought it in the way of many thoughtless youths'.[11] His travels took him as far north as Schleswig-Holstein, approximately 750 kilometres from his birth-place.

In the midst of this disquiet and turmoil, Schwarz was one night lying in his bed when he found himself reflecting on Paul Gerhardt's hymn, 'Commit whatever grieves you',[12] especially on the verse:

On him place your reliance, if you would be secure;
his work you must consider, if yours is to endure.

God is not moved to giving by self-tormenting care,
or anxious sighs and grieving; all must be gained by prayer.

Suddenly, he says, his eyes were opened to the grace and glory of Christ, and this became a life-changing moment for him. Then and there he resolved to express his gratitude to God by offering himself 'for the service of the Lord in the mission field to bring the light unto the benighted souls of the heathen'.[13]

Schwarz's initial intention was to enrol in the Basel Mission Society in Switzerland (founded in 1815 and known at that time as the German Mission Society), and he set off literally to walk to Basel, approximately 900 kilometres away. However, along the way 'in a rather unexpected way his steps were guided to … Hermannsburg' instead.[14] One cannot help wondering whether the fact that Hermannsburg was only 200 kilometres from Schleswig-Holstein might have had something to do with his change of mind!

At Hermannsburg, Schwarz enrolled in the same class as Kempe (1870–75), graduated at the same time, and was designated for mission work in Central Australia. Others in that class also designated for Australia, but as pastors, not as missionaries, were Jürgen Bode, Dietrich Georg and Heinrich Wiese. In addition, Christoph Dierks, Wilhelm Kowert and Heinrich Loose were also in that class, and were sent to New Zealand. All these people feature in the letters and reports that follow.

Also like Kempe, Schwarz needed to find himself a wife before he left. He subsequently became engaged to Dorothea Wilhelmine Charlotte Schulz from Wöhningen. This couple, too, were separated until Schwarz, with Kempe, had arrived in the Australian Centre.

Louis Gustav Schulze was a member of a family with generational roots in Saxony, Germany. He was born in Kleinvoigtsberg, near Freiburg, on 1 March 1851. His father worked in a silver mine. Altogether there were ten children in the family, 'but half of these the Lord took unto Himself again'.[15] The family was devoutly Lutheran, and Louis was baptised eight days after birth, confirmed when he was 14, regularly attended church, and was raised with daily devotions as a natural part of his life.

His schooling was a somewhat unsatisfying experience. In part, this was due to the multiplicity of teachers 'from whom,' he says, 'I learnt little or nothing at all'. But it was also due to the family moving home to the town of Seifersbach, 30 kilometres away, and the young Louis having to change to a school in which his teacher 'did not understand how to teach'. 'Under him,' Schulze reflects, 'I lost practically all inclination to learn'.[16] Not surprisingly, Schulze left school at around the same time he was confirmed.

Being raised in a family that extolled the virtue of work, it was natural for Schulze to take on a variety of casual jobs during the last years of his schooling. In 1866, once he had left school, he immediately sought employment. He found this as an apprentice tailor in the city of Hainichen.

Though only ten kilometres from his family home, Hainichen was a world away from the kind of life to which Louis was accustomed. 'The peaceful, healthy and pleasant life in the country I now had to exchange for a noisy, unhealthy and unpleasant city life', he recalls. 'Friends for strangers, the dear family-circle...for a group of many brazen-faced tailors... [And], worst of all, instead of encouragement in God's Word...I was discouraged in it, leading me to seduction into evil ways.'[17]

For almost all the four years of his apprenticeship, Schulze existed 'in this state of lukewarmness', as he describes it.[18] He completed his apprenticeship, but then experienced a thwarting of his plans for full employment afterwards. Somewhat disillusioned by his situation and the life he was living, he went home to his parents in mid-1869 and, during this visit, 'the Lord ... accepted me again in His grace, and restored to me inner quietness and true peace'.[19]

Even in his younger years, Schulze had had a vague notion that he would like to be a missionary 'when he grew up'. Now that notion became a yearning and, with the support of his parents, his pastor, his siblings and friends, he set his mind on enrolling in the Neuendettelsau Mission Institute. His parents, however, desired that he attend the Hermannsburg Mission, and he acceded to their wishes on this.

Schulze arrived at the Hermannsburg Mission Institute in late 1869. Because he was too young to begin theological studies immediately, he found work with a tailor and commenced his preparatory studies. At first he was unhappy about the 'unchristian atmosphere'[20] in Hermannsburg; but once he was accepted as a candidate in late 1872, he happily settled into the community and his studies. He graduated in May, 1877 and, together with Gardus Bertram, Johann Hoopmann, Heinrich Meyer, H Niemann, Wilhelm Peters and Johann Thiessen, was designated for unspecified mission work in Australia. When he left for Australia in June, he was engaged to Charlotte Gutmann, of Wittingen, and she would follow him three years later, arriving at Adelaide in August 1880.

The Colonists/Settlers

Supporting the missionaries in their missionary undertaking was a constantly changing band of non-ordained men. There were wagon drivers, shepherds, cattle handlers, masons, carpenters, handy-men and others. As well as attending to their specific designated assignments, these people were expected also to share in such tasks as cooking, cleaning, general maintenance, and the like.

These folk are generally referred to in the reports as colonists or settlers. The two terms are so closely linked that they are virtually identical.

In almost all cases, the Australian settlers were well-established lay members of ELSA congregations and they simply wanted to assist in the mission work of their Church amongst the Aboriginal people. They either volunteered their services or were asked. The first such lay missionary was J E Jacob who accompanied the first missionaries to Killalpaninna in 1866.

There were many more settlers/colonists who made a similar commitment to Hermannsburg on the Finke. Among those appear such names as:

Bähr, J C
Hämmerling, G
Hübbe
Hunt, J
Meyer, H
Mirus, George
Nitschke, Carl F
Pohlner, Alexander

The Hermannsburg Institute also contributed to this pool of lay missionaries. Like their Australian counterparts, these were lay members of the Church who had an interest in mission work, but on the international scene. In personal e-mails with him, Hartwig Harms says that all these people were called 'colonists', but that the term had nothing to do with colonialism. Rather, it was a term used of anyone in Germany who settled in a new place. Hartwig prefers to call them 'lay missionaries'.

As was the case with the ordained missionaries, the German lay missionaries always had a trade, (farmer, shepherd, builder, etc). Almost all of them were men who desired to be ordained missionaries, but were unable to be admitted into the Hermannsburg Mission Society (HMS) training program because of their lack of academic qualifications. Nevertheless, under a scheme possibly proposed many years before by a Professor Hofmann in Rostock, Ludwig Harms supported the practice of sending lay people out with trained missionaries. But then, to cite Hartwig Harms once more, 'The only condition was that they spent some time in Hermannsburg before being nominated—normally at least one year, serving or working as a craftsman with one of the local craftspeople or as a helper of a farmer. So Louis, and later Theodor, Harms could observe them and get enough knowledge about them in order to decide if he wanted to send them as helpers together with the missionaries'.[21] If accepted, they were then assigned and commissioned for their work.

Not everyone was enamoured of the idea of lay missionaries. For example, the first Hermannsburg superintendent in South Africa, August Hardeland, claimed that the colonists were not worth the salt they added to their meals.[22] His comment referred to the practice of mission personnel living in community where lay missionaries needed more of the income than the ordained staff, because often they had larger families and so—according to some people— were using up too much of the resources of the mission. Consequently, in time the practice of lay missionaries diminished, and most lay people simply stayed where they were, got other work, and formed Lutheran congregations. In much the same way in Australia, missionaries and lay people also formed themselves into congregations, and thus contributed to the growth of the Church.

Altogether, HMS sent 11 lay missionaries to Aboriginal missions in Australia. The first of these went to Killalpaninna: Hermann Heinrich Vogelsang (in 1866), Friedrich Wotzke (in 1867), and Wilhelm Koch, a teacher (in 1869).

Those who were assigned to the mission on the Finke were (in order of arrival):

Holtermann, Heinrich Friedrich (1877)
Jürgens, Heinrich Georg (1877)
Tündemann, August (1877)
Wolf, Johann Heinrich Christoph (1881)
Baden, Heinrich (1882)
Eggers, Christian (1882)
Freiboth, George Christoph (1882)
Koch, Heinrich (1882).

Each of these people has their own story to tell, and those stories deserve to be told. At the end of *Missionaries, Madness and Miracles* is a section on *People*, and this contains some elementary information on many of the settlers. From time to time they come to the forefront of the story—sadly on too many occasions when they clash with the missionaries—but then fade quietly into the background.

The colonist/settlers/lay missionaries were indispensable for **the economic well-being of the mission community.** As is stressed in many places in the reports, the establishment of Hermannsburg on the Finke was both a mission enterprise and a business enterprise. The undertaking had as its focus the bringing of the message of Jesus Christ to the Arrarnta people, but those engaged in that aspect of the project were not totally romantic idealists. The mission needed to be nurtured within the practicalities of a sustaining and sustainable environment in the desert. Hence the sheep and cattle, horses and bullocks and poultry and dogs and seed they took up with them. Hence the need for skills of building and tending, digging and sowing, blacksmithing and baking. Hence the need for workers others than the missionaries. Hence also the expectation that eventually the Aboriginal people, too, would be included in that workforce.

Hence, too, the need for **financial accountability.** Money from Germany and the Church down South was being poured into Hermannsburg on the Finke, and Germans were scrupulous in keeping track of that money. And of the stock and other animals. And of the work on the land and in the garden. And of the buildings. So, really, there is no cause for surprise when in the reports and letters the writers seem to put a lot of effort and time into this aspect of their enterprise.

The Wives

Almost all the missionaries and colonists who went up to the Finke in those years of establishment were single men. However, these were not monks bound by vows of singleness and celibacy. Far from it! No surprise, therefore, that either before they set out from home they were already engaged, or soon after they arrived in the Centre they were anxious to obtain a partner for themselves. And so the fiancées and wives began to arrive—a group of people who warrant accolades above all others, and whose devotion to the cause takes one's breath away.

But they are also the people most hidden in this story. Most commonly referred to simply as 'the fiancées', 'the wives', or 'Mrs (n)', or

'Sister (n)', the European women of Hermannsburg on the Finke rarely get a look in. One senses them always there in the background, cooking, sewing, helping in the garden, having babies, and engaging with the Aboriginal people, especially the Aboriginal and other white women. But who they really are, and what they are really like and what they actually do all day are matters very much left to our imagination.

Even where they originally came from is, unlike with their husbands, information not easy to come by. I still cannot, for example, discover much more information about my great-grandmother, Dorothea Queckenstedt, than that she was born on 30 October 1853, that she was twenty-two years old when they engaged in 1875, and she came from Knesebeck. And I know nothing of Schwarz's wife, apart from her name, Dorothea Wilhelmine Charlotte Schulz, and that she was originally from Wöhningen, Hanover. A little more is known of Schulze's wife, Charlotte Henrietta Elizabeth Gutmann, born on 9 March 1855 into an established and highly respected family in Wittingen, Lower Saxony, the third of five children, daughter of a tailor and his wife, devout Lutherans.

This is not to say that further information is not available on all these women. Rather, what is told us about them in the reports is meagre and unsatisfying, and far more research remains to be done on them. Traynor claims that Dorothea Queckenstedt/Kempe and Dorothea Schulz/Schwarz were the first white women to live in Central Australia.[23] One cannot help wondering what it was like for them to come from what were often well-established and comfortable homes in Germany to the wilderness, to the primitive and basic conditions of the Centre, to a totally foreign culture, and devote their lives to a life and cause they would never have dreamt of as little girls.

And what was it like for them to tend to their special needs in the dust and the drought, what like to give birth and raise children in such a hostile land? When I think, for example, of my great-grandmother coming out to the Centre as a young woman of 24 years of age, literally taken up to the Centre of Australia in a cart, giving birth to seven children up there (one of whom died at the age of six), and then herself dying at the age of 38 years after the birth of the seventh child, being buried in the lonely Hermannsburg cemetery and left there when the rest of the family left, my heart bleeds. I have no doubt her story would echo within the stories of all the Hermannsburg wives.

The Arrarnta People[24]

Kempe and Schwarz, their helpers and animals arrived on-site at Ntaria in June 1877. The Aboriginal people who witnessed their arrival—the Arrarnta people—had arrived there something like 60,000 years before that.[25] The gaps between the two groups were huge.

The Arrarnta people were one of approximately 500 Aboriginal tribes or clans in Australia, between them speaking more than 250 languages incorporating up to 800 dialects. The estimated total Aboriginal population in Australia at the time of the arrival of the British varies between 315,000 and a million, with a figure of approximately 750,000 seeming to be the consensus. The Australian Bureau of Statistics estimates that at 30 June 2021 there were 984,000 Aboriginal and Torres Strait Islander people, representing 3.8 percent of the total Australian population.[26]

It is possible to make only a guesstimate of the population of the Arrarnta people. The Alice Springs Aboriginal Art and Culture website states that, regarding the Arranta, 'at the time of European contact there were about 126 "tribal" groups having all or most of their territories in the Northern Territory, with an estimated total population of 35,000. These people were hunter-gatherers who lived in small family groups of 15 to 30, called bands. Bands were the basic residential and economic unit. Groups of bands formed larger social units that anthropologists have called "communities", "tribes", or "culture blocs", depending on whether a political, linguistic or religious perspective is taken.'[27]

The geographic area occupied by the Arrarnta was extensive, several hundreds of kilometres in every direction from Alice Springs. It has been estimated that in the desert regions of the Centre, population densities were as low as one person per square kilometre. Thus, the actual number of Arrarnta people who occupied Ntaria would have been relatively small, and the letters and reports in this book indicate that, in the beginning, there were probably no more than several hundreds of Aboriginal people at most who came into contact with the Hermannsburg mission.[28] Naturally, as the Finke River Mission grew, so, too, did the number of people associated with it, and today it is estimated that there are something like 7,000 Aboriginal people connected with the Mission.

The land in which they live is harsh, desolate, arid. Rainfall is sparse, and there have been occasions when no rain at all was recorded during a year. Severe heat and drought are common; yet during the wet season flooding can occur, and in winter temperatures fall below freezing point.

Nevertheless, for millennia before the missionaries arrived, the Arrarnta had lived quite successfully in this, their country. They had their own language. They had a complex and sophisticated kinship (family) and social system which was important for regulating whom they married and how they related to each other. They had their own hunting, feeding and watering grounds, and moved from one to the other of these as they needed—a habit that frustrated the missionaries who were hoping for a settled and regulated relationship with the Aboriginal people, especially when the missionaries looked to the locals to provide them with a reliable workforce.

Contrary to what the first missionaries believed when they initially encountered them, the Arrarnta had their own religious beliefs and practices which provided them with their understanding of their world, the land and themselves. That religion also governed the lives of their people and incorporated ceremonies and rites that were important to the social and spiritual well-being of their people. They practiced their own form of medicine and healing.

Despite their isolation, even before the missionaries arrived in Ntaria, the Arrarnta people were not unfamiliar with Whites in their territory. From the time Arthur Phillip landed in Botany Bay in 1788, the Whites had been spreading along the fertile crescent of the eastern and southeastern coasts of this land they were 'discovering'. In 1836 the colony of South Australia had been founded, also comprising at that time what was later named the Northern Territory. Soon after that, white people were moving further into the Centre to explore and settle. Between 1858 and 1862, John McDouall Stuart led six different expeditions to the North, on the fourth trip taking in the Finke River and MacDonnell Ranges, and ultimately, on his sixth journey, reaching Darwin. In the early 1860s, Burke and Wills traversed the country from south to north, including Coopers Creek in their itinerary. Ten years later, between 1872 and 1875 explorers William Gosse, Ernest Giles and Peter Egerton Warburton put their footprints on the countryside around Ntaria. And between 1870 and 1872 the Overland Telegraph line from Adelaide to Darwin was constructed.

Accompanying these various White intrusions were the pastoralists. The first leases for a cattle station were granted to the Undoolya and Owen Springs stations (east and west of Alice Springs respectively) in 1872. Later, other leases developed as outgrowths from repeater stations of the Overland Telegraph line (e.g. at Peake and Charlotte Waters). With the completion of the Overland Telegraph Station at Alice Springs in 1872, white settlement began in that location, the town originally being named Stuart.

Thus, by 1877 the Arrarnta people were familiar with white people encroaching upon their land and colonising it. Nevertheless, as the Hermannsburg missionaries slowly made their way along the Finke, one cannot help thinking that the locals might have been bewildered and bemused by the sight of these few white men and their wagons, 3000-plus sheep, a few hundred cattle and horses and bullocks, dogs, a handful of hens and a rooster literally plonking themselves down on the edge of the river, and immediately beginning to construct fences and sheds and other buildings for themselves and their animals. Here are two lots of people chronologically divided by tens of thousands of years, originally geographically divided by thousands of kilometres, and in terms of culture and education divided by gulfs just as huge: What on earth are they to make of each other? This is the decisive story in *Missionaries, Madness and Miracles*.

What, if any, negotiation occurred between White and Aboriginals as the former thus settled themselves in this land is difficult to ascertain. The British presumed ownership of the country by sovereign right and arrogantly granted land leases to pastoralists, missionaries and others as the government saw fit. The Aboriginal people were simply pushed aside, displaced and replaced. Little wonder that tensions between the two groups arose very early in Australian colonial history, and that skirmishes, clashes and killings occurred from the outset of the White take-over. In Tasmania, for example, occupied by the British in 1803, it became legal in 1804/6 for the white settlers to shoot Aboriginal people. In South Australia-Northern Territory, despite the appointment of a Protector of Aborigines at the same time as the colony was founded, there were regular clashes between Whites and Blacks, one of the responses to these being the formation of a Native Police. This book also tells this sad story as it unfolded in and around the Finke mission.

The extent to which the Hermannsburg missionaries were offenders in the brutality against the Arrarnta people and their neighbours is a further touchy discussion point in *Missionaries, Madness and Miracles*. The Finke River Mission rightly makes much of the facts that there was no stolen generation in the Hermannsburg Mission, and that there were no massacres perpetrated by the Mission.

Nor did the Mission take the land from the Aboriginal people. Even though the early Germans gained their land from the South Australian government, they never saw themselves nor desired to be a part of any great British plan to colonise this country. Rather, for the Hermannsburg Lutherans the land was gift from God insofar as it was a place leased to them in and from which they might undertake their mission work. Certainly, they brought up their sheep and cattle and poultry, their wheat and barley seed, their fruit trees and vegetable seeds, and they sought to cultivate the land and grow their crops. But they did so purely for the purposes of sustaining themselves and the mission station. They desired to be self-sufficient, to build a community around their station that would support the mission and in which Aboriginal people could share with the work, production and benefits of this self-sustaining community.

Paul Albrecht talks about the land on which the Whites established their mission as land lent to the mission by God only for the time it took for the mission to be established. Once the mission believed that point had been reached, it set about the unique task of returning that land to the Aboriginal people, but in close consultation with the Aboriginal people themselves, and according to their laws and customs. This happened between 1972 and 1982, and by that time five separate Land Trusts were involved in the process, comprising five languages: Arrarnta, Pitjantjatjara, Luritja, Alyawarr and Anmatyerr.[29]

Thus, in terms of land, the Hermannsburg missionaries have always respected the land as under the custodianship of the Aboriginal people, and—even if not always perfectly—have done their best to ensure the Aboriginal people in their area maintain the land and are regarded and encouraged as the custodians of that land. When pastoralists and others sought to remove Aboriginal people from their land, or to take their land from them, those same missionaries advocated for and stood alongside the Aboriginal people as they fought to retain custodianship of their land.

Despite this positivity around the inter-action between the Hermannsburg missionaries and the Arrarnta people, there is much about the missionaries' relationship with the Aboriginal people that is disgraceful, embarrassingly so. There were times when Vic and I were working on the translation that I felt so ashamed of how the missionaries (including my great-grandfather) spoke about the Aboriginal people and mistreated them, that I just wanted to hide, or even destroy, those parts of the translation. They are shameful.

However, we have chosen not to do this, because that would be to deny truth. We cannot and ought not ignore what actually happened.

As painful as it may at times be to speak of these things, it is critical for our understanding of each other that we do so, as truthfully and objectively as possible. So, the bad, sad, ignominious material. *Missionaries, Madness and Miracles* takes us into all these various aspects of the relationship between the Arrarnta people and those first missionaries. There are always a number of stories at play as the narrative unfolds. At times those stories collide and divide, at other times they blend and merge. At times the two groups speak past each other; at other times, wonder of wonders, they connect. What is important in the telling of these stories, as well as in coming to terms with them, is that we are realistic and honest with each other, balanced and fair in the telling and the listening, and that we work respectfully and lovingly with each other as we seek to reconcile in the process. So that, out of all that, there emerges a new story, our story—a story that can authentically speak about this place as our place.

I was recently invited to submit a creative response to studies being undertaken by scholars interested in the notion of de-colonisation. The question put to me was something like, 'What did those first missionaries think about the Aboriginal people, and what did they intend on doing, when they first set foot in the Finke?' Here is my response to that request.

Confused Together

They did not understand the land,
those first missionaries who in 1877
came into that land known as Ntaria
and called it Hermannsburg.
They did not understand the land.

Not like the first peoples of that land
who understood the land
like the back of a black hand,
But who did not understand
these men with white faces,
who came into the land
speaking of a man called Jesus
who could truly save them.
They did not understand.

And because they did not understand
one another
they spoke past each other,
And stood
looking at one another
in mutual confusion.

Thus shall it ever be
until someone proposes,
'Let us stand alongside each other
And learn to speak truthfully to one another
in each other's language'.
Then might we understand
the other.

The Lutheran Church

Brief History of the First Lutherans in South Australia

The first major group of Lutherans to settle in South Australia arrived at Holdfast Bay on 18 November 1838.[30] There were approximately 200 of them, and they had sailed to their new country from various points of Prussia in two ships, the *Prince George* and the *Bengalee*. Their leader was Pastor August Ludwig Christian Kavel, and the venture was sponsored by George Fife Angas of the South Australian Company which greatly contributed to the British peopling of this new colony. A third ship of Kavel's people, the *Zebra* captained by Dirk Hahn and with another approximately 200 people on board, arrived in Port Adelaide at the end of December 1838; and a fourth ship, the *Catharina*, brought about another hundred in late January 1839. Journeys took approximately four months, and it was not uncommon for passengers to die along the way (e.g. on the *Prince George* voyage, 14 people died, seven adults, seven children).

The second wave of Lutherans arrived almost three years later, on 28 October 1841. They sailed on the *Skjold*, and in this lot there were some 270 people, led by Pastor Gotthard Daniel Fritzsche. Some 50 people died on this voyage.

Kavel's people had settled in Klemzig, Hahndorf, Glen Osmond and Langmeil/Tanunda. Fritzsche's people settled in Lobethal, Bethany and Blumberg/Birdwood. Wherever they settled they quickly established their homes, farmlets, gardens and, naturally, churches. From the beginning, they also established schools. They grew in number, and the details of the enthralling story of their settling into their new country may be accessed from various of the books and other resources listed in the *Bibliograpy/References*.

Why had these people come here?

Without a doubt there were those among them who emigrated for what they perceived to be a 'better life': new country, new land, new opportunities. Britain was still looking to expand its territory, but by 1800 there were those who had become somewhat disenchanted by the penal colony approach used to establish much of the east coast of Australia. Instead, they had a mind to establish a colony of free settlers somewhere else in the land, with the central southern part of the country a most obvious possibility. Two of those people were Edward Wakefield and Robert Gouger who, between them, sparked the formation of the National Colonization Society (1830) and the South Australian Association (1833). Allied with them were George Fife Angas and the South Australian Land Company (1835), and all of these combined to promote the establishment of the new colony of South Australia which was to be founded on the basis of free government, free trade and freedom of religion. The South Australia Act of 1834 brought these plans into reality. Thereafter, this new venture was publicised overseas, and new settlers began to arrive in the place which was named Adelaide in 1836.

Among those who got to hear of this new colony in the South were the Lutherans of Prussia. Before long there were those among them who were keen to make for themselves a new life on the other side of the world. However, what made this prospect particularly appealing to most of these people was not simply the desire for the 'better life'; they were genuinely motivated by a yearning for religious freedom.

Ever since the Protestant Reformation in Europe in the 16th Century, the religious scene amongst Christians had been a fractured one: Roman Catholics, Greek and Russian Orthodox, Lutherans of one form or another, Reformed of one form or another, Baptist, Enthusiasts, and more. Such, too, was the scene in Prussia at the beginning of the 19th Century, with the Roman Catholic, Reformed and Lutheran Churches forming the three predominant groups.

At that time Friedrich Wilhelm III was king of Prussia. One of his dreams was to bring greater unity between the churches in Prussia, especially between the Lutheran and Reformed. Already in 1798 he had had published a new book of worship orders (the *Agenda*) which amalgamated various liturgies from both traditions, and which he expected to be used in all Lutheran and Reformed churches. Most, the Lutherans in particular, ignored it. But then in 1817, coinciding with the 300th anniversary of Luther's Reformation, Wilhelm resolved to force the issue. He decreed the formation of a Union Church, consisting of all Lutheran and Reformed Churches in Prussia, and the *Agenda* was to be used in all churches.

Wilhelm's decree was the spark that lit a bourgeoning flame of opposition to this Union Church among Prussian Lutherans, especially among those in Silesia, who became known as the Old Lutherans. They were not only resistant to the union, but actively disobeyed orders to comply with it. As a result, they experienced push-back, repercussions, harassment and persecution from government officials. Lay people were removed from offices they held in the Church. Some were fined for their disobedience, others felt driven into exile, and yet others had their possessions and property seized. Some pastors were suspended or removed from office. Some were imprisoned, as were numbers of lay people. Some churches were locked so that members could not access them, with soldiers at times called in to enforce the lockouts. Pastors went into hiding, and lay people caught sheltering them were fined or jailed.

These folk could have complied with the new situation but chose not to. For most of them, this situation was a matter of faith and conscience, and, in the end, many of them felt compelled to leave their homes and their homeland. The opportunity to migrate to the free State of South Australia was for them a Godsend, an answer to prayer.

So, they came. And they settled. And they spread.

Unfortunately, Lutherans are an argumentative lot. Whether or not as a homogenous group they are any different from similar groups might be a matter worth exploring; but there are no two ways about it that from the time of the Reformation, Lutherans have established a consistent pattern of coming together and then breaking apart. Even on the various sea voyages of those first Lutherans from Germany to Australia arguments and divisions occurred amongst various passengers, some of those ending quite acrimoniously.

Thus, it may come as small surprise to many that within five years of Fritzsche's arrival in Australia, and with only two pastors and several congregations comprising the Synod at that time, the Lutheran Church in Australia had split. This happened at the Synodical Convention of the Lutheran Church (such as it was) at Bethany in 1846. The arguments that led to the split are variously described. There were issues about chiliasm (the expected thousand-year rule of Christ on earth): some believed it to be a teaching of the Church, others did not. In 1839 Kavel had produced his *Apostolic Constitution* (a Church constitution he believed to be prescribed by Scripture), and this claim was disputed by some members. In 1846 Kavel had also produced what he called his *Protestations*, a list of points where he disagreed with the *Lutheran Confessions*. This, too, was a contentious issue for the Synod. Finally, Fritzsche had invited three missionaries from the Dresden Mission to attend the synod at Bethany, and there were those (Kavel among them) who claimed this to be an act of 'sinful unionism'[31] and objected to the presence of these men in their midst.

A huge argument ensued, voices and tempers were raised, and Kavel and his followers stormed out of the synod. Quite likely, though, much of the split had to do with the differing personalities and psychology of the two men. They simply did not always get along, and rubbed each other up the wrong way until matters came to a head. In much the same way, issues in the Lutheran Church today, if the truth be told, are not always issues of theology and Biblical interpretation (as we like to pretend they are), but rather issues of psychology and personality.

The split that occurred on 18 August 1846 led to the formation of two Lutheran Synods in Australia—the first of a variety of splits and Synods that have plagued Lutherans in Australia ever since. One Synod, followers of Fritzsche, named themselves the Evangelical Lutheran Synod of South Australia (soon after, the Evangelical Lutheran Synod of Australia – ELSA), and the other Synod, followers of Kavel, became known as the Immanuel Synod. Each Synod, in its own way, grew and developed from there until the eventual amalgamation of those two Synods 118 years later, in 1966.

Such was the background to the Lutheran church scene that greeted Kempe and Schwarz on their arrival in Australia almost thirty years after that original split.

The Lutheran Church and Aboriginal Mission
In our religiously diverse Australia, super-sensitive as it is to discrimination and political correctness, the notion of Christian mission is, for many, anathema. For them it is offensive, even abhorrent, to criticise the beliefs of another and to attempt to impress one's own beliefs on them instead, this being the popular view of what mission is about. And those so minded will be quick to point out the atrocities and abominations that

over the centuries have been committed by Christians in their pursuit of the conversion of others to the Christian faith. Many times, sadly, Christians have deserved such derision.

That aside, one cannot escape the fact that mission outreach to people outside the Christian fold is embedded within the DNA of Christianity. Where anyone believes that Jesus is *the* Christ, the One in whom alone any other person can have and enjoy a full and proper relationship with God, and where one has received a mandate from that One to 'go into all the world and preach [this] gospel to every creature', there Christian mission is inherently inevitable.

Thus, when Lutherans in Australia took the decision to undertake mission work to Aboriginal people, they were doing nothing more or less than what Christians around the world had been doing for centuries. And in the mid-19th century they were just one of many churches involved in a renewal of missional fervour throughout the world. All of it as natural to Christians as breathing.

Unhappily, there is a dark side to Christian mission; there have been abuses inflicted on others through the misguided zealotry of many a Christian mission and missionary. However, before we would inflict upon these missionaries any eternal judgement of the same ilk as we perceive they inflicted upon people of their time, we do well to step back, take a deep breath, and do them the courtesy of seeing them as people of their time—in exactly the same way as we are people of ours. *Missionaries, Madness and Miracles* deals with history, and none of us can change history, change what actually happened. We may not like what we read. We may not always agree with it, and our first response may be to disown that history. But, like it or not, our first obligation is to read and hear the history, the story, to seek to understand and even appreciate it in its own context. Then we might be on the first step to being able to make some initial objective and respectful observations as to what this history has really been about.

Mission outreach—in particular, mission to Aboriginal people—has been an integral aspect of the work of the Lutheran Church in Australia from its beginning. The first such Lutheran missionaries were Clamor Wilhelm Schürmann and Christian Gottlob Teichelmann of the Dresden Mission Society. They arrived in South Australia on 13 October 1838, five weeks, in fact, before the first of Kavel's people. They worked among the Aboriginal people in Adelaide (the Piltawodli/Pirltawardli people). In 1840 they were joined by two other Dresden Mission Society missionaries,

Heinrich August Eduard Meyer and Samuel Gottlieb Klose, and between them the Adelaide work expanded to include mission undertakings in Encounter Bay and Port Lincoln.

By 1846 this mission work had begun to diminish, and by 1853 all four missionaries were no longer engaged in mission work. Instead, they had each accepted calls as pastors to various congregations in South Australia and Victoria,

The relationships between the two Australian Synods and their various iterations were often mixed, and even paradoxical. There was animosity and division on the one hand; but at the same time there was a degree of cordial collegiality on the other. Even Kavel and Fritzsche, it seems, maintained a kind of friendship after their split. At times there were half-hearted overtures for a reunion between the two Synods, but never anything really serious until the mid-20th century.

All of which leads to Killalpaninna.

Killalpaninna

In the spirit of that strange inter-Synodical accord just mentioned, the two Lutheran Synods in Australia were quite open to a challenge put to them in the early 1860s by former missionary to India, J F Meischel, to engage together in mission to the Aboriginal people in the Australian interior. Recent explorations in that region had expanded the Whites' awareness of the land and its people beyond the fertile coastlands, and a spirit of faith and adventure impelled the Churches to take up the Meischel challenge.

Consequently, at a combined mission festival at Blumberg on 6 March 1863 the Lutherans resolved to undertake a mission venture among the Dieri people in upper South Australia. They formed a 'confessional union', elected an inter-synodical mission committee, and negotiated with the South Australian government for land in the Coopers Creek/Lake Hope area.

Finding personnel for the enterprise presented a number of difficulties, and in the end the two Churches approached the Hermannsburg Mission Society HMS) in Germany for its assistance, in the belief that this organisation was most closely aligned with their theology. Ludwig Harms was the HMS Director at the time, and he was prepared to send both missionaries and pastors for the work in Australia.[32]

So it was that in August 1866 the missionaries J F R Gössling and Ernst Homann arrived in Adelaide from Germany, freshly-ordained.

They were accompanied by H H Vogelsang, a lay helper destined for the new mission. With them arrived G A Heidenreich and C G Hellmuth, assigned as pastors for ELSA.

By 9 October that year, wagons, supplies and personnel were ready for the 1,000 kilometre journey to the Coopers Creek area, and, after a huge farewell service at Tanunda, Gössling, Homann and Vogelsang, plus layman J E Jacob from Mt Torrens, set off on their history-making trek. It took them three months, often experiencing rocky and fluctuating fortunes along the way. And when they reached their destination, they found it already occupied by a group of Moravian missionaries who had arrived several weeks before them.

Undeterred, at least at this stage, the Lutherans moved on to Lake Killalpaninna where by February 1867 they had set about the task of establishing their mission, which they named 'Hermannsburg'.[33] Sadly, though, things went badly almost from the start, with the Aboriginal people quickly becoming resentful of—even hostile to—this white intrusion, and with living and working conditions taking a greater toll on the missionaries than they had anticipated. The Moravians, too, felt under threat from the Aboriginal people so that, despite the presence of a reinforced police force in the area, they moved across to Killalpaninna as well.

Matters did not improve, however, and within six months of the commencement of the mission, all the Lutheran missionaries, except Jacob, had returned down South for their own well-being, resolved not to return until the police could assure their safety. But Gössling had had enough, resigned as a missionary, and accepted a call to the Jindera congregation in NSW.

Homann and Vogelsang returned to Killalpaninna in January 1868, taking with them their brides, and a teacher, W Koch. Their labours over the next few years bore some fruit, including the development of more harmonious relations with the Aboriginal people, and the translation of a catechism and Bible history into the Dieri language. Nevertheless, a severe drought, continuing shaky relationships with the Aboriginal people, and discouraging results for their efforts persisted. Homann became so dispirited that he left in 1872, and the Moravians also left, moving across to Victoria. C H Schoknecht then became the missionary, in 1871, but he left in 1873. Colin Jericho says that 'the years 1873 and 1874 were described in reports as years of utter misery, want, and hardship beyond all description'.[34] All of this took its toll on the few workers who were left, and the mission was becoming unsustainable.

Little wonder, then, that in 1874 the two Lutheran Synods that had undertaken this project, dissolved their agreement. The ELSA partners pulled out of Killalpaninna completely. But the Immanuel Synod battled on, renaming the mission 'Bethesda'.

Such, in brief, is the story of Killalpaninna prior to the commencement of events in *Missionaries, Madness and Miracles*. It is not, however, the end of the Killalpaninna connection with the 'new' Hermannsburg, and the ongoing threads of that connection are picked up as the new story unfolds.

Before we return to that story, however, it is necessary for the cohesiveness of our narrative to backtrack a little, and briefly fill in the details of one of those other stories: the story of Hermannsburg in Germany.

Hermannsburg Mission Society and Institute/Seminary[35]

As the infant Lutheran Church in Australia began to grow, the question of continuing pastoral supply to its congregations also began to loom large. Within the ELSA, the first response to that challenge was for the Church to develop its own supply of pastors from within its own ranks. Kavel also favoured this approach, and as early as 1842 he and Fritzsche were personally instructing a group of five potential candidates for ordination, using their homes as the learning centres.[36] After the split in 1846, they continued this approach, but each in his own Synod.

In 1845, prior to the split between them, Fritzsche and Kavel shared in the building of the Lobethal College for the purpose of pastoral training.[37] This remarkable little undertaking enjoyed varying success, its most notable graduates eventually each becoming presidents of ELSA: Carl Hensel, Phillip Oster and Adolph Strempel. However, when Fritzsche died in 1863, the training of pastors in this place and way 'was left in abeyance', as Brauer puts it.[38]

This is the point at which the Hermannsburg Mission Society enters the picture. It was also the time when the Immanuel and ELSA Synods were beginning to think about the possibility of a joint mission venture to the Aboriginal people. On both fronts—congregational and missional—there was a sudden need for staff: pastors and missionaries. Hermannsburg in Germany was able to provide both.

There were, of course, other mission societies and seminaries in Germany that could have been approached. Indeed, several of these did provide personnel for the Australian Lutheran scene over the years. The

Dresden missionaries (Schürmann, Teichelmann, Klose and Meyer) in South Australia, for example. As well as the Basel and Gossner Mission Societies, and the Neuendettelsau Mission Society.

But it was to the Hermannsburg Mission Society that the ELSA and Immanuel Synods turned in this initial time of need. They probably did so because of personal connections that Church members still had in Hanover, and also because of their knowledge of Hermannsburg and their closer affinity to its theological and confessional stances than to other similar societies.

That brings us to the Harms family, the people responsible for the establishment of the Hermannsburg Mission Society and Seminary.

George Ludwig Detlef Theodor Harms, called **Louis Harms** (1808–1865). He was the second son of a Lutheran pastor, Hartwig, and his wife, Lucie, in Walsrode on the Lüneberg Heath, Lower Saxony. At the age of nine the family moved to Hermannsburg (also in Lower Saxony) as a result of his father accepting the call to be the pastor there.

Louis received an excellent education at all levels: primary, secondary and tertiary—the latter at Göttingen University (1827–30). His time at university was particularly challenging to his faith, and he claims that at one stage he lost his faith in God. However, at the conclusion of that period in his life, and as a result of his personal daily Bible study, he returned to the Christian faith more committed than ever. More Lutheran than ever, too, it would seem, with Regina Gantner maintaining that 'Harms subscribed to a narrow Lutheran confessionalism'[39], evincing a 'theological thinking [that combined] Lutheran faith and pietistic revival pietism'.[40]

Politically, Louis, as well as his brother Theodor, were supporters of the monarchy, specifically of the Hanoverian royal family. References to those loyalties turn up here and there throughout our records. Anything to do with a nationalistic, democratic republican movement (such as the 1848 revolution, for example) was anathema to them. This mindset might well explain the rather authoritarian approach Louis often adopted in his dealings with others, notwithstanding that there were those who experienced him as having a 'beautiful disposition and gracious character'.[41]

The two passions in Louis' life were (1) a commitment to his understanding of the Bible and the Faith, especially to the Confessionalism of the Lutheran Church as he understood it, and (2) his fervour for mission, especially overseas mission. Already in 1834 he had been involved in the formation of the Lauenburg Mission Society, and in 1836 of the North German Mission Society.

For a time Louis worked as a tutor in Lauenburg. But when his father became ill in 1843, he returned to Hermannsburg to assist him as his curate. He was ordained in 1844, and admitted to the pastorate of the Hanoverian Evangelical Lutheran State Church in 1849, the year that his father died. There were two Lutheran congregations in the town, St Peter's and St Paul's.

From the outset of his ministry in Hermannsburg, Louis set about reviving the faith and Church life of the community through his passionate preaching, engaging Bible studies, and hands-on pastoral care. He was a gifted speaker, and '[by] the 1850s Hermannsburg township had become a tight-knit Lutheran congregation supporting heathen mission with liberal donations, spurned [sic] by annual mission festivals'.[42] Up to 6,000 people attended these festivals.

Louis Harms was also responsible for the instigation of the *Hermannsburger Missionsblatt*, one of the primary sources for the materials in this book. Harms regarded this publication as a way of informing and instructing its readers about the happenings and thinking of the Hermannsburg Mission. It was also a means of enhancing the sense of unity and fellowship between all those involved and interested in that mission.

The Hermannsburg Mission Society and Seminary was established by Louis Harms in 1846. Its purpose was two-fold: (1) to train men[43] for ministry as pastors and missionaries in the Lutheran Church, and (2) to establish and maintain overseas mission fields.

There were special features and requirements about the training of students at HMS as distinct from other similar institutions. This is not to say that those features were unique to HMS.

1. HMS was especially intended for those wishing to engage in mission and pastoral work, but who did not have the educational qualifications normally expected of those entering the world of theological academia. In many cases, this was probably due less to academic ability than to the lack of previous academic opportunity and to lack of the necessary funds. Nevertheless, Reller says that '[it] is clearly the case that the first Hermannsburg missionaries were not academically educated theologians', and Harms himself agreed that the Hermannsburg missionaries were less well educated than those of other societies.[44]

2. Despite that, Hermannsburg students were subjected to a rigorous, if somewhat modified, theological study program of four years. Their subjects included Scripture, Dogmatics, Church History, German and English (Latin was introduced in 1861), General Studies (including world history, geography, arithmetic, music), Catechetics, Homiletics and Pastoral Theology.[45]
3. The course was very practical, in that students were expected to bring with them, or acquire, some practical expertise or experience. Kempe was a blacksmith, for example, and Schwarz a baker. Schulze was a miner. Others were masons, carpenters, farmers. As well as being theologians and pastors, missionaries needed to be handy, self-sufficient, self-sustaining people.
4. Missionaries also needed to be capable of engaging and navigating other cultures, languages and natural environments than their own. Thus the ability of Kempe, Schwarz and Schulze to work in the Arrarnta language, for example, to begin to know something of this new and different culture, and the capacity to catalogue the flora and fauna of their new home in the Centre.

The Harms brothers divided the operation of the Mission between them. Louis was the Mission Director, and he appointed his brother, Theodor, to be head of the Seminary. Their first class comprised 12 students, and their first graduation in 1853 saw 16 new missionaries headed for South Africa. They sailed there on the *Candace*, a ship that the Institute had built for the sole purpose of transporting personnel and goods to Hermannsburg mission stations.

Louis never married, and he regarded the Hermannsburg students as his children, insisting that they address him as 'Father'. Theodor also adopted this practice. Life at the Seminary/Institute was rigorous and strict, with an insistence on students being obedient to Harms, and subservient to his worldview. Independent, critical thinking was not encouraged.

Louis died in 1865, the year Lutherans in Australia were beginning to make their acquaintance with the HMS. Thus, Louis never really had a lot to do with the development of the Lutheran cause in Australia beyond his educational inter-action with the very early Hermannsburgers who came out to this part of the world. The closer relationship between the Lutherans in Australia and Hermannburg in Germany was with Louis' brother, Theodor.

Carl Friedrich Theodor Harms (1819–85) was Louis' younger brother by 11 years. He enjoyed a similar education to his older brother, completing studies at Göttingen in 1842. Louis immediately appointed him as Director (or Inspector) of the Hermannsburg Seminary. Between 1857 and 1866 Theodor was also the pastor of St Laurentius Church in Müden, about 10 kilometres from Hermannsburg.

After Louis died, Theodor took responsibility for the whole of the Hermannsburg Institute: i.e. as head/inspector of the Seminary and Director of the mission program. Under his directorship the institution and mission expanded, with missions in India, Africa, Australia and New Zealand. Theodor did marry, and he and his wife had three children. The second of these was Egmont, who became Director of HMS after Theodor's death in 1885.

Because Theodor plays a major role in the establishment of the mission on the Finke, he constantly appears in the pages of this book. Hence, information on him at this point is kept brief. However, there are two further aspects of his directorship that are worthy of immediate note.

The first is the physical expansion of the mission complex in Hermannsburg, Germany. Originally students were housed and taught in The Old Mission House (erected in 1849), and later known as Ludwig Harms House. This is where Kempe, Schwarz and Schulze, as well as Heidenreich, received their training. In 1879, however, the New Mission House was erected and opened, and references to the 'New House' spasmodically occur within our story.

The second item of note is Theodor's entanglement in the various Church-State tensions that were at play in his time. Firstly, there was the 1866 annexation of the Kingdom of Hanover by the State of Prussia. This move posed a threat to the continuing existence of the Hanoverian royalty to which, as noted above, the Harms' brothers were intensely loyal. But it also threatened the Hermannsburg Lutheran Church with the possibility of the Prussians enforcing a Lutheran-Reformed Union upon the Churches. For Harms, such an act was abhorrent, and served only to increase his commitment to a strict Lutheran Confessionalism.

Secondly, was the *Kulturkampf* (Cultural Struggle or Conflict) between 1872 and 1887. This was a struggle between the broader Church in Germany, including the Roman Catholics, and the State, the latter represented largely by Chancellor Bismarck. The concern on the part of the State was that the Church had accrued too much influence in the affairs of the country. The concern on the part of the Church was that the State wanted to diminish the power of the Church, especially in matters of education and marriage. The possibility of this happening horrified Theodor, and his response to it occupies its own space in *Missionaries, Madness and Miracles*.

As remote as these events in Hermannsburg, Germany, may be to Australia, they did have their impact upon the Lutheran Church in this country and, therefore, upon the mission on the Finke. Consequently, it is helpful to be aware of these faraway events and of their appearance from time to time in this book.

Finke River Mission

After they had withdrawn from the Killalpaninna venture, the ELSA was compelled by circumstances to make decisions about its future participation in any mission work among Aboriginal people in Australia. Not the least of those extenuating circumstances was the substantial financial and material investment the ELSA had made to the original endeavour. How was this investment to be sorted out?

Even though there was uncertainty for a while about the best way to proceed, both Synods nonetheless each still retained some heart for continuing their mission endeavours. Immanuel decided to hold on to Killalpaninna. ELSA would look elsewhere. ELSA leaders had, for example, held discussions with the explorers W C Gosse and E Giles on the likelihood of a mission undertaking in the MacDonnell Ranges area. The South Australian Surveyor-General, George Goyder, offered to set aside 200 square miles of land in the James Range and Finke River region for a possible new mission station.

In early 1875, the ELSA resolved to take up this offer, with the original lease of 200 square miles later increased to 900 square miles. However, the new development would only transpire on the understanding between all parties that the new mission was to be owned and operated by the Hermannsburg Mission Society in Hanover.

Director Theodor Harms was not altogether happy with that arrangement. He was prepared for the Institute to supply missionaries for the work, but on condition that these would remain under the oversight of the Hermannsburg Mission Society through a Superintendent in Australia. He was also prepared to train and supply pastors for the Synod, but only on condition that the Synod would share in the support of the mission, financially, materially and prayerfully. The Synod eventually agreed to this.

The two Australian Synods also agreed that the property on the 'old' station at Killalpaninna would be valued and distributed between them. Immanuel would retain one-third of all animals and equipment, plus the buildings; ELSA would receive two-thirds of the livestock and equipment. After a number of meetings and considerable discussion, final decisions on these and related matters were made at a special meeting at Rosenthal on 4 August 1875. These decisions included details on the immediate implementation of the plan to begin the new mission in the Centre.

The first task was to tidy up arrangements in Killalpaninna. On 13 August a group comprising Immanuel Synod President Rechner and lay helper R Graetz, together with ELSA representatives Pastor G Heidenreich and lay helper H Drögemüller left for Killalpaninna to effect those decisions. Concurrently, three other lay helpers who the day before had been commissioned for service in the Centre also headed for Killalpaninna. They were George Mirus, a shepherd from Bethany; G Hämmerling, a contract worker from Light Pass; and J C Bähr, a driver.

Together they carried out an inspection of the property that began on 6 September and lasted several days. Of special interest in relation to the 'new' Hermannsburg was the fact that the livestock comprised '49 horses, about 120 goats, 29 head of cattle, and 4674 sheep'.[46] Among these were those destined to make the exacting trek to the Finke.

Once the inspection was completed, the Synod representatives headed back home. The lay helpers (Mirus, Hämmerling and Bähr) remained in the northern area to await the arrival of the new missionaries.

Those new and young missionaries were already on their way. Kempe and Schwarz had graduated and been ordained in Hermannsburg, Germany, in June. They had been assigned to mission work in Australia and had departed their country on 21 July.

Thus, it seemed, all was in place for the plans to be executed. Those arrangements included the appointment of the man who would be the Superintendent of this new mission: Georg A Heidenreich.

Georg Adam Heidenreich (1828–1910) was the fourth member of the group of ordained men who established Hermannsburg on the Finke. As the Superintendent of Aboriginal Mission for ELSA, he was involved in a different way, however, from Kempe, Schwarz and Schulze, and that involvement was frequently controversial, as our reports and letters demonstrate.

Georg Adam was born on 28 September 1828 in Tiefenort, Saxony, and we know little of his early life. After primary and secondary school he obtained work in the Hanover mint. During this time he was influenced by the preaching of Dr L A Petri of Hanover, resigned from his job, and in 1861 enrolled in the Hermannsburg Mission Seminary. He graduated in 1866, and soon after was ordained in Hanover in the presence of George V of Hanover and the royal family. Typical of the Hermannsburg graduates, he immediately had to find a wife, and did so in the person of Anna Meyer. They were married in April of 1866, and soon after sailed to Australia, arriving in Adelaide on 24 August. During the course of their life together, the Heidenreichs had nine children.

Classmates who came to Australia with Heidenreich were J F Gössling, C G Hellmuth and E Homann. They were the first HMS graduates to be assigned to Australia by Director Ludwig Harms, and thus, by virtue of the formation of this bond with Hermannsburg, Germany, they hold a unique spot in Australian Lutheran history. In his reports Heidenreich in particular frequently alludes to a special kinship he claims he had with Harms, and one cannot but wonder whether his background and relationships generated within him a sense of seniority in respect to the later missionaries.

It is noteworthy that Gössling and Homann were designated for mission work (to Killalpaninna), whereas Heidenreich and Hellmuth were assigned to congregations ('Church') and only ever served in parishes. What makes this fact noteworthy is that one of the recurring, contentious issues around Heidenreich was the question of his role or status as 'missionary'. Every now and then he gives the impression that he believed he could flip-flop somewhat between 'Church' and 'mission', whereas the evidence indicates that he was actually commissioned to serve as a parish pastor ('Church'). And when he made noises about wanting to serve as 'missionary', that inevitably caused friction between him and the designated missionaries. It is also noteworthy that Heidenreich never spent one day in actual 'mission' work in Hermannsburg. His rare visits there were always as Superintendent, administrator.

By the time Kempe and Schwarz arrived in Australia in 1875, Heidenreich had been the pastor at Bethany for over nine years. He was a busy man, serving the large congregation at Bethany, plus several smaller, outlying congregations (Krondorf, Neukirch, Dalkey, Hummocks and Rheinthal). During his ministry, a second new church was built in Bethany (in 1883), as well as a new school (1888). He had instigated a Lutheran Young Men's Society in Bethany (1868), and an early off-shoot of this was the Bethany Brass band, of which he was very proud.

Beyond the parish, Heidenreich served on the District Church Council and the Mission Board. The Bethany congregation was one of the main driving forces behind the formation of the Finke River Mission, and in September 1875 Heidenreich was appointed Superintendent, or Provost, of that mission.

South Australia and Northern Territory

The last of the inter-weaving stories within *Missionaries, Madness and Miracles* is the story of South Australia and the Northern Territory. These are the larger geographical canvases upon which all else coalesces. In turn, the South Australia and Northern Territory stories are a part of the even broader Australian story, with the larger, all-encompassing Aboriginal story embracing them all.

When Captain Arthur Phillip raised the British flag at Botany Bay in January 1788, there were estimated to be something like 750,000 Aboriginal people on the continent, their history extending back some 60,000 years. On that day (or very soon after) there were already clashes between the new arrivals and the ancient inhabitants of the land, with the number of Aboriginal deaths reportedly varying between several and several hundred. Since that day the European settlers had quite quickly spread south, north and west across the land.

So, by the time in 1875 when Kempe and Schwarz trundled their wagon out of Bethany and headed for the Centre, European Australia had 90 years of its history behind it. Hobart had been established in 1804, Brisbane in 1825, Perth in 1829, Melbourne in 1835 (although Port Phillip had been settled in 1802). The transportation of convicts to the country had ceased in 1868.

The white Australian population was around 2,000,000. Pastoralists had occupied much of the east coast. Rural towns were developing. The various colonies had postal systems and the beginning of telegraph and railways. Freight and passenger-carrying services using horse, bullock and (later) camel power were in place, as were coastal shipping services. Gold and other minerals had been discovered, and mining developed. The British pound was in currency, and branches of the British Royal Mint had been established in Sydney (1853) and Melbourne (1872). Tasmania had effected its infamous Blood Line by which it proposed to rid itself of its total Aboriginal population (1830).

South Australia was a latecomer to the European Australia scene, having been proclaimed a British colony only on 28 December 1836. In addition, by 1875 the colony had somehow come to include the Northern Territory as well. Cross says:

> In 1863 the representatives of the struggling colony of South Australia acquired a huge tract of so-called wasteland which they called the Northern Territory. But when the question was raised, no one seemed to know with any certainty how the idea of taking over such a large area of land had come about. 'The thing has grown upon us', wrote the Advertiser columnist.[47] It had grown until it was too much trouble to turn back.[48]

Port Darwin had been visited by the *HMS Beagle* in 1839, and named; and Darwin had been officially established in 1869. By 1875 the white population of the whole of the Northern Territory was probably around 2,500.[49] The histories of South Australia and the Northern Territory were linked until the North was transferred to the Commonwealth of Australia in 1911.

South Australia prided itself on being a colony of free settlers, as distinct from other colonies that were heavily involved in the convict trade. It also prided itself on its inclusion from the beginning of the rights of Aboriginal people. For example, the Letters of Patent issued in England in February 1836 authorised the establishment of this new colony, 'provided always that nothing in those our Letters Patent ... shall affect or be construed to affect the rights of any Aboriginal Natives of the said province to the actual occupation or enjoyment in their own persons or in the persons of their descendants of any lands therein now actually occupied or enjoyed by such natives.' And in his Proclamation speech in December of that year, the Colony's first governor, John Hindmarch, stated:

> '[It is] my duty to apprize the Colonists of my resolution, to take every lawful means for extending the same protection to the Native Population as to the rest of His Majesty's Subjects and of my firm determination to punish with exemplary severity, all acts of violence or injustice which may in any manner be practiced or attempted against the Natives who are to be considered as much under the

Safeguard of the law as the Colonists themselves, and equally entitled to the privileges of British Subjects. I trust therefore, with confidence to the exercise of moderation and forbearance by all Classes, in their intercourse with the Native Inhabitants, and that they will omit no opportunity of assisting me to fulfil His Majesty's most gracious and benevolent intentions toward them, by promoting their advancement in civilization, and ultimately, under the blessing of Divine Providence, their conversion to the Christian Faith.'[50]

South Australia was the first Australian colony to legislate for a Protector of Aborigines, in 1836. The first to hold this office was Matthew Moorhouse. How effective this position was, and how successful the government policy on Aboriginal people, are contentious questions, given that in 1856 the office of protector was abolished and that by 1860 most of the reserves designated for Aboriginal people had been leased to pastoralists.

Adelaide and beyond

Compared to conditions when the first white settlers occupied South Australia, by 1875 Adelaide and its surrounds were quite developed. The population of the Colony was approximately 210,000, and of Adelaide and its suburbs around 100,000.[51] The accompanying map[52] (over page) shows the spread of European settlement out from Adelaide between 1836 and 1886 and as far as the so-called Goyder Line.[53] The South Australian white population had also settled south of the capital (in Encounter Bay and Kangaroo Island [early settlements], and Mt Gambier [established in 1854]). In the West the explorer John Eyre had made his famous exploratory journeys to Lake Eyre and Albany between 1838 and 1841, and Port Lincoln was proclaimed a port in 1839.

Kempe and Schwarz arrived to an Adelaide that had already filled out into its familiar grid-like structure. It had its own tram, train, telegraph and postal systems that increasingly extended throughout the Colony. It was well served with schools, churches and hospitals. And it was one of the main hubs for the wheat, wool and mining industries that were being developed in the Colony.

Thus, the freshly-minted missionaries landed in a healthily established, albeit small, city and colony, a suitable springboard for the beginning of the enormous task that faced them. All the amenities they required to remain linked with their German homeland via letters,

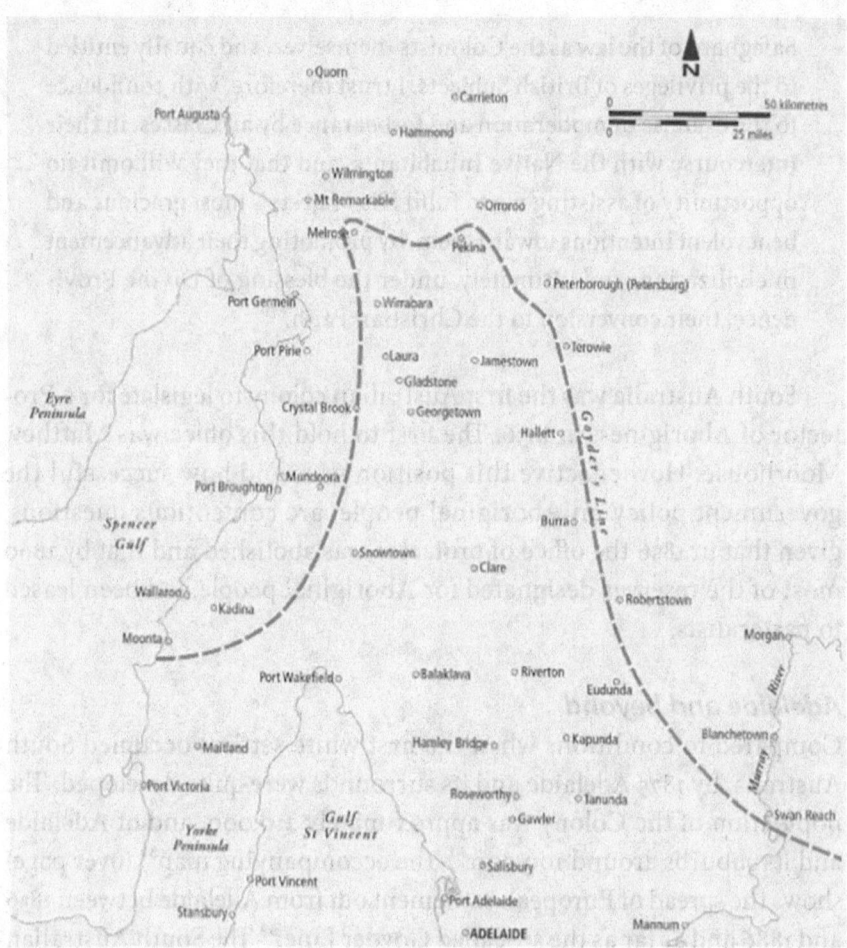

Map of South Australia, showing extent of the Goyder Line

parcels, and other goods were available to them. All the facilities to equip them for what lay ahead were in place.

North of the Goyder Line, however, life was a different matter. This was essentially desert land, the place in which the Aboriginal people were very much at home, but in which white people struggled to exist. Nevertheless, white explorers, settlers and pastoralists had gradually begun to trickle into that part of South Australia and the Northern Territory as well. The Hermannsburg missionaries were a small part of that movement. But without a doubt, one of the greatest, if not the greatest, contributor to that early influx into the Centre and North was the establishment of the Overland Telegraph Line.

The Overland Telegraph Line

The idea of connecting Australia with the rest of the world by means of an international telegraph line was a dream held by many people ever since the introduction of the electric telegraph into Australia in the mid-1800s. However, the chief proponent for the proposal that this line should run from Adelaide to Darwin was Charles Todd, South Australia's Superintendent of Telegraphs. His vision, and that of his colleagues, was that from Darwin the line would connect to Java by way of an undersea cable, the Europe-Asia telegraph system having already reached that far.

Two other colonies, Victoria and Queensland, also vied for the right to construct this line. Among those associated with these ventures, the most notable were probably Robert O'Hara Burke and William John Wills whose expedition in 1860-1 set out to map a possible telegraph route between Melbourne and Darwin, Sadly, their total party of eight, except for one, perished in the desert in the process.

Around the same time, John McDouall Stuart was exploring a possible route between Adelaide and Darwin. In the end it was this route that won the day, with the South Australian government effectively muscling all other contenders out of the race by agreeing to pay the cost of the whole venture—estimated to be £128,000.[54]

The line was built in three sections: from Port Augusta in the south, Darwin in the north, and the third within the Centre. Work began in late 1870. The route ultimately taken by the line was often determined by Aboriginal tracks and waterholes which Stuart had notated.

Logistics for the project were mind-boggling. Workers and supplies were transported into each site from a variety of locations across the country. Conditions were harsh, bordering on atrocious. The maintenance of supplies of both materials for the line and the sustenance of the work crews were punishing, involving innumerable bullocks, horse-drawn wagons, Afghan cameleers (later famously immortalised in the Ghan railway), and ships and boats.

At times the weather, especially in the northern section, threatened to sabotage the whole project. Despite that, the line was completed on 22 August 1872. Construction of the line consumed 36,000 posts (wrought iron and timber), 3,000 kilometres of galvanised telegraph wire, countless insulators, and copious batteries (there being no electricity supply at the time).

The line also required repeater stations. Technology at the time restricted the distance that each message was effective to approximately

300 kilometres. This necessitated the cumbersome task of each message being transmitted, received, transcribed again and then re-sent many times. Altogether 12 such stations were built (including the ones at each end of the line in Adelaide and Darwin). The other ten were at Port Augusta, Beltana, Strangway Springs, Peake, Charlotte Waters, Alice Springs, Barrow Creek, Tennant Creek, Powell Creek, Daly Waters. Many of those names will become familiar to the reader. Each repeater station required a telegraph operator, accommodation, and other facilities for family, other staff, equipment and supplies.

The line was an extraordinary achievement, and Todd's name is worthily celebrated with it through the naming of a river after him, and of a town after his wife, Alice.

When the Hermannsburg missionaries set off on their great trek, the Overland Telegraph Line had been operational for three years. Thus, it was well established, and in a number of ways it played an important role in the establishment and running of the mission.

1. Those who built the line had already paved much of the way that the missionaries would follow. Therefore, the mission personnel were not pioneers moving into land not before trod by white feet and without maps: a significant number of people had gone before them. This does not in any way diminish the enormity of the task they did undertake, nor the ground-breaking moments along the way. But we need to view all that within the context of earlier accomplishments by white people in the Centre.
2. Because of those who had gone before, the missionaries had assurances of regular places of respite and support along the way. Within our letters and reports, we regularly encounter people with whom the missionaries connect and who help them. At times that help is provided by staff at a repeater station. At other times it is by a pastoralist or someone from a station run. Some of these people are station owners or lessees who set up business in the Centre. Yet others of them are workers from the construction of the Overland Telegraph Line who stayed on in the Centre after the work was completed. Some of them gained employment in the maintenance of the line. Others sought work on the stations, or other allied work (e.g. freight or bullock drivers, or in support industries and businesses as settlements and towns slowly developed in the area).
3. The telegraph line became an important means of contact with the rest of the world for the missionaries, both as they journeyed

between Adelaide and the station, and for more urgent messages while at the station. For the latter, of course, they had to travel either to Alice Springs or Charlotte Waters, or get word to either place through someone else. But for the former, the repeater stations were important travel supports along the way.

The Pastoralists

A second major contributor to the growth of Northern-Central Australia were the pastoralists: stock-owners and crop-growers. These had a huge impact on the expansion of white Australia and the decimation of the Aboriginal people. The Whites simply assumed they had a right to the land, and that they could either take it outright or 'procure' it for a pittance. Ultimately, though, the government in each colony claimed ownership of the land and administered the leasing of the land to white settlers. It was under that understanding and arrangement that the Lutheran Church was granted its lease for the mission on the Finke in the first place.

The ownership and management of the properties leased or acquired by pastoralists could become quite complex. In the earlier days of white settlement, squatters and especially illegal squatting were problematic. Gradually, though, the government moved to legislate and regulate the white ownership of land, its sale and use. Consequently, in South Australia, by the time one of the last pieces of such legislation had been enacted—the Strangways Land Act of 1869—all such matters were under government control.

Nevertheless, the pastoral situation remained complicated. There were clashes with Aboriginal people. Some of the pastoral lands were bought by absentee land- or leaseholders down South, and then administered by a manager. Others were bought and then run by the owner. Instances of all of these occur in *Missionaries, Madness and Miracles*, and the reader is referred to the section on *Places* at the end of the book for further information on many of these properties.

As a rule of thumb, by the 1860s pastoralists had established themselves north beyond the Goyder Line as far as the southern edges of Lake Eyre. So, when in 1865 the first lot of Lutheran missionaries began to make their journeys to and from Killalpaninna and to mention places like Beltana, Farina (Government Gums) and Muldowdna, they are referencing areas that had been occupied by pastoralists some ten years before. And when ten years later Kempe, Schwarz and Heidenreich journeyed through here, they were travelling in tracks and calling in on landowners that were, relatively speaking, reasonably established. Heidenreich in particular was familiar with the route and many of the pastoralists and managers, so often had he made that journey.

Beyond that point around the south of Lake Eyre, however, pastoral development was only a short step ahead of the first missionaries to the Finke. And, as mentioned earlier, much of that development was linked with the construction of the Overland Telegraph Line. The line itself attracted certain people who were seeking to buy and develop pastoral lands in the area. In other cases, people who had worked on the line then stayed on after it was completed, also purchasing and developing pastoral lands.

Properties that came into these later categories—all established between 1872 and 1875— included, for example, Strangway Springs, Dalhousie Springs, Peake, Charlotte Waters, Horseshoe Bend, Henbury, Undoolya and Owen Springs (closest neighbours to Ntaria-Hermannsburg missionaries). Again, more detail is available on these, and others, in the section on *Places*.

There was considerable inter-action between the Hermannsburg missionaries and a variety of pastoralists. These connections are well documented throughout the letters and reports that follow. In the majority of cases, those inter-actions were positive. On the first journey, for example, the missionaries often depended on one pastoralist or another for assistance. In fact, there were definitely occasions when the missionaries were saved from the harshness, horror and even death that confronted them in this hostile, untouched desert by the goodness of various pastoralists.

Furthermore, most of the pastoralists were respectful of the missionaries, even if they did think they were misguided and even crazy. They co-operated in the provision of supplies, mail and cartage to the mission. They were friendly and neighbourly, and we read of many examples of this throughout the letters and reports.

On the other hand, there were times when relationships between pastoralist and missionary became strained. There were those pastoralists who regarded the missionaries as pests, a blight on the Central Australian landscape. There were occasions when they refused to support the missionaries. And there were instances when missionaries and pastoralists were bitterly opposed to each other over the treatment of Aboriginal people.

The Currency

The two main currencies referred to in *Missionaries, Madness and Miracles* are the British pound sterling and the German mark. There was no Australian currency at that time, this only being developed well after Federation (1901).

Finances play a prominent role in our story, so much so that the detail given to them can become somewhat boring. Consequently, in the book that detail has been reduced to a certain extent. However, it is fully retained in *The Translation*.

For some readers, one of the tantalising questions about the currency is its value in comparison to present-day currency. This is not an easy matter to settle, as different sources provide different information. Also, over the 19 years covered in this book, the value of any currency changed from the beginning of that period to the end, thus making it impossible to give any single figure that covers the whole period. Nevertheless, readers interested in this kind of detail will find it helpful to have at least some ballpark figures around the amounts of money mentioned.

An *ad hoc*, informal group think tank from among economically-qualified people within my own acquaintances estimated that UK£100 in 1875 equates to around UK£10,000 in 2024, which equates to around AU$20,000. Using that information as a base line, it is possible to calculate the broad equivalents of other amounts given in British pounds.

The group found the Deutschmark more difficult to ascertain, because of various complications within the German system (e.g. periods of hyperinflation, periods of fixed or floating exchange rates, and the transition to Euro currency). However, they submitted the suggestion that all German DM amounts be converted to their 1875 UK£ equivalent. That is, UK£1= DM20.45. Thus, DM100=UK£5 in 1875, which in 2024 equates to UK£500, which is AU$1,000.[55]

Another resource is the National Archives (UK) Currency Converter which can be found on-line at https://www.nationalarchives.gov.uk/currency-converter/ This one, though, is somewhat restricted, showing the purchasing power of the currency. Thus, for example, in 1880, according to this site, £100 could purchase three horses, or 10 cows, or 200 kilograms of wool, or pay the wages of a skilled tradesman for 300 days.

Finally, a couple of sites that have developed simple tools for making currency (and other) conversions. One by a certain Thom Blake at https://www.thomblake.com.au/secondary/hisdata/calculate.php

According to this site, for example, UK£100 in 1880 is worth AU$19,500 in 2024.

And another tool by Professor Rodney Edvinsson of Stockholm University, at https://www.historicalstatistics.org/Currencyconverter.html This one is somewhat more complicated, and readers are invited to play around with it!

So, as can be seen, reliable currency equivalencies are difficult to ascertain. Nevertheless, as stated earlier in this section, this information at least provides resources to shed a degree of light on the world of currency around the time of the beginnings of Ntaria-Hermannsburg.

Source Material and Abbreviations

Almost all of the translated material in *Missionaries, Madness and Miracles* has been accessed from three main sources, two of them being Church papers.

The first of these is the **Hermannburger Missionsblatt** *(The Hermannsburg Mission Journal)*. This monthly publication was established by Ludwig Harms in 1854 in the interests of the Hermannsburg Mission Institute and the Hermannsburg Lutheran congregations. Its purposes were to impart information and instruction to its readers, as well as to foster a sense of unity between them.

The second source for our primary material is **der Lutherische Kirchenbote für Australien** *(The Australian Lutheran Church Journal)*. The first edition of this ELSA church paper appeared in 1873. Prior to that, the two Lutheran Synods (i.e. the ELSA and Immanuel) had made a number of attempts to produce a joint publication for the distribution of church news and opinion among their members. However, none of these productions was remarkably successful, and so the decision was made by each synod to produce its own publication.

The first *Kirchenbote* editors were Pastors Ernst Homann and Adolph Strempel. The paper was published monthly. An account of its early struggles—including the problem of slow or non-paying subscribers—may be found in Joyce Graetz's *An open book*.[1]

Pastor Oster replaced Homann as editor in 1878, and in 1880 Pastors R Ey and G Bertram took over the editorship. Printing was done in Adelaide.

By 1883 the paper had become unviable and was discontinued for a short time. However, by the end of the year it had found a new home in Hochkirch (Tarrington), Victoria, and a new publisher, Oscar Müller. Pastors C W Schürmann of Hochkirch and W Peters of Murtoa were appointed editors. When Schürmann died suddenly in 1893, he was replaced as editor by Pastor E Darsow.

The third major repository of primary source material are the **original, handwritten reports** of the authors of the letters and reports in *Missionaries, Madness and Miracles*. These materials are stored in the archives in

Hermannsburg, Germany. A microfiche copy of them is available in the Australian Lutheran Archives in Adelaide, a gift from Hermannsburg, Germany, to the Lutheran Church in Australia. Almost all of these materials had never before been published or translated into English.

Within this publication, the following are the abbreviations used in connection with these source materials:

Rev	Revised
Transc	Transcribed
Tr	Translated
CJP	Carl Julius Pfizner
DAP	Dorothea A Prenzler
MA	Max Altmann
RJK	Robert John Kempe
VCP	Victor Carl Pfitzner
ELSA	Evangelical Lutheran Synod of Australia (formerly ELSSA, the Evangelical Lutheran Synod of South Australia)
HMS	Hermannsburg Mission Society [Germany]

Readers may note an occasional inconsistency in the referencing of numerals in the text. This is mostly due to the fact that we have retained the designations given in the original texts for these numbers. Some times the fault may well be ours.

Source Material and Abbreviations 51

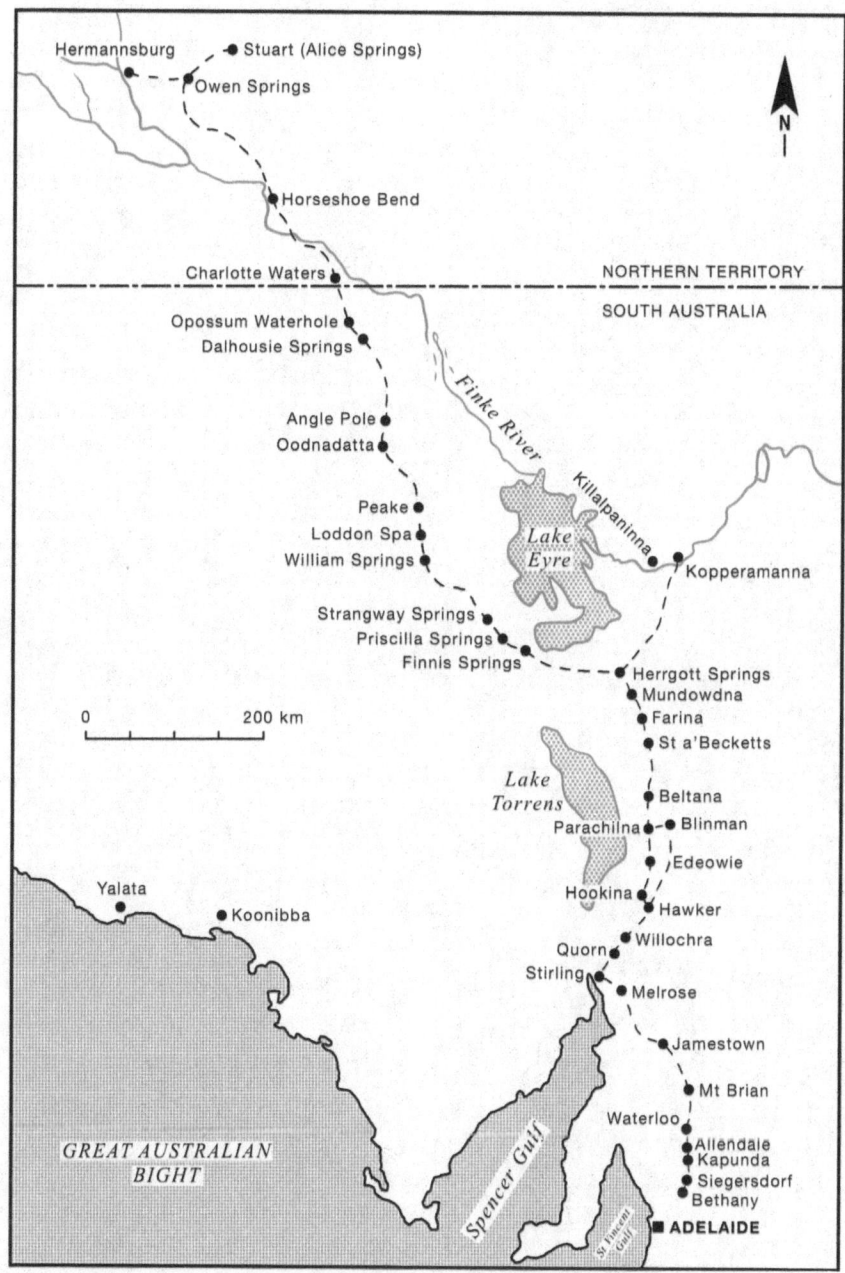

Map of route taken by first missionaries between Adelaide and Ntaria [James Geue, modified]

1.

Arrivals and Commissionings

Missionaries, Madness and Miracles is an epic tale. Two young men in the prime of their lives—herding 3000 sheep, several hundred horses, cows, bullocks, dogs, hens and a rooster, accompanied by their helpers and, at times, a superintendent—travel something like 2000 kilometres into the heart of Australia by foot, horse and wagon through what is mostly desert, all to establish a mission station in the Centre. They take 20 months to complete the journey, and along the way battle dust, floods, drought, thirst and death. They have never before been out of their home country of Germany and are complete strangers in a totally alien land. Their plan is to use their new station as a base for mission work to the local Arrarnta people, but also as a place where the Aboriginal people might work, earn a living, and become a part of the new Australian society that is gradually engulfing them. How foolish they were! Yet, what a great tale!

When Kempe and Schwarz stepped out of the gates of the Hermannsburg Mission Society House in Germany for the last time, they surely could have had no real idea of what they had let themselves in for, despite their fine education and training for mission. One cannot help wondering how they were feeling. No doubt, excited, pumped by the prospect of the adventure before them. Filled with faith and fervour, and therefore confident that God would bring them success. But surely also at least a little apprehensive, and maybe even afraid. Sad to be leaving home and loved ones.

The reports in *Missionaries, Madness and Miracles* are factual, but sometimes almost dull, statements of the realities of life for the people involved in this tale. There is a good and healthy objectivity about them. Nonetheless, both between the lines but also screaming within the lines, there is a great passion as well. Those engaged in this drama are really just ordinary human beings, like any of us, and, like us, they hurt and cry and struggle and laugh and bleed.

* * *

30 September 1875, Bethany[1] *(Kempe to Th Harms)*

'My soul is still before the Lord who helps me.' PSALM 62:1

Dear Pastor!

I wish we could really do what this text says. I wish we could be really still before God, for that is what we need. The future lies darkly before us; we do not know what we will encounter on the journey into the interior of Australia that is soon before us. From everything I have heard, I only know that all kinds of lack and deprivation await us. But I entrust myself to the gracious care of our God. He has helped us so far. He will help us further. We have indeed been permitted to experience his help, his grace and faithfulness in rich measure on our trip, and we have cause only to praise and thank him.

As you know, we left Hermannsburg on 21 July and already on the Thursday boarded the *Wega* that was to carry us to England. After two days of pleasant travel, we reached London where, already on the Sunday, we were picked up by the dear Behns and driven on a carriage through the city to the fairly distant Hammia Villa, the home of the dear Behn family. The entire, large city lay in deep silence, and people looked at us amazed to see us driving through the city on a Sunday. Finally, a difference between here and any other city in Germany when the peak of activity is precisely on Sundays. We were shown wonderful hospitality that made us forget the deprivation soon to be experienced on the ship at sea.

At midday on 28 July we travelled to Southampton in the company of G Behn who brought all our belongings in good order. On 29 July we put to sea. My brothers were soon badly affected by sea sickness, especially Brother Bode who could not get over it and is still quite weak. Otherwise, it was pleasant on the ship. The food was excellent, and no one prevented us in any way from conducting our devotions and our Sunday services in the cabin that, at our request, our fellow travellers were happy to vacate.

On 3 August we entered Gibraltar Harbour where we had the opportunity to view the famous Pillars of Hercules which I had imagined as being much more impressive. From there we entered the Mediterranean Sea and then passed through the Suez Canal into the Red Sea. On the trip we put in at Malta, Port Said, Ismael (situated on the Bitter Lakes) and Suez, all of which I will not describe here, since Brother Baunothe[2] has previously done that. There is nothing special to report on the trip through the Red Sea since it was night when we passed the most important site, the Sinai Peninsula, and thus could see nothing. It was very hot, so most passengers camped on the deck at night, including myself.

By God's grace, on 18 August we passed without tears the Gate of Tears, or Bab el Mandab, and arrived safely at Aden. This does not look at all like an Eden; there is nothing to be seen but bare rock, no trees or shrubs or green blades of grass, with terrible heat. Going ashore we were surrounded by swarms of beggars, large and small, Jews, traders and the like, offering us their ostrich feathers.

The ship sailed off again that night, and I was happy that we were again on the open sea, since Aden was so hot. We then travelled through the Arabian Sea, and every day I looked forward to seeing the highly praised island of Ceylon where we could hope to eventually have a day of rest.

On 26 August, very early, we could glimpse the coast of Ceylon, so we hurried to get our possessions in order because we had to board another ship in Ceylon. The *Bokhara*, on which we had travelled to this point, was booked to sail to Calcutta. At 9:00 in the morning we sailed into Point de Galle Harbour, and soon there was a veritable annual market on board. All sorts of wares were set out for sale: precious stones, rings, ivory, ebony objects and the like. We gathered our seven purchases together and, as fast as we could, transferred them on board the Nubia that was due to sail to Australia. Brother Wiese and I went ashore, while Brothers Schwarz and Bode stayed behind because of sickness. We caught up with the former in the afternoon and went on a small tour of the island, to the so called Cinnamet Gardens[3] where we had the chance to see the magnificence of a tropical forest. Here the Lord God seemed to have a veritable storehouse. Trees everywhere: coconut palms, banana, cinnamon, nutmeg and breadfruit trees were growing together in profusion.

In the evening we also visited the marketplace in Port de Galle and were not a little amazed at the colourful throngs of people of various colours and languages. It was rather late and time to get on board, which we then did.

Next day the ship set off and we made good progress since we had a favourable wind. We had many new passengers on board and tried to make ourselves known to them. We were happy to find a German-speaking man. He was a senior Catholic priest, rather, a bishop, by the name of Bugnion, born in Switzerland, but now at sea for no less than the sixtieth time. He was a dear, devout man, with whom we often conversed, though we could not agree with him on matters of religion because he had some quite strange views.

Another Roman Catholic priest was also on board. He urged me to join him in going to Schiffer-Inseln[4] to preach the gospel to the godless Germans there, an urgent task. I granted him that this was so but told him it was not in my power to decide.

Our journey proceeded well and quickly. Already on 11 September we could see land and entered the Albany harbour, called King George Sound, at about 8 o'clock. Together with Brother Wiese and Mr Bugnion, it did not take long to go on shore in Australia for the first time.

With a prayer for God's guidance, we set foot on our new homeland, though it did not appear very inviting. Wherever one looked there was nothing but bush, low shrubs and scree. Only in the village of Albany itself had the inhabitants, with a lot of effort, laid out some beautiful gardens. But lunch tasted quite good, for it was again something German that we could enjoy. In the afternoon we climbed a fairly high hill, but even there we overlooked nothing but desolate stretches.

On 12 September, a Sunday, the last on the ship, we again sailed off and were very happy to see the town of Glenelg before us on Thursday morning, 16 September. We quickly packed our things together and went ashore, where we first had a coffee and then, with the help of an Englishman travelling with us, got our things toll-free through customs, and went by train to Adelaide. Here Brother Homann[5] kindly met us at the railway station and received us into his home.

The brothers had not been expecting us. When Brother Homann received our telegram from Glenelg, he thought we were some other brothers.

Great now was our joy, and we were glad that the faithful God had brought us safe and sound to our destination after such a brief and felicitous voyage. To him be praise and thanks for that! He has brought us so far and will help us further.

Next day Brother Heidenreich came to fetch us, but nothing further happened that day because he first introduced us to the English Minister and Protector of Aborigines and presented his petition for rations for the Blacks, all of which was granted.

You will have also seen from Brother Heidenreich's letters that we have received 900 square miles instead of 200 for our mission. That made me glad. However, I believe that if the mission is to be a success, we must work hard to obtain a loan because the journey will cost a lot. As I heard and saw at the general assembly of the mission community that took place yesterday evening, one cannot hope for much help from the local congregations. However, I think that if the soil is to some degree good there, and especially if good water is available, as Mr Gosse assured us when we were with him on Monday the 27th, the station will later not cost much.

We have already sought to become familiar with the language.[6] I have found that it is not at all easy, especially because of its great lack of concepts. Yet I do not want to trouble myself with that at the moment. With the Lord's help we will get over that problem; everything depends on his blessing.

The first difficulty we face is the long, arduous journey that will soon take place and will probably take 19[7] weeks. In due course I will report how things go.

We want to place ourselves in God's hands and trust in his grace. May he bless our going out and coming in and give us truly firm and lively faith so that we learn to be quiet in God who helps us. Pray faithfully for us ...

H Kempe

* * *

Even as Kempe and Schwarz are getting underway on their journey in Australia, Theodor Harms, through the pages of the *Hermannsburger Missionsblatt*, is reporting on their progress to church members back in Germany. In this next letter, he feeds back information from Heidenreich to the Hermannsburg community and, at the same time, recaps something of the transition from the mission at Killalpaninna to the mission on the Finke.

In this report Harms also makes a point of the fact that Heidenreich is accompanying the missionaries on the trek. This immediately raises the issue of the exact nature of Heidenreich's brief for the journey itself and, indeed, his assigned role in the actual establishment of the station. It seems that, even before Kempe and Schwarz arrive, there has been consultation between Harms and Heidenreich which resulted in Heidenreich deciding that he, too, will journey to the Centre on this trip. Already in August, a month prior to the arrival of Kempe and Schwarz,[8] the Bethany congregation had

> ... declared as being in accord with P(astor) Heidenreich, that he as director of the missionaries ... should accompany them on their journey ... and that during his absence one of the itinerant preachers ... should take his place for the temporary carrying out of the local office of preacher.[9]

Again, the report indicates that the initiative for this decision originated with Heidenreich, and was then endorsed by the congregation.

One cannot help wondering why this decision was made, why it was made at that time, and why it was made without any consultation with the missionaries themselves.

Of course, there were sound practical reasons for others with more experience of the Australian conditions to accompany these young German novices on this daunting mission. There is no disputing the fact that Heidenreich did solve many a problem for them, as future reports demonstrate. Nevertheless, and as future reports also demonstrate, Heidenreich's personal involvement in the trek and the establishment of the station seem often to be something he desired for himself. His presence was not always conducive to happy experiences or harmonious, healthy relationships, and was therefore a debatable, and debated, decision. It is telling that when reflecting on this matter in his later autobiography, Kempe comments that only a day after their ship landed in Adelaide, Heidenreich

> ... picked us up ... and informed us—that is, Schwarz and myself—that we were to commence the trip to the Finke as soon as possible, that he himself—alas!—was to be the leader of the party, and that he wanted to be back again in his congregation by Christmas.[10]

Kempe wanted to delay the journey to a more propitious time of year and to provide more time for preparation. However, he says,

> ... in spite of every—yes, every—effort at dissuasion on the part of those who knew something about travelling conditions in the Interior, the good Superintendent insisted on having his own way, so that a start was made with the journey from Bethany on October 21.[11]

*   *   *

4 October 1875, Hermannsburg, Germany; Bethany[12] *(Th Harms, Heidenreich)*
'My soul extols the Lord, and my spirit rejoices in God my Saviour; for he has done great things for me, he who is mighty and whose name is holy. Amen.'

With these words Brother Heidenreich begins his report of 4 October, just as he is about to set out with the brothers, Missionaries Kempe and Schwarz, to take possession of the territory assigned to our mission by the English government in the interior of Australia and to found a mission station. Brothers Homann and Schoknecht had declared that it was impossible to continue the mission at Killalpaninna and had returned to the Colony, with my permission. Homann had become the pastor in Adelaide and Schoknecht in Horsham, serving in the Lutheran congregations there until I might call them to missionary service among the heathen. They left because the lack of water in those sandy deserts made life impossible for the missionaries and the stock, and so we gave up the mission station at Killalpaninna.

A section of mission supporters in Australia believed another attempt ought to be made to keep the mission at Killalpaninna. A debate between them and us thus became necessary.

The loyal Brother Drögemüller—may the Lord bless him for his great love and faithfulness—attended to the peaceful and amicable division of the mission property. We were left with 33 horses, 17 head of cattle, 50 goats, 3100 sheep, a wagon, 10 sets of harnesses, 2 riding saddles and a pack saddle, and some further things to the value of some £20.

We had now given up the mission at Killalpaninna, but had not given up mission as such in Australia. The Lord must compel people to undertake mission, but also to give it up. The Centre of Australia has been opened up and thus the path to mission among the poor heathen has been made clear. If we Hermannsburgers are here, according to God's will, to be pioneers and to open up the fields, we will, speaking with Father Luther, be totally content to do so. We place the results in God's hands. A true supporter of mission does not pay homage to success but is a faithful servant to his Lord who leads his people in wondrous ways, but always with blessing. It is quite possible that this undertaking of ours will not be successful in the way we want, but in no way will it be in vain, since it is begun in the name of the Lord Jesus.

Brother Heidenreich, pastor at Bethany near Adelaide, has taken on the management of the local mission and has set off for Central Australia with the Brothers Kempe and Schwarz, leaving Brother Bode as the pastor in charge at Bethany until he returns. He writes:

'Several days ago I received from the Minister of Lands, Boucaut, an answer to my petition. The Australian parliament has given to us as a grant 900 English square miles on the Finke, MacDonnell Ranges, for all such time until we or our missionaries have totally abandoned this place for two years and it is thereby to be regarded as surrendered. May the Lord graciously prevent that and preserve the place as a sanctuary in their homeland for the heathen who become Christians.

Since the Minister has given us no information about the usual rations for the heathen, and I had earlier promised to introduce our missionaries to him,

I immediately made arrangements that we might pay our respects to him on the same day. I thanked him sincerely for the gift of the 900 square miles for the Mission, but also asked him at the same time not to give away any of the 2000 square miles I had asked for until I had been on the place myself and examined everything in detail ...

I then asked him immediately if he was willing to grant the usual rations for the heathen. The dear man then replied: "They will get all that I can give them." He then addressed Brothers Kempe and Schwarz in a very cordial manner, and when the conversation was finished to his satisfaction, we said our farewells, highly delighted. May the Lord bless the Minister with his grace.

We then went to the Protector of Aborigines, informed him of the promises made by the Minister for Lands and of our intentions to declare the gospel to the heathen, and requested his help. This gentleman also received us in a friendly manner and directed us to make an application in written form. He will do his best for us.

We thank God that our queen, Victoria, has such ministers and advisers that assist God's kingdom in such a commendable way, like the Minister for Lands Boucaut, the Surveyor General Lendes, the Protector, many important men in parliament and our advocate, Mr Angas. The Minister for Lands has stated in an open session of parliament that he would double the 900 square miles as soon as it was necessary and appropriate for the heathen and the government.

So, we should not be sorry that we have given up our old station at Killalpaninna, as is clear from a conversation which our loyal representative Drögemüller had with Pastor Rechner on the spot. Drögemüller said: "Pastor Homannn has given us a completely accurate picture of this sad station". Pastor Rechner replied: "He should have told the Committee and the General Assembly that he would not go onto the station unless Commission members were sent with him". Drögemüller: "Homann often and at length said that at the General Assembly at Rowland Flat, but people did not believe him". Rechner: "Yes, yes, that is true, and the place is now of little value as a sheep station". Drögemüller: "I believe that is why Director Harms could no longer be confident about the previous mission, because people did not have confidence in his missionaries". May the Lord bless the new beginning in Central Australia.

At the Feast of St Michael we had our annual mission festival in Rowland Flat. Brother Strempel preached the main sermon. It was replete with divine truth and a clear message for blessed mission work from all points of view. It was a wonderful testimony.

Then our Brothers Kempe and Schwarz preached, to the comfort and joy of all God's children and in defiance of the devil and to annoy and slander him. They spoke on the basis of their texts used when they were commissioned in Hermannsburg. The entire service was rich in blessing.

In the afternoon I announced to the assembly: "After receiving from Director Harms the office of leader of the mission, I herewith assume it before God with all his duties and rights, as they are contained in the Director's letter to Pastor Oster of 15 October 1874". I promised faithfully to carry out my duties for the Church in mission, to the extent that the Lord God will give strength and grace in my weakness.

Then I outlined the steps recently taken to continue our mission, and then accepted the assistance of Brothers Ahrens, Drögemüller and Schmidt as lay members of the Advisory Council, for which may God be praised, honoured and thanked. The spiritual advisor has not yet been determined. However, if the faithful Lord provides our honoured Senior Hensel with physical strength, he will take on the office, to my comfort and joy and certainly to the mission's blessing...

Preparations for the journey to the new station on the Finke in the MacDonnell Ranges cannot be put off due to the present lack of finance. I have to buy a stallion, a year's provisions for seven or eight men, tools, a pair of bellows for the smithy, compasses, and many other things necessary to protect lives and possessions. Then comes the establishment of the station itself. Thus, I can do no other than ask you to send 500 pounds sterling. We will in future have a significant asset if you could send us Christian, single men as fellow workers on the mission. Their sea-fare here would be free, and I would send their permits as soon as I knew that you had the workers to send to us.

With God's help the commissioning of our missionaries will be on 20 October in Hahndorf, and in the same week they will begin their journey into the Centre. I will accompany the young Brothers Kempe and Schwarz to inspect the place where we have to establish the station. But the Lord is travelling with us; I fully trust him and am directing everything so that his name is honoured through us. Brother Bode will meanwhile take my place in my congregation that has willingly granted me permission to travel...
Heidenreich'

*   *   *

Prior to the departure of the mission party, there was a great deal of preparation for the journey. A wagon, horses and supplies needed to be put together. The ecclesiastical necessities had to be attended to. Arrangements had been put in place for the gathering of the livestock from the 'old station'.

In the research into material *Missionaries, Madness and Miracles* we found no extant letter or report that provided insight into what was involved in the provisioning of a venture like this. However, in his later major report (see Chapter 15), Kempe does provide such a description, and it is fitting—both for continuity of the story and purely for interest—to extrapolate that part of the report from there to here.

* * *

[From the report of March 1880][13] *(Kempe to Th Harms)*
Much care has to be exercised in preparing for such a journey, lest something of vital importance be overlooked. A six to nine months' supply of flour, tea and sugar is essential, but of meat only as much should be taken as will last until fresh meat can be obtained at a cattle station. Cooking utensils must be taken: a kettle for boiling the billy, a three-legged cast iron cooker with lid, known as a camp oven, for frying, cooking and baking, a water bucket, drinking utensils, knives and forks, articles of clothing and soap for washing, combs, horse-shoes and nails along with a hammer, pincers and rasp for shoeing the riding and wagon horses; furthermore saddlery equipment and leather for possible necessary repairs to the harness, also needles and thread for repairs to clothes. And it is wise to take along some medicine. Smokers must think of tobacco, pipes and matches. Those who can afford it will take along some dried fruit, potatoes and vegetables, in order to provide the stomach a change of diet should sickness intervene. It will be evident, that when all these things are loaded onto a wagon there is not much room left for anything else. The usual weight is two to three tons, a ton weighing a hundredweight.[14]

When all is ready the journey may begin, but 'always at a slow pace', for in this country the advice of Eulenspiegel[15] is very much in place: he who travels slowly will reach the goal first. Usually one travels from 10 to 15 English miles a day, but when good water and pasture are found, the draught horses or bullocks are given one or more days rest so that the average miles per day amounts to 6 to 8 English miles. Many a one may think: Surely that is very little; the animals can easily endure that! But please note that the animals do not get grain or hay as in Germany, but only grass, which they have to seek for themselves, and the horses are hobbled by a short chain which is fastened by two strong leather straps to their two front legs, to prevent them from running away. And then it happens that very little and very poor grass is to be found, and the situation can become so gloomy that one has to marvel that the animals can survive at all. For example, on our first trip inland the position was so serious that the horses nibbled the wood off the bushes. Even when the trip is made in good times, the bleaching carcasses of draught animals and riding horses lying in the hot sun provide ample testimony that much worse conditions have obtained at some other time.

When a day's journey has been completed, camp is struck, usually a place where water is available, but not always. In the latter instance it is necessary to carry water for human needs. This water is carried in casks or in a sack made of sailcloth. The first task is to unharness the draught horses or bullocks or the riding horses, to take them to water and to hobble them and let them go, sometimes driving them to a place where the best pasture is found. Then wood has to be gathered for a fire over which the billy water is boiled for tea, after which the meal may begin, for meat is seldom cooked or fried right there and then, but salted meat has been cooked in advance to last for several meals, and this is eaten cold with bread.

And now we can hop into bed, can we not? Oh no; we are not yet ready for that. First of all, meat has to be cooked for the following day and bread has to be baked, the so-called damper[16] which is prepared in the following manner: Dough is stirred in a basin, or in the absence of one, on the pocket of a pack-saddle, when travelling with horses, or on a saddle cloth, in a mixture as stiff as possible. This dough is then laid into hot ashes and completely covered by them. If the ground and the ashes are hot enough, the damper is fully baked in an hour. Even so, this is only an emergency operation.

When time permits, bread is preferably baked in an iron pot. Only when these things have been attended to, and no repairs to harness or clothing are necessary, may one retire for the night. A place near the wagon reasonably free of stones and bushes is sought out. Then the bed-clothes are spread and the sleeper takes his rest. A bundle of clothes, or a saddle, or a few twigs take the place of a pillow. In summer nights the heat can be most unpleasant, but a greater nuisance are the mosquitoes which often permit no sleep whatever. The only way to combat them is to lie under a net well-spread, or to have cattle dung smouldering nearby, which while spreading a rather evil odour is still preferable to the stings of the mosquitoes

When morning has come the draught animals have to be located and gathered. This is usually the task of one or two of the Aboriginal people, who are specially suited to this task, because they have excellent sight and are more experienced in detecting the tracks of animals and following them than we Europeans.[17] In the meantime breakfast is prepared, and when this has been consumed, everything is again packed away. If there are draught animals, they are immediately harnessed and the journey continues. Not infrequently the draught animals wander far away, which calls for patient waiting until they are returned.

Because only a few wild animals are found in these parts, the enjoyment of a hunt comes but seldom. A dish of wild ducks or pigeons is about all that can be gained.

There is little change in such travels from day to day. What could cause a change? At best a strong shower of rain. This, indeed, does bring about a change, for apart from the routine tasks the wagon has to be covered with a large sail-cloth, here known as a tarpaulin, which every driver must of necessity take along with him. And the individual traveller will try to shelter in a tent that is set up or seek some other way of keeping dry.

It will be realised that such a journey is exceedingly monotonous, and anybody who might consider it a great adventure could be very much disenchanted. One is truly joyful when the yearned-for destination is finally reached.

* * *

On 20 October 1875, the missionaries were commissioned and farewelled during a special worship service in Hahndorf. Kempe and Schwarz were not ordained during this service: that event had already taken place in Hermannsburg, Germany, before they departed their homeland.

The introductory paragraph in this next report captures something of the parochial theological mindset of those early Lutherans. 'Neuendettelsau' and 'Iowa' refer to a Lutheran community and Synod in Germany and the USA respectively; 'Schwärmerei' is any person or group of a dodgy, wishy-washy theological bent.

20 October 1875, Hahndorf[18] (Kirchenbote *editor*)

Ordination and Commissioning

Dear *Kirchenbote*![19]

I hope you will not take it amiss if an old friend asks you to carry the following report with you on your next errand. I want to tell you about a happy event: the ordination of pastoral candidate Heinrich Wiese, and the commissioning of the two missionaries Hermann Kempe and Wilhelm Schwarz. Both are proof that the Lord of the church still looks upon us with grace, and that our dear Evangelical Lutheran Synod in South Australia has no need to contemplate its extinction. If we simply remain true to our Confessions, the Lord will also acknowledge us. Let us guard against the inventions of the Neuendettelsau and Iowa people, which can break through the solid wall of our Confessions and create all kinds of back doors through which every possible Schwärmerei and error can slip in. For then the Lord will remain true to us, despite all the shouting of our opponents, as if we were on the path to dead orthodoxy, indeed, even to Rome.

But now to my task!

This time it was St Michaels Church, Hahndorf, in which, on 20 October, the double celebration described earlier took place. In front of the altar, especially adorned with garlands, sat the ordination candidate Wiese, who had passed a theological exam on the preceding day, and to his right and left sat the Hermannsburg missionaries, already ordained in Hanover. The ordination of the former[20] had not taken place, because the Hanover Church Council, according to ecclesiastical order, does not ordain pastors[21] for foreign countries.

Present from those professionally qualified were the Pastors Hensel, Strempel, Oster, Homann and Ey, and Bode, the pastor designated for Victoria. Pastor Appelt was prevented from taking part since his invitation reached him too late. The festive service began with the hymn: 'Come, Holy Spirit, Lord God', whereupon the local pastor, Strempel, took the liturgy at the altar and read Psalm 100. Then the first four verses of hymn 1920 were sung, and the hearts of all worshippers were certainly united in prayer for the ordinand as the words rang out: 'I fold my hands, and may my beginning, middle and end, my Jesus, be truly blessed!'

During the singing of the last four verses of the hymn, Pastor Oster had approached the altar, and he gave the ordination address in a moving voice. Proceeding from the psalm text, 'A day in your courts is better than a thousand, etc', the preacher developed the thought that this text suited all festivals of the Lord, but especially the present one in which a brother was to receive consecration for the holy office and two missionaries commissioned for service among the poor heathen of this land. Then, turning to the ordinand, he preached on the glorious and very fitting verse, Jeremiah 15:19: 'Therefore, thus says the Lord: Where you stand by me, I will stand by you, and you shall remain my preacher. And where you teach the upright rather than the evil, there you are my teacher. And rather than you submit to them, they submit to you.' The theme was: The threefold demand and promise of the Lord to the servants of his Word: 1) with reference to the dignity of the office; 2) with reference to the teaching and 3) with respect to its defence.

After the singing of the five following verses of the main hymn, Pastor Oster, assisted by Pastors Hensel and Strempel, conducted the solemn rite of ordination according to the Lutheran agenda of the Missouri Synod. Candidate Wiese knelt at the altar and pledged himself ready to do the work of God and to be faithful to all the confessional books of the Lutheran Church. With the laying on of hands by the three ordaining pastors, he was consecrated for service in the Lutheran Church, and together with hearty exhortations and words of comfort was extended the following greetings: Pastor Hensel: Isaiah 41:10, 'Fear not, I am with you; do not waver, for I am your God. I strengthen you, and I help you; I uphold you with the right hand of my righteousness.' Pastor Strempel: 1 Chronicles 29:20,[22] 'Be strong and courageous, and do the work. Do not be afraid or discouraged. God, the Lord, my God, will be with you, and will not withdraw his hand. He will not forsake you, until you have completed all the work for the service in the house of God.' Pastor Oster: Revelation 2:10, 'Be faithful until death, and I will give you the crown of life.'

With that, this uplifting rite was concluded, and may the Lord richly fulfil for the dear brother the promises contained in these words of God, and may he recall them for his comfort when he learns, from his own experience, the burden of his office.

After the singing of verses 10 to 12 of the main hymn, the second rite was conducted, led by Pastor Heidenreich. At the altar he preached the commissioning sermon, based on John 14:6, 'I am the way, the truth and the life; no one comes to the Father except through me.' In the introduction the speaker noted that both missionaries present had already been commissioned in the German fatherland, but he considered another rite necessary to bind them closely to our local Church and Synod. At the conclusion he directed this thought to both men being commissioned in the form of a question, to which they responded with a loud 'Yes'. Kneeling down, they were blessed after the Lord's Prayer had been loudly prayed over them.

May the Lord now be with them, protect them on their dangerous journey, and bless their activity. That prayer was directed to the Lord also in the closing hymn, No 1235, 'May God be gracious to us, and grant us his blessing.'

After the first two verses were sung, Pastor Strempel conducted the closing liturgy, and then during the third verse the festive congregation gave their thanksgiving offering for the blessing received. The pastors and missionaries present united in the communal joy of receiving the Lord's Supper, and for everyone that was surely an experience to revive the heart...

A festival participant.

2.

The Journey: Bethany to Hergott Springs

The journey begins. Kempe, Schwarz and Hübbe, their driver, get their laden wagon underway. The wagon was probably drawn by four horses, several spare horses tagging alongside. As they move off, Heidenreich provides Harms with an insight into his own busy preparations. He darts from place to place, mind and energy devoted to the mountain of concerns that confront him: tidying up his parish pastoral business, arranging for someone to stand in as Bethany pastor while he is away, concerned about the quality of those he has to work with, attending to pastoral supply issues in both New Zealand and Australia, sorting out finances, finalising necessities for the journey.

Yet again there is the question of the need for him to be going, the need for him to be so in charge. Were the missionaries and their helpers as inept as Heidenreich at times makes them appear? Or perhaps the expedition was put together under pressure, so that matters became too messy for the missionary party to resolve by themselves, and as a result Heidenreich felt compelled to become more involved than even he had originally intended. At the same time, there are indicators that Heidenreich may have found it difficult to delegate, despite the facts that the missionaries were more competent than he gave them credit, and that there were qualified and competent lay helpers available to assist, but not called upon to do so.

It is noteworthy that in this next letter Heidenreich concedes mistakes were made in setting up the party. At times there is a sense of haste in the way they went about their preparations, with a consequential smattering of chaos as the journey commences. Not a good feel so early in the venture.

* * *

*4 November, 1875, **Ragless' Hut**[1] (Heidenreich to Th Harms)*
Venerable and much-loved Father!
 Delivered out of great troubles with the Lord's help, I have now arrived at much greater ones. Yet I hope that, when the Lord has rescued me from

six afflictions, evil will no longer touch me in the seventh. Therefore, I am concerned only with doing the will of him who is so merciful. May he still my heart so that it does not forget that, in joy and grief, it moves in, out of, and by means of mercy.²

Brother Wiese will himself have written that he has been examined and ordained. For the time being he is standing in for dear S Hensel who is doing more study, especially in dogmatics, where his results were poor. I have greatly regretted that he wrote down a lot but had little in his head.

It is a pity that current students are not taught to familiarise themselves with the brief and nicely formulated summary of *Schmidt's Dogmatics*, which is complete enough for our present circumstances. The treasured content is retained, as I know from experience. In addition, most students do not have the kind of gifts that our dear Kempe has. It is thereby not my intention in any way to find fault with the industry and faithfulness of our dear, precious Inspector,³ but to honestly say what is necessary and useful here.

Until I return, Brother Bode is to act in my place as pastor, with the approval of the Church Council and the acceptance of my congregation. Then he goes to Schoknecht, into the congregations that had sent a call to you.⁴

These church matters proceeded with many a difficulty, but very peacefully. Only, it is a pity that two more pastors were not immediately available. As I wrote to you, one will perhaps have to come from New Zealand, or Gössling should stay in Albury until you send another deputy. I also do not know where I am to find his travel fare at this time, since I have already borrowed £300 to equip the mission here …

After our missionaries were commissioned on 20 October, they set out on the Friday from Bethany, fully equipped with provisions and other things. Already on Saturday an injured brother from one congregation came back; his task was to handle a young stallion for a stretch but he said that as a draught horse it was of no use to anyone; it had struck him and one of the missionaries. I was coming from hearing confession, and next day had the installation of Bode's assistant, the reception of an English woman into the congregation, and confirmation of 26 children, as well as the distribution of Holy Communion to 200 communicants. When I got home, sad news awaited me. Our missionaries were said to be going from one hotel to the other and arguing with people on the street. I said, 'Those are despicable lies.' However, when I had got together my entire Church Council, I was unanimously advised to follow the missionaries as soon as possible, to buy a new horse, and set off.⁵

Fortunately, Pastor Rechner⁶ arrived to discuss with me the parcelling out [of funds]. He pointed out to me the difficulties involved in any immediate and total distribution and offered to pay £300 into my mission account until he was able to settle everything else. I accepted this offer because it was sensible. Therewith the last remaining problem with my trip was removed.

I went to my dear, precious Anna and told her I would be going away early next morning. She got a shock but acquiesced. Next morning she took me to the closest train station. Oh, the parting from this precious and faithful soul was difficult for me. May the Lord grant us a happy reunion on earth, or in heaven.

I then hurried to Carlsruhe where the missionaries were just arriving. They complained to me about their woes, and I complained to them about mine. To my joy I ascertained that the evil rumours were baseless, purchased a new horse next day, and sent the bad one back to its original owner. Thus, it was in good spirits that we travelled on from Carlsruhe on Wednesday. I remained with the missionaries for two days, with the horses going well.

Then I went to Port Augusta with the mail coach, where the other wagon and eight horses were.[7] I there had to pay some large accounts: 65 pounds to Schmidt and the wagonmaker, 18 pounds to the saddler and 12 pounds at the hotel for feed and for putting up the worker and a heathen from the old station,[8] quite apart from the serious bill I had to pay for my own hotel stay. Pulling a face did not help, so I paid and energetically loaded up and drove away. It was on the third day that I succeeded in travelling on with this wagon.

The journey through the hills from the sea to here is terrible. When I reached the hills I vividly recalled my native hills in Thuringia with the proud Wartburg, because one hill towered up similarly like a cone, only the impressive, venerable castle was missing. After staying for a night in Soltano,[9] I camped with the worker and the Black in a tent on dear mother earth. Sleep deserted me since I did not know where our missionaries were and whether they had received my letter pointing out a better route. I also thought of you and how far their superintendent[10] had now come, so that he was sleeping on the earth where the grasshoppers gave him no rest, instead of in the nice soft bed of his precious wife. Yet I also thought of the success and blessing of the mission and slept until I happily awoke.

Next morning, after our devotion and breakfast, the horses in the bush were rounded up, watered and harnessed. With eight horses this took about an hour before setting off. But behold, our horses were work-shy, leaving the wagon stand on level ground after pulling it over high hills the previous day. Then the old teaching about patience had to take over, and an hour later they briskly moved forward.

It is a pity we have the eight horses from up here; they are as lean as hounds and do not have the strength to make this long journey on saltbush, without grass and fodder. Were we to take fodder with us they would not be up to hauling it and we would have to turn back halfway along the track and fetch new fodder.

Now for the fourth time in rapid succession we have to make this journey; yes, we have to go 600 miles further than previously.[11] That causes me deep distress, but there is no way out of it. The Lord will strengthen the poor animals also with saltbush so that they can continue to serve. Experience on this trip will tell more accurately whether I can make better arrangements in the future for our poor animals and workmen. That is why I am travelling with them, so that our entire management becomes better, more certain, and successful in all its aspects, by God's grace.

I can already see some foolish mistakes made in planning, but when working things out practically,[12] how will I find things when the new station is finally established? We have always honestly and accurately weighed up financial matters but have still done foolish things with good intentions. May the Lord forgive us also for that and preserve me from further such foolishness.

Yesterday we arrived here at the Ragless' Hut but received no news of our missionaries by post or wire. What should I do? If I go one way, they will go by another! For two days we have lived on bread, jam and tea; provisions on the new wagon are plentiful but my workman has become sullen and bad-tempered. Satan assails me with his miserable taunts, asserting that I am spending my time and energy for nothing, that I am deserting my precious sheep and lambs, my brave wife and dear children. Who knows but that the missionaries have already turned back. Now I could go further in my folly and complete the measure of my foolishness. I read and prayed, wrote letters to the Church Council, to Gössling and various members of my congregation, and finally began this report to you. That helped.

While in the process of this writing I am summoned to lunch. I go outside to call the workman and the Black and on returning see, to my great joy, Brother Kempe arriving with Hübbe's riding horse.[13] Lunch could wait! I hurried to meet him and asked how everyone was and received the reply, 'Good'. But they had not received my letter.

We were all happy that we were together again, and that the four horses purchased and the young stallions were in such good condition. This was great joy for me, as Satan had to leave me, and my faithful Saviour turned all my sadness into joy. Stupid me; I can be cross at myself for allowing the devil to torment me so; I know how he burdens me with his attacks, and I still let him in...

G A Heidenreich

[In the margin: Have you already sent me the £500? Otherwise, we will have to turn back since my finances are used up. What am I saying? You and the Lord will take care.]

* * *

Heidenreich follows up this letter with a similar letter in the *Kirchenbote* to all ELSA members.[14] In that letter he briefly reports on the commencement of the journey, and encourages Church members to provide support to this undertaking through their prayers and financial gifts.

Meantime, Th Harms replies to the above Heidenreich letter with two letters which are not included here because their main focus is New Zealand.[15] This is a not uncommon occurrence in our letters and reports: New Zealand Church and mission business are intermingled with Hermannsburg mission matters. As much as possible, the New Zealand focus is minimised in the body of *Missionaries, Madness and Miracles*: that is a tale in its own right. It is enough to be aware that New Zealand business is always there in the background, and that it does have an impact on the Finke Mission. A chapter on the critical connection between the Finke and New Zealand missions is provided later in the book (Chapter 36).

Now, however, we turn to the first of the missionaries' account of their trip. It is an extensive report, signed by both Kempe and Schwarz, but in Kempe's handwriting in the original. The account of their journey was written as a diary, as they travelled, with the last report in this first posting headed as being written at Mundowdna, roughly 600 kilometres (375 miles) along their way.

Reading between the lines, there is a fair amount of naivety in the way the young missionaries go about their travel tasks. It is obvious they have done nothing like this before, and when Heidenreich does eventually join them, there is an impression that his intervention is something of a rescue mission.

October-November 1875, Australia[16] *(Kempe to Missionsblatt)*

… We commenced our journey into Central Australia at 4:00 pm on 22 October. It was not possible to leave earlier because the packing and equipping of the wagon took so much extra time. Before we set off, teacher Topp came with his children and sang the song: 'Jesus, go before us on life's path',[17] all of which was sung very sincerely from the heart. The farewell was difficult for me; one did not know what all lay before us on this long journey. We first drove to Tanunda where the wagon was further packed with horse fodder, eggs, sugar, and so on. It was our intention to travel as far as Neukirch, 12 miles away; however, we got only as far as Siegersdorf to Brother Hagen, where Brothers Heidenreich and Schmidt said goodbye.[18] We, however, stayed there overnight.

23 October. We hitched up very early because we wanted to get as far as Waterloo, about 28 miles. But our horses did not want to start moving, and so Hagen had to help. A farmer by the name of Graetz accompanied us a little further. That was also very good in that he could immediately see how difficult the going was, particularly when a small mare lashed out so violently that one was in fear of one's life.

In Kapunda we met the man who sold us the horse, with whom we had a little dispute. We were only able to travel 2 miles further, as far as Allendale where we stayed, bringing the horses into the paddock of an Englishman by the name of Lewis. When he heard that we were missionaries, he gave us back our money[19] and wished us God's blessing. He then prepared our beds on the wagon.

Sunday 24 October. We had to remain here today because there was no Lutheran Church in the area; and so we held our divine service as best as we could in the hotel. It was very boring, but we occupied the time as well as we could, partly by reading, partly by writing.

Monday 25 October. We hitched up early and today travelled to Waterloo. Everything went much better and more orderly. We arrived at around 5:30 in the evening. Pastor Ey came to us with the news that Brother Heidenrich would soon be arriving because he had heard of our misfortune and had already set out. We all lodged with Pastor Ey where once again we enjoyed an evening of singing, and then all of us, tired and weary, went to bed.

Tuesday 26 October. We bought a new horse for £40 sterling. In the afternoon we packed the wagon, and then we stayed there because it had become too late to leave.

Wednesday 27 October. We now travelled in the company of Brother Heidenreich, past Saddle Hut to Burra Burra,[20] 27 miles away. We arrived late in the evening, hungry and tired, and lodged there in the hotel.

Thursday 28 October. Today was very warm, dry and windy so that often one could see neither horse nor wagon because of the dust. We travelled past Mt Bryan to Willogoleche, where we put the horses out to paddock and stayed in the hotel. Here we met a Black of the Dieri tribe who spoke fluent English and could conduct himself as well as any European.

Friday 29 October. Brother Heidenrich travelled with the mail coach to Port Augusta, and so on our own again we travelled the 22 miles via Canowie Station to Jamestown. Immediately after our departure we got stuck in a waterhole and had to fetch extra horses. We were able to go further only after 11 o'clock and arrived at Canowie at 2 o'clock. Here we asked how far it was to Jamestown and whether there was water on the way. We received the reply: 'It is 15 miles to there, and there is no water on the way.' That meant we had to push on hard. Fortunately, we arrived at the specified place at 7 o'clock in the evening, brought our horses into the paddock, and spent the evening on or alongside the wagon.

Saturday 30 October. We drove off early and ate something along the way, but it did not taste good since there was a hot wind blowing, so that our lips became very cracked. In the afternoon there was a thunderstorm but no rain. When we got to Stone Hut[21] we were unable to get a paddock, and so we travelled 2 miles further until we came to good water at a place called Rocky River where there was also good fodder. So, we decided to stay there. The horses were unhitched, hobbled, and let loose to go wherever they wanted to. The driver Hübbe saw to all that and, while Brother Schwarz brewed coffee, I fried eggs and took care of everything else necessary for housekeeping. Then we sat down on the ground and ate our evening meal with relish. Soon thereafter we conducted our communal devotion and went to bed.

Sunday 31 October. Today we held our divine service in the big church, that is, in God's open air, and we edified ourselves as well as we could. We spent the rest of the day reading, writing and going for a walk. At 6:30 in the evening we held devotion and had reason to thank the Lord that he had refreshed us even in this wilderness. However, I could not get to sleep for a long time; my thoughts dwelt on Hermannsburg. I longed to be there again in the church.

Monday 1 November. Cool and bright. Temperature at midday 90°. When we had got our horses together, we left at 7 o'clock, and at 3 o'clock in the afternoon arrived at Mt Remarkable—Melrose—which is 2500 feet high, and which we had already had in view for five hours. Brother Schwarz decided to climb the mountain; I on the other hand preferred to climb onto and ride the horse as Brother Schwarz had previously done.[22]

In Melrose we received a message to go to Stirling where Brother Heidenreich was expecting us. We camped 2 miles beyond Melrose. Because Brother Schwarz stayed away too long, we ate alone and went to bed. Brother Schwarz got back very late.[23] Apart from a few slips and torn trousers, he had descended quite happily.

Tuesday 2 November. Bright and warm. We drove off at 7.30, got stuck along the way, and because the horses turned too short, the whole front of the wagon became unhitched. There was nothing else we could do except unload and then hitch the wagon on again. However, as we drove off the horses again veered to one side, the wagon drove over a crate of eggs, and the entire contents lay scattered on the ground. Fortunately, only six eggs were broken. These Brother Schwarz put into a bowl, and made an omelette from them for the evening meal.

Wednesday 3 November. Bright and warm. As we were leaving, the horses would not pull, but later things went better. Our route went through nothing but hills that reached up on both sides to the heavens; only a narrow pass went through them.[24] In most places it had been hewn out and was so narrow that only one wagon could get through. That was truly romantic. As we drove through, I thought to myself: Cl Böhmke[25] ought to be here, here he could study Romanticism. Seven miles before Stirling the pass ended, and we now entered a thoroughly doleful plain. Nothing but sand and stones were to be seen. We stopped in Stirling, since there was still so much to attend to, and we could no longer reach the next watering place. Here we received the news that Brother Heidenreich was already ahead at Ragless's Mud Hut with another wagon and awaited us there.

Thursday 4 November. Very warm and dry. We drove off at 8 o'clock, reached Piche Richi Pass at 3 o'clock in the afternoon but did not stay there. We travelled further for another 3 miles, as far as Bingerton, where we camped. Altogether we covered 19 miles. The whole night there were severe thunderstorms, but little rain.

Friday 5 November. Very hot and humid. We travelled for nine hours, and reached Ragless's Mud Hut without difficulty, where we met with Brothers Heidenreich and Bähr, and also with a Black from Mundowdna. A very poor area; nothing but saltbush and sand. May the Lord our God help us further. He alone can help us. In the evening Brother Heidenreich told us that he had a tent there on the wagon. I had nothing more urgent to do than to set it up, for I thought it would be much better to sleep in the tent than under the wagon. But alas! We had hardly lain down for an hour when the wind blew up, alarmingly whistled through the tent, and had already pulled out a few pegs. I made them firm again but had hardly lain down again when a very heavy gust of wind came, and with one jerk had made the tent significantly narrower. I did not see Brother Heidenrich any longer. He was lying outside of the tent, but soon came back to us in the now reduced tent; and so we finally got back to sleep. Thanks be to God, it had not done us any damage.

Saturday 6 November. Clear. Dry, biting wind. We drove off at 8:30. First our wagon with four horses, and the stallion alongside, then the other wagon hitched with eight horses, but all in very poor condition. On the plain we met Arabs[26] with four camels; even though they kept a hundred paces distant, our horses still became flighty. At 3 o'clock in the afternoon we reached Tike, where we camped. We hobbled the horses and let them loose, although there was no fodder there. Afterwards Hübbe and I went hunting, and we shot three wallabies, during which time Brothers Schwarz and Bähr baked two dampers. We tried them out that evening and found them to be very good.

Sunday 7 November. Clear and warm. During the morning Schwarz informed us that the sorrel mare Fanny had a foal. That was not good news for us. After we all had seen the foal, we decided to let it live. At midday we had barbecued wallaby, but it did not taste very good. At 4 o'clock we held divine service under a tree.

Monday 8 November. We drove off, leaving the mare with the foal, together with another grey horse since it was too weak to follow after the wagon. At evening we arrived late at Hookina, and so we had covered 24 miles. Here we had to feed the horses, since there was no pasture.

Tuesday 9 November. Ready for departure at 10 o'clock. Very warm. Hot wind, which often brought huge dust clouds, so that we looked like Indians. We travelled via White Well where we rested for a little while, then to Moralana Creek, where we camped. There was not a stalk of fodder here. The horses ate the leaves of the bushes. That hurt my soul. I would have preferred to go hungry, if I could thereby help the horses.

Wednesday 10 November. Clear. Hot wind, as yesterday. After we had found them, we gave the horses a little bit of feed. While they were eating we also ate our breakfast and then drove off to Edeowie. We arrived there after a while, tired and dispirited, because here too we were not able to give the horses anything apart from a little chaff and bran. In the afternoon we split up. Schwarz climbed a hill, Heidenreich wrote letters, Hübbe likewise. Only Bähr and I are at the wagon.

Thursday 11 November. Last night I well and truly froze. Today we again had to hitch up extra horses to the front on account of the sandhills. At 2 o'clock in the afternoon we came to Bunyeroo Creek, where we gave the horses a drink, ate something, and then drove on. At evening we arrived in the vicinity of a creek, where we camped. But there was no water there. We had to eat from the provisions we had brought with us.

Friday 12 November. Dry, hot wind. Temperature 104° F, in the evening after sunset, 80°. We had to search for the horses until 10 o'clock. Today we travelled to Parachilna Creek where we had to stay, since the next water hole is 16 miles away. We drove the horses 2 to 3 miles for pasture. We expected rain in the evening, but instead of that a terrible dust storm blew up so that we could not even see the nearby hills.

Saturday 13 November. Clear and warm. A very sandy track, because of which we again had to hitch up extra horses, and as a result only arrived at Blackfellow Creek late in the evening. The water here was meagre and took three-quarters of an hour to fetch. Today we set up the tent in the evening because tomorrow is Sunday.

Sunday 14 November. Clear and warm. After coffee and devotion we wrote, Schwarz to Inspector von Lüpke, I to the *Australische Kirchenbote* and to my fiancée. The others walked and relaxed. At 4 o'clock in the afternoon we held divine service. I thought a lot about Hermannsburg, where today the anniversary of the death of the sainted Father Harms was celebrated.[27]

Monday 15 November. Dry, hot wind. 9 o'clock departure. Arrived at 2 o'clock in the afternoon at Breakfast-time Creek. We hoped to find fodder there but there was nothing. We first led our horses to the well but lost both our buckets. I then took them to the creek, about 5 miles further on, and found some water but no fodder. I left the horses there even though camels were grazing nearby, because I did not know what better to do. When I came back the others had fortunately fished the buckets out again.

Tuesday 16 November. Biting, dry wind. At 3 o'clock in the afternoon we arrived at Blinman Well. Our foal did not want to go further. We had to kill it. At Blinman Well we bought ourselves some hay for £6/10/0 sterling., which the horses ate in a night. And so in this night alone they cost 43 thaler 10 groschen in German currency. Here we also received letters, Heidenreich six, I one, and these made us very happy. Heidenreich hired yet another man here, to drive the cattle from the old station to the new.

Wednesday 17 November. Clear. Dry wind. After we had completed our business, and also somewhat lightened Bähr's wagon, we left at 10 o'clock and travelled without any difficulties to Windy Creek, 18 miles away, where we camped. Along the way Schwarz had an altercation with a cow that was lying on the track, and was unable to go any further, and then reacted very angrily, especially to the horses. As he struck the cow with the whip, she butted his horse; he fell off, and then the cow also went for him. But everything turned out well in the end. We found water there in a well.

Thursday 18 November. Today we only travelled 9 miles as far as Leigh Creek, where we stayed because there was considerable fodder there, and also water that was necessary for the horses.

Friday 19 November. Clear and warm. Afternoon temperature 100°F. We travelled only 12 miles today, and stayed in Brown's Camp. We had to drive the horses 5 miles further for water and fodder. We had taken something along for our own use.

Saturday 20 November. Had to wait a long time for the horses which two of our people looked for, but in vain. Bähr then went out, and when he did not come back, we all went out to search but found nothing. They had already been diverted ahead of us. Then the Black came and told us that the horses had been found, apart from one, upon which we instructed him to find it, and either today or tomorrow to bring it to St a'Becketts. Almost two hours had already passed when we drove off, forced to do so because we had no more water. We reached St a'Becketts, which should more correctly be called Sandy a'Becketts, late in the evening. Once again, we had to abandon one horse along the way.

Sunday 21 November. Dry wind, the same as yesterday and every day. It was a gloomy Sunday for us. We had to spend nearly the whole day looking for our horses which had wandered a long way away. The Black came in the afternoon, but without the horse. It had already run back to Leigh Creek and was not to be brought back from there. However, the manager at St a'Beckett station promised us to take care of the horse.

We held divine service in the afternoon, and we edified ourselves greatly through a sermon on the Gospel reading on the ten virgins. Thus did the Lord bless us even in the wilderness.

Monday 22 November. We had to look 5 miles further for the horses, that's how far they had run away even though they were hobbled. We were finally ready at 10 o'clock and drove off to Government Gums, 12 miles away, and reached there at 2 o'clock in the afternoon. There was good water there. We occupied ourselves with writing, washing our clothes, and with hunting ducks, but did not find any. In the evening we sat for a long time around the fire and thoroughly enjoyed the beautiful, still evening.

October-November 1875, Mundowdna[28]

Thursday 25 November. After breakfast and devotion I again went hunting and shot two doves, and along the way I put my trousers in water to soften them up. Then I took up position underneath the wagon in order to write the travel report to Hermannsburg, which pretty well kept me occupied until the evening. Then I again went to the water to wash my trousers but, alas, a herd of cattle had come along—around 600 head—and had not only trodden my trousers into the slime so that I could not find them again, but had also made the water so mucky that the whole thing was nothing but slime. For that reason we had to dig a pit just to get some water into our containers, for we knew that we would not reach water until the next day. However, the water was so strongly mixed with cattle dung that it stank terribly. And yet rainwater that has run together like this is still the best; people can conclude for themselves how bad the state of the water can be. Towards evening the old horse died.

Friday 26 November. When we found our horses, we hitched up and set off at about 10 o'clock, as far as the wagon located in Paradise,[29] where we divided the horses and drove further. But we soon came to sandhills and therefore harnessed all the serviceable horses to one wagon, left behind the two hills on our right, and drove about 6 or 7 miles towards Mundowdna where, because we arrived too late, we had to make a stop. It was very warm today with the temperature climbing to 114°, and yet we were unable to give the horses any water because we had none.

Saturday 27 November. We had to search for the horses for a long time. Five of them had strayed 6 or 7 miles away to look for water. Bähr and I eventually found them. Heidenreich had gone on ahead while we slowly followed, and we reached Mundowdna at 1 o'clock in the afternoon. It is a very bleak place, and the water here is brackish—at least what is in the well is unfit for human consumption. We may well have to wait here for 6 to 8 days because Heidenreich wants to ride to the old station[30] with two other men to fetch the horses and the cattle. So, we have to wait until they come back. There is such a hot wind today that it is almost unbearably warm.

With that I will close my daily notes for now since our arrival here completes one phase of our journey. It is only the first part, about a third. We are now about 500 miles from Adelaide,[31] English miles, naturally, as all mileages are given according to English reckoning. There is certainly not much good news in what I have written, but I cannot write anything else than report the truth. How gladly had I rather written nothing but good news. Yes, our mood often sinks low. I have often been tempted to cry out with the prophet: 'It is enough, Lord; so now take my life from me, for I am sick of living.' But then I again reproach myself that we are in the Lord's service, that he has sent us and will be with us all our days, until the end of the world. He will also know why he deals with us in this way and that this is the best for us even if we do not yet understand. Yes, one often experiences just that.

One example is this. On 20 November we were at Browns Camp and could not find our horses and were only able to set out at 2 o'clock in the afternoon. I said to Heidenreich in the morning: 'What might the Lord have in store for us today?' We were soon to find out. As we were standing near the wagon, all of a sudden a revolver discharged and started a fire, but we were able to put it out immediately. If that had happened while we were travelling, how easily the bullet could have hit one of us, or indeed could have burnt the whole wagon! And so we had the Lord to thank that we had not found the horses earlier. So, we are to be silent before the Lord and put our hand over our mouth when we are not able to understand what the Lord is sending us. Oh, if only by his grace we can win some souls, even if it were only one, that would be a rich compensation for all the trouble and work, travail and danger that we have had to endure up to now, and still have to endure in the future, for the most difficult experiences are yet to come.

I would here like to add the request that you, dear Father, especially think of us in your prayers, publicly, as well as in your own private chamber. Also, I would like to ask the whole mission community to be fervent in prayer for us, that the dear Lord Jesus would richly bless us and further the work of our hands. Finally, dear Father, I would like especially to ask you for everything I can ask in making the plea that you are able to send more brothers to Central Australia, and to send them at least two months earlier.[32] If that cannot be done, then I would still like to request the same thing for our fiancées, for it is too awful to travel here in summer...

Yours, in childlike love,
H Kempe, W F Schwarz

* * *

The next letter, addressed to the different audience of the Australian Lutherans, repeats much of what Kempe has just reported. It does, however, contain a few comments of interest different from the above, and these are worth including.

* * *

14 November 1875, Blackfellow Creek[33] (Kempe to ELSA members)
Dear *Kirchenbote* readers!

... From Willochra we travelled together to Hookina, Edeowie, to here. Our order in travelling is as follows: the lighter wagon is up front, drawn by a team of four horses, driven by Brother Hübbe. The heavy wagon follows, driven by Brother Bähr with six horses (there actually should be eight, but two horses have become disabled: one is too weak, the other has fortunately endowed us with a foal—or, rather, burdened us). Then one of us rides at the back driving the disabled horses. Finally, we take turns in helping with the wagons, share all other work apart from cooking and baking, which Brother Schwarz has taken on.

The region here from Port Augusta to Beltana looks sad and desolate. Nothing but bare rocks and dry plains, no grass or other kind of fodder, only saltbush. The tracks here are very bad, despite it being summer. What must it be like here in winter, when the wagons cut 2 feet deep, as the deep ruts still left attest?

Traffic along the whole stretch was very busy. At first we met lots of wagons loaded with wool, but now we are meeting large mobs of all kinds of stock, almost all travelling to the MacDonnell Ranges. The hills are already giving us lots to think about. I have discovered that the line of hills that we first had on our left, and then to our right, form a great chain with those near Adelaide, with many offshoots. Perhaps that is why the English call them 'the backbone of the colony'.

That is how the Lord has helped us to this point. May the faithful God help us further, for without him we can accomplish nothing. Amen.

H Kempe

* * *

Schwarz now picks up the story. It seems that he and Kempe took it in turns to keep their diary up to date and to ensure it was forwarded to its various intended recipients.

In this next section Schwarz personifies the *Kirchenbote*, the publication of which apparently experienced difficulties in its early days. These problems were probably connected with the mixed reception the magazine received within the church, split along the lines of the two Synods. Like a messenger on horseback, the *Kirchenbote* carries in its saddle satchel various dispatches to its readers. The German text is not always easy to fathom, and Schwarz's attempts to be humorous and clever may feel somewhat forced to 21st century ears.

* * *

6 December 1875, Mundowdna [34] *(Schwarz to ELSA members)*

If we will trust in God to guide us
and hope in him along life's way,
we'll know his wonderful protection,

through cross and sadness, every day.
When we are led by God's strong hand,
we build on rock, not sinking sand.[35]

Yes, dear mission friends, the above hymn verse and its contents are what have to this point strengthened and preserved our souls that were weary to the point of death, so that now with God's help and gracious protection we have reached the station of Mundowdna last Thursday. The faithful Lord will grant us strength and endurance also for the further journey through the arid, desolate plains, until we catch sight of our desired destination. This he will do to your joy, to his honour, and for the salvation of the poor heathen who need salvation. He will certainly not let those who trust in him come to ruin.

It is now our duty, dear mission friends, and our love for you compels us, to give a true and honest report of what has happened on our journey, just as we promised you in a holy setting.[36] Now there is someone else urging us with the demand for a thorough report: the *Kirchenbote*. It has earlier (at least one-half of it) experienced the troubles and difficulties of such a journey in Australia, as well as the aversion against the writing of long reports on such a journey. Its demands are modest and it is satisfied with dry-as-dust reports. However, it seems that it is trying to get us to write that way so that it has even more in its messenger's satchel for you, dear readers. We gladly comply with such a request. One such request has spurred us on to Paradise (not a heavenly one but one genuinely Australian, situated 25 miles south of Mundowdna), and coming into our hands in the form of a faith-strengthening letter together with other letters and the precious *Hermannsburger Missionsblatt* has given us a much joy.

Now I move to the actual report which, at the request of dear Pastor Heidenreich, I must give this time. We heartily thank the dear sisters and brothers, especially in the Bethany parish, for all the gifts of love that they gave us for our travel needs in the form of produce. It is my special office as chef and cook to handle all this. Our domestic duties involve handling the many gifts of eggs, butter, honey, jam, ham, bacon, dried fruit, etc. There are seven of us people, and at first we had a good appetite which was lost due to the effects of the heat. But by now our supplies have significantly diminished. The last and biggest ham, given to us by the dear Eckermanns in Waterloo, is now to be attacked. We have eaten at hotels whenever we came across them on our journey, and occasionally received fresh mutton from the English, either purchased or for free. We also dined on wild roast duck killed for us by Brothers Kempe and Hübbe.

Following are diary entries on other happenings on our trip.

Brother Kempe has reported up to 14 November when we had reached Blackfellow Creek.

On the morning of the 15th we set out at 9 am with 98°F and reached Breakfast-time Creek at 2 pm where we hoped to find fodder for the horses. There was little fodder but plenty of water, since there was a well 2 miles left of the track. Both buckets fell into the depths while we were drawing water, so we had to drive the horses 3 miles further to fetch them water and fodder. We fortunately fished our buckets out of the well, held our evening devotions, and went to bed.

Next day we set off early and reached Beltana at 1 pm (one could call it the Australian Turkey because of the Mohamedans and camels there). We travelled on a bit further to Blinman Well. Here we hired an Englishman for 25 shillings a week whose first job, with Brother Hübbe, was to fetch the stock from the old station.

The track so far followed was marked out clearly by stock that had fallen dead. Our vehicles often had to make detours because of dead horses and bullocks lying on the track. Especially when we looked at the miserable horses in front of the large wagon, our thoughts were, 'How long will it perhaps be before we have to pay the same price, given our frequent lack of fodder and water.' So it happened that we had to abandon our ten-day old foal before Blinman Well. Next day we lost a four-year old grey mare. Another grey, that was driven from Browns Creek with the other horses to Mortel Station for water and fodder, knocked up, and so had to be left to its own devices. It is questionable whether we will see the horse again.

A third grey belonging to the large wagon left us at a waterhole, a day's journey from Government Gums, not far from Paradise. It was exhausted. We drove 2 miles back with the small wagon, hoping the horse would recover, but it died two days later.

So, we have had one trouble after another in recent times. We found it especially difficult to get to Mundowdna with the wagons and exhausted horses, as the track was often nothing but deep sand.

On 27 November we arrived at the last named place with the small wagon and all the horses. Brothers Kempe and Bähr brought the large wagon only on 2 December, and with the greatest of troubles at that.

On 29 November Pastor Heidenreich, accompanied by Brother Hübbe, the Englishman Joe, and a Black[37] set out for the old station to fetch cattle and horses from there to here. I spent the time with the wagon and made a stockkeeper excursion with the overseer and people from the station to a waterhole 15 miles away on the way to the old station.

On the station here we have sighed a lot, and will offer many a sigh more. We are in a difficult position. The tracks in all directions are very sandy, but we have to take one of them. So, both Brothers Kempe and Bähr, who searched for the best route out, returned quite discouraged because they could not find what they were looking for.

Today the brothers are in better spirits after Pastor Heidenreich came riding back yesterday 5 December in the evening, just as we were holding our divine service. He brought with him good news, namely that the 20 head of cattle and 19 horses that still belonged to us were in good condition and would arrive next evening. He enjoyed being on the old station, was received well by his people, and given most friendly hospitality. He also expressed joy over the students there, who had already made good progress; he had found a hundred adult Aboriginal people there.

Today, 6 December, we have made necessary purchases in the store. Pastor Heidenreich and Brothers Kempe and Bähr are busy repairing the pack saddle while I am finalising this report.

W F Schwarz, Missionary

* * *

In the midst of all that, Heidenreich would have been aware of a letter from Bode, the pastor taking care of his parish in Bethany, to Th Harms. Bode is facing problems which in some ways may sound rather petty to modern ears, but which for the Church at that time were serious matters. One cannot help sympathising with Heidenreich as he is called upon also to deal with these kinds of concerns in the midst of the huge struggles along the desert road.

2 December 1875, Bethany[38] *(Bode to Harms)*
Dear, precious Father!
... When I came from Schönborn two days ago, I found a telegram here, containing the following:

'G Heidenreich. Can you tell me the pastor who is designated for Maryborough?[39] Answer. Hellmuth.'

I have now written a letter to Hellmuth and discussed the matter with him, arguing that I was the pastor set to go to Maryborough. That is what you had decided, dear Father, and that would have been right also with me. That

Brothers Homann and Heidenreich thought it necessary that I should go to Horsham was also acceptable. They also said, dear Father, that you determined this the last evening we were with you. They thought that was the case, but that the brothers were to make the final decision. The matter can now not be really changed, because it has been arranged here that I should go to Horsham and the congregations there are longing for my arrival.

What do you think on this matter, dear Father? Please write to me about what I should do ...

Then I also want to ask if you will send me the call from the congregations in the Horsham district ... I would have preferred to serve the Lord in the mission. But it was not his will. So I must be satisfied. I will go where God leads me.

... J Bode

3.

Around the 'Old' Station

By late November-early December 1875, just over five weeks into its journey, the mission party has trickled into Mundowdna. Since leaving Bethany, the numbers in the party have increased to seven: the two missionaries, Heidenreich, Hübbe, an Englishman called Joe, an unnamed Black helper, and one other. A second heavier wagon pulled by six horses has been added to the caravan. Heidenreich and two helpers in the lighter wagon, pulled by four horses, have arrived earlier than the second group, reaching Mundowdna on 27 November.

Meantime, up in Killalpaninna (some 160 kilometres away) there awaits the unfinished business of dividing up the assets of the 'old' station between the Immanuel Synod and ELSA, as already agreed upon back in August. By September, three lay helpers—Bähr, Hämmerling and Mirus—had been sent up to sort out the various groups of animals (horses, cattle, goats and sheep), in anticipation of handing these over to the Kempe-Schwarz party on its way to the new station on the Finke.

In order not to waste time, Heidenreich decides not to wait for the rest of the party to pull into Mundowdna. Instead, he gives himself a rest day, and then heads to Killalpaninna to get everything organised up there. Hübbe and Joe go with him. On arrival at the 'old station', he meets up with lay helper Vogelsang and teacher Meyer and enjoys a catch-up evening with them. Over the next day or so, 3100 sheep are culled from the mob and, droved by Hämmerling and Mirus, begin the long trek to the new mission in the Centre. Heidenreich is left with 20 horses and 20 cows to look after, and a day or so later he, Hübbe and Joe head back with them to Mundowdna.

Heidenreich arrived back in Mundowdna on 5 December, all of this activity in relation to Killalpaninna having occurred in just under six days. While he was away, Kempe, Schwarz and the rest of the convoy had arrived at Mundowdna on 2 December and were waiting for him.

* * *

6 December 1875, Mundowdna[1] *(Heidenreich to ELSA members)*
Precious *Kirchenbote* readers!

... On my return yesterday I encouraged and comforted the brothers by the Lord's grace, so that new love of life and desire for travel might be awakened in them. I had hardly done this when a letter arrived from Brother Hämmerling saying that, as a result of the great heat and a lack of water, we had lost 700 sheep over a stretch of 40 miles. Yesterday evening a stockkeeper arrived and confirmed the sad news. We ourselves cannot remain here any longer and want to travel 6 miles further to Colana where we will find fodder and water for some time. From there I want to travel with Brother Hübbe to the sheep to see whether we can do anything to save them. During that time the brothers here are to break in four of our draught animals (in addition to which I must purchase two old ones), as well as several saddle horses. When we return and the Lord gives us rain we intend to continue the painful and difficult journey in the Lord's name. That all this causes much pain to heart and head, and costs much in money and time, is clear to anyone who is prepared to understand. So I will speak no more, because God is speaking and calls you to fulfil your duties in this holy undertaking as you experience harsh and difficult realities...

G A Heidenreich

* * *

Despite the difficulties and hardships the travellers had experienced to this point, they were going along quite well, comparatively speaking. They were supplied with what they needed for the journey, were safe and well and, even though the going was slower than the unrealistic pace they had originally set, they had successfully achieved most of their goals to date. Although, Kempe does say that 'we arrived in Mundowdna ... in very quick time—in fact, too quickly. Our horses were so worn out that they had to be spelled for quite a while'.[2]

However, from Hergott Springs on, things begin to go worse. Drought conditions set in, and the care of the animals becomes a major headache. In fact, conditions become so bad that on the advice of some of the local pastoralists and others, the Hermannsburg parties decide to stop in and near where they are until the late summer rains come. That imposes upon them a halt of several months, and requires a great deal of sorting out of people, supplies and animal care—an inconvenience thrust upon other parties that were traversing the area at the same time as well.

Consequently, the sheep have been settled with food and water on the Peake station, almost 400 kilometers away. The cattle and horses are being cared for at Mundowdna and Hergott Springs, with the overseer of Mundowdna, Mr Ireland, providing generous grazing grounds for the animals, and water available at Hergott Springs. The wagons and supplies are also at Mundowdna.

All this has required a lot of running about and resulted in stress and loss of energy. Heidenreich is doubting whether or not the whole venture is worth it. Kempe says he does not want to talk about it at all: 'it [has been] too tragic'.[3]

Then, in the midst of this instability, and after conflicted consultation with himself, Heidenreich decides to return home for Christmas. It seems pointless to him simply to twiddle his thumbs during this enforced stop. Besides, he wants to organise a number of matters pertaining to the mission, and to rustle up further support from local congregations, and believes he can do that best by going home. He also wants to serve his congregation over Christmas. Possibly, though, he simply wants a break from the hardships of the track. Possibly, too, matters are not always smooth within the travelling group.

This next report is written by Heidenreich during his break in Bethany. There are times in the report where he makes reference to matters concerning Bethany. There are other times when he refers to matters relating to the travellers, also reflecting on what was happening up North before he left.

It is easy to detect these various threads in the letter. Occasionally the accounts become a little confusing. However, rather than endeavour to sort out all that confusion in the commentary, it is largely left to the reader both to experience the uncertainty, and perhaps to make sense of those parts for themself.

* * *

27 December 1875, Bethany[4] *(Heidenreich to Th Harms)*
Venerable, dearly loved Father!

At Ragless' Hut I promised that I would report further to you when I was at the old station. Herewith I carry out my promise, faithfully and truthfully. Until we reach the new place, Brother Kempe will supply you with reports on events as they take place. Thus I will not rob you or myself of time over the same matters because we have little time on earth. Instead, I will try as best I can to provide you with something profitable, a clear insight into our internal and external management.

... The Lord [has been blowing] the fire of tribulation so hot that its heat penetrates bone and marrow, and I have myself already said to him: 'Lord, it is enough, take my soul to yourself!' But he desires our life, not our death, so he again strengthens and comforts us richly by his Spirit, Word and prayer, with the result that in this desert and wilderness I have experienced the most miserable and also the sweetest and most pleasant days of my 10 years in Australia.

What can and should I say? Moaning and complaining? No, I must praise and thank the Lord for all his goodness, faithfulness and marvels for us ... All true Christians know that nothing in this dark heathendom is accomplished by our might, strength, wisdom, money and resources, but only with the gracious working of our God and of the Lamb... As for our financial management, mountains of obstacles stand in our way before it can be on a sounder footing ...

I owe you a small insight into these difficulties. I already informed you last time that our mission horses pulling the large wagon are terribly overworked. My suspicion has been confirmed; two of them have died, three are useless for heavy hauling. Also, the new draught horses are in poor shape. We have had to take a longer rest at Hergott Springs where in the surrounds the Lord has provided water and good grazing for horses and cattle. We cannot go further until it rains, since we can find no more water for 400 miles. We and all the cattle must perish if we, like Jacob, did not take rest and travel on at the Lord's command.

In addition, we have to traverse high sandhills and long stretches of sand on unmarked roads, for which our draught horses do not have a third of the strength needed at present. I have the debts of an army major and £200 is far too little for putting on new workers. We cannot do anything about gaining heart, but the one who can is our Counsel and Strength, our Champion, the Eternal Father and the Prince of Peace, who must help us out and rescue us from death, and who will not allow his honour to come to naught in dealing with us ...

So that we can, by his grace and mercy, set idle hands and tired knees to work, I have bought four good draught bullocks which we have broken in and added to our four young, strong bullocks. We harness these eight bullocks to the large wagon in front of the two horses, so as to master the sand and stone hills, with God's help. We have eight more draught horses for the small wagon. For rotation, we want to break in three more of our steers, as also two saddle horses for riders.

Meanwhile, I have received sad news in a letter from our shepherds who are already 200 miles ahead of us: in two days about 700 sheep have died of thirst and great heat ...I have to accept that not only the whole herd was close to death, but also the three shepherds. I quickly resolved to chase after them for the 200 miles on horse-back to try to save what could still be saved.

On this journey I have learned to ride like a wild man. But I first had to buy the four draught bullocks, going from Mundowdna to Colana ... so that our workmen were occupied and could bring the wagons to the main road, to follow me when there was sufficient rain. So I first went to [? unclear] with Hübbe and bought the bullocks that day.

In the evening a rider approached from the direction of our sheep and gave me the comforting news that no more sheep were lost, but that they now were at Mr Bagot's[5] for three months and had been given fodder. This made my trip superfluous. We spent Sunday in Colana.

On Monday we wanted to go to our people with the bullocks ... Hübbe wanted to go out to fetch them and came back later in the evening with one. I impatiently paced to and fro and mulled over our whole situation: that I was not needed to deal with bullocks and breaking in horses, like the other workmen, and that I was needed down South, ordering, guiding and leading matters relating to the mission, the Church and the congregation, so that things would not again be in a mess. So I wrestled long and mightily with the Lord, that he would show me the right thing to do. I wrote out some directions to be followed in this rest period, divided the tasks among the missionaries and workmen, until the journey could continue after rain, news of which they were to immediately give me. I was just finished with this when Hübbe came. We had to stay the night.

In the morning we first got the other two bullocks, and I then loaded the iron harness for eight bullocks on a pack horse, saddled my horse and rode ahead of Hübbe to our people who were already thinking that I had gone off to Peake to the sheep. I informed them of everything: that I had sold the young stallion for £25, and therefore paid only £23 extra for the four bullocks, also that before I left Mundowdna I would buy the large, fine stallion for £50. I read out my directions which they were happy to comply with and handed them over to Brother Kempe. We then chatted in cordial fashion for several hours, until we held devotion, then slept, had breakfast and again held devotion. Then I had my horse saddled and set off to [? unclear] where I had a lot to do on the journey home. On the way back I covered about 600 miles, four days on horseback, three days and two nights by mail and three hours by train.

It was approaching Christmas when I returned to my beloved congregations and household, where I really enjoyed the three festival days, with Word and Sacrament and household joys. I preached every day and held two meetings in my congregation. I hope in 14 days to have everything here again in order, so that I can without delay hurry to my brothers in the wilderness, following the same route on which I came down. We then intend, in the Lord's name and with his gracious help, to hurry to the goal we are fervently longing for. If it is at all possible we will report to you with every mail how the Lord is living and active among us, since every letter from us will warm your hands and heart. It is just a pity, that we will soon be cut off from all postal connection and will have no post for 400 miles. I will do what I can to see that at least each month you get my telegrams ... I will direct mail to you only if the new place proves useless and unfit for a new mission station. In that case I will sell the whole expensive business[6] and use the proceeds for New Zealand, until I receive different instructions from you. In that case this mission will be finished.

Our gracious God will surely prevent that and, rather, I am certain that we are engaged in a profitable venture, and that he will open up for us a wide door. Just that you know what I intend to do if the worst does happen and the place cannot be retained, that you will receive a telegram from me that you can reply to by return telegram, so that the lives of your children and flocks are not placed at risk. In that case I have to act promptly...

* * *

It is astonishing that Heidenreich seems ready to throw in the towel on this whole endeavour at this stage. He sees it as a sponge soaking up money that could be better used in, say, New Zealand. They have only just begun! He is obviously fearful for the party's safety. And yet one wonders what is really going through his mind, and just how committed he actually was to the endeavour.

In the next section of the letter it is difficult accurately to ascertain the issue Heidenreich is working through. It seems he still had hopes, even ambitions, that the 'old' station might be regained as a mission of the ELSA. It also seems that he had discussed this possibility with Meyer and Vogelsang on the recent detour to Killalpaninna. However, in ways difficult to discern, he feels he has been thwarted, even betrayed, by people like Schoknecht, (a previous missionary), Rechner (the Immanuel Synod President) and Vogelsang, and so his dreams for this place have been, if not shattered, then at least put on hold.

* * *

[7]Now I have to turn to a difficult task, and had I not promised you a report on the old station, I would prefer to say nothing, for the news will be as unpleasant for you as for me. Now I have to tell you the truth, as I saw, heard and experienced it.

We have been deceived. It is true that the committee has treated our missionaries irresponsibly; but it is no less true that our missionaries have acted in the same way to you, me and the poor heathen. I was filled with the thought of fully bringing to light our missionaries and their ... nature to you ... through my own observation, because I had placed all my hopes on Schoknecht's fidelity, as you yourself fully know. We went there with our eyes open; I not only saw that the place was very good for grazing cattle and capable of being made habitable for humans. Further, I saw that it was a place full of hope for the conversion of the heathen. There were ... pupils there who eagerly read, wrote, prayed and sang in the English language. Their teacher Meyer attested their good morals, and some of them made such a good impression on me that I uttered a deep sigh. There were lads, youngsters, and seven girls. All were in a camp of over a hundred and were very well behaved. I can no longer describe my feelings as I compared the difficult work of our missionaries in Zululand with what I had to see here: where we had sown in tears, others were reaping with joy. I bitterly reproached myself that, unwittingly, I had allowed myself to be misused by the missionaries to give you false information, and that I had not kept Schoknecht in my congregation after his wedding, as Bode is doing now, until I had viewed the place for myself. My only comfort was that you and I had never seriously given up the place, but that it had been taken from us by force by Rechner and there was still the prospect that 'property wrongly gained will not to the third heir be attained'.[8]

At this point Vogelsang had no more to do with me, nor I with him, and I cannot hide that fact. I accused him of treachery, and he replied that the letters had been forced from him by Rechner who told him that Hermannsburg was now seriously undertaking the mission. In addition, the reports in the journals were not true; he had not offered them his service, though challenged several times to do so, and there were other matters over which he had to reach clarity with Rechner. We then put aside our personal agendas; who knows why God has allowed all this to happen. If I can ever regain this station with honour and dignity, I will grasp it with good conscience and confidently install one missionary, with your permission, since Meyer is a good teacher.

That the sins of people follow on their heels, I can clearly see with Schoknecht. When I recently exhorted him to support the mission, he replied that he would sooner do nothing until he saw results. I kept my silence with the crass fellow and thought, 'He will change his mind'. Then I come home and Bode gives me a letter from him in which he asserts in return that he does not want the matter addressed through private correspondence, but be approached personally.

Oh, you poor young fellow; I fear that you are falling lower than your poor wife, since the mission, your mother, has become a private matter to you. May the Lord soon enlighten the eyes of your understanding. I am glad that I wrote to him already at Beltana, giving the full impression I now have of the old station. I hope that what I said hits home and he honours the truth...

Very cordial greetings from your loyal and heavy-laden son,

G A Heidenreich

* * *

Elsewhere in the world – 1875

At the same time as this small band of Lutherans was slogging its way into the dreary wasteland in the Centre of Australia, the rest of the world went about its other business. For example, in 1875:

- It was ten years since the American Civil War had ended (on 9 April 1865) and Abraham Lincoln had been assassinated (15 April 1865).
- Alexander Graham Bell made his first telephonic transmission (May).
- Bizet's *Carmen* had its premiere in Paris (March).
- Matthew Webb became the first person to swim the English channel (August).
- Albert Schweizer was born (January) and Hans Christian Andersen died (August).
- The Ottoman state declared itself partially bankrupt (October).
- Albert, Prince of Wales, made an extended visit to India.
- An earthquake in Venezuela and Columbia killed 16,000 people (May).

* * *

1876

As supporters of the Finke Mission in Germany and Australia considered the new year, here is what the editor of the *Missionsblatt* anticipated lay ahead:

January, 1876, Hermannsburg, Germany[9] *(Missionsblatt editor)*
... we have a difficult year before us, with heavy spending on equipping 16 missionaries that has cost thousands of thaler, with new beginnings that will cost thousands of thalers. If we calculate with reason, it says: 'It does not add up'. And if we ask the world, it says: 'You are fools, it is impossible'. But if we look to the Lord and his Word, he says: 'I am with you every day until the end of the world'. And he further says: 'Go into all the world and teach all people and baptise them in the name of the Father, the Son and the Holy Spirit'. Accordingly, we do not want to hold with reason, nor with the world, but with the Lord Christ, as the true God and our brother, and with his Word.

And yet, reason and the world should also serve us. Reason should be our treasurer so that the books in which income and expenditure are listed are accurate to the penny; and the world should be auditor, checking that everything is honest and law-abiding. May the Lord grant that neither treasurer nor auditor can ever say anything else than: 'The pious are a somewhat clumsy people who do some things wrong, but they are honest folk who are not looking for what belongs to you'.

* * *

From the comfort of his home in Bethany, over Christmas Heidenreich reflects on his decision to go home for a while, and makes plans for heading back to the party. At times this next report, too, becomes a little confusing as Heidenreich moves between events up North (where he is not), and events at Bethany (where he is). The repetition of information is due to the fact that the two reports are to different recipients. The previous letter of 27 December 1875 was to Director Harms. This next letter is to the ELSA members.

January 1876, Mundowdna/Bethany[10] *(Heidenreich to ELSA members)*
Dear readers of the *Kirchenbote* have heard of our sad situation from the last report from Missionary Schwarz and me.[11] For many of you the anxious question may have hovered on your hearts and lips: How is this going to turn

out? Will our whole enterprise finally come to nothing halfway along the track? For you and us it was undeniable that our future was dark and difficult; we were in a fierce battle, one piece of sad news following another. No sooner was I able to say concerning the 700 sheep who had died, 'The Lord has given, the Lord has taken away, his name be praised,' when I read in the news that all herds of cattle and sheep ahead of us had to stop, all vehicles from the Northern Territory had to stay beyond Peake, and even the mail driver had lost two horses.

What were we now to do? Should we carry on with our undertaking, wear away our last reserves of strength for travelling further and so cut off all further possibility of a successful journey? That was not on.

We enquired of travellers, station managers and other people to choose the best and easiest of all the difficult ways out. Mr Ireland[12] gave us the decisive advice not to move from the Mundowdna run before rain arrived. He kindly pointed out for us an excellent place for grazing our horses and cattle on the River Frome.[13] The condition was that we water the stock on the government reserve at Hergott Springs. It would have been tempting God not to follow this advice and offer, and wrongly opted to move forward. Our old draught horses were so exhausted that, as it was, we had to give them longer rest and recovery in order to gather new strength for the sandhills and sandy tracks that lay ahead of us. We intended to make a trial run. At my request, Mr Ireland and his people drove the two wagons, one after the other, for 2 miles through the Mundowdna sandhills with ten strong draught bullocks. In addition, our people had harnessed the best two draught horses into the shafts. It was late in the evening before they got through with the last wagon, often driving them all to the point of being dead tired.

At 10 pm I arrived at the station, also dead tired and hungry from driving the horses and cattle, and met Mr Ireland and his people as they were eating their evening meal. They could not relate enough of the burdens and troubles of their day. Once again we got valuable advice, for Mr Ireland told me that not for all the world would he again help me with his bullocks. We now harnessed all our horses to the small, light wagon to get the 6 miles to Coolong Springs to our other people and the remaining stock. As long as I live I will not forget this track through the terribly deep sand and through the deep trenches of the Frome.

Next day Hübbe accompanied me to Colana to Mr Russell[14] to buy draught horses, and thereby be able to break in our four strong bulls. For £48 we purchased four middle-aged bullocks, together with the harness for them and four more, and sold our stallion, so that we could set out for our destination with eight bullocks and twelve horses in the shafts in front of the large wagon. Here I received news from a traveller that our people with the sheep had received plenty of feed and water for three months at Mr Bagot's beyond Peake. That made my intended stay there with Hübbe superfluous.

Next morning I sent Hübbe for the bullocks we purchased, so that we could then catch up with our other party[15]. By midday he was not back.

Worry and boredom plagued me. I mulled over all the work ahead of us with the bullocks, with the draught and riding horses, and with breaking them in, how our wagons were scattered, how much time we needed to get them to Welcome Springs where we would again join the actual road north.

Furthermore, I considered the great cost of completing our journey, as well as the miserable state of our finances. Because our stock was supplied with feed and water at both places, I reached the conclusion: You have to go back to Bethany, summon a mission assembly, clearly explain our situation, and petition for generous, extraordinary assistance, since you can hardly expect to receive money from Pastor Harms within two months, money you need immediately.

However, man proposes but God disposes. There arrived what I discovered to be a harvest from way back,[16] and I had to give up my aim to summon a mission gathering. However, my presence here has not been useless. We have peacefully agreed with the Immanuel Synod on the final distribution and withdrawal of the last funds from the common mission treasury…

I am happy to have received a report from our dear missionaries in which they give thanks for God's spiritual blessing at the precious Christmas festival and report on the workers, that they all have their hands full so that there will be plenty of work for me and the two men who have been taken on, Heinrich Meyer from the state of Hanover, and Alexander Pohlner from here. Both are experienced bush men. When finished with equipping the party in the South, we want to set out in God's name and hurry on to the second party that is 200 miles further on. With the Lord's help we will join forces to capture the citadel of Satan in dark heathendom in the heart of our land. On 21 January I will, God willing, travel from here[17] to the North…

* * *

Heidenreich was the most vociferous writer among the four men involved in the mission venture, and with his finger in the variety of pies already mentioned, he has a lot to say about many things. One of these is his relationship with others, in particular with his peers and colleagues. A distinguishing trait he displays in many of those relationships is his animosity towards them, as well as his criticism of them. He frequently expresses a feeling of being a minority of one in what he sees as heroic battles.

We see one example of this in the next letter.

20 January 1876, Bethany[18] *(Heidenreich to Th Harms)*
Venerable and much-loved Father!

A lot of bitter, sharp and hard thoughts have again passed through my mind in this short period while I was travelling, caused for me by Oster and Homann, with Gössling and Schoknecht. Thank God that he drove me back in order to rip a great hole in this web of lies so that both 'heroes', who have assaulted you and me so despicably and without any justification, will lose their standing with their own friends as well as in the Church. For the God of old still lives; he gives success to the upright despite the envious and the haters. But it disturbs me deeply that I must everywhere be the killjoy who alone is to blame for all misfortune and perversity, and as such is made abominable to his own brothers ... by false brothers and, what is more, with the result that God's Kingdom is not built, neither in the Church nor amongst the heathen.[19]

Nevertheless, I will not allow myself to be alienated from Jerusalem[20] whether in good or bad times, since I have a good conscience in everything, in that I seek only the welfare of our Church and of the heathen, the salvation that God will grant me through his only begotten Son without first asking those people for advice on whether they are not more worthy, more able and better than I...

Pray faithfully for our mission, that we can climb over the mountain of difficulties. The decision on distribution of funds with Pastor Rechner has been amicably settled in my house on the 17th, and we are still to receive £200. Our total share in terms of cash amounts to £5000, with stock and harness valued at about £3000. The mission brought in as much as was paid in by both Synods.

Notwithstanding that Hermannsburg was to get nothing, God however gave it two full shares, and the other(s) received only one. I am happy that I can use the £200 to plug up the largest holes until I receive the £500 from you that, I think, is coming in February, otherwise we will be over our head in debt. I am setting up an extra collection in our Synod that should bring in a nice amount. For God will not allow us to be put to shame.

There is much work to be done for the mission down here and when I am away, Homann has refused to you, and Oster to me, to take on supervision of the mission. So I have nominated Pastor Hensel in the *ministerium* as spiritual member and he has been voted in. Thereby a host of Amalekites have been slain and I have gained a loyal assistant in the Church and mission. In the process, the leaders of the two parties are linked together, and those with divergent views will not help either side with their noise. Thus, my proposal struck the hearts of pastors like a lightning bolt. May the Lord crown us with rich blessings in our common labours.

So, the work of the superintendent is for the time being divided between two pastors and three laymen, but the different tasks have not yet been allotted. I wanted to leave your hands free until matters in … have been settled. I am letting them all work freely, doing everything along with them until you later assign specific tasks after matters have been clarified with me.

The reports of our dear missionaries from the North are good so far, only they are too unacquainted with the nature and conditions of this country. They will have to learn often to later change their opinions and judgements. We first want to let them go their own way and note their good intentions.

The work with breaking in the wagon bullocks and saddle horses is almost finished, so tomorrow I will again set out on the journey to them, for the brothers from Germany have still not yet arrived, and it is time to go since we do not later want to be stuck after the heavy rain on the lower Finke that we have to cross over four times. An amazing land! At one point one is dying of thirst from a lack of water, at another one is drowning in a flood, or is marooned with cattle and wagon. And a person who is not an omniscient God and no prophet is supposed to manage everything properly and expediently— here where all years and months are different.

My absence from here causes sacrifices for myself, my household, congregations and the Church. But it is only for a short time, and the Lord can quickly change things into joy and blessing for all. I would prefer to stay here had the bitter necessity [of my going] not become more apparent. My love of travelling has long since been lost; it has become boring. And yet I am going into the centre of this land at the Lord's command and know that no hair of my head falls without his will.

So I again take my leave of you in the hope that I am able, with the next mail, to report on an important section of our further journey…

G A Heidenreich

* * *

The Mound Springs

As is glaringly apparent, water is the critical factor in the survival of the Hermannsburg venture, especially for the animals. A certain amount of water could be carried in barrels on the wagon for the humans. But for the animals it was impossible to supply their needs in that way. For them, it was what could be found naturally in rivers and creeks and springs. This is why the so-called mound springs became an essential source of supply for the precious stock.

Beneath the surface of the route the Hermannsburg expedition took lay the Great Australian Artesian Basin.[21] It is one of the largest groundwater basins in the world, underlying something like 22 percent of the Australian mainland. For much of this area of inland Australia, it is the only source of fresh water. In places the table is up to 3000 metres deep, and the water temperature varies between 30°C and 100°C. The water has heavy mineral content but, when cooled, is drinkable.

Because of artesian pressure forces, in many places water from the basin naturally discharges to the surface and thus becomes a source of readily available water for all. In some places where this happens, small mounds form around the water outlet—hence, mound springs.

By the time the Finke mission party travelled through these parts, the locations of many of these springs were well known, and it was a relatively easy task for them to tap into this knowledge, even if only as they went. These springs became natural stopping spots, and so their names occur throughout our narrative. Thus, Hergott Springs, Coolong Spring, Finnis Springs, Priscilla Springs, Strangway Springs. At Peake it was Freeling Springs.

The daily output from the springs is not always huge, sometimes little more than a trickle. Nevertheless, it is usually enough to quench thirst. Until, that is, one reaches the magnificent Dalhousie Springs which has a daily output of an estimated 14 million litres.

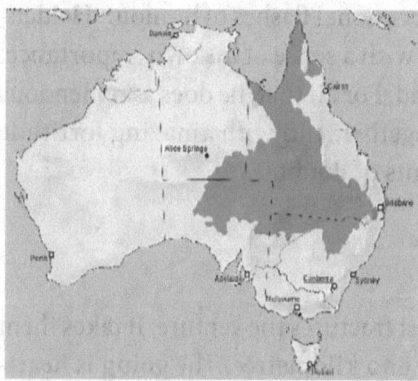

Shaded area indicates the extent of the Mound Springs. [Justin Costello, 2015]

4.

The Journey: To Dalhousie Springs

With three individuals involved in writing the reports for *Missionaries, Madness and Miracles*, there are occasionally two or more reports on the same event or series of events. The happenings in this chapter are one such occasion.

Rather than present these reports separately and in chronological sequence, they have been collated into groupings under the names of each author. In this way the reader is provided with an unbroken and cohesive account by each of the authors in turn, thus making it easier (a) to gain an over-all, unified sense of that author's recalling of these events and (b) to provide greater exposure to the character of each of the writers.

This latter point is one of the exploratory tasks of *Missionaries, Madness and Miracles*. What sort of people are these who undertake something like the founding of this mission station? What are they like?

Readers will draw their own conclusions to such questions. But, generally speaking, Kempe gives an impression of a down-to-earth, perceptive person who writes in a no-nonsense, straight-forward and self-effacing style. Schwarz appears as more of a scholar, and his writing is denser and more verbose, but with occasional flashes of humour. Heidenreich is focussed on detail, absorbed with a sense of his own importance, something of a legend in his own mind. For all that, he does a tremendous job in keeping the whole venture together, and with amazing fortitude and persistence—despite his moments of doubt.

* * *

This next section of the journey almost fractures the venture. It takes them just on five months to travel almost 600 kilometres. The going is heart-breaking, the heat and drought conditions are horrendous, and the party becomes disheartened, split into varying numbers of groups. There is a great deal of toing and froing between groups, and members of the party feel like leaving, and some in fact do. These are the times in the narrative when one cannot help thinking that these people are insane. To subject themselves to such heat and hardship, to push animals and vehicles to the limit through miles and miles of sand, to cling stubbornly to the belief that what they are doing is some kind of divine mission—all these and more are the actions of the possessed and the mad, one might think.

We pick up the story as Heidenreich returns from his Christmas-New Year stay in Bethany. He brings with him three extra helpers.

* * *

Heidenreich's Account

Heidenreich is the most prolific and detailed of the four chief authors of our reports. He is also the most loquacious and bombastic, all of which makes his writing quite colourful. One is left in no doubt about what Heidenreich thinks and how he feels. Now and then he offers insights into inter-actions between people, and these add an appealing human note to the story.

Because of the amount of repetition with the reports of the others, a number of Heidenreich's accounts have been omitted or curtailed. These can, however, be readily accessed from the electronic version, *The Translation*.

Heidenreich wrote two reports on his return back to the missionary party in early 1876. Despite the great similarity between the two reports, there are enough subtle and interesting differences to make worthwhile the inclusion of them both.

12 February, 1876, Mundowdna[1] *(Heidenreich to ELSA members)*
On 21 January I set out from Bethany for the second time on my trip to our mission party. At my request I received as helper, Karl Nitschke, from Krondorf for the further journey from the camps mentioned in the previous report to the Finke-MacDonnell Range. We travelled by train and mail to Kanyaka; here we parted. Nitschke travelled with our things to Beltana; I travelled with the mail to Blinman to carry out business. Unfortunately, one horse after another had to be exchanged on this night ride, and from the penultimate station I was forced to walk because the last two horses refused their services due to exhaustion.

Exhausted and suffering great thirst, I reached Blinman in the morning at breakfast time, and found Alexander Pohlner with three horses ready to fetch me and our purchases to Beltana. Arriving there next day we found Nitschke waiting for us. We had to put heavier loads on the horses. I rode the one chosen to carry our packs; Nitschke and Pohlner alternated in riding the second and third horses.

Late in the evening we arrived at Myrtle Springs[2] and were warmly received by Mr Murray. One horse that had been left behind when we first travelled through here had strayed and was not to be found, despite much searching on the part of Pohlner. It has probably returned to the old station.

What should we do? On this day the heat was almost unbearable. Already the previous day Nitschke had terrible headaches because of the heat and thirst. We could not burden our horses with large water containers, so we decided to travel at night and reached The Gums as the sun rose, our horses dead-tired. Here our horses were to get rest, but I rode to our people ahead on one of the horses that had been rested. Ten miles from Mundowdna I met the mail rider from the North who informed me that Hämmerling had left the camp and set out to travel on, and that Bähr and Josef had gone after him from the Finniss with six bullocks and two horses, but one bullock died and the other became lame.

Next day I was on my way to the Gums early, and there met our Missionary Kempe in the evening. I went with him to Missionary Schwarz at Hergott Springs. From there we set out with the smaller wagon to which he had hitched six horses. At evening, after all sorts of difficulties, we reached the dangerous elevation of Welcome Springs. So as not to drive our horses too hard and demand too much of them, we agreed that on the first day Nitschke should travel with both missionaries to Salt Springs, on the second day 8 miles to Davenport Springs, and from there about 9 miles to here at Finniss Springs, where I am writing this report on 12 February.

I went back to Collana where Hübbe, Meyer and Pohlner were to drive the free horses and cattle into a yard to stop them from running back. It was midnight by the time this had taken place and our people had eaten at the table of Mr Russell.

Next morning the riding and pack horses were saddled and we drove the cattle via Welcome Creek to the second camp of our wagon. The Springs contained only pure salt water; only on one side was there a small source with potable water, barely enough for us four people.

I advised that we should take turns guarding the cattle during the night so that they would not stray. But my people replied: 'The cattle are tired and won't wander off'. I gave in, and we lay down to sleep on white salt crust.

Waking up during the night, I became aware that the animals had strayed off; only some old horses were still near us. My suspicion that the following day would be doubly hot with its strong solar heat proved correct. We spent the day searching for the animals; the moon was shining brightly by the time Pohlner arrived with the last animal.

Though dead-tired, we had to trek on during the night. Sunday at noon we arrived at Finniss, suffering terrible headaches. Here we refreshed ourselves listening to a sermon of Luther.

On Monday we wanted to drive with our loaded wagon over the sandhills that lay in front of us, but it was obviously impossible. So I asked Mr W Coulthard[3] for an old dray which we twice loaded with part of the things on our heavy wagon, and succeeded in driving it through the terribly deep sand, with God's help. With a lot of effort and trouble on our part, and the strength of the draught animals, we succeeded in getting the heavy wagon through.

Nitschke and our loyal and hard-working missionaries had outdone themselves, and almost worked themselves to death in the indescribable sandhills. As a result Nitschke lost his nerve and all hope, and at my request and encouragement did not stay any longer, but walked the return journey with the heavy load of his things. He had done what he could, held dear and treasured by us all. He will be painfully missed, especially by me.

Since we could not stay here at Finniss Springs because of the lack of water, we mutually lamented our crisis, steeled ourselves, and decided to go on. But before it came to that, most of our horses strayed off again, but now with God's help have been found again by Pohlner and Hübbe...

G A Heidenreich

4 March 1876, Peake[4] *(Heidenreich to Th Harms)*
Venerable, much-loved Father!

... On 21 January I travelled with my church chairman, Nitschke, partly by train and partly with the mail, up to Blinman and Beltana, 350 [miles] from Adelaide. I had sent off Pohlner with three horses to Blinman where I had to make several purchases. From there we went to ... then after ... to Meyer. From here I travelled ahead via Mundowdna to the stations of Coolong and Hergott Springs to arrange everything to be bought for the next journey. Here I found that my plans had to be scrapped: the bullock wagons and two drivers had gone off to the sheep,[5] so now I had no driver. So Nitschke had to take over the wagon and the missionaries had to help him drive.

On the first day travelling I stayed with them, then I went back to Colana, where I had sent Hübbe, Pohlner and Meyer with the loose horses and cattle, so that we could put the animals in a yard for the first night. Meyer came with some of the horses, while Hübbe looked for the rest at Coolong. Pohlner came with the cattle.

Next morning we drove 3 miles further to the second camp place where our wagon was,[6] and in the evening Hübbe arrived with the rest of the horses. Since there was no drinking water there, I said: 'Let us take turns keeping watch tonight, so that we have all the animals together tomorrow, but it should not be necessary'. However, next day the horses, including ten old ones, and all the cattle had gone back to … Springs, some of the horses even further. None of us could believe it.

I sent Hübbe and Pohlner after the runaways and Meyer to the wagon with the old horses and the packhorses. When neither Hübbe nor Pohlner turned up, I saddled up and followed their tracks. After riding 6 miles, one of our cows came up, looking for its calf. Now I knew that we faced lots of trouble and work. I rode off and saw Pohlner with some of the horses and cattle coming from Welcome Springs. Hübbe also came from another quarter and told me where the rest of the horses were, but he could ride bareback no further. I gave him my saddle horse and took his without a saddle, and drove horses and cattle to our night camp, sent Pohlner away after the cow and calf and then waited in vain for them until the end of day.

I cried out to the Lord for help; on my own I could no longer keep the young horses and cattle together. What would now happen at night? In addition, we had no provisions. Finally, Pohlner arrived without cow and calf. I questioned him and said, 'Go off there, perhaps she is there, and come straight back. Tonight we have to drive through to … so that we get something to eat'. He went off and slowly pushed on until he arrived with the cow and calf. Then I took the horses and he the cattle, driving them until the next day at midday to Finnis Springs and our wagon. Here we found food, drink and church, for it was the Lord's day…

On Monday the wagon was to cross the frightful sand dunes in burning heat. I said, 'You are not going to get through with the whole load. Let us first drive ahead with a cart', and that is what happened. On Wednesday the wagon was meant to get through but remained stuck. I again asked for the cart to be fetched from the station; this happened with some reluctance.[7] This time I also crossed over, and when we came to the almost empty wagon, I had to go to the other animals that Meyer was looking after alone. He asked me to follow the wagon with the cattle, since they did not like being driven with the horses. I said, 'I will guard the horses here until Hübbe and Pohlner bring up the strays'.

Then Brother Schwarz arrives with the empty cart, bringing Nitschke's belongings with him. He says to me that he [Nitschke] wants to go back. I said to him, 'What, again?' I tell him that he should at least stay until a wagon comes from up North.⁸ He can leave with that. However, next evening Nitschke comes with Kempe, saying he is staying no longer. 'The devil made this country; the mission will not eventuate; people and animals will die, all for nothing; I should go back to my congregations and family.' I earnestly and lovingly tried to convince him to stay, but no, next morning he set off on foot to cover the 600 miles. After an honest discussion, I again prayed for him. During that he took off and I hurried after him on foot, walking several miles with him. But I had to turn back with a heavy heart.

Brother Kempe then again went with the wagon on the condition that he would again drive the stock; he had had enough of driving the wagon. I said, 'You can do whatever you want.' ... I thought to myself ... Here I was again, driving horses, and I do not want any other person to experience how the devil now attacked me in the wilderness with his hordes of sad and frightening spirits. It became so bad that I drove into the station at noon, and said that when Hübbe and Pohlner arrived with the horses they should come after me to the wagon. I reached the wagon during the night. Kempe had fetched water, Schwarz and Meyer were off looking for fodder and water. Finally we got together for a meal and devotion.

In the morning, ten of the horses I had brought were missing. Meyer and Schwarz said that they had gone back to Finnis. I saddled up and went after them, but they were not there. So I waited to see whether they or Hübbe would come during the night. And that is what happened. When I arose before dawn, I saw Hübbe and Pohlner sleeping in front of the yard with the strays inside. Pohlner and I then went with these to the wagon, with Hübbe driving the strays.

Next day Pohlner, Schwarz and I drove half of the wagon load from the ... Spring over three high sand dunes. Schwarz then stayed with the things while we travelled back and loaded up next day. Since Hübbe and Meyer had now found the horses, we went on further over the second sand dune, where there was good food and water. Pohlner and I were with the wagon, Meyer with the cattle, Kempe and Hübbe with the horses. We led the way, Meyer following us, with the horses meant to bring up the rear.

Night fell and I wanted to fetch water for tea and to prepare our evening meal. But I got lost and had to stay awake during a cold night. Next morning I rose early, got to the wagon, found Kempe and Hübbe and heard that there were more horses missing. Pohlner arrived with the draught horses and said that there was good fodder and water at Priscilla Springs. We should let our animals rest there, since our draught horses had become exhausted in the sand dunes. I sent Kempe there with ... horses, and Hübbe was to bring the others. I was to return in the evening with the draught horses. At this point

Meyer went off in a defiant mood. Schwarz and Pohlner were with the wagon, Hübbe bringing up the horses, and we had some peace.

Rumours of deaths now spread across the country in all directions. Stock owners had lost hundreds, and all prospect of our travelling further was written off. What I again then suffered I will record in my secret account! ...

G A Heidenreich

* * *

The above report was written as a personal letter to Director Harms. What his 'secret account' was remains a secret, though one might speculate it has something to do with the petulant Meyer.

Heidenreich also wrote an account of this part of the journey for the *Kirchenbote*. In places it is a fuller version of the events recorded above and, for that reason, the latter part of that report is attached here. At the beginning, there is a slight overlap of events between the two reports.

2 March 1876, Peake[9] *(Heidenreich to ELSA members)*
... Leaving Finniss Springs where Nitschke left us, our missionaries drove the wagon 6 miles further. We stayed there for several days to finally gather together all our stock. Travelling on we had to cross over even higher sandhills than at Finniss until about 5 miles from Stuarts Creek. Missionary Schwarz and Pohlner remained there, the latter making wedges for use under the wagon wheels, while Kempe went off with the horses to Meyer who on the previous evening had driven the cattle to Priscilla Creek. I followed him there with the draught horses and provisions. In the evening Hübbe also arrived with the horses that had again strayed. Mr Miller was very friendly and gave us some of his best fodder and water and extended to us all sorts of other kindnesses. Though the external emergency was removed for now, the concern about how things would go in the future became even greater.

Meyer left us.

News about sheep, cattle and horses that had fallen dead spread widely. In addition, news arrived that our sheep had to leave from where they were because they had no more feed. Mr Miller's people advised me to telegraph from Strangways to Mr Bagot at Peake, to ask him to provide us with water for our sheep, horses and cattle. I talked it over with Kempe and Hübbe, who considered this to be good advice.

So, I myself set out for two days of riding along the long trek to Mr Bagot. He was not at home but was at Pinkley Springs, 60 miles from Strangways. I decided to go there, too, and came across the plain where our 700 sheep had died;[10] I surveyed that with a heavy heart. I wondered how it was possible that sheep that had good fodder could have died here. It could well be, as the station managers and their people told me, that our people had droved them in the sun's heat and in packed flocks instead of at night and spread out. I shall not allow myself to come to any definite judgement before I have received precise information from our people.

Next day I went from Lotton to Humbom, previously called Mount Margaret, where I saw the ruins of the once impressive station and thought: 'The founders of this station were deceived by the water holes that were once amply filled with rainwater but are now completely dried up, just as we were deceived at Lake Killalpaninna.'

I had been told that a Black was living here at Humbom; he would be my guide to Mr Bagot at Pinkley Springs. So I called out but got no reply. I did not know whether to go right or left. Then I saw a cairn of stones that I approached on foot, while my good and faithful three-and-a-half year old black and brown, Hannibal, grazed. I knelt in the shadow of this little cairn and cried out to my God for help. After I stood up, strengthened and comforted, I saw a stockyard not far away and approached it with the intention of meeting the Black. This I did not do. Instead I noticed a cart trail that I followed, after first filling my water bag and watering my Hannibal with my tea mug.

After covering 7 miles this cart track brought me to Mr Bagot. I received a friendly reception and for two days negotiated with him and his younger brother for help out of our dire situation, like the Canaanite woman with the Lord Jesus. Though ready to assist us, he himself lacked water.

Next day he rode with me the 18 miles to Hope Springs, but there too everything was dry. He told me he could only provide help at Loddon-Spa Springs where we would have to make stone troughs for ourselves. But he could grant us this assistance only under the condition that he found two months' supply of water in Sandy Creek, and that we were willing to pay six months' rent of £50. At this I was again at a loss.[11] What was I to do? Should I drive the sheep for 70 miles without water back over the old field of death, or bring them forward for 50 miles without water? That is what went through my mind and heart.

I set out on the track to our sheep at Peake 50 miles away to see what could be done. After traversing those 50 miles where there was almost no grazing, I decided to go forward again to the large Dalhousie Springs; in the last week Gabes had driven there with 500 cows, Murray with 1300.[12] They had waited there for rain, but none came, so they travelled on, and we want to follow them. We suspect that there will be a long dry period, for only summer rain falls here. I have before me the rainfall reports of the policeman Flynn and the telegraph manager Chandler. They show that for many years the rainy months are December to March, that winter rains are sparse or not to be counted on. I am now satisfied as a result of what I have seen with my own eyes and heard with my ears from both of these men. In addition, I have received other detailed information and a survey of the road that lies ahead of us, for which I heartily thank God...

G A Heidenreich

* * *

The amount of running around on horseback that Heidenreich does is astonishing. Were the situation not so serious, his frenetic activity would border on farce, the more so in this instance simply to catch up with someone he is not even sure is where he is said to be to ask about provisions for their party. Refused his request, Heidenreich decides to push on to Peake alone. He calls in at a post office on the way and sends the rest of the party a note—evidence of an operational postal service as distinct from the Telegraph Line. He also dashes off a disconsolate note to Director Harms, once again on the verge of quitting the whole undertaking.

24 February 1876, Strangway Springs[13] *(Heidenreich to Th Harms)*
Highly respected, much-loved Father!

My soul lies in blood. Because of the pain I cannot speak of all the evil, attacks, and insults of the people who should help and advise me to reach my goal. Also, I am now finished, spiritually and physically I am weak and over-worked. And yet it would be unconscionable for me to give up the goal before I see it; and even if I now also die in the process, I want, if God wills it and leads me on the way, to see it, and then write to you the irrefutable truth, that I still exist by God's grace.

How it will be in the near future I do not know. As soon as matters are clarified to some extent, I will give you the news. I wanted to do so today. I have telegraphed Mr Bagot for water, and also to the Synod which is now in session, and if the mail does not go before I get an answer, I will write to you some more. I comfort myself that day and night you are wrestling with God on our behalf...

G A Heidenreich

* * *

According to his later account, Kempe arrived at Peake on 27 March to find Heidenreich waiting for him. So, by the time he pens this next letter Heidenreich has probably spent a couple of weeks in Peake. Who Gössling is in this report is unknown: possibly a misprint in the original letter. It does not really matter. Whoever he is, the sheep are in a bad way and dying fast.

3 April 1876, Peake[14] (*Heidenreich to Th Harms*)
Venerable, much-loved Father!
... I have to report to you about the sheep, that they unfortunately already ... and many of them are dying in this terrible heat. According to Gössling's report that is before me, we still have 20 percent of all the sheep, apart from the lambs that have survived; I will account for them later. If I could sell half of them at a good price and buy horses and cattle instead, I would gladly do that, for there is not much profit from sheep. I leave the decision to you, and also to the advice of my [advisors]. However, if I can act to our advantage I will do so, but up here there is not always an opportunity.

I am painfully waiting for money from you. Despite being thrifty, our journey has already cost over 1000 pounds sterling and can cost as much again if the Lord does not give us rain. Ten sacks of flour cost our L.H. (?) and £60 in freight to haul it up here. Then, consider what the many tools, harness and other necessary things cost by themselves, plus freight. If the old station, a third of the distance away, cost over £6000, you can easily see that in the first years you (will) have to send large sums of money [for the new station]. This investment will certainly bear fruit a hundred and thousand fold, for if our missionaries manage things reasonably well, this mission will be a lucrative business for Hermannsburg. The closer we get to the place, the better are the reports we hear about the country, the water and the heathen. It is thus worth the toil and sweat to hurry on to where the Lord will grant more than we can comprehend.

I am sharing my experiences with you so that you have a faithful and true testimony, should this be my last earthly journey before I go to heaven. Then you can run everything well in future...
G A Heidenreich

* * *

Gradually the scattered group is brought together and, once again, Heidenreich does a great deal of running about in the cart in the process.

Schwarz has been down at Strangways with the wagon; Kempe in Peake, presumably with the other stock; and the sheep are already in Angle Pole, north of Peake.

Easter was on 16 April in 1876, and the whole party was able to enjoy something of a 'holiday' around the celebration. The driver who 'left' at Strangways is not named, but was probably another for whom the going has become too arduous.

Despite Heidenreich's earlier musing at Peake about selling off the sheep, the party has decided to push on to Dalhousie Springs. Exactly what Heidenreich has in mind when he envisages a 'subsidiary' station at Angle Pole is not clear. Surely not a second station, somehow subsidiary to the Finke?

Heidenreich's account of the journey from Angle Pole to Dalhousie Springs is straightforward, and so there is no need to make further comment on it at this point. Except to note again all the running around Heidenreich continues to do—an activity exacerbated by the need at one point to ride all the way back into Peake when a station owner is not prepared to 'loan' the party some supplies.

14 May 1876, Angle Pole[15] *(Heidenreich to ELSA members)*
When Kempe and I last wrote to you from Peake, Schwarz was still 100 miles back with the wagon. So I set out with a cart and two horses to fetch him and the wagon. When I arrived the driver left our service.[16] I telegraphed Kempe and had someone else come, and now spent quiet weeks and Easter in Strangways with Schwarz. We set off again on the third day of Easter and drove quickly to 20 miles beyond Peake. There I handed the cart over to Schwarz so that he could drive with the wagon to Angle Pole, while I went back to fetch the incoming mail. Then I rode in two days to here. Schwarz also came with the cart to the Neals,[17] but arrived here at the camp only four days later. Now for the first time the whole group, including the livestock, was together, and I heartily thanked the Lord for that.

Yet we always go from one crisis to another. We wanted water to get to Dalhousie and heard that between nine and eleven groups were already there, whose stock had died, not because of thirst, but hunger. That is why I decided to stay there until the last drop was consumed. I offered our people a pound to whomever could find more water, and together with Kempe took the greatest care to find a good well. For during this stay it almost seemed to me that we should establish a subsidiary station here, and I had already made preparatory steps to go down South.

However, we found no water, but from the 9th to 11th the Lord gave us beautiful rain from heaven and closed the door to further travel. And so, as the Lord wills and grants grace and life, the third big departure for the last 400 to 500 miles will take place on 16 or 17 May, via Charlotte Waters toward Alice Springs.

And since you will soon settle your accounts for the mission festival, I also wish to place mine immediately on record, as far as I can in this travel time.

We were given 33 horses, and in addition I bought 9, and 2 foals have been born to them; that makes 44. Of these, 5 draught horses have died, and 4 foals; we sold 3 and lost 1, so altogether 13; so that now there are 31 horses left.

We were given 17 head of cattle, in addition I bought a cow with a calf and 6 draught bullocks. Of these, 2 draught bullocks died, leaving 23.

We received 3100 sheep, and of these almost 1000 have died, 2056 are still alive. In addition, 356 lambs came from these, so 2400 are left.

In addition, you have to take into account that, if the counting of the sheep is not quite accurate, we slaughter a sheep every day. I could more accurately say that each week 9 are used in the kitchen for Whites and Blacks. What the 2 wagons, the cart, and the harness cost I can only tell you after I get home,[18] since I sent all accounts back home. And so we now set off anew with 31 horses, 23 head of cattle, 2400 sheep, 5 dogs, 4 hens and a rooster. Since we are now all together again, I have limited our party to only 4 workmen, of whom 2 are with the sheep and 2 with the wagon. Furthermore, some Blacks want to come with us from here, and the missionaries and I help where necessary.

Our living provisions have dwindled to three-quarters of a sack of flour and one-quarter of a bag of sugar. Since we cannot fetch anything from the South under four or five months, we are inclined to ask: Where do we get bread in this wilderness? But the Lord will take care of us, and I will have to borrow bread until ours arrives. These are bad conditions which no director, superintendent and mission community is able, with the best of intentions, to change. In everything we are now happy and confident and have the certain hope that we will reach the goal that is set before us. How glad we will be if we are on our place at the time of your mission festival. Then I will release you from all your anxiety with a telegram and gladden you as well as the festival gathering…

G A Heidenreich

May, 1876[19] *(Heidenreich to ELSA members)*
… When I ended my last report from Peake it was the most difficult time for our journey and the hardest test for our hearts. It was a matter of our

mission in the far North either succeeding or failing. Our physical and mental strength was broken, the expedition was divided into four groups, large stretches of 50 to 80 miles without water lay ahead of us, the sun burnt over our heads, so people and animals were not up to doing anything, and our provisions were running low. Some spots behind us were drying up and there was no goal to look forward to. Through his spirits of the desert and sorrow, the devil painted our position significantly worse than it was. My heart was often very fearful, but what comforted me was that the work we are pursuing is not ours, but God's.

I went from Peake to our sheep at Angle Pole that were lambing. This caused me some perplexity because many of the lambs born on the glowing, hot earth perished in the first three days. If we did not want to run the risk of losing them all, we could not push on with the sheep in the great heat and lack of water for five or six days. Nor could I follow the advice that we should kill the lambs to save the ewes, and so commended both to God.

I arranged to separate the ewes from the large flock and to preserve them that way, then hurried to Macumba to Gilbert's Station and to Mr Hart to learn whether there was water for us to travel further. I found everything in a favourable state but of course had to abandon the plan to investigate the track that we intended to follow to our place or destination and see if fodder and water were available. I was advised to stick to the usual track because fodder and water greatly varied in this region.

All the people up here who have seen our holding and are familiar with it say that it is excellent for the mission, which is why we have already experienced some hostility.[20] Comforted, I returned to Angle Pole, listening to the horrible howling of wild dogs. After separating the sheep, I counted 2374 that were left for us. The rumour that we have twice lost sheep is not true. Rather, they all died at one time, over 900. Our people were not to blame. On the contrary, they did their best, everything possible, to preserve them. The great lack of water, the heat, the burning sand and stony plains caused their death.

Missionary Schwarz and Brother Häse are not yet here at Angle Pole with the small wagon since the horses have been so damaged by previous drivers that they are not in a condition to want to haul a ton of weight. Kempe and I have had a lot of smithing to do here. We have to fit a shaft to the large wagon and mount it in such a way with iron that we can drive only with bullocks. With two horses in the shaft and bullocks in front it has cost us dearly, since the drivers Bähr and Joseph have thereby lost a large strong horse and two of the best bullocks. A third they left lame at Angle Pole. He is now shod and has enough fodder and water to recover here.

Though there is enough rainwater here for a considerable time we cannot stay here any longer because the Macumba that lies ahead of us may well be dry, and we would then have to travel 80 miles without water. As soon as the wagon is in order and the bullocks are shod, we intend to set out and with God's help proceed to Dalhousie Springs, 160 miles away...

I must also note that Angle Pole is the centre of the Wadloo[21] tribe of Aboriginal people. The tribe is healthy, strong, industrious and adaptable...

G A Heidenreich

8 June 1876, Peake[22] *(Heidenreich to ELSA members)*
Dear esteemed Mission Community!

...On resuming our journey, Pohlner carefully and cautiously drove the bullock wagon to which we had hitched eight bullocks. After Hübbe had decided on his own volition[23] to leave us, I drove the horse wagon to which we had hitched six horses. I was happy to see that our draught horses were not as bad as they had been made out to be by good and bad drivers. Although I am not a professional driver, I have driven the wagon through fairly long and deep sand stretches, and over hills, almost without at all using a whip, as we have previously had to do. Granted, the horses now had ample fodder and water, and God was with us. On the last trip[24] we not only did not lose one animal, but also in the last days before Dalhousie, Kempe and Hämmerling rounded up seven runaways. Of these we have broken in the leader to serve as a pack horse.

Unfortunately, we lost the rainwater[25] along the way, and our flour ran out. So, I rode in a great circle to look around for feed and water and found everything better than I had first thought. I gave the order to set up camp and immediately set out on the terrible track back to here, since Mr Murray's manager at Dalhousie loaned us no flour, but directed us to his store at Peake to pick up two bags of flour and one of sugar.

There is no stretch on the north-west road that I have not had to ride along three to eight times,[26] either on horseback, with the wagon, or on foot, sometimes ahead, sometimes in the middle of the procession, sometimes behind it. What no one else wants to or can do usually falls to me, and I am not able to say: 'I will not or cannot do that'.

So, in eight days I again travelled the 150 miles from Dalhousie, and then back again. I took a Black with me to hitch and unhitch the three horses harnessed to my cart, but he deserted me already the next day. Now I was completely alone in the wide world, and in the morning I often had to look for my horses 3 to 6 miles away, and leave God to guard the cart and my few possessions.

On the holy festival of Pentecost[27] I sat by the fire in the creek and sadly thought of former times when I proclaimed the mighty deeds of God in my dear, precious congregation. I prayed to God for a speedy Pentecost blessing for the local heathen. Tears welled up in my eyes; this tough fellow had learned to cry and wail on the trip North.

But God the Lord had enough of my howling, for via the postmaster Chandler at Peake he sent me 14 letters and a telegram to turn my deep sorrow into bliss. Because the telegraph line was broken, both telegraph masters travelled to me from Peake and handed over the letters like dear couriers. I did not have time to read them straight away, since I had to cook some meat and make tea to host my dear guests. I was happy that they liked the taste. I took up the letters when I was alone again …

G Heidenreich

8 June 1876, Peake[28] (*Heidenreich to Th Harms*)
Venerable, much-loved Father!
… You will now be surprised that I am again writing from Peake, but everything with us is proceeding as it should. I wrote to you from Angle Pole how the Lord granted us rain and with what stock numbers we set off to our desired goal for the third time. We did so in this order:

Pohlner drove the wagon with eight bullocks, Hübbe and I the wagon with six horses; Schwarz drove the cattle on horseback the first and second day; on the second day the two shepherds set off with two flocks and Hämmerling with the cart and kitchen. On the second day I drove the horse wagon with Schwarz and let Hübbe join Kempe and the loose horses to muster them together from all four directions, in readiness for setting off.

All went well with the wagons; and I let both rest on the third day so that the draught animals might retain their strength. I rode back to the camp site to help with the loose horses. I came across one flock of sheep, and then the other, in good order, also across Hämmerling with the kitchen but no Kempe with horses. When I came to the old camp, a pack horse stood there tied up, with things lying on the ground, and remnants of a fire; otherwise, nothing was to be seen or heard.

For a while I let both of my horses graze. After climbing a hill I could see neither Kempe, nor Hübbe, nor horses. I made tea, ate, drank and made ready for the other two. Kempe finally arrived with one lot as the sun was going down. I let him eat and drink, and we saddled a young horse for him. Then Hübbe arrived with the other horses, and while he ate and drank, we decided to go on since the horses were restless. I chased after a few runaways and suddenly heard Kempe cry out. His horse was bounding towards me without rider, and I took fright, so that my horse first plunged forward to the ground, then backwards. I stayed in the saddle and Kempe came up on foot. I first mustered the horses together so that he could once more catch and mount his horse. Then Hübbe arrived and we drove deep into the night so that we got away from that place. Otherwise, it would have taken us all day.

Next day we arrived at the wagon. Here Hübbe left us, and I took over the horse wagon on my own, and had the cattle driven by some heathen, and the horses by the two missionaries. The sheep were now ahead of us.

This was how things were up to Macumba. Prior to that, seven horses had run away and were chased by Kempe; Schwarz brought in the others. When Kempe arrived and explained that he could ride again only in four days because he had chest pains, I put Schwarz in charge of the cart with the kitchen; Kempe was to go with him and rest. I sent Hämmerling after the runaways, while Pohlner and I drove on with our wagon. After the horses were found, Kempe and Hämmerling remained at Macumba to break in the lead horses for riding. Both of them arrived with the horses only on the last day before we came to Dalhousie Springs.

Everything else went smoothly. We had water and fodder everywhere. Humans and animals were happy and were gaining strength. This was the best section of our long trek. We thought we would be at our place in time for the mission festival. Suddenly, we were brought back to earth as the rain dried up and we were not able to borrow any flour at Dalhousie. Now what were we to do? We had enough water, and after riding a circuit, I found the fodder better than I had thought. So I gave the order to camp there until the Lord gave us more rain and more favourable conditions. Since we had enough bread for only three days, I had no other option than sadly to go back with the cart and three horses, in order to fetch two sacks of flour and one of sugar in Peake, as directed at Dalhousie.

Eight days ago I went back, taking a Black with me. Next day he left me and I was all alone, at the mercy of the funereal spirits in the wilderness. I was now everything: driver, cook, servant and guard. I wish you could have seen me with my ... hat with its fly net, my long beard, blue woollen shirt, leather belt with pistol, long knife, small leather pouch for tobacco and matches, large boots with nail studs, and torn trousers. You would have cried rather than laughed. I do not understand why ... there are so many who envy and hate me, for I truly have no presence or comeliness.[29] But I was happy at heart and sang so that the bushes swayed. Only one thing displeases me, that in the morning one has to search for the horses, often up to

6 miles, in all directions. One is always a bit anxious until they are back at the cart, so that one has not strayed from there a further 2 or 3 miles. One can be brought to despair when things sometimes go wrong, but by and large I had a good trip...

From here I intend to set off in the next days so that I am not cut off from the brothers by a lack of water. At Dalhousie we wait on the Lord, and when the clouds again lift we will continue our travels. In 10 to 12 days I hope to be with the brothers again. Otherwise all is good, and our place is excellent, as an eyewitness has again testified[30] ...

G A Heidenreich

(In the margin:) Yesterday God gave us a baby daughter; mother and child well. Hallelujah! Amen! Dear Father, accept these gifts from me from the bushes and ... of Australia. I give what I can.

* * *

The group actually arrived in Dalhousie on 29 May. The two previous Heidenreich letters were sent from Peake when Heidenreich made the trip back there for those needed supplies that he was unable to procure in Dalhousie. His reference to 22 June in this next letter is the date he arrived back at Dalhousie after that trip.

26 June 1876, Dalhousie Springs[31] *(Heidenreich to Th Harms)*
Venerable, much-loved Father!

Although I still have no letter from you, the love of Christ for you compels me to write again, for I know that you are with us in eager expectation of events, and that you will not hold a bit of foolishness against me.

By God's grace I arrived here with our brothers on 22 June with the cart loaded with provisions for a couple of months. Nothing particularly new took place on the journey; it bore entirely the Australian stamp of monotony. Only, without my knowing it, I did have the honour for the last three days of my return journey of having the ringleader of a band of murderers of about forty men as my loyal and industrious servant. I was not a little surprised when our people told me this. I myself questioned the cook of Gilbert's Station here, on whom the band had made the attack two months ago, and he confirmed the above statement. So, praise and thanks be to the Lord for his protection and cover against all evil.

We have to remain here without moving until the Lord's cloud rises with rain, allowing us to set off. Meanwhile, the three of us, Kempe, Hämmerling and I, want to begin a trip on horseback to examine the track, fodder, water and our place, starting on 28 June. I wanted to avoid this trip and its costs, but since we now have time, it is really advantageous for the sheep shearing and our entire stock, as also for the supplying of rations by others, that I acquire a thorough knowledge of everything, in order to arrange for everything to proceed properly...

G A Heidenreich

* * *

Kempe's Account

Kempe's account of the journey from Hergott Springs to Dalhousie is much meagre than Heidenreich's, and in working through that account we of necessity back-track to places and information we have already visited. But, from a different perspective.

This first Kempe offering on this part of the journey is a pitiful cry of despair in the debilitating wilderness. The precise location of Pricerla Watercourse is not known. Scherer says that it is not Priscilla Springs, but probably Gregory Creek,[32] which is about 20 kilometres, or 12 miles, from Finniss Springs. The date is also fuzzy, and is probably meant to be 11 February, or even a little later. According to Heidenreich and other accounts, the Kempe-Schwarz-Nitschke group left Finniss Springs some time after 4 February. Thus, they have taken something like a week to travel those 20 kilometres with the small wagon and some horses. Before they left Finniss, they had already been subjected to some of the most gruelling of human conditions imaginable—heat and sand and dust— and were on the verge of exhaustion already at that stage. From there, the situation has only gotten worse.

On top of all that, the whole expedition has become divided and separated into five different groups. Kempe, Schwarz (and Nitschke?) are stuck in the sand at Pricerla watercourse. The sheep, shepherded by Mirus and Hämmerling, have already arrived somewhere north of Peake. Bähr and Joe are driving the large wagon with its food and other supplies up to the shepherds. Heidenreich is still back at Finniss Springs with some horses. Pohlner, Hübbe and Meyer are still further back from Finniss with the cattle and some other horses. The venture has become a nightmare of chaos.

7 February 1876, Pricerla Watercourse[33] *(Kempe to Th Harms)*
Dear Pastor!

... This letter is not meant to serve as a report but only as a call for help in our present need, a plea for your and the whole mission community's intercession. Our journey, like the journey of the apostle Paul to Rome long ago, proceeds with great difficulty or, if you will, does not even proceed. Every day it gets worse, every day there are new plagues and troubles, so that we are often close to losing our mind and courage. Until now we were still reasonably together, but now we are separated into five groups.

The sheep are already 60 miles beyond Peake but can go no further, because there is no water there. Already 1100 head have died of thirst.

The big wagon has followed those who are with the sheep to bring them rations, since they have nothing more to eat.

We are sitting here in the sand with the other wagon and cannot go any further because our horses, since they have no food and also have not had water for a long time, are too weak.

Heidenreich, together with a number of horses, is behind us at Finniss.

There is still a herd back there which we are awaiting with anxiety, but one day passes after another and they are still not coming.

Adding to this misery there now comes the terrible heat; the temperature reaches up to 130° Fahrenheit, and as a result of this everything is dry. It has not rained here for 12 months.

In such circumstances it is easy to see that one just has to get to a bad state physically. One always has to lie on the ground and does not have enough water to wash, though thoroughly dirty. Further, one is not used to the heat, becomes continually weaker, and is required to make superhuman efforts, as I and Brother Schwarz have felt with dread in recent times. One also becomes spiritually exhausted, for even though we always hold morning and evening devotions, that cannot replace the divine service which we have already now gone without for four months. In addition, one only too often utters words in anger and annoyance, which shocks us, and often we have poured out bitter tears over our circumstances ... Also, one cannot hope to make further progress for some time, unless the Lord soon graciously sends us rain. In respect to this, human thought offers little hope, for the heavens are always clear and one day after the other the same dry, hot wind blows.

You can see from this, dear Pastor, that we have the greatest need for your and the mission community's intercession ... When this letter arrives, I think that we will be in the worst possible position. Yes, I can say that it is terrible, cruel, to travel here in summer. In Germany no one, even if they imagine the worst, can have even an approximate idea of such a journey. One cannot even describe it; it has to be experienced. If one takes only one matter, the lack of water, what that means can only be experienced when one gets into that situation...

H Kempe

N.B. This letter was written under the wagon, because I could find no shady place. Therefore, please forgive my scrawl. Also still to be mentioned is that Brother Nitschke, whom Heidenreich had brought with him for support, has turned back yesterday out of desperation. It was too much for him to bear.

* * *

About six weeks later Kempe and Schwarz arrive in Peake, to find Heidenreich already there. The stay here provides them with some breathing space, and Kempe uses part of the time to pen a letter to Director Harms. It is the first time he has had the opportunity to do so for quite some time.

In this letter he recapitulates much that has already been reported. Again, though, it is worth now seeing those past experiences through his eyes.

1 April 1876, Peake Station[34] *(Kempe to Th Harms)*
Dear Pastor!
... our experiences have been quite strange, contrary to our wishes and desires, yes, completely contrary to what we thought the Lord expected us to experience, as far as human eyes can see. We have often asked, 'O Lord, why are you doing this?'

At this point the Lord's words ... have comforted me: 'You do not know now what I am doing. But later you will understand.' I have then again patiently surrendered myself to the Lord's will, hoping that in the end he will let us see his glory ...

Here in the wilderness the devil is particularly active in leading us away from our faith, and I can say that I have never so felt his nearness as here in the Australian wastelands. But thanks be to God who has given us the victory through our Lord Jesus Christ. He has helped us and strengthened our faith so that, by his grace, we have reached this far. He will, I believe, help us further and allow us to reach the goal of this journey, even if not within the time we had desired and hoped for.

Now to the report. I had discontinued this report upon our arrival in Mundowdna. We did not stay there long, but soon after that went another 6 miles further to Coolong Springs where we wanted to take a break for a few weeks. People had advised us at first not to travel further, but to wait for the summer rains which come in December and January, because almost all the waterholes were dry. Furthermore, no fodder was to be found there. However, Superintendent Heidenreich left, because nothing was to be achieved by remaining stationary. Special circumstances in his congregation and elsewhere urgently demanded his presence, and so he went back to Bethany and arrived there on Christmas Eve. We others had to celebrate the precious Christmas festival as well as the New Year in Coolong, and even in the wilderness the Lord Jesus was amongst us.

We sensed that, and heartily rejoiced both over the beautiful Christmas tree which Brother Schwarz provided and on which, lacking candles, he had placed the lantern and some Stearin lights,[35] and also over the wonderful Christmas songs which we sang together until late into the night. Also, we were not totally inactive during the week but have broken in four bullocks and made harness for them, broken in two horses, made a waterbag, and so on. There would still be a lot more to report, e.g. about our hunting parties for turkeys, kangaroos, and such-like, except most of them are still running around with their limbs intact.

Our stay there lasted until about the middle of January. I cannot say exactly how long, since I have left my diary in the wagon which is about 100 miles back. Then we transferred with the wagon a further 6 miles northwards to Hergott Springs, while the stock remained at Coolong. On 25 January I was just on the verge of riding to Coolong to see to the stock, when Superintendent Heidenreich arrived back again and brought with him another man from the Colony by the name of Nitschke, who was to support him, and also two other men for driving the stock.

After we had finished making the necessary preparations and consultations, we left Hergott Springs on 1 February, first of all for Welcome Springs, which was in no way welcoming for the water stank terribly, and then to Wangianna and Davenport Springs. The first of these, however, had such salty water that even the horses would not drink it, so that we were forced to draw at least some water from a small hole with a small container, even if not sufficient. And the second spring lay so concealed in a deserted gully that it seemed to me as if the evil spirits had made their home there. At least, though, the springs had some drinkable water.

From there we drove to Finniss Springs where we stopped for several days, because we had to wait for the stock which, because they had strayed several times, were still lagging behind us. Fortunately, after some days they all eventually caught up so that we could now again continue our journey.

The Finniss Springs lie on the south-eastern corner of the great Lake Eyre, and while up to this point we had always travelled towards the north and north-west, the route here turns towards the west, for it goes around Lake Eyre. It is only 35 miles further at Mount Hamilton that the route again turns north-west, because the lake likewise turns towards north-west.

From Finniss we had a difficult stretch of track to negotiate, namely 5 miles of sandhills. These are long, narrow series of hills, one behind the other, and always a small valley in between, here called a flat. They consist of loose sand that has been blown together and are about 30 to 60 feet high. We therefore loaded half of the cargo onto a cart, and took that to the other side of the sandhills. Next day we tried to fetch the wagon with the rest of our things. However, we could not even accomplish that, so that we once more had to load the cart and then fetch the empty wagon.

In the evening we took the horses back to water, and next day we loaded the cargo onto the wagon, hoping that things would now work out. But already in the afternoon we were again stuck.

Brother Schwarz rode out to look for water and came back only at evening. Nitschke, who had imagined that the travelling here would be much easier, took his things and went back home. I, too, had become so discouraged that I also turned back and in Finniss asked Superintendent Heidenreich to let me drive the horses, since I could no longer bear the struggle and at this time suffered greatly with headaches. My request was granted, and from then on this became my job.

The next day we travelled to Tinditindina where there are some particularly good springs. We remained there a few days because we were again waiting for the horses that had stayed behind. However, here we again had to lighten the wagon because we had to negotiate a further 3 miles of sandhills. Only at the second attempt did we also drove the stock—I with the accompanying horses, and Meyer with the cattle. I arrived at the wagon at 12 o'clock midnight but found everything quiet. Only after calling out for a long time did Hübbe answer. He had been out looking for horses.

Next morning I was just on the point of making tea when Heidenreich also arrived and told us that he himself had got lost in the evening while he was looking for water, and had to sleep in the bush. I now drove the horses to Priscilla Waters where we received permission to stay with all our cattle for some weeks, during which time the wagon which was still stationary on the salt lake called Lake Phibbs was brought, and was to be held there until

Superintendent Heidenreich would write to us.[36] He had ridden to Peake Station to ask whether we could access a spring there, while we waited here[37] with our stock for the long hoped-for rain.

However, man proposes but God disposes, and so it was in this case. What we all desired and hoped for came to nothing. But the Lord did open another door. We learnt that 160 miles from Peake there was a big spring called Dalhousie, where we could go with our stock and wagon.[38] We also gained permission to stay at Angle Pole, a big water hole, until our party was together. Accordingly, Superintendent Heidenreich wrote to us to follow as soon as possible. He himself, however, had to go to Angle Pole and Macumba to see if there was sufficient rainwater there, so that we could drive through with our stock. He found about six weeks supply of water. So we had to hurry to meet up. But first of all the wagon which was completely broken down had to be fixed. We drove it to Mt Hamilton station, where there is a smithy. After we had first of all shod all the horses and got a forge burning, I fixed the wagon with the help of one of our people. During this time we had gotten our stock to Stuarts Creek where there was still reasonable fodder.

After completing all this work, we set out again. Brother Schwarz was on the wagon, I, together with Hübbe, was with the horses, and another man drove the cattle.[39] Our route went northwards, always along the telegraph line, via Blanche Cup (a hill that looked very similar to a sugarloaf, around about 50 feet high, with a strong-flowing spring at the top, and which was probably a volcano, for close by there is also a hot spring) and via Kewsen and Beresford Spring. We arrived there late in the evening almost at the same time. This spring lies on a hill between two other high hills which also, as one can clearly see, were once volcanoes long ago. In general, all springs here are situated more or less on high hills, which is also a little piece of Australian geography.

We again stopped there for several days because there was good fodder which our stock needed. On 20 March we decamped and in the evening reached Strangways Springs. Besides cattle yards, there are also a post- and telegraph-station here, but with such bad water, the like of which I have never drunk. There Brother Schwarz received a huge letter from his fiancée, in which there were several small gifts. This caused great joy, especially since it was his birthday.

Because of the bad water and lack of fodder, next morning we drove off everything that could travel, but we only took two days supplies with us, since we hoped we would again soon meet up with the wagon. Although there were another 7 to 9 miles of sandhills there, we nevertheless thought the horses would pull the considerably lightened wagon through, especially since we had inquired about the easiest route and had set out on that. Consequently, we drove with the horses to the Emily and on the next day to the William Springs, where we first of all took a short rest of about four hours. We had to go from there for 35 miles without water but could not travel in the heat of the day, which the stock could not endure. Instead, we set out towards evening and drove through the night to Douglas Creek. There we first gave the horses and ourselves a small break, and then early in the morning again travelled further, so that through God's grace we fortunately arrived at Loddon Spa already at 12 midday. On the way there we also saw the decaying remains of our sheep; on this stretch over 900[40] had perished from thirst.

Here we hoped to meet up with the wagon again, but our hopes were dashed. In the evening of the same day—Thursday 23 March—Brother Hämmerling arrived, sent by Superintendent Heidenreich. He was supposed to relieve me because, together with the latter, I was meant to get the cart into good order at Peake Station; it was wobbly all over. Since I had brought nothing with me except the clothes I was wearing, I also wanted to wait for the wagon that, according to our reckoning, would soon arrive. But instead of the wagon, the carter arrived next day alone and, together with provisions, brought the sad news that the horses had failed in their service, and Brother Schwarz had gone back with the wagon to Strangways to wait there for rain.

At this point nothing else remained for us except to drive off with the horses and, indeed, immediately the next morning on Saturday, 25 March, in order to reach Peake as soon as possible. I will never forget this and the following day. Already in the morning cloud banks rolled in from the north-west, and became ever higher and higher, so that we certainly hoped to get rain. But instead, such a terrible dust-storm arose in the afternoon that it became quite dark. It blew throughout the whole night so that after we arrived in the evening at Fountain Spring, and because it was pitch-black, the horses had to look after themselves. We could not sleep all night because of the frost.

Even though the next day was beloved Sunday, we could not stay there because there was not a stalk of fodder there. Instead, we had to drive the horses a further 3 miles beyond Outside Springs, into Bulldog Creek, where we spent the night. For me it was doubly hard to work on this Sunday since it was my birthday, but I surrendered to the will of the Lord. May he not count it as a sin for us to have worked on this day.

Next morning we drove off early, and towards evening reached Peake Station where we met Superintendent Heidenreich who was waiting for us. I was quartered there in the telegraph station. Heidenreich was also there, and it felt quite strange to me to sleep once more under the cover of a roof.

Mr Chandler, the telegraph master, is a very friendly man and, in general, reached out to us with a helpful hand. May the Lord God repay him richly.

On Tuesday the two other men drove the horses on to Angle Pole, while, together with Superintendent Heidenreich, I had to spend the whole week industriously employing my noble skills as a blacksmith. We not only fixed the cart but also made 68 bullock shoes, shod three bullocks, and made a mounting for a bullock shaft.

Today now, on Saturday 1 April, we have pretty well completed our work, and now want to wait further because, before anything else happens, the wagon must be here before we are able to go further.

At this point I want to finish my report for now, to continue it further later. God grant that I can do it at our place. There are not a lot of happy things to report, but I can write no other than what is the truth. If we often do not understand why the dear Lord puts us to the test so hard, and deals with us so strangely—e.g. that he has still given us no rain, so that it is extremely difficult for the old Adam—nevertheless I firmly believe that it will all work for our good, for in the Christian life we only reach the crown via the cross.

It was also difficult for us when we looked into the future and at our shrunken stocks of food, and could not anticipate when and in what way we would survive. We also still do not know when the rations which have left Port August will arrive into our hands. In addition, there are the terrible heat—the thermometer rose up to 126°F—the troublesome flies and mosquitoes and all kinds of creatures, such as ants, from the smallest up to the bulldog ant which is up to an inch long, lizards, snakes and so on, so that one often becomes sick and tired of life. Nevertheless, the Lord has helped us. He will also help us further, and I have received new hope and joy especially because I have heard from all who have seen our place that it is very good, and also because I have here seen a lot of Blacks, who are physically well-built. They belong to the tribe of the Wadlu …

H Kempe

* * *

The reference to the Wadlu, provides another example of the unexpected and intriguing connections made with so many other people in the course of translating and writing this material. In October 2019, the South Australian Crown Solicitor's Office on Native Title Claims contacted me regarding a native title claim on which they were working. The Office was investigating the validity of a claim appertaining to the traditional, legal Aboriginal custodians of land around Oodnadatta. Somehow, the Crown Solicitor's staff had heard of our translation work, and were wondering whether the missionaries made any reference in their reports to the names of the Aboriginal tribes in that area at that time. Any such reference could lend credence and validity to one or the other of the contenders in this particular claim.

We did find such references. The first was the one above, by Kempe, to the Wadlu people. Then in his corresponding report of May 1876 (see above) Heidenreich denoted them as the Wadloo people. In an earlier report (7 April 1876) Schwarz had referred to the Monkarapana tribe, but they appear to be located further south than the area under investigation by the Crown Solicitor.

So, this information was passed on to the Crown Solicitor, and it proved to be determinative in the Crown Solicitor's Office decision to grant the Dieri people native title to the land in contention.

* * *

Kempe's report above was written to Director Harms and the Hermannsburg community in Germany. Only later in May does he get the opportunity to write a report of his own to the Lutheran community in Australia. That report (below) contains so much similar material to the above report that much of it is here omitted. However, towards the end of the report Kempe moves on to new information, and that material is now included.

19 May 1876, Stuarts Camp[41] *(Kempe, Heidenreich to ELSA members)*
Dear Mission Friends!

... On 8 April Pastor Heidenreich set out for Strangway Springs with the cart, to fetch the wagon. Since Häse did not want to go further, Pastor Heidenreich telegraphed a message to send Hübbe here, and he responded to the call. I, on the other hand, packed my things together and rode with two horses to the camp site, where I arrived on the Sunday before Easter and was able to celebrate the precious Easter festival in the company of our people.

Here there was much work for me. I had to make a shaft for the bullocks, to shoe horses and bullocks, to make yokes, etc.

On Friday, 5 May, Superintendent Heidenreich arrived with the news that the wagon would already be at Angle Pole, so Pohlner took the bullocks to meet the wagon and fetch it here.

On Tuesday, 9 May, all arrived safely, so finally we are all together, soon, God willing, to continue our journey together. On the 10th and 11th the Lord mercifully sent rain, so we hope soon to get green feed. The stock then needs less water. Despite the rain, the waterholes are still empty...

H Kempe

[Heidenreich adds:]

I must add to this reliable report only that, God willing, we intend to set out from here to our place on 16 and 17 May. Since we are at last all together, I have reduced superfluous staff to two shepherds and two drivers. Our hard-working missionaries do everything else, together with some Blacks and myself. We are taking from here 33 horses, 24 head of cattle, and 2420 sheep. With God's help and care we have saved 600 ewes and 356 lambs. In addition, we have 5 dogs, 4 hens, and a small rooster. Fiedler's large one died. We want to go out from the station[42] to survey the country, the road and water.

* * *

At last everyone and their animals arrive at Dalhousie Springs where there is an abundant supply of grazing and water. It is also a busy place, with several other groups sharing the area with the Hermannsburg mob. Among these groups were possibly some of those the missionary party had met earlier along the way. Their optimism about a speedy conclusion to their journey unfortunately proves to be misplaced, but at least at this point helps to bolster their spirits.

This next Kempe letter is actually written after the reconnaissance trip to the mission site on the Finke, the story which occupies the next chapter. Kempe returned from that trip on 30 August, and so there is a substantial gap of several months between the events he describes here and his recounting of them.

Though it receives the briefest of mentions in his letter, Kempe's reference to his reunion with Schwarz is touching. 'I was glad to see them all again, especially my colleague Schwarz'.

29 September 1876, Dalhousie Springs[43] *(Kempe to Th Harms)*
Dear Pastor!

... In order to link up with the last report, I have to go back in my thoughts to the telegraph station in Peake, from where I wrote that report. If I am not mistaken, it was 2 April when I ended it. I remained there until the 12th of the month. During my stay there I had to drive Superintendent Heidenreich back to Strangways Springs with the cart in order to fetch up the wagon that was still there, and with which Brother Schwarz was staying.

On the 12th of the month one of our workers, Hübbe, arrived with three horses to fetch me to Stuart's Camp, where the rest of our people were camped with the stock. In the afternoon, however, Superintendent Heidenreich telegraphed that Hübbe wanted to come to Strangways Springs because the previous driver did not want to go any further but had hired himself out elsewhere. He therefore rode off on the same evening. Since I wanted to celebrate Easter in the company of our people, nothing else remained for me but to set off on the same evening, the Wednesday before Easter. I rode until 12 o'clock mid-night, when I lay down for a little while in order to wait for the day, since I had never come this way before. I then resumed my journey the next morning.

On the Saturday before Easter, with the Lord's help, I arrived safely at Stuart's Camp. As painful as it was for me to have to ride on holy Good Friday, nothing else remained for me but either to do that or celebrate the sacred Easter festival all alone along the way. I preferred the first.

We experienced a truly joyful Easter festival with each other and could really sense the blessing of the divine Word, the risen Christ in our midst.

Brother Schwarz celebrated Good Friday communally with Superintendent Heidenreich at Strangways Springs, but Easter partly at Beresford.

Hübbe arrived on Tuesday. They caught the horses the following night, and on Wednesday came to Strangways. On the same day the journey resumed, for Mr Hogarth had the kindness to drive the wagon 20 miles further with his horses.

After the festival I had a lot on my hands because there were various things to do for the onward journey. Each day we waited for the other brothers with the wagon and often looked out to see whether or not they were coming.

Finally, on 5 May Superintendent Heidenreich arrived on horseback. He had waited for the arrival of the post at Peake and had ridden straight to our camp. He brought us the news that the wagon was already at Angle Pole. But it was only on Thursday the 9th of the month that the brothers arrived with the wagon. That was the first time that we were all together in one place. I was glad to see all of them again, especially my colleague Schwarz.

This place lies on a large creek, called Neals Creek by the English, and Eringa by the Blacks, and is about 50 miles distant from Peake.[44] It was as if the Lord wanted to say: 'Now is the time that I am sending you rain', for it began to rain on the same evening and kept going until the next evening, but did not produce much water. Yet we thanked the Lord God from our hearts for it and at the evening meal sang from full hearts, 'Praise to the Lord, the Almighty,' because we were now in a position to be able to travel further and to complete all the necessary preparations for the onward journey.

On the 16th of the month the wagons were able to leave, and the flocks of sheep also left the next day, while I still had to stay behind with Hübbe in order to gather together the loose horses which had run off in all directions, because they now had water. On the 18th of the month, towards evening, we had them together again.

As we joined the last of them, we found Superintendent Heidenreich waiting for us, and the same evening we drove still further. The next day we again joined the brothers. Here Hübbe left us. Up to this point he had been in our service; he now went to Peake. We continued our journey, and on 29 May we safely arrived at Dalhousie Springs, where we set up our camp at a place somewhat removed from the track, since at the spot closest to the road there were already three parties. They had camped there partly because of the shortage of water on the way, and partly because they had fled to here from their stations.[45]

*　*　*

Schwarz's Account

The Schwarz material on the part of the trip covered in this chapter is the least of the three contributors. Perhaps there is more material elsewhere. But perhaps, too, this is all there is. Schwarz gives the impression of being the quietest of the trio, happy to stay in the background while the other two more vocal members of the group see to it that the word gets out on how things are going for them.

As classmates and colleagues, Kempe and Schwarz have many years of shared experience, and one detects that they worked comfortably and cordially together. Sadly, that relationship appears not to have lasted, and we hear more of the fracturing of their relation especially at the end of their time on the Finke. However, in the reports they submit at this stage of the story, there is a sense of collegiality and collaboration.

In the following accounts, there is reference to 'the mission festival'. Each year in Hermannsburg, Germany, the community gathered for several days for their mission festival. People came from far and wide, engaged in worship services each day, and heard reports from the Hermannsburg mission fields all over the world. It was customary, then, for proceedings at the mission festival to occupy almost all the space in the two editions of the *Missionsblatt* following the festival.

Schwarz's first letter below is one example of this practice. The letter would likely have been read out at the festival, or at least referred to, and then published. In his presentation, Schwarz sounds a little embarrassed that the mission party has not made the progress folk back in Germany might have hoped.

7 April 1876, Strangway Springs[46] *(Missionsblatt editor, Schwarz to Th Harms)*
The Brothers Kempe and Schwarz are at the moment undertaking a terribly difficult trip into Central Australia, in order to take possession of the more than 900 square miles of land which, as you know, the English government has granted our mission. The dear brothers are demonstrating a genuinely heroic spirit on their journey. It has not rained there for 12 months, and everything is dried out; 1100 of the 3000 sheep which our mission gave to them have died. And the brothers themselves have so little water that they have not been able to wash for months at a time, so that sometimes worry and loss of courage have threatened to overtake them. But they have ever and again prayed themselves out of this mood, and so they are travelling on happy and confident.

But now I would like to ask all of you with all of my heart to pray especially for these Australian brothers: they are now enduring the most terrible conditions in our entire mission. Both of them are equipped for this kind of work, for both of them have become used to this heat in a special way, the one as a blacksmith in the forge (Kempe), the other as a baker in the bakehouse. Yet sometimes the heat gets too much for them, for there the thermometer often reaches up to 150° Fahrenheit. I now leave it to you to clarify with your pastors at home how many degrees that is on our Reaumur thermometer.[47]

Now to my great joy a letter arrived yesterday from Brother Schwarz, which has been written with the purpose of reaching us in time for the mission festival. So, I heartily greet the precious, large mission community on behalf of our dear brothers. And I think I cannot do better than to present the letter here; that will give the best picture of their needs, but also of their faith. The letter runs as follows:

'Those who sow with tears will reap with joy.'

'Dear Pastor!
I first greet you in the name of the Lord, together with your dear family and the Hermannsburg community; and since, as I think, this letter will get

to you for the mission festival, I feel free to ask all the dear mission brothers and sisters assembled at this blessed festival to present greetings from us, your brothers living temporarily abroad, and also especially to ask for their prayers that the Word of God cited above will also soon be fulfilled by us in Australia. It is true that we are not yet fully underway with the sowing of God's Word among the poor heathen of Australia. Yet we are almost six months on the way towards that goal, and insofar as nothing is gained without tears, so there may be even more of them later on the mission field. But to God be thanks for everything. May the Lord later, out of pure grace, allow a rich harvest to follow, to his praise, for the salvation of the heathen and to the joy of all of God's children. I have no doubt that he will allow and grant this to take place.

As already mentioned, in 14 days we will have been six whole months on the trip to the Centre of South Australia, and have travelled 600, 700, yes almost 800 English miles. Note that for a good 14 days we have camped in three[48] groups in different places. The people who are driving the stock and the unladen horses, are around about 200 English miles beyond Strangways Springs, while Brothers Heidenreich and Kempe are 100 miles ahead of me at Peake Station, to where they have ridden. I, on the other hand, together with the driver, the wagon and eight draught horses, am here at the station, which is 600 miles distant from Adelaide. The reason for this is just as much the inability of our horses to pull as it is the lack of desire to do so. I find myself in a tight spot and involuntary imprisonment but hope soon to be released from that.

However, this is what happens on such a long, toilsome, exhausting trip in hot Australia, with all sorts of privation, sweat and temptation, and what unfortunately is still worse, not always without sin. This you can clearly imagine, dear Pastor, as well as can each Christian brother and sister, if you are in touch with your own natural heart.

So, as a result of all this we have accumulated not merit, but rather much guilt. May the Lord nevertheless have mercy on us and prepare us further on the journey, so that we become and be more zealous when he eventually places us in the full-time work of his vineyard. It will be three full months before we reach our desired goal. We could indeed reach it already in time for the mission festival, if we were to ride there; but this is not of any use, because we do not have enough provisions and hand tools to take with us until the wagon arrives. It is also necessary that several men go ahead on horseback in order to determine the track for the wagons to the mission territory.

The poor heathen in South Australia at least awaken in me a firm hope for success. During our trip we saw heathen from different tribes, of which there are 14 in total, as I learnt only two days ago from a heathen, indeed from the chief of the Monkarapana tribe. The last of the 14 tribes is divided into two main families.

Amongst all the heathen whom I have seen so far, only four adults were entirely naked. However, no woman was amongst the four. The children without exception all go naked. However, that these Australians, too, are capable of education is proven by the skill with which many of them speak the English language, and the care that they take with the work entrusted to them. And so they do not need first of all to become human, as the 'monkey prophets' allege. And certainly, sooner or later, the faithful Lord and Saviour Jesus Christ will, because of their entry into the kingdom of God, put to shame many thousands of nominal Christians...

W F Schwarz'

* * *

Having reached Dalhousie, it is Schwarz's turn to write the *Kirchenbote* report for the Australian Lutheran community. He repeats the news Kempe earlier mentioned about Hübbe leaving the group and returning home. This must have been a sad event especially for Schwarz and Kempe, because Hübbe had been their wagon driver from that very first day when they set out from Bethany, six months previously.

31 May 1876, Dalhousie[49] *(Schwarz to ELSA members)*
Dear Mission Friends,

First of all, we greet you in Christ Jesus, and ask that you do not hold it against me that this time you receive only a few lines from my hand. To your joy and comfort you will learn from my letter that the Lord has heard the urgent prayers for us and has wonderfully helped us. Brother Kempe has already informed you that the faithful Lord granted us two days of blessed rain before our departure from Stuart's Camp. And I now happily write that we, and especially our stock, have been able to taste the full blessing of those days of rain on our journey from Stuart's Camp to Dalhousie.

On 16 May, immediately after the midday meal, we set out from Stuarts Camp with two wagons, and drove the cattle soon afterwards. The flocks of sheep and Brother Hämmerling with the cart followed days later. The spare horses could move only on the third day, because it was hard to get them all together. In those days they had found feed and water all over the place.

On 19 May we met together again 4 miles beyond Angle Pole. Here Brother Hübbe parted from us, but Aboriginal people helped us drive the cattle and horses. On the way up here to Dalhousie Springs we had ample water and feed, both on the right and left.

On 29 May at about 2 pm we reached Hart's Camp and pitched camp about 2 miles northwest from there. There was plenty of water and feed in the area.

So far everything would be fine except, unfortunately, tomorrow Brother Heidenreich must begin the long and difficult trip to Peake to purchase some sacks of flour and other necessities and bring them up here. Our supply of flour is down to a few pounds…

W T Schwarz

5.

Reconnaissance Trip

Between 28 June and 30 August 1876, Kempe, Heidenreich, and Hämmerling undertook a reconnaissance trip from Dalhousie Springs to the proposed mission site on the Finke. They took with them a dray to carry their provisions, a spare horse, and a dog. Kempe and Heidenreich both wrote reports on that trip, one each for *Missionsblatt* and *Kirchenbote*. While there is a considerable degree of repetition in the reports, there are sufficient differences to again make worthwhile the publication of all of them.

As in the previous chapter, the reports of each writer have been collated into discreet groups. Once more, this has been done to provide an unbroken account of each author in turn, to more easily be able to see the variations in the accounts, and to gain further insight into the character of both Kempe and Heidenreich.

* * *

Kempe's Account

31 August 1876, Dalhousie Springs[1] (Kempe to Kirchenbote)
Beloved brothers in the Lord.

Shortly after sending off our last report from here, Pastor Heidenreich, Brother Hämmerling and I set off for the Finke to survey our future mission area, and also to search out watering places on the way there. We left here on 28 June with the cart and one riding horse, but managed only 14 miles because it was already fairly late.

The following day we travelled further and reached the telegraph station of Charlotte Waters on Sunday 1 July. Things went well to there since we fortunately found just enough water for our horses between Hughes' Hole[2] and Charlotte Waters in a small claypan. This made us all the more happy since we knew of the water shortage at Charlotte Waters. We at first got permission to stay the one day, Sunday, but already on Sunday morning the local telegraph operator informed us that we had to leave there since there was enough water for only two days.[3] So we went on despite it being Sunday, because we had to, and camped for the night in thick scrub with which the whole track was fairly well covered.

Next day we reached Goyder Creek where the government has had a well dug but, as we later saw, no water is to be found. We did find sufficient water for us and our horses in a native well.[4] On 4 July, we rode on and, after traversing the sandhills, reached the Finke at noon. We rested there before riding on a stretch in the hope of reaching water. But it got dark, and we were forced to spend the night there. It was only on the return trip on the next day that we found water at Crown Point, i.e. 'tip of the crown', getting its name from the pointed rocks that are nearby. We spent the day there and made a tour into the mountains where we were amazed by the high sandhills, some of which are about 200 feet high.

On Thursday 6 July we went on, crossing the Finke after going back about 10 miles. We kept the river to our right and came to Mount Musgrave. Here we granted the horses a rest day since we had to supply ourselves with meat that we got from Mr Warburton.[5]

From there the sandhills caused us many difficulties. Before we got to Horseshoe Bend we had to pass a very high one. At that spot we obtained enough water by digging down in the Finke. We came across the hardest sandhills on the way from the last place to Old Depot, which we reached on 10 July. At this point the Hugh River joins the Finke. Here the latter goes straight westwards, our track follows beside the other.

We left Old Depot on the 11th and reached Mount Burrell on the 13th where we found water, but only by digging. That was a tough stretch of track. On the one hand it was very sandy, and on the other hand we had to be very saving with our water supply. Thirdly, the horses did not want to go forward, especially since we had to travel the third day without water. So they drank all the more at that place. I have often been amazed how much water a horse can swallow.

We now gave them a day's rest, driving off only on 15 July and arrived in the evening at the so-called Deep Crossing where we found ample water, though mostly salty. Only one slightly larger waterhole was somewhat better.

Since the next day was Sunday we stayed there and held our service in the evening.

From there the track almost always closely follows the Hugh. It is only where the track goes through the James Ranges that the creek seeks another passage. One meets it again only when it breaks through the second chain of hills belonging to that range.

On from Deep Crossing we had to camp for another night without water since we found none either at Doctor Hole's or at Doctor Stone's property.

It was only next day that we reached McClore's Springs (if one can even call water seeping together a spring) where we found water for our stock in a depression. We had to dig a hole for ourselves because the first one stank horribly. The water in the creek is close to the track, just as it leaves the James Ranges.

Now we had the Waterhouse Ranges before us and, towering over them, we could see the MacDonnell Ranges. We would have preferred to travel further the next day but had to wait because Mr Conway was away.[6] So, we climbed a mountain hoping to see the Finke from there. But we were not able to. In the evening Mr Conway arrived and we discussed our travels with him.

On 22 July we rode off with another pack horse.[7] We made about 18 miles, up to the last projections of the Waterhouse Range and, on the following day, to the confluence of several creeks, all coming from the MacDonnell Ranges. There we found a wonderful waterhole and, because it was Sunday, we stayed to hold divine service. The confluence of these creeks forms Ellery Creek which flows on from there to the James Ranges in a south-westerly direction. The gorge that it flows through may well be our eastern boundary. The area is overgrown with grass and thick mulga scrub almost to the Finke which we reached next day, camping in the river bed.

Next morning we separated. Pastor Heidenreich rode to the right, I rode left up along the Finke, Hämmerling in the creek. At midday we met together at the foot of a hill. On the way we had found no springs, but many, and some very big, waterholes in the Finke. It is very wide there with much fine feed on the plain. After eating we rode on and passed through the narrow gorge through which the Finke flows. On this track we saw the first Aboriginal person, but he was very shy and wild. In the evening we had to camp in the MacDonnell Ranges, close to the Finke where there was lots of water, but brackish and salty.

Next morning, 26 July, Pastor Heidenreich climbed a hill. From there he saw that behind the hill and just before another hill the Finke divided into two arms. The one goes east to Mt Giles, the other goes left towards Mt Sonder. From here we were unable to get through the gorge because it was full of water, so Pastor Heidenreich considered it best to ride 10 miles eastwards, on the plane where we were, to look for a mountain that could serve as our boundary marker. Several miles south we found a mountain with two peaks. We took note of this as the assumed southern boundary, and rode back, passing the point of egress taken in the morning. We reached the hill where we met on 25 July and stayed there.

Next day we rested, doing all kinds of things such as mending, washing, baking and the like. At noon Pastor Heidenreich climbed the hill with Hämmerling. We called it Three Miles Hill because it was situated 3 miles from the narrow pass. From there one had a panoramic view of the plain that lies between the MacDonnell and James Ranges.

On 28 July we rode on over stone hills, plains and sandhills with lots of growth, thickly overgrown with a kind of sheoak. At evening we came to Gilbert Springs where there was lots of good water, the best I had drunk until now in Australia. Next day Hämmerling rode back to look for the lost cooking pot—and found it. Pastor Heidenreich likewise rode off to look for the map lost yesterday evening. He did not find it, but lost a knife as well. However, he found many springs along the creek, right up to the mountains, about 20 in all, with good but also partly salty water.

In the afternoon we rode on westwards and after 10 miles came to a creek that we followed up and down without finding water. So we had to camp in the evening without water.

Though the next day was Sunday, we were forced to ride on, first of all 5 miles south where we climbed a mountain from which we thought we could see reeds about 2 miles away. But on riding to the spot we were disappointed to see that it was nothing but fairly high spinifex.

We now had to hurry to get back to Gilbert Springs. We got there in the evening and made Monday our day of rest because it was not possible on the Sunday. I stayed in the camp to get something together for the devotion we wanted to hold in the evening. Pastor Heidenreich and Hämmerling went for a walk during which the former found his lost knife and map, as well as many springs and a waterhole besides which wonderfully green bushes and some fig trees grew.

Next morning, 1 August, we rode off from Gilbert Springs and met a creek 5 miles on that flowed out of the ranges in several arms. There was no water, but tall tree growth. We followed the creek and in the evening arrived at the Finke. To our astonishment it was exactly at the place where we first came across it. We rode along it for another 6 miles and found a large waterhole where we spent the night. Unfortunately, the water was really salty. We followed the course of the Finke further, after 6 miles coming to the gorge through which the river flows into the James Ranges. We were hoping to see the palms mentioned at Mount Giles. Since the track was very sandy and partly rocky, we turned back and rode east along the creek that goes into the Finke about a mile below our last camp. We found good feed and soil there and returned to our last camping place because the sun was setting.

On 3 August, we began the return trip, first following the Finke, then along the James Ranges, crossing Ellery Creek where it cuts through the James Ranges. Next day we came to MacClore's Springs. On the way there we almost lost our dog. He could go no further because of thirst, and we had no water to give him, having none ourselves. However, Hämmerling later brought him water and fetched him back.

On 5 August, we came again to Owen Springs and next day, Sunday, conducted our divine service on a hill not far from the station. We stayed on the station until Wednesday 9 August, when Pastor Heidenreich arrived back from Alice Springs where he had gone to send a wire about rations. During those days I did some smithing, partly for ourselves, partly for Mr Conway.

On Thursday 10 August we finally drove with the cart back to Dalhousie Springs, arriving yesterday on 30 August, safe and well by God's grace. The trip up north had been dry enough, the trip down was worse. From Goyder to Hugh's Hole we had to travel without water for 64 miles. You can imagine that the horses were not galloping but let their ears hang down noticeably. If rain does not soon fall, the previously mentioned waterhole will dry up in four weeks. Then there will be a stretch of 110 miles between here and the next supply of water. God grant that everything we have done serves to the glory of his name, and soon graciously grant us rain.

On arriving here we found everything in its previous order. All are cheerful and, as far as I can see, contented, though the brothers here have had no bread for 14 days, having only meat, tea, and assorted vegetables. Now that we are here, we also have to adapt to what is unavoidable—though I on my part would rather live without meat than without bread. But this lack will only last two to three weeks, we hope, until the camels get here ...

H Kempe

* * *

The above report was written by Kempe for the Australian readers of the *Kirchenbote*. It is quite brief, and the next report—written for the German audience, via Th Harms and the *Missionsblatt*—is even briefer. Kempe deals with events in an unassuming and direct way, not given to using more words than he needs to. He is distinctly different from Heidenreich, his style no doubt reflecting the character of the man.

29 September 1876, Dalhousie Springs[8] *(Kempe to Th Harms)*
... After Superintendent Heidenreich arrived back[9] we at first were not able

to consider travelling further. After gaining accurate information about the track and watering places, he then decided to travel with a light wagon to the place assigned to us by the government. He wanted to see if it was suitable for the establishment of a mission station, and at the same time get to know the way there. Because the place lies 50 miles west from the north road, we ourselves first have to find a suitable way. Hämmerling and I went with him.

On 28 June we set off with the cart and with one spare saddle horse, and on 19 July we reached the station of Owen Springs, which is situated on Hugh Creek, 285 miles from Dalhousie Springs.

We left the cart there and took our provisions on a pack horse. We rode from there on the 20th of the month to our place, and after we had ridden across it in various directions, we again returned to Owens Springs on 5 August. We were able to do that with calm and happy hearts, since we had satisfactorily convinced ourselves that the place is good. There is flowing water, a lot of good fodder, and also splendid timber growth in places. In this respect, nothing at all stands in the way of establishing a mission station. Only experience will teach us how things will go with respect to missionary work. We have seen only a few heathen at this place, and these were partly so shy and wild that they hardly came close, but hid themselves as much as possible. Time will tell whether we will be able to farm fruits and crops. This is why I want to refrain here from further description. However, I intend to report later in detail. Also, one cannot form a proper judgement with just a brief overview. Besides, I am not well acquainted with the conditions of the Colony, weather, soil conditions and such things. But we all think that the dear Lord in his grace and mercy will not withhold his blessing from us, and then all will go well.

So, on 10 August we again left Owen Springs, after Superintendent Heidenreich had first of all been to the Alice Springs telegraph station and had received the news of how things stood with our provisions. On 30 August we arrived back in Dalhousie, with thankful hearts that the faithful Lord had so wonderfully helped us. For despite the fact that it was a pretty difficult and dry trip, everything again went well, contrary to our expectations.

Several times there were minor events that were less enjoyable, e.g. several times we had to dig for water in small springs that had been made by the Aboriginal people. Once when we had almost finished doing that and wanted to give a drink to our horses, the well collapsed, and we had toiled for nothing. Another time we had again laboured to dig out a well, but there was so little water in it that we were only able to give each horse four buckets of water. On the next morning, this one also collapsed…

H Kempe

The Heidenreich accounts of the reconnaissance trip now follow. Like Kempe, he wrote two lots of reports, one each for his German and Australian audiences. They are written in the typical Heidenreich style: in detail. Thus, Heidenreich does, indeed, provide the reader with a more fulsome and colourful picture of events than the rather laid-back and under-stated Kempe.

* * *

Heidenreich's Account: the *Missionsblatt* Version

5 August 1876, Owen Springs[10] *(Heidenreich to Th Harms)*
Highly respected, dearly loved Father!

From 29 June we, namely Kempe, Hämmerling and I, together with four horses, a cart, saddles and harness, have come from Dalhousie Springs to our place and back to here on a reconnaissance for water, food, and the route to and from our place. God be praised and thanked for everything that happened and that we experienced as follows:

From Dalhousie to Charlotte Waters we had enough water and fodder to go another 60 miles to water in the Goyder. When we came to the Finke we hoped to find water, but found some only at the foot of a hill. I climbed this hill with Kempe with great difficulty. We found a place clear of stones, and on it I planted a cross with the words: May this be a sign of the Son of God and of Mary planted in the far north.

As we climbed down the other side of the hill, we saw all sorts of images and figures of animals and birds in the soft sandstone, like a picturesque grotto, something like a pagan temple. We had to leave, unsure whether these had been made by the hands of God the Creator, or by heathen hands. We had enough joy just seeing this in the desert.

As we went further along the Finke from there, we found water and good fodder every day and enjoyed looking at the beautiful big gum trees until we had to leave them and follow the watercourse of the Hugh. Several times we had no water for the animals for two days, the nights were terribly cold, and the earth beneath us was like ice. Until two days ago we had to light a fire at night for warmth, and in the morning our blankets were frozen white.

Finally, we came up to where we left our cart and other things, and 14 days ago yesterday we set out for our place without any familiarity with the country, everyone on horseback and with a pack-horse for provisions. So, everyday all three of us were able to ride on, otherwise one would have had to remain with the cart and the other two return each evening. But that would have meant too much loss of time and we would not have been together as a group. So it worked out for the best, and I am happy that I did not allow myself to be separated from the others.

We went along the north side of the Waterhouse Range, but found water for us and the animals only at midday on Sunday.

I had to preach,[11] and in Ellery Creek right on our boundary I proclaimed the gospel message of the power of God's kingdom through the teaching and example of Christ. We wanted to bring both to the heathen in the nearby Finke valley, hoping that by God's grace they would be accepted in faith and evidenced in life.

No Christian will blame us for having hearts full of expectation of things to come, after all the hardships we had endured.

On Monday we got up early. As we came into our block (place) the fodder and the land became increasingly more beautiful and better. We came through outstanding little valleys and had before us a small range of hills running from the north to the south. I continually rode ahead in the lead, and then Hämmerling followed with the pack horses, and Kempe after him, in order to check if anything had been lost in the bushes and undergrowth.

When I reached an elevation, there now spread out before me a plain 30 miles wide and 17 miles long. Filled with wonder, I did not know how I should extol, praise and thank the Lord. For my soul was now completely silent before God. However, the brothers joined me on the hill, and I had to get back to work again.

We now saw the beautiful and mighty Finke 5 miles in front of us. It snakes through our entire territory from the MacDonnell Range to the James Ranges, and contains very many gum trees. We saw that our Lord God had bordered this place with four ranges. The eastern border was the small range on which we had stopped. It still has no name, and I want to let you give it a name when you next write. The southern border is formed by the incredibly long and broad James Range, the western border by the Gosse Range, and the northern border by the MacDonnell Range with its high hills.

It was an entrancing sight to be able to see and to overlook everything from one point. I have not found anything like that since. Then we went down into the beautiful Finke valley with happy and joyful hearts. From a height I looked at the tallest tree, rode directly towards it and saw around me an abundance of the best grasses. I arrived at the tree I had seen in the middle of the Finke valley. I joyfully drew my long knife out of its sheath, and in the name of the Triune God I cut into the east side of the tree, with its three equally tall tips, the sign of the Son of Man.[12]

Meantime, the brothers rode off for water in the two arms of the Finke. I, on the other hand, went into the third. Here I found two large waterholes and called out to the brothers to come. We and the horses happily drank our fill of the water we had found, for one learns early in Australia to really value this precious gift of God. We then sent our horses out for good fodder, Kempe shot a duck, and Hämmerling made the evening meal. After devotion we fell asleep in the sandy bed of the Finke, which the heathen on account of the white sand call the Milky Way of the earth. The Milky Way of the heavens, which they call Lara-Binda, has its origins in the Finke.

The next morning I had for our devotion the psalm: 'Make wide the gates and lift high the portals of the world, so that the king of glory may come in!', and also a victory song of the church. Then I left Kempe on the right and Hämmerling in the middle of the Finke to ride up to the MacDonnell Ranges to look for water. I myself rode on the left in order to look for springs near the Finke. We met together at midday. Kempe and I had not found any springs. On the other hand, Hämmerling had found many, as well as large waterholes. I believe that on our place there is no point in the Finke where, from one end to the other, we are ever further than a quarter of an hour away from water.

We now went into the hills through fearful gullies, over timber, boulders and stones, through water and very deep sand, until it got so bad I had to make a halt. Kempe and I immediately climbed a hill, but it was too low. Since I could not from here make out the borders of our place, from north to east, south and west, I fervently asked God in our devotion to give me full clarity about this.

The next morning I got up early, climbed the highest hill, and by means of compass, map and telescope located our border. However, I could not locate it within a mile in these mountains before consulting with the surveyor Goyder, so I named the hill below me Warteberg.[13] Two miles in front of me, where the Finke divides into two arms, I named the dividing hill Drommelberg;[14] and the valley at my feet, which on account of the amount of water in it made it impossible to go on, I named Amathal.

It later turned out that this Wartberg[15] is not ours, so we will not have our earth brought there as did Louis the Springer,[16] to have 12 knights stick their sword into it and swear false oaths, as happened at the Wartburg. However, our thinking should be that of the other hero of Wartburg who sang, 'Take they our life, goods, fame, child and wife, the kingdom must still remain ours'.[17]

Then I climbed down the hill, had breakfast and held a devotion. I went 10 miles further eastwards along a valley, and with Kempe later climbed a hill and found twin peaks as our north-eastern border. We then went back 3 miles, right up to the range.

About 3 miles from the MacDonnell Range we had gone far enough, for it is of little use to us. From the foot of the range we now went south-west into the middle of our territory, up to the James Range, to the source of the Gilbert Springs. Right away I climbed a mountain and lost my best map. The next morning I went to look for it and lost my only knife. Now I thought: 'It's enough to have two bad things happen. Good things come in threes and more.' I went back along a watercourse and within a mile found that there were more than 20 good springs. Then we went to the west-north border and found it confined within a long tongue of hills of the James Range, running from the south to the north beyond the Gosse Range.

We found outstanding land, feed and timber, but no water, and had to go back to Gilbert Springs on Sunday, which we celebrated on Monday.[18]

Since I was now terribly missing my knife and map, I decided to climb the mountain for the third time, and in a wonderful way I found both.

Hämmerling came from hunting up onto the mountain, and we built a cairn of stones on the peak. I named the mountain The Mountain of Lost and Found. Then Hämmerling said that he wanted to go to a different high peak to hunt, and I went with him. At the foot of this mountain we found a large water reservoir, adorned by nature with a splendid grotto of creepers, oleanders and other flowering bushes. Along the rocky walls above, the swallows had built their nests and I was in a wonderful mood.

We went still further. I heard an emu hen calling its young and said to Hämmerling, 'Can you hear the emu?' Immediately afterwards, the hen came with a flock of young ones. He shot one, and we also caught three. With the good roasting meat in our hands we then went to Kempe in the camp. He was to preach.

I went along a watercourse which came from the last hill, and to my unspeakable joy found new springs. Within a length of 2 miles there could be hundreds. They come out of basalt rock, and go along something like stone troughs between 2 and 20 feet wide, and 2 miles long. I have never drunk such good water in Australia as I did from these springs.

I then once again looked at the grotto mountain, how it lifted its head regally over the others around it. So, I called it King Mountain. And since the most recently found spring had its origin in the mountain, I called it Mary's Spring. I did this out of thankfulness, since I earnt the money for my studies at Hermannsburg in the currency of his majesty King Georg V of Hanover. I have also not yet forgotten the parting words of the great king in the Knights' Hall at Herrenhausen after our ordination, in which he deeply regretted the death of our blessed Father,[19] spoke of his joy over the mission in his land, and promised to pray for us with his family. He had also not been mistaken in his hope that many of my brothers would pray with me for the beloved king, that God would eventually elevate him.[20]

From Gilbert Springs we headed east past Karmel[21] into a creek that comes out of the mountains in three watercourses and presents a complete view of the Hermannsburg mission. Standing there were the old healthy gum trees, with branches broken by the storm, standing like honorable chiefs among those in full virility that stretched their crowns freshly and vigorously into the air. Then came the long, slim, young branches and the countless small saplings. Never in Australia have I seen such a beautiful grove as this one.

We followed the very good grazing land right up to the Finke, and I gave it the name Theodor Creek. Its entry into the Finke is exactly where we first of all came to the Finke. This is also the best place for the station, with the most water allowing distribution of cattle on all four sides. However, the soil is not as good as in a flat further towards the James Range.

Today I have not yet come to a decision as to where to build the station but am still weighing it up and testing it before the Lord.

We then went 6 miles along the Finke into the James Range; but since our provisions were all used up, we went back to good fodder, and from there to here in three days.

So far the Lord has helped us. We now want to spend a few days making a track with the cart, to sow and plant some things, and then with God's help begin our return journey to the brothers at Dalhousie, in order to travel with all those who will stay on our place, after the gracious rain has been sent.[22]

In two months I have received no more news, and another month may pass. On the other hand, we have God's Word, and with that we have enough of everything old and new for our holy calling.

I am now satisfied that the site has exceeded all my expectations in every respect with every thing that is physically necessary for the existences of a blessed mission. The heathen are also very numerous, but they are very shy, so that we were able to speak only with six. They made a good impression on me.

The most difficult matter is the very expensive cost of freight and the high salaries for people. However, that can eventually be alleviated through the breeding of stock, and even be eliminated. If only we could apply a few thousand pounds to the purchase of cattle, we could soon have surpluses in the main account. From our place we have a double market. If we are unable to link with Adelaide, we can go to Port Darwin where the fat cattle fetch a higher price, and there is more water along the way.

Do not allow yourselves to be shifted off course, for the Lord has got us on the right path. I only regret that I have to travel home too soon ...

Kempe greets you heartily...

G A Heidenreich

31 August 1876, Dalhousie Springs[23] *(Heidenreich to Hermannsburg, Germany)*
[Missionsblatt editor writes:]
Finally, after unspeakable toil and hardship, our dear brothers Heidenreich, Kempe and Schwarz, together with their colleagues, have arrived at our mission site in the middle of Australia.[24] To the Lord be praise, glory and thanks, that he has graciously preserved our faithful brothers, has protected and blessed them, has heard our prayers, and has brought our cares to nothing. He has helped and will also help us further. Hallelujah, Amen.

[Heidenreich reports.]
Dear, precious Mission Community!

On the day of our arrival at our place, we came from the east. I always rode ahead, then came Brother Hämmerling with the pack horse, and Brother Kempe behind him. A chain of rocky hills, from the MacDonnell to the James Ranges, lay close to our border.[25]

I rode up a hill to look at the course of the Finke. What a wonderful view of our area presented itself to my eyes. The great, broad area assigned to us lay before me as if God himself has set the boundaries with these four mountain ranges. In the north the MacDonnell, in the west the Gosses, in the south the James Ranges, the last named by Mr Giles as the Krichauff Ranges. The range on which we found ourselves formed the eastern border.

Before me there lay a plain, not very bushy, with low elevations and sandhills, stretching 17 miles long and 30 miles wide. It is traversed by various watercourses on which grow tall and short gum trees. On the sandhills there exists a kind of sheoak tree, which we later found to be up to 80 feet high and 2 feet in diameter at the trunk.

Throughout, the Finke River shimmered brilliantly and beautifully with its wide bed of sand and rich growth of gum trees. At that point my soul was again quiet before God, this time out of joy, as previously out of pain. Then the brothers came after me, the quietness was gone, and after they had enjoyed the view, we rode along a 4 or 5 mile flat towards the Finke which we found overgrown with the best of grasses and bushes for fodder that we partly knew and partly still did not know. With every new discovery of the goodness of the Lord my heart became lighter and lighter, until I came to the highest and most prominent gum tree on the Finke. The strong, slim tree had three similar tips. I drew my knife, and from my horse I cut, in the name of the triune God, the sign of the holy cross so that here now Jesus Christ the Lord will become more glorious every day.[26]

During this time the brothers rode in two of the Finke's watercourses to find reeds; where they exist there will probably be water. I then rode further along a third watercourse and found two lagoons. Joyfully I called to the brothers that I had found water. Without any skill and wisdom on our part, but only by God's gracious leading, we were not only in the middle of the Finke River, but also in the middle of the stretch of land that had been assigned to us. Here the station will be built, as the Lord wills, and when my dear advisory council approves the choice. No other location as good as this one commends itself for the establishment of a station. Everything is to be found here for its maintenance, the protection of the station from the natives[27] on account of the clear view, and for agriculture in all directions.

G A Heidenreich

* * *

Heidenreich's Account: the *Kirchenbote* Version

31 August 1876, Dalhousie Springs[28] *(Heidenreich to ELSA members)*
Dear precious Mission community!
... The day we arrived there[29] we came from the east. I always rode ahead, then came Brother Hämmerling with the pack horse, and Brother Kempe behind him to look for anything lost travelling through brushwood and bushes. A chain of rocky hills from the MacDonnell to the James Ranges lay close to our boundary.

I rode up to one of the highest hills to see the course of the Finke. What a wonderful view of our district opened up to my eyes. The large, broad area assigned us lay before me as if God himself had set its boundaries, with its four ranges. In the north the MacDonnell, in the west Gosses, in the south the James Ranges, the latter named Krichauff Ranges by Mr Giles. The range on which we stood formed the eastern border. Before me there lay a plain overgrown with few bushes of lower height, and sandhills stretching a length of 17 miles and 13 miles wide. It is crossed by various watercourses where tall and shorter gum trees grow. On the sandhills there is a kind of sheoak tree that we later found to be 80 feet tall and 2 feet in diameter around the trunk.

Through all that, the Finke River with its white bed of sand and rich growth of gums shone out brilliantly. At that point my soul was still before God, this time for joy whereas previously often out of pain. The brothers followed me, so the quiet moment was over. After they had enjoyed taking in the view, we rode on to the Finke over a flat 4 or 5 miles long. We found it densely overgrown with the best grasses and fodder bushes, some of which we recognised, others not. My heart swelled and grew lighter with every new discovery of God's goodness, until I came to the highest gum tree on the Finke that I picked out. The strong, slender tree had three equally long tips. I drew out my knife and, still on horseback, cut the sign of the holy cross in the name of the holy Trinity to show that from now on Jesus Christ the Lord would here be glorified forever.

Meanwhile, the brothers rode in two watercourses of the Finke to look for reeds where they could suppose there was water. Doing the same thing, I followed the third course and came across two lagoons. I happily shouted to the brothers that I had found water. Without any skill and wisdom on our part we were, by God's gracious direction, not only in the middle of the Finke River but also at the centre of the stretch of land assigned to us. It is here that the station will be built, God willing, our choice having been approved by our dear advisors.

No other place is more suitable for establishing a station than this one. Here can be found everything needed for the maintenance and protection of the station. There are also good prospects for extensive agriculture. My main concern about working with the heathen by living close to their camps has been raised through conversations with experienced local people: the heathen would certainly desert their camps if we built a station close by.[30]

I have also given up my thoughts about a road to here, surrendering my hopes to others with my conviction that we could make a new road along the Finke through the James Ranges. We lack the strength and time for that. Another attempt to settle next to the James Ranges and on from McClore Springs is out of the question because we found a 50-mile stretch of deep sand, no water, and very rough rocks and stones in some parts.

There remains nothing else to do, meanwhile, than keep to our original track. So our station has to be established in the area first indicated, the more so because it has to be built on the right side of the Finke River. Driving through the Finke is difficult even now in the dry season when springs hold water and the horses already sink deep into the soft ground. How could we traverse it in wet weather?[31]

The Finke is an absolutely wonderful river. It has white sand in its bed all the way from its confluence in the MacDonnell Ranges (about a mile from our place) up to 40 miles before Dalhousie where it divides into many arms and disappears into the sand. The Aboriginal people call it *Lara Binda* and are of the opinion that the stars of the Milky Way migrated from this *Lara Binda*.

Some Englishmen think that the Dalhousie Springs and some other springs to the south-east are the Finke showing up again.[32] Others think it goes to Lake Eyre, though hidden in the sand. I can only hold to the first view. The Finke River has very different water from beginning to end, especially sweet, salty and brackish, and often so close together that water sites which neighbour each other have different water in the middle from that on both sides. In our area we have an inexhaustible supply of water with the Finke River. It is not even half a mile between the MacDonnell and James Ranges before we come across water in one of the three watercourses. Sometimes there is water standing or flowing in all three. We are quite content that God has made no exception of us but has given us brackish and salty water along with the good and sweet.

Enough of that. We now want to turn to the boundary markers. We were able to locate them easily following the government map of the MacDonnell Ranges. That was to be our first task. I had a wonderful panoramic view from the high mountain that I climbed; it was here that the explorer Mr Giles had viewed the whole mountain range. At the time he could travel no further because of deep water.

With four rocks I made a table to set up my compass and checked the surroundings with the map. I found the boundary of our mission property about half a mile away. Since I could not be sure whether it was to be sought at the confluence of the Finke River (it forms two branches there) or at the hill that lies before this confluence, I named the hill on which I stood Wartberg (until I got 'Certainty'[33] from the surveyor general). I named the valley at my feet Annenthal so that the Wartberg would have its proper surroundings—just like the Wartburg home at Eisenach. It is well known there that it is the Annenthal that lies at the foot of the [Wartburg] mountain.

About 10 miles away we subsequently found our north-east boundary at a double mountain. Lacking water, we could not get to the north-west, so we diverted from the MacDonnell Range to Rudalls Creek to delight in the luxuriant grass that (in view of this year's drought) testifies to the fertile, fruitful soil of this valley. We then reached Gilbert Spring via Gilbert Creek and followed along the James Range until we could make out, from the above-mentioned mountain, our south-west boundary marker in a long offshoot of this range that reaches beyond Gosses Range.

Returning to Gilbert Springs, I went off again to search for my best map and my only knife, the loss of which I could not get over. To my great joy I found both and thus named the mountain 'the Mountain of Loss and Recovery'. I saw Brother Hämmerling building a stone cairn on the other side of the mountain and went to him to lend him a hand. When finished, we approached another mountain, to do a bit of hunting and shooting something to eat. At the foot of the mountain we found a considerable waterhole and a beautiful grotto in the mountain adorned with fresh oleander bushes and dark green creepers. The swallows had made their nests up in the roof.

Going on we heard a hen[34] calling to her young. We looked around and along came the adult with a flock of chicks. Hämmerling shot one. I caught two by hand and he a third; the mother escaped with the rest.

With our booty in possession, we set off to Brother Kempe, going up a dry watercourse. There we found new springs in a tributary running down from the grotto mountain. They contained a great amount of water, stretching for a long way up and down in large basalt basins, 6 to 20 feet long and wide and at a considerable depth.

We went together for about 2 miles beside the water and enjoyed looking at the many small fish playing therein and at the splendid water troughs that allow water to flow from one to the other. They will be extremely handy for watering the stock. Here God himself has been the master builder, I thought; he has saved us much cost and work. We do not have to worry about stock foundering here.

I again looked at the grotto mountain from the water side, seeing how it raised its head majestically over its surrounds, and named it King George. Since the wonderful springs with their rich supply of water surpass in goodness the Gilbert Springs and have their origins precisely under the mountain, we called them the Mary Springs.[35]

Next day we passed by a solitary mountain that Brother Kempe named Carmel. We came across a new creek with three arms that comes out of the James Range. It is surrounded by a beautiful grove full of countless young and strong secondary growth in the middle of the old honourable chiefs with branches broken by a storm—a not unfitting image for the Hermannsburg mission. We named it Theodor Creek. We went along it for about 10 miles, as far as the Finke, hoping to find the Doctors Springs marked on the map. We did not find them so we assume that they must lie still further to the right. We now undertook to cross the James Range in order to find the southern boundary. After riding for 6 miles I decided to defer this trek to a later time because we still had no idea of the range's breadth, and we had provisions for only three days.

As for the heathen on our new mission field, we spoke at various places with six. They understood almost no English, but know tobacco, which they call 'backo'. This surprised us until one of them from the MacDonnell Ranges brought us a bundle of green tobacco the like of which I had hardly grown in the manse garden at Bethany, it was so large and good.

The Aboriginal people are very timid. Whenever we got close to larger groups they fled. But there must be a large number of these poor people here who need our help, since we found footprints of men, women and children everywhere, often so plentiful that they resembled the tracks of flocks of sheep on the move.

The young generation among them here in the North are numerous, as we had occasion to observe at Owen Springs, and I likewise at Alice Springs with the so-called 'tame Blacks'. If I were to draw general conclusion from the latter for the Blacks in our area, I could well assert that, 'for the present', these poor people are not folk for the kingdom of God—the old ones are dull, lazy, and like to eat. But I hope for future success with the strong youths and children. Yet our missionaries will leave nothing unventured also with the adults.

If any mission in South Australia has prospects of lasting success it is our 'Hermannsburg' on the Finke-MacDonnell where the Lord has given us not only the necessary 'spiritual powers and gifts', but also the physical means and gifts needed for the task, if the might of Christendom is to be brought to bear on the social and daily life of the heathen and have a truly blessed affect on them.

From the outset it has always been the chief thought of the Hermannsburg mission's work to bring culture and morality to the lost heathen through the influence of the gospel. That should remain the case, by God's grace. Drawing together the total results of my investigative journey, I must say that we have enough and more than enough of heathen, pasture, wood, water, fertile soil, clay, limestone, sandhills and stone hills etc, of all that is good and bad. To be sure, we have found no traces of gold, silver or copper mines that would repay effort; they may be present for later diggers.

But that is fine, as is the fact that our station is 45 miles away from the main road, so that the Blacks remain spared from the negative influences of the many white visitors who bring only harm to the Blacks.

So, I can conclude the report with the words: Dear mission friends, you who have wept, struggled, and prayed with us, and offered up your gifts, rejoice with me—what am I saying—with us all who here in the wilderness by God's grace walk with you in one Spirit and faith. God is faithful; he grants success to the upright. Amen...

A Heidenreich

* * *

The next letter is a personal communication from Heidenreich to Director Harms, and the change in tone from the immediately previous communications is remarkable. It is also again apparent that there have been more of these personal communications than we have in our collection.

However, this next one provides sufficient insight into the troubling experiences of the party. It is written just a few days before the arrival back in Dalhousie of Kempe, Heidenreich and Hämmerling. Heidenreich is fretting about supplies as well as about the sheep and about people who are attacking him. He does not specify who all these people are, but he does mention those 'in our party'. It seems there is tension in the group, and one surmises that especially includes between Heidenreich and Kempe. He is disturbed by pastoral ruckuses in the Church down South, though one wonders why he might feel any responsibility for addressing those: these are surely matters for the President. Yet again, he is worried about the financial viability of the whole venture, obviously feeling the pressure to make it a successful business venture as well as a mission endeavour. And he continues to be torn between returning to Bethany and personally taking over the whole mission endeavour on the Finke.

All in all, things are in a bit of a mess. Earlier Heidenreich had complained about the poor organisation of this venture, the rushed nature of its planning. Quite possibly the expedition is now paying the price for that lack, and the party has been somewhat caught out. What plans, for example, had they made before they left for the shearing of the sheep? Also for supply of provisions, especially the further north they went? Had Heidenreich thought through all the running around he has ended up doing? And he had obviously not thought through how they would dispose of the wool from the shearing.

* * *

26 August 1876, Charlotte Waters[36] (Heidenreich to Th Harms)
Venerable, much-loved Father!

Man proposes, God disposes. Since I could not get any provisions, we had to turn back.[37] We have arrived here safely with everything, praise and thanks be to God. Brother Schwarz told me by letter that they baked their last bread on 14 August and we did so the day before yesterday. Here, too, we can get no flour but are to have beef on our three day journey to Dalhousie. In three weeks the camels with our provisions will finally be with us, if God so wills and gives grace. If that is not his will, he has to do something else. What is true with him is true for us, namely, his word of promise: 'I will not leave you nor forsake you'. If he still has long, thick ears, I will have to institute proceedings against him so that he takes back his word. But I will stand or fall by it according to his will and pleasure, as long as his promise stands.

Thus I am not worried about what we will eat tomorrow, or drink or put on, but I am completely happy and confident, by his grace and goodness, to the amazement of all those who hate and envy us. I now am truly experiencing this: the greater the crisis, the closer God is.

You already know that not everyone in our party thinks like this. May the Lord give me wisdom, patience and endurance for all the complaints, attacks, questions and myths of others, so that everything best serves his sacred work.

There is still no rain.

I am working here by telegram, seeing whether we can still make a small profit from our wool. Our next job will be to shear the sheep so that we can move on after it rains. Perhaps I will send our horse wagon to Peake to fetch flour and the boxes with the tools, since our things have arrived there.

We are all well and the food is tasting much better, because we do not have much. This is nobody's fault, since no one can see into the future. The Lord will soon set us free from all evil; in every need I am and will always remain joyfully certain of that.

To my great joy I here received your dear, precious letter of May, this year. Kempe has his letter and Bode[38] will soon receive his by return mail. To my sorrow I see that all my letters on the trip and Kempe's report from Peake are not yet in your hands. That is because of the poor postal system and the great distance to be covered along various tracks. I have faithfully reported all important matters every month, or two at present, with all our sorrows and joys. If you have not received our letters, the Lord has spared you much deep worry. Most of it was complaints, tears and blubbering on our part, and I know that our suffering is your suffering, and our joy is your joy, so I have blunted much of the hard and bitter news so that you do not hear one sad story after another, although I have given you factually true reports. Later I intend to give you an exact geographical survey of our place; that is why I have not emphasised this aspect in this report. Fortunately, it has again come to hand so you will at the same time get a fuller report.

Things look sad in the poor Church. Jakobson, Gössling, Schoknecht and Bode contribute a lot to the confusion, and I am settled on fixing what they have wrecked. Gössling is proceeding with such presumption and acting so imperiously that I do not want to know where it will end. I am not sure about the unauthorised dealings between Jakobson, Schoknecht and Bode, but will under no circumstances get involved in all that, especially since Jakobson, as Drögemüller says, has taken malicious joy in blocking young Hansen's study in Hermannsburg, and is complaining to Pastor Hensel and the Church Council about Gössling's rough dealings. As much as I am needed there, I cannot make any decision before moving in with everything onto the mission field here, because the loss to the mission could not be made up, given the present situation. So I am not relying on my own thinking or that of other people, but will wait on the Lord from one morning watch to another, until I can with a good conscience return to my precious family and serve the Lord in the Church. I would prefer to stay among the heathen for the good of the mission, but I have no will except that God's will be done in everything and for everything that pleases him...

G A Heidenreich

* * *

A Personal Reflection: Heidenreich I

I have developed a real liking and admiration for my great-grandfather. I like the way he observes and engages in the world he is discovering for himself without a whole lot of palaver and wordiness. I like the glimpse of an intelligent mind that expresses itself quite simply. I like his doggedness, his unpretentiousness. And yet I imagine him as quite strong-willed, not afraid to tell how he sees things. He would not always have been easy to get along with.

I know for a fact that he and Heidenreich did not always get along well with each other. There is already evidence of that, with more to come. The fact is, though, that Heidenreich did not get along with a lot of people, including peers and colleagues. So, what was it really like at times for him and Kempe (and Hämmerling) as they made this two-month trip where they virtually lived in each other's pockets?

There is no doubt that Heidenreich worked hard, was conscientious in his role as superintendent, and was zealous for mission work, and he is to be admired for that. But as he goes about that work, he regularly comes across as opinionated, self-centred and grandiose, bordering on the narcissistic. I get the feeling that he views the Finke mission as an imposing and dramatic undertaking of personal kingdom building in which he is the heroic leader, the fearless explorer who grandly splashes his favour and nomenclature on this new land he is claiming. Here and elsewhere he obviously regards himself as superior in various ways to Kempe (and Schwarz and, later, Schulze), is at times condescending in his respect of them, and at other times even a bully. But that is typical of so many of his relationships, it seems. He would have been a very difficult man to work with, especially if you had a mind of your own.

In his account of the Hermannsburg missions in Australasia, Hartwig Harms says that Heidenreich was 'not exactly diplomatic' in many of his dealings with others.[39] 'His heart burnt for the mission', Harms states. 'Unfortunately, it burnt so strongly that it lacked steady thinking and careful judgement. His zeal was occasionally hectic, leading to impulsive decisions not popular with the young missionaries. And in his attempt to ensure lasting support for mission work in his Church, he was not always open and adept, so that he was accused of lack of clarity and, occasionally, dishonesty.'[40]

It is also significant how often he refers to being torn between his congregation at Bethany and the mission on the Finke. On the one hand he revels in the challenge of administering the new mission undertaking, and in being very 'hands on' in matters related to the mission, frequently to the point of giving serious consideration to moving to Hermannsburg itself and running the whole mission on site—a thought that appears to horrify Kempe and Schwarz! On the other hand, he also talks more than once of missing the Bethany parish and yearns for them and his family during his travels to and in the Centre. He would rather be home. It is an understandable dilemma. But I wonder how aware Kempe and Schwarz were of it. One would think they at least had an inkling of it, and I can imagine that, in part, it was discouraging for them: Heidenreich's heart was not always in this venture. It is also obvious there were times when they wished he would just go home and leave them to it.

For all that, I do feel for Heidenreich and the tremendous burden placed upon him by this daunting task. I can appreciate that the close relationship he claims with Director Harms was important to him, and that letters such as the next one were of special value and encouragement to him.

21 September 1876, Hermannsburg, Germany[41] *(Th Harms to Heidenreich)*
My very dear Heidenreich,

After a very long, serious illness that has kept me in bed for eight weeks, I am again writing to you with heartfelt and thankful joy that our faithful God and Lord has heard our fervent prayers and graciously helped you dear people through so much trouble and deprivation, and preserved your good spirits and joy in believing. He will continue to be with you and, with our prayers, will bring you into the land that he has given to our mission. Your journey ... active participation and fervent prayers rise up to his throne from many, many hearts, just as we pray for you, especially every Sunday. The Lord strengthen your faith so that you do not lose heart but remain joyful and confident. In such times we have really experienced the wonder of the statement in the Creed: I believe in the communion of saints. Built on the Lord and standing on one foundation of faith, with heaven open, the holy angels protecting us, and sure that our prayers offered in faith are heard, how should we not happily continue along our pilgrim way and struggle, until suffering and time come to an end.

You have your battles and we have ours. I have refused to use the new marriage liturgy and will continue that stance, but have to await being removed from my pastoral office. But come what may, the Lord is with us as long as we keep our conscience pure and undefiled. May his kingdom remain ... An open, honest war is better than an easy peace. The Lord will not desert Hermannsburg as long as it does not desert him.

The small sprig of flowers in your last letter was such a precious, warm greeting from the desert. Oh that the hearts of the heathen might be bound together in faith to form a lovely, sweet-smelling bouquet for the Lord.

The difficult start of our Australian mission should make us joyfully hopeful that things will turn out with blessing. May the Lord bless you dear pioneers and walk with you step by step...

Th Harms

6.

Waiting at Dalhousie

Altogether, the expedition spent almost 11 months at Dalhousie Springs (30 May 1876 to 9–10 April 1877). There were a number of reasons for this lengthy halt, the most important of which were the need to wait for rain which would provide food and water along the way for the animals, and the need to shear the sheep. That latter task required the erection of shearing facilities and the procuring of shearing clippers and wool bales (which they had not thought to bring with them). There was also the need to return all the way back to Finniss Springs to collect some of their goods and chattels which had been left behind there on the way up. In addition, time was taken to ensure supplies for the humans in the party, and to attend to repairs and other maintenance on the vehicles.

Two of those months were, of course, spent on the reconnaissance trip. Whether this trip was pre-planned or only decided on the spot is not absolutely clear: more likely, it was a decision made along the way. It seems that quite a few decisions were made in this way.

* * *

31 August 1876, Dalhousie Springs[1] *(Heidenreich to ELSA members)*
By God's grace I have now completed the main task that I undertook with my mission travels. I have personally inspected our new mission field and been able to assess that it has turned out to be excellent and suitable for our work, as far as human eyes can judge. I no longer have any doubt about the specially fitting location for the founding of the new station that is to be called Hermannsburg, according to the express wishes of Director Harms.

I would now be within my rights to return to my 'dear Bethany' with all the circles that are dear to me—what would I rather do than that? But I know that both congregation and family do not want me to leave my work half-finished. Thus, because of the present external needs, I am prepared before the Lord to stay here for a while, as long as I have to, until he grants me the grace of installing our entire mission staff on our property. This assumes that my dear congregations and family agree to the delay on which they, next to God, have the right to decide. I await their reply.

There is again plenty of work here. Today our large wagon with the ten draught horses will be made ready for Peake to fetch the things we off-loaded there. Those left behind have to build a shed for shearing sheep and then shear them.

Meanwhile, the camels with our freight should arrive. Some will stay here, others will be sent on, as soon as dear God sends us a good rain like the last one. One like that helps us on the spot with our caravan.

When we have about 120 miles behind us and reach the Finke, we will have enough water supply for the rest of the journey, and our precise knowledge of the way to grazing and familiarity with watering places gained on our last trip[2] will bear fruit for the draught animals and herds...

G A Heidenreich

* * *

This next letter from Kempe is a mixture of reporting on life in the Dalhousie camp and reflections of a personal nature. He also explains some of the principles under-girding the approach to this mission. The personal reflections are quite moving. And his justification of the need for the number of animals they took with them is revealing of the consideration that, despite some appearances, had gone into at least this aspect of the venture. There is the double-headed desire to make the mission as self-sufficient as possible, as well as to create a business enterprise that would make the mission financially independent. In the longer term there was the hope that the mission might make sufficient profit to plough money back into general Church funds. As matters transpired, these were rather lofty ambitions at the time, but laudable.

29 September 1876, Dalhousie Springs[3] (Kempe to Th Harms)

> 'But the desert and the wasteland will rejoice, and the open country will be joyful, and will bloom like the lillies.' ISAIAH 35:1

Dear Pastor!

When the prophet spoke these words above, it did not seem to Israel, the people of God, that they could ever be fulfilled. In spite of the many and urgent sermons of the prophets sent by God, the children of Israel by and large remained steeped in idolatry, so that even such a pious king as Hezekiah could in the long run, through his reformation, delay only for a short time the ruination to which the people were rushing. Nevertheless, the prophet here foretells better times, rich in blessings, still awaiting the people from the hand of God. Of course, this could be grasped and understood only by a person whose spiritual vision the Lord had opened up through living faith.

So, it is my opinion that we can happily and joyfully, by faith in the Lord Jesus Christ, also apply this word to ourselves and our work, although we now see nothing—in fact, even the opposite. For it is the work of the Lord which we do. He has sent us and also will neither desert nor neglect us, but after this long and difficult journey will again send us a time of refreshment and will grant us his blessing on our weak efforts, according to his promise.

Even if we do not see great success—which is hardly to be expected of people who have sunk so low—it would be blessing enough and our work richly rewarded if only a few souls—indeed, even one—were led to him through our poor service. The Lord make us ready and able for that.

Before I now continue the report, I would first like to allow myself a few remarks. It may perhaps have struck one or another of our dear mission friends that we have so much stock for our mission, and they may have asked themselves: Why do you take such a lot of cattle with you? Is this really necessary for the establishment of a mission station?

To this I answer: Here in the centre of Australia it is unavoidably necessary. I was also at first of the opinion that it was not necessary, but I have come to a different conviction, for here it is not as in other mission territories where European settlements, if not altogether close, are nevertheless not far away. Here we have to reckon with hundreds of miles. The next place where we can buy provisions, at least flour, is no less than 700 miles distant from our place. So, in order to be in a position where we do not have to buy everything, we as much as possible have to take everything with us, both to build anything as well as to have meat and milk on the station. You cannot go with money in hand to the first best merchant or farmer to get something, because they are just not there. That includes cattle, as well as working horses and bullocks, also dairy cows and animals kept for meat. For the latter we also use sheep.

At the same time, the communication systems between the Northern Territory and the Colony[4] are so meagre and expensive that even now and also in the future we will have to do everything by letter ...

The Lord God has so far wonderfully helped us because, contrary to all expectation, everything has happened quickly and well. But here[5] he has again given us the command, 'Halt!' For further north, as we discovered, there were long stretches with no water. On top of that we also had no flour, and so we had to decide to remain here, as difficult as that would be for us.

These Dalhousie Springs lie 140 miles from Peake and 60 miles from Charlotte Waters. It is a fairly large area, about 50 to 60 miles in circumference, where the springs lie scattered about, large and small. Some flow so strongly that they would be able to drive a mill, while others no longer give any water at all but have become overgrown over time. All without exception are warm springs. The one on which we are situated may well be 20°R[6], others are probably even warmer. The water is thoroughly good but contains a rich mixture of minerals, saltpetre, magnesium and so on. Otherwise the surrounding area is rather desolate, as the English people say: 'a stony desert'. Since it has not rained since 9 May, and in the meantime the winter frosts have pretty much taken away the grass, you can easily draw the conclusion that now in September things no longer look very pleasant.

Nevertheless, we have to be happy, and that we are because we can stay here for at least there is no lack of water here ... During this time we have occupied ourselves with all sorts of things, as is usually the case in such an encampment. By and large it is very boring.

When we arrived back here[7] new difficulties confronted us. The brothers here had already been without flour for 14 days and so Superintendent Heidenreich prepared to travel again to Peake in order to fetch some sacks of flour and a box of tools which were waiting there for us, since the driver who brought it had unloaded it there. In the meantime, we borrowed another 50 pounds of flour which we now had to ration until either the camels bring us flour or Heidenreich comes back again. In addition, we also have dried fruit, rice and raisins, so that, thank God, we are now able to satisfy ourselves each day.

On 2 September Heidenreich set off on the road to Peake with the large wagon, eight horses, and another man. It was a difficult trip since many of the creeks were dried up, and so they often had to travel for many long stretches without water. After an absence of 26 days, by the mercy of God they again arrived back here happy, except that Superintendent Heidenreich was rather exhausted and suffering from a throat complaint and rheumatism.

Already before the arrival of the brothers, on Tuesday 26 September, the camels arrived and brought us ten sacks of flour and the mail but, unfortunately, nothing of the other things that we had ordered. The camels had already met Heidenreich along the way, so that he already knew how things were with us. He had already ordered the six bags of flour to be brought to Charlotte Waters. We were glad that the dear brothers were now here again, and with good reason, for on the wagon they brought not only nine sacks of flour, the mentioned tools, and some government supplies for the heathen, but also some pieces of clothing and other things that can serve for our upkeep.

And so the dear, faithful God has wonderfully helped, and shamed our lack of courage, so that we are now able to look forward to the future without worry. Oh, if only we poor, stupid human beings could let go of our cares and diligently make use of the privilege that has been given to us as Christians, namely, 'Do not worry', and 'Cast all your cares on him for he cares for you.' So it must be and remain our daily prayer: Lord, strengthen our faith.'

During the absence of the brothers who went off to Peake, we here in camp have also not been completely idle. Since we intend to shear our sheep here, we have built various sheep yards, a shed and a wool press, while Brother Schwarz has officiated as cook, baker and butcher.

Today I want to bring this report to an end so that, God willing, I will continue it from our place.[8] I only have to add that today, with the help of Heidenreich, I have built a forge in order to be able undertake some emergency work.

Now, looking back on this whole time, despite all troubles, tight spots and difficulties, we can only offer praise and thanks for all the underserved love and mercy that our faithful God has shown us. For not only has he kept us well and given us everything that we needed, so that we suffered no want; he has also comforted us and revived us in our loneliness by his dear, precious Word which has ever and again refreshed us, comforted us, and strengthened us when we were in danger of losing courage, and the spirit of worry tormented us. He has also done this through many precious letters from those nearby here and from the dear homeland. From these we have been able to see that we do not stand alone, but that many dear Christians lift up praying hands for us. May the Lord bless all the dear letter writers in soul and body.

So, we certainly hope and believe that God does not neglect the prayers of so many of his children, but will hear and guide and lead us according to his counsel, and will also finally accept us with honour. For even if things are sometimes strange, they are always blessed. He also leads us by way of the cross and tribulation, which also serves us for the better, and we know that this time of suffering is not comparable to the glory that is to be revealed to us. Thereby we become ever more like our highly-praised Saviour whose path also went through suffering to glory, through cross to crown.

Mission and passion must always belong together. Therefore, whenever something oppresses us, we always want to cling to God and his promises, and to sing with Luther: 'And whether it lasts into the night and again in the morning, my heart should not despair of God's power nor be full of care. This is what the true Israel, born of the Spirit, does, and waits on its God.' ...

H Kempe

* * *

Heidenreich's next letter addresses ongoing issues relating to the mission in New Zealand, in particular the extent to which Heidenreich is to be involved there. Even in the midst of the desolation of the Centre and the problems he needs to resolve there, he is distracted by problems in an entirely different part of the world. Also, he continues to dilly-dally around the 'stay-go' question. And still has the time to toss in the odd disparaging comment on Kempe and Schwarz. His criticism about their personal issues is gobsmacking. It is also hypocritical, given the yearning for 'home' he himself expresses on occasion.

3 October 1876, Dalhousie Springs[9] *(Heidenreich to Th Harms)*
Venerable, much-loved Father!

Through the Brothers Gössling and Kowert I received the news that I am to have nothing to do with the New Zealand mission, which would be fine with me also. However, you earlier commissioned me to put everything in order in the mission in New Zealand, to establish the first station and give it a name. And since, writing in your own hand, through me you again called Gössling for mission work in New Zealand and Schoknecht in Central Australia, you said in a letter: 'You must by all means be the man to take everything in hand'... I will be very thankful to you if you limit my mission call to South Australia...

Now I am coming to you like a beggar with his sack. First, I ask that you send three hardy colonists who will receive all provisions and a salary of 200 [Reichskrone[10]]. After faithful service in the Lord for a number of years, this amount should be increased. The best people are labourers, shepherds, masons, carpenters and smiths, able to do work capably. You will receive their shipping fare from Schmidt, and so you can send us helpers very soon. I have had to pay off a shepherd and a driver because of drunkenness and misconduct. Though I am thereby placed in an embarrassing position, I prefer to put up with everything except tolerate such bad behaviour.

Can you send us a bell like those in the Old House?[11] Here they cost too much. Then also 2000 revolver cartridges No 9 from ... Ahnert, two revolvers, a good double-barrel shotgun, and one or two long sabres, since these are cheaper and better back home. Here it is the other way around, with gunpowder and lead cheaper. With everything flowing into and out of your treasury, I will save money wherever and however I can. I am happy at the good offerings coming in from the congregations, and that, despite the terrible expenses for people's wages and food, we still have a small reserve. The Lord is visibly blessing what we have in our sack.

Are you able to send us £500–1000 for the purchase of cattle? That would be great gain for the main treasury, though I do know to some extent your many expenses and look forward to the time when with, God's help and blessing, I can send you something instead of receiving.

How much longer I can now remain on this journey depends on God and my congregations from whom I have asked permission to stay away for a longer period. I must carry out the main task given to me: to reconnoitre the place and choose a site for the station.

Believe me, it was necessary that I came with the expedition, and it is no less necessary that I stay on. The young brothers are not up to the great task, and I have every cause to express to them my reservations that this mission, too, will sooner or later be crippled if it does not proceed step by step with great faithfulness and patience. This is a hard and difficult field for which not one in ten men, otherwise able missionaries, is equipped.

I find the necessary endurance lacking with my dear brothers. They have too great and lofty things with which to concern themselves: bringing their fiancées up here by carriage, being independent, and what not else. Out of love I will not point this out; perhaps God will give them grace so that they improve.

Given all that, we are not yet over the high mountains of obstacles that soon lie before us. The time has come when I must either rush off home to Church as fast as possible, to the detriment of mission, or I must stay at the mission and Dierks[12] will succeed me in my pastoral office. That is the iron necessity we are facing, and I am inclined to either, and so am unable to reach a decision. I ask you to decide whether I go back to the Church or from now on remain entirely in the mission in the Far North. I sincerely ask that the faithful Lord gives you the right answer for me, and that I can then go my designated way full of trust and confidence...

G A Heidenreich

* * *

31 October 1876, Dalhousie Springs[13] *(Kempe to ELSA members)*
Our camp is still at Dalhousie Springs. The mission staff members here on 1 October were the same as mentioned in the last report. However, next day the shepherd J Hunt and the driver A Pohlner left. To take the latter's place Superintendent Heidenreich has taken on a new driver, an Englishmen by the name of George Carlin.[14] The vacancy left by the shepherd has not yet been filled,

since we intend to dispense with one shepherd because Brother Mirus took over the large flock and we intend to hand over the supervision of the small flock to the Blacks. Superintendent Heidenreich set out for Finniss Springs with the new driver to fetch the things that had been left there and, perhaps, to bring some other things from Peake. For this purpose he took with him the small wagon with eight draught horses and also a saddle horse. That left only Hämmerling and Mirus in the camp, apart from the two missionaries.

Activity. Brother Mirus looks after the large flocks, while the missionaries have to attend to the other work. From mid-month onwards the latter have had to take on the supervision of the small flock, taking turns a week at a time (for reasons mentioned below) and will continue to do so.

State of health. Thank God all are well apart from Brother Hämmerling who still suffers from an ulcer on the leg. The weather was consistently dry with lots of wind. In the middle of the month there were some thunderstorms but only a few drops of rain.

Special observations. As mentioned above, we handed the small flock over to the Aboriginal people. After a few days it emerged that they had slaughtered sheep. Naturally, we cannot use such shepherds. We dismissed them from their posts and must now look after the flock ourselves.

* * *

Despite being able to access around 400 letters and reports in our research for this book, it is obvious there is still an unknown number of those documents 'missing'. Whether they have been destroyed or buried in some yet-to-be-located hideaway is a moot point. It would be a wonderful thing, however, to be able to locate them, for that would help to fill in the obvious gaps in the reports of October to December.

Heidenreich has left Dalhousie, purportedly to return to Finniss Springs to collect the things they had left there on the way up. Incredibly, that is a return journey of well over a thousand kilometres, and one again wonders how that situation came about. On the journey Heidenreich (probably travelling also with the Aboriginal lad 'Bobby') has to contend with drought, government officials and a broken-down wagon. But, even as all this is happening, it is easy to detect under-currents of other unsettling things going on, but what those are is not spelt out.

3 November 1876, Finniss Springs[15] *(Heidenreich to ELSA members)*

… Last time I informed you that I wanted to go from Dalhousie back to

Finniss to collect the remaining bits of our possessions. The next day, the Lord graciously granted that George Carline entered our service, coming from Port Darwin. Now that all was in order for the camp and the journey and that the horses grazing far off had been found, we two[16] and a Black set off with nine horses.

We were hoping to find water on the second day, but everything was dried out and our thirsty horses had to go another 12 miles before we found water. There, at the Macumba, we encountered two government parties, one of which went to Alice Springs, the other with us to Peake. There were another 35 miles to the next water, and from there just as far to the next source where I gave our horses a rest for three days, and I went ahead to Peake with the government people, to send off a wire for shears and wool sacks.

Though we had struggled through without loss, we all came to the conclusion that, in a short time and until it rained, the return trip to Dalhousie would soon be out of the question. If I had speedily received from Finniss the things absolutely essential for us to travel further, as well as the shears and wool sacks, we would have immediately turned back as a matter of life and death.[17]

However, the Lord prevented that, and we were soon to experience why. He made it clear to me that, whether we got rain or not, it would be impossible to move out from Dalhousie. If heavy floods arise one can make no further progress on the track; if they do not arise, it is absolutely impossible. In this bad period we can still be satisfied that our stock are there richly supplied with water and the necessary fodder. The owner of that place cannot send us away because he cannot stock his run until the rain comes.[18]

In the present state of affairs, I see myself as a superfluous, even burdensome person, who for a long time has not been able to do anything here but could be doing a lot at home. I had received by telegraph the answer to my letter to my congregation about me staying on longer. But since it [i.e. that answer] did not relate to the present circumstances, I sent a telegram to my congregation for advice repeatedly expressing the wish that I should stay until the station was founded.

Against my better knowledge and understanding, I accepted the supposed[19] will of God, as also my congregation saw it, and continued my journey to Finniss.

I suggested to two government officials who intended to go to Beltana, that they could travel with me to Finniss if they were willing to bring me from Beltana the shears and wool sacks to Finniss on the cart that they were to fetch there. They gladly accepted this offer and provided their own food.

On the way[20] the heat became worse every day, scorching all the fodder. Our wagon had been standing in Dalhousie, during which time the white ants had eaten the hubs under the remaining paint, and Missionary Kempe had not discovered the damage. When I set out[21] he told me that the wagon was in good order for travel. I also did not discover the damage before the wheel fell to pieces. How good it was that I had not gone back from Peake. We would have been stranded on the road with our goods, unable to move on because there was no wagon available there. We applied all our bushman crafts and, on the worst wheel,[22] we made two new spokes between every two existing spokes and arrived in Strangways with God's help.

From there the government people went off to Beltana with a cart, and Mr Hogarth showed us great hospitality. He tied the wheel together and gave us free lodging for a week. May the Lord reward him. However, when being tied, the rotten wheel rims fell apart and we had to resort to iron wheel rims and bolts.

I was in a terrible situation, and the usual reliable telegraph reply of my fellow council members wisely left me again carrying the whole load on my own. After again and again considering all possibilities and making inquiries and calculations, I was left with no better or faster solution than to fetch a new wagon from the South in the best and fastest way possible.

In my mind I can already hear the self-appointed judges saying: 'The mission is finished! As soon as he comes home he is not going off again, and the others will soon follow him. That will be fine with God, too, since he [God] can carry out his work without us.'

It is true that our mission is not alone in fighting to succeed against failure; everyone beyond Peake, including all animals, will be involved in a life and death struggle. A year ago the situation was already bleak; now I can hardly describe for you the present state of this region. The fearfully hot winds destroyed all green growth eight days ago, the dear sun rises every morning in a silver-white haze, covers itself by day in thick clouds of dust, and goes down in the evening sparkling fire. People and animals are exhausted and weak, and birds fall lifeless from the sky during the day. It is a very big question what the near future will bring us...

We also do not hide from you that our party at Dalhousie has sufficient provisions for nearly a year, and that in three weeks' time a good supply will be added for the future. This has made my joy twice as great that I could at the eleventh hour fetch our things with the large wagon before the terrible time that I mentioned occurred.[23] Unfortunately, I suffered a fall from the wagon and ongoing infirmity would almost have cost me my life on the return journey, had not God and his angels protected me. The dangerous crisis that came upon me allowed me no rest by day or by night.[24]

In case I am misunderstood and my worries are wrongly construed, I must say that I again am happy that neither the government nor other parties have so looked after their people as our people have, because they missed acting at the right time and left their hands lying inactive in their laps.[25] God piled good things on us,[26] and had I understood him completely I would have gone to Peake the first time with two wagons.[27] You will now hopefully say with me: To God be the thanks for what has been given and done.

Instead of laying the foundation stone of our station on the Finke as you and all of us would wish, I am at present sitting idly at Lake Eyre, a miserable region. I really do not know whether I should and can travel north or south since, as things stand, any movement can have very negative consequences. I have already often asked the dear, faithful Lord to take my soul to himself, but he might still want to use me because I have too much flesh and blood that he must first crucify and kill, if I am finally to gain my inheritance with him.

Nothing unusual comes my way when I understand what I have deserved because of my many sins and great misdeeds. Despite that, I remained faithful to him and my only comfort is that God is gracious, merciful, patient and utterly faithful… Up to the present I have received no report from the brothers at Dalhousie, nor have any arrangements been made[28] …

G A Heidenreich

3 November 1876, Finniss Springs[29] *(Heidenreich to Th Harms)*
Venerable, much-loved Father!

… I believe that I have already reported to you that I wanted to gather all our things on the road from Dalhousie to Finniss. We began this journey in God's name but discovered that the water dried up so quickly in the heat that we had to push on with great urgency and effort to Peake, with nine horses. Since there are regularly full sources of water from there on, we could have gone further, but the hubs of our wagon were eaten by white ants under the remaining paint. It could not be used, and tying things together in Strangway did not help to make it further usable. There was nothing else to be done except to fetch a new wagon from 600 miles away. Given the lack of fodder and water, that is no light matter.

I found myself in a new struggle, protesting, 'Lord, hear my pleading'. Attempts to go home and wait for rain were shattered by two telegrams expressing the wish of my dear congregation and my precious wife that I should stay here until the station is founded. So, against my better knowledge and insight I complied again with God's will as it seemed to be expressed by the congregation. Today God has shown me that I do have to go home, against my will. What he has in store for me I still have no idea but will find out later and let you know.

It will greatly reassure you if I describe our present situation at Dalhousie as accurately as possible. Our flocks have plenty of water and the necessary fodder for a lengthy period, if God still does not want to give us rain because of our sin and lack of faith. We are thus at a place where we will, by God's grace, suffer no great loss of stock. Our missionaries and workmen have a supply of the most necessary food for up to a year in the camp and have six sacks of flour ahead in Charlotte Waters. If rain comes, we can move on. If no rain falls again this year—which the faithful Lord forbid in pure grace and mercy—they have at Peake, 150 miles behind them, 31 sacks of flour, eight large cases containing sausages, dried fruit, ... rice, five bags of sugar, clothing and shoes, in short, enough of everything for a happy and comfortable settlement at the lovely Finke. I got this together at the eleventh hour down south, with the help of my council members. In this respect—I do not mention other matters—we are better supplied than the government people and squatters.

My heart revived in the midst of our troubles on the way to Mount Hamilton when I met the driver George White with his two large bullock wagons that are to be loaded with our things at Peake in three weeks' time. If rain comes, he is willing also to take on our ten sacks of flour, sugar, large bales of blankets, axes, hatchets and to bring everything to Owen Springs, 45 miles from our place. That is what I have arranged with him.

If no rain arrives, the whole of the North will be in jeopardy, not to mention the horrible desolation and loss of human life. In that case neither he [i.e. White] nor any other traveller can budge. Should this happen, I have directed our dear missionaries to bring no supplies to Charlotte Waters by bullock wagon before it rains, but to wait on the Lord's direction. If rain does not come according to his will, and their food stocks are almost eaten up, the bullock wagon should first fetch supplies from Peake, before the journey is resumed. That is the description of our present situation from which I am cut off, until the Lord again raises up his gracious clouds. May he do what he desires and what is good for us and further our holy undertaking. For there is no one else who can help ... He must bring our work to a victorious conclusion, even if it takes our death. For he has commanded us to preach the gospel to all creatures and there are many up here in the North. He has let me see that with my own eyes, to hear it with my own ears and to touch it with my own hands. If he continues to stretch me further on the rack, beyond human endurance, I will, like Luther during Melanchthon's sickness, throw my beggar's sack at his feet and, like Luther, say to him, 'If you let my Phillip die, you can do your work yourself'. For I too will soon have had enough, and more than enough, so that I can at the moment simply not pray any more, and no Word of God clings to me. I can no longer endure it; my eyes are a well of tears, and my strength has deserted me... What my heart now desires and feels I cannot do and do not want to say, out of love for my Saviour and for you. You have enough and more than enough to put up with, without my croaking, and you cannot say, 'I do not want anymore. I cannot take anymore'. Thus, I am willing to regard these my thoughts as disgraceful and shameful, and not dwell on them any more...

G A Heidenreich

* * *

Heidenreich is at the end of his tether, absolutely discouraged, and torn with indecision. There are also unknown factors contributing to his depressive mood, and one would love to know what those are. Then, in the midst of all that miserable detail, Schwarz submits the following, almost desultory, report:

30 November 1876, Dalhousie Springs[30] *(Schwarz to ELSA members)*
   Camp. Dalhousie Springs
   Staff. Two missionaries and two labourers, four men in all.
   Activity. Brother Mirus continually tends to the large flock while we missionaries take turns in looking after the other flock. The person not shepherding played the role of cook. In the first week Brother Hämmerling was busy building a hut (with a reed roof and mud walls), but he now has to search for the horses that ran away some time ago.
   Special events. The weather is very changeable. Extreme heat, heavy storms with huge dust storms, but accompanied by only a few raindrops.
   In recent days it has been more cold than warm, so that we had to get out our warmest clothing.
   State of health. Good, thank God.
   Losses. One horse perished from old age.
   W F Schwarz, Missionary

* * *

Then, suddenly, almost out of the blue, this from Heidenreich:

4 December 1876, Bethany[31] *(Heidenreich to ELSA members)*
Dear precious mission community!
    The faithful Lord has again brought me back spiritually and physically well to my dear congregation and to the precious members of my household—whether for a shorter or longer period depends on when he sends rain from heaven to make further travel possible. So I ask you now to join me in thanking the dear Lord for all his faithfulness, grace and mercy shown to us all and to me in the past. Yes, it is a precious thing to thank the Lord and sing the praises of his name...
    With God's protection, our new driver, George, will arrive in Bethany in four to six weeks' time, with a Black, six horses and the broken wagon.
    In addition to the already numerous and high transport fees with camels and wagon, we now have the extra expense of a new wagon and for its transport from here, a considerable expense which, humanly speaking, could cause us many a headache...
    G A Heidenreich

He provides no detail on what has led to this unexpected and dramatic decision. He claims it has to do with the weather; but, in view of his earlier dark mood, it is more than that.

In my anecdotal recollection of events around this time is the claim that Heidenreich had eventually approached Kempe and Schwarz regarding his indecision about staying with the mission party. More than that: he shared with them his desire to head up the mission on the Finke once they reached their goal. Then he asked them what they thought he ought to do. And they told him to go home. They did not want him being so involved in the whole project.

If this story is true, it helps to explain the devastation he is experiencing. It also explains his decision to go home as an unwanted member of the party.

In addition, there is the fact that Heidenreich never went back to the Centre as a member of the Finke group.

* * *

Thus does this troublesome year draw to a close. Yet, there is one more shocking piece to its sad tale that will be revealed only in the new year.

Meantime, though, in the first of the final two reports for the year, Schwarz is painfully justifying his deplorable failure to properly address Director Harms. His explanation provides fascinating insight into the way relationships were played out amongst the Hermannsburgers. In the final report, Heidenreich is anxious about financial matters. He is also alarmed by the looming Missouri infestation, on which there will be more in future reports. He says not a word about his previous personal dilemma and pain.

16 December 1876, Dalhousie Springs[32] *(Schwarz to Th Harms)*
Dear cherished Pastor and Director.
... I sincerely ask you to be lenient with me for not previously addressing you as Father, which I would very gladly do if I did not feel conscience bound by the Lord's words.[33] Hopefully, you will not for that reason be angry with me. May the Lord also be powerful with his strength in my weakness so that I prove faithful and am daily more conformed to his image. So my wish and plea to your cherished, worthy person is that you continue to remember me in your prayers to God, though I do not doubt that you have previously done this conscientiously.

Though I have so far not been given the task by our esteemed Superintendent Heidenreich with being permitted to write the usual quarterly report, for which I have less skills than my dear Brother Hermann Kempe, I am still very happy to write an occasional letter to you to indicate my thanks to you for all the love you showed to my poor person in dear Hermannsburg, as also now here in the Australian wilderness, with your faithful intercession and scriptural comfort in your precious letters and issues of the *Missionsblatt*. Yet I must confess that I would gladly have written more frequently had I not, as noted previously, been so anxious about how to address you and, furthermore, not knowing whether you already had a lot of work without reading superfluous letters, since Brothers Heidenreich and Hermann Kempe faithfully report everything that comes to pass.

Dear cherished Pastor, we unexpectedly and quite suddenly gained an opportunity to send letters to the Post Office at Peake. I know of no other way of sending you a short letter still this year than to cease writing out in full the letter to you that I drafted some days ago and to simply send you the draft itself. Please forgive me that it is in a very rough state...

Your unworthy, W F Schwarz

28 December 1876, Bethany[34] *(Heidenreich to Th Harms)*
Venerable, much-loved Father!

...With God's help I am again back home. Rain has still not fallen in the North, and our brothers remain stationary at Dalhousie with everything. Our driver with the broken wagon will also be here in 14 days.

To my horror I see here down South that we already have about £300 of debt from the terrible freight costs for camel and other wagons. And so my counsellors have asked me to ask you for a generous amount of money for our upkeep, and that you let us have this as soon as possible.

Since we are not able to earn much from the wool, we have to meet our many expenses from the cattle. I have already taken steps to do that. Up North animals are too dear, so I made this offer to Mr Worland at Mundowdna: he is willing to sell us 400 to 500 young cows at £4 to £4/10 a head. For the mission he will include the calves up to a year old that are running with the cows, and the necessary mustering horses. There is so much to be said for this purchase. The animals are a third of the way to our place and are accustomed to the bush fodder and spring water of the North. I have seen what that means in that a station owner has already lost 120 of the 500 cows that he bought down South in prime grazing conditions. They died here where we are making our purchase.

We cannot make single purchases very cheaply here; for so many we would have to pay £600 extra, and it would cost us another £100 to drove them here. Taking into account unavoidable losses, this purchase with calves and horses offers us a profit of more than £1000 at the moment. My advisors have realised this, and we are now in written negotiation with Mr Worland. He has verbally promised to allow us credit for half of the money at 6 percent for an extended period.

We know that we cannot take this step without you and your help, also that it must be taken. For as soon as the long-awaited rain arrives, the deal must quickly be closed so that the party driving the animals can connect up with the wagons that leave from here, so that they have food supplies; otherwise that will later again involve large expenses.

Thus, I will try to borrow £1000 pounds from friends until we can meet the total cost after you send us money and we acquire earnings from the cattle. However, the purchase will only happen before you reply if sufficient rain arrives, and I receive news by wire that our brothers are proceeding to our place. Otherwise I will wait for your approval.

My advisors have rejected the purchase of some camels—11 young, strong cows and a bull—from Mr Elter[35] whom I contacted on my way home. We cannot do that at present. I do not have to insist on it; we still have close to two years of provisions for the journey. I know that we will have to buy camels later, just as I know that through using camels we can make a lot of money from the government and other stations with low incidental expenses. For all occasions and circumstances we have active, fast carriages for our men and their wives for their essential travel up North. So I will wait for the right time when the Lord also supplies money for that, since he knows better than I do that the purchase of camels is necessary for the future.

Have you found workmen for us, and when will they arrive? I wish they were already here, travelling with the wagons and driving them; otherwise I will have to take on others.

Otherwise everything is quiet at present and I am needed more by Church and mission here than I thought I was up North where, as a rule, I received only good news from here.

Now I have to take axe and shovel in hand to remove the Missourian growth from our Synod and to restore a more open path for our mission finances. I am very anxious about our synod this year, but pray that the Lord will give me grace, strength and patience for everything, so that in everything I can discern and do his will. What changes and disorder have arisen in my absence! It is becoming ever more clear to me that I must remain in my pastoral office to ensure the continuation of our mission and supply of money. One must say to the shame of the old Hermannsburgers not only that they have been lax in giving for the mission, as the receipts in the *Kirchenbote* show; they have also in many ways divided and weakened our resources, while still insisting that they are the best and most loyal Hermannsburgers...

G A Heidenreich

* * *

Elsewhere in the world – 1876

- American librarian, Melvil Dewey, published his Dewey decimal library classification system (March).
- The future Pope Pius XII was born in Rome (2 March).
- German engineer, Nicolaus Otto, filed his patent for the four-stroke internal combustion engine (17 May).
- Truganini, the last surviving Aboriginal person in Tasmania, died (8 May). In the USA former slave, Harriet Scott, also died (17 June), and gunfighter Wild Bill Hickock was killed (2 August).
- Montenegro declared war on Turkey (3 July).

- Johannes Brahms' Symphony No 1 premiered in Karlsruhe, Germany (4 November).
- A huge cyclone killed 200,000 people in Bengal (31 October).

1877

17 January 1877, Hermannsburg, Germany[36] *(Th Harms to Heidenreich)*
My dearly beloved Heidenreich.

God be praised that he has so faithfully and graciously helped you, has borne you, us and our sins with patience, and will certainly help and bear us further. May he give grace so that you will soon be on your place with the animals so that you can take on the mission work there. Your description of our place has moved us to tears of thanks and joy and drives us to greater zeal and prayer that the Lord may continue to look on us with his grace. Also, the names Königsberg,[37] ... grotto, have pleased us very much, and our dear king will also be delighted.

However, let us not express overly bold expectation. There will still be many disappointments in the future, and things will turn out contrary to what we thought, for that is what one experiences in the kingdom of God. But God has made a start and will continue to help, for an undertaking involving so much work and prayer cannot be in vain. Continue to work with confidence, pay attention to the hand of the Lord, be patient and peaceable...

I can imagine that you have no end of troubles, yet not as many as I have. So, let us comfort each other and trust the Lord whose strength is mighty in weakness. Be confident and undaunted... There is nothing you can do about the talk and squabbles of others. I cannot determine whether it is best for you to stay there or to return to Bethany. Yet I believe that, unless the Lord determines otherwise and indicates the opposite, you must remain in Bethany as pastor and superintendent of the mission... If it does turn out that it is better for you to stay in the Centre, I will accept your offer with great joy... Also, do not let the disturbances in the congregations there trouble you too much. The eyes of the Lord and his hosts are watching over you ...

You have invited me to name a range. I suggest Wolfengebirge[38] so it is named after our precious king ... and therefore also along with Königsberg and ... grotto. I also approve of the faithful Theodor's[39] name being used, though in deep humility.

I commit you to God, my dear Heidenreich. May he bless you and the dear Brothers Kempe and Schwarz and keep you humble.

In confident, fatherly love,
Yours, Th Harms

* * *

The next three letters are from Kempe and Schwarz to Director Harms and are among the saddest in the whole saga. Kempe is at his wits' end over the situation in which they find themselves, and he feels overwhelmed by the responsibility being placed upon him. His relationship with Heidenreich has reached rock bottom—in fact, is threatened with irretrievable damage. He agonises over his own actions, wrestles with inner demons, and must surely at times have been in deep depression.

Those letters are presented below in their entirety, and they speak for themselves.

3 January 1877, Dalhousie Springs[40] *(Kempe to Th Harms)*
Dear Father!

Greetings in God and comfort in Jesus Christ.

Because children place unconditional trust in their father and, without holding back, can tell him everything that is deeply troubling and distressing them, I have thought to act in a similar way towards you. True, I am no longer your child in the sense that we were while staying in the Mission House, but that should not hinder me in complaining to you about my distress. For I know that at our commissioning you said that you wanted to remain our dear father and in the future, as previously, could entrust you with everything. That gives me courage.

At the moment it is not physical need that moves me to write to you. Though our present situation is not enviable but pitiful, I do not want to complain about it because I believe that the Lord will finally help us to get through it, because his honour is at stake and it would bring shame on himself were he to allow us to perish. So, one gets used to the worst situation. Moreover, we have in that respect cause for praise and thanks that the Lord has kept us safe to this point, which is really a miracle in view of the terrible heat that we had at Christmas and again have now, with only a few days somewhat cooler.

It might have been time to write another report, but what should one write? It is easy to tell our situation; we are still at a standstill, waiting for the longed-for rain without which we can go no further. So, life here is rather monotonous and there is little to say apart from that we are at present shearing the sheep. Schwarz and I are looking after them, taking turns week by week. Inspector Heidenreich will write more about how he is getting on.

While shepherding, we have plenty of time to prepare sermons and to study God's Word, but in the process I sense the power of the devil and experience in a real way how true your opinion is, one that I previously doubted, that the desert is the habitat of evil spirits. I can sense their presence.

With that I come to what I wanted to bring to your attention.

I am frequently beset by the most horrible and most blasphemous thoughts. It is clear to me that it is the devil getting at me in very different ways. He readily points to our previous and present situations, and says:'You see that there is no gracious and merciful God, for have you experienced nothing on your journey other than trouble, suffering and misery? There may well be an Almighty God, but his only pleasure is in tormenting you and the stock; why else does he send you no rain? He could do that but he does not want to. Give him up and make an end of it.'

Added to that, one sometimes utters words in resentment and anger that one later has to regret with tears. This gives the devil occasion to reproach me for my sins, saying: 'You are not up to being a missionary. How can you want to convert others when you yourself are unconverted! Give up this mission; you can serve the Lord in other ways.'

Then there arises doubt in God's Word and promises, so that I do not know what I should do. I have already said to my dear Brother Schwarz that I would pull out if things do not change. For how can I preach to the heathen and to ourselves if I myself doubt? I would be a hypocrite. I have often thought that it is my sins that bring on us all our suffering, and have asked the Lord to remove me with a blessed death so that the entire work is not hindered because of me. Then there are again times when I find comfort in my Saviour and in the forgiveness of sins, but soon I am back again [with doubt], more harshly than before .

That is my extreme need that I need to bemoan to you, dear Father; I would really like to hear your fatherly advice in this matter, and earnestly ask you to write to me advising me what I should do. I will gladly do everything that you recommend.

I ask only that you do not make this letter public.

I also ask forgiveness for not sending it directly to you but forwarding it as an insert. I would gladly send you more by way of enclosure to save money, but do not want to give you more work, knowing that you already have enough to do and that your time is precious.

I wish from my heart that we could soon escape from this mental inactivity and take on a lot of work. That is where I am at my best. This, next to God's

Word, is the best way to keep the devil at bay. God have mercy and bring us soon to our goal so that we can begin our work among and with the poor heathen.

I also ask for the help of your intercessions.

Finally, I have another request. Is it possible to have the sermons on the passion story in print? I can remember them fairly well but would really like them firmly fixed on paper. Please take my request into consideration.

I still have no news about when and how our dear fiancées are to arrive. It is all the same to me, but I here again express the wish that they come early enough to be able to travel in the cool season.

I want to finish this letter today, on 3 January. We celebrated a blessed New Year and can sense that the faithful Lord is with us also in this wilderness. However, already on the second day of the new year, we unfortunately had the sense and experience that the devil is not asleep also in this year but continues to seek out someone to devour. He caused a rift in our small company of four men. One of them, Gottlieb Hämmerling, sneaked into the hut while I was shearing and drank all the brandy. As a result he was drunk the entire day and unable to shear.

He will leave us. Indeed, we actually have to dismiss him because we cannot put up with this kind of behaviour in the mission. However, I think he will exclude himself out of false shame, since the devil has him so firmly in his coils that he can only get his freedom by genuine repentance. God have mercy on his poor soul and make us ever more vigilant and move us by this incident to ever more prayer so that it does not ruin us and the whole undertaking, as the devil wants, but rather brings blessing. May God by his grace bring that about.

From this you again see how much we need your intercessions, yours, dear Father, and those of the entire mission community. So, we all ask for them again.

Cordial greetings from my dear Brother Schwarz and me to you and your entire family, the mission houses and the whole community. God will see to it that things turn out well. We are making our way to Canaan on a new track through desert sands.

I am and remain your obedient son,
H Kempe

18 January 1877, Dalhousie[41] *(Kempe to Th Harms)*

'Before they call I will answer, while they are still speaking I will hear.'
ISAIAH 65:24

Dear Father

When I wrote my last letter to you and indulged in so much complaining and moaning, none of us thought or suspected that the Lord's help was so close at the door. It was as if the dear Lord waited until we had reached certainty amongst ourselves and purified us of all filth, for when we removed the villain from our midst, it began to rain that very night and rained very heavily with brief breaks until Thursday. We trusted the Lord who could and had to continue to help us even without the man of whom I wrote at the end of my other letter, and who left on the same Saturday. It rained so heavily that we got to see such floodwaters as we had not previously seen in Australia. The flood rose above the old marks reached by the last flood. I, a doubting Thomas who could not and refused to believe that the creeks could ever run, witnessed this to my shame. It began to rain on 7 January, the festival of Epiphany, and we were able to celebrate it with happy hearts because the faithful Lord has finally opened up for us the gate and doors to the land assigned to us. May he also grant that his Word finds ready soil and ground in the hearts of the poor heathen with whom we are to labour.

Since the feast of Epiphany is now also celebrated as the church's mission festival in our dear homeland, we thought that on this day many prayers for us poor desert pilgrims would be ascending to the Lord in heaven. How wonderfully the dear Lord has heard these prayers, since we here in Australia, fully nine hours ahead in time, were celebrating Epiphany while it was still Saturday for our dear ones back home. So the Lord here fulfilled his promise literally: 'Before they call I will answer, while they are still speaking I will hear.' Help had already arrived before our loved ones at home presented our great need to the Lord. His Word is reliable, and he certainly delivers what he promises. May his holy name be praised forever.

We, too, in our weaknesses, have praised and thanked him, and have heartily sung: 'Praise to the Lord the Almighty etc', this despite having a great deal of work to do because our stock had strayed in search of water and, furthermore, because we two, Brother Schwarz and I, are quite alone, apart from the shepherds, and we have lost 300 of our sheep as a result of the deluge. Despite all this, we have offered praise and thanks for the blessing and our Lord Jesus has not allowed us to suffer ruin but has given wonderful help so that we have all our animals together again, and the sheep, too, are recovering with the fresh, green fodder.

We firmly believe that the faithful Lord will help us further and will send us people so that we can move off, since he has promised: 'I will never leave or forsake you'. So we are already preparing to set off on our journey. The Lord grant that it can soon take place.

Humanly speaking, now is the best time to journey on. First, it is cool after the rain; secondly, there is plenty of water everywhere and, thirdly, also fodder. So, we do not have to be in too great a hurry and so overwork the stock.

However, our hands are tied, for in the first place we lack workers and, secondly, the Superintendent is not here. In October he went off and is again in the far South, leaving us in the lurch. The pretext was the wagon: it was suddenly supposed to be of no use. But this did not make a journey right down South necessary, since another was available in Blinman.

With that I come to a topic that I have long wanted to write to you about, dear Father, but will actually do so now, not for my own sake but for the sake of our undertaking. I fear that such further maladministration will cause it harm.

Firstly, looking back over the whole journey so far, it has all been for nothing, I have to say. It has already consumed huge sums of money, quite apart from the loss of horses, sheep and other things. If we were setting off from down South now, after it has rained, we would at present take half as much time to get to our place at a quarter of the cost and possibly without losses. Why was the advice of experienced people not listened to before we set off down South? That advice was that we should sell most of the sheep, and also that we should not begin the journey before receiving favourable reports from the North that one can receive day by day.

And when we arrived at Coolong Springs and *had* to recuperate there because the horses were senselessly worn out, something that experienced people had also warned us against, why did Superintendent Heidenreich go off and leave us sitting there for eight to ten weeks, when four weeks were certainly *enough*?

That is how things are again proceeding, to our sorrow. It is no minor matter to be dawdling around on this route for two years without being able to do anything and, moreover, to be languishing physically and spiritually.

All that would still be tolerable if love and unity prevailed among us, which is not the case. Rather, I have to admit that I have lost all respect for Superintendent Heidenreich, because he treats us not as brothers in the Lord, not even as salaried people, not even as a man of the world, one of the roughest, treats his subordinates. Rather, he treats us like a drover treats his obstinate bullocks, which shows at the very least meanness and narrow mindedness.

I ask, has Superintendent Heidenreich a right to act this way?

I do not want to supply examples; my pen resists writing down cases of such mean behaviour. I will mention only one case where, in anger, I allowed myself to be so enraged that I threatened to shoot him.

That was the time when Heidenreich was away at Peake fetching a sack of flour that an Englishman[42] did us the favour of selling at cost. We previously often had to ask the English for a favour and were given what we asked for. During this period the same Englishman who gave us the flour came to us and asked us to lend him our wagon for several days. He wanted to fetch some wood from a yard, but his wagon was in bad repair. We believed that we could not refuse this request and gave him the wagon. When Heidenreich got back, enquiring after the wagon, we reported what happened. He raised such a hullabaloo in front of our people and the heathen that it was disgusting. He scolded us as unreliable people who played fast and loose with mission property and did not stop berating us, so that he foamed at the mouth. That so enraged me that I was carried away to make the above-mentioned threat. May God graciously forgive me.

That would all not really be so bad, since it concerned personal matters and could do little harm at the end of the affair. But I must add an important point which has already and continues to cause much trouble, and will do so in the future, if the evil matter is not eliminated. I refer to the strange double way of controlling affairs.

When Superintendent Heidenreich went away as [he did] last year when we were at Coolong, he handed things over to us, but also to the workers, especially to one person who was to have total control. When we heard that the people with the sheep lacked provisions, this person proposed that we should send off our one wagon with provisions, which we did after hesitating for a long time. When Heidenreich came back, he told us we had got the whole matter totally wrong: *nota bene*, there was never a reason to do what we did!

Why should the people who earn a wage be in control?[43]

When Heidenreich went off from here he had set things up in just this way; he even said to the man whom we let go after New Year: 'If the missionaries tell you something that does not seem right to you, simply say that you [missionaries] cannot tell me what to do.' That is what the workman told us when we wanted to give him an order. This very same man stirred us up against Heidenreich when he was here, but cited his authority in this way when Heidenreich was away.

Can any lasting good come from such dual control?

It becomes a dangerous thing to allow our workers the slightest amount of authority, for in the bush there are few respectable people. Most of them are drunkards, blasphemers and the like who have no desire to work. That is why they go bush, to earn a lot of money by doing nothing.

Heidenreich has already told us that he would, in any case, allow the workers to give their advice when we are on the station. Then, again, he planned to set one person as administrator, who was to seek the missionaries' opinion in difficult cases.

I cannot go into these two matters any further and, *for my part, herewith renounce all participation in matters of administration under such conditions.*

Given that we are up North and everything is running smoothly, and Heidenreich is finally down South again, will there not often be instances where quick action is needed, thus making it necessary that responsibility for administration rests in the hands of one person, one who is himself on the station, since the connection by mail and all communication is very deficient? What good does it do us if we have an administrator down South in the colony? In that case Mylius in India could be our administrator.

Would it not be better to appoint one of the old brothers, perhaps Schoknecht,[44] as our superintendent up North on the station so that we know who we are to follow? For the worst thing is that when something happens, we are called on to act responsibly, even while in reality we have no say.

We are by no means eager to take on administration. On the contrary, I will fight tooth and nail against that, but we feel forced to write about this for the sake of our enterprise.

We would gladly place ourselves under Schoknecht if he were to join us. It was not for our sake that Heidenreich wrote to you that Schoknecht is unable to serve in the Australian mission because he cannot be placed over us who endure the hardship of the journey. Nor did he [Heidenreich] write with our approval but only in his own interests, because he knows only too well that Schoknecht would not tolerate the kind of base behaviour that, unfortunately, often comes up; he knows him enough as an energetic man who has a mind of his own.

I do not know whether G Heidenreich has already written any letters to you about these matters, in which he has tried to present the very same thing quite differently. Let him do what he wants; I have not written any untruths but presented everything as it happened, as Brother Schwarz can attest in support of me. I have also written on his behalf.

I will say it again: we have not been motivated to write of these matters out of dislike for him personally. If that were the case, we would have preferred to stay silent and let it all pass over us. What drives us to act is only love for our sacred cause in which we are involved and work, and also love for you, dear Father, since we know you already have enough to worry and vex you. We are eager to do our best to prevent damage which must inevitably come if this kind of oversight is continued. We saw ourselves forced to take this step and write to you about the matter after we had given long thought to how it could be raised. So please credit us with sincerity, dear Father. We would have never reached our decision had we not known that we could tell you everything that weighs down on us and troubles us.

May the Lord God in his grace and mercy grant that his holy undertaking proceeds further, in spite of our many sins and foolish ways and make us faithful in watching and praying and working for him. May he bring glory to himself with these poor, deeply sunken people so that he brings many of them to salvation. Yes, Amen.

Hearty greetings to your entire dear family and to the whole mission community from

Your obedient son, H Kempe

also W F Schwarz, who hereby certifies that everything about our situation reported in this letter by my dear Brother Hermann Kempe is absolutely true.

In particular, I mention that Superintendent Heidenreich has, completely without my knowledge, written the letter stating the impossibility of Brother Schoknecht serving on the mission here. I remember expressly opposing Superintendent Heidenreich earlier when he wrote the letter in question from Peake. It was actually already at Lake Phibbs where I was alone and he tried to bamboozle me with all kinds of ideas on this matter. Upon which I roundly declared to him: 'I sincerely wish Brother Schoknecht would come here'.

Today, on 28 January, all are well. Please take utmost care with the attached letter,

H Kempe

Dear Father!

I have to bring you up to date on one thing that still causes me great distress. We have let the man called Hämmerling go; rather, he has gone of his own accord, since he did not accept the conditions we *had* to impose after his lapse. These were 1. acknowledgment and confession of his sins, 2. the promise never to do it again, 3. loss of pay for the week because he did no work until Friday, and we could not throw away mission assetts for such things, and 4. loss of the usual brandy at breakfast during sheep shearing.

Both of us suspect that Heidenreich will do as much as he can to bring this man back because he has placed far too much trust in him. He has already caused offence for our cause down South by being drunk for several days at every hostelry, as people have told me, and with my own eyes I saw Heidenreich forced to pay his boozing account of £7 at Beltana that he had rung up on the mission's account. So if Heidenreich brings this man back with him, we cannot for conscience sake and because of God's Word that says: 'Keep away from such people', remain in the mission up here, but will in that very hour leave the place, as long as the situation remains unchanged.

This Hämmerling was also alone to blame for the death of many sheep, as our workers assured us. Do not be surprised, dear Father, if you receive news of this nature. We can act in no other way.

We ask you for your advice by return post, as to how we should proceed in all these matters.

Your obedient son, H Kempe

11 March 1877, Peake[45] *(Kempe to Th Harms)*
Dear Pastor!

In about mid-January we received your valued letter which strengthened us anew in our difficult situation, and for which we sincerely thank you.[46] Now that Superintendent Heidenreich has deserted us, our position is doubly difficult since we alone have to keep things in order and are still held responsible for everything that is undertaken. As a result I had to make the long trip to here to settle the business with the rations which the driver who brought them off-loaded, not wanting to bring them further. With God's help I hope to settle everything.

Only, I have become really annoyed by the lack of understanding on the part of the people down South who sent the flour in simple and, what is worse, really bad sacks so that nearly all are damaged, and we will presumably lose much of the contents. Everyone knows how far things have to be transported and how the sacks suffer damage on the way, so that all flour should be sent off in double sacks. We now have to listen to the English say that the mission is wasting money. We cannot refute this because it is true.

Another reason for my trip here is to look around for workmen, because every week longer that we have to stay down here is the greatest disadvantage for us because we should actually be getting the station ready in winter.[47] In the summer heat we can do half as much work as in winter. I have already written to Heidenreich. Whether that is of any use, I do not know. I have the prospect of gaining two workmen here.

Then, if the Lord gives his grace, we can soon set off, so that with his help we can perhaps be on our place at Pentecost or soon thereafter. May the Lord help us and give us success. May he bless our going out and coming in, and allow us to find access into the hearts of the poor heathen with his Word.

When we are on our place we can, in my view, establish several stations because the place is large enough and has multiple suitable sites. I would like to hear your opinion on that, dear Pastor. And if you are of the same opinion, I ask you for assistance at the next commissioning: for one workman, perhaps Doppe or someone else, since we have to do most of the work ourselves. I hope that you, as our dear Father, will not refuse this request.

Schwarz and I are at present reasonably well, thank God, but we have to put up with a lot after the rain. This is partly because of the annoying flies that are worse than ever, and partly because of stomach weakness, so that we cannot digest any food, and partly because of sore eyes that are still causing us trouble. While we were travelling they were so bad that one morning I had to search for the tracks of my horse by getting on my knees to find them. On another day I met some drivers who gave me some eye lotion that did me good. Schwarz's eyes were also bad when I set off. Yet I hope to God that he will in due course take this problem away. It is a climatic ailment that the English call sandy blight. It is uncommonly painful.

Hopefully, this is the last letter you will get from us as we are travelling; God willing, we will next write from our place. How delighted we will be to again have regular activity. We thank and praise the Lord for all that he so far has done for us. I firmly believe that he will give us his blessing, that we can be confident of your prayers and those of the entire mission community and certainly that the Lord cannot allow the prayers of so many of his children remain unheard. May he make us faithful to the end.

Cordial greetings from Brother Schwarz and me to you, your dear family and the whole community.

I am and remain your obedient son,
H Kempe

* * *

In his autobiography penned towards the end of his life,[48] Kempe pays scant attention to the journey to the Centre. But he does single out Heidenreich's departure, his plan to drive back to Finniss Springs. 'But', says Kempe, '(Heidenreich) did not return. We had anticipated this, and were not particularly sorry about it either.' (12) The hurt and pain in relation to Heidenreich obviously lasted for life. Schwarz's feelings and thoughts on all of this are less well known, but he, too, obviously felt betrayed by Heidenreich.

It is noteworthy that Heidenreich never returned to the Centre except for matters of business, in particular the two inquiries that were later held in regard to the mission. Despite his earlier stated dream of living on the mission itself and running it, he never spent a day in actual mission work. It is almost as if his and Kempe's explosive falling out killed off those dreams, and he settled for managing the mission from afar. It is regrettable that this approach later became a further bone of contention between him and the missionaries.

Curious, too, is the lack of any specific mention in Heidenreich's letters and reports (at least, as far as we know) of the break-down of these relationships. He refers to tension and inner torment, and does not hold back from criticising the missionaries from time to time. But he never directly addresses what must have been for him a terrible series of experiences up there in that desolate place. It is almost as if he slinks away in pain from it all, and hides in his beloved Bethany.

Meantime, those left up in Dalhousie are compelled to get on with the task for which they originally set out.

Personal Reflection: Heidenreich II

As a descendant of one of the conflicting parties in this sorry tale, it has been a sobering experience to work through this element of that tale. But, in the process, the exercise has also thrown light on what has long been a mystery, at times almost a secret, in my own family. I referred earlier to the silence in my family around the great-grandpa story; and part of that silence was connected with Heidenreich. Before ever becoming really interested in Hermannsburg, I recall my father once making passing reference to Heidenreich. I had never heard of the man; and when I asked my dad, 'Who are you talking about?', he cut the whole conversation short by simply saying, 'Hmph! Heidenreich!'

However, it is not just in my family that I hear the silence around this dark part of the Hermannsburg story. I hear it also in the wider Church community. The story is usually framed as this heroic undertaking by gracious Christian people. Undoubtedly, there is a degree of justification for that framing. But these people were also frail and flawed human beings, often not very gracious to each other at all. And we tend too often to gloss over that. Like, possibly, for example, in Scherer's comment on the 'threat to shoot' incident, when he says: 'In later years Kempe related how tension on the journey once rose to such a pitch, that one man threatened to shoot another. This incident very likely involved one of the assisting laymen on this section of the journey'. (11) Did he, and others, really not know the true story? Or, did they know, but even in knowing, dilute the reality?

And then I wonder how other descendants of the players in this tale might think and feel about what actually happened between our forebears. Extended family feuds have been sparked off by lesser events than this. I would trust, however, that we might have the strength of character to be real about these ancestors of ours. And also the grace to be gracious and forgiving on their behalf.

7.

The Journey: Arriving at the Mission Site

By the beginning of the new year, 1877, there is a stirring among the party: they are organised and ready to make the final big push to the mission site some 350 miles (560 kilometres) away. Everyone is anticipating an easier run on this last stretch, and not without justification, given the comparatively easier travelling conditions ahead. Nevertheless, how long this last leg will take is something of an unknown, particularly in view of the fact that, as for the whole of the journey so far, not everyone in the group can travel at the same pace. The sheep only manage 8 to 10 miles (13 to 16 kilometres) per day, the cattle, horses and the wagon around about 25 miles (40 kilometres). All that is needed to get going are the rain and the opportunity to stock up on supplies.

Down South, Heidenreich is settled back into his parish. The New Zealand venture continues to cause headaches. Finances all round are stretched and he has to send out an appeal to members of the ELSA to dig deep and give more. So, there are still glitches, but also optimism.

* * *

20 March 1877, Bethany[1] *(Heidenreich to ELSA members)*
The long requested flooding rains arrived from 6 to 11 January. Large and small animals are said to have cried out pitifully in fear of the torrents of rain and loud rushing waters, giving our brothers an idea of the bellowing of all animals in the Flood. Unfortunately, the flood took away 150 of our sheep, and besides them another 250 died because of the wet conditions, leaving us with only 1900 who have recovered well with the green fodder. The horses and cattle are now also in good condition.

But the damp air also has its drawbacks: our brothers are suffering from vomiting up all food, and the small flies in their eyes and those of the horses are so bad that one can barely write.

As to when our people can now set out from there, this depends on the arrival of other people and the driver White who brought freight for us to Peake from Port Augusta for £26 per ton, and who now is to bring a load from Dalhousie and Charlotte Waters to our place at £24 for six tons. Our bullock wagon is to travel with him, together with the entire expedition. I have handed over to the missionaries the planning for and direction of the trip, since I lack the strength for a repeat trip.

The new wagon[2] here is finished, three draught horses have been purchased, and the others have made a good recovery. We have purchased things to load. Fodder for the wagon horses to last for a 500 mile trip has been ordered at Melrose. We have taken on a man who is to travel with the previous driver who is now breaking in the horses. Then we load up and, God willing, set out from here next week.

* * *

The Missionaries' Reports

For Heidenreich, details matter. All must be in order, and it is important that he has control. Now there are hassles with the New Zealand missionaries (and probably also the Hermannsburgers) not properly attending to their reports. There were two lots of reports they had to submit: one to Germany, many of which were published in the *Hermannsburger Missionsblatt*, and the second to Adelaide/Bethany for the ELSA for possible publication in the *Lutherische Kirchenboten für Australien*. Here is his little complaint about that:

4 April 1877, Bethany[3] *(Heidenreich to Kempe, Schwarz, Heine*[4]*)*
Not only are duties laid on me; I have also been given rights, and God is a God of order. So I again ask you to send me the reports for publication and to share with me the internal developments of your endeavours, like your views and wishes. The truth will set us free as long as we act truthfully and are not greedy for empty honours. I have to go to great pains to stress that with you, so I am writing to you, in this instance, what Father Harms commanded in the Founding Statutes, where it says in paragraph 5, literally: 'The local church in mission is to be kept continually informed on the state and progress of mission work by the mission superintendent, not by the missionaries'. The reports to Father Harms should also go through my hands. Here I have ordered things to avoid duplication of labour: the brothers send monthly reports for the Church conducting the mission and quarterly reports to Father Harms. I take material from both for the local church and then send everything to Father. If the brothers have private concerns, they address them only to me. In this way the one protects the other.

The monthly reports are passed on in sequence, but so far only Brother Kempe has reported to Father Harms. I have no objection if you want to appoint one of you to make these quarterly reports, otherwise you have to observe this same procedure as with the monthly reports. If it is easier and preferable for you, and Pastor Heine accepts my request that he becomes my representative among you, I will, after receiving your reply, give specific instructions on sending your reports to Father Harms, and you can send them through him. But I must have the monthly reports sent to me by you so I can best do my duty for the mission there and here.

* * *

Meanwhile, up North, one can almost sense Kempe, Schwarz and the rest of the group straining at the bit to get going. During their stay at Dalhousie they had met up with other parties and travellers on their way to various places. As these people left they no doubt created a restlessness in the Hermannsburgers to be on the way, too.

31 March 1877, Dalhousie[5] *(Schwarz to Th Harms)*
Since our English neighbours left Dalhousie we have had many travellers visit our camp. Trooper Flynn from Peake was recently here with three men and brought letters from you. He informed us that the driver, White, would have set out from Peake with our things and would arrive here in 14 days. Mr Flynn returns again in a few days and will take with him my report and a letter to you from Brother Mirus.

We have taken on an English labourer with whom Brother Kempe has broken in two draft horses and two riding horses. So, we are now ready to set off. We do not yet have a bullock driver and Brother Kempe wants to take over the wagon for the time being. Brothers Kempe and Mirus are unfortunately very weak and exhausted, especially since Brother Kempe returned from Peake; he travelled there on 5 March and came back on the 18th.

It has often rained, and on 17 March the creeks were running again. At present we have plenty of fodder and water here. At the same time the flies are very troublesome by day, the mosquitoes by night. They are a real plague for the eyes.

* * *

Then, at long last, they are on the way again. On 11 April the sheep head the expedition off in a staggered start. Altogether there are eight men, plus animals, in the group. The men are the two missionaries, Kempe and Schwarz, with Kempe designated by Heidenreich as the leader. Mirus is in charge of the sheep, Thomas Mills is the teamster, George Spence is also a drover. F Stone (appropriately named) is a mason! They are very aware of the building task that lies ahead. There are also two un-named Aboriginal people with them, serving as general hands.

15 April 1877, Hughes Hole[6] *(Kempe to ELSA members)*
We are now travelling again. Thanks be to God. We were very worried that we would have to stop longer, but the Lord destroyed our cares and showed us once more that he alone can and wants to help us further.

Shortly earlier, before driver White reached us, two more people joined us, and so we could prepare to set off after we had broken in the horses. Thomas[7] and I took the crates by road, together with the goods that White was to load, while the two men who joined us, George Spence and Thomas Mills, broke in two steers for pulling the wagon; Brother Schwarz had to pack the crates and cases and repair sacks.

On Tuesday 10 April White arrived, and Wednesday morning Mirus set off with the sheep, at noon our wagon left, and in the afternoon Brother Schwarz with the cart. We stayed behind with the horses since we had to help White with the loading; in the afternoon he also drove off.

Next morning we set out and were all together again at Opossum Hole. We stayed there with the horses and wagon for one day to allow the sheep to get ahead. We all joined up here on Saturday, with other wagons as well, so there were nine teams here on Saturday and eleven on Sunday. There is now a lot of activity up and down the road.

Our stock numbers are 1900 sheep and 25 head of cattle, but we will have to buy a pair of draught bullocks. Besides that we are driving 22 horses.

Thus the Lord has done all things well, yes, even more than we can comprehend, since he has sent us people at exactly the right time. He will continue to help. Yes, Amen, and he will bring us finally to the place set apart for us. May he ever help us and bless our going out and coming in...

H Kempe

* * *

Heidenreich Travel Notes

From his study in Bethany, Heidenreich follows the progress of the travellers as best as he is able. There was by now an established, if not always reliable, mail service between Adelaide and the areas into which the missionaries were moving in the North. The telegraph system was well and truly operational. And settlers took whatever opportunity they had to send mail and parcels back and forth with travellers along the way.

Heidenreich provides some interesting travel notes on the route and scenery that the party can expect to transverse between Dalhousie and the mission site. In between those notes he also provides glimpses of day-to-day organisational mission matters, in particular concerning the anticipated arrival of the next group of Hermannsburgers, including Schulze and the fiancées (the letter of 16 May).

14 May 1877, Bethany[8] *(Heidenreich to ELSA members)*
Dear Readers!

You will perhaps be happy if I make some additional comments about tracks, watercourses, ranges and natural features in the region that is being traversed, with the assistance of the travel reports that keep coming in. The track from Dalhousie leads along Mount Crisp through Christmas Creek, then in a long creek covered with red-barked mulga, first over rocky hills then over stony plains up to Opossum Hole. Twenty-two miles further to Hughes Hole there are 12 miles on a good track until one is through the sandhills. This is a good spot for people and animals, so it is a place where travellers rest and gather. I will never forget how we arrived there one Sunday afternoon with our horses dead-tired after travelling for three days without water, and how our horses, after drinking copiously, did not want to get out of the water.[9]

It is 6 miles from there to Blood's Creek where the telegraph line borders the road for another 100 miles. There is a wonderful vista on this great stony plain. On all sides one sees large ranges in the far distance, especially up to the Finke valley on the right. Then the track becomes terribly rough up to Abminga Creek, 20 miles from Blood's Creek. The Abminga has many deep waterholes but rarely has water; it runs into the Finke where it soon disappears in the sand.

For the 23 miles from here to Charlotte Waters, one has the Franz Range on the left. Then one travels over a tableland to this telegraph and police station.

We have received news from our travellers up to this point. In the next report I intend to give more information about the border between South Australia and the Northern Territory.

Matters became so muddled with regard to the recently dispatched wagon that Brother Schmidt followed, paid off all three people, placed the wagon with the load, three horses and Bobby Boy with Brother Hampel and the other three horses with Brother Ossig[10]. At that moment we then had no usable people to send.

Then there suddenly came news from Director Harms that, with God's help, he will in the New Year send three colonists with the fiancées. Since this wagon could no longer help the missionaries on their travels, and we again had to provide transport for those still arriving, we preferred to leave the wagon inactive for a short time, to save a lot of money in wages and other costs...

G A Heidenreich

16 May 1877, Bethany[11] *(Heidenreich to Th Harms)*
Highly honoured and dearly loved Father!
... We sent off the new wagon and three workmen on the day after Easter. That cost about 120 marks, but I economised by sending council member C Schmidt after them to pay them off so as not to jeopardise everything. He housed the wagon with the horses and the black lads with German farmers, until the fiancées arrive with the three settlers. They were then to undertake the journey to our place with the wagon. For the present we were unable to get good workmen; in any case, this wagon was not of any help for our missionaries to travel further. The worst was, if the fiancées and settlers had arrived [with the wagon gone], we would again have had to pay out dearly for a new wagon, horses, harness, which we could not afford...

Heidenreich

11 June 1877, Bethany[12] *(Heidenreich to ELSA members)*
Dear precious Mission Community.
... I [now] add the following about the track from Charlotte Waters up to Mount Musgrave. The track first goes through a lovely wooded area on moderately sandy ground until one comes to our old South Australian border after 15 miles. It is striking how even nature marks the border with different trees, bushes, spinifex and grasses appearing. There are another 15 miles from the border to Goyder, partly over a terribly rocky track, partly long flats. The area has lovely ranges to the right and left, and the Finke can often be seen to the right from elevations of the track. The Goyder has a broad bed, deep sand, and thus also water in the driest times. It has large gum trees on its banks, and good pastures on both sides.

From there the track becomes more sandy and the sides so wooded that one sees nothing more than the sky above until one comes to the Finke after 16 miles. There the track goes around a small round mountain and proceeds close beside the river bed for 10 miles on a charming flat without bushes until another small hill appears on the right. The track leads to the elevation of this hill which offers a wonderful view out over groups of sandstone formations ahead of and along the track. In appearance they resemble old ancient ruins of knights' castles. I was vividly reminded of my home in the Thüringen forest.

From there the track goes down and follows along the Finke in a mighty stand of gums whose shade and pleasant scent now give real refreshment for some miles after the previous long hardships. Then come the burdensome sandhills again to rob man and beast of previous joy, until the Finke again appears at Kronenberg. We have climbed this mountain and at that time described the most notable features.[13] It may be 8 miles from the last mountain to this one.

From there one again goes up-hill and down-hill for several miles on sand and stones on a plain 8 miles long, up to the crossing of the Finke valley which is a mile wide. The track before, during, and after this point is difficult and bad for several miles, then becomes better between high sandhills along a plateau with the mighty Musgrave Range to the right, until one comes down at Mount Musgrave to the Finke on the left. After crossing the Finke it always remains on one's left side, though the track later often borders on the river...

G A Heidenreich

July 26, 1877, Bethany[14] *(Heidenreich to ELSA members)*
Finally, I want to still describe the last stretch of track our brothers had to travel along. We had last arrived at Mount Musgrave. From there the track goes over the creek into a level flat between two round mountains. Behind them to the left, a mile further down the Finke, lie Grant's and Stock's stations. The track passes over Horseshoe Bend (resembling a hoof shoe) up to Old Depot, over large sandhills, long flats, occasionally in the Finke valley through the runs of the above-mentioned gentlemen. From here the Finke flows to the west, the Hugh joining it to the north-east.

Immediately behind the entry of the Hugh there is a well preserved house, built earlier by the telegraph party. Here, for the first time, one has to drive through its deep sand bed. Before one again crosses it ten miles further on, the highest sandhills have to be climbed over. Then there are two double crossings in the next 12 to 14 miles. The river stays on one's left after the last crossing, but the track is difficult until it improves beyond Francis Creek.

From Mount Burrell, which lies a mile to the west and where we first found water for our thirsty horses in the Hugh, the way is hilly and rough. Then come nice flats until one reaches Deep Crossing between hills, where Brother Schwarz broke the wheel.[15] From here sandhills again occur.

I have often been amazed how things regularly change in the North: sandhills, gibber plains, then sandhills or ranges—continually changing.

Then one sees the first line of the James Ranges. After passing over these, a good track goes down over several creeks to the second row of mountains through which the Hugh has broken, and the track crosses the river several times.

Then come more open surroundings once more, until one reaches a new crossing of the Hugh through thick scrub. Ten miles on Doctorhool lies on the right and Doctorstone on the left. These two rocks are a remarkable phenomenon, standing there in a large sand plain, majestic on all sides. Then one travels in and beside the Hugh through the last arm of the James Ranges, on to Mount Clare Springs.

From there one can already see over the Waterhouse Ranges to the MacDonnell Ranges. The track now goes for nine miles over easy sandhills in and along the Hugh through the Waterhouse Ranges where there are large springs, then over terrible rocks and deep sand until one finally sees the Owen Springs station close in front of one. Back then we rode down from there close by the Waterhouse Ranges but could not find a driving track there. To my joy I heard from Mr Gilbert that he and his people later made a road as far as Ellery Creek, and so our dear brothers only had a 10 to 14 mile drive to the Finke and our place...

Heidenreich

* * *

The Account of the Trip (cont.)

Back on the track, things are going quite smoothly—well, comparatively so for this group! From here to the arrival on the Finke, we simply listen to the voice of the missionaries as they tell the tale.

3 May 1877, Mount Musgrave[16] *(Kempe to ELSA members)*
Dear precious Mission Community.

... I have already written how we fared up to Charlotte Waters. All went well from there, except that the wagon shaft broke at Goyder. Next day we made a new one and two more yokes for the oxen. Yesterday we all reached this place well. When we arrived at the Finke we were not a little surprised to find it flowing, and at a fair breadth of about 30 yards. Our surprise turned to joy when we heard that this water came from the Hugh, since from Olderpool we have to continually follow up that river; so soon we were able to find water everywhere, even for the sheep, which has not always been the case. This gave us new courage and happiness and our hearts were filled with praise and thanks to the faithful God who has done everything so well, yes more than we even asked for or could understand. Our wagon and the bullocks in front now form a mighty team and I am delighted with the people who take pains looking after it. All our stock are in good condition, the horses almost too fat; even the work horses grow fatter. You would barely recognise some of them...

H Kempe

24 May 1877, Mr Gilbert's Station, Owen Springs[17] *(Kempe, via Heidenreich)*
Dear precious Mission community!

... Already on 24 May Missionary Kempe was on Mr Gilbert's station at Owen Springs with the horses that had to be driven, in order to attend to various business matters there. He ... reports on various things as, for example, the steps he has taken to acquire a new wheel for the cart that was damaged on the trip; the stallion has died and he advises that another be purchased; negotiations with the driver White about the rejection of his demand for £25 more; about the present supply of provisions and those to be sent again at the next opportunity and their use; that the lambing has begun, which has forced them to hurry to get the flock to our place; finally, that they hope within three months to finish a house needed for shelter and protection of their things. His writing evinces the vibrant and happy spirit of a conqueror after much struggle and hardship.

27 May 1877, Owen Springs[18] *(Schwarz to Heidenreich)*
Dear Brother Heidenreich!

Since it is already the end of the month and I must report, I will do so immediately since Mr Conway (the manager on Mr Gilbert's station) intends to fetch the mail and take this note with him.

God be thanked for everything. Since 1 May we have with God's help put behind us the stretch from the Finke Crossing to here. Just this moment Brother Mirus has arrived with the sheep and our wagon. White is also close behind. We number seven persons (five Whites and two Blacks) and are all well, thank God. Brother Kempe has already mentioned that the stallion is dead and the lambing has begun. I note only that we have had to kill 41 lambs in order to save the ewes, also that one draft bullock and two sheep died of poisonous fodder near Old Depot, and that I had an accident with a spring cart at Deep Crossing. Tomorrow, God willing, we intend to travel on...

W F Schwarz

24 June 1877, Finke, MacDonnell Ranges[19] *(Kempe to Th Harms and ELSA members)*

... We have already written to you from Owen Springs about how things have gone for us up to that point. It only remains to describe the short stretch from there up to our place, and what we encountered there. I want to do this in somewhat more detail, since not many people know about this stretch of the journey.

We left Owen Springs on 29 May. First of all, Mirus with the sheep, which he drove around past the paddock. We also went the same way with the horses, while the wagon and the cart which Mr Conway loaned us drove through the paddock, following the road. He [Conway] had already made the trip to Ellery Creek, since he had brought his stock to that place and had struck camp there just shortly before our arrival.

On the evening of the same day we all arrived at a small creek, about 5 miles from Owen Springs, where we found plenty of good water. Wagon and cart arrived fairly late because they had taken a wrong turn. From here the road goes all the way along the Waterhouse Ranges, right to the end of them, and then again westerly up to Ellery Creek. That is, however, a stretch of 34 miles and we had to prepare ourselves for that.

On the next day Brother Schwarz helped Mirus to drive the sheep, and at the same time intended to look for water, but he found none and rode back in order to camp with Mirus. However, he could not find him, because he had camped at the rocks to the left of the road and, to our amazement, arrived back with us late in the evening.

We had stayed behind, in order to ride off first thing next morning and bring Mirus water and rations. We gave instructions to the man who had the cart to drive until he caught up with the sheep, while the one with the wagon was to drive as far as he could. We who were with the horses, i.e. one of the people and I, drove the unladen horses, reached the sheep at mid-day, and then drove with Brother Schwarz, who now also helped us, as far as Ellery Creek, where we arrived just on sunset and refreshed ourselves eating the water melons which Conway's people had sown there.

Next day[20] we rode out, one man going back to check on the others, Schwarz and I driving to our place to find, if possible, a short way through the northern parts. However, we soon realised it was impossible to get over the hills with the wagon; they stretched in a long line from north to south.

Arriving back in the evening we found that the cart had arrived, and late in the night Mills also arrived with the bullocks, but without the wagon which he had left 4 miles back. On Saturday I rode back and helped Mirus to drive the sheep. We reached the camp in the evening.

On Monday 4 June we travelled further. Brother Schwarz helped to drive the sheep while I rode on ahead to show the cart driver the way, and another man followed with the horses. We all arrived at the Finke on that same day, Schwarz arrived late in the evening with Mirus, and in the vicinity of the sandhills where, in the previous year, Pastor Heidenreich had twice camped with us.

On the next day the wagon also arrived. Schwarz and I rode slightly northwards to look for a place to establish a station, but we could arrive at no decision because the place did not seem suitable to us. So the next day we all rode out along the right-hand side of the Finke until we came to the MacDonnell Ranges, and then back on the other side. We realised that there was no suitable place there, on the one hand because it is remote, and also because the track is so bad that the wagon could only get through with the greatest of difficulty—indeed I can say: it is impossible. And secondly, the whole area is a swampy lowland.

In the evening we had a festive meal consisting of fish which we found in the waterhole, and water melon which we had brought with us from Ellery Creek...

So far everything has gone very well, and we now have reason to thank the Lord for his faithfulness and grace. However, I do not want to stay silent about the bad experiences, or at least those that appear so to us. It seems to us that the Lord has wanted to show us that we are not to place our trust in cattle or any other creature, but alone in him; for not only have many of the lambs died during frosty nights, and already one bullock has fallen dead, but there also appears to be an epidemic in the whole herd of cattle, for they all look very thin, much worse than when we were driving them.

But we also want to thank the Lord for that, even though we do not understand it right away. May he continue to help us and further the work of our hands, and now open for us the doors to the hearts of the poor heathen, that we may lead some of them to him.

H Kempe

* * *

Thus does this great, arduous and eventful journey end, and in what has become the under-stated manner in which he tells his readers about it, Kempe simply reports their arrival in a fairly matter of fact way. We arrived. We got to work.

Nevertheless, it is not at all difficult to detect the relief and the gratitude that he and the others did feel as they called a halt at that chosen spot in their place—the place where he expects he will die. He writes:

24 June 1877, Hermannsburg[21] *(Kempe to Th Harms)*
'The Lord's portion is his people, Jacob his allotted share. He sustained him in the desert, in the arid, howling wasteland. He led him and gave him the law. He protected him as the apple of his eye. As an eagle carries its young, and hovers over them, he spread out his wings, and took him, and carried him on his wings.' Deuteronomy 32:9–11

This word of God has come true in full measure also for us, so that we now have every reason to praise and glorify the name of the highly-acclaimed God of Zion who has led us out of the arid wasteland by graciously giving us plenty of rain. He has protected us on our way, and has carried us as on eagles' wings and finally, after such a long, long desert journey, has brought us to the place assigned to us. Here, unless his will that we do not question for a moment be otherwise, we are to work, and perhaps here also our life's course on this earth will end …

* * *

Even as this momentous moment has arrived for Lutherans in the Centre of Australia, back in Germany Director Harms has over-seen another series of events that will have their impact on the ongoing Lutheran story in Australia and New Zealand.

2 July 1877, Hermannsburg, Germany[22] *(Th Harms to Heidenreich)*
My dear Heidenreich.

Fourteen days ago, seven missionaries, Peters, Bertram, Hoopman, Thiessen, Schulze, Niemann and Meyer set out to sea from Hamburg on the sailing ship *Peter Godeffroy*, bound for Adelaide… The fiancées of Kempe and Schwarz, as well as Kowert, Loose, Dierks and Georg are coming on the same ship … I eagerly await news whether the expedition has arrived at our place…

Th Harms

* * *

And what were the first impressions of the Aboriginal people to this intrusion into their world? Barbara Henson recorded this personal recollection from one of the Arrarnta people whom she interviewed:

> The first time my grandfather saw the missionaries, it was morning time. He was hunting kangaroos, and he saw this dust coming. And he run to high hill, look down, something coming here, hide in the bush. He don't know what's coming. Then run back to the camp and tell everybody, they went to the sandhill and stopped there, crying and frightened. Sheep and white people coming, but they don't know what that is. After that they saw the people, Aboriginal workers, they brought with them. They come to Henbury, stop there, two, three days. Kill six sheep for them people, give them flour, they throw it away, they don't know tea and sugar. Then they boil tea, show them how to make tea. They never drink it, frightened. My grandfather was young fella. They thought they was debbils, they don't know whites. They reckon this white is a ghost one, come from the dead. And the Aborigines said, those ones from further south, no, this not debbil, only the skin different. From Henbury, they come to Hugh River, come to Owen Springs, then to Hermannsburg.[23]

8.

Setting Up

Water

The official date for the founding of the Hermannsburg Mission on the Finke is 7 June 1877. Though the missionaries, their accompanying settlers and all the animals had arrived in the area a few days prior to that, it took several days before they were able to decide on the best location for the mission headquarters. The deciding factor was water.

Water would always be a major issue for the mission. When the Finke flooded and flowed there was plenty. As the waters receded, there were residual waterholes, some large, some small, and these were critical to the survival of humans and animals. But the only assurance for a regular water supply for the mission staff and their residences was through the provision of well water.

Consequently, one of the first things the group did was dig a well. However, in time even a well became ineffective. It would silt, become salty (or saltier), and become undrinkable. So, another well would be dug.

Over time, water supply to the mission became an increasing problem. In fact, people even died because of the foul quality of the water. In addition to the increase in daily usage of the available water and to dry and drought seasons, there was also the polluting of water by the animals. Churned up by mud and excrement, so much of the natural water on which the Aboriginal people had relied for centuries became contaminated. Moving the animals from one watering spot to another only compounded the problem.

The Hermannsburg community struggled with this difficulty for years. Only in 1934–5 was a significant remedy found to easing the problem, when a pipeline was laid between the Kuprilya Springs and Ntaria, a distance of 7 kilometres. The Hermannsburgers now celebrate the gift of that pipeline and its water every year on their Kaprilya Springs festival day; and it is customary for the babies of the community to be baptised together on that day.[1]

For now, we return to the beginning of the mission days on the site. The new settlers waste no time in making their place habitable for the animals (who appear to take precedence) and themselves.

* * *

24 June 1877, Hermannsburg[2] *(Kempe to Th Harms and ELSA members)*
... On the next day[3] we rode down on the right and left of the Finke and convinced ourselves that the southern plain would be suitable for the establishment of the station. It was only a matter of us finding water. On the other side we found a long 'hole' (i.e. depression), about 2 miles long, but on this side absolutely nothing. We then decided to dig for water on the next day, and if we were to find good water there, this would determine where we would establish ourselves. We commended the matter to the dear Lord's heart and next day began our work. Already by midday we had beautiful fresh water. Then on the same day we transported everything to this place. It is situated approximately a mile from the James Range, where the Finke cuts its way through, and 48 miles from Owen Springs.

Now there was plenty to do. Above all we had to make sheep pens and soon began to cut timber for this purpose. Yesterday, on 22 June, we completed the big sheep pen, 50 cubits square, made of nothing but stakes. We have also carted enough timber for a hut; in the morning we can begin building that. During this time I want to go again to Owen Springs with the wagon in order to fetch another load of things that White has brought for us.

* * *

A few months after their arrival, in October, Schwarz wrote an extended report on those early days and months. In that report he also provided his and his colleagues' first impressions and experiences of the Aboriginal people in the region. There is evidence in this report that within three months of their arrival, the missionaries had begun their language work with the Arrarnta people.

31 October 1877, Mission Station on the Finke[4] *(Schwarz to Th Harms)*
Dear Pastor!
... we are now able to write the first station report from here to you and the whole precious mission community. By God's grace alone ... we have come so far with the establishment of a mission station right here in the

heart of Australia... It is my strong opinion that Brother Kempe and I would never have reached this place had your prayers not surrounded us like fiery walls, and had your premature thanksgiving for our supposed arrival made it impossible as it were for the dear Lord to delay us any longer. I can hardly believe that God has ever been played such a Swabian prank,[5] so to speak, as happened with the reports of our premature arrival.[6]

Already at Dalhousie we read in letters, and soon thereafter in the dear *Missionsblatt*, that we had arrived; while Brother Kempe and I were still camping with heavy hearts in Dalhousie Springs and waiting for the rain to stop, the dear brothers and sisters on the other side of the ocean were full of joy, praise and thanks to God. When I received that message at Dalhousie, I immediately said to my dear Brother Hermann: 'There's no doubt about it; the Lord is now obligated to establish us on our place as soon as possible, for he cannot take the thanks without deserving it.' ...

On 4 June the gracious, merciful and faithful Lord brought us and our herds safe and well to the fresh water and pastures of the Finke...

Towards evening on 4 June we met in the mission territory and camped by a large waterhole on the Finke. For evening devotion we sang with joyful hearts: 'God has brought me this far,' read the last three psalms, and thanked the Lord on our knees, as well as we poor people could. After the devotion we lay down on the ground as usual to sleep under God's free heaven.[7] During the night, as on the previous day, soft rain drizzled down on us, and the thunder of the Lord rolled in the clouds. We went to sleep happily and by God's grace again woke on the next morning, well-renewed in strength. A thick fog (such as I have never seen before) covered the whole area until midday, and the same also happened on the morning of 6 June.

After the midday meal Brother Kempe and I, together with one of our people, saddled the horses in order to inspect the area upstream on the Finke, and to search for a suitable place for the station on the large plain there. However, we found the track there to be too difficult for the wagons, so we decided that on the next day (as on 6 June) we would inspect the plain that was situated a lot closer, and returned back to the camp.

In the evening we caught a meal of fish from the nearby waterhole with a fishing rod and cooked them over a large fire for breakfast the next day. I notice that there are many fish in the Finke; they taste magnificent, and we have since prepared many a meal of them.

On the afternoon of 6 June we inspected the nearby lower plain, which greatly appealed to us. One has a wonderful view from this plain, and at this time of year, at least, the horizon is bordered by fresh green. If one directs one's gaze from here directly to the north, one sees the plains covered with bushes, and sandhills that are likewise overgrown. In the background, over 20 English miles from here, we have the James Ranges before us. In the south, 3 miles distant, we have before us the highest point of the James Ranges, at the foot of which the Finke has cut a way through the ranges. Towards the east the horizon is bordered by a row of bush-covered sandhills that extend south to the James Ranges, and these consist of red sandstone, just like the MacDonnell Ranges in the north. Westwards, however, we have a part of the plain, as well as the Finke, with a forest of beautiful gum trees.

As much as this plain appealed to us for the establishment of a station, we were not without worry about water. The bed of the Finke is very broad at this point, and all the water is on the far bank and so is too far away. After we had inspected the area a little bit more, we returned to the camp dissatisfied, and consequently were still unable to reach the desired conclusion today. We commended our concerns to the Lord anew, and asked for his advice and his help. We also agreed that on the next morning, 7 June, armed with pick and spade we would walk to the plain below to dig for water on this side of the bed of the Finke. We did that, and after just one hour's work the Lord let us find good water. This led us to reaching the decision for our present station.

Already on the afternoon of 7 June everything was brought here, where we now by God's grace and with his help have already begun to establish the first mission station on the Finke, to the honour of the Lord, to the joy of his children and angels, to the blessing of the heathen, but to the defiance and annoyance of Satan and his followers.

The name of this first station is Hermannsburg. However, the Aboriginal people do not know what to think of this foreign word, so it is good to name this station also with a word of their language that has the same meaning as the German. If you, dear Pastor, agree with this, then the name of our station here is to be the following: *Ilta quana arkuinta uma*, which means the camp, place or dwelling of the person who sets me free, in short, the Liberator. Anyway, in the next report Brother Kempe will place the correct name of the station on the letterhead in case the above is not the correct one.

For the sake of brevity I now trace the work done so far on the station, with the Lord's help, and other events in the order in which they happened.

In total we were eight persons as we entered our mission territory, namely six Whites and two Blacks, the latter born 400 English miles from here. Of our six Whites there were Brother Kempe, Mirus (shepherd), and I, as Germans; F Stone (mason), Th Mills (bullock driver), and G Spence (stockman), as Englishmen or born in Australia.

When we had found water on the morning of 7 June, Brother Kempe remained back at the site and, while waiting for us to arrive with the wagon, built a chicken shed out of bush and grass, for we had brought four hens and two roosters with us. These therefore were the first to receive a roof over their heads. However, the most beautiful hen was stolen a few days later by wild dogs.[8] The whole area was full of them. Now they are fewer, since we laid poison, and our hens have multiplied, for we have 11 little chicks.

On 8 June a small sheep pen was built, for our sheep were beginning to lamb.

On 9 June the first 200 stakes for the large sheepfold were cut; besides that, I also built a dog kennel. When we arrived we had three dogs, but now we have six, two large whippets, the others cattle and sheep dogs.

On 21 June the large 150 foot square sheep yard was completed. It is built out of 7 foot high stakes which are driven into the ground, stake upon stake next to each other. Now at last the sheep have their permanent home.

On 25 June Brother Kempe, together with the bullock driver and team, began a trip to Owen Springs to fetch a load of our things from there. G Spence left us and went back with him.

On Saturday, 30 June, Stone and I drove into the ground the first ten posts of our present dwelling.

On 14 August our shelter was ready, and we thanked the faithful Lord from the heart that he has helped us thus far. Our dwelling is 18 feet long and 24 wide, built from nothing but timber, the roof out of reeds from the Finke, and the floor laid with sand-stone slabs.

In the period from 25 June to 14 August, the merciful God and Father has done a great thing for us; for he has not only brought back Brother Kempe with the wagon, healthy and safe, from Owen Spring, but has also preserved him on the next trip to Alice Springs. He travelled there and back in the days from 13 to 21 of July to fetch nails and tools for building…

Furthermore, on 4 August the first heathen in the region came to us. They were two striking, powerful men who stayed with us for two days. We received them with joy and gave each of them a shirt by way of a welcome, since they, like all the heathen living here, were naked. They received this gift with joy; they also did not reject the food served to them. However, we first had to bite into it as proof that there was no poison in it, for they also know poison and its effect.[9]

Since the visit of these two men, probably 70 to 80 others from every age group have already come and gone among us, but still no women.

For now, I am refraining from giving any further report on the local heathen, their life and customs, since we have hardly begun to learn their language. However, they are no apes but real people, and I have to write that with absolute clarity. Like us, they have a clear language, and in a few weeks they learn so much English[10] that they are able to make themselves understood with us. Also some of our Black brothers in this area have a striking similarity to this or that European known to us.

In addition, I note that the Aboriginal people everywhere here make a good impression on us. Hardly a dozen of them who have visited us have come away unshaven. They do not like hair either above or under the teeth, so they asked us to free them from it. The local heathen would stake their lives on their whiskers and goatees should their existence ever be in jeopardy. Not infrequently, two other men used their hands to cover the beard underneath the scissors, just as another did for himself, anxiously covering his beloved whiskers.

After some time, however, they were a little less fearful; for they learnt to know us as good barbers who respected their beards. The boys allowed their heads to be shaved. We gladly did this to free them as much as possible from nits, which they also do not like. May the Lord give them grace so that they likewise willingly allow themselves to be cleansed from sin by faithfully taking up and accepting his precious and salvation-giving gospel. Amen...[11]

Now that on 14 August we were finally under cover, we felt at home. It was no small thing to camp for almost two full years under the open sky, by day and by night, in heat and in cold. It was vey cold here this winter, for it froze regularly with ice for four weeks, with the exception of some nights.

Our next period was now taken up with the building of a so-called stockyard in order to create a home also for our cattle and horses, for up to this time both roamed wherever they liked. However, they got into no neighbour's corn because our nearest neighbour was 50 English miles away.

It took three weeks to construct this 80 feet long and 50 feet wide cattle yard, which is necessary for catching, branding and breaking in (getting them used to work) the cattle and the horses.

Around this time our neighbour 50 miles away paid us a visit and brought us letters and papers.[12] Note that since our arrival here we have already received mail four times. We offer you, dear Pastor, as well as all worthy brothers and sisters in God, hearty thanks for your love which has revived us up to this point through many a comforting letter...We give you special thanks for the esteemed *Kreuzblatt*.[13] May God bless its going out and coming in everywhere.

In the middle of August two English people came here, both of whom we took on because it was near sheep shearing time.

On 30 August we received two more neighbours, graziers who had settled at Ellery Creek, seven English miles from here. Mr Barker, as one of them is called, has already visited us twice.

On 1 September Brother Kempe started writing up a station diary.

In the course of the following week we made a start on the shearing; this began on 10 September and lasted for three weeks. The number of sheep shorn is 1700. We retained a number of unshorn sheep for slaughtering. In all we probably have 2200 head of sheep here on the station, and around about 80 goats, 25 head of cattle, and the same number of horses. We have already received up to 500 lambs since arriving here, but unfortunately are not getting any more because of the current heat and lack of decent feed, while the other stock flourish magnificently.

During the shearing, my dear Brother Kempe was permitted to play David again, because we were compelled to form three different flocks; he looked after one, Brother Mirus the other, and two of the heathen the third as well as the flock of lambs.

In the middle of the shearing a German by the name of W Meissner came to us looking for work, which he immediately received. He says that his parents were born in the Harz, but he does not know which confession they belong to. However, this W Meissner is a faithful and industrious worker, and has taken over driving the bullocks. Even though, since the beginning of October, there are only four men here, and indeed only Germans, the building work is progressing joyfully. To the Lord be thanks for everything.

It is not necessary to write that Brother Kempe and I long for our dear fiancées and brothers to be with us as soon as they arrive. Up to the present we do not know if they are still at sea or already on Australian soil. But I hope that their faithful companion, namely our Lord Jesus, is with them wherever the dear ones happen to be; also that he will soon bring them to us safe and sound. Whatever the Lord does, his will is always good.

At this point I should finish my report, since I only had to report to the end of September, and Brother Kempe on the last three months of this year. Today is already Wednesday and the last day of October as I write the conclusion of my report. So please, dear Pastor, I beg your gracious forbearance. I do not want to make excuses for my tardiness in providing reports. But I promise, with God's help, to improve, and this is surely necessary in all matters. Turn me, O Lord, so I will be turned. Amen.

Because it is already 31 October, I will report only briefly that by God's goodness and grace we are all still well, and although all the English left us already three weeks ago, we will nevertheless begin to erect a stone building next week. We already have 40 loads of stone. A lime kiln is already built, and an oven full of lime has been fired and removed. In addition, the limestone for the next firing is already crushed, and today Brother Kempe and W Meissner are cutting the wood for that.

I would also like to report that we actually have a palm valley in our vicinity, only 6 English miles from the station, and downstream on the bank of the Finke, or according to the language of the Aboriginal people, the *Larapinta*, where it breaks through the James Range. Last week Brother Kempe and Meissner rode there and found up to 30 specimens of magnificent palm trees standing in the most beautiful bloom. Some of them must have been up to 70 feet high. On their return they brought a young palm with them and a frond which was 10 feet long and almost just as broad. Brother Kempe planted the young palm close to our dwelling on the bank of the creek, and last Saturday the Lord gently watered it through a welcome rainstorm...

Your most humble
W F Schwarz

* * *

2 August 1877, Finke, MacDonnell Ranges[14] *(Schwarz to ELSA members)*
Dear mission brothers and sisters,

... On 17 July the barrel of my gun exploded an inch in front of the cock as I was firing. The whole load shot out backwards, but I remained unhurt under angelic protection and remain well to this hour, together with Brother Kempe. Since 5 June to the end of July he has already made two trips, one to Owen Springs, the other to Alice Springs. Brother Mirus and the two Englishmen, together with both Aboriginal people, are likewise well, by God's grace. The Lord be praised for that.

On the other hand, we are not lacking work. Indeed, we have more than we can handle with our small force since we total only seven people, and Brother Mirus and one Aboriginal person are always guarding the sheep, and have no end of troubles, since the lambing with all its difficulties is not yet over. The job of the younger Aboriginal person is to keep a constant eye on the horses and cattle, whether here on the property or on the road, as in recent days when he was out with the bullock wagon that within the space of four weeks had driven twice to Owen Springs and had brought White's cargo here to the station.

So, there was only one man who could be occupied full-time with building because I constantly had to look after the wagon, as has long been known, and thus could give little help. But thanks be to God, for he has also blessed our house building. In the four weeks of July we have finished so much of the wooden structure that we have only the thatching to complete. The reeds for this are already cut. The building is 24 feet wide and 18 feet long, and strong enough for use as a regular dwelling. I am very much looking forward to finding shelter in it soon, especially when it is so cold, as it was from the 15th to the end of July. With the exception of three days we had heavy frost at night so that in the morning the water was covered with about half an inch of ice. The last two nights we have had no ice, meaning it was all the hotter by day. Thank God that he has helped us to this point, and with his help we will soon be under cover.

As for our horses, sheep and cattle, I can report that all is in good order since there is no lack of fodder and water. God be thanked for everything.

I could finish here since I basically have nothing further to report. However, I can just imagine some dear mission friends, on reading these lines, softly murmuring: 'What kind of a mission report is that, with no mention of the poor heathen and even less about their conversion?' Dear friends, just be patient, believe and pray that the Lord in his own good time will graciously grant that reports can be written such as you like to read. The work of mission demands first faith, then work, and thirdly patience.

Since our arrival at the mission territory I have not seen a single one of the natives who live here.[15] That they approach us is even less likely. From this you must not draw the conclusion, dear friends, that our place is unsuitable for a mission station because we are not yet surrounded by a crowd of poor heathen. I am not of that opinion, but freely admit that it is better for us that the local natives are still holding back because, as it is, we have our hands full with constructing the station. That Aboriginal people do otherwise stay here is proven by the deserted campsites; and the smoke we see rising around our place proves that the natives are not far away...

W F Schwarz, Missionary

* * *

30 August 1877, Mission Station on the Finke [16] *(Kempe to ELSA members)*
...Brother Schwarz has already mentioned in the last report that we have finished our house and thus are adequately protected against sun and rain. The rest of the time we have worked on a stockyard and have reached the point where we intend finishing it tomorrow. It would not have taken so long had we not had to fetch the rails from Ellery Creek, 6 miles from here. There are

plenty of gum trees for timber here on the Finke, but the trees are too thick and large to be of use for our purposes. I am extremely happy that this job is finished. My hands bear testimony that it was almost too difficult for me. There is also much to annoy one in the process, as you can easily imagine, especially people who are intent on making a lot of money, working little, and eating well. Two weeks ago we took on two men like that but soon had to fire them.

Otherwise we are all well and hard at work, thank God… This time I can also report that today a small group of 15 Aboriginal people visited us, nothing but tall, strong figures with quite imposing beards. Today they left again, giving us to understand that it was to fight people in Alice Springs. Not far from here they made a large fire that is still visible in the night sky…

H Kempe

The reference to the Aboriginal people going off to fight another Aboriginal group raises a sensitive, but nevertheless not-to-be-ignored reality about life among the Aboriginal people. In a number of conversations I have had with people who know the Aboriginal world far better than I do, the point has been made that these early missionaries totally misunderstood the extent to which the Aboriginal people were violent towards each other (*Missionaries, Madness and Miracles* confronts us with many such incidents.) The inter-tribal aversion and hatred were strong, and the various groups were constantly at war with each other. To under-estimate this reality is to diminish one's understanding of the Aboriginal people.

*   *   *

By October, three months after their arrival, the community is taking on something of an established shape, in terms both of the actual buildings and in their daily life and work. The following are snippets from Schwarz's and Kempe's reports for the month, all to the folk down South.

7 October 1877, Finke, MacDonnell Ranges[17] *(Schwarz to ELSA members)*
Dear mission community!
… each day we begin our difficult work in high spirits and, with God's help, complete as much as we can. We strive to finish as quickly as possible all the external tasks that immediately present themselves, so that we can finally begin the actual work of mission amongst all the poor heathen. In the course of recent months more Aboriginal people than ever have shown

up here, and at this very moment as I write these lines, a lad we have named Tommy' is calling out to me: 'Lightfellow, come up.'[18] He worked hard with us the whole time we were shearing sheep. Three imposing, strong men have recently arrived and make a good impression on us, as do all the Aboriginal people of this tribe who have come near us...

Until now, the Aboriginal people come and go with us, as is their custom, but we hope that they will gradually settle down with us for a longer period, even if it is only the men at first who are here. So far no female person has put in an appearance. Meanwhile we must practise patience and, in any case, we have plenty of work.

Thank God that we have shorn our sheep for this year. We had, of course, to pay £1/10 per 100 sheep shorn. The lambing season is not yet over; the flock has now increased by 500 lambs. On the station we number seven Whites and seven Aboriginal people.

Now we can start burning limestone in order to erect a stone building before the wet season, if possible.

This month we unfortunately lost two head of cattle through pleura;[19] the other one[20] is in good condition, as are the sheep and horses. However, a young mare in foal also died, as did a sheepdog from rat poison that had been laid. In all these losses I am comforted by knowing that it is the Lord who allows such things to happen and knows why he allows them to come upon us...

Since 30 August we have gained neighbours at Ellery Creek. God grant that they are good neighbours...

W F Schwarz, Missionary

31 October 1877, Hermannsburg[21] *(Schwarz to ELSA members)*

Since the two last-mentioned Aboriginal people visited us, about 70 to 80 others of every age have come and gone but still no women-folk. I am refraining from writing a report on their life and customs; I have to be sure about what I write. In a few weeks they learn enough English that we are able to communicate with them.[22] In that they bear a striking resemblance to some Europeans known to us. In general they make a good impression on us; the adults take a lot of care with their thick beards. We have shorn the heads of the lads to free them of bugs that they find troublesome...

October 1877, Hermannsburg[23] *(Kempe to ELSA members)*

Dear mission community!

... Brother Schwarz has already mentioned ... that sheep shearing has begun, and we finished the work on 7 October. After this we now want to really get going on the construction of a second house. Meanwhile on Tuesday we had to release two of our labourers, the mason St(one) and the bullock driver M(ills), so that apart from Mirus we are retaining only one German by the name of Meissner and one Englishman whom we let go on the following Monday—rather, he himself decided to go. We were happy with this since he wanted a high wage but did little work. We naturally cannot stand for this, preferring to do the work ourselves. We are not allowing ourselves to be intimidated but are pressing on. Meissner took over the bullock wagon, while I broke stones.

Now, with God's help, we have reached the point where we can start building in the next days. We have 40 loads of stone in place and have already burnt lime. All depends on God's blessing, and that is what we have been granted to experience. I do not believe we would have achieved much more had we still retained the three labourers.[24] ...

We always have enough Blacks on the station that come and go, but until now no woman has been here. Naturally, we cannot yet speak of any actual mission work since we have our hands full as it is.

We received a special treat when I rode down the Finke with Meissner and found the palms mentioned by Giles about 6 or 7 miles away.[25] The way there is somewhat difficult. There is only enough space between the cliffs for the breadth of the river, and one cannot ride everywhere because of the water. Yet the sight of the palms richly made up for our troubles. They are magnificent trees, growing up as straight as candles; the tallest may be 60 feet high. We counted 30 large trees standing close together and many small ones. We took a very small plant and a frond with us; the latter was 10 feet long and 7 to 8 feet broad. The palm's blossom consists of a strong stalk about 3 inches thick and 5 feet long from which the yellow-green flowers hang, like grapes. Judging from the sound, the wood must be very hard. When struck it sounded like beating on an iron rod.

Eight days later, Brother Mirus rode there and viewed the trees. Brother Schwarz will have to wait for that until our help-meets arrive; he is officially tied to the kitchen...

    H Kempe

*　　*　　*

Meanwhile, down in Bethany, Heidenreich appears to be feeling somewhat isolated from unfolding events. On the 5th and 6th of September he wrote two almost identical letters to Director Harms, the first he has written to him since May. Why he wrote two such similar reports we are not told.

Because of the similarity of the two letters, only that of the 5th is published here. Heidenreich complains that he has not heard from Harms for almost a year. Given the close bond he claimed with Harms, this would undoubtedly have been painful for him. He also has complaints about New Zealand, the next lot of new arrivals for the mission, the mission itself, the ELSA. It is noteworthy that he never complains about his congregation: he obviously was content in his ministry there, a fact he consistently makes clear in his letters. And, despite the complaints, there are moments of happier things.

5 September 1877, Bethany[26] *(Heidenreich to Th Harms)*
Highly honoured, dearly loved Father!

I still have no answer to my many requests and questions about the money so necessary for the mission, the sending of three to four pastors, and the request of our Synod to you concerning those you send remaining in the services of the Church. I hear and read in letters that you have quickly made changes in New Zealand, whereas in January 1877 you directed me to keep the superintendency in my hands. You have also suddenly called Dierks away from here.

That has brought me derision and insulting letters from the New Zealanders ... Now the missionaries there are writing reports to the church papers that they are reporting what they are told to report! I have given him no such order but have said to Homann that he should accept no reports for the *Blatt* until the matter is settled by you. However, because it is still continuing to happen, I asked our president, Oster, whether the Church Council, as representative of the Synod, had commissioned these reports. He replied: 'To my knowledge, no!' So, one can only conclude that you gave them the instructions, which I doubt. So now we have the wretched situation that I tried for so long to prevent.

... That I am left without knowing what to do, is easy to understand, also that I have little joy in this situation. In such affairs not even Satan has anything to celebrate and in this web shows me the reward for all my struggle for precious mother Church and for my sacrifice of life and property. Had the Lord's Word not always been my comfort, I would have already gone away, or sold my bits and pieces here and emigrated to a different country. I would thereby make many people happy, but not me, my household, God and his upright children. The struggle rages in my heart back and forth to the point that I am unable to do anything, not even write to you. If I decided to do a bunk, you would not readily give me a licence to do so.

However, tall mountains lie before me. I have not received from you so much as one letter of the alphabet about the whole company that will be here in a few weeks, even though I am responsible for all provisions in the Church and mission. That is likely to cause a great loss in time and money, if not more, and great trouble and blame for all the work [that will need to be done] ...

On 6 June, by God's grace and faithfulness, our brothers arrived with everything at our place. Praise and thanks to him for that! They are healthy and happily at work, have finished a large sheep yard, and are erecting a dwelling house, having chosen for the station the second site examined by me at the James Range after the rain. They unfortunately report heavy livestock losses. The expensive stallion is dead, two bullocks, many lambs, and a contagious infection has broken out among the cattle. Unfortunately, as I wrote to you earlier, we have been unable to acquire any workmen. Apart from two, they have all left again. If only the dear brothers would wise up from experience.

No report for you has yet been sent to me. For many reasons and for the good of the mission, I again request that you direct the missionaries to have the reports pass through my hands. Early reports have caused unspeakable damage because of incorrect presentation. That is also the way you promised things should go in superintending matters. The brothers are all wrong in saying that I am demanding reports on my own initiative because you said nothing to them about that, even though your letter about setting up a superintendent was printed in both church papers here. Though I have told them that they can report to you on personal matters, as much as they want to and have time, Schwarz especially has always some objection.

The most difficult matter is now finances. There are no workers up there, and if you have not sent a large sum with the people who are coming, we cannot send off the eagerly awaited help. For that we need £1000... I fear we have several hundred in debts ...

... Kempe does not believe that the new party[27] will get through before the next winter. It may be possible for the men, but it is almost impossible for me to get the fiancées through the wilderness with rough characters, such as the local drivers. Due to physical weakness, I am unable to accompany them; also, the new men need to be placed in the Church. If there is one to spare, I will send him North as a missionary, unless you have already decided otherwise. It is a pity that Dierks did not remain here; as a married man he could have taken the fiancées with him, and a young man could take the fiancées to New Zealand. So, I am totally in the dark how things will proceed ...

I do not know how I am to understand that Major von Rauschenbusch[28] has sent Homann directions for payments into and out of our local treasury. Homann himself is surprised and writes that he already wrote to you years ago that he no longer wished to work in the mission in an official capacity. This causes me embarrassment. Only recently[29] you wrote that I should take no notice of all that others say and write. So, I do not know what to make of the letters I have not yet seen. I have been considered faithful in all matters, and thus request that in future you yourself have all such matters sent to me if you yourself do not have time, and so put to an end all the pointless questions and messages going to and fro. For the moment, nothing more can be done about this.

Four pastors are to find placements here ... The worst is that I know nothing of what you have decided for the arrivals. I can make no definite arrangements while everything is hanging in the air. I readily believe that it is not possible for you to write, given all your work, but it is extremely necessary [that you do] for our cause here.

Hoping that the travellers are bringing everything needed, I conclude this time with a wish that the faithful Lord makes everything turn out well ... Every mail from up North brings an invoice for loans and other urgent things, one amounting to £123, then again several for £60... Then we still have to pay about £100 for freight. To this must be added the cost of the new purchase of two tons of flour, four bags of sugar, the necessary tea, ... biscuits and so on, with the terrible cartage costs that this time will come to £600 to £700, since we cannot get a ton from Port Augusta to our place for less than £60. Think how many chests and cases the missionaries still have here and then all that the fiancées and settlers are bringing.[30] That all has to be transported. The brothers write that they have brought it for this life; in the next they will no longer need it!

When I survey what can be seen, I become quite dizzy, but that does not help ... Pray for me that I do not become faint-hearted with everything ...

Your true son, G A Heidenreich

* * *

A few weeks later, and Heidenreich's tune has changed. The proviso he mentions in this next letter relates to Th Harms' insistence on having the final say on where pastors and missionaries sent to Australia would eventually be placed. Not everyone in Australia agreed with this proviso/condition, and it was consequently the cause of another extended ruckus in the ELSA.

4 October 1877, Bethany[31] *(Heidenreich to Th Harms)*
Highly respected and much-loved Father!

... Shortly after sending off my last letter, I received your lovely, prized letter of 15 June 1877. May the faithful Lord reward you for removing my doubt and lack of faith with a hefty and timely jolt that eliminated almost all of my recent complaints. I also ask your forgiveness for my last letter where I let myself be side-tracked into uncertainty by a variety of events ...

I will try to put into effect in the best way possible the new trust given to me, taking into account your stated proviso about the missionaries to be placed in church service here. This proviso is no small matter for me or the local Church Council. So that this point might be finally resolved, I had to make a request contrary to your wishes on behalf of the Synod in Blumberg, namely, to drop this proviso for our Synod. I did that, paying careful attention to all the main issues. I will have to contend with the old and new difficulties at the next session of the Church Council. Above all, I have to counter the jibes people make here: that you have wanted to hang onto a supreme power over our Synod by means of this proviso. So, I am forced to refute this baseless idea, using my experience, words and actions ...

Through Major von Rauschenbusch I received a bill of exchange for £300 from the London bank and a letter for Pastor Homann. On behalf of our beloved and worthy head treasurer I thank you for both and ask you to tell me if in future I should deal with the Major to relieve you of financial matters ...

It was a difficult task this time, but the Lord has supplied help and even blessed us with a nice surplus. I am a novice in drawing up financial statements on such a large scale and ask that, if the forms are not to your liking or detailed enough, or in too much detail, you advise me of a better method. It puts me at ease if the accounts are faithful and exact; and, so that at any time anyone can closely check our calculations, bank books, especially our income and expenditure, I will keep everything in a special box so that they can be used as a record also after my death ...

I have not yet received a mission report for you ... I reminded Kempe months ago about the report for you, but as yet have no reply or report. Thank God that they are now at the place, and that everything will now be better and easier to set up and supply.

It seems to be absolutely necessary that we send up one of the newly arrived missionaries with the fiancées for protection through the wilderness, and to provide encouragement for the settlers. Up North he will be fully occupied in the regular course of things without any duties being added. To send the people up later would cost a great deal. A final decision has not yet been made. I first want to consult the fiancées and settlers, and if the need arises, then whoever we consider to be the most suitable will go with them. I trust that you will be in agreement with us ...

I have waited until this last moment so as to be able to tell you of the arrival of our dear brothers and sisters, but the Lord has still not given me this joy. At that time in the past we had travelled for 15 weeks; they have already been at sea for 24 weeks.

I feel sorry for the brothers and sisters going up North. It is questionable whether we can send them off immediately. We will have to send up provisions in advance, and that should really happen at the same time to save expenses and supplies. But the matter is now urgent, and I have to send an order to Port Augusta so that the rations are sent off. I am glad that the fault this time lies with the Church Council, as I today learn from the letter of Major von Rauschenbusch that was sent to me by Homann. Otherwise the blame would again be laid on you or me, as it was on Simon the cross-bearer ...

With warm greetings and blessings for your silver wedding anniversary so that you live together in marriage with divine blessing until your golden wedding.

I remain, your true son,

G A Heidenreich

9.

The Arrival of Schulze, the Fiancées, and Others

A week or so after the missionaries arrived at Ntaria, the sailing ship *Peter Godeffroy* set sail from Hamburg, Germany (16 June 1877), arriving in Adelaide exactly four months later, on 16 October. On board were 135 passengers (one of whom, a child, died *en route*), and among those passengers was a further contingent of Lutherans bound for a variety of destinations. There were settlers for South Australia, missionaries and fiancées for New Zealand, pastors for various congregations in the ELSA, and personnel for the mission in the Centre. These latter included the fiancées of Kempe and Schwarz (Dorothea Queckenstedt and Dorothea Schulz), and the laymen Jürgens, Holtermann and Tündemann. Also among them was the young pastor who would become the third founding missionary on the Finke, Louis Schulze—except, when the *Peter Godeffroy* dropped anchor, he did not know that would be his future.

Once again Heidenreich finds himself a very busy man, called upon to arrange everything to do with these new arrivals' accommodation, travel to new homes, food and other necessities for their well-being. Also, finding the necessary finances for all of this. He is a little flustered, and on 2 November complains to Director Harms:

> Everything is happening so quickly and with such confusion in Church and mission matters that I cannot write about them calmly and clearly... Our money reserves have completely disappeared, and I must urgently ask for another considerable amount to be sent, for the new party is costing much and at this time one can expect little income.[1]

Despite the challenges, everything is organised in a reasonably quick time, and by mid-November—a mere month after their arrival in this new world—the group assigned for the Centre is on its way. A week later, Heidenreich has caught his breath, and he is able to reflect on what has happened in the past month. Yet again, it seems that many vital decisions about the arrangements for the mission are made on the run.

* * *

26 November 1877, Bethany[2] *(Heidenreich to Th Harms)*
Highly honoured and much-loved Father!

Now that the newly arrived, beloved brothers and sisters have vacated my house and it has again become quiet around me, I can briefly report on recent events, actions, deliberations and business.

When the *Peter Goddefroy* finally came in sight after long waiting, I received a telegram from Pastor Homann, immediately travelled to Adelaide, and then to the ship next morning. There followed much talking, many questions and, above all, much work. It turned out, since I could not guarantee church work to the party of missionaries, that the missionaries' fiancées and the settlers would receive a spiritual guide for their trek through the wilderness. Kempe had written to me that there was enough work on our place and, if I was able, I might like to send another missionary …

4 December 1877, Bethany[3] *(Heidenreich to ELSA members)*
Dear faithful congregations in mission!

… So, when the ship arrived my first task was to read Director Harms' letter of July to the six new missionaries, to inform them of my proposal. Since they were all equally dear to me, each one of them would have to consider whether he was favourably disposed to travelling to our difficult mission field, and to inform me of his decision after a set time to think it over.

To my joy our dear senior and spiritual mission advisor, Pastor Hensel, also came onto the ship. With him I could discuss how to handle the matter in question, together with the advisor H Drogemüller who was also present. Brother Schulze volunteered,[4] while the others did not want to nominate themselves. In the presence of Pastor Homann, who had come with us to meet the ship, I asked whether the others considered Brother Schulze suited to be a missionary in the far North. They answered 'Yes', whereupon in the presence of the other brothers I declared Brother Schulze to be a missionary in South Australia.

Now we could undertake further measures for all the others, fully preparing the fiancées for New Zealand, arranging their travel and looking after their belongings. After Pastor Homann and I had initiated these matters, I then put Missionary Peters in charge, had the other things put into a store and laid siege to the large accommodation of Pastor Homann. May the dear Lord richly bless him and his hospitable hostess for their love and sacrifice.

The following days brought a lot of work because of the necessary equipment we had to purchase for the long trip. Toasted, long-life bread had to be prepared, many things bought, packaged, or even shipped. The dear people of Bethany, Schönborn, Friedenberg and others brought gifts in kind—ham, butter, sausage, cheese, jam and the like...

[5]Because of the summer heat, we had to hurry so that the mission party could leave as soon as possible. There was a lot of work for everyone. The women baked cake from a sack of flour, and this was dried and packed into tin chests. A large crate was filled with cut ham, sausages and bacon... As well, letters and telegrams [were sent] for the procurement of carts from outsiders to take these things up to the mission station.

By 6 November everything was ready. The commissioning service in Bethany took place in the presence of all who had arrived together...[After the service,] I read out the arrangements for the journey. They were brief and logical, as follows:

'Dear brothers and sisters, on this journey you have Missionary Schulze as your spiritual carer, and you are to love and honour him. Dear sisters, take on the cooking and everything connected with it. Brother Jürgens is to be in charge of the wagon, and Holtermann and Tündemann are to help with the other tasks along the way. When you have, with the Lord's help, arrived at our station Hermannsburg, Brother Schulze and all of you are to submit to the older missionaries. You are to discuss important matters communally, then report to me in detail so that, if it is necessary, I can gain the approval of our dear Father.'

... Next day was the wedding of Pastor Georg and Marie Radehorst, with an even larger congregation assembled...

[6]On the same night [as the commissioning service], our treasurer Schmidt set off with the colonist Jürgens for our wagon[7] near Port Augusta. Missionary Schulze and the fiancées of Kempe and Schwarz, and the colonists Holtermann and Tündemann, stayed with us until the morning, after Pastor Georg's wedding. They then travelled via Adelaide, stayed for a few days with dear Pastor Homann, and then travelled with their belongings by ship to Port Augusta. Brother Schmidt, together with Jürgens, Bobby Boy and the wagon, met them at Port Augusta on Monday. Brother Schmidt reported to me that he had found our wagon and belongings in top condition at Mr Hempel's place where he had to pay off the wagoners after Easter—a blessing for us;[8] he also had found the horses with the Ossig and Hamdorf families in especially good condition. May the faithful Lord richly reward the kindness of these souls, especially Mrs Hempel, for looking after my loyal Bobby Boy so well.

Also in Port Augusta everything went better than expected. On the first trip we had many sad experiences on account of the wagoners we had hired, so we wanted to avoid anything similar. However, the situation was such that we might create those same difficulties, for if we hired an experienced wagoner our mission personnel would be his servants; but if we sent one with them for only part of the way, the horses would be pampered, and we would have to pay heavy return travel costs. If we sent our people alone, even with the best instructions, the danger was that they would come to grief on the road.[9]

In contemplating these problems, we were agreed from the outset that, wherever possible, our party should be attached to the freight wagons that were to bring our belongings from Port Augusta to our Hermannsburg station. But that would not be altogether advisable either. All things look easy on paper but turn out difficult in reality; so also here.

However, the Lord fulfilled this wish too. Driver Brown[10] took on most of our cargo, and by the time Brother Schmidt arrived, he had already loaded and sent off two of his wagons. He himself was waiting with a mount at Port Augusta for the arrival of our people and wagon in order to escort our party joined to his.

In Brown we have a fine, loyal driver who is not only known in the North as an honest man but has also rendered me outstanding service on my trip. He knows where I left the horses so they would not starve to death and where our belongings had been left at various stations. He had promised Brother Schmidt to take them with him and to pull out our wagon if it became bogged. He also knew exactly where to find water and fodder in the far North …

Brother Schmidt has had to hire a third wagon to take our belongings from Port Augusta; this wagon is following ours.

After all purchases had been attended to and the things had been loaded, our wagon drove off, accompanied by Brothers Schmidt and Brown up to Stirling. There the former left our dear brothers and sisters in a happy mood.

Our three heavy bullock wagons and our horse-drawn wagon are thus travelling through the wilderness.[11] From Edeowie and Beltana I received news from Missionary Schulze that so far all had gone well, but they had lost a horse from death before reaching Beltana. The horse had previously been sick and had probably eaten too much sand on the trip, as often happens in the North.

May the faithful Lord accompany the travellers further with his fiery steeds and chariot and give them happy hearts and joyful courage. May he make us ever more faithful in the service of the holy mission so that, with your loyal help, we again meet the new heavy but unavoidable expenses. Since the hire contract with our labourers is soon coming to an end, our maintenance costs will be less. This year we hope to earn money from wool, since the contract cost for cartage will be reduced by half...

G A Heidenreich

* * *

The Case of a Missing Letter

Around the time of the arrival of the *Peter Godeffroy* contingent, there is a fascinating and revealing correspondence between Heidenreich and Director Harms about a missing letter. As recounted in the previous chapter, in his letter dated 5 September Heidenreich grumbles to Harms that he has not heard from the Director for about a year. Eight weeks later, in his reply of 1 November to this complaint, Harms assures Heidenreich:

> My letter to you was sent off a long time ago. [On 15 June, as it turns out.] In it I replied to the questions in your letter of 5 September, but did not send the money ... Either it came into your possession very late, or it has been completely lost. The one thing would grieve me as much as the other... In the event that my above-mentioned letter does not reach you, I repeat for you the answers to the questions you raised...[12]

Meantime, in a letter of 4 October (i.e. between his letter of complaint of 5 September and Harms' reply to that on 1 November) Heidenreich is over the moon that he has received Harms' letter of 15 June, the letter 'sent off a long time ago'.

It is obvious that the 15 June letter somehow went missing for a while—taking something like 16 weeks (to 4 October) to get from Hermannsburg, Germany, to Bethany. In the interim the two letters of 5 September and 1 November have somehow crossed over each other.

It is all somewhat complicated, and may (possibly) be simplified thus:

- 15 June: Harms writes to Heidenreich, but that letter somehow goes missing.
- 5 September: Unaware of the letter of 15 June, Heidenreich complains to Harms over lack of contact.
- 4 October: Heidenreich writes to Harms, rejoicing that the lost has been found.

- 1 November: Harms replies to Heidenreich's complaint of 5 September, not yet having received the news of 4 October.

What is revealing about these incidents is, first of all, the complexity and unreliability of communication at that time where there are such great distances, and hence delays, between one person's letter and another's.

The second revelation in this incident is that it took, at that time, something like eight weeks for a letter to travel between Australia and Germany, and *vice versa*. How difficult it must have been, in the best of circumstances, to engage in extended dialog. How frustrating, too, when dealing with difficult matters requiring urgent attention.

* * *

Meanwhile, up in the Centre, news has come through of the new arrivals in Adelaide. This next letter from Schwarz is a classic example of Schwarz's writing style and of the piety with which he and quite likely his peers were imbued.

30 November 1877, Hermannsburg[13] (Schwarz to ELSA members)

> 'I long for you, Lord; I hope in you, my God. Do not let me be put to shame, so that my enemies do not exult over me; for no one who waits on you will be put to shame.' PSALM 25

First of all, sincere greetings in the name of the Lord Jesus, my only mediator and chief shepherd, to whom be honour for ever. Amen.

In these days another month is coming to an end, so we deem it our duty to inform you, dear mission friends, how the faithful Lord has directed us with his grace and help, so that you join us in thanking the Lord and faithfully give further assistance to his kingdom work, as you have in the past. May he richly reward you all in body and soul for time and eternity. Amen.

Brother Kempe and I sincerely thank you for all the love and kindness shown to our brothers and to their fiancées who recently arrived in your midst. May the faithful Saviour richly bless you for that, and grant that you one day joyfully stand at his right hand, together with all the elect.

May the gracious and merciful God also grant that we, together with you, share this blessed joy with a host of these poor heathen brothers. He has shed his holy, precious blood for all people, and desires that all be helped and come to know the truth. So, we want to carry out our work on the station joyfully, despite the devil, world and our own reason which continually whisper into our ears that these heathen are sunk too deeply to ever be able to become true Christians and children of God. But we hope in the Lord who alone can give a new heart and a new and right spirit to make the dead live. His promise remains true: The last shall be first. So happily continue to believe, pray, work and hope, for no one will be put to shame who waits on him.

We four men, Mirus, Meissner, Kempe and I, were permitted to experience this also this month. We have all, without exception, been in good health, despite the great heat. We had many storms, strong winds and lots of dust, but three times the Lord granted us refreshing rains.

This month the heathen came and went, almost too much, so that we barely had the shepherds we need.[14] An old Aboriginal man who was lame in both feet was with us for several days. We gave him food, medicine and a new blanket. The probable cause of his condition was that three younger Blacks brought him to Ellery Creek, took away his blanket, and left him lying in misery. But then, they are foolish, blind, poor heathen.

Our entire stock is in very good condition. We have received two foals, castrated 140 lambs, laid out a new foundation, carted wood and burnt lime. Brothers Kempe and Meissner went to Alice and Owen Springs and brought the repaired cart and young stallion from Gilbert.[15] They brought a hen and young cat as a travel gift. We make good use of the latter against the many mice and rats.

We are very happy to receive news that brothers and fiancées are already on the way. There is said to be plenty of fodder and water along the track. May the Lord keep them in good spirits and graciously bring them here safe and well. There is no lack of work for them here…

W Schwarz

* * *

And as this second year of this undertaking draws to a close, Heidenreich frets about money, business, food and people.

Undated – (assumed) December 1877[16] *(Heidenreich to Th Harms)*
Highly honoured and much-loved Father!

You will forgive me if, in addition to the report for the *Missionsblatt*, I present you with some other matters. The missionaries on the station write that the sheep would produce no profit, only a loss. The stated reason is that the pay for the shepherds is so high, and meat would be much cheaper if each month they were to buy a fatted bullock for slaughter.

So, the sheep have to be driven South or sold up North for 12 shillings on average.[17] Those are calculations without expert advice. For in the first place, the sheep will no longer be looked after by paid personnel; as soon as Holtermann[18] is there, he can take on one or two heathen as assistants. ... Wool, unfortunately, will bring no profit, and ... can make over £200 income.

Secondly, fresh meat is much healthier than salted. Therefore, we also intend to slaughter bullocks ... The missionaries and I have often seen with our own eyes how people on other stations slaughtered a fatted sheep in the evening, which then after dawn the next morning had to be buried, or had gone off in the salt barrel in the first eight days, depending on a change in the weather, and ... sheep bad, so that the loss of a sheep is not as bad, because it amounts to only shillings, compared to a bullock that costs pounds...

... We lost as many sheep on this journey as on the first,[19] and the rest brought in less than the droving costs. And so our fine flock of 3561 head has been greatly diminished. If we keep and maintain those that we have, we not only have a continuous supply of good, wholesome meat, but our income grows with 50 percent profit so that we can later buy and rear a herd of cattle. Thus, I have given Kempe permission to give fatted sheep for slaughter to the neighbouring station in exchange for young cows, if the neighbours want to eat mutton for a change, and our people want a fatted bullock in exchange.

I say again, the management of the station cannot develop in a proper way unless a prudent and experienced man is put in charge...

Dear Father, I very much regret that you sent Peters.[20] He is well on the way to giving you and Hermannsburg a rotten name[21] after entering a congregational school with Homann, Strempel, etc., and in my presence, he defamed you ... among the young brothers, ... and made accusations against you and strong allegations against the brothers. I chastised him on the spot but so far one senses no improvement. May the faithful Lord grant that I do not have to report in the next mail that my misgivings have had the outcome I fear. At first I did not want to send you the letter from ... and also did not want to write that last [bit]. But I am mortal and have to this moment not hidden from you both joy and pain ...

Having overcome this mountain, we hope things get better. We no longer have the terrible loan repayments and will soon earn something from the livestock. But please immediately send money... Our treasurer Schmidt has returned from his trip to Port Augusta and reports, to my joy, that when Jürgens and our wagon arrived, they not only found everything in good order, but also the heathen lad[22] and our horses in excellent condition ... The horses were so flighty that they swerved offline when they set out and were reined in only after a considerable time. Soon enough they will go slower. Jürgens seems to be developing into a good driver and we have all come to hold him dear...

(Schmidt) left our dear travellers in excellent spirits in the hands of their driver. In a few days they will have arrived at their wagon. They will soon have overtaken the third wagon, so that our desert trek this time takes place with three teams of bullocks and our team of horses. This is a bullock expedition, equipped and maintained by so many new people that they will make many ... It causes me considerable grief that I have to stay home for the sake of some church work ...

Your true son, G A Heidenreich

* * *

Elsewhere in the world, during 1877:

- Queen Victoria was proclaimed Empress of India (1 January).
- The Great Railroad Strike, leading to rioting and upheaval in the USA, in Baltimore, Pittsburgh and St Louis, occurred during July.
- The first test cricket match between England and Australia began on 15 March in Melbourne (Australia won); the first Wimbledon lawn tennis tournament began on 9 July; and for the only time in its history the annual Oxford-Cambridge boat race ended in a draw (24 March).
- The dancer, Isadora Duncan, was born in San Francisco (26 May), and the Mormon leader, Brigham Young, died (29 August).
- Thomas Edison demonstrated his new invention, the phonograph (29 November).

* * *

1878

With the arrival of the additional personnel for Herrmansburg on the Finke, another voice is added to the mission narrative: that of Louis Schulze. The next letter is his first to Director Harms from Australia and, although it repeats some of the story already told, it nevertheless has value in hearing that part of the story through this new voice.

9 January 1878, Beresford[23] *(Schulze to Th Harms)*
Dear Pastor,

First, I offer you cordial wishes for a happy and blessed New Year. When I look back in my mind's eye I have to exclaim with the poet, 'Oh how the years run by, how our time vanishes, etc.' At the end of my last letter to you I told you that I would be going to the interior as a missionary. It seems only a few days ago, but already ten weeks have passed and, with God's help, we have journeyed on with many a burden and with much trouble, as you may have learnt from the letters of Brothers Kempe and Schwarz. Half the journey is now behind us, and I will now briefly tell you about this.

After we had packed everything necessary for such a long and difficult journey, Superintendent Heidenreich and Pastor Georg blessed us for the task in the church of Bethany on Tuesday 6 November. The following day we attended Georg's wedding in Bethany and departed on 8 November from Bethany for Adelaide. We lodged again at Pastor Homann's and got some more items for our trip. Saturday morning we travelled by train to Port Adelaide and from there by steamer to Port Augusta. Our crates were sent 14 days earlier, so, apart from our crates with provisions, we had only five crates belonging to Brothers Kempe and Schwarz.

There was still a lot to do before everything was in order with these crates. Brother Peters and Pastor Homan's son, Bernhard, were true helpers indeed. We arrived at Port Augusta on Sunday evening and did not know where to stay overnight as all the hotels were full. The captain of the ship, an Englishman, kindly allowed us to stay on board overnight.

Next day we had to take the oath of allegiance and I had the pleasure of meeting two Germans, one a coachman from Pomerania, the other a policeman from the town of Hanover. Both took me into their care.

On Monday, Mr Schmidt, a member of the Mission Committee, arrived with Jürgens and the coachman and Bobby, a heathen lad whom Superintendent Heidenreich had brought down South with him from the Interior. They arrived from Melrose with our wagon drawn by six horses, having travelled there by rail and mail coach.

On Tuesday we bought some more things needed for the journey, packed the wagon and departed in God's name on the same day with our mobile desert dwelling. Some were sitting inside, some standing in the doorway, and others walking alongside. We travelled to Stirling which is a very small village by German standards. We lodged there for the first time with our new house under the stars. The horses were unhitched, watered, and put out to pasture. One does not have to pay for this in this land of freedom. The pasture is dry, only after rain is there green grass or saltbush. In some places it is very desolate so that nothing will grow. We passed through areas where for great distances there was only stony rubble or sand.

The country from The Gums to Peake does not even grow real trees but only low scrub. One can imagine green, grassy places, but can find none.

I must not digress too far. While some of us looked after the horses, one fetched or looked for wood, another got water. Later we brewed tea in a big iron pot, half as deep as wide, with three legs, called a camp oven. Such a camp oven is used for everything—both for baking bread and for frying and cooking. So you see how practical the Australian cook or chef is, or has to be.

Last week a horse kicked out with its hind legs and broke the camp oven in two. It happened to be standing on the front of the wagon. What a calamity for us; we cannot buy one up here, so we have to cook in tins. Fortunately, we can still use it for baking.

When the tea was ready, we ate our supper which, besides the tea, almost always consists of meat, bread, sausage and cheese, except that the last two are sometimes missing. After supper we talked for a while, then looked for bags to spread on the ground and after devotion lay down to sleep.

Next morning we looked for the horses, watered them and had a drink of coffee with bread and meat for breakfast. We then harnessed up, placed the goods on the wagon, and after devotion drove forward in God's name.

So that is how it mostly goes, day after day, mostly. We halt at midday, have a drink of the extra tea that has been brewed the previous evening and eat something with it. When the heat is too great, as it is today, we sit quietly in the shade with the sweat dripping off us, and then drive at night by moonlight.

We cannot cover big distances up here as we can down South, where we travelled 20 to 30 English miles (5 to 7 German miles).[24] Here we average 10 to 12 miles[25] per day, with a day's spell now and then, otherwise man and beast would not be able to bear it. At the beginning of the journey we were anxious to get as far as possible each day, but now everyone is glad when I say: 'We will stay here for the day'.

If at all possible we stay where there is good water, as most of it is salty, and we have become ill several times after drinking the bad water. For instance, at The Gums we hoped to have a rest period after many days of very heavy journeying but, lo and behold, the water was so salty that we hurried on and had another difficult trip of several days.

How good it was for all of us when we arrived at Welcome Springs on the Wednesday before Christmas, where we found good water and a little green, grassed space. We stayed here until the day after Christmas. But our joy was soon to be clouded for on Thursday Holtermann was to return from looking for the horses which were grazing about an hour's distance from the camp but he did not arrive. To assist him, we kept a big fire burning at night from 8 to 11 as a beacon. I fired three shots, but all in vain. On the following morning I rode out to search for him and found him after a short distance; he was lost in the scrub.

Our hearts were filled with thanks and joy as we celebrated the much-loved Christmas festival. A little hut built of branches and twigs was our living and bedroom as well as our house of God. There the Lord blessed us richly with his Word and Sacrament.

As I consider our journey so far, I cannot but thank the Lord for all he has done for us up till now. Even though we had some very bad days, we overcame them all with the help of the Lord. We had one such bad day, for instance, at Hookina. A strong wind blew up so much dust that we could barely see each other a few paces away. In the morning we were covered with dust and dirt. Our spirits were terribly low, and we were glad to leave that place in the morning.

That evening we reached a lovely place, compared with that of the previous stay. There was little water, but it was good, so we stayed the night. One must carefully search out beforehand where there is water and, if necessary, camp there even if it is noon. At times we have journeyed into the night to get there. We always have to carry some barrels of water with us, for at times we have to halt where there is no water. The horses have had to be taken one to two hours distance to water, or have had to wait till the next day when we have reached a waterhole. Among the local drivers who drive up and down the track, and whom we have often met down South, the main conversation revolves around the places where there are good water and feed.

At waterholes we found stock, such as sheep, goats, and horses. The Government or the towns people have dug big wells in some places and built water tanks, and a man is employed to maintain them. The traffic coming down on this track here in the desert is by no means light. The railway may even get up to The Gums from Port Augusta in three years' time; that is about 100 English miles from our old station.[26] That would bring significant relief for us too, because a ton, that is 20 hundred-weights, costs £60 sterling in freight alone from Port Augusta to our station. That is 400 thaler.

Travelling with us now are two wagons, and one is coming up behind, each one carrying three tons. For the moment we are remaining with the first two wagons because the track is too sandy. So, now and then the bullocks have to help us out, because we have only six horses, not enough for up here. Last week we had to cross sandy hills near Finniss. We hitched up 20 bullocks and even with them had difficulty getting over the sandhills. If Mr Brown arrives today with his two wagons we will consider journeying to Strangway tomorrow where there is a post office and telegraph station.

Concerning our inner life, I have to confess that here in the desert it especially holds true: watch and pray. The evil enemies, the devil and one's own evil heart will not leave one in peace. Yes, I believe I am correct in saying that it is worse here than anywhere else. But it is as [Scripture] tells us. 'All things work together for good to them that love God' (Romans 8:28). The devil always comes off the worse for it if only we watch and pray. Therefore, I beg of you most earnestly, pray for us fervently, you and the whole mission community. It seems to me that the devil's fiery darts are directed especially against the mission in this country. How painful it is to see people die in the chains and bonds of Satan. In many places along the way we have met groups of 15, 20, or 25, a mixture of adults and children.[27] They make themselves a small hut of twigs in which they live. Their main nourishment is lizards, mice, snakes and worms, etc., apart from food they get now and then from Whites, for gathering wood or carrying water.

What grace it would be if help could be given these people too, before it is too late, and if we could be the instruments for this in the Lord's hand. We must all pray for this.

Cordial greetings to you, your dear family, as well as to the whole mission community from both the fiancées of Brothers Kempe and Schwarz, as well as from the three settlers and myself.

Your obedient servant, Louis Schulze

The above letter is another example of the typically minimal references made to the women in our letters and reports, not just by Schulze, but by all the writers (men). Earlier, Heidenreich, at least, was concerned about the well-being of the two Dorotheas on the looming trip North, and he saw to it that they were cared for and protected. In fact, the safety of the women was one of the main reasons for Schulze's inclusion in the party in the first place.

However, on the account of the journey itself, everyone else (even the goats!) get a mention. But not the women. What wagon were they travelling in? How were they coping? What considerations needed to be, and were, made for their special needs? What did they talk about? And with whom?

Not a word.

* * *

As we have already noted, apart from the challenges of the Finke mission, Heidenreich is involved in matters relating to the mission in New Zealand, and to the placement of Hermannsburg (Germany) pastors in congregations in Australia. Invariably, these people and related concerns get under his skin, and he complains about them to Harms.

At times, though, Harms chides Heidenreich for his oft-critical attitude towards others. So, for example, in a letter of 1 November of the previous year,[28] Heidenreich has obviously been unhappy about certain matters in New Zealand, and even about Th Harms' response to those and other affairs. In that letter, Harms says to Heidenreich:

> I am only acting in your interests, and those of the mission, in separating the superintendencies of Australia and New Zealand as independent offices that, naturally, offer help to each other in love. I thank you heartily for standing by me so faithfully in all respects, and know for certain that the Lord will richly bless you for it. But you must not forget, my dear Heidenreich, that some confusion is inevitable in the case of such new and complicated undertakings. Do not lose courage. I know for a certainty that you will not break off connection with me.[29] That you must not do for the sake of the Lord and his Kingdom. You have only half as much work, care, conflict and struggle as I have.

And this reminder of the importance of love and consideration for others occurs more than once in the correspondence between Harms and Heidenreich.

To his credit, Heidenreich responds positively to Harms' cautions, as the next letter demonstrates. But, then, in the letter after that, almost as if he cannot help himself, he is once again peeved by the actions of people like Schoknecht and Oster, and is vexed by the possibility of a split in the Church.

24 January 1878, Bethany[30] *(Heidenreich to Th Harms)*
Highly honoured, much-loved Father!

... I thankfully accept your paternal advice that I should be a milder overseer of the missionaries, for it is true: 'A stubborn person makes a wise one resentful and destroys a gentle heart', but 'the heart of a wise person knows the right time and manner'. May the dear Lord also grant me that; he knows, has seen and has heard everything, and by his grace I know that in me and with me there is nothing good, so that I barely have the will to accomplish anything. But the Lord will help me, so that your advice does not fall to the earth.

We also need your admonition to be thrifty...I am glad that you have given this salutary advice, for it protects me. I can also gladly tell you with certainty that our brothers up North are gradually coming around. May the Lord give further help.

Our dear travelling party has made quick and safe progress; on the 18th of this month they were close to Strangway. The horses are said to be fat and do not want to pull properly in the sandhills. That is the old problem, and it is good that they have the bullock wagon to help.

This year the heat here was terrific with many suffering sunstroke. I hope that our dear brothers and sisters are still well and in good spirits despite the almost unbearable heat between the sandhills. I also have pleasing news from the station and things seem to have settled down. Thank the Lord for that.

In the Church things are again gloomy, and there could be a split in our Church if the Lord in his grace does not avert it. The Oster party, to which Gössling, Homann, Schoknecht, Peters have attached themselves, tries everything possible to stir up strife with Hermannsburg. You know full well that I do not belong to them ...[31]

* * *

Heidenreich's reference to the 'Oster party' in the letters above and below is another of those puzzles for which he provides no answer. The most likely scenario is that some doctrinal issue has been raised within the Church and people have taken sides on the matter. In 1877, for example, there were disputes between the various Synods in South Australia over the use of a certain, shared catechism (*Boeckh's Catechism*), in particular over what were perceived by some pastors as questionable understandings of the doctrine of Christ. Brauer lists Strempel, Hensel, Oster, Ey and Homann as one side, or 'party', in this debate.[32] It could be that this is the dispute Heidenreich is here referencing.

Likewise, the reference in the letter below to the antipathy of some of the surrounding property owners towards the mission is ultimately a little short on detail. Many pastoralists believed that the missions were treated too favorably and that they ought to be reined in and more heavily controlled. But what specific instance Heidenreich has in mind is not stated as clearly as it might be.

26 February 1878, Bethany[33] *(Heidenreich to Th Harms)*
Highly honoured and much-loved Father!

My heart is full of matters here and in the dear homeland, but I have my hands so full of work that I can write to you only what is most necessary ...

A deal is again being worked through between Bode and Peters regarding a position, as Bertram told me yesterday. I know nothing of all that but, in light of his own words earlier, I consider Peters capable of anything. I once wrote to you my opinion about him, and that appears to be coming true all too early.

Schoknecht is said to have been with Homann for 14 days. Although they invited the other pastors and conferred with them, I heard of this only third hand after Schoknecht had left. The apparent outcome is that Schoknecht has formed a synod with the pastors in Melbourne ... In addition, Homann and Schoknecht are trying to work at getting the later brothers[34] for the Church Council against your proviso ... The Oster party can fish in these troubled waters, yes it can press for a decision that is very disagreeable to me, that the rest of us Hermannsburgers form a synod by ourselves ...

The devil is angry at the mission, and the large cattle owners look greedily at our mission property, so that they have had a law passed in parliament that all mission societies ... must enter into the same lease agreement as they. These 'lies' have been circulating for 21 years, and can be renewed for as long again. The lease holders up here with us have to pay ... per square mile annually. From what has been sent to me, it is not clear whether or not we have to pay for our lease...

Hopefully, that will not be eaten as hot as it is served up. We will take all possible and necessary steps and consider all options to see whether we will do best with a proper lease, or one so-called, and whether we can choose what is best for ourselves. If I knew that George V was now king in England, I would write to him that he should persuade our Queen Victoria to grant us our place in perpetuity...

* * *

In the next bracket of four letters, the predominant note is one of joy and thanksgiving. True, the weather is hot and draining, the need for water constant. Yet, at the mission station itself life is becoming more settled, the community more established. But the big news is the pending arrival of the new party—including a third missionary—and, especially for Kempe and Schwarz, the arrival of their fiancées.

By mid-January the travellers are somewhere in the vicinity of Strangways, heading for Peake, still anything up to 1000 kilometres to travel. The going is tough, but bearable. Nevertheless, to assist this group over the last part of the journey, Kempe and Schwarz decide that Kempe, accompanied by Meissner, should head down South and meet the party somewhere near Peake. They take extra horses and wagons with them.

So, there was a practical reason behind this dash to meet Schulze, the fiancées and the others. But I imagine that my great-grandfather was so excited about the expectation of meeting up with Dorothea and about their prospective marriage that he would have been happy to make this trip, anyway. One can almost hear his smile as he tells Director Harms about the planned trip.

Once the parties meet, the two are married, almost immediately. The reason for that quick wedding is mostly about propriety. They wished to avoid any possible later accusations about improper conduct between an engaged couple.

In the midst of all that, one cannot help feeling a little sorry for Schwarz who had to remain behind on base to take care of the sheep, lambs and cooking.

* * *

1 February 1878, Mission Station on the Finke[35] *(Schwarz to ELSA members)*
Dear precious mission family!

… By God's grace we are safe and sound to this hour, Mirus, J Roger and I. We hope that Brother Kempe and Meissner, who left here on 15 January, are the same as they travel to meet the brothers and fiancées who are on their way here. May the Lord bless their going out and coming in and bring them all safely to us.

As for work, there is not much to talk about this month. For one, the heat was so great that it reached between 102 and 106 degrees in our cool buildings. Then our people had bad eye ailments, so that first Kempe and then I had to undertake shepherding duties. Our well had to be dug deeper and lined with stones. While this was happening, limestones were broken up, building timber cut down and driven to the station. Soon afterwards the lime kiln was filled and fired. When Kempe left I was busy in the kitchen and Roger had to help Mirus guard the sheep because of his weak eyes. There was a little or no actual building work done, though we hope to have the new stone building ready for the arrival of our brothers and sisters.

We have received very little rain this month, but lots of storms, wind and dust. We are thus longing for rain, not only because of the bad dust but also to provide fodder for the stock and produce in the garden. The garden produce was first nibbled at by rats, now the ants are everywhere. Otherwise everything has come up very well.

There were usually seven heathen here, all engaged in work, except for two.

The cattle, horses and sheep are in good condition, but longing for the refreshment of rain which God seems about to give us, since dark clouds cover the sky all around...

W F Schwarz, Missionary.

3 March 1878, Dalhousie Springs[36] *(Kempe to Th Harms)*
Dear Pastor!

You will certainly be surprised to read a letter from me with the old familiar address at the top, 'Dalhousie Springs'. You will think that we have even retreated again. That is not the case.

The reason I am here is to fetch our long-awaited and longed-for brothers and our fiancées. I had to make the decision to come because they continually wrote ... that my coming was necessary. However, it would not at all have been necessary, and I received only the first two letters and telegrams mentioned, because I was already underway when the last arrived.

After tossing back and forth what was advisable, both Brother Schwarz and I decided it was necessary that we travel to meet them, for we learned that they did not have a driver who knew the track and, as we often enough experienced on our own long trek, lack of familiarity with the track can often cause delays and losses. So, I set off with a man, three wagon horses and two riding horses. Brother Schwarz could not leave the station because he was mustering.

No rain had fallen at the time when we left; it seems that this year will again be dry. Thus we did not follow the track but rode 200 to 250 miles[37] along the course of the Finke, down to Charlotte Waters, where we again met the track. At this last mentioned place I learned that they were still below the Finke, and that I had to extend my pilgrimage. Because of the lack of water, I did not again follow the track but the course of the Stevenson to examine the watering places and then, when necessary, struck out along the track with the wagon. But the dear Lord took away our cares by sending us enough rain to allow us to travel along the track.

So, I met them, fiancées, settlers and my dear Brother Schulze, on Sunday 10 February at Peake Creek, 3 miles north of Peake Station, with all hale and hearty, by God's grace. Those were overwhelming moments, seeing each other again after such a long separation, so overwhelming that I could barely say a word.

Despite needing a rest after such a long and exhausting ride, I could not think of that with so much else to do immediately. Besides, in my dehydrated and poor state I was supposed to relate our experiences and more such things in one go ...

I considered it appropriate to get married while on the journey, since Brother Schulze had a marriage licence. This was partly for my sake, partly for the sake of the people there on the wagon, and partly for those down South in the colony. So we were married here in Dalhousie Springs on the previous Friday, 1 March, with Brother Schulze officiating.

Though there was no church, not even a house, but with the event taking place in a tent, we experienced blessing and sensed the Lord's presence. He [has been] and remains our one and all, the centre and Lord of our hearts.

I do not intend to write anything at all about our further journey, since Brother Schulze will do so at the appropriate time in his report. But this I must confess and say to God's honour, that the dear and faithful Lord looked after us like a father caring for his children, and always supplied us with fodder and water at the right time, often answered our prayers wonderfully, and put me thoroughly to shame because of my worries and doubts while travelling down. It gave me much to think about and ponder over, especially when comparing this trip with our first one. Now, on 10 March, we are in Charlotte Waters and I hope to reach our station in five weeks.

I now want to speak about another matter, not as though the earthly ... but only to give closure and certainty concerning it. The point I raise concerns our salary.

Dear Pastor, when we set out, you said that we were to be treated like other missionaries. But Provost Heidenreich was of the opinion that we should receive £8 in each of the years until our fiancées arrived, but then, £12 after marriage. I did not object to that, but both Brother Schwarz and I are of the opinion that that cannot be accepted if we are to avoid living in a ragged and shabby state. This cannot be your opinion and no Christian could ask that of us.

For £12 ... in Germany is not nearly as much as 12 thaler. I really do not need to explain that no one can get by with that, even given that all our clothing is supplied which, incidentally, is not the case and which we are not demanding, because we would thereby be made dependent on the kindness and benefaction of the congregations down South ...[38]

11 March 1878, Charlotte Waters[39] *(Schulze to ELSA members)*
When I review our journey and, in particular, compare it with that of the Brothers Kempe and Schwarz under the direction of our Provost Heidenreich, tears of joy and thankfulness well up involuntarily in my eyes and those of Brother Kempe and the others in view of the fatherly way our faithful God has dealt with us, his ill-behaved children. My dear Brother Kempe has now and then told us about his trip; he met us on 10 February at Peake Creek, to my great joy and the joy of us all. We have truly not deserved such gentle treatment...

When we arrived at Peake everyone told us: 'You cannot possibly proceed further, because the water has already dried up in many places.' At the same time, I also there received a telegram from Brother Kempe that finished with the words: 'Pray for rain!'

Furthermore, in the telegram he promised to come immediately to Angle Pole. What were we now to do? We set out on our journey again, trusting in the Lord who had so far helped us through many a difficulty. Just as we were leaving, the Lord granted us a good shower of rain for the journey as a pledge of his further help. We drove up to Peake Creek.

Already on the next day Brother Kempe came to meet us. Joy at seeing each other again was great, but there was still concern about progressing further since, as Brother Kempe reported, water had dried up in many places.

Nevertheless, we dared to travel on and, behold, the Lord gave us plenty of water at just the right time and place, so there was nothing to stop us resuming our journey. We stayed for several days at Dalhousie. There I was asked to marry my dear friend and compatriot, Kempe, on 1 March.

The external aspects of the event were not very impressive in a festive, celebratory and uplifting sense. Our tent served as a church, and we set up an altar using casks and cases. Schwarz's fiancée provided decoration with green branches. I took Proverbs 31:10–12 as the wedding text. The wedding was certainly a meagre affair, but we had a delightful time, and spent the evening happily singing and telling stories. That is how the Lord is able to bless and refresh one in the wilderness ...

Yours, Louis Schulze

11 March 1878, Charlotte Waters[40] *(Schulze to Th Harms)*
Dear Pastor.

We all arrived here safe and well the previous Saturday a week ago. We can only thank and praise the Lord for our journey because he has given us beyond what we could pray for and comprehend.

On 10 February Brother Kempe met us at Peake Creek, 3 miles this side of Peake. As bad as the situation with water was at the time, we risked travelling on, trusting in the Lord. At the right time and at the right places he gave us enough water and with it also fodder for our 13 horses, so that we were free to get back on the track. And so we now hope to celebrate Easter on our station.

Precisely on my birthday, 1 March, Brother Kempe had me conduct his wedding at Dalhousie. It was not in the dear house of God, but in a tent where we had erected an altar made of casks and cushions, covered with a rug. Schwarz's fiancée even decorated the tent with a variety of green branches. I used Proverbs 31:10–12 as the text for the wedding address. Of course the wedding breakfast was not such a grand affair, but we were all extremely happy...

Louis Schulze

* * *

Schwarz has obviously dated this next letter incorrectly. From its contents one can imagine him entangled in a welter of emotions as he waits for the new arrivals, especially for his first sight of a fiancée he has not seen for over two years. That happy occasion occurred on 11 April. Until then he has to send off this report from a place where 'nothing much has happened'.

19 April 1878, Hermannsburg[41] *(Schwarz to Th Harms)*
Dear Pastor,

... With God's gracious help we have again begun a new year and already lived through a quarter of it, so the time has come to report on it to you. Yet what should I report when one day is much the same as the other and nothing much has happened, at least in the period I am writing about. Thus, I need only write briefly.

Apart from a few poor heathen, there have been only five persons on the station: an English worker called Roger, together with Meissner, Mirus, Brother Kempe and I. When Brother Kempe and Meissner set off from here on 5 January to meet the dear brothers and sisters, only three of us remained on the place, and had our hands full with looking after sheep, building and the like, with the poor heathen giving excellent help so that, with God's help, we could complete the most necessary tasks, though one after the other suffered an eye complaint.

God be thanked for everything, especially for the nice rains that he has sent us in this quarter and particularly on 22, 23, 24 March. We have high hopes of gaining some garden produce this year. Our cattle, horses and sheep are in good condition, and lambing has already begun. There is no lack of fresh green feed and good water and we owe God thanks for doing everything well ...

Natives[42] were present in varying numbers in the last quarter, but never more than 12 to 28, and only males. Unfortunately, little progress has been made in language study. God grant that it will soon go better, but there is little hope of getting to it in the immediate future, because we are short of workers. Thus, our greatest wish in this respect is that more brothers and sisters can soon follow us from Europe, and that our dear fiancées, Brother L Schulze, and the dear colonists will arrive here safe and sound on 11 April ...

W F Schwarz

* * *

The following is Schulze's account of the arrival of the new residents at Hermannsburg on the Finke. One can imagine the joy, as well as the sense of consolidation, many of them would have experienced over the expansion of their little community. But one can also imagine the bewilderment and apprehension of others as they surveyed this new home in this lonely desert—the home that at that point they likely expected to be their home for the rest of their lives.

It is worth noting that the journey for this group took only five months, compared to the 20 months of those first travellers.

19 April 1878, Hermannsburg[43] (Schulze to ELSA members)
Dear mission community!

With God's help we have now finished our long and difficult journey. As you will see in the heading of this letter, our station shall henceforth be called 'Hermannsburg', at the directive of our dear Director Pastor Harms.

In my earlier letters I could only thank and praise the Lord for his fatherly, indeed, wonderful guidance, so even now I cannot do otherwise than raise songs of praise and thanks. At all times we were able to proceed unhindered on our way.

When we needed rain to make further progress the Lord provided. After the rain he gave us a very beautiful view, for now the usually desolate, grey and barren land has begun to bloom. A veritable carpet of flowers has spread over the fields. So, for instance, the Opossum and Ufes Holes were completely covered with lilies. It was not only a feast for the eyes, but the body was to have some nourishment too. A herb called Mansheroo[44] was also growing there, and we used it to stew soup or prepare for salad.

But the Lord put the rod alongside the apple, as it is always the case if we want to go to heaven. Already before Strangways Springs we suffered to varying degrees with sore eyes, and especially this side of Charlotte Waters the faithful Lord afflicted us, especially me, with eye complaints. I could hardly see anything for a fortnight, and even now my eyes are not quite right. Just as well Kempe was with us so that our journey could proceed up to here without hindrance.

On Wednesday 10 April we got to within 20 English miles of our place. Brother Kempe and I hurried to reach the station on that same day and arrived there at 3 o'clock in the afternoon. Brother Schwarz welcomed us with great joy.

Next morning Brother Schwarz rode out to meet the wagon while Kempe and I decorated the little airy, wooden hut inside and out with palm fronds which Brother Schwarz had the heathen gather from the Finke River on the day before. We were hardly finished when our wagon arrived, and I had to hurry to get the rubbish out of the hut. Brother Schwarz was not among the arrivals, having missed the wagon, but he arrived soon after. The joy of seeing each other again was of course not little. We had fish caught by the heathen for our welcoming meal...

May [God] continue to look down upon us in grace and, above all, give us access to the hearts of the heathen, for which we continually pray, and which we must never forget...

L Schulze, Missionary

* * *

As indicated a few letters ago, one of the muddy questions that occasionally arises is whether the land on which the mission was located was allocated to the Church as a grant or as a lease. The fact that Heidenreich and the missionaries refer to this place as 'our place', plus other ways and places in which they refer to the land, infer that they regarded Hermannsburg on the Finke as a grant. This is especially so when comes the time at the end of our story for a decision to me made about the future of the mission.

However, on other occasions the mission land is definitely spoken of as a lease. That is the case in this next letter where Heidenreich expresses concern about possible changes to the lease—in fact, about even the retention of the property at all.

Also in this letter he takes up the thorny issue that Kempe earlier raised about the missionaries' salaries. At this point they were paid nothing much more than board and lodgings. This, too, becomes a matter that occupies their vexed attention for some time, especially as the settlers/colonists are receiving greater pay than the missionaries.

The Chinese mission to which he refers was located in Melbourne. Peters, one of the latest new arrivals, had been sent there to develop that work, but it has fallen through—a fact that will hardly help to enhance Heidenreich's already poor opinion of Peters. Likewise, it seems, of Meyer, another of the new graduates just arrived.

And then there is the matter of the bell…!

18 May 1878, Bethany[45] *(Heidenreich to Th Harms)*
Highly honoured, much-loved Father!

Good reports have come in from the Centre concerning the physical situation of the mission. The gracious Lord has been with the travellers and they have probably celebrated the Easter festival with the whole community on our place. Also, from the government I have received the promise that we can be free of worry about the possession of our place, since the new land laws do not extend to the Northern Territory where our place is situated. Handing things over to leases will bring greater security and more rights, as far as I understand. I wait daily for the reply of the new Minister for Lands to my new submission and will later send it to you. The difference will probably be that originally the place was handed over for the mission until the time we did no mission work for two years and also had no intention of doing any more, but now we will have to ask the government to renew our lease every 25 years for a further five years.[46] If it happens that we have to give up the mission we can use the new conditions … for … years to our advantage by including the value of buildings, etc. The new documentation will make that perfectly clear. Nevertheless, I am pleased that I can this time share as much as this with you.

Brothers Kempe and Schulze are sending along what is enclosed through me. I regret that Kempe's writing is so unreadable and so I will explain the main point in a few words. It is the question of a fixed salary. The missionaries appeal to the fact that you promised them that. At the beginning I asked them how much per annum you had promised them. They did not know, and I told them that I was also in favour of a fixed salary but 'I cannot act on my own authority, and so I think it best that, until the matter is regularised, you receive what the earlier missionaries got on the old mission here'. They were happy with that for the time being and we have remained true to our word.

It is now time that this difficult matter was regulated for the betterment of the mission and its workers. The mission will have to carry the cost of everything belonging to their upkeep, so the question of finance can relate only to salary and clothing; though I doubt whether this latter should also be covered. The missionaries would like more money, as much as the colonists are now paid.

We had a good [harvest], but we have nothing but debts and more debts, and I am sorely waiting for you to send money. What are we to do? To promise something and not keep to it only makes matters worse. So, I am again placing the matter of the missionaries in your hands and hope to God that you will make a decision so that our people remain contented in doing their work ...

The Chinese mission is at an end. Peters has off his own bat submitted himself to the Church Council for a transfer, first by letter, then orally. With much effort we were able only to persuade him to take up ministry in the Church with your proviso. He has at last done that but does not otherwise want to know about the proviso, and agrees entirely with the document that was sent to you by the Church Council with the last mail. This makes my head spin and hurts my heart.

But enough. It is now in your hands and will certainly be answered by you. Peters justified his position by asserting that you did not want him to do mission work, otherwise you would have sent him to Africa. He then claimed I was not willing to give him financial support. At the conference I told him that I could not promise a fixed salary ...[47]

All is well with the young brothers apart from Meyer who has incurred much hostility by introducing innovations. I feel sorry for him since he otherwise seems to be a decent man. The Lord will sort it all out.

I have a special request: My congregation at Bethany wants to order a new bell from Germany, to weigh a hundred-weight without any iron or woodwork for fixing it in place ... Since you often need small bells for the heathen, would you be so good as to order me one, to be well packed with all attachments and sent here to my address via Hamburg. It is best if you ascertain the amount for the bell and freight to Hamburg when you order it. Write and tell me what the bell costs and when it will be sent off so that I can send you the money.

We would like to have it soon because our old one is cracked. For the time being we have purchased a small one weighing 14 pounds; We will send it to our Hermannsburg station in the north when the new one is here...

    G A Heidenreich

27 May 1878, Bethany[48] *(Heidenreich to ELSA members)*
... The three loaded wagons[49] are expected to arrive at our station in only one or two months' time, stopping to at least give the draught bullocks rest and relief after crossing the sandhills. I am very glad that we still have a short period to pay the £600[50] for freight. Until then the faithful Lord will manage matters. From where, I do not know. If I look to Germany I see no hope of any door opening up to such a sum. If I look at the various claims for money in our Synod, I am inclined to say that the people have done everything possible and shared in the mission in a praiseworthy way...

    G A Heidenreich

10.

Settling In

A striking feature of the next couple of letters is the quick and calm way in which, after the arrival of its new members, the community settles back into what feels like an established routine. Even though he is a new-comer, Schulze in particular gives the impression of easily slipping into life in his new home. There are indications that inter-actions with the Aboriginal people are slowly developing. And the community even has its mail delivered every six weeks! Back in the mother Church in Hermannsburg, however, there are rumblings that all is not as well as it might be.

* * *

30 May 1878, Hermannsburg[1] *(Kempe to ELSA members)*
Dear mission family.

The month of May has already flown by since writing the report for the month of April, but I can and must excuse myself because we have mail service only every six weeks. Looking back over the recent time, we have every good cause to cry out with the psalmist: 'Praise the Lord, O my soul, and forget not all his benefits'. Yes, the Lord has done good things for us; therefore we are glad.

At the beginning of April I was still travelling to fetch our dear ones here. Brother Schulze has already reported this, also that we arrived here on the 11th of this month safe and well. All that remains is to give the rest of the report, which is fine with me, since the hard building work makes my fingers quite stiff for writing.[2]

After our arrival we had to spend some days putting everything in order, and then celebrated Palm Sunday as a community on the station. Then we had to hurry to get the small house ready so that the women did not need to cook in the open, and Brother Schwarz's fianceé had somewhere to live before the wedding. The Lord gave his blessing to the building so that we were able to cook in the new house already at Easter. There was nothing more for us to do than to put up the roof and bring in the floor paving, using large stone slabs.

On Maundy Thursday we celebrated the Lord's Supper as a community and refreshed ourselves with God's precious Word on the other days,[3] so that we could very easily sense that the risen Saviour was in our midst in the wilderness.

After the days of rest we first fetched in all the horses, branded them and brought them all up to the Finke. After that we began building a shed about 80 feet in length, partly to contain a dwelling for the settlers and partly to house the freight of the wagons that were on the way, so that things were at least protected from the sun. You can easily imagine that we all had our hands full with this work…

H Kempe

30 May 1878, Hermannsburg[4] *(Schulze to ELSA members)*
Dear mission community.

Since this month ends tomorrow, I will provide a report on it. In reviewing these four weeks in my mind, I can only thank and praise the Lord because everything has proceeded at a steady pace, and in one's Christian life that is the best thing.

This month we finished building the shed that we started in the previous month. The only thing missing on the settlers' living quarters is a proper roof, because we could not yet cut grass, so it is covered only with bushes. After finishing this we went out breaking and carting stones for the actual dwelling. We are still working on it and are not yet quite finished; something always turns up to interrupt the work.

We had a lot of trouble with the lambing of the sheep and goats. Then Mr Hartig[5] arrived last week with Mr Brown's load of freight. That gave us new tasks with unloading, unpacking and sorting. Hartig packed the previous year's wool onto the empty wagons and we sold it to him.

As for the heathen, they are constantly on the move. At one time there are many here, then few. On Sunday 11 May five heathen women came here with six children; after a few days they disappeared again. While the men on average are strong and imposing in stature, these women were the opposite. The children also looked wretched. If these people do not soon receive lots of help, they will die out after a short time. May the Lord have mercy on them before they perish, and at least save some by means of our feeble service. Let us together pray to him for that…

L Schulze

* * *

The Aboriginal people being constantly on the move would be for purposes of hunting. Times have been a bit tougher than before, and there is a need for them to seek their supplies as well.

Together with its customary worries about finances, the following letter from Heidenreich contains the first serious reference in *Missionaries, Madness and Miracles* to the consideration of a second Hermannsburg mission station somewhere in Australia. In later reports, further occasional mentions are made of this possibility, not only by Heidenreich but also by the missionaries. The discussion is usually presented in vague terms, indicating their diffidence around this prospect: it might, or might not, be a good idea.

Heidenreich's reference to 'the Hermannsburg split' alludes to the issues around Th Harms which are spelt out more fully in the next chapter. Unfortunately, they turned out to be more than rumours.

12 June 1878, Bethany[6] *(Heidenreich to Th Harms)*
Highly honoured, much-loved Father!
… [May] God be thanked for all that he has done for and through our dear travellers. My only complaint is that the brothers, despite having the help of four men and two women, still keep paid workers. They have been advised by us several times not to keep on any other workers at present. Given the good building material on the place, we consider this expense unnecessary. The old station was built with almost half the workers using poor building materials that had to be transported from far away.

I still have no answer from you concerning my question about establishing a second station. I could only support that proposal if you were able to send us £1500 annually. But if that is not possible, it is our opinion that no more colonists need come from Germany for the time being. We fear that the increase in personnel would only cause more unrest on the station and here in the congregations. The dear brothers do not seem to be fully aware of the need to grow provisions and increase the number of livestock, so the mission will cost much for a long time still.

I have painfully looked in mail after mail for a letter and money from you. We have already borrowed £350 at 6 percent to avoid paying 10 percent at the bank. With the last mail £150 arrived from the station via Kempe, and in the next days £290 will come in from Port Augusta. At present we have £390 in debts, apart from the considerable amount of outstanding pay for the workmen and for freight for one wagon of our things that has not been unloaded on the station. Two wagons have been properly uploaded by the brothers who are not doing so well, according to the mail today.

So you see, dear Father, that I am caught in great financial need and have long been in need of calling on your trust. However, I do not intend to make use of that unless there is no other possibility... [Nevertheless,] if you have not already sent any money, please send me at least £600 with the first post so that I do not get into debt and our enterprise that is going so well suffers an irreparable setback. For our people up North must be sustained, so that in the process our joy is also sustained...

The articles in our *Kirchenbote* on the Hermannsburg split do not concern me and several of my brothers. That is a rumour of the editor and his assistants. They would like to transfer the struggle to here, but I will not let them and will keep silent until the next Pastor's Conference when the writers and their assistants will have to identify themselves and their shallow actions, if God so wills and helps us. Some brothers have called on me to write to you a statement in support of your noble struggle for pure Lutheranism, and have it signed by the faithful brothers. I like that very much, but the dear brothers find it hard to keep their mouths shut and may divulge our strength without meaning to before we can meet here. I do not know whether I should prepare this statement for you and send it off without further signature. For here, as in Germany, if something is to succeed, one person acting alone must protect his back. That is nothing new, and I am not afraid to stand before God for it, but the statement should also be of profit, improve things and be helpful. I have collected material and, with God's help, intend to think of points from the holy scriptures, the practice of the church, and from world history, and do so clearly and intelligibly but also as briefly and as succinctly as possible. Where I fail to achieve this goal, please add what is needed and cut out what is superfluous, if you find it helpful for the situation there. I will not be finished [with the statement] this time for my classroom work is piling up all the time... Do not let anyone deceive you; you have firm ground under your feet. The Lord will preserve you, and certainly suppress your enemies...

G A Heidenreich

8 July 1878, Bethany[7] (Heidenreich to ELSA members)
Dear precious mission congregations.
... Large bills have arrived with this mail and we expect even bigger ones in the next. So I beg my dear fellow pastors and the other brethren who administer the mission accounts in our congregations to send to our General Treasurer, C Schmidt, as soon as possible, all the money available so that our other overdrafts do not become too large...

G A Heidenreich

* * *

The rumblings around the suspension of Th Harms (next chapter) are very unsettling to the missionaries in the Centre—as they will have been to all Hermannsburg graduates. They have a close bond with their Director, and an unsettled Hermannsburg in Germany raises the spectre of an unsettled Hermannsburg in Australia.

In this next letter Schulze refers to 'the old Christianity', by which he certainly means the Old-Lutherans, as they were known. As recorded earlier, these were the Lutherans in Prussia who opposed King Friedrich Wilhelm III's imposition of the Union Church upon them. The 'old Lutherans' regarded themselves as the genuine Confessional Lutherans and were those who first came to Australia with Kavel and Fritzsche.

It is also of note that Schulze's description of the missionaries' impressions of the Aboriginal people is the first written instance of such observations with any detail. As time goes by, those observations increase in number and size. Their perspectives also change as the missionaries and Arrarnta people better get to know each other. As the report from Kempe then indicates, there is pressure on the missionaries to produce some converts. After all, they have now been on site for over a year.

8 July 1878, Hermannsburg[8] *(Schulze to Th Harms)*
Dear Pastor!
With deep sorrow and heartfelt compassion I read in the *Missionsblatt*, and in several letters, of your suspension and of the separation of the greater part of the active members of the congregation from the Hanoverian State Church. May the Lord give open eyes and keen consciences to all Christians that they may not fall into the snares and nets of Satan and his allies but evade them as long as they are still able.

Looking at the old Christianity, one sees with great pain how the sun of righteousness sinks more and more into the evening sky, and how the little band of believers is pushed to emigrate. By contrast, looking at the world of the heathen, one's heart is filled with joy at the rising of the Son of Life here and there.

The Lord grant that here, too, such a ray of light may shine so that at least a few turn to him. There will not be many, for there are not many heathens here to begin with, as the tribe here consists of about 100 souls. Further up the Finke River, where we would like to establish a second mission station, there are more tribes. Many of these people have degenerated physically; they live like beasts, and go about stark naked, eat rats, snakes, worms, roots and the like, and live under open skies during the hot summer as well as the cold winter. They protect themselves from the cold of winter by making fires on both sides of where they lie and at their feet. So they are not as silly and degenerate as the civilised world thinks.

Concerning their physique, they are sound, even very imposing persons, and compare well with Europeans. There are some talented people among them who are quick to grasp things. One sees no trace of religion, so to teach them of a higher being will be difficult.

Concerning their marital relations, they live in a free and easy community. Some men have several wives, and some women have several husbands. Parents are very proud of their children but, unfortunately, they have few.

They bury their dead.

Their only weapon is an 8 to 10 foot long wooden spear which they know how to throw very well. A hollow tray in which they carry their food is their only kitchen utensil. Our food, like meat, bread, and tea, is not despised by them either. Those who work for us get food and drink and some cast-off pieces of clothing now and then, of which they are very proud. Almost all of them do not last very long at work, and before one realises it they disappear, but come back sooner or later. There are times when there are many here, then again only a few, sometimes none at all.

One just has to love some of them for their good natures; with others, again, one occasionally has to be very strict. Effective punishment for them is to disregard them and to give them no food. They like to work a little, for then they know they get something to eat. We are house building just now and some do help quite well, now and then. Only, one often has to stir them into action, usually with the following words: 'You get no tucker if you do not want to work.' That often helps. But then they are so smart that as soon as they have had their meal of mutton, bread and tea, if one does not look out, they are gone with the wind, only to reappear shortly before the next meal to qualify for some more food. One has to be very alert to see who has worked well, who little, and who not at all, to feed them accordingly.

Our previously mentioned house is being built of stone and roofed with reeds. We have sufficient building materials, such as stone, lime, clay and wood, but the latter is rarely straight or sound, therefore not very suitable for building purposes.

As for efforts in the garden, this year all our care and hard work have been futile. On our arrival in April the sweet corn, lettuce, cabbage, melons, etc. grew really beautifully, but were quickly destroyed by the oncoming cold. At times it is so cold at nights that the water freezes into ice. Winter clothes are very acceptable, especially in the evenings while sitting still, reading and writing. In the mission house, we know how to deal with the cold, as we have a good fire going. However, we lack the best thing—an oven.

As the rain came only in March this year, it happened that the seed of the plants did not ripen before the arrival of the cold. If the rain had come in the wet months of December and January, we certainly could have had a good maize harvest. The scarcest commodity in this country is water; if it rained more often, the whole countryside would be a beautiful flowering garden, but most of the time it looks somewhat desolate and bare. Even now there is not a blade of green to be seen far and wide. At times it looks like rain, but it does not or hardly ever comes, except during the rainy season.

May the Lord bless our physical labours in gardening, building and in raising animals, etc., and especially bless his spiritual work done by us, as well as with these poor people who are still sitting in the shadows and darkness of death. What joy it would be to see only one of them released from this. May the Lord grant that this soon comes to pass…

L Schulze

10 August 1878, Hermannsburg Mission Station[9]
(Kempe to ELSA members)
Dear mission community!

… We are not now able to complete the building quickly since we have let both Englishman go after we were told to do so, with the instruction to be extremely thrifty. We want to do what we can, but our friends down South must be very patient when we cannot quickly report on actual mission work. We intend to work on contentedly, commending our labour to the Lord. He will see it through.

Otherwise, there is little to report about the last month. All our efforts were required for the building work. When the house is finished I will attach the plan. Our Black brothers have faithfully helped us, and we would not have finished so quickly without their help. Naturally, we had to feed them. In general, we must say that the majority of Aboriginal people make good workers, with the right direction. In this respect, as in others, they are not as unintelligent as some think.

I hope to God that we will soon have better news to write. If you bear the cause on praying hearts, God's blessing will not be lacking, also earthly necessities. The mission is a work of faith, patience and prayer. Think of that often and do not grow weary, but grow in the Lord's work since your work in the Lord is not in vain...

H Kempe

* * *

The following briefest of letters from Schulze is a little gem for the glimpse it provides into marriage customs at the time. Coupled with other similar references in *Missionaries, Madness and Miracles*, it appears that there was as much likelihood of a marriage being arranged, very much as a matter of convenience, as there was of a couple falling in love and choosing to marry.

31 August 1878, Hermannsburg[10] *(Schulze to Th Harms)*
Dear Pastor!

Forgive me for sending you just this note. For, when we had already finished our letters, Holterman arrived, opening up on a request.

He asked whether I would write to you on his behalf, asking if you would be so good as to send him the daughter of the widow Kuhlmann to be his wife, if she was in agreement. He spoke to the mother before he set out on his journey, and she had no objection. The widow Kuhlmann is the mother-in-law of Wilhelm Kruse. He does not know the daughter by name. Can you please send news to Holtermann or to me...

L Schulze

* * *

From this point until the end of the year, the mission staff are very focussed on the completion of the mission buildings. That focus has been evident in earlier letters. However, there now seems to be a greater urgency to get this work done so that they are able to move onto other tasks, especially their mission work with the Aboriginal people. The contact with the Arrarnta is increasing, though the 'walkabout' issue has already raised its head, and will continue to do so.

22 September 1878,[11] **M St Hermannsburg**[12] *(Kempe to Th Harms)*
Dear Pastor!

Once again a quarter of a year lies behind us ... [We] have now pretty much completed our external work and can now in the near future start learning the language. We have certainly had to work extremely industriously during this time, for here in the bush there are not many people, so it is a matter of applying ourselves to the job. We have all faithfully done that, as much as has been in our power.

Brother Schulze had already mentioned in the last report that we had begun the construction of our homes. It would now take me too far off the track to describe all the details of the building, and it would also be pretty boring. So I only want to mention briefly that on 7 August we had finished all the stonework on the walls, so that we were then able to lay off both Englishmen whom we still had working with us, since Provost Heidenreich had exhorted us to be extremely thrifty.

It was now up to us first of all to put the roof on, and this work has occupied us to the end of this month because we had to fetch timber for both the rafters and slats, as well as reeds for the ceiling from a good 14 miles away. So we have now also completed a little house for the settlers...

In addition, I must mention that on 25 August our crates finally arrived, as well as a load of flour. And so, after three years and some months we have at last again set eyes on our belongings. The carter who brought this load has now undertaken the shearing of our sheep; but since it is such a long and difficult journey to Port Augusta, about 750 miles away, we will be able to get only a modest amount for the wool.

Finally, I can also report with a thankful heart that between 28 August and 4 September the dear Lord has granted us gentle rain. Each day there were larger or smaller showers. It is something very rare for rain to fall at this time, for the actual rainy season is in the months of January to March. Green grass is now growing vigorously everywhere, but whether the rain will be of much use for our gardens is greatly to be doubted, for the hot, dry wind quickly scorches everything, unless further rain soon falls again. We have spared no effort, but during the rain have sown a variety of seeds in the earth. May the Lord give his blessing to this so that at least something is saved.

During this time the heathen have constantly gone off and then come back again. Some of them have given us good service in our building; however, the innate desire to go walkabout does not allow them to stay in one place for long. Even if they have got plenty of everything, they nevertheless have to give into this desire from time to time. One of the main driving forces behind this is probably also the lassitude, the main vice of almost all indigenous peoples.[13] The nomadic searching for game, as well as their national dances, mean much more to them than work.

We recently had opportunity to see one such dance. For this purpose they paint and decorate themselves with feathers, grass, and foliage, which in their opinion is meant to be beautiful but which rather gives us the impression that they are somewhat demonic. Those who are not dancing sing and provide the beat with two wooden sticks. However, whether these dances and what they are singing with them have their basis in heathen superstition, we have not yet been able to ascertain...

H Kempe

N.B. Since our old shepherd,[14] who has been with us for three years already, is leaving us in the near future, and we therefore have to take on his work, we would like to ask you to send us another settler as a shepherd. He does not have to be an experienced shepherd, for that can be soon learnt. A married man would be best for us. We all again ask that you grant us this request that they come as soon as possible with the fiancées.

* * *

Most of the material in this next letter was presented in previous letters. Only the last paragraph has extra information to report.

22 October 1878, Hermannsburg[15] *(Kempe to ELSA members)*

...We have now recently discovered the Bagot Springs; they are only four miles from here in the James Ranges and contain a magnificent amount of water. It is only a pity that the way there is so rocky that the stock cannot get there. Reeds 14 feet in height stand there. We have found other different sources of water in the mountains and plenty of palms, so we can show you many interesting things when you eventually come to inspect.

* * *

Every now and then there is a letter from one or the other of the settlers. As mentioned earlier, these were lay workers who worked alongside the missionaries. Some were members of congregations from down South, others were graduates from Hermannsburg, Germany, but not ordained.

3 November 1878, Hermannsburg[16] *(Jürgens to Th Harms)*

Dear Father!

When we set sail you told us that you did not require a letter from us until we were at our destination. So I have conformed to your desire insofar as I have not written too early but, on the contrary, have been too negligent. I ask you for forgiveness, dear Father; I thought Brother Schulze's travel diary was valid for us all.

But now I want to write something today, and not on behalf of our station or the brothers and sisters, but only from me personally. I want first to tell how the Lord has protected me. You will already have heard that my gun exploded. Yes, it was so blown to pieces, dear Father, that not one piece of the mechanism is usable. Despite that, I suffered only an arm wound, though I was thrown to the ground.

After that I was bitten by a centipede which is a poisonous worm, but the bite did me no harm.

Then, while shoeing a horse, I once finished up lying under the horse without being hurt.

Later, I twice fell from my horse without being injured.

With all this the Lord has thoroughly chastened me, but in all that I can see his forbearance, patience and loving kindness.

The main purpose of my writing is to inform you how I now am in my innermost being. The restlessness about which I once often complained to you is gone, and I am quietly at peace with my calling and station which soothes all privations, troubles and toil. But the spiritual trials are not over. One has hardly overcome one than a person is stuck in another.

Now, dear Father, we will see each other again 'up there' and will tell face to face what the Lord has done for us. I know what you have to endure, but you will overcome everything through him who overcomes all. May the Lord keep us faithful to the end. Amen.

Your thankful, H Jürgens

* * *

This next letter from Schwarz is another classic Schwarz. It is lengthy—he loves words. He is ponderous at times, and obviously thinks carefully about what he is saying. He also has a wonderful sense of humour, and it is easy to detect that humour bubbling away as he tells the famous story of the parrots and the snake. Like Kempe, he, too, is anxious to finish with their demanding building projects so they can get on with their 'real work'.

17 December 1878, Hermannsburg[17] *(Schwarz to Th Harms)*
Dear Pastor!

With thanks to the faithful Lord and with hearty best wishes for your worthy, much troubled person and family, as well as for the dear *Kreuzgemeinde* and mission community, I begin this report in the heart of Australia amongst the poor heathen who until now have sat in darkness and the shadow of death, and have heard nothing of the love of God in Christ Jesus, his only-begotten Son. However, by God's grace an Advent season has now begun for them in which we hear the message: Repent and convert, for the kingdom of heaven is at hand, and: Jesus and his kingdom of grace will now find room among you. Yes, may God, Father, Son and Holy Spirit bring this to pass. Amen.

Up to this point we have not yet progressed as far as being able to preach to the heathen in their language, but with God's help we are well on the way to getting there, because in the last two months we have been able to devote ourselves to studying the language much more than earlier. The large amount of building and other work completely took up all our time and energy. We are not lacking in ongoing physical work, but the actual main building construction is now considered finished insofar as the interior fitting out of Brothers Kempe's and Schulze's residence is by and large completed, so that they could move in shortly after New Year, unless, because of the clay floors, the brothers want to wait until after the rainy season.

Altogether there are now five buildings on the station, two of which are built out of red sand-stone. The smaller one covered with iron[18] serves as the station kitchen and supply room, the larger reed-thatched roof one as the missionaries' residence.[19] The other three buildings are made of timber with reed-thatched roofing, and the larger and oldest of these so far still serves as a dwelling for Brothers Kempe and Schulze, as well also for communal worship and as a dining room. Another building is the communal residence of our settler brothers, while the last is the station smithy and equipment room.

Apart from these buildings there are the necessary cattle yards and a considerably large wagon shed. We have two wagons as well as a two-wheel horse cart and a nice iron plough. We have already made good use of the latter, and with the help of the horses have ploughed up two pieces of land. Except for one small part, these have also already been completely seeded, mostly with maize. We have also sown a bit of barley and oats, together with a little wheat as a trial.

In addition, we brought all sorts of fruit kernels and fruit stones, as many as were available to us, as well as field peas and lentils, together with all sorts of melon and garden seeds. We hope they will flourish under God's blessing, for without this all of our effort is totally in vain, and no amount of skill helps, neither does manure, which is usually supposed to be most effective, according to the scientific experts of Europe.

Now, concerning our mission brothers and sisters, who now number nine, we have plenty of reason to thank the Lord; for by his grace and goodness we are up to now healthy and well. All of us brothers, as well as Brother Kempe's and my own dear wife, are each able with God's help to carry out the daily work that is required of us, even though recently we have had not inconsiderable heat which our dear wives felt even more, working at the fireplace. For weeks now we have had only a few days under 30 degrees,[20] but several days between 30 and 40 degrees even in the shade of our pleasantly cool homes, though summer has only begun this month.

However, we do not want to complain about all this, but thank God for everything. In these last weeks he has refreshed us greatly through thunderstorms and some pleasant showers of rain. Therefore, we confidently hope that the Lord will send us more storms and give us heavy rain. The rainwater is a very welcome drink for us, and rain is greatly needed if our ploughing and sowing, undertaken in hope, are not to be ruined.

The Lord is faithful ... Up to now he has carried us as on the wings of an eagle and safely led us, and has daily granted us his dear precious Word, pure and undiminished. He has often and richly refreshed us through his holy sacrament during this quarter, according to his faithful promise: Behold, I am with you! He has also been by and with us every day, and has blessed our work and our leisure, and has comforted and strengthened us in our wilderness. What more could we want? For us, nothing more than that he also keeps us faithful, and finally, when our little hour[21] comes, grants us a blessed end and graciously receives us...

We especially remembered you and the dear *Kreuzgemeinde* at the dedication of the station here. This took place on the evening of 30 October. We chose the evening, the time after dinner, so that as many as possible of all our brothers and sisters could celebrate and pray with us, for by day there are always two out with the stock. The foundation stone was laid with 1 Samuel 7:12, Ebenezer, applied to our station. Under this theme, 1. we remembered the faithful help of God, 2. were exhorted to thankfulness and faithfulness to the Lord, and 3. encouraged to continue in joyful trust in God.

In our final prayer we commended not only this new Hermannsburg but also especially the dear, dear old Hermannsburg with its dear shepherds to God's continuing protection and faithful care...

What we must now briefly mention from here is that since last week our flocks of sheep have had to be taken about 5 miles up the Finke because the feed near the station has gone. So, in the first weeks of this month the necessary preparations for this have been made, and pens have been made for the flocks, as well as the necessary shelter for the cook and two shepherds.

The site of this sheep station is very lovely, for it is surrounded by beautiful trees. It also has a lot of good water in the immediate vicinity, and there are many tasty fish to be found in it. But the many ants which are in and on the trees, and whose proximity makes for a lively existence, are indeed annoying companions for the brothers.

As small as our community already was, it is now also a scattered one, and we can have a communal celebration neither for the day of repentance tomorrow, nor for the approaching valued Christmas festival. But the brothers hold communal morning and evening devotions. Brother Jürgens, who as cook looks after the bodily needs of the dear brothers Mirus and Holtermann, also serves as house father. Also, every Sunday and festival day evening the brothers are served with the preaching of God's holy Word, with Brother Kempe, Schulze and I taking it in turns to visit them …

Finally, I want to share with you a little story that played itself out on our station last Friday evening and partly still on the following morning. It caused us all grief as well as joy and thanks to the dear, faithful Lord that out of grace he averted greater harm.

Some considerable time ago some of the heathen brought us four young parrots that Brother Kempe especially took in hand. However, two of them soon died, while the last two increasingly flourished and proved themselves very teachable. Brothers Kempe and Schulze then made a fairly large bird cage for these, our two little darlings. This was placed outside under the open verandah near the kitchen on a large empty wooden box which stood upright with the open end facing the wall. Close by it was a small box with kitchen cutlery, which at the same time was used by our dear wives for cooling down food and such like. They had to be particularly busy near this box and the bird cage, also because the meat safe and water containers were located there. In recent times Sister Kempe had also taken care of both beautiful green birds, while I twice had the good fortune to recapture the fleeing rascals.

Meantime, they gave us much great joy with their comical natures and diligent repetition of the song which had so often been whistled to them by Brother Kempe and myself: *If I am sad at times*. They imitated this tune with a clear voice, singing rather than whistling, especially early in the morning, as soon as we started singing our morning song in the building opposite. We all rejoiced together, and every day they became more dear to us.

Last Friday, however, our previous joy was turned into sudden sorrow. This was caused by a green, poisonous 5-foot long snake that had for a long time already taken up residence in the kitchen and then eventually in the box under the verandah. Strangely, not a single one of us thought last Friday morning to pay a visit to our darlings, as was usually the case. However, after the devotion Brother Kempe and I went together to the kitchen verandah where our dear wives were engaged in their work. One of them was preparing breakfast and the other was sorting out the fresh milk. This was done on the small box.

While we now chatted with one another, we all noticed the deathly silence of our pets. We looked in the bird cage and, to our deep sorrow, became aware that the dear songsters lay dead on the floor of the cage. After breakfast, attempts were made to determine the actual cause of this small misfortune. We soon came to the unanimous conclusion that a snake must have perpetrated this double murder, for one bird lay with its head towards the wall outside of the cage, and from the beak up to the wings was pretty well squashed and slobbered on.

Naturally, we took serious measures to discover, if possible, the murderer and to render it harmless in the future. However, all our efforts seemed to be in vain until, after an hour, my dear wife told me that she had taken the box on which the birdcage stood outside and had cleaned it a bit. I was now to bring it inside under the verandah of our home so that it might serve us as a bench. I set about the task and had moved it a considerable way from the spot and examined it. The box was lined with tin and in it lay an old sack with some straw. I couldn't discover anything, but as I tipped the box over several times, I heard a strange rustling in it. I then examined it once again and immediately saw the snake, which was old enough [to have killed the birds], and which was gladly transferred from life to death by Brother Schulze and me.

We all rejoiced at its death and thanked the Lord that he had preserved us, especially our dear sisters, from its deadly poison. Thus was our slight sorrow turned into great joy, thanks to our faithful Lord.

However, it is not only this snake that has lately done us some harm, but also the people here who are still under the power of the old serpent. The local heathen, our poor black brothers, have too great a love for our small stock, less love for looking after them, and much more for frying and eating them. Because of this they have probably stolen and consumed well over 20 head of sheep and goats in a quarter of a year. At lunchtime in October they stole no less than six head from the flock while we were eating, but we hunted four of them down when the animals had just been killed and taken away.

During dinner two weeks ago two heathen again stole a sheep from the flock and slaughtered it on the hill nearby. However, they immediately put us on their trail because of the fire they had made for roasting the sheep. We hurried to the spot and gave them a very unwelcome surprise so that they left everything behind and fled as swiftly as an arrow. We took the dismembered sheep back with us as food for the heathen who were working on the station who number between four and six.

We do not wish for the poor people the kind of end that we joyfully provided for the snake, but we do desire from the heart the end of their enslavement to sin. We confidently hope that in this matter the dear mission community is of one will with us, and therefore entreats the Lord so that it may also soon be said of this people: The night is over, the day has come. Yes. Amen. O Lord, help; O Lord, bring success.

Dear Pastor, if it is at all possible for you to send to this station some clothing for the heathen, we would like to ask mainly for shirts and trousers. It does not matter what colour or material—everything is acceptable...

W F Schwarz

* * *

If that last letter of Schwarz's is typical, so also then are the final several letters and reports for the year from Heidenreich. He continues to be bothered by recalcitrant pastors, Missourians, and money. The proviso that Hermannsburg pastors designated for mission work in Australia might also serve as parish pastors is something of a thorn in his flesh. He is concerned by the possibility of a split in the Church, and ELSA members are becoming critical about the lack of converts in the Centre

4 September 1878, Bethany[22] *(Heidenreich to Th Harms)*
Highly honoured, much-loved Father!

I am herewith sending you a report from Missionary Schulze. So far he is managing well, except he still has too little experience in building with wood and relating to the heathen ... He shows his lack of knowledge in claiming that the heathen women have several husbands. That is not the case up North, nor here in the South. Men do have several wives, and that can be the case also on the Finke. The future will tell; his assumptions rest on hearsay, since barely six women have been on the station for some days.

Despite being sent letters and telegrams to the contrary, our dear brothers keep outsiders on as workers during these difficult financial times. That causes me much displeasure as I face my council, the congregations, and the pastors, since we have already borrowed £400 and still have debts of £300. I did not want to pressure them at a miserable time and, with the council's approval, have postponed the letters of exchange until next month. If the incoming mail brings no money from you, I will have to bite the sour apple and send you an account for £400 ... It is very necessary that you direct the missionaries not to take on outside workmen, otherwise my Council members will shed all responsibility for them. So far they have faithfully helped me and have loaned me most of the money without interest, so that I was able to go easy on your reserves. Not so much comes from the congregations anymore because of the school. Also, the reports of the brothers do not encourage people to give.

We here, unfortunately, have too many worshippers of success who immediately want heathen converts and are themselves as a rule not yet properly converted. Otherwise, they would see how much work they have caused the dear Lord, and still do. But one has to listen to their old grumbling and does best to remain silent.

I anxiously await your reply to the letter addressed to the brothers and Church Council about your proviso ...

The machinations of Homann, Schoknecht and Peters have suffered a severe blow ... There is to be a session of the Church Council a day before the mission festival where I will again, with a sad heart, be able to see behind the brothers who have become Missourians, how sin strikes its own masters.

With the other brothers things are tolerable. Meyer, with his innovations, has caused much damage from the beginning which he will feel for many years, and Thiessen is somewhat too reserved in dealing with people. Yet, both have already made good friends...

The dear Lord has again given us a baby daughter. Her name is Bertha, and all are well...

G A Heidenreich

10 October 1878, Bethany[23] *(Heidenreich to Th Harms)*
Highly honoured, much-loved Father,
... You will be wondering how we have already spent so much money but I can assure you that I have been extremely careful with the finances and have thus incurred much hostility from the mission people, whom I patiently put up with to the honour of my Saviour and of the mission.

Apart from finances, it is otherwise well with the mission. The congregations have, in an admirable way, contributed financial support, as you can see from our accounts, despite all resistance from their pastors...

The text at this point became so corrupted as to be indecipherable. Heidenreich is apparently referring to what he would consider to be good, faithful Hermannsburgers. But then ...

On the other hand, [there are] Hermannsburgers who teach on marriage, absolution, and false interpretation of scripture according to everything Missourian, to gain the majority of votes against me and Georg. Until now I have restrained them by my silence, but [my patience] seems to be at an end. I will have to speak up, and then we will be faced with a division of our Church that I want under no circumstances ...[In] these years I have experienced so much abuse that I have often regretted that I did not carry out your directive to the letter of the law, come what may.

The quarrelsome spirits have become more defiant ... because of the proviso. My considered opinion at the time was that once the young brothers belonged to the Synod, they would loyally side with me. But I was badly mistaken...

Another sad piece of news arrived yesterday. According to one report, Pastor Niemann is on his death bed without hope of recovery and, according to another, he has died. Homann is said to be with him, since he lives next to him, but I have not yet received reliable news from Homann. That would be a heavy blow for us. God grant that it is not true. Niemann was in Lobethal. We slept there in one bed, though we got little sleep; our hearts were too full. He worked here very well and gained the love and loyalty of his congregations and of the Synod, so he would be painfully missed. It would be really hard for his fiancée even if she is not yet on her way here. It would be better, if she is still at home, that she waits until there is certainty about the rumour...

I sincerely thank you for the £200 I received in the last mail. We have to send £400 to Port Augusta for cartage and half of that arrived as requested. For the other half we are overdrawn at the bank until you send us more money. It is so unfortunate, financially, that you also have money problems at home. Yet the Lord will provide, so I learn to let him do the worrying. I acutely share your church struggle and am glad that you are rid of von Lüpke, who also had his supporters here, to our detriment...

G A Heidenreich

25 November 1878, Bethany[24] *(Heidenreich to ELSA members)*
Dear, precious mission congregations!

... The [year] just past was in many respects difficult and costly ... You will easily understand that we have thus not lacked worry and care in continually withdrawing large sums of money from our bank account. But the faithful Lord has helped us through everything. Even if he has not given us all the money, he has created hearts willing to loan what is necessary, and without interest. May these people be truly recompensed by him in his own good time with rich blessings for time and eternity.

You have considerably lightened our burden with your prayers and generous gifts... On behalf of Hermannsburg and ourselves we sincerely thank you for helping to bear the work of mission out of genuine love. At the same time we ask you not to grow weary in the work assigned to us. Mission is always a work of faith, love and hope...

It is also a work requiring patience. With you we would gladly see and hear that our dear missionaries were fully engaged in spiritual work on the hearts of the poor heathen. But let us remember the mountains of physical difficulties and labours our brothers have had to overcome in three years ... As soon as [they are able] our missionaries will apply themselves to the greater task, after the lesser work, of converting the heathen, helping them to be saved...

There was a lot of damage from a hail storm over Hermannsburg...

Yours faithfully, G A Heidenreich

*   *   *

This final letter of Kempe's for the year is very revealing for the glimpse it provides into some of the behind-the-scenes thinking on two important issues. The letter is private, with only Heidenreich privy to its subject matter—though one would assume that Schwarz and Schulze were included in the discussion as a matter of course.

The first issue is the possible establishment of a second mission station, a discussion begun earlier and set to continue. The rationale provided by Kempe is of great interest. And the second issue relates to the future of the Aboriginal people and is chilling.

Also of note is another reference to hostilities between various Aboriginal people, further indication that the missionaries were aware that these were occurring.

In the original document, the first page is completely illegible. There is obviously a 'first point' Kempe has been making with Harms, but we have no idea what that was. Now he comes to the next point:

31 December 1878, Hermannsburg[25] *(Kempe to Th Harms)*
... As to the second point, namely the founding of a second station further north on the Finke about 18 miles from here, I have already written to the Director.[26] However, I want to present you with the reasons why that is necessary, yes, I would say, absolutely necessary.

It is certainly not presumption on our part that determines our view. We experience daily and see it ever more clearly that two things make it necessary, 1) the well-being of the mission and 2) the existence of the livestock.

It is necessary for the mission because the Aboriginal people in the MacDonnell Ranges are hostile against those who are here,[27] and thus they do not associate with each other. If we want to get close to those who are there with the preaching of the gospel, we have to have a station in the vicinity, even if only a small one for two families at the most, a missionary and a settler.

In addition, we can count on better agriculture there rather than here, since the soil is more fertile and, again, it rains there more than here; all thunder showers generally follow the mountains here. Thus, before rain arrived here this year, there was already grass 2 feet tall up North.

It does not have to be a station as large as Hermannsburg, only that a place is manned and we can make use of the wonderful area there. At the moment we have only a few horses up there.

Secondly, it is necessary for continuing to keep the livestock. It is almost impossible to keep sheep, cattle and horses at the one place. Because the sheep eat up everything around the station, the other animals have to go out for miles to find fodder. If one wants to get to the horses and bullocks one first has to go out at quite a distance, and that wastes a lot of time. So we have to have horses and cattle on the second station to look after both properly.

Finally, that set-up would be also better insofar as we would be on our own up there and would not fear our animals getting mixed up with those of the neighbouring cattle station.

I think these arguments make sense. If you give your assent, I earnestly ask you, dear Pastor, to write as soon as possible to Provost Heidenreich so that we can receive further instructions from him.

I also want to inform you about something we have long considered and wanted because it would be a benefit to the station, namely, increased numbers of livestock. It is not the mission's business to seek earthly treasures but, because we have the land, it would be good for us to use it. At present this is not the case.

Incidentally, that would not entail much work; two men can well look after a herd of cattle numbering 600 to 1000 head. If we bought 100 cows at £5 sterling a head, we could with the Lord's blessing in five years' time easily sell several hundred and do that annually. Then at least this station could serve to maintain other stations that have no income as in India, for example.

I do not think we will achieve much with the heathen here. I do not mean that they would be incapable. No, no, because that depends alone on God.

I only mean that as a people they can no longer be helped precisely because they are no longer a people but only remnants of a people. So, the mission has to do no more than glean what is left and lead some to the Lord. The tribe that lives near here may possibly number a hundred souls but are divided into innumerable clans.

In our view it would therefore be good if we could also do something for other mission stations that cannot maintain themselves. If we could just achieve some profit here on this station, much could be gained, with God's help.

Thus I want to ask you, dear Pastor that, when you send money, to designate it for the purchase of cattle. We ourselves will not gain from this; rather it will cost us some toil. Nevertheless, we really want to take on this work if we can thereby profit the mission.

I hope you do not take my letter amiss, but treat me with forbearance, especially since I intend nothing but good for the mission...

H Kempe

* * *

Meantime, in the rest of the world in 1878:

- Greece declared war on Turkey (2 February).
- Gilbert and Sullivan's *HMS Pinafore* premiered in London (25 May).
- Telephones were introduced in Hawaii (20 July).
- Actor Lionel Barrymore was born in Philadelphia (28 April) and Joseph Stalin in Gori, Russia (18 December).
- Catherine Beecher, champion of education for women, died (12 May).
- Inventions introduced to the world included Vaseline (14 May, in the US), and the first moving pictures (race horses in Palo Alto, California, 15 June).
- Cleopatra's Needle was installed in London (12 September).

11.

The Removal of Theodor Harms

In 1876 the Prussian king, Wilhelm I, legislated compulsory civil marriage, as distinct from marriages performed by the Church. As well he introduced a new marriage liturgy. Both innovations were recognised and adopted by the Hanoverian State Church. However, for reasons of conscience, Theodor Harms refused to accept either. Consequently, in 1878 he was removed from the State Church. He was followed by the majority of the Hermannsburg Lutheran community, and on 13 February 1878 they established the Lutheran Church of the Cross, independent of the State Church. At the synod in Hermannsburg on 30 April 1878, under the chairmanship of Theodor Harms, pastors and representatives of the independent churches of the country founded the Hanover Evangelical Lutheran Free Church.

Although these events occurred quite independently of the Lutheran churches in far-distant Australia, they nevertheless were noticed and felt in Australia. In particular, they had immediate implications for the mission work in Central Australia. To what extent, if at all, would the Hermannsburg Mission Society continue to support the Finke mission? There was the matter of the longer-term implications for the relationship between the Lutheran Church in Australia and the German Lutheran churches: would, and could they continue to be in fellowship with each other?

In the January, February and March *Missionsblatt* editions of 1878, Theodor Harms published three reports on his removal from office. Only excerpts of these reports are included in *Missionaries, Madness and Miracles*—sufficient to provide a comprehensive account of proceedings without becoming bogged down in wearisome detail. The full versions of all reports are available in *The Translation*.

* * *

January 1878, Hermannsburg, Germany[1] *(Th Harms)*

My Suspension

On 22 January my suspension, that is, my preliminary removal from office was delivered, thereby instigating a disciplinary trial against me to which I have to present myself before the superintendents and the chief officer in Bergen[2] on 24 January.

The reason for my suspension and the eventual removal from office is my consistent refusal to use the new marriage order. That is the sole reason why I look to my removal from office happily[3] and confidently but protest against it loudly and solemnly. I am a poor sinner and not worthy of the sacred preaching office, but before men I am not aware of being worthy of such a heavy punishment, for there can hardly be a more grievous thing for an upright pastor than being removed from the office that is the most wonderful and precious of all offices. I have preached no false doctrine but have always been seen as zealous for pure doctrine. I have not lived a godless life that would be in contradiction to the doctrine I have preached. I have gladly and willingly risked health and life for my difficult twofold office.

... I maintain and will do so until my end that true marriage belongs to the Church, that is, the joining together of the bride and groom in the name of the Triune God, so that the bridal couple become married people by means of the church wedding. Thus, in every instance where Christians leave the registry office where the marriage has been made valid for society, they still remain a bridal couple.[4] They become a truly married couple only by means of a church wedding and may thus live together as married people...

I could have accepted the new marriage order and in carrying out my pastoral office changed and garbled it, as some are said to do ... and thus made good in the eyes of people. I could have soon afterwards continued to work with the old formula, as would be popular. But that would have been hypocrisy and cowardice ... So, I have considered it better to follow the path of honesty and say to the authorities: 'I cannot and will not accept the new marriage practise because it is against God's Word, according to my knowledge and conscience'.

Since for this reason I am not worthy to remain in my pastoral office in the State Church, I must leave ... I intend to leave ... without grumbling or hatred, the dear, dear age-old Church from which streams of blessings have flowed out over the entire world, the age-old and honoured sacristy in which Urban Rhegius, Hildebrand, Walther, Johann Arndt prayed, in which my father, brother and I many a year bent the knee, under whose roof the palms and cypress garlands hung which my precious, ancestral king lovingly placed on my brother's coffin, from the familiar manse, where my family lived for 61 years, where I was born, where I lived as pastor for 11 years, where my sainted brother lived, prayed, struggled, wrote, suffered and died and in which I also would like to have died.

My consolation is that I am permitted to stay in my beloved Hermannsburg, God willing, and may remain as pastor of a free congregation, free of the state, free of the State Church in which I can and may no longer remain ... I leave in God's name, I stay in God's name. Christ is my life and to die is my gain. Amen.

February 1878, Hermannsburg, Germany[5]

My Removal

On 4 February the document of my removal from office was delivered, and I was later informed that I had to vacate the manse by 1 March ... I say again before God that neither self-will nor desire for separation has driven me to refuse to acknowledge the new marriage order but my conscience that is freed in and by God's Word. Thus, I joyfully move out of my street, though with tears, and find solace in the mercy of my God. I am gaining no wealth, possessions or honour. I leave my profitable office behind and endure much shame, derision and mockery before the world. Before me lies a dark time, full of toil and concern, but over me there arches the sky of the goodness and mercy of my God ...

As soon as I received the notice of my removal, I gave notice of my resignation from the State Church. If I am unworthy of being a pastor in it, I can no longer be a worthy lay person. I have been told: 'Give up your office voluntarily and withdraw to the mission'. However, a large part of my congregation can accept the new marriage order as little as I. Had I voluntarily surrendered my office, I would have, in my view, deserted and betrayed my congregation that says to me: 'Where you stay, we also will stay'. I have also been told: 'Let another pastor conduct the marriages, then you do not have to do anything that you say is against your conscience'. But, as long as I was in my office, the church was mine, and I cannot let others do what I consider to be a sin.

So, I have let myself be removed, but before God and my loyal congregation I do not consider myself to be removed ... Thus, I acknowledge myself now as before, as a pastor of Hermannsburg, and the section of my congregation that thinks as I do says: 'You are our pastor'. If we, pastor and congregation, can no longer stay together in the State Church, this can and must take place outside of it in a free Lutheran congregation, one that is free of control from the State Church...

Some may be angry at me for rashness, stubbornness, and a desire to be separate, and so on; let them write and say what they want. For me it is crystal clear; I know for sure: this is God's will and way and that is enough for me ...

We are separating from the church government, not from the Hanoverian Lutheran Church ...

So, you dear brothers in the Hanoverian State Church, do not reject us, do not turn away from us who have been brought so far by the Lord God ... It is often said and written that we pushed and agitated for separation. Come and see for yourselves that no one is being manipulated, no one is being cajoled. We do not hate or rage, we do not scold or berate those who think differently from us. Each person must follow his own free conviction so that he can gladly and willingly bear the suffering that will certainly come upon us heavily ...

We offer you sincere fellowship in faith and love but do not shy away from the honourable struggle. However, should some of you remain our opponents, let us be honest, open opponents, not using lies, not complaining in the courts, not using force, but standing with the weapons of the Spirit with each other and praying for each other in our private room, we who seek to serve one Lord and one truth...

As a result of me leaving the State Church ... will not the existence of the Hermannsburg mission be placed in question? I do not fear that for, in the first place, I am leaving the State Church, rather, I am leaving the State Church's governance of God's way and will, as I do not doubt.

In the second place, the committee members who are not leaving and are remaining on the committee and getting on in a great way with those who are leaving are working with each other in the one faith in the holy undertaking, as I do not doubt, since our mission is a purely private matter, and our missionaries have nothing to do with the governance of the State Church and have never done so. What my sainted brother occasionally wished for, that the Hermannsburg mission might be placed under the Consistory, that it might occupy a similar position to that of the parishes and pastors, fortunately never happened.

Thirdly, our mission stands on the firm ground of our Church's full confession, as well as on Luther's orders, and has never wanted anything to do with union and false doctrine.

Fourthly, and this is the main thing, the Lord is in charge. If the Church authorities want to deny us the church collections ... we will painfully request these, but will hopefully manage without them, for our Lord Jesus has lots and lots of money and has at all times been our treasurer, not people. They may no longer allow us to examine and ordain our students in the Christ Church ... We will, with God's help, set up exams and ordination elsewhere ...

Apart from the obvious opponents of the mission, I firmly believe that the Hermannsburg mission will in these days have to endure a hefty blow so that it will be thoroughly shaken, but also that it will stand firm in struggle and crisis ... If it is unable to endure the storm, well then, it might fall and I with it. We mission people, however, are resolved to take a good look at our hearts and homes to see where anything is lacking and must change. This time is to be for us a real time of repentance. We intend to limit our expenses as much as possible and I will write to the missionaries that they should limit themselves as much as possible, [too]. We will all pray and do what we can and be of good cheer and confident, always aware of the words: 'Go to the whole world to preach the gospel to all creatures'. We intend to limit ourselves but not the work of mission. Pray, work, be busy and frugal, but do not go looking for handouts or begging, but trust the Lord. That is how we have acted and will continue to do so ...

March 1878, Hermannsburg, Germany[6]

Our Separation

When I received the notice of my removal from office on 4 February, I declared in writing on the same day my departure from the State Church, and verbally on 8 March after the legal four weeks had run out. Thereby I was legally dismissed from the State Church.

It is easy to understand that a large part of my congregation was deeply affected by my removal, and many told me: 'We will not leave you, Father Harms; where you stay we also will stay'. Many resignations followed, and these continue. Everyone can attest that I never demanded in my sermons that the congregation separate, and never tried to move anyone to leave, and still do not. When someone questions me, I advise him and explain as much as I can and leave it to his conscience whether he leaves the State Church or stays in it. I want it to be a matter of conscience for every person, as it is for me. One can then be confident and happy, come what may. I have not even persuaded the members of my family, had no need to do so, least of all my small, brave wife. From the outset, they were of the same mind as I, ready to bear the cross that I had to take up.

... On the days that we have services, ... I continued to conduct services in my house, as many as it could hold and, since we had no venue, my loyal brother, Inspector Sültmann, was able to gather the faithful together in the new Mission House. I would not have believed that the manse could have held many hundreds of people. It was amazing. The police left us undisturbed so we could edify ourselves in total freedom. I had quite openly made our intentions public.

How we later longed to be able to serve and worship the Lord together, for after my leaving we were not able to celebrate the Lord's Supper through lack of a place. But they were precious days, very precious, the services so moving, and the spirit of faith and love filled the hearts of people as I had never before experienced. The mood was one of happiness. One Sunday afternoon, while instructing the children who thronged around my pulpit, I ended by asking them to memorise the following statement: 'Be happy and well behaved at home, honorable and decent in the streets, humble and devout in church, strong and sensible in the fields, pious and honourable everywhere, always in the fear of God—that is the best'.

At this my friend Nagel from Hamburg, who was sitting with me, cried out loudly: 'The child that next Sunday can best recite the verse will get a thaler from me to go toward the building of the church'. As much as it could be understood, this caused great glee. Those standing at the back said, half aloud: 'What did he say?' and later learned the necessary details about the silver incentive. In the evening my dear friend Nagel gave me a thaler for the most industrious child and another for the laziest, namely, for himself, since he could tell me with absolute certainty that next Sunday in church he would not remember one syllable.

Next Sunday, while teaching the children, I conscientiously gave both thalers to two children, one as a reward for the child who recited the verse well and the thaler intended as punishment for a child who also well remembered the verse, in place of the lazy Nagel who could not recite the verse. However, both children gave up their thaler, with beaming faces, for the building of the church.

This is how we celebrated in separate houses; the love increased, also the desire to worship together. When I legally left the State Church on 8 March, and hundreds had previously left, nothing held us back, for love had erected a church in 14 days. One of the faithful who followed me to freedom, the landlord Georg Brammer, placed his large barn at our disposal, over 100 feet long and 36 feet wide. The Lord God bless the dear man and his household for his great love and faithfulness.

With amazing speed the barn was quickly transformed into a church, and what a church!—so nice and roomy, so richly adorned with garlands and flowers as to make one's heart skip and beat, when one sees it empty, and still more when one sees the nave and the gallery full, even up in the attic where one can hear everything even if one can see little. On Estomihi[7] Sunday we gathered for the first time in our Bethlehem. There were 2000 people and more in the assembly, with three brass bands, with 50 to 60 instrumentalists that were not too loud. Our congregation's choir sang beautifully. This Sunday belongs to one of the most wonderful days of my life.

The church dedication was on Invocavit Sunday and I installed the seven signatories elected by the congregation and the deacons (in charge of giving alms). Two hundred people took communion. Again, a wonderful day. Reminiscere (Sunday) brought us new joy: 326 received the sacred Lord's Supper ... On 13 February the house fathers gathered and constituted themselves as a free Lutheran congregation, independent of State Church governance ...

But what is the mood of the *Kreuzgemeinde* and what is its thinking? Does it complain and berate? There is nothing of all that. It is happy and contented to be free without raking up matters and agitating. There is no politicking, as is stated in lies. It is a purely church movement, a new awakening, as 30 years ago, in highly favoured Hermannsburg. The blissful feeling of freedom filled our hearts. The Lord grant that we do not misuse it and become unworthy of it.

If someone asks: 'Where have you been staying?' I answer: 'Before 1 March I had to vacate the manse. On 27 February I left the treasured rooms with my family. An indescribable pain filled my soul. We bent our knees in my study for a final prayer and then moved into our new small dwelling, not far from the mission complex, that the good Lord had kept available for us. That is where we now live, happy and contented ...

Two-thirds of my former congregation (I cannot be more accurate) have so far followed me, about 2000 souls ...

In times of trouble I have received many proofs of the love that the Lord wanted to richly bless and reward but hardly not one that so revived me as the following letter of a child.

'Dear Pastor Harms! Because you have been dismissed, would you please be so kind as to come to us and be my father's assistant preacher? We have enough room for you to bring your wife and children too. I have such a huge doll's bed that your smallest child can sleep in it, and there is enough room for the others. Please greet your whole family from me.'

Thus, we continue to work hard and are very, very happy. The loyal landlord Heinrich Witte has presented us with a place for a church and the loyal landlord Georg Hiestermann a place for a manse, and I have a room in the latter hospitable house where I can speak to my congregation's members before and after divine service, since I live 20 minutes away from our church. It is a lovely refuge also on Sundays between the services. The building of the new church is already well under way. I hope that it will again become clear what faith and love can do, and that the Lord gives success to the upright. To him alone be the glory. Amen.

* * *

By July 1878 it appears that Harms has become well enough settled in his new situation to be able to devote himself again to matters relating to the mission in Australia. The Mission Society continues on, but how well, and for how long?

There are two main issues with which Harms is immediately confronted. One is the ongoing question of the *proviso*, and on this he is prepared to make concessions. The second relates to the salaries of missionaries, and about this he is in a quandary.

26 July 1878, Hermannsburg, Germany[8] *(Th Harms to Heidenreich)*
My very dear Heidenreich,

So now I have again moved into the old mission house and will stay there as long as God wills. Banished from the manse on 1 March, I have until now made do in a small dwelling and have now returned to my old home that I had 20 years ago. A time of great calm has begun for me. The formation of the congregation is completed, and things have become clearer, and I will be able to attend to my correspondence better than previously. A difficult and critical time now lies behind me but also a time of blessing. The congregation has been renewed and rejuvenated. May the Lord grant that it is found preserved and faithful in the oven of affliction.

Pastor Oster has written to me on behalf of the local Synod asking whether I might finally transfer to the Church Council the right to loan to congregations the brothers who have been sent out. However, I promised the brothers when they left that I had no intention of releasing them from mission service. Now, one cannot see, either in the immediate or distant future, whether they are able to be used to serve the mission to the heathen, but I want and must keep my word.

So, I hereby determine that all the missionaries who want to stay as pastors in the local Lutheran congregations, should once and for all be released from mission service, but on the condition that they remain members of the Synod that supports our mission as theirs, and that the congregations be obliged to pay their travel costs—previously paid by the mission—back into the mission coffers. I hope that I have acted rightly and appropriately.

I am unable, and do not want, to decide the matter of our missionaries' salary. I believe that it is better if they are not placed on a predetermined amount but are given as much as is needed to live a decent life. Let us keep their complete trust, dear Heidenreich, and not be miserly, but also resolutely oppose excessive demands. If it later turns out that a pre-determined salary is better, make your suggestions to me. Yet I must here inform you that we will be able to do little for Australia this year. We are allowing you £300 sterling that you can draw on our account by exchange 30 days after September ... and there will possibly be estimated installments of 150 pfennigs. When the Lord clears our debts, which he will certainly do soon, we shall ask for more. The African brothers have agreed to a 20 percent cut in salary, and we are here being as thrifty as possible.

Our Lord is faithfully standing by us in our Church struggle. We remain calm and joyful in faith. Pray for us.

The Lord will stand by you. Take comfort and do not despair. Greet your dear wife and all the loved ones.

In true, fatherly affection,

Yours, Th Harms

Top: Schwarz, Schulze, Kempe; Bottom left: Heidenreich; Bottom right: Th Harms.

Top: First Australian Lutheran Seminary, Lobethal. Middle: Engagement of AH Kempe & Dorothea Queckenstedt, 1865; Bottom: Hermannsburg Mission Institute.

Top: L Schulze & wife, Charlotte Gutmann. Bottom left: G Heidenrech, wife, Anna Meyer, and child. Bottom right: Engagement of WF Schwarz & Dorothea Schulz, 1865 (?).

Top: Departure to Killalpaninna from Bethany, 1865.
Bottom: Killalpaninna Mission Station (sketch) Date unknown.

Top left: AH Kempe. Top right: WF Schwarz. Bottom left: Original Kempe letter to Th Harms, from Pricerla Watercourse, 7 February 1876. Bottom right: LG Schulze.

Top: Baron von Müller. Middle: Hermannsburg cattle. Bottom: Acacia Kempeana (witchetty grub bush), with author.

Top: Drought.
Middle: Finke in flood.
Bottom: The Swan Taplin Inquiry, 1890 [Stipendiary magistrate Henry C. Swan seated on camel in foreground, probably Mr Charles Eaton Taplin (centre) and Police Inspector Bryan Charles Beasley (extreme right)]

Top: Peake Telegraph Station. Middle: Palm Valley.
Bottom: Dalhousie Springs

12.

Language, Weather and Mumblings

1879

By the beginning of 1879 the mission has been on site for just on 18 months. Now that the essential building work is complete or in hand, life is progressing from the 'settling in' process to the business of everyday routine. That routine has a three-fold component. First is the task of the physical upkeep of the station, including care of the animals and the provision of food and other daily bread for themselves. On account of the erratic weather, that activity is made more difficult than they would like it to be. Secondly is learning the language and beginning translation work. For these tasks they require assistance from the Aboriginal people—aid that is not as reliable as they would like it to be. Thirdly is the concern around conversion to the Christian faith, where little, if anything, seems to be happening.

20 February 1879, Bethany[1] *(Kempe to ELSA members)*
Dear mission congregations.
    … With God's help we have begun to learn the language and work at it every day. This does not go quickly, since we have no manuals to assist us and we have to learn every word from the mouths of the Aboriginal people. Besides, we have a heavy workload but so few people. Anyone with any knowledge about this can easily imagine what is entailed in learning a completely foreign and undeveloped language, especially one so lacking in grammar as that of the Aboriginal people in Central Australia. By comparing the language here with the grammar book of the blessed Pastor Meyer and the one that Pastor Homann gave me in the Dieri language, I have discovered that they are similar in linguistic structure, but vary from it at many points. The vocabulary is quite different. At least I have not yet found any words with the same meaning. One can hardly have any idea how hard it is to explain something to the heathen when it comes to abstract concepts.[2] There is almost no one who understands some English, which was certainly the case down South. Yet nothing is impossible with the Lord. He will also give us success in this matter, and next time I will be able to report more.

Otherwise, everything has proceeded as usual. The Lord has kept us all in good health and faithfully guarded and preserved us from all danger. In addition to his blessing of Word and Sacrament, may he kindly grant us rain so that our physical sowing succeeds. May he have mercy on the poor heathen who annex (i.e. take for themselves) one head of small stock after another; in their craftiness they are just as clever as civilized thieves…

* * *

Kempe's report above and Schwarz's report below were both submitted to Heidenreich for publication at the same time. While Kempe is interested in the linguistics, Schwarz is interested in the land, in particular in the ploughed sections of land they have just prepared for sowing.

20 February 1879, Bethany[3] *(Schwarz to ELSA members)*
[Our fields] lie quite close to the station, have good soil, and retain moisture for a long time. Even in the greatest heat they still had some green cover, and the first green grass always showed up there after every rain. That is the reason why we chose that area to sow grain …

About three weeks ago we felled a palm and brought to the station a piece 8 feet long and 15 inches thick. We are thinking of cutting it into boards. The wood appears to be very soft. The heart of the crown of fronds is very tender and tasty. One can eat it either raw or cooked. I tasted it straight after the palm was felled and took a good portion home. We all found its taste very good when eaten raw; the taste is like that of the kernel of a nut.

We prepared a portion as a vegetable and it tasted like asparagus when cooked. We boiled the rest in water with a bit of sugar and let it ferment. It smelled like raspberry juice but soon became sour as vinegar.

* * *

Then, in a couple of reports later, both Schwarz and Kempe provide happy updates on weather and crops. The station is looking lush, the setting idyllic. They must surely feel as if their choices of site and task were exactly right. In the good times, optimism is high.

12 March 1879, Hermannsburg[4] *(Schwarz to ELSA members)*
… [God] """has richly blessed us with frequent rain so that we are totally happy. It is green and blossoming everywhere. The grass is growing mightily,

the weather is pleasurably cool, for 14 days no more than 23 degrees Reaumur in the shade, the birds are singing happily, the sun and the moon are mirrored in the torrents of the Finke which has been flowing without a halt since 12 February. The high water did not reach the most recent peak, but we thank God that this year he has again richly supplied feed and water for the animals.

Water twice covered our ploughed land, but only for a day, and did no damage because there was nothing growing there. Our first seeding came to nothing at all, partly because the seeds were eaten by vermin, while the rest rotted in the soil and then dried up. We have now sown everything again. The field peas look the best and about 100 beans have come up, with some already in flower. Melons and cucumbers seem to be going well.

H Schwarz

14 March 1879, Hermannsburg[5] *(Kempe to ELSA members)*
… in a space of six weeks the whole region looks transformed. Six weeks ago everything was still bare and dry; now everything is adorned with green. Though the rain came fairly late—the first on 9 February—since then it has fallen almost daily, more or less, so that the Finke has not stopped flowing and actually rose fairly high on 14 February, though we here on the station did not have heavy rain, but certainly up in the MacDonnell Ranges.

So we cannot sufficiently thank the Lord that we have feed for our stock and no longer have to cart any. We also hope to get some melons and other ripe produce from the garden. We have to wait and see if the field crops of maize, oats, barley and wheat ripen, but we wanted to try out some seeds. From almost all the seeds that we sowed, such as varieties of cabbage, beans, radishes and the like only a few plants came up. The seeds were no good. We thus request various seeds for next year, especially potatoes. [This request has already been met.]

The rain has brought an unwanted situation: the *wanderlust* of the Aboriginal people has again awoken, so that we do not have a single one at present for language class. The pause that has come is partly due to the amount of work we have, and partly due to the return of summer ailments: bad eyes and nausea …

H Kempe

* * *

In the midst of this activity, Heidenreich has some good news to share with Harms and with the mission staff in the Centre.

22 February 1879, Bethany[6] *(Heidenreich to Th Harms)*
Highly honoured, much-loved Father!

... I have approached the government once more, earnestly seeking free rations for the heathen. It seems that this time we will be successful. Our mission will then have an annual subsidy of at least £300 from the government. That is worth our prayers and thanks. I am increasingly happy with the missionaries. They appear to be conscientiously learning the language. May the faithful Lord add his blessing through his Spirit. My councillors are on the same page as I am ...

G A Heidenreich

* * *

Then the question of a possible second mission station again raises its head. This time, though, there is much more substance to the discussion than previously. One also senses that the matter is causing a degree of disagreement among the various parties, as the following three letters indicate.

First up is Schulze. Among the points he makes is the allusion to the possibility of his being the missionary to leave if they do open another station and reduce the number of missionaries on the Finke.

13 April 1879, Hermannsburg[7] *(Schulze to Heidenreich)*
Dear Pastor.

... We have always been of the opinion that the three missionaries for this station are too many. But we were hoping that a second and then also a third [station] could soon be established, even if not in our area with this tribe. The heathen on this station come and go, so we should go to another tribe. We are fully convinced that this has to happen, if the mission is not to limit itself to this tribe alone. To ride out from here to the next tribe is at least 50 miles, so one could look for days before finding a person.

As for the relationship to one another, the tribes are constantly on a hostile footing, so that no one dares to step across his boundary without running into danger. It is only a few years ago that our tribe had a feud with the neighbouring tribe, one that cost lives.

With the Christmas mail we received news from our Director that we were not to think of founding another station for a long time because of debts. So, in good conscience, we had to point out in the next mail that three men serving as missionaries is too many for this station. They must put workmen in our place, since the number of labourers cannot be reduced if everything is to be run properly. We missionaries do not want to be always doing nothing but physical work.

In the next mail, Pastor Hensel, church councillor and chair of our mission committee, wrote making the suggestion and request that I should change places with Brother Thiessen after some congregations left their Synod. The congregations were not happy with him because he lacked the gifts for the task but had nothing else against him. I felt very sorry for Brother Thiessen.

In the case of Brother Meyer, the situation is worse than with Brother Thiessen, since his congregation not only complains that he is not up to the task, but also complains about other matters. Pastor Hensel does not seem able to speak well of him. However, this old gentleman wields great, perhaps the greatest, influence in the church down South.

From all this you can see why Brother Kempe can say in his letter that they will probably not let me come up here again when I travel South to fetch my fiancée. This would not be an easy step for me since I, for one, really want to remain a missionary and, then, have deep reservations about being a pastor of a congregation that had not been happy with its previous pastor. We must wait to see what our Director says in his reply ...

Louis Schulze

* * *

Heidenreich is not sure what to say or do on the matter. So, he refers the question to Director Harms. [Unfortunately, portions of the original text are so corrupted that we could not read them. However, we have translated what we could. The sometimes messy result is included below, in the hope that readers can for themselves catch the drift of Heidenreich's response.] We also get further little insights into Heidenreich's opinion of the missionaries—not always flattering, but typical.

The 'two older brothers' Heidenreich refers to are Kempe and Schwarz. If what Heidenreich hears is accurate, cracks are already beginning to appear in the relationship between these two colleagues and friends. Their wives also seem to be caught up in the tension that now exists between the two couples. These are worrying signs within a fragile community.

18 April 1879, Bethany[8] *(Heidenreich to Th Harms)*
Highly esteemed and much-loved Father!

... I have a decision to present to you about a request from the missionaries, since it is a point that you alone can decide. I will let you see my own preliminary answer to our missionaries and then want to attach our opinion on it for you. I wrote to the dear brothers as follows:

'Bethany, April 1879... Dear, precious Brothers. All three of you have written to me in your own hand: "If no new station can be established in another area, two missionaries are then too many on the present station. It would be better to use one at another place because of the training costs."'

This, in brief, is what I am presenting to you for a decision ...

I wrote: 'Dear Brothers, you know as well as I do, that I can make no decisions to call you away to be used elsewhere. Our dear Father Harms has expressly reserved this authority for himself. If there is to be a change, that can happen only by his or his successor's authority.

If this is clear to you, I can proceed further. You are to present your reports and concerns first to me and a decision is my responsibility as far it is my right and duty. For anything beyond that I have to consult a higher authority for a decision. In this way you and I preserve proper order.

So that this matter is not drawn out ... I and the honourable Church Council will send off with the next mail a short summary of your reports and later send you the answer as soon as it arrives. Yet, dear Brothers, listen now to my non-binding preliminary reply and give it some consideration. Dear Brother Kempe, so that you three missionaries [might work effectively together ?]... one of you can thoroughly learn the language, and then the other can apply what has been learned in the school. In this way you work mutually, hand in hand, and will by God's grace have the joy in these difficult times of seeing some gathered for eternal life. For the time being I consider it appropriate that two of you, Kempe and Schulze, devote your entire energy to learning the language and that Brother Schwarz begin teaching lessons as soon as possible, because desire for work grows while one is working...'

So far my reply to the brothers. They are still making suggestions for the establishment of a second station away from our place, but as much as I desire an extension of our work, I cannot achieve that with our meagre resources, and heartily thank God for preserving this mission to the present. I believe that when he has allowed us to find a firm footing in the land of Australia he will give us the means and the energy for that. In the present, I am in no way inclined to begin another undertaking while allowing the first go to ruin in the process. Rather, we first want to await his path into the hearts of our heathen but at all times stand ready for the nod from him to work among other groups.

I now want to share with you my attitude to the conduct of the brothers. I hope you will receive with goodwill what I wrote to them without letting it determine your own position. However, I must add two points for your consideration before you make your decision. The first is the easiest to put into effect. If you are able to give us £500 annually for a new station, besides the money already assigned to us, we here will make arrangements to carry out the plan.[9] However, this does not seem to be possible even for your treasury at the moment, so I will immediately move onto the second point, namely, to the question: Are all the missionaries necessary on our present station? In view of the situation that has now emerged, to this we say, 'No, two are enough'.

But it is up to you to decide who should stay and who should be used elsewhere. It seems to me to be my duty to give you some insight into the relationship of the brothers ... at work. Unfortunately, the two older brothers do not get on well and the two wives seem to have made things worse. That is a bad thing for you and me. Brother Kempe I cannot give up because of the language (work), and I cannot give up Brother Schwarz because of his management of external matters. Both have great qualities for the work but also great deficiencies, so that neither of them could successfully supervise the operation. However, on the other hand, they possess such good talents that I do not want to be without either. Kempe flutters all over the place, wants this one moment, something else the next. What he thinks is good today, in a short time becomes a defect to him.

Schwarz cannot hold his tongue even when he knows that he is wrong, but he is more consistent and thus does not alter his position even if it costs him his neck. He faithfully looks after the management. Brother Schulze would work more collaboratively with Kempe, but he is still too young and too easily ... Here I am confronted with a mountain and do not know how we are going to get over it. One thing I do not want to do is to try to get Kempe to stay with Schwarz. You know from the last report that a shepherd station has been set up, where Jürgens and Koch stay. If Kempe wants to move to the shepherd station with his wife and concentrate mainly on the language, with his wife cooking for the people ... a dwelling ... Schwarz can run the school on the main station and keep attending to the administration. Both men are valuable for us, so I want to remain patient with their weakness and help where I can, so that they get on. I wanted to tell you this first. Incidentally, one of them could find work here in the Church if they could not get employment elsewhere. But I will not make a move before I get your decision, especially since the Church Council has got on its high horse at the synod, as much as they might humbly ask for help when it suits them to do so ...

* * *

Finally, Kempe has his say on the matter. He sounds a bit frustrated, not sure that they can even maintain the present station, let alone start another one. There is something of a contradiction here, because the earlier reports indicate that Kempe was included in the request for a second station. Regardless of that, what Kempe is here advocating is, above all, the requisite lay assistance for the maintenance of the station. If they have that, the Finke would probably work all right with even just one missionary, Kempe himself being willing to leave to make that happen.

21 April 1879, Hermannsburg[10] *(Kempe to Th Harms)*
Dear Pastor!

I have been intending to write to you for a long time, but was still hoping that the situation about which I want to write in this letter would be clarified. However, after much thought on the matter I saw no other way out.

I have already submitted a report on this to Pastor Heidenreich, and also want to let you know about the matter. It concerns our conditions here as missionaries.

For a long time it has seemed to us that neither you nor the Kingdom at large are hearing anything about our mission work. We have been unable to do anything about this, our hands being tied, so to speak. However, I can no longer remain content about this and have to let you know what the situation is, even if there is no change and no prospect of things being different. So, I will try to clarify our situation for you as best as I can.

1. With reference to external matters. Apart from us three missionaries, there are here on the station three settlers and one shepherd, Mirus, who will soon be going away when Schulze travels South[11] and, most probably, will have to stay there. We will then be five men. Two must continually tend the sheep, leaving one workman apart from the missionaries.

There is much work, like bringing in horses and cows, and sometimes looking after them as well as a third flock of sheep, fetching wood, picking up the mail, repairing the various yards, erecting different structures, shearing sheep. One cannot list everything that comes up in a camp like this. In addition, we have made every effort imaginable to grow crops, but so far without notable success.

Who is there to do all that? It is obvious that we missionaries have to work hard from morning to evening without being able to think of studying the language and other things. Now, we in no way refuse to work, as we have shown. But to be occupied just as workmen is unsatisfactory for me because we were sent out as missionaries. I consider it wrong of the mission to use missionaries, who have cost so much, as workmen.

I would no longer be annoyed if one could see an end to this, but the situation will not change unless we get more settlers. I have thus already written to Pastor Heidenreich that either the livestock numbers be decreased or several more settlers be sent. I cannot with a good conscience carry on as things are.

2. There is another factor why we cannot achieve much as missionaries, namely, the nature of the land and the people who belong to it. At the most there are here in this area perhaps 150 to 200 souls belonging to the local tribe. But by far the majority of them are not on the station, and cannot be, because nothing grows here, nothing can be cultivated, forcing them to make a living away from here by hunting, fishing and the like.

And even if we wanted to feed them, not many would stay here, since they far prefer their rats, mice, roots, snakes and the like to our food, especially since they can get them without working,[12] whereas we are forced to get them to work if they are here. Some can be kept here during a dry season, but nothing can hold them back when rain arrives. After the rain we at present have only one [Aboriginal] person here, so three men have to look after the animals, work which is otherwise done by the heathen, even if we have to supervise them because they would otherwise reduce the size of our herds and flocks ...

I would say that if we had an average of 10 to 20 workmen here on the station, one missionary would be enough and more than enough. For, apart from the great distances, the nature of the people prohibits us travelling to other family groups, since they constantly roam far and wide and have no permanent residence.

I have written about this to Pastor Heidenreich and applied for the removal of two missionaries since the resources can be better used ... I was sent out as a missionary, so would like to use my energy following this calling, which I cannot do here.

3. Finally, I must speak about the matter of expenses. To this point we have always hoped that we could do some farming ... so as to reduce costs. This year we are having a really good season ... one that could not be better as far as the weather goes, and yet we see that the crops have not ripened. The seeds sprout ... and green growth is vigorous as long as there is moisture in the soil, but the dry, biting wind dries everything up. This year we have nothing ripe apart from several kinds of melon. That does not mean that we could not get a year when we could grow some maize; it grows well here when it has moisture and the rain falls at the right time, in January at

the latest. It then becomes ripe before the winter frosts, but we cannot rely on that happening.

If it is true, as letters from the South always tell us, that the station cannot be retained without farming, there remains nothing but to give it up. We cannot count at all on cropping.

We are certainly in a difficult situation, since every year we have to transport all our food up here. Counting just us ... that comes to £5300 sterling. It will be very difficult for the congregations down South to raise that every year; likewise, the expenses for Hermannsburg. Just the freight costs a massive amount that could be put to good use elsewhere.

If the mission is to be retained here, nothing else needs to be done except either to reduce the livestock to what is essential, thus allowing a reduction in the persons employed, or we have to have more people, workers, and if possible increase the number of animals significantly, especially the cattle. This is the safest move, as I have already informed you, also writing this to Heidenreich several times. In the course of several years we could then make a profit ... but that costs a lot of money and labour. In three to four years time some profit could be gained from the sheep, but we would have to wait patiently for that to happen. That requires work, and work requires workmen. All that is obvious, as anyone can see.

We live as frugally as we can, and for this reason have been content to waive a salary and are happy with what we are given, so that we are no burden for the mission. But we are not happy to stay here simply as labourers. So, I sincerely plead with you to give us your opinion. I hope Pastor Heidenreich has already written to you about this matter. I am sorry to bother you with such things but cannot do anything else. I must act for the sake of my office and for the sake of the mission and not give cause for slander. Enough slander is already directed against the mission from the world.

In circumstances such as these there can be no thought of beginning a second station. For that reason alone one missionary is enough for such a small number of heathen. In any case this person must be able to discharge his office and not be required simply to be a workman. I have already written to Pastor Heidenreich expressing my willingness to be called away from here, though that is not an easy step and would be the cause of much worry, work and unpleasantness. Yet, for the sake of the cause, I am ready for that to happen to me and allow myself to be sent somewhere else, whether New Zealand or Africa. All I want is to serve my Lord as a missionary.

But I place this entirely in your hands, dear Pastor. I am writing this so that you do not think that I am longing to get away from here to serve as a pastor.[13] That is in no way the case; I much prefer to remain in the service of the mission...

H Kempe

* * *

So, the year moves along. Schulze bemoans the absence of Aboriginal helpers, Heidenreich is pleased with the government support being provided to the mission and shares some of his impressions of the Aboriginal people, while Kempe is working on his first book on the Arrarnta language. And the Schwarz family make history with the birth not only of their first child, but of the first child of the mission.

23 April 1879, Hermannsburg[14] *(Schulze to Harms)*
Dear Pastor,
... After the first heavy rain, this usually bare and bleak earth was covered in the loveliest green. What a pleasant sight for us! We had not seen the like of it for a whole year. Immediately after the rain, even during the rain, we put our seeds into the ground and some sprang up very soon, others not at all. Much of what germinated dried up after several days, so in spite of all the rain we have little to harvest. Melons are the only things that grow well. So we have, if but little, nevertheless something for which to be thankful to the Lord.

There is sufficient feed for the stock, even though, for the most part, it has already dried up. ... Because of the heavy rain it is as if all the heathen have been swept away except one, and now we ourselves have to do all the many jobs they were able to do, particularly during the lambing of the sheep. We had plenty of physical labour before, but all the more work now, and so we cannot properly exercise our calling as missionaries. Even if we had a mere hour or so to spare, the Aboriginal people are missing, so the study of their language is not progressing properly and not every heathen is useful for this. Before the rain came we had somewhat settled on one Aboriginal person, and he would have stayed on except that the others came and dragged him away to be circumcised. Circumcision marks the change of status from childhood or boyhood to the status of manhood...

Louis Schulze

30 April 1879, Bethany[15] *(Heidenreich to ELSA members)*
Dear mission congregations.

... You all know that we entered the current year carrying heavy debts. Thus we were obliged to cut costs where possible in staff requirements and other supplies ...

[Also] in the annual report to our government we presented the petition that our Aboriginal students be assured of free rations ... I asked MP Mr Krichauff and Pastor Homann to take steps to see the matter through. Both have faithfully done their job and brought our request to a conclusion: the praiseworthy government is this time delivering up to five tons of rations to our station, with no freight charges. If one calculates all the rations granted for the running of the station—food, blankets, clothes, tools, kitchen utensils, tobacco, soap and the like—plus the freight—it must come to £500 in value. That brings a lot of honour to our esteemed government ...

The missionaries have worked hard at learning the language by alternating with each other mornings and afternoons, so that they have half a day to study the language from the mouths of the heathen and can use the other half for writing it out on paper. If they make real progress there is no doubt that their wish and ours will soon be fulfilled, namely that they can relate not just short sentences to the heathen but whole sections ...

Also, since the dear Lord has attended to their material needs, the heathen have gone walkabout. Sometimes no one is present for a language lesson. They will surely come back when they are tired of roaming about, as they generally do after they have had their foolish escapades. It is dreadful to see how they run away after rain, armed with spears, small shields, boomerangs and axes, a round cudgel with a flint stone attached to the thick end. With this they not only make their weapons and basins but also cut down trees and telegraph poles.

The men usually wear all their ornamentation: a white bone or wooden stick through the middle of their nose, and a tall circular crown on the head, woven from the hair of their wives' heads that they regularly cut so that it does not get too long. When the group of able-bodied men move out with the healthy women, who carry their provisions in bowls and firesticks in their hands, the adults make off with the larger children. At the rear hobble along the sick, lame and nursing mothers. These often have a child at the breast and carry one on their back, while leading another by the hand or pushing it along at their feet. One hears the first lot happily shouting, while the second group complain, moan and cry. The first lot run around wildly like loose horses and cattle, while the second group can barely move from the spot, and the hard-hearted men are little concerned about their wives who carry such burdens, and about their little crying children.

Their heathen character becomes really apparent at their heathen festivals, arousing both divine and Christian pity.

I cannot say whether the heathen on our station have the same customs and same kind of weapons; I have witnessed the above only with a tribe between Peake and Dalhousie. This is the tribe from which I took the heathen lad, Bobby Boy,[16] who unfortunately stayed at his old home on his return. I not only regret that, but chiefly the fact that we were prevented by lack of resources to do mission work with the entire tribe that was healthy and strong.

I also regret that all the land around here has been taken up by pastoralists...

G A Heidenreich

*3 June 1879, **Hermannsburg**[17] (Kempe to ELSA members)*
... At present I am busy preparing a primer but am naturally making slow progress. This demands we go deeper into the language. I often come across blocks and boulders lying in my way that first must be removed. I have several times ridden out and persuaded the heathen to come to the station. Though they promised to come, they did not. They like the free and unrestricted life more than anything else. That is what I know to write about them up to this point...

Now, a bit about our animals. We have castrated seven young horses in these days and still have nine foals too young to castrate. This year we gained 800 lambs...

Research and Publication

Kempe's mention of his work on an Arrarnta primer underscores the fact that, in addition to their work as Christian missionaries, pastors and labourers, he and his colleagues were also—in their own unique way—scholars. They went into this new world of theirs as students, learners intent on researching the land, the people, the language. And as they immersed themselves in their studies, they produced workbooks and grammars and other resources in the language of the people. They then aspired to have those published for the benefit of the people and anyone else interested in their world.

- Kempe's **primer** was the first of those Arrarnta publications. He completed his work on this by year's end, and makes references to its progress in later letters. The manuscript was published in Adelaide in

1880 under the title *Aldolinga angaxa*.[18] A second edition was produced in 1888.
- In his book on Western Arrarnta literacy, David Roennfeldt alludes to a **German-Arrarnta wordlist**, or mini dictionary, that Kempe produced in hand-written form around the same time as his primer.[19]
- Coinciding with the work on his primer, in 1880 Kempe worked on a **major paper on the Arrarnta people** for publication in both the *Missionsblatt* and *Kirchenbote*. It is likely Schwarz collaborated with him in this work. The first English translation of that paper is reproduced in Chapter 15 of *Missionaries, Madness and Miracles*.
- The year 1880 was indeed a hectic and productive year for Kempe's writings, for by October he had produced a paper for presentation at the Royal Society of South Australia. The paper is titled **Plants indigenous to the neighbourhood of Hermannsburg on the Finke River, Central Australia**. Only eight pages in length, the paper is remarkable for the depth it displays of Kempe's knowledge of this topic after such a short time in the Centre.[20] Immediately following Kempe's paper in this same publication is the announcement of the naming of a new species of plant discovered in South Australia: the *Justicia Kempeana*.[21] At some other time in botanical history, Kempe also had another plant named after him: the *Acacia Kempeana*, otherwise known as the Witchetty Grub tree.

There is then a ten-year gap between publications from the Finke missionaries. This is not to say that they ceased their research work: it is obvious from our letters and reports that their studies continued throughout their time in the Centre, but with little public output except for their reports and letters. But then, in 1891 there is another flurry of published materials.

- In December 1890, Kempe had another presentation before the Royal Society of South Australia. This is his 54-page **Grammar and vocabulary of the language spoken by the aborigines of the MacDonnell Ranges, South Australia**. This grammar also incorporates a dictionary of 1750 Arrarnta words, an expansion of his earlier wordlist. Hartwig Harms claims that there were approximately 5000 known Arrarnta words at that time.[22]
- In April 1891, Schulze had a paper presented to the Royal Society of South Australia. His is titled **The Aborigines of the Upper and Middle Finke**

River. The Royal Society report on this paper notes that it was translated by botanist and naturalist, Mr. J. Tepper.[23] Because the paper was previously published in English, it is not reproduced in this book. A copy is available, however, in *The Translation*.

- Finally, by 1891 Kempe had completed his work on the first Arrarnta **devotional and worship book**. It was published in that same year and consisted of 156 pages. Within its pages were Luther's Small Catechism, selected readings from Scripture, 53 hymns, and prayers for a variety of occasions.

There is an interesting link between the hymns in this book and the formation in 2015 of an Aboriginal women's choir that became known as the *Song Keepers*. Members from six central desert choirs were brought together into a single choir with the intention of making a thanksgiving and cultural trip to Germany. Hymns from Kempe's hymnal were (and are) still in use amongst the Arrarnta people, and the community wanted to take these hymns back to Germany and sing them to the German people who were responsible for bringing them to the Centre in the first place, but in their own Arrarnta language.

Thirty-two members of the choir made this journey, and most of them had never been overseas before. They were away for a month during May-June 2015, performed 14 times, and visited a number of historical sites in Germany including, of course, Hermannsburg. A documentary film called the *Song Keepers* was made of the whole experience, and this was shown in cinemas around Australia.

* * *

***3 June 1879, Hermannsburg*[24]** *(Schwarz to ELSA members)*
What I must still tell you is cause to praise God. On 19 March the Lord gladdened us with the birth of a healthy daughter. Mother and child are safe and well to this hour. In holy baptism our baby daughter received the Christian names Caroline Rosina Dorothea. The entire mission family here is safe and well. God be thanked for everything.

13.

Mixed Blessings

18 June 1879, Bethany[1] *(Heidenreich to Th Harms)*
I am happy to report that we have finally succeeded in getting from the government free rations for students and aged heathen. This time our gift is for over £600. So the dear God is helping us through unbelievers, when believers do not want to help.

G A Heidenreich

* * *

Land and work – Aboriginal Spirituality

In this next chapter, and throughout *Missionaries, Madness and Miracles*, the missionaries repeatedly complain about their difficulties in getting the Ararnta people to work—at least, in the way the missionaries expected 'work' to be done. They also bemoan the Aboriginal laziness, their bad habit of running off all the time, and their theft of the mission's animals.

From the missionaries' perspective, all of this is simply bad behaviour, immoral, in some instances. The mission has set up this station to be worked according to their German, Lutheran customs and work ethic. It is a business within which the Aboriginal people might have a job and earn a living. These people ought surely to welcome that. Why wouldn't they? Why don't they? And why do they repay us with ingratitude and theft of our animals? To the Whites it is all quite baffling.

What the missionaries failed to grasp was that these attitudes and actions of the Arrarnta people were as embedded in their Arrarnta worldview and spirituality as the attitudes and actions of the missionaries were embedded in their Christian worldview and spirituality. They also failed to appreciate that the two worldviews were worlds apart.

However, any non-Aboriginal person wading into the waters of Australian Aboriginal spirituality does so at peril, for this is a vast, complex, sophisticated and sensitive topic, with secrets. It is not to be lightly played around with. Thus, I am loathe to attempt even a brief introduction to it.

On the other hand, little is achieved by backing away from each other on spiritual concerns. Rather, one hopes that taking the risk of engaging in an encounter with each other's spiritual understandings, even at a basic level, opens up the possibility of authentic connection. A multitude of resources are available for such a task, and some of those are listed in the *Bibliography*. As a beginning exploration, I would suggest Paul Albrecht's *Relhipperra: about Aborigines* which can be accessed and downloaded online[2].

In both Christian and Arrarnta spirituality, the practice of work is closely associated with the understanding of land. In traditional Christianity the land, the whole universe in fact, exists as a result of the creative action of God. All was gift, and all was in perfect harmony, each part of creation a blessing to the other. However, on account of the so-named Fall, the creation, including the land, becomes a cursed blessing, and the weed and thorn-infested land now has to be beaten into submission through hard, sweat-browed toil. Humans almost have to drag the things of the earth from the earth in order to enjoy them. Hard labour becomes the norm, and only through this hard work do humans earn the right to enjoy the rewards of the earth. They also earn the right to be paid for their toil. Those not prepared to do this—lazy people—deserve nothing. In briefest form, that is the spiritual basis from which the missionaries came.

According to Arrarnta belief, the earth is eternal, and within it have always dwelt the ancestral spirit beings. In the time of creation, what came to be called the Dreamtime or Dreaming, these ancestral spirits emerged from the land and formed and shaped the things of the land. Those same ancestral spirits now reside in the land and in all of the creation that forms the land: in the flora and fauna, in thunder, lightning and rain, in the sun, moon and stars, and also in the humans to whom the spirits give birth.

People, land and ancestral spirits are all connected with each other in a complex network of dynamic relationships. Associated with these connections are the mysterious *tjurrunga* and other sacred objects and sites, chants, dances and other rituals. It would be impossible (even foolish) to attempt to delineate all of these in a brief introduction such as this.

Nevertheless, put as simply as possible, the crucial basic points to make for our immediate purposes are that

- the land exists in order to sustain the people,
- the ancestral spirits who created the land are those who sustain the land, and
- the ancestral spirits undertake their task only through the proper conduct of the rituals, words, songs, chants, dances and so on, in association with their corresponding *tjurrunga*.

That final point is what the Arrarnta people classify as work: the proper attendance to the proper rituals by which, ultimately, the land [creation] is sustained. As can be readily seen, that is a totally different understanding from the missionaries as to how the world works! And when the missionaries criticise and berate the Aboriginal people for their heathenish views and behaviour they are often actually attacking the heart of Arrarnta spirituality and life.

But there are other related Aboriginal beliefs around land and work that exacerbate the spiritual difference between the two peoples. One of these is that the land is not owned in the way the Europeans understood ownership: as something somehow purchased and possessed by an individual or group. For the Arrarnta the land was a trust to the people, its custodians, and its resources were to be freely shared by all.

So, when the Arrarnta first saw a group of white people walking onto their land with a mob of sheep, that for them would have been a consequence of the ancestral spirits having been awoken and having done what they were meant to do. And this 'gift' would have been gift, to be shared by all. So, why not help yourself?

The final observation to make in this section is that the Arrarnta also believed that they only needed enough for today, and that they were in fact provided with enough for that day. There was no need to hoard or to save. Provided the proper rituals were enacted, the ancestral spirits would sustain the land, so why worry? In many ways, the Aboriginal people were exemplars of the injunction of Jesus: 'So do not worry, saying, 'What shall we eat?' or 'What shall we drink?' or 'What shall we wear?' For the pagans [heathen] run after all these things, and your heavenly Father knows that you need them... Therefore do not worry about tomorrow, for tomorrow will worry about itself. Each day has enough trouble of its own.' (Matthew 6:31,32,34, NIV. See verses 25–34.) Yet, when the Arrarnta did that, the missionaries called them lazy!

* * *

Each of the three missionaries submits a report during the second half of 1879. Taken together, these provide a comprehensive over-view of all their work at this stage. All missionaries comment on the weather and the crops. But then each of them selects one or two different matters for their specific attention. Their work is becoming increasingly complex and demanding.

July, 1879, Hermannsburg[3] *(Kempe to Harms)*
I recently read all the *Missionsblatt* reports on the old station at Killalpaninna to gain clarity on one point, and I found there that there was always sad news about the station and very little happy news. The same goes for this station and will probably remain the predominant theme for quite some time. I do not doubt that the Lord Jesus wants to make the heathen of this land children of God, ruined though they may be. Rather, I firmly believe that. We see that on the old station the first 12 heathen have at long last been incorporated into his kingdom through holy baptism. May the Lord keep them in the faith, true to the end, to the praise of his grace and to the shame of all who previously maintained that the heathen were incapable of accepting Christianity, and that all work amongst them was futile. I also believe that here, too, the gospel will not disavow its nature as yeast.

True, we have not progressed to the point where we can fully preach the gospel to them, for we lack familiarity with the language. We can tell them short Bible stories with simple sentences, but one soon finds that one still has too few words, especially when dealing with spiritual concepts such as sin, grace, holy, righteous and so on. For these we have so far found no words; they seem to have no concept of these. To create words demands caution; one first must know and discover what they think of thereby. Often when one thinks to have found the right word for something, one later learns that they think of something quite different with it.

Also, there are times when one can do no language study for the simple reason that no heathen are here. Thus it happened that all the heathen left the station after rain in February and returned only at the end of May, allowing us once more to continue our language study, which we had to postpone for a full quarter of the year. In this period I rode out several times and pressed them to come to the station. The last time I found some who promised to come, but that is where it stayed. The first time I did not find a single one.

This restless wandering is what makes it impossible to find them. That is the case nearly all the time, but we can do nothing about it except to pray diligently that the Lord may prepare their hearts and bring them to become aware of their miserable condition, especially the latter. For, despite everything, they consider themselves to be quite fortunate. The devil has so blinded their hearts that they do not feel their own miserable state.

Now, in earthly terms they are not needy. After rain, something can soon be found for the stomach. Moreover, they are not fussy and can soon find as much as they need. The rest of the time they lie around lazily. Thus, as long as there is something to be found outside the station, they do not like to come to it, because we feel compelled to get them to work. One would wish that we could give work to many of them, but there is little prospect of that.

Hope of growing grain crops here is always diminishing, since all attempts so far have failed. We only wish and hope that, as I recently read, it is our lack of familiarity with the soil and climate that is to blame so far...

As for our relationship to the heathen, we can say that we have no cause for complaint. They cause us no trouble beyond some occasionally stealing a sheep because they do not want to work. They often go about this quite cleverly, even if not so cleverly that we cannot catch them and take back the sheep from them. So far they have shown no antagonism toward us. That is not to say that it does not lurk in their hearts, for their continual skirmishes among themselves show they are capable of hostility. It exists in every person's heart, so how should it not be in the hearts of these heathen who have for so long been ruled by the devil.

In general, they show how deeply people can sink when they turn away from God and serve Satan. They have lost all awareness of a living God and know only how to tell foolish fables of evil powers that get them by the scruff of the neck. Noteworthy is that they believe that the soul lives on after death, though in a distorted version of the Christian belief in the resurrection of the dead and eternal life...

We are otherwise all sound and well, praise and thanks be to God, and here in the desert that is the greatest earthly gift God can give us. But the dear Lord has also blessed us spiritually; we have his precious Word and Sacrament and can meditate on it and enjoy it as often and as much as we want to. What more could we want? Even if we have to fight many an inner battle and have to put up with all sorts of privation, we can patiently bear all this, knowing full well that this time of suffering is of short duration. Yes, we learn to treasure everything more here than at home where everything is plentiful, also earthly gifts.

To mention just one thing, we are, for example, very happy if we can have a meal of greens made from thistles. Thus it is our eager wish to grow green vegetables, and we are really thankful that this summer we have brought to ripeness some melons and a kind of gourd called a pumpkin. Unfortunately, frost ruined all other produce; it came very early this year...

H Kempe

P.S. Dear Pastor, we also want to ask, in case you send a crate of clothes for the heathen, that you kindly include one or two carding combs that are not available here. Our women would like to spin some wool but have no tool to do the carding.

I also want to note that if a married man can still not be found to serve as a shepherd, a single man is acceptable. I wrote earlier about a married man only because the brothers later usually want to have a wife. To bring one out later always involves high costs. I wanted merely to indicate that if the wife is sent only later, there are many expenses, which are not incurred if a man either brings a wife with him at the outset, or does not wish to have one at all.

3 October 1879, Hermannsburg[4] *(Schwarz to ELSA members)*

... The Lord has also richly blessed us with rain. Within three quarters of a year the Finke has flowed four times for long periods, even in the riverbed on this side (a bit further up from the station it has three beds). As for the last flood on 2 August, this caused us more concern than the previous ones. We had established a garden close to our well on the river bed this side. We were still unaware that the floods also submerged that spot and did not think that the otherwise dry and sluggish Finke would soon become active again with such unusual force. The planted seeds were already doing well and we were looking forward in hope to the future delicacies.

At the beginning we rejoiced over the heavy rain. But when the torrents approached our garden we prayed the Lord to stop the rain. But he let it continue. For two days and two nights the flood waters flowed around the garden, but the Lord's hand stayed them so that they were not able to do the slightest harm. Praise be to the dear heavenly Father because he makes his children anxious and afterwards doubles their joy.

We have now already enjoyed many vegetables from our garden; one can barely notice this because the garden is very productive and things continue to grow. Also in the small garden near the station everything is fine and gives cause for hope. Most of all, the fruits of the field invite us to 'taste and see that the Lord is good!' Our wheat is standing up magnificently and the maize continues to grow. The barley and oats are also excellent. It would be desirable to have many acres of such wheat but our wheat field is only 120 paces long and 9 paces wide. This is our fourth trial planting and we have no seed left. We had about given up all hope since the three previous attempts completely failed. But now the Lord has clearly and distinctly shown that his name is called 'Wonderful'. The green growth of the maize previously looked fine, but the corn was destroyed by the frost. This time that will not be the case.

As far as our stock numbers are concerned, the Lord has also richly blessed us in this area. The sheep have increased by 800 head, the horses and cattle in corresponding numbers. Horses and cattle are up to their bellies in pasture. For a year we have had good grazing and plenty of water. The wilderness is green and blooming like a paradise, in garden and field. God grant that the arid hearts of the heathen here will soon become green and bloom to the honour and praise of his name.

He has also blessed our activity. With this mail, Brother Kempe is sending off a manuscript in the *Aldulinga*[5] language, and this is to be printed. It is meant to be a future exercise book[6] for the heathen and is designed for this purpose. May the Lord graciously grant that this initial gift to the heathen here will produce rich blessing. May he daily make us more faithful and diligent for our holy calling.

Unfortunately, there were only a few heathen here for months at a time, which made our language studies very difficult. For some weeks now more and more have been coming and going. At the moment there are about 30 here. They have again stolen some of our rams, probably for a wedding feast or similar celebration. We expect the government rations to arrive next month and hope that through their daily, regular distribution the heathen will stay more permanently on the station... [and so] give up their vagabond existence.

As far as other work is concerned, we have finished a new building for the sheep shearing and, as well, a wool store. A section is designated as accommodation for the shepherds, and Brother Holtermann is already living in it. We have fenced a piece of land comprising 15 acres, making the smaller part arable, and have ploughed it. We have still to clear the rest and plough it. If God grants more rain and and success and we get enough seed at the right time (February and March), we can harvest enough for our needs ...

To be noted, finally, is that we have felled timber and cut boards to extend the dwellings of both Brothers Kempe and Schulze. In addition, timber has been felled, carted to the station, and partially cut...

F W Schwarz, Missionary

December 1879/2 January 1880, Hermannsburg[7] *(Schulze to Th Harms)*
Dear Pastor,

... Following the beautiful and frequent rains during the winter months, the wheat grew quite splendidly. The few handfuls of barley and oats sown also bore richly. The kitchen or vegetable gardens supplied us with quite a number of beautiful meals during the months of September and October. Thank the Lord for this gift of first fruits. But the sun rose even higher in November and December, and because it did not rain after 17 October, nearly all the plants dried up, despite all the watering by hand and covering them with shade. The sweet corn which we put in at the end of August shot up and flowered superbly, but because of the intense heat it was unable to set any grain, or little. In some parts it dried out, so that at best we got our seed back.

In the middle of December the heat became really intense. We had not previously experienced anything like this up here. Some days we did not know where to stay, at night as well as by day. We ate hardly anything but drank all the more.

The thermometer rose to 53°R[8] in the sun. The result of the heat followed soon enough; one after the other began to feel ill. Kempe began with it and we saw little of him. He was hardly well enough to be seen about now and then. Then I had to lie low for a few days. Jürgens and the wives also crept quietly about. It did not affect Tündemann, but he chopped himself in the leg and had to rest also. These were our circumstances with the beloved Christmas-tide approaching. Schäfer and Schwarz began ailing, too. The latter had to go to bed on the third day of Christmas and even now is unable to do anything. The dear Lord helped us through in that we were not all laid low at the same time.

Although it remained very hot up to the first holiday, and most of us were ailing, the beloved Christmas was a very beautiful one for me. Prior to Christmas we wished for a lovely rain as a Christmas present. The Lord granted this wish to the extent that, since the second festival day until today, he covered the very hot sun with clouds and let a cool breeze blow. One can breathe afresh again, and with the exception of Schwarz, we all have recovered again. The head and stomach are the areas everyone complained about. Thanks be to the Lord for this, too.

Regarding the heathen, I can give you encouraging information.

The long-awaited two wagon loads of food rations for the heathen given by the government arrived on 21 November. With them came a considerable number of heathen who had previously heard of this along the way. After some days we counted over a hundred of them. According to the orders of the government, all the old, the sick, the frail, and the pupils receive one pound of flour, some sugar and tea. Because much flour was lost this way, we built a bake-oven, and baked the bread for them, which they liked even better. In general, they are great friends of work that is done for them!

Since 25 November we have started to conduct school for them every morning before distributing the rations. The lessons consist only of reading and writing. One cannot speak of big advances in such a short time, but we have already come to know that they are not incapable of being educated.

Unfortunately, this was disputed for a long time by the ignorant and by enemies of the mission. Some [of the Aboriginal people] write the letters quite nicely and know the five vowels, too. It makes me really cross to read or hear disparaging judgements about these people. They have certainly sunk deep spiritually, for despite all our efforts we have found no trace of any religious rites among them. Nevertheless, they are Adam's children, as the first glance indicates. With their beautiful slender bodies, 6 feet tall, as well as their mental capabilities, they in many respects even excel many Christians. They do not burn their dead but bury them. Although both sexes go quite naked, there is a sense of modesty and they always move around at a certain distance from one another. How good it would be if we could give them each at least a shirt. Doubtless, polygamy is the rule as almost each has two wives; some have even three, but we have not observed any adultery or fornication.

Each lad is circumcised on attaining manhood. Then they are no longer *wura* (boys) but *atua* (men). During the circumcision ceremony the blood vessels in the arms are pierced in three places so that the blood spurts out. This is kept secret from their womenfolk. We hope to find out if this is a religious act. Apart from eating, drinking and sleeping, their main amusement is dancing. They are completely taken by this. They celebrate many of these festivities during moonlit nights. I once went to have a look at such a celebration. It was as if I came upon a mob of devils. Their bodies were painted with many patterns, and upon their heads were big bunches of feathers and such-like. The actual dance is simple; the women and most of the men sit there, singing a short verse and repeating it again and again while beating time on their naked legs. Some of the young men move forward and backward in time with the beat, stamping their feet to make the earth resound with noise. This dance is called *iltada*, and that is what they call our divine service too.

We gathered them around the Christmas tree in our yard on Christmas Eve, the men on one side, the women on the other side, and the children in the middle. Afterwards Kempe told them the story of Christmas in their language. I might mention here that for some time now we have been telling them Biblical stories in their language as well as we can. We gave them two small cakes boiled in fat. The children got some meat besides and the diligent pupils were awarded an extra cake. We then sang some songs and dismissed them. During all this time they were very quiet and attentive, the children

most of all while eating. Already the next day they were asking when we could put on another *iltada*, they liked it so much...
L Schulze

* * *

Heidenreich then rounds off the year with a series of good news items for the Australian Church. These items relate to finance and progress with language work.

24 November 1879, Bethany[9] *(Heidenreich to ELSA members)*
Dear mission congregations.
   By God's grace we have now completed another year of mission work... We entered the financial year just completed with almost £1000 of debt, without any prospects of immediate sizeable income either from here or from Germany, and with fearful hearts and lack of trust in God's help. Our financial report has already shown everyone that the faithful Lord has worked mightily with us. We have not only been able to pay off our debts up to a capital debt of £450, but we have also made financial provision for nine mission brothers and sisters and an additional shepherd in the far North, deliberately taking a debt of roughly £4 into the new financial year. Everyone can see what we see: this is God's blessing, grace and favour shown to his sacred mission work.
   But the blessing of him coming to our aid in the past year is not the only thing for which we praise and thank God. Rather, he has showered us with blessings from the old year for this current year. The approved government rations, worth £500, benefit us for the first time this year. Our missionaries report that these will reach our station in one or two months.
   In addition, the loving Lord has opened up two new sources of blessing that flow into our mission's new year, one material and one spiritual. He has given us a glorious earthly blessing in terms of crops in the field and gardens. In a grain sample sent to us, I counted 120 grains on an ear of wheat, 125 on an ear of barley and 130 on an ear of oats. If the yield in a poor year is only an eighth as good, the work is still worthwhile and saves us a lot of money.
   Yet the greatest blessing we have so far is a treatment of the *Aldulinga* language in a manuscript of 23 pages sent to me by Brother Kempe. This is to become the first primer for teaching the heathen. It begins with an alphabet of 20 letters, moves to spelling, lists grammatical rules, progresses then to sentence construction and telling stories, and finishes with hymn verses. I really like both the content and the stated aim of the booklet.

With God's help there will soon follow a larger one with Bible verses, catechism and key hymns. After consulting and reaching agreement with Pastor Homann, we will get the manuscript printed and some of the copies bound and sent to our missionaries for use in the school...

G A Heidenreich

* * *

Elsewhere in the world in 1879:

- Albert Einstein born (14 March), in Ulm, Germany. Also Knud Rasmussen, Polar explorer (7 June), in Jakobshavn, Greenland; Margaret Sanger, nurse and birth control proponent (14 September), in Corning, New York; and Marxist revolutionary, Leon Trotsky (7 November), in Yanovka, Ukraine.
- Bernadette of Lourdes died (16 April), in Nevers, France.
- Steam motor trams trialled in Sydney (23 September).
- The British invaded Zululand in South Africa, beginning the Anglo-Zulu War (11 January).
- Henrik Ibsen's play, *A Doll's House*, premiered in Copenhagen, Denmark (21 January).
- First edition of the Jehovah Witness magazine, *The Watchtower*, published (1 July) in Pennsylvania.
- The longest ever professional bare-knuckle prizefight took place in Mississippi, lasting 75 rounds (8 July).

14.

The Flint Report and Afterwards

1880

People have been bad-mouthing the Hermannsburg mission. Heidenreich describes them as 'enemies of the mission',[1] but provides no detail on who these people are. John Strehlow surmises they may have been neighbouring pastoralists and like-minded folk who were both curious about and envious of the mission's success with the land. Or perhaps people critical of the government for providing rations to the Aboriginal people.[2]

Notwithstanding who these 'enemies' were, the Minister of Education and Commissioner of Crown Lands in South Australia have commissioned an investigation into the mission. These were the people who had administrative oversight over land and settler issues in the Northern Territory. They appointed a certain Ernest Flint to carry out that investigation.

__Ernest Flint__ first appears in newspaper accounts of the massacre at Barrow Creek in 1874.[3] At that time he was the assistant telegraph station master there. On the evening of 22 February 1874 Flint, together with station master John Stapleton, five other white men and an Aboriginal lad were sitting outside the station having a cigarette and a chat. Suddenly they were attacked by a large group of Aboriginal men with spears.[4] Why they were attacked is unclear, but the common reason given is that there had earlier been a dispute between White and Black over the distribution of rations.

The station staff fought back with guns, and the melee that followed resulted in the death of Stapleton, the death of a linesman, John Frank, and the wounding of the Aboriginal lad, Jimmy Maroni.[5] Flint was also wounded by a spear thrust into his leg. On the day, at least two of the attacking Aboriginal people were killed. However, in the reprisals that followed 'reports suggest that the number of Aboriginal lives taken ... was between 50 and 90, possibly higher'.[6]

Following the massacre, Flint was transferred to the telegraph station at Charlotte Waters. He moved from there in 1878 when he was appointed Commissioner of the Peace in Alice Springs. In 1879 he was appointed as the telegraph station master in Alice Springs. It was in that capacity that he made his way out to Hermannsburg in late August-early September 1879. His report was submitted in November 1879 and made public in the new year of 1880.

* * *

18 February 1880, Bethany[7] *(Heidenreich to ELSA members)*
By order of the Minister for Education, the following report on the mission station on the Finke was dispatched through the Master of the telegraph station in Alice Springs.

Alice Springs, 12 November 1879
Dear Sir,

In accordance with the instructions sent to me on 19 August 1879, I have visited the mission station on the Finke and now have the honour to submit the results of my observations.

Since my visit and its object were completely unexpected,[8] I found everything in its normal state. The site chosen for the station is excellent, both for raising animals and for agriculture. The improvements consist of one main building 100 feet long and 30 feet wide, built of stone and covered with reeds. This is divided into three equal rows of rooms for the comfort of the families that live therein. Separated from the main building, there are other permanent rooms containing the men's dining room, bedrooms and kitchen. The usual things necessary for a sheep and cattle station are also in evidence: permanent sheep and cattle yards, pens, wool scales and the large, roomy paddock only recently fenced.

This year the missionaries have attempted to sow grain on a small scale, looking for increasing success. To judge from the results, this has turned out to be a highly successful enterprise. One must consider, however, that the past year has been outstanding in terms of rain. Since 1872 no rainfall such as this has been noted; and it is still to be proven whether such wheat and other crops can be grown in a normal year and with minimal rainfall, as is normally the case between the months of March and November. In this matter the missionaries seem to be very confident in their intention to seed a hundred acres with wheat, barley and so on next year. If their expectations are fulfilled, the time is not far away when settlers in Central Australia will produce their own flour, and indeed at less than half the present price. I have carefully packed up some test samples of wheat, barley and oats grown on the mission station which, I trust, will reach you safely. Quite apart from their value as local products, they should raise some interest in view of the fact that they are the first agricultural products to be grown in the heart of the continent. The samples have not been picked out but randomly taken from the harvest and before becoming fully ripe.

When I arrived, I found nine adult male Aboriginal people on the station, and learnt that the number hovers between 3 and 50. This section of the MacDonnell chain of hills is extremely fruitful with all kinds of inland food. The surrounding land through which the Finke cuts, with its great many fish, offers a profusion of wild life of every kind: yams and edible roots grow in profusion. However, it must be noted that this makes it difficult for the missionaries to keep the Aboriginal people on the station. The ones here belong to a tribe different from the one in the vicinity of Alice Springs. Since the region has only recently been taken into possession, very little interaction with Europeans has previously taken place. Thus, the Aboriginal people are shy and reserved. In view of these difficult circumstances it will take some time and much effort before the missionaries succeed in relying on regular visits by the Aboriginal people.

Some sheep were slain by the Aboriginal people, and the missionaries are of a mind to punish them. But they rightly explain that if one were in future inclined to take harsh measures and initiate punishment, the mission would then be forced to close.

Without expanding further on this matter, I would note that I am of the opinion that the missionaries are doing everything in their power to convert the natives. They have certainly had a hard time until now and will continue to do so. However, I think that their efforts will finally be crowned with success.

The residents of the mission station are subject to other disadvantages. There is the difficulty of adopting the use of the English language, but they are quickly overcoming this barrier. Indeed, they are now already able to speak English with a degree of fluidity and, without question, the Aboriginal people understand communication in a simple, childlike English better than in the gurgling German language.

Mr E W Parke of H Parke and Walker owns a cattle station 7 miles from the mission station. He speaks in very laudatory terms of his neighbours and explained to me that they are very obliging. He certainly believes that they strive hard and persistently to fulfil the tasks assigned them.

Finally, sir, I must admit that I gained a very favorable impression from my visit. Previous falsely held opinions were completely removed. I would therefore respectfully advise that the mission station continue to be supplied with reasonable amounts of food provisions and clothing for the use of the Aboriginal people.

I am, etc., Ernest E Flint

* * *

Heidenreich submitted a copy of the Flint report also to Harms. At the end of that version of the report he expresses his delight at the outcome, and appends some brief comments on the superiority of German efforts in mission work. He also provides a succinct summary of Hermannsburg mission principles—quite significant observations for the understanding of the Hermannsburg venture.

18 February 1880, Bethany[9] *(Heidenreich to Th Harms)*
We are very happy to be able to share with you such a favourable report about our undertaking, the beginning of which provided exceedingly great difficulties. Our joy is all the greater because it was begun by Germans, and to all appearances will be carried out successfully, for which we sincerely offer our best wishes to the brave missionaries who in this way are genuine pioneers of civilisation. Up to this point all the many mission undertakings in each Australian colony have more or less completely failed. They have partly not met the justified expectations, even though they worked with significant government support. It is all the more cause for joy that now German people, who obviously have begun in a proper way, should successfully see through a noble pioneer undertaking.

It seems to us entirely right that such undertakings initially do everything to first of all establish their settlements firmly and soundly, and to adhere wisely to the main object only as far as is necessary, instead of from the outset working at the civilisation of the natives through teaching and instruction.

Thus, they must set these people a strong and compelling example which gradually gains the trust of these wild children of nature. And when they have won that, then the scattered spiritual seed will grow with the same success as that which one's hand has sown in virgin soil.

* * *

Kempe and Schwarz make no mention of the Flint visit or report, at least, not in the material to which we had access. Any hiccup the report may have caused is quickly put behind them, and they get on with the work at hand. Schwarz's next letter gives a peek into his classroom of Aboriginal children. His comments raise the question of the extent to which the missionaries linked attendance at school with the provision of rations. That there is a link is not in doubt. But did they make the one (the rations) conditional upon the other (the attendance)? There are times when they apparently did—but whether they always did that is a question up for debate.

29 January 1880, Hermannsburg[10] *(Schwarz to ELSA members)*
A general malaise has set in with us. It manifested itself in extreme debility, pain in hand, foot and knee joints, associated with strong headache. Rain fell on 5, 6 and 7 January, but it was soon just as hot as previously. The maize harvest has yielded nothing this time; it shrivelled up as a result of the heat and dry conditions. The melons can take the heat better and grow luxuriously, but the mice are so crazy about them that recently we have hardly had one undamaged.

The Lord has finally granted us the great joy for which we have long yearned. I mean the large number of poor heathen who have been living here on the station for a good two months. They are daily being given lessons by us. True, it is not the desire to learn that draws and keeps them here but the rations. Be that as it may, it is good that they are here and, thanks to the government rations, that we can give them more and more of what is most needful, apart from food. In this way we want to make them stay here and learn.

Handing out rations takes place at about 9 am as soon as school is finished. The latter begins at 7 am straight after breakfast. Then the lads, girls, and children over five years that are present receive instruction, first in writing then in reading. Each one gets a slate tablet, on which the letters or syllables have already been written out, and a slate pencil. When the pupils have written on both sides of the slate, their tablets and pencils are taken from them and work continues in front of the large blackboard on the wall to teach them to read phonetically. Naturally, the pupils usually find the same letters and vowels on the blackboard that they previously wrote, and they are often called out during dictation and reading. Brothers Kempe, Schulze and I have a lot to do, dictating and checking the writing of the pupils. At present two carry out this work while one of us, usually Brother Schulze, has for the last eight days taken some of the pupils, especially the girls, to start reading then writing.

The number of students varies between 26 and 30. Today we had over 30, and we must say that they are making fairly good progress. For some days now, old and young are receiving practice in learning off by heart. The brothers have translated some Bible verses that the heathen recite after finishing reading and writing. They repeat word for word in their own language; this takes place individually and with all who are present.

When the lesson is finished, the daily portions of government rations are shared out. At this point all eyes light up with joy—the work has been mastered and there is something to get their teeth into. The old men get their share first, then the pupils. They should actually come last, but one knows how children are. The last are the old and frail women and nursing mothers with infants under 12 months.

On average about 50 persons daily receive rations on the station. We give the pupils their share right at the beginning and will continue to do so as long as we have rations; this is the only way to keep them here and to urge them to pay attention. If they do not apply themselves well in school hours they are punished by getting a smaller portion or by having one completely withheld for one day. This has proved to be very effective; it allows us to satisfy more people with less, something we have already begun to do. We bake the flour into bread and share it amongst those who qualify. This causes much more work but it saves a lot.

Missionary Schwarz

* * *

The faithful Mirus, who has been a part of the whole project from the time even before Schwarz and Kempe arrived, is looking to leave the station. His departure raises the matter of his replacement. What kind of person ought that to be? And ought there be two replacements, not just the one? Kempe heads off on a mini-mission, one made the more urgent by problems with a reluctant Tündemann.

17 February 1880, Hermannsburg[11] *(Schulze to Th Harms)*
Dear Pastor!

Hearty thanks for your kind letter that we received yesterday. Our Provost immediately noted that he should be straightaway informed how many settlers we had to have. For that reason Brother Kempe wants to ride at once today to Alice Springs (80 English miles) in order to telegraph the details to him.

We would like to have two settlers, single men, one as a shepherd, since our old shepherd Mirus would like to leave soon, and it is impossible for Holtermann to look after the sheep on his own. Another man is needed for the rest of the work, chiefly for riding, since one often has to ride out to the horses and cattle. We want this other person urgently because Tündemann has no desire to be here. I ask you to write to us about how we are to behave towards him as he wants to leave.

Please send us the kind of settlers who are motivated by nothing but the love of Jesus. It is no paradise here as some suppose, so I am told, and are eager to come here. When they come, they are very disappointed and then it does not work out. Only the motivation to serve the Lord through these poor people is able to overcome the difficulties here and to make uncomfortable living conditions tolerable. Here one has to do without natural beauty spots and earthly pleasures, which sometimes makes things hard for the old Adam. This is what moves us to speak to you about the colonists...

We are fairly well, apart from Brother Jürgens who has a bad leg which is getting better...

L Schulze

18 February 1880, Owen Springs[12] *(Kempe to Th Harms)*

Since I am now on the way to Alice Springs and have to stay here[13] today and tomorrow because it is too hot to ride during the day, I want to add just a few more words and at the same time emphasise how vital it is that only such settlers are sent here who want to serve the Lord Jesus. I want only to recall on this trip something from which it is easy to draw conclusions about the rest.

Indeed, there is no trace of paradise here. Yesterday evening I rode away from Hermannsburg and spent the whole night on the track since I can no longer endure the heat on my head. This morning I arrived here after riding 45 miles. I am dead tired but cannot count on sleeping during the day because of heat and insects. Now I must cover the same distance to Alice Springs, but again wait until tomorrow evening and ride through the night. The same on the way back. Anyone can easily imagine what exhausting travel that is, quite apart from the lonely, tedious riding in the wilderness.

You may ask: Then why do you cover such long stretches in one night? I reply: I would gladly divide these stretches and prefer to take two days, but I have to do it in one as there is no water in between.

Add to that the almost unbearable heat without any prospect of change. Hot east wind, clear sky, and one might call it the angry sun sending down its scorching rays—that has been the weather for 82 weeks.

How disappointed one must be after convincing himself that he will here find pleasant days and a virtual earthly paradise. No, nothing like that is here. Our lot is troubles and great privation of all kinds. We are not complaining about this but want to prevent dissatisfaction in the future. It is better to acknowledge and speak the truth than to exaggerate with great enthusiasm and actually spout lies.

We say this so that we later have our backs covered, for, as much as we need two people, if they come here with such expectations, they would not lighten our load but increase it. We already have our own burden to carry.

People like Jürgens and Holtermann are what we must have...

Please excuse, dear Pastor, that I have been so wordy but my intentions have been good. May God soon bring me back safe and sound...

H Kempe

* * *

Then comes this letter from Kempe, demonstrating how far the missionaries have yet to go in their understanding of the Arrarnta's spiritual world and in their ability to enter it.

22 March 1880, Hermannsburg[14] (Kempe to Th Harms)
Dear Pastor!

... [It is] painful for us Christians that so many heathen still sit in darkness and in the shadow of death. Such thoughts inevitably arise as we look at these so deeply-sunken people among whom the Lord has placed us. It is true. No person could sink deeper, both spiritually and mentally, than is the case with them ... That is in the first place because they have no need for something higher[15] and, secondly, because their language has no terms for things that are imperceptible to the senses, which naturally follows from the first point.

In the case of other peoples there is still something with which the missionary can connect, an awareness of a higher being, even if it is dim and muddled. All of that is missing in the case of these heathen. They feel fortunate and totally contented if they can fill their stomachs. We have recently told them several Bible stories. For example, I have told them the passion story as best as I could. They understood it all, but it does not occur to them to ask me any questions, and it makes not the slightest impression upon them. And why should it? They know nothing at all of sin, injustice, divine punishment, guilt, etc., so how could they long for a Saviour? I cannot insist that my opinion is correct. But I hold that the law must be preached to them before anything else. Hell must be made really hot for them, so to speak, so that they at least learn to recognise that they are sinners and need a Saviour. They do know that it is wrong to have stolen but only because we ordered them not to, but they consider it to be a heroic deed.

The only thing to note with them is that they are frightened of punishment. There, too, we come across difficulties that we did not previously foresee, for one must then explain who God is, against whom they have sinned. About this they have not the slightest idea. All that must first be taught and explained. For this the necessary words have to be found, and that is difficult. For example, we have long enquired whether they have any word at all for 'punishment', but so far in vain. Likewise, we really wanted a word to include the concept 'to believe, trust', 'to consider as true', but could find none other than the word they use for 'to think, to mean'.

However, there is this word *etunga* that deviates from the rule. Whereas other words can be conjugated, this one remains the same in all tenses. They possibly possess no other word, and we finally have to use this one.

They have enough words for earthly concepts, for things that belong to their daily life, often two or three for the same thing. Thus, e.g. they have a special name for each type of spear, though they differ little from each other. On the other hand, they do not know concepts of morality. The single word for good, *mara*, must also stand for 'proper, right, beautiful, acceptable', etc. For 'bad' and for everything that is not *mara*, they say *kuna*. How little one can come to grips with such a word is clear when one sees that what we call *mara* they describe as *kuna*, and vice versa.

Given this situation, should we now lose heart and throw in the towel? Yes, that is what the old Adam would all too readily like to do. Our disheartened spirits often say to us: Why do you still wear yourselves out for the sake of a few heathen? It is all of no use.

Well, viewed rationally, that is perhaps true. I say perhaps, since other experiences we have had indicate that it is not certain. God's Word tells us something quite different, namely: Go into the world and preach the gospel to all creatures. Now, no-one can deny that these heathen are also rational creatures. So we must persist and be patient and wait for the Lord's help. God's Word is always effective; we hope and pray that it will eventually soften their hard hearts and bring about blessing for them.

Some, especially children, make good progress in other, earthly matters, such as writing and reading, so one cannot ask for more. Others lag behind, finding it very hard to learn, having barely learned the five vowels. They can copy them down but have no idea what they have written. One finds such people everywhere.

Generally speaking, almost all of them have a talent for writing and drawing. This can be observed from the way they paint their bodies when they hold their dances; they often produce very decorative patterns.

The worst thing is that we are unable to give them enough work. Were we to employ and feed them all, it would cost the mission a great deal. Yet there is no other way to keep them on the station, and they are soon forced to make a living and go out to where they can do that most easily, in or near the ranges. We have often discussed among ourselves how we might avoid this bad situation but have still found no solution. I do not doubt that they would easily learn some craft, but the question is again: how are the products to be personally delivered, given the sparse population of this land? We would be happy to find a way out of this dilemma.

Physically, things have gone well. The Lord has graciously kept us free of serious sickness so that we have stayed well, apart from minor summer ailments consisting of stomach pains and rheumatism. Praise and thanks be to him! Only Brother Jürgens had to stay in bed longer than a week. He had erysipelas[16] on his leg from the long dry spell.

The lack of fodder resulting from the drought forced us on the 12th of this month to shift our sheep to the outstation Alkarabanta, where we have to stay during lambing. Lambing is now fully underway.

Hopefully, the Lord will also send us drenching rain, which is doubly desirable for the sheep and for the cattle, and also because we still hope to sow some wheat. We were able to pick only melons from the garden; heat and dry conditions seem to do them no harm. Otherwise things look very desolate and sad, which is not surprising since we have had only one good shower of rain in the last five months, not enough to produce grass. The temperature rose to 50°R in the sun.

May the Lord continue to grant us what we need physically and spiritually, especially that his Word proves fruitful in our hearts and those of the heathen...

H Kempe

This is another illustration of the dilemma, the bind, in which the missionaries constantly and frustratingly find themselves. They care about the well-being of the Aboriginal people, both physically and spiritually, and desperately want to connect with them. But the Aboriginal people do not seem interested in anything but the rations. The missionaries want to do what they consider to be the best for them, but others say the missionaries ought not be wanting to do anything at all. They should get out; and there is that in the missionaries that agrees with this. But there is always that 'Go...'!

To us the problem is blindingly obvious. So long as the missionaries approach the Aboriginal people as superior to them, as the bearers of things that the missionaries are convinced are needed, as the mouthpieces and deliverers of truth and right... as long as this is the missional attitude there can be no real, mature and authentic connection between the two, White and Black. That connection can only be made when, instead of patronising 'telling', there is genuine listening, mutual and trusting engagement.

15.

Kempe Major Report

The following report was written at Hermannsburg by Kempe between March and December 1880. It is the first of its kind in relation to the Arrarnta people. It was commissioned by Th Harms, and is remarkable for the insight gained into Ntaria, its people, its geography after only twenty-two months from the time of the arrival of the missionaries. Schwarz signed off on the report and no doubt assisted in its production.

A similar report was written by Schulze over ten years later (1891), and that report was read at a meeting of the *Royal Society of South Australia* in April of that year. A copy of that report has been included in *The Translation* [Chapter 16].

Here, now, is Kempe's report, without comment and with minimal endnotes.

Part I[1] *(Kempe to Th Harms)*
Since you, dear Pastor, have requested me to supply a detailed report on points which you yourself have set forth, and Pastor Heidenreich has asked me to oblige, I will endeavour to the best of my ability to fulfil this task.

Since, however, we are still gaining many new insights in our work among the Aboriginal people, may I be permitted to alter somewhat your suggested outline and report later on the people themselves, lest I now write something which I later find to be incorrect.

I will now try to give you a description of

1. The geography, the mountain ranges, their height, their extent and direction, etc.
To help you in your orientation, especially with regard to our mission station, I have prepared a plan on a small card.[2]

Probably everyone knows that the large inland area of the Australian continent is largely unexplored; a look at a map of Australia makes that abundantly clear. It would, of course, have become better known long ago if it were more fruitful, and not so very barren and unproductive, as it now is. But the fault lies not with the soil, which in places is very good, but with the lack of rain and water.

The whole area is a large plain, crossed by only a few relatively low mountain chains. The chief wind throughout the year is a dry south-east trade wind, and even thunderstorms or a general rain change the direction of the wind only briefly, and the south-east trade-wind soon regains its supremacy. There is really no regular rainy season, but most rain falls from January to April. The Australian inland has been opened up somewhat by the erection of the telegraph line from Adelaide to Port Darwin and by the trips by a number of explorers, who from various points of departure have crossed the territory to the east and west, frequently not without heavy losses, sometimes with the loss of their own life, or at least hazarding their life because of the waterless deserts which they had to cross. Owners of cattle, too, are pushing ever further inland, so contributing to the discovery of the unexplored inland.

When, for example, we arrived here in 1877, there were only two cattle stations nearby, apart from the telegraph station at Alice Springs; now their number has grown to five, and when conditions are favourable, that is, when rain has fallen, considerable traffic is found on the main road from Port Augusta to Port Darwin. But by 'main road' we must not think of a paved highway, but rather of a very ordinary road which, in the main, follows the telegraph line. The distance from Port Augusts to our station is 900 English miles, and the only means of transport consists of wagons drawn by horses or bullocks. If all goes well, such a journey takes from 5 to 6 months, but in dry years it can take 8 to 10 months, and even longer, before the freight reaches us. A ton (20 hundredweights) now costs 60 pounds sterling, the equivalent of 1200 German marks. It should be mentioned that the country between Port August and here varies considerably. From Port Augusta to Government Gums, to which point a railway is being laid, a distance of approximately 250 miles north of Port Augusta, we have the so-called lake area, in which water is to be found only in the beds of rivers or creeks, and so water soon becomes scarce. From here on to Peake, 500 miles north, springs abound to provide water, but frequently feed for cattle is very scarce. From here a stony desert extends to Charlotte Waters, 700 miles to the north. Here again, water can be found only in water channels, and it soon becomes scarce. In this regard this is the worst stretch of the road, because travellers often have to go for 60, 90, or even 100 miles without water. The stretch between Charlotte Waters on to the MacDonnell Ranges, known as the Sandy Desert, is better. Although here, too, water is to be found only in the beds of creeks, the fact that they are sandy means that water can at least be accessed by digging in the sand.

Our mission station, to which the government of South Australia has directed us, lies between 132 and 133 degrees longitude east of Greenwich, and the 24 degrees latitude passes almost through the middle of it. To the north the MacDonnell Ranges stretch in a straight line about 300 miles from west to east. They begin 60 miles to the west from where the Finke issues forth from the above-mentioned ranges, but then extend another 240 miles to the east. Its highest points rise to 4000 feet above sea level, and the hills consist in part of red sandstone, as the ranges in the south, and in part of granite, as in the ranges in the north.

This mountain range is of special significance because it constitutes a dividing watershed between South and North Australia; all the water of the southern half flows southwards, and that which falls on the northern half flows northwards. To the south lies the James Range, which is not as high nor as long as the aforementioned, but it is approximately 20 miles wide and consists of red sandstone. Its highest peaks may lie about 2000 feet above sea level. About 35 miles north-west of our station lies the Gosses Range, which stretches from north to south but is of no particular significance. The Welfen Heights[3] are broad at the northern end and run southwards to a point near the station on the Finke. From a high point, known as the 'Ernst-August-Heights', one has a delightful view of our whole area.

With regard to the rivers, it must be stated that actual rivers do not exist, but only river beds, which are dry for the greater part of the year. Only in the rainy season or when thunderstorms suddenly arise are they filled by raging torrents of water which, however, soon disappear. The Englishmen call all such watercourses 'creeks', and only the big ones do they honour with the proud name 'River'.

Such a river passes through our place, and it is indeed the greatest inland river, called the Finke River. It has its source in the MacDonnell Ranges and is formed by the confluence of a number of smaller creeks, on one of which the cattle station of Glen Helen is situated. The river then breaks through a narrow gorge of the above-mentioned ranges and flows southwards towards the James Range. Our station Hermannsburg is close to the place where this river makes its entry into these ranges. Although this Finke River is nothing more than a large river bed, water often lasts for a considerable time in many deep sections or in springs, but in times of drought the water becomes salty and bitter. In rainy seasons this river can really become quite a stream. Why, last year we saw it overflow four times, and when it does it is as wide as the Elbe at Harburg.[4] East of the Finke flows Ellery Creek, which likewise rises in the MacDonnell Ranges and enters the James Range 7 miles east of our station and links up with the Finke. At the entry into the James Range, 7 mile from here, the cattle station of Messrs Parke and Walter is situated.

West of the point in the MacDonnell Ranges, where the Finke has its source, another creek comes forth out of the same ranges, namely Rudalls Creek. It flows westwards and then joins the Finke 15 miles north of Hermannsburg.

Apart from this there are many other smaller channels, all of which feed the Finke, that is, if they manage to reach this river and do not lose themselves in the sand, even as the larger creeks, and the Finke itself, finish in sand. Very few manage to reach another river, or a lake, or the ocean. In addition, we have on our station the rarity of springs in two places, namely the Gilbert Springs, 20 miles to the west, and 5 miles west the Bagot Springs, both situated against the James Ranges and providing small flows of water; but the water issues forth out of rocks. (In front of the Gilberts Springs is located the Königsberg (literally King's Hill) and beneath it the Grotto of Mary. Round about both of these are found growing in the sandhills 'flowers of Mary', usually in the shape of a heart, up to three-quarters an inch in size, white and yellow like the colours of Hannover. After every rain they can be seen in their glory, standing in honour of the royal couple.[5])

North of our station, where the Bagot Springs Creek joins the Finke, we have our out-station, called Alkarabanta, to which we take our sheep when feed is scarce here, especially in the lambing season.

2. Concerning the Europeans who live here, their occupation and number, our postal service and the colonisation of this land

It is difficult to give an exact number of the European population in our parts, but an estimated 100 living between Peake and the MacDonnell Ranges would not be far out. Right now I will refer only to those living in our immediate neighbourhood. In my references to the creeks I have already mentioned two stations. Apart from these, three others must be mentioned. Forty-five miles to the east from here, at the northern point of the Waterhouse Ranges, lies the Owen Springs station of Mr Gilbert, right on the track to Port Darwin. There we collect our mail, which hitherto has come every six weeks but, as from 1 April 1880, will be available every month as it passes by *en route* to Alice Spring. But the postal delivery is made per horseman, and so only letters, papers and packets up to one pound in weight are accepted for delivery, since larger packets or packages would necessitate the use of four or more packhorses instead of the two used at present. But it should be noted that the Post Office where our mail is posted is not Alice Springs, but Charlotte Waters. Another 45 miles to the east of Owen Springs, in the MacDonnell Ranges lies the Post and Telegraph Station of Alice Springs, and another 12 further to the east the Undulja cattle station of Mr. Tennant.

The mention of 'cattle stations' already indicates the occupation of these people: they are engaged in raising sheep, cattle and horses, which alone is profitable in these parts because the rainfall is too low for agricultural pursuits, and even if this were not so, the very limited population and the heavy cost of transport would render this impractical. Even if it were possible to till the soil, as is the case further south, it would not be pursued here for the owners know full well that if the land were suitable for cultivation, the government would reclaim the land and have it subdivided for farm allotments which would greatly advantage the government treasury.

As it is, the pastoralists pay annually a mere six pence per square mile of land.[6] This enables them to lease large tracts of land, up to 10,000 square miles of land, and more, which has caused them to be referred to as squatter kings. Squatter, by the way, is the colonial expression for a pastoralist who rents a large tract of land so cheaply. That the raising of stock is highly rewarding is evident from the fact that the owners mostly reside in the colony down South or in England where they live very comfortably, even though they have to pay high prices for foodstuffs and high wages for those employed on their properties. In addition to his keep, an ordinary labourer receives 30 shillings, that is, 30 German marks in wages per week. Unfortunately, this high wage does not really benefit most of these workers very much, for when they have worked for a few years they make another of their trips to Adelaide, 'to have a spell', as they say. What they really want is to enjoy some compensation for the hardships encountered in the outback. And so their hard-earned savings are usually used up after only a few weeks of merriment and celebration.

They are not a bit interested in religion. This becomes evident from the following: I once met a young man of about 15 years of age who happened to be the son of a station owner who had probably sent him into the outback because he was ashamed of him down south. He was asked which religion he acknowledged. To which he replied: 'I don't know its name.' When I went on to ask him how many sacraments his church had, he answered: 'I don't know that either; no one has ever asked me such a silly question, but I believe it would be at least from 8 to 10.' This is not intended to imply that all are like this, but it would apply as a general rule, since most of these fellows have run away from their parents and their school.

Part II[7]

From what has been said so far the deduction could easily be made that there is no such thing as colonisation in our inland. Although the pastoralists themselves, who need have no fears of farmers intruding into their areas, have tried to cultivate some vegetables and fruit trees, the results so far have been negligible. We, too, here on our station have tried in various places and at various times to grow maize, wheat and garden produce, but usually without success. In the spring of last year the maize looked most promising, but just when the plants were flowering it was so dry and hot that the fruit would not set and we barely regained our seed. The wheat grew well, but it is doubtful whether we shall again receive as much rain as last year, but we live in hope. Of garden produce, melons, various kinds of cabbage, root vegetables and a small kind of bush bean appear to do best. But, as we have said before, the trouble lies not with the soil but with our weather alone, the long periods of drought and the great heat. Summer comes at the end of the year. Most rains fall in the months January to April. There is no gradual transition from one season to the next; it is normally a case of extremes, either too much or too little.

For the greater part of the year nature is as dead, but there is no 'winter-sleep', as in Germany; it is rather the barrenness of the heat of the sun. The earth becomes yellow, the hills become red. The heat becomes unbearable and the atmosphere is like the heat out of a heated bake-oven. The earth is glowing hot; even the dogs are afraid of putting their feet onto the hot sand, yes, the sand become so hot that when bullocks are used by day they are prone to lose their hooves, and so the drivers usually operate by night. Majestic whirlwinds pass over the land, raising dust high into the sky, until finally thunderclouds appear on the horizon. Often these merely raise great clouds of rolling dust, but sometimes they do bring rain. When this occurs, a transformation immediately takes place. Everywhere seeds germinate, and everywhere one is stepping on flowers or grass. Unfortunately, however, all this glory soon departs and the dry and arid conditions return, or, if the rain comes late, overnight frosts cause all fresh growth to wither.

The soil, which is usually found near waterways or on adjoining plains, consists of red sand, or of clay, or a mixture of both. The latter is by far the most productive. But we also have large tracts of sandhills, embracing hundreds of square miles, and they are no good for anything. They do not even grow any grass, but only the notorious spinifex (*triodia irritans*), a kind of grass with sharp, penetrating points, which even the cattle try to avoid, let alone eating it. To ride in such sandhill areas is very monotonous, for the scenery never changes. As soon as one reaches the top of one sandhill the same drab view is repeated, until finally a watercourse or a stony ridge relieves the sad sameness and provides a different even if not much better view.

Similar to these sandhills are the limestone hills which also occupy large stretches of land; but they have at least the advantage that, when the soil in the plains is soft in rainy seasons, the cattle can retire here, knowing that there is luxuriant grass growth between the hills. But despite all this, there would always be sufficient land available for cultivation, if only, as I said, we had more rain at regular intervals.

In good years we have a rainfall of from 12 to 14 inches, in less good years maybe 5 to 6 inches. But times have been when not even two inches have fallen in a year. I would really like to know how many inches of rain fall in a year in Germany. This could easily be determined, because the measurement is quite a simple matter: One simply places a funnel into a jar, which at the bottom is of the same width as the widest part of the funnel, and then measures the water in the jar, finally adding all the inches or parts thereof gained during the year at the end of the year.

This would help everybody to gain an idea of conditions out here, not forgetting to take into account the dreadful heat (the thermometer rises to 112 degrees Fahrenheit in the shade and to 168 degrees in the sun) in comparison with the moderate and damp warmth in Germany.

3. Buildings on the mission station, their number and construction, and the people living there

In order to provide a better overview, I have included a ground plan, but please take note that building No 7 does not stand where it is indicated on the plan, but to the left of Nos 1 and 2 and approximately 200 steps removed from them.[8]

At present we have six buildings on the station, or seven if the fowl house is included, and I will refer to them briefly not in accord with the numbers given on the plan, but rather in the order in which they were built. No 3 was the first house which we were still able to erect in 1877. It was originally built of wood, 24 feet wide and 20 feet long, covered with reeds and consisted of only one room, which had to serve a wide variety of purposes. But now we have removed the wooden walls and substituted stone walls; on the southern side we added another 6 feet and erected a wall through the middle, so that the house is now 24 feet wide and 26 feet long and contains two rooms, of which the first half serves as a dining room and place of worship, plus storeroom, while the other half accommodates the two Jürgens.

We have in mind, however, to erect, as soon as possible, a building to serve as church and school, so that the former room may be used exclusively as a storeroom for our provisions. Our next building was a kitchen (No 2), built of stone in 1878; it was covered with galvanised iron and was 20 feet long and 15 feet wide. When our wives and the colonists arrived on 11 April of the same year, we at least had a covered kitchen. Even so, Brother Schwarz and his wife had to live in it for some time in considerable discomfort, since the greater half of the kitchen was in constant use, and because the iron roof generated a lot of heat. But now we were also concerned about building a home for the colonists and a shed for the wagons. Whereas the house was made of wood and rushes for roofing, and brush-work was used to roof the wagon-shed, we were able to complete this project (No 5) by 9 May. The whole building was 45 feet long and 14 feet wide, of which 16 feet of the length applied to the house, which at present is occupied only by Brother Tündemann. The henhouse (No 6) Brother Schwarz built while I was absent to fetch the brothers and sisters.

Our next task was to build a dwelling for ourselves, and this we took in hand immediately. After we had brought together the required materials, such as timber, stones, lime and clay, we were able to lay the foundation on 24 June of that year, and by 7 August the walls were already completed.

But most of the work still remained to be done. For instance, the roof, for which we had to fetch the timber 9 miles and the reeds 12 miles; the inside wall had to be erected, etc., so that Brother Schwarz was able to dedicate the building on the basis of 1 Samuel 7:12 on 30 October 1878, and now was able to leave his rather restricted quarters.

My dwelling was next on the list, because hitherto I had lived along with the others in the old house. But so many other duties intervened, e.g. the building of a smithy (No 4), built of timber, 16 feet long and 12 feet wide, which we completed in November of the same year, 1878. And then we had much work with our stock, particularly the sheep, which we had to remove away from the station, and for which we first had to provide yards and a hut.

And when lambing began all of us had plenty to do, so that I was able to enter my new abode only on 9 April 1879. Brother Schulze, however, remained in the old house and took over the room I had so far used. Only on 18 October of the same year (1879) his house, too, was completed, and ready for habitation. This home (No 1) is 66 feet long and 25 feet wide and contains three sections, one for each missionary. Brother Schulze's section contains four rooms: a) kitchen, b) living room, c) study and d) bedroom. Schwarz's section 2 is the same as section 1, but my section 3 has only three rooms in that study and bedroom have been combined. The outside walls are of stone, but those on the inside and the ceilings are constructed of timber and clay.

In this year we erected another dwelling for the shepherd Holtermann, with a wool and shearing shed adjoining, made of timber and the roof of reeds (No 9). It is 45 feet in length and 45 feet wide; 12 feet of the length belongs to the Holtermann home. To these buildings must be added the sheepyards. Some of these were erected already in 1877, but last year they had to be enlarged. The total length is now 240 feet by 150 feet wide. Their construction is partly of upright posts and in part of bush-timber; the latter appears to provide better overall results. The pens for horses and cattle were in part erected in 1877, but these, too, have in this year, 1880, been enlarged by 40 feet in length and 24 feet in width. The original dimensions were 56 by 72 feet in width and length. The enlargement was essential for the purpose of branding and castrating the horses and cattle, for these operations require strong fences or yards. The animals are naturally rather wild and become very restless, and when a particular animal is frightened or infuriated it will snap a rail of from 4 to 6 inches in diameter like a stalk of straw. But the law requires that every beast be branded, and non-compliance is met with heavy fines.

Our stock numbers at present are: 1) sheep, 2400 – shepherded in two lots; 2) goats, 100, which together with the rams are usually cared for by one person; 3) cattle, apart from the 8 work-bullocks another additional 32 head; 4) horses: in May of last year we had 52, work-horses included; since then we have not had them all together, since they, like the cattle roam around in a wild state and are only brought in when branding takes place. Even so, their number may by now have reached 60. 5) poultry, perhaps 25.

We have two wagons, a bullock-wagon and a horse-wagon, plus a two-wheeled cart, also horse-drawn, but which because of age wobbles hither and thither and will soon have to be replaced by a better conveyance, since we urgently require such a lighter vehicle.

But let us now leave the station and survey the world of nature and cast a fleeting glance on the world of plants.

4. The world of plants

Let us begin with the trees. We need not go far, for only a short distance down from our house we find in the Finke the most common gum tree (*Eucalyptus rostata*). It grows in all small and large watercourses, but only in these, so that it provides the surest indication of a watercourse, when one sees in the distance the fresh green of its leaves. It grows up to a height of 80 feet and provides the best building material and useful timber in these parts. However, the trees must not be felled in summer, but during winter, because otherwise the white ants soon begin their destructive work. The family of eucalypts is rather well represented, but at present I am not yet in a position to give you the names of the other varieties. And the same applies to the other trees and plants; most of them are still unknown to me. But I will make mention of a rarity: these are the Fen Palms growing in the James Ranges called *Maria*

Livistona. This is a majestic tree, with its stem 60 to 70 feet high crowned with a cluster of leaves from 10 to 12 feet long, which resemble very much the fans attached to a long stick.

The fronds are 5 to 6 feet wide. The fruit hangs on a bunch 5 to 6 feet long. These grow out from between the stems of the fronds and are about the size of a large grape-berry, but they have very little flesh, because they contain a large round and very hard stone. One has the impression of being transported to quite a different land when standing under these delightful trees.

In addition we have another palm-like tree, which, however, is not really a palm but belongs to the Cycad family and is called *Eucephalortos MacDonnellii*. The flower and fruit are more closely related to the conifers, and so this growth could be called a 'palm-conifer'. Apart from this we have only one other conifer, the so-called pine, *Callitris verrucosa*, which grows only in the ranges and is very misshapen or crooked. Most widely represented are the acacias, but all of these appear only in bush-form, and only a few achieve a thickness of from 5 to 6 inches. However, most of them have very beautiful flowers and would be a worthy adornment to any German garden.

If we now proceed into the sandhills we find there a most unusual tree, from 30 to 40 feet high, topped by a thick round crown, whose leaves, really more like needles, hang down a long way. This is the so-called sheoak, *Casuarina glauca*. The name sheoak is no doubt an unfortunate choice, for apart from its name the tree does not have the slightest resemblance to an oak, and its seed is more like that of the pine. The wood is very solid and hardy but difficult to work. It is best suited for building purposes because of its resistance to harsh weather conditions. In some places among the sandhills is found the so-called grass-tree, but this belongs to the *liliums* (lilies), despite its difference in appearance, because along with its flower it attains a height of 12 feet. It is called *Xanthorhoea Australis*.

I by-pass other trees which are seen but rarely and because their names are not known to me; and of the other plants I can only give you the families to which they belong, for it would take us too far afield, should I attempt to give you the names of every particular kind. From experience I have gained till now the families of trees include: the banksias, geraniums, *Malvaceae*, *Violaceae, Zygophylleae, Sterculiaceae* and *Sapindaeue* in various kinds. Well represented are the *Droseraceae, Chenolea, Amarontaceae* and *Polygonaceae*. The grasses which grow here are mostly unknown to me, and really good pasture grasses are few; it would therefore be good if various new grasses could be introduced and tried. In particular, it would be desirable to find a grass that can overgrow the notorious *Triodia irritans*.[9]

It is remarkable, too, that the land produces so few edible fruits and plants, which in other lands are found in great abundance. Apart from an orange-like fruit and another similar to a fig, only a few kinds of berries are found, but I am assured that if these were sent to Germany, everyone would find a taste more than enough. This is probably one of the reasons why so few Aborigines live in these parts. But before we go on to speak of them, we will briefly survey the animal world.

Part III[10]
5. The animal world

Very little is to be said of mammals. Apart from the animals with pouches[11] I know only of rats and mice, of which there are far too many, and of the wild dog (dingo)[12], which is no less cunning than the fox, and whose weird howl seems to be especially appropriate to this land.

On the other hand, birds are well represented. The largest is the emu, which attains a height of 6 feet. Its dark-grey and bristly feathers hang long and low. The wings are hardly visible and it propels itself forward with his legs only. The dark-green eggs laid by the hen weigh a pound each. It is a very exciting scene to watch a flock of emus waddling across the plain. They are easily tamed if caught when young, but can become a real plague about the house, because they take and swallow whatever they can find, even nails, keys and the like. Another bird to be seen on the plain is the 2-feet high wild turkey, ever on the alert, whose meat is a delicacy.

And the various kinds of wild pigeons, when fried, are not to be despised. They are in part very lovely birds, with splendid plumage and an upright and pointed crest. Only the large brown-feathered pigeon does not possess the latter.

But whatever is that flock of dark fellows with the beautiful red tail-feathers? They are making an unholy racket. They are black cockatoos, wild fellows and real desert-dwellers. No-one has so far succeeded in taming one. Their plumage is a shining black, with red tail-feathers, and taking into account their crest, they measure from 18 to 20 inches in size. But in order to study the birds at their best, we will do well to watch them on the water. Here we find plenty of life and very colourful activity. We see the pelican, with his one-foot long beak, swimming along majestically, now and then dipping his beak into the water to snare a fish. We see the various kinds of ducks, cormorants and snipes swimming together in their wide variety of colours. While the heron slowly wades near the bank the water hens with their copper-red legs dart hither and thither, until the night calls us to rest and we hear only the monotonous call of the owls and other birds of the night; but this, too, is often so chilling, that one lies awake all night when spending the night in the open. And when these cries are joined by the howling of the dingo, it creates a veritable hellish concert, and one is strongly reminded of passages of Holy Scripture, as Deuteronomy 32:10; Isaiah 13:21–22; 34: 11–15.

However, towards morning, even before daybreak, life begins anew. Quite early in the morning the various singing birds come for a drink of water. Then come the small slate-grey parrots with the beautiful red spots on both sides of their beaks, and then the various very attractive green parrots which, when they have drunk their fill, fly away chattering. In swarms of thousands come also the scarce four-inches long green shell-parrots,[13] almost covering the ground around the water, all the while making such a screeching din that one cannot hear one's own voice.

And finally come the not-to-be-forgotten crows, which here are just as grey-eyed as at home, plus the hawks and vultures[14] which at opportune times strive to gain a good meal.[15] And, oh, what life there is in the bushes! What a multitude alone of the small and delicate birds which are hardly as big as our German hedge-wrens, what a variety of colours and differences in sounds!

But the insects of our land are just as numerous. From the tiny sand-flies, hardly visible to the eye, able, however, to torment the human species considerably, to the voracious grasshoppers (or locusts) and the loathsome and to some extent poisonous spiders—what a mighty array! Indeed, what a host of ants alone, from the small impertinent, pesky black ants to the bulldog ants, one-and-a-half inches long, which sting like a wasp!

Of reptiles we have only lizards and snakes, but both in abundance. The Aboriginal people have already given us the names of 13 different kinds of snakes, most of which are poisonous. We also have many lizards, the largest 6 feet long. The most remarkable is a small one, hardly 6 inches long, covered over and over with prickly points and changing its colour several times a day. It looks most attractive when it is yellow with brown spots. The Englishmen call it a mountain-devil. It is quite harmless.

Because of the lack of water it is but natural that we have few fish and amphibians. Our largest fish weigh a pound. It is a kind of herring, called sweetwater-herring.

[16]Travelling in the bush

We have mentioned earlier that transport within the interior of this land is possible only by the use of wagons. It may be of interest to you to describe such a trip in the Australian bush. But it has to be noted that the word 'bush' does not mean a thick forest, but rather the uninhabited and uncultivated area of this land, and it can happen that one can come across places in this so-called bush where there is not enough wood to make a fire and one has to resort to cow-dung instead. Earlier reports have referred to our journeys, but only in dribs and drabs. The nature of the trip will depend greatly on whether one rides a horse or travels in a wagon, whether few or many constitute the party. But I will try to deal with all these cases ...[17]

Part IV[18]
6. The Aboriginal people

There could hardly be another people on the face of the earth concerning whom such varied and often almost contradictory opinions are more widely spread or are so diametrically opposed to each other than the Aboriginal people of Australia. In books and periodicals one can read the most fantastic reports concerning them. This may in part be due to the limited acquaintance with these people, but there are probably other reasons which I had better not state here.[19] I can of course not give a description of all the Aboriginal people of Australia, but must confine myself to those which I have before me every day. Nevertheless, the difference, especially with regard to external things, would be slight. It is impossible to state the number of Aboriginal people living on the Australian continent; it has not even been possible to determine into how many tribes they are divided. In our vicinity alone we have five different tribes, each of which would probably number slightly above 100 souls. The tribe among which our station lies calls itself Altolinga. We will consider it first.

The nature and outward appearance of the Austral-negro, or, as they have recently been called, 'negritos', ie, 'negro-like'. This name is certainly more fitting than the former, for apart from the colour of their skin, they have nothing in common with the negro of Africa. They display nothing of the curly, woolly hair and the thick upturned lips of the negro. The colour of their skin is really more dark brown than an actual black, and one has to have had association with them for some time in order to be sure of this, because they often smear their bodies with red iron-ochre, ashes and fat, so that they then appear brown-red or quite black.

Their hair is not so much woolly as stringy, always hanging down and black in the case of the older persons. As a result of so much smearing of themselves with fat and so much lying in the sand, it sticks together more and more, so that it seems as though they have only clusters of hair. In a book I actually read recently that the Australian negros have no hair but only tufts of hair that hang from their heads. To prevent it from hanging into their face they bind it with yarn made from the hair of opossums,[20] either at the back of their heads or on top. The latter mode is used by women and children. The men lay great store on their hair and their beard, and I believe that one could not punish them more severely than to deprive them of both, not merely because they would be robbed of their adornment, but also because they would be despised by their fellows, since a full beard counts as a man's very important adornment.

A moustache, on the other hand, is not much favoured, and they often come to us and ask us to shave it (remove it, actually, cut it off), but while we are obliging them they are so concerned about their chin-beard, that they hang on to it firmly with both hands. Their outward appearance is by no means as ugly as is often said. They are slender of build, frequently reaching, and even exceeding, 6 feet in height, and in every way well proportioned. Often I have made comparisons between them and us Europeans, but cannot find that they are much different from us in their physique. The only things in which they differ from us are the receding forehead and the thin legs, so that one hardly notices a calf of the leg. But this may be the consequence of their poor diet, and I know a few who have worked for Europeans from their youth, and have as a result received a nourishing diet and have developed strong calf and arm muscles.

Clothes are unknown to our dark people; the warm climate enables then to manage without. Even in winter, when the nights can be very cold, they walk about naked. They try to warm themselves by day by holding a fire-stick near their body, and when they sit they keep as close to a fire as possible, while by night they sleep between two or three fires. And because like all indigenous people they sleep very soundly, it often happens that while they are sleeping they suffer unbelievably severe burns. So, for example, we have a woman coming to the station every day with her small son only a few months old, whose knee-flesh has been burnt away to the bone. Of course the child cried, but neither the mother nor anyone else heard it.

However, in their association with Europeans the Aboriginal people learn to appreciate the benefit of clothing. One can, of course, see them walking around in very odd outfits. For example, if one has the good fortune to have two pants or two shirts, he will wear both, and possibly a heavy coat over both, however hot it may be.

They possess neither clothes nor houses. Whether they sleep or are awake, they are under the open sky. A tree or shrub will provide shade against the sun, while for protection against the wind they merely place a number of bushes on top of each other. Only for protection against rain they have huts, but those are of the simplest construction. They are similar to a roof or beehive resting on the ground; accordingly, they are very low and have but one entrance and exit. A few branches are simply pushed into the earth and tied together at the top or merely propped against each other. Then leaves or grass are strewn over it and several pieces of wood placed onto it to make it firm. But these huts are used only when it is raining; as soon as it is dry they again camp under the canopy of heaven.

On the whole they are a peaceful and harmless race; murder occurs very seldom, and they are actually very good-natured in general. When they have a quarrel, which is but natural, and much noise and disturbance results, it usually does not last long, and they seem to bear no great ill-will. The big noise seems to be what matters most. It does happen that someone will spear another man, but they know full well which parts of the human anatomy are the most dangerous, and so they avoid them and usually aim for the thigh.

We have had no sign whatever of cannibalism; on the contrary they are often much too kindly disposed towards their children, so that we often felt moved to punish their children, when we saw how the little ones were striking their elders, throwing things at them or even biting them out of pure temper. They are not much concerned about the future; free of worry, they live one day at a time. They are a lighthearted people, happy and making the most of life. Quite unconcerned about the affairs of the world, they sing to themselves, with no thought for what they are going to eat or drink the following day. There is no need to impress upon them the words of Matthew 6:25. And how wonderful it is that along with their lack of anxiety they are also contented, and ready to make do with whatever is edible, because their land certainly does not offer them much.

They divide all their food into two classes, namely meat foods, which they call *gara*, and plant foods, called *mana*. But to these names of the class of food they add the particular kind; e.g. a kind of marsupial they call *putaia*, and so the meat of the animal is accordingly called *gara putaia*, i.e. flesh of a *putaia*. On the other hand, the small onion-like bulbs, slightly larger than a pea, which are to be found in great abundance under the earth and very pleasant to the taste, they call *injirkna*, but when they want to fetch them and eat them, they always refer to them as *mana injirkna*.

Australia has very few quadrupeds, and so they eat all they can get hold of; even rats, mice and bats are welcome. Only the wild dog (dingo[21]) they avoid, though they tame some of them. They likewise eat practically all kinds of birds, even crows when they have nothing better. But they make an exception of hawks and some water fowl, whose flesh tastes altogether too oily. Snakes, lizards and wood-worms[22] are a particular delicacy. Large specimens of the latter are frequently found in gum[23] trees. They know exactly which snakes are poisonous and will not eat them until the venomous fang has been extracted and the tail has been cut off, since they have the peculiar idea that all poisonous snakes can also kill with their tail.

They even eat the voracious caterpillars which often cause so much devastation. They are collected into a small tray and then eaten after they have been slightly roasted in hot ashes. In this connection two observations should be made: firstly, that contrary to many reports they do not eat their meat raw or semi-raw, but to the contrary, they cook or roast their meat very well and will turn down the most delicate beef if any part of it still shows a trace of red.

Their manner of cooking is very simple. They make a hole in the fire-heated sand and place the meat into it without removing the skin, because they hold that thereby the best juices would be lost, and then they cover the meat with hot ashes.

And, secondly, it should be mentioned that the women receive little of the meat. Hunting is the men's business and so they consume most of their catch. Only when they have been particularly successful do the women receive a small portion. The women are responsible for plant food, not only for themselves and the children, but also for the men, for they love to lie down as much as possible.

The chief nourishment consists of the above-mentioned small onion-like bulbs, of which they often carry with them a large supply. Then there are various seeds of grasses and some species of *acacia*, which are in part eaten raw and in part roasted and then beaten with stones or rubbed and baked into bread. This, too, is done by means of the hot ashes. Also growing here is a fruit about the size it of a medium-sized pear, called *lankua*, whose thick peel when roasted tastes somewhat like potatoes. But only the peel is edible; the inner part consists only of unpalatable seed. Unfortunately, this fruit is rather rare. Here and there are also some species of wild berries, wild oranges, figs and peaches etc., but only a few and they are not very palatable. However, in times of drought they even resort to the roots of reeds and rushes. But this constitutes a real 'bread of misery' and becomes edible only when it has been hard-roasted and beaten with stones, and even then it consists mostly of fibre and peel.

Their favorite means of nourishment is wild honey. However, this is not always available, and even in good years supplies are limited. Nevertheless, they are prepared to walk long distances to get it. Generally speaking, they love sweet things more than anything else, which is why they also believe that, after death, they will always eat aki, which is a small, very pleasant and sweet-tasting berry, similar to the blueberry which grows in our hills.

They have to live with these few means of sustenance, and there may be many days when they cannot satisfy their hunger, but this does not prevent them from being happy. When they have nothing they eat nothing, and they are able to endure this for a long time, but when they have food, they are able to consume considerable quantities. If, for example, a messenger is sent somewhere with a supply of food for the way or even longer, he will probably eat the portion immediately, considering it is much more comfortable to carry it in his stomach than on his back.

Naturally, there are no villages in Central Australia. Its people wander hither and thither; today they are here, tomorrow somewhere else. Only when they conduct their dances does a larger number assemble; and when these are over, they disperse in all directions. There are always certain places where one or more persons usually stay and from which they seldom depart for any length of time. In most instances these are their places of birth,[24] and this accounts for their particular love for them.

It is just this nomadic kind of life which constitutes one of the chief difficulties in serving them with the Word of God. The very nature of their country forces them to live in dispersion, because they are able to exist only in and on the river valleys and wherever else there is water, and because they have no idea and no opportunity to engage in agriculture or the raising of cattle. And so, in order to help them spiritually, we must also provide material assistance. We first attempt to convince them that they should work for their own physical support, for without this they will remain as they are. But how and in what manner, here in the inland and so far removed from communications and commerce, we can offer them useful and financially rewarding employment—this is a question we have often raised and discussed, but so far without finding any solution.

And it remains a great need, for, as with all heathen people, so also with them, laziness is one of the chief vices. They love most to sit or sleep in the shade by day and to sing and make a noise by night. In addition, they are to a degree intrusive, and are masters in begging and stealing.

They are unbelievably adept in denying everything that suits their purpose, and even when they are caught in the act, they still declare their innocence with a most innocent mien. If anyone has been successful in hunting, he has to share with others of the same camp. Of course, he keeps the best and most for himself, but he is compelled to hand over to the others and does it without demur. Whether this is a kind of law among them or plain good-naturedness, or whether, as the Germans say, they are thereby 'using the sausage to throw for the ham',[25] I have not been able to determine. We often observe, that, when for instance, the old people receive something, they share with the younger, or when the children receive a portion, they give some of it to the old people. Soon I hope to reach greater clarity on this matter.

Part V[26]
Weapons and various utensils (including tools and personal effects)
If the proverb is true: 'The wise man carries all his possessions with him', then our Aboriginal people are surely the wisest, for they almost always carry all their property in their hands, or if they cannot handle everything, on their head. It is easy to realise that all their effects, including their weapons, have to be of a very simple kind, because they have no tools, but have to content themselves with the use of flint[27] as best they can. In their natural condition the use of a hatchet or axe is completely unknown.

For their work in fashioning wood they use an instrument which is similar to a carpenter's chisel. They call it *mera*, and it serves a double purpose, namely, one end is used as a chisel and the other for the throwing of spears. It consists of a very smooth and hard piece of wood, about 15 to 18 inches long and from 4 to 6 inches wide. This is made very thin and gradually pointed at both ends, also slightly hollowed, so that it resembles a small, flat tray. By means of resin and sand a sharp piece of flint is now fastened at one end, and this end is now used for the shaping of wood, while on the other end a small barb or hook, made from the sinews of marsupials, is attached, which is used for the thrusting of spears, so ensuring greater power and sureness of aim.[28]

The spears are mostly made up of various pieces, because they seldom have the good fortune to be able to make them from one piece, because straight wood is very scarce, and they frequently have to look for days before they find a piece that is suitable. The tip of the spear is usually made of one piece and fastened with kangaroo sinews, because the tip must needs consist of very hard wood, whereas the shaft may be made of softer wood. By a similar process some spears are equipped at the tip with a barbed hook.

In addition to these two weapons, and to have a full complement of arms, every warrior must also be equipped with a shield and an *alburinja*. The first consists of a piece of wood about 2 feet long and a foot wide, rounded off to the outside and somewhat deepened within, with a grip in the middle in order to hold it firmly. Although they always carry this about with them, it is but seldom that they have need to use it; ordinarily it serves as a seat when they sit down. The *alburinja* is a piece of wood very much like the crook[29] of a butcher, but it is made very thin and flat, which they are able to throw with incredible skill and dexterity. In Western Australia I saw several Aboriginal people throwing the *alburinja* in such a way, that, after it had risen high into the sky, it began to whirr around in spiral-shaped arcs, which, the further the *alburinja* descended, became tighter and tighter (circles) until it hit the ground near the feet of the thrower.

Apart from these weapons every man possesses a stick pointed at the bottom. This they use for the digging up of roots and the opening up of tree branches, if they suspect the presence of a large wood-worm, and they have such a trained eye, that they seldom undertake the exercise in vain. When they find such a worm, they extract it by means of a stem of grass and then hang the living specimen to a string tied around their hand.

They really have no proper idea or taste as to how to decorate themselves. The only decoration they carry is a brightly-burnt piece of wood or a small bone to which they sometimes attach the tail of a rat or a few feathers. This they either wear in the hair at the back of their head or through a hole in their nostrils, which is done to all males in their boyhood.

Only when they hold their dances do they use all their skill to decorate themselves—but more of that later. The women, on the other hand, possess nothing apart from several small and larger trays or bowls for the ingathering and preservation of various kinds of seeds, fruits and roots. They are used, too, for fetching water, and if they have small children, they serve as a bed or a cradle for the little ones. With these few possessions they can naturally go from one place to another without much bother and trouble. Of earthly possessions, house and home, and all that is mentioned in the explanation of the Fourth Petition and The First Article, they have neither need nor any idea, and consequently no words in their language for 'rich and poor', for in their community everybody is equally poor and rich.

The social life of the Aboriginal people
There is probably no freer community in the whole world than that of the Aboriginal people of Australia. They have no king, no prince, no chief ruling over them to whom they owe obedience. Everybody is free-born and does as they please.

To some degree, the wives and children will obey the word of the father, but not always. Their life together has so little of the usual essence of a marriage that the bonds of family life are rather loose. It can happen, and it often does, that a man will live with a woman at the station, while the other woman is no one knows where, and the children, if old enough to look after their own food, may have their abode somewhere else. If, however, a number are together at the same place, the oldest among them usually says and commands what is to be done, but most of them will only comply when it suits them.

In a camp everything follows a certain order. The men and grown lads sleep separately, and likewise the girls and women with the children. Only now and then will an older man sleep together with his wives and children; young men seldom do. So also, when they come to the station, the men will sit on one side of the house and the women on the other, and no man can be prompted to fetch or do something which would require him to pass close to the women; he would rather make a long detour, so that he does not see the women and they do not see him. This bashfulness naturally disappears gradually when they begin to wear clothes.

An exception takes place in the case of a person being seriously sick or when someone has died. Then all of them, men, women and children sit close together and howl and wail. This is a kind of lamentation for the dead. In recent times we had opportunity to attend burials of Aboriginal people, three of whom had died in a relatively short time. The first was the child referred to earlier which had died of the burns received near an overnight fire when the mother had failed to awaken to the child's cries. The next to die was an old blind woman. She was soon followed by a man still in his best years, but completely paralysed. He had been taken from one place to another in his poor condition. We observed that the customs and ceremonies used were not always the same, but varied according to the person who had died. We saw, for example, that when the blind old woman had died, they were quite indifferent towards her and did not bother about her, so that we finally took a spade and went to bury her, whereupon in the end an old man accompanied us and took over the task. But he accomplished it in such haste that all was done in scarcely half an hour. There was no lamentation for the dead; on the contrary they seemed rather pleased to be rid of her, due, maybe, largely to the fact that they had had to feed her in her old age and blindness, a responsibility they would no longer have. The attitude of the people was quite different in the other two cases. Before the departed had actually died the men, women and children sat together and began to howl and to cry in such a heart-rending manner as to send a shiver down one's spine. They did not really cry, but screamed and bellowed. Only in a few cases could one observe that their crying and sorrow came from the heart.

I attended the burial of the child. After they had wailed for a time, several men went to the mother and took the child, which she was still clutching in her arms, from her by force, whereupon the howling and screaming really increased. It was indeed heartrending. The mother attacked the other women as though insane, but was overpowered by them. One of them took a bowl full of glowing coals and ashes and threw them onto the head of the mother, so that her hair began to go up in flames.

I now followed the men, who with the young corpse in their arms, were hurrying to the grave, to see where and how they would perform the burial. The prepared grave was near the camp; it was a narrow grave about 4-feet deep. The earth had been carefully put aside in a heap. The child was placed naked in the grave, with its face turned to the west and the legs pressed upwards against the abdomen. Then they pushed the edges of the grave with their feet and used other loose soil to fill the grave, carefully removing all grass. The heap of earth which had resulted from the digging of the grave they left untouched. When this had been done they said to me *'wala una la'*, i.e. 'You go home!' which I did, for I had had enough of it.

Here we have an example of what it means to die like the heathen, who have no hope. And I would pose the question: 'What remains of the highly-praised happy condition of the heathen, about which some people enthuse?'

Surely such happiness is not to be envied. The howling and wailing by the men is continued on the following day, and by the women in the mornings of several more days. They also observe many strange customs. In the case of the last-mentioned death, we noted that all the men marched in single file to the hut of the deceased, where they all threw themselves into a heap and screamed and howled. Then they went to the grave, accompanied by the women, where one of the women poured a bowl of water on the grave, whereupon the wailing and screaming began all over again, and sand was thrown into the air. Furthermore, after the women had left, all the men took a piece of wood which they held against the back of their necks with both hands, dancing around the grave several times while making grunting sounds.

Still shrieking, they threw themselves onto the mound of earth, and then cast their piece of wood onto other dry pieces of wood with which the grave had been covered. Finally, they left the grave one by one and the women set fire to the hut of the deceased. It is also worthy of mention, that both men and women did not speak aloud during these days, and the women went without food on the first day.

The men manifest their mourning by making a white mark across their forehead, while the women smear white colour over their whole head, hair and face. It is a custom, too, for the nearest relatives of the deceased to cut off their hair, the women completely, and the men at least in part. On the following day they all forsake the camp where the death has occurred, probably out of fear of the *vanja kuna*, the evil being which, according to their idea is responsible for the death, and likewise for sickness and evil in general.

A similar wailing ensues when someone has suddenly come to harm, as we experienced when a lad had fallen from a horse and sprained his ankle. As soon as this became known, all and sundry came along to howl, which I forbad, whereupon they dispersed, but some still carried on in secret.

It is surprising to find among heathen who have sunken so deeply that there is still quite a deal of love on the part of parents towards their children, especially since the children seldom return this love to them. Of course, this love often degenerates into a blind doting love, so that the parents find it impossible to punish their children, in consequence of which they later earn nothing but worry and trouble. This is, of course, only natural, for no child can prosper without proper discipline.

It is further to be noted, that the whole people are divided into four classes, each with a different name. This may remind one somewhat of the Indian caste-system, but actually it has nothing in common with it, for while there the various castes are very strictly separated, so that they may not even eat together, let alone take a wife from another caste, the exact opposite is the case here, for they needs must take a wife from another class. The names of these four classes are *Bunanke, Baltare, Kumare* and *Burule*. But it is not a matter of indifference out of which class, for example, a Bunanke man takes his wife, but it is all prescribed, and it never happens that these rules are ignored, but they are rather observed with the greatest of care.

So, too, the children which result from such a marriage, do not belong to the class of either the father or mother, but to another, and indeed, girls as well as boys to one and the same. The relationship is as follows:

A man who is a:	Can only take as wife:	And the children are:
1. *Bunanke*	*Burule*	*Baltare*
2. *Baltare*	*Kumare*	*Bunanke*
3. *Kumare*	*Baltare*	*Burule*
4. *Burule*	*Bunanke*	*Kumare*

Apart from these there are various sub-classes, but these extend so far that even the Aboriginal people themselves become uncertain and confused when asked about them, and often cannot keep themselves from laughing about it.

This classification has a number of consequences. One result is that the grandchildren of a father re-enter his class, and that the classes 1 and 2, and 3 and 4, are always changing their names, but even so, for example, a *Kumare* can never come from a *Bunanke*, and vice versa. It also follows that the men already know in advance who is to be their wife. But it can happen, for example, that all *Bunanke* men have no girls; what then? Well, then the *Kumare* have to wait until a *Baltare* girl becomes eligible for marriage. Sometimes it happens that the men come to each other's aid and go to a neighbouring tribe, or that someone steals a wife for himself from a neighbouring tribe, but this usually leads to fighting. But if there is no other solution at hand, the poor fellow just has to wait.

We have with us, for instance, a *Kumare* who, though well up in years, is still single. We had here two *Baltare* girls who according to the rules were his by right. But they did not want to stay with him. Several times he went after them, brought them back and gave them a thorough hiding, but both of them ran away to Englishmen at the nearest station, and have not returned to this day. In the end he seems to have accepted the situation, but not without bad feelings towards the Englishmen, because they kept his wives and did not chase them away.

Right here it ought to be noted that polygamy is rife among the men, and each of them tries to gain as many wives as possible. But in this connection the class system forms a healthy barrier, for without it they would take a lot more wives. One is soon convinced that here as everywhere polygamy is the cause of much mischief and discord, but when one tries to impress this on the Aboriginal men it is very difficult to convince them. They will probably answer: 'Oh yes, it is good for you white men to have one wife, but for us it is good to have two or three!' And if one enquires further why they consider this good, they will answer: 'Well, they have to supply us with *mana* (plant foods); we men provide the *gara* (meat food)', although that is usually not very much. The women have to do the most. The lordly men love to sit in the shade and sleep. I once asked a man (*Baltare*) whom they had to consult when they wanted a wife and what was expected of them? He looked at me in surprise and answered: 'We do nothing. I simply go and say, 'your daughter is a *Kumare*, and therefore she is my wife, because I am a Baltare'. And that is that. He simply takes her, and she is his wife, provided she stays with him.

A final consequence of this classification is that, of necessity, all people of a tribe must be related among themselves, and every grade of relationship has its particular name, but all this is bound up with their system, and it is therefore very difficult to determine the names of the grades of relationship as we understand them, for in individual cases they seem to have a quite different way of looking at it. To date we have not succeeded in our endeavour to clarify all these names with regard to their real significance.

Concerning the intermingling of the members of a tribe among themselves, as also of the neighbouring tribes among themselves, it must be said that this is as good as could possibly be expected of heathen people. Frictions and brawls do occur, but only seldom, and in many cases it is chiefly a matter of making a big noise. Wars involving whole tribes one against the other are rare, nor do they care for an open, honest fight, but prefer to get the better of their enemy with cunning, and they are masters in the art of pretence and hypocrisy.

The language of the Aboriginal people

A unique characteristic of the language of the Aboriginal people of Australia is that it is so very fragmented, so that one could almost say that there are as many, if not languages, then certainly dialects as there are tribes and smaller tribal divisions, for every tribe does not merely have a different dialect but also different words. The fundamental structure is the same in all cases, and one may therefore probably assume that originally they were all one people, but in most cases the words are quite different. I have here a vocabulary of the language of the Aboriginal people at Koperamanna and surrounding area, and another of those who formerly lived at Encounter Bay, but have now died out, but I have not yet found a single word which agrees with the Altolinga language apart from the word for husband or wife (*noa*), which is used here in exactly the same way as at Koperamanna.

How did it happen that this people has been so greatly divided and fragmented? Furthermore, how come that their numbers are so few over the whole of the great island when, after all, they have lived here for a very long time? These are questions which have occupied my thinking a lot and which must concern every thinking observer. If cannibalism had been rife amongst them, or they had been engaged in large-scale warfare, this would provide the explanation, but that just did not take place. Nor can one say that frequent sicknesses of epidemic proportions took a very heavy toll of their numbers. What may be the cause of their very limited numbers? I must admit that I am able to give no other explanation that that which the Scriptures provide in Proverbs 14:34, 'Sin is a reproach to any people'.

As things stand at present one cannot really speak of the people as a *nation*, but only of dispersed remnants of a people, scattered over the whole wide island. To some degree, no doubt, the nature of this land contributed to their enforced dispersion, for no one can live in the great waterless deserts, and this may be the reason, too, for the fragmentation of the language along with the people, and this becomes the more understandable when one considers how far apart the various watercourses are. As in every area of mission work, especially among uncivilised people, so here we have one chief difficulty which first of all has to be overcome, the learning of the language.

What Missionary Büttner wrote in the *Allgemeine Missions-Zeitschrift*, Vol VII, 208, I endorse wholeheartedly, for day by day we experience more and more how difficult it is to proclaim the mysteries of the kingdom of heaven to the heathen in their own language. I cannot do better than to quote the words of the above-mentioned, who says:

> And so it is not merely the task of the missionary to learn foreign and hitherto undeveloped languages, and then quickly preach in them, as a German missionary might preach in Lithuanian or Polish, but whereas they will have to use the heathen language not only to speak of bullocks and sheep (here kangaroos and lizards), of murder and theft, but rather to preach the law and gospel, they immediately find themselves forced to work hard on the language in order to express totally strange concepts, and how much that really has to be said, if the true significance and the real essence of Christianity is to touch the heart, much has to remain unsaid, because for the time being it seems quite impossible to express those things in this language. Only one who has tried to speak about the mysteries of the Kingdom of heaven in such difficult languages will understand how long ago the Roman missionaries to the barbarians believed that it was possible to speak to them of the Christian faith only in Latin.

And that is our position here, and at this time we see no other way out of our predicament than this, that we either speak to them in parables or paraphrase or express the truth or lesson in terms of their understanding.

Just an example: we want to tell them the parable of the Rich Man and the Poor Lazarus. Immediately, we have a difficulty with the words 'rich' and 'poor', of which they have no idea nor any words for them; among them everybody is equally rich and poor. And if we try to explain this by reference to ourselves (we are rich when compared with them), they simply say: 'You are *knira*, i.e. big, we are *gurka*, i.e. small.' What have we gained thereby? Or take words such as these: king, kingdom, power, rule, Kingdom of heaven, etc.; these simply do not exist for them. Whence should they have acquired such a concept? After much hard work we are now able to speak with them, but the further we advance the more one realizes how limited their language is, and how much work is still required before one is able to speak it fluently. In order to teach the children to read we have had printed a primer, not a reader; a long time will elapse before we will be able to provide the latter. Nor are we going to hurry such a publication because, for the time being, the mouth of the missionary is the best Bible and reader.

It is not the linguistic structure of the language nor the lack of concrete terms that makes learning the language so difficult, for the structure is very simple and they have enough concrete concepts, far too many, in fact, so that they name each thing in great detail. No, it is the lack of abstract and especially moral concepts of which they have no idea whatever. The two words *mara* (good) and *kuna* (bad) are almost the only ones and are used for almost all situations.

The structure of their language is simple enough. They decline, e.g. all substantive things in one way, and this declension is very simple, because they have no plural for nouns. The declension is as follows:

	WORD STEM & ENDING	
Nom and Accus	*atu(a)*	the man
Genitive	*atu(ka)*	of the man
Dative	*atu(nga)*	to the man
Vocative	*atu(ai)*	oh, man!
Ablative	*atu(la)*	from the man

Part VI[30]

All the adjectives and pronouns are declined in the same way, but it is difficult to distinguish which is the actual personal or possessive pronoun, since they often use the latter in a personal sense. Adverbs are formed by attaching the syllable *la* to the adjective. If an adjective stands near a noun, only one of the two, usually the noun (substantive) is declined. All words are altered at their ending, never at the beginning, and that by adding syllables or words. These attachments, since they are very much like our prepositions, might be termed postpositions. There are many of these, e.g. *ela* or *lela* = along with (accompanying), where, to; *una* = to, up, in (indicating direction); *ka* (indicates possession and direction); *wane* = in; *kwana* = within, inside; *nda* = only; and still many more. Somewhat more complicated is the conjugation of the verb. They distinguish between 1. transitive and 2. intransitive verbs, and the difference lies in the use of the first person of the personal pronoun, which in transitive verbs is always *ata*, e.g. *ata atuma*, I strike; but in the case of intransitive verbs, *jinga*, e.g. *jinga lima*, I go. Because, however, many words do not only end in *a*, but also begin with the same letter *a*, and it becomes difficult to say clearly the two vowels which are so close together, they do without the one and contract both words. So, for instance, they do not say *ata atuma*, but *atatuma* (N.B. A footnote says that they often omit the opening a altogether and say: *tatuma*, I strike.)

Of numbers they distinguish between three, singular, dual and plural. They have no passive but try to compensate for this by having a third kind of verb, namely the verba reciproca, which can be formed from every other verb by slipping the syllable *li*, e.g. *ilknima*, to wash; *ilkni(li)ma*, to wash oneself. In other instances *lu* is slipped in, perhaps also *la*, e.g. *atu(lu)ma*, to strike or hit oneself; *gama*, to cut; *ga(la)ma*, to cut oneself.

There are only three tenses: present, perfect and future, but they do have various forms of perfect and future. Apart from the indicative and conjunctive mood, they have also the imperative, passive, supine and optative. In addition they have a special form for the expression: 'If I do this or that', which we call conditional, and also a form of announcement: 'Else I will do this or that', which we call denunciative. The auxiliary verb 'to become' is formed by the addition of the word *rima*, or *irima*, which is probably identical with the verb 'to see', *arima*, e.g. *menta*, sick; *mentirima*, to be sick; *kuna*, bad or sick; *kunirima*, to be or to become bad or sick.

The conjugation of the verb is very simple; one merely has to observe the proper use of the pronoun. By way of example I will conjugate one verb in its three tenses and numbers:

PRESENT TENSE

Singular	ta airima	contracted	tairima	I see
	unda airima	"	undairima	you see
	era airima	"	erairima	he sees
Dual	ilina airima	"	ilinairima	we both see
	mbala airima	"	mbalairima	both of you see (you both see)
	eratera airima	"	eraterairima	they both see
Plural	anuna airirima	"	anunairirima	we see
	arangara airirima	"	etnairirima	they see

PERFECT TENSE

Singular	ta airaka	contracted	taraka	I saw
	unda airaka	"	undaraka	you saw
	era airaka	"	eraraka	he saw
Dual	ilina airaka	"	ilinaraka	we both saw
	mbala airaka	"	mbalaraka	you both saw
	eratera airaka	"	eratararaka	they both saw
Plural	anuna airireka	"	anunarireka	we saw
	arangara airireka	"	arangarireka	you saw
	etna airireka	"	etnarireka	they saw

FUTURE TENSE (*x* spoken as *tj*)

Singular	ta airixina	contracted	tairixina	I shall see
	unda airixina	"	undairixina	you shall see
	era airixina	"	erairixina	he shall see
Dual	ilina airixina	"	ilinairixina	we both shall see
	mbala airixina	"	mbalairixina	you both shall see
	eratera airixina	"	eraterairixina	they both shall see
Plural	anuna airirexina	"	anunairirexina	we shall see
	arangara airirexina	"	arangarairirexina	you shall see
	etna airirexina	"	etnairirexina	they shall see

In no way do we desire to claim that we have to some extent mastered the language, even though we are able to converse with them, for much remains which we have not been able to fathom, and how true our first assertion is becomes very clear when we try to translate something into their language, as has been mentioned previously. Again and again it becomes patently clear that much more research has to be done. We have worked very hard on the problem, how to form a noun from any form of the verb, but it appears that nowhere do they do this, and yet how is one to get along without it. For, of necessity, one must have a goodly supply of words if the gospel is to be proclaimed in their language. One continues to hesitate to introduce words from other languages and goes on hoping to find reasonably fitting expressions out of their own language, but I nevertheless believe that eventually we shall have to resort to it. But this, too, has its problems, for while they do not possess the letters f, a, c, sch, q, we would have to prepare them for their use and then explain them. We missionaries find our task doubly difficult because we are dependent on our own limited knowledge and insight and have no aids to help us,[31] nor have we anyone who can support us with advice, help and correction, but rather such as afterward may well find fault with us and criticise us.

Finally, I must add that the enunciation of words by the Aboriginal people usually leaves much to be desired; one speaks this way, the other differently. Some understand us quite well, while others adopt a stupid attitude and suggest that they understand not the slightest. But although we are often fearful we do not despair, but put our trust in the Lord. May he give us the right wisdom in all things and help us, too, to overcome the language barrier.

Finally, I append an example of their language with a literal translation underneath, but must immediately add that I will be grateful for any corrections.

MARK 7:31–37

Atua urbuqa ninta atua Jesuka inirirexika, nana janauka
men some one man to Jesus have brought. he could not hear,

aragalta manta naka. Etna Jesunga inkaka ilqa ekurela tananga
the mouth blunt was. They Jesus asked the hand his on the same

inbaraxika. Jesus nana erilla arbuninga ararakala ilqa ekura
to lay. Jesus the man from the others took aside, the hand his

ilpaka irbuka, boliukala, alinja inbukala, algiranga raka
in the ear placed, did cry, the tongue did touch, into the heaven looked.

alomelamanga hepata! Nana nima: iluai! Iparpa ilpa ekara
saying Ephatha! that is: be loosed! Immediately the ear his

kabula kala alinja iluka, mara era ankaka. Erilla
was opened, his tongue was loosed, well he has spoken. Men

inkaraka tnulkurirekala ankamanga: Jesus irkaraka marilekala
they all startled (amazed) saying: Jesus all done well,

janauriremanga aumanga era lilama, janau karirimanga aukamanga
those unable to hear hearing he makes, those unable to speak speaking

era lilama.
he makes.

Part VII[32]
The religious situation of the Aboriginal people

Many readers will doubtless shake their heads at the above heading and think that it is much too early to submit a definite judgement in the matter since, on our own admission, we have not as yet researched the language sufficiently. I share this opinion and want to make it clear from the outset that this is in no way to be an exhaustive treatment, but that we are here setting forth only as much as we have been able to establish thus far. It is not easy to gain definite facts in this field, not only because of lack of knowledge of the language, but also because they take especial precautions to keep it secret. Since I have already been made aware of this point through several articles in the *Allgemeine Missionszeitschrift*, and am also already the wiser through my own experience, I wish to refer here only to what we have so far recognized as correct, and reserve the right to supplement this section at a later date.

A mere outward observation of the life and activity of the Aboriginal people could lead one to believe that religion is something entirely foreign to them. Even when one has lived among them for a time, one could still be led to have this opinion.

However, that is by no means the case. A closer inspection will reveal traces enough, and the assertion still put forward by some, that there are whole peoples entirely devoid of any religion, is a myth, for even among this so deeply sunken people there are present notions and forebodings of the existence of higher and spirit beings on whom they are dependent. Not only do they believe in the existence of an evil being, concerning whom they have the most peculiar notions and to whom they ascribe all evil things, such as sicknesses and deaths, and so on, but they also believe in the existence of a good being, as we recently learned in a discussion with them. This good being they call *alxira*[33], and ascribe to him the creation of heaven and earth, declaring, too, that he lives in heaven, is favourably disposed towards people, or at least would do them no harm. Here and now I wish to retract and correct my opinion set forth in an earlier report.

This, of course, gives them scant comfort, for they seem to think of *alxira* as sitting still in heaven, while only the evil being, *ranja kuna*, involves himself in the destinies of people in that, as already stated, he causes sicknesses, death, etc, and so they live in constant fear of him. Whether they do anything in an attempt to gain the favour of the evil being or to conciliate it, perhaps through a kind of sacrifice and the like, we have not yet been able to discover. But even these weak notions and premonitions reveal that it would be wrong to describe them as without religion.

Moreover, there is still more to it, for they also believe in the soul living on after death, and in their opinion the soul goes to a place in the north, called *laia*, where they reside in peace. And when they declare that these souls no longer eat *gara*, that is, meat foods, but only *mana*, plant foods, and indeed only fruit, that animals are present there but are not eaten, rather remain always alive—this, in my opinion, is still an idea of paradise lost, even if only residual. Besides, one hears also all sorts of sometimes quite silly fables from them, which they believe with all seriousness, as they are in general very credulous and superstitious, so that there is nothing so monstrous that they do not believe it, especially if one of their own has told it.

So, for instance, they believe, that the two nebulae in the southern sky are two old men with large white beards, who are very angry with all dark people and that they throttle them to death. And when in February of this year the comet was visible, they were in great fear, saying that he wanted to kill them. But we need not be too surprised at that, for even among Christians one finds similar superstition.

Another faint glimmer of religion is to be found in the circumcision of their young men and in their dances. With regard to the circumcision, it must be noted that the boys are not circumcised when they are small children but when they are considered to have reached a mature manhood, that is, when they are from 10 to 12 years of age. No one is permitted to marry before this rite of initiation. We have not had an opportunity to witness such, and it is difficult to gain access, because they are very secretive about it. They do not even speak about it with their own people, women and children, but usually go to a spot that is kept strictly secret. We have learned only this, that those who are circumcised have to stay there until their wound is completely healed; if they run away, they are brought back by force. They have told us, too, how the young men cut an artery on their arm with a stone, and that the old men drink the squirting blood, which is supposed to make them strong again.

After this operation the artery is bound up. Several men showed us a number of such scars.

The dances, in which occasionally women and children may participate, are more public and, depending on whether men alone or men and women together participate, each dance has its particular name. On these occasions they do their utmost to decorate themselves. In our opinion it is no real adornment, but then tastes vary. A detailed description would take us too far afield and would not help much since it is hard to visualise the scene without having actually witnessed the proceedings. The chief points are: firstly, they are able to gyrate their bodies and limbs with great gusto and adopt the strangest of poses; secondly, the stomping of their feet on the resounding earth; thirdly, their singing or, better, their weird noise, while dancing. There is very little music in their singing, for it is really only a sing-song kind of speech; what matters is the rhythm. If the women take part, two choirs are formed, the men on the one side, the women on the other. The women always sing an octave higher, sometimes two. The dance is usually performed by from 4 to 8 men; all the others sing, or they keep the beat with the *mera* or another stick. When their singing has gone lower, so that they are unable to continue, they switch over to an octave higher. Herewith a sample of such a song:

[1. is repeated freely, 2. is repeated in G.
3. is repeated in C. Below line = The same as 1.]

When they have sung this long enough in the key of C, they begin again, as mentioned previously, an octave higher. 'But what do the words of the song signify?' many a person will ask. And this is the strangest thing: they themselves do not know. They have learnt it from their forefathers, but no longer know what they are singing, and one looks in vain for the words in their language. They have many such songs, and a different one for every dance. If, e.g. they have slain an emu,[34] they use a particular song, and, again, a different one when someone has died, etc.

When considering all this, certain questions involuntarily arise: What is the origin of all these notions of higher beings, of the continuation of the soul after death? Where do all these customs and practices among them come from? Whence come the dances and songs, and the peculiar circumstance connected with them, that of all the tribes I have come to know, all know and sing the same songs without knowing what they are saying? My opinion is this: No doubt these people must have immigrated into these parts in very early times as one people and only in later times were fragmented into innumerable tribes and sub-tribes because of the nature of the land. Furthermore, they must have at that time had a higher degree of culture, which was gradually diminished as the body of the people disintegrated and the people were scattered, and so, too, their language suffered accordingly.

In all likelihood their dances and songs initially had religious significance, but along with the cultural decline followed the loss of the religious meaning of these songs; only the word-sounds were inherited by tradition from one generation to the next.

Similarly, circumcision originally would probably have had a greater religious significance than it has now. In fact, all the customs and practices, not only those alluded to here, including the class system are, in my opinion, remnants of an earlier culture. In addition, it is also possible that as we gain a better knowledge of their language we will gain new insights into these matters, including whether any tradition has been preserved, from whence their forefathers came—matters which have not been clarified so far.

One can also clearly see in these people how deeply the need of religion is impressed on the human spirit, along with the truth of scripture: 'Sin is a reproach to any people' and 'Considering themselves to be wise, they became fools.'

Finally, it should be mentioned that men are to be found among them who profess to have knowledge of healing, but unfortunately their art is limited to a few surgical experiments, and these are so childish and silly that one needs a lot of superstition to ascribe to them any success; they are actually nothing more or better than conjuror tricks which make one laugh, even against one's will. Since I have referred to this in a previous report, I can refer you to that.[35]

To work among these people, to bring to them the blessings of the gospel of Jesus Christ—this is our task. Will this not prove to be a vain undertaking? Seemingly, yes; but we will not lose heart, but continue faithfully with the Lord's help. The work is, of course, very considerable; it is as though we first have to provide the soil into which the seed is to be sown. First of all we have to teach them the very simplest truths, and that demands patience and much hard work. May the Lord preserve us from working in vain and grant us fruit in his good time; and even if here the words of our Lord in John 4: 37, 38 should apply, our weak effort will not have been in vain.

7. Our missionary work and other circumstances

Since we have begun our real work among the heathen barely a year ago, and because of our limited knowledge of the language and its imperfections, so that our actual mission work has had to be conducted in a rather clumsy and rudimentary manner, surely everybody will excuse me if I express myself briefly in this matter, especially since I have already here and there mentioned these things in other reports.

Much remains to be done in linguistic research before one is able to proclaim to them freely the mysteries of the kingdom of God. Often it seems to take too long, but impatience will not help us and here, as always, any rash or precipitate action would do no good. So far we have concentrated especially on the rising generation. We have instructed the children in the requisite primary subjects of writing and reading, and have begun, too, with memorising and singing; and we must say that, contrary to our expectations, they have made good progress. Lately we have drawn in to a greater extent the adults and told them simple Bible stories from the book of Genesis and also some from the New Testament. At first we were very discouraged because they seemed to grasp nothing of it at all; but lately there have been signs of improvement. We have not yet begun to preach, for apart from lack of fluency in the language, we realise that this would not be worthwhile. First of all, if I may express myself this way, we have to teach them to listen. This we try to achieve by asking them questions on the stories we have told them and by discussing the story with them. For us this has the added advantage that we are the better introduced into the language. Since Brother L Schulze is absent at present, this work has especially fallen to me, while Brother Schwarz has especially taken care of the school, but we assist and support one another in both areas. Recently we instructed them in the basics of geography, which seemed both very strange as well as interesting to them; after only one day's instruction most of them came to know the five world continents and are able to point them out on a map of the world. They were very surprised to learn that there were other lands apart from their own, and that there was so much water in the world when their own land has so little. This, too, must serve to help them in their understanding of biblical truths, as they observe that God who has created all this must indeed be a mighty being.

And so it is with everything. The many things other children already know must first be taught. So, e.g. they have no system of reckoning time because they can only count to two, and whatever exceeds this number they call either *urbura* (some) or *njara* (many), the latter being used when it exceeds the number of their fingers. Accordingly, we have taught them the numbers from 1 to 10, on which they are now able to build further, and now we are busy teaching them divisions of time into weeks and months, because these are often mentioned in Holy Scripture, and because without such knowledge it is difficult to make the relevant stories clear to them.

And, finally, a little on our own circumstances and conditions. As in the homes of all genuine Christians, so here every day begins with a communal morning devotion and closes with an evening devotion consisting of a hymn, scripture reading, prayer, creed and the apostolic blessing. Every Sunday we conduct a forenoon divine service, using the liturgy of the Lüneburg Church as far as this is possible in our small congregation. However, as soon as our brothers and sisters arrive, we intend to use the worship service in full. We take it in turns to preach. On Sunday evenings we assemble for Bible study. At present we are studying a chapter of the prophet Isaiah on each evening. A harmonium accompanies us in the singing of our hymns, both in our divine services and our devotions. For a long time we had to use an ordinary room for our divine services, but now we have our small church and are able to edify ourselves therein. The whole church and school building is 30 feet long and 16 feet wide. It is built of timber frames. The Aboriginal people helped quite well with the plastering of the walls and with the whitewashing of the walls and ceiling. This was pleasing because for the greater part the building was erected for their special benefit, more so since the school takes in the larger portion, being 18 feet long and 16 feet wide, whereas the church section is only 12 feet long. The church is called 'Bethlehem'.

Nothing more remains to be said, but if I should have overlooked anything or failed to describe anything in sufficient detail, I would ask you to draw my attention to it, for I am willing to make amends.

And now I would ask you, dear Pastor, to remember us faithfully in prayer, that the Lord would strengthen us in our difficult task with his strength, that he would give us wisdom in all things, and, above all, love towards the poor depraved heathen, which we often lack, and that he would in his own good time crown our weak efforts with his rich blessing.

H Kempe

Hermannsburg, 23 December 1880

16.

Business Matters, More Arrivals, New Church and School, Christmas

Financial Management

Heidenreich is happy. Financially, in the first part of 1880 the mission is in a healthy position, due to the ongoing faithful support of the Hermannsburg community in Germany, generous giving from the Australian congregations and the subsidy from the government.

Heidenreich was a meticulous accountant, constantly ensuring that his financial figures and books are accurate to the last penny. On the mission station itself the missionaries were the same, and it seems that Kempe shouldered most (if not all) the financial responsibility. Any discrepancies or shortfalls in the accounts were embarrassing.

This attention to financial detail was regarded by Heidenreich and the missionaries as no more than right Christian living. However, they were also aware of the eyes of the outside world upon them, and more than once speak about the good witness they need to demonstrate to that world by their honesty and accountability in matters financial.

The mission was also handling quite substantial amounts of money. It is not always easy to determine the particular currency one or the other of the writers is referring to when citing figures. Mostly, though, they dealt in British sterling.

Nor is it always easy to determine the value of money then in comparison to now. For an attempt to provide at least some idea of the equivalents, see under *Currency* on Page 47.

15 April 1880, Bethany[1] *(Heidenreich to Th Harms)*
Highly esteemed, dearly loved Father!
It is with a thankful heart that I notify you that I have received the draft of £200 sterling through Major Rauschenbusch, as well as a record for £50 sterling from teacher Topp for our printery, as also other small sums from Pastors Georg and Wiese, all of whom I have given receipts. We are also collecting for the repayment of the principal debt; I will ask Major Rauschenbusch to publish and acknowledge the amounts in the *Kreuzblatt*, and

will enter it here in our ledgers as having been received from Hermannsburg. I consider that to be the simplest and most proper procedure for you and for us.

Thanks to God, generous donations are coming in from the congregations here despite all resistance, so that we have covered all expenses to the present, including the new purchases of over three tons [of provisions for the mission], £115 sterling, and we have paid for three years of the so-called pocket money for our missionaries and colonists. The last thing gives me the most joy; for it is a mere £12 sterling per year for a married missionary, £8 sterling for one unmarried, and £6 sterling for a colonist.

With our meagre resources we have retained the rate of payment from the old mission; but it will give me great joy if in time we are able to raise that. Despite that small amount, after the deduction of what they have received, we still have the amount of £132 sterling and several shillings. As said, all of that has been paid for out of revenue from the congregations.

Yesterday, in the Mission Council, we discovered we were so well-off that we decided to pay off £150 sterling of our capital debt, to put £100 sterling in the bank on interest, and to attempt with the rest to pay off the new freight charges of £180 sterling as well as the travel costs of the fiancées who are coming. The faithful Lord must certainly still bestow much more in addition. He will also supply us for the other debt of £300 sterling on top of that, for he has plenty of gold and silver, for which I am happy…

G A Heidenreich

* * *

In other good news, Heidenreich receives assurances of government support through the Minister for Education, who is responsible also for the administration of Aboriginal affairs. All of this support is immensely helpful in the mission's efforts to become self-supporting and self-sustaining.

20 April 1880, Bethany[2] *(Heidenreich to ELSA members)*
Dear mission congregations,
    … I can this time report on God's continuing gracious help in our mission… The government had earlier granted significant aid for the use of our pupils as well as for sick and weak heathen, likewise for the blind, lame and crippled generally, who are also to be found among the Aboriginal people of our land. In meeting the lack of material assistance we are afforded the

opportunity of sharing spiritual blessings. Despite their inborn wanderlust, the Aboriginal people now stay on the station...

The first large consignment of food and blankets, etc. could not last long in view of the large number of Aboriginal people. Our Missionary Schwarz therefore submitted a request for another shipment in due course... [Mr Krichauf MP and I met with the Minister for Education in Adelaide.] He received us very cordially and we had a good discussion with him. He spoke most warmly in favour of the proposal and stressed that our missionaries had proved that it was possible to pursue agriculture in the far North. It was of such great importance that, even if only a little wheat, barley or maize could be farmed, significant expenditure, currently £60 a ton, could be saved. As soon as our missionaries have made it possible to grow enough grain to make bread, he was willing to supply them with a hand-mill of the latest construction that he had seen at the Sydney Exhibition. With this mill enough flour could be prepared for Whites and Blacks that, in quality, would be the full equal of so-called second-class flour. We expressed our sincere thanks for this offer and assured the Minister everything would be done by the superintendents and by the mission personnel to reach the goal of growing grain for making bread on the spot.

I had to report in detail to the Minister how much new land had been prepared for agriculture, how things stood with physical work, as well as with missionary work, and furthermore supply an inventory of everything on the station, and such other things. We asked again for the Aboriginal people to be supplied with four tons of flour and corresponding amounts of tea and sugar, likewise blankets, shirts and dresses and other things, stating that we were not in a position to pay for the freight, since we had only recently sent off a load of provisions to our mission personnel and had to meet the high freight charges. He agreed to consider this and to support it at the ministerial council. I have now received the written reply that our petition has been granted.

I can also happily inform you that the school booklet in the Aldulinga language has been produced in the government printery after Missionary Kempe checked the proofs. The booklet is very valuable, and pupils can now have it in their own hands as a primer and reader...

G Heidenreich

* * *

Heidenreich is also concerned about the legal status of the mission station. This, too, is an issue that crops up from time to time and it relates to both the property itself and also its buildings and accoutrements.

22 April 1880, Bethany[3] *(Heidenreich to Th Harms)*
Highly esteemed, dearly loved Father!

... Only one thing is lacking, and that is a registered title from me with our government of all the property, possessions and livestock, that guarantees Hermannsburg its rights for ever. This legal title can be filed in court only by me under certain conditions, which you must first sanction. I have to lodge a certificate here so that after my death everything is placed in the hands of my advisory board until a new superintendent named by you, or the respective director, takes my place.

It is my intention that we both settle this important matter while we are still alive...

G A Heidenreich

* * *

Schulze, too, is happy with the agricultural and pastoral endeavours on the mission, despite the dry season. However, the school has its unique challenges.

23 April 1880, Hermannsburg[4] *(Schulze to ELSA members)*
Dear mission congregations!

... From February to November last year, the Lord frequently visited our land with wonderful rains. Our hearts rejoiced, and the desire was awakened in us and also expressed to the Lord in prayer to grant us such rains every year, allowing us to sow and reap plentifully, so that the burden for our mission congregations might be diminished. It would be a small thing for our Almighty Lord to water our land, but he has again not done that. Why not? Here the Lord's words apply: 'His counsel is marvellous, etc.' The Lord thinks this is the best thing for us. If we do not yet understand that this is so, he will reveal it to us, and we will have cause to praise him.

Now to the situation with agriculture this year. If we turn our attention to our breeding of animals, our heart is again joyful. The horses now number some 60 (66), the cattle some 40 (43) the sheep and lambs number over 3000 (3500), though we have used a good number of sheep as well as bullocks for our kitchen in winter.

Lack of feed forced us to drive the ewes at lambing time to Alkarabanta, the sheep camp of the previous year. That was not what we wanted, because we could not conduct our communal divine services there. Furthermore, an extra man had to go there as cook. Yet we are happy that the Lord has richly blessed us with lambs despite all the dry fodder. We now have as many as in the previous year (800) and hope for more.

Going on to actual mission work, there also joy and pain alternate when working with the poor heathen. One is happy about this one and that one in the classroom, but then suddenly one of them is completely gone. When he returns after a short or long time, all that was learnt is forgotten, and the progress of others is held up. If one takes them to task they laugh and say: 'What's the point of schooling? Why must we always be learning to read and write?' They are unfortunately comfortable in their old state and do not want anything better...

L Schulze

* * *

The under-current of chafing between Heidrenreich and Kempe resurfaces in this next letter. What was it between these two men, one wonders. Different personalities, different backgrounds, differences in age, perhaps. The reference to Saxony and Hanover is curious. Both men came from Saxony; but in some way there is a superiority in Hanover with which Heidenreich has coped, but Kempe has not. There is something ironic about his reference to 'self-important people'.

12 May 1880, Bethany[5] *(Heidenreich to Th Harms)*
Highly honoured, much-loved Father!
... Missionary Kempe has begun to write an extensive report to you.[6] On the whole it is good, but could be better and more succinct, yet it is still a commendable piece of work by him. In some places I had to make improvements, and it is good that these appear in parenthesis in the relevant places. He is a Saxon and Hanover has never become his second home. To give a clear insight into our entire mission territory and my earlier report I have had our treasurer Schmidt's daughter draw up for you a detailed map, which will be very welcome to you. I do not like meddling with the work of others, and so I thought the best was a new map with exact details...

I am also sending you a draft of the statutes that I ask you to proof-read... I must tell you that I would never have surrendered the local mission to the State Church. Nor would I ever do so for, until now, this mission has a legal identity only in my person, and therefore it had already become such a heavy responsibility for us not to allow you or me to hand it over to the bloated spirits of self-important people.

However, because to this point the mission [i.e. the mission site itself and all matters relating to the government] depends so much on my person, it is possible that in the event of my death my successor could unwittingly let the mission again fall into the hands of the local Church. That is why I have drafted the statutes, want to have them included in the deed, and ensure that I can establish the rights of the Hermannsburg Evangelical Lutheran Mission Corporation with the government. Then every successor will have to observe the statutes, or can, without damage to the mission, be dismissed by the directors. I am now aiming for that goal, and when everything has turned out well, by God's grace, I can lay my head to rest. Hurry, for it seems to me that I have little time left on earth.[7] ...

G A Heidenreich

* * *

30 June 1880, Bethany[8] *(Heidenreich to ELSA members)*
Dear Mission congregations.

Our faithful God and Saviour has in recent times ruled over us with graciousness and discipline, as the letters to me from our dear missionaries show. To the divine visitation there belongs, in particular, the increasing indisposition of almost all the mission folk caused by scurvy. Different medicines have had no effect, so we have now sent new ones with the mail, and they must consider changing their diet. This sickness comes with a second visitation of God in the North with the extreme dryness. Our brothers and sisters could sow nothing, either in the garden or paddock, so they have no vegetables, the best medicine for the above malady...

Our people do not lack work. They are hard at work building a large school that they also want to use as a church. All the material was already on the place: stone, lime, wood, etc. Missionary Kempe was, for a time, cook for the shepherd Holtermann on the outstation. While doing his literary work, he also cut reeds for the kitchen roof; they just had to be fetched with the wagon...

Missionary Schwarz has journeyed about 30 miles into the MacDonnell Ranges to a cattle station, but has found our place ten times better than that one...

G A Heidenreich

* * *

[Undated] July-September 1880 (?), Hermannsburg[9] *(Schwarz to Th Harms)*
Dear Pastor,

I earnestly ask you not to hold it against me that I am this time writing somewhat briefly; for some weeks I have been suffering more than usual with my sore eyes and so can barely read and write what I have to.

As far as we know and understand, what the faithful Lord has done with us in the last three months is as follows:

First, he has preserved all us mission brothers and sisters sound and well, so that everyone could carry out their assigned tasks.

In addition, he has preserved and graced us daily with his pure and undefiled Word, and granted our bodies what they need, even if not all at the one and self-same table, since two of us have to be on the outstation to look after the sheep. Since 14 days ago we are divided into three groups, for on the 2nd of this month[10] Brothers L Schulze and Jürgens started on their journey with the wagon, to bring the fiancées, a trip that well may take about a year.

Secondly, the Lord has continually blessed us with the presence of the poor heathen, both grown-ups and children. They have remained fairly constantly on our place, so that in this quarter we daily had an average of 15 students. This gave us much joy, for learning is now more a pleasure than a burden for them. I could tell many a praiseworthy thing about this cheerful bunch, but must unfortunately refrain from doing so.

Thirdly, the Lord has increased our holdings of both small and large animals. The sheep increased by 900, with horses and cattle increasing according to their number. May he who has granted this blessing also see to it that he provides the animals with fodder, since already there is no longer any fodder for the herds both here and on the outstation. If God does not soon send sufficient rain, we will be forced to establish another sheep station.

This year it is dry everywhere. Since New Year it has rained only moderately on one day (namely 25 July). As yet we have noticed no benefit from that, since early August the present continuing cold weather prevents growth and, besides that, the dry east wind has already dried everything out. Far and wide there is no vegetation or grass to be seen, least of all in our gardens.

Everything is desolate also on our agricultural land because the severe drought did not allow us to sow seed. Consequently, this year we cannot count on harvesting any grain.

The Lord's counsel is, however, wonderful and he carries it out gloriously. He is the source of our confidence, so he will look after us also this year. The Old Man has to learn patience, which is a good thing, though difficult.

Fifthly,[11] with respect to our other work, this consists of building a church and school for the station. Today we are already completing the erection of the roof. Next summer we hope to use the building for its intended purposes.

So, we are not lacking physical labour. In fact, we have more work than ever since the journey of the brothers leaves us with two workers less...

W F Schwarz

* * *

Kempe wrote the quarterly report to Harms for July to September, and in it he included brief information on the dry weather, their stomach complaints, progress in building the new school and church, and the absence of Schulze and Jürgens as they head South to collect their fiancées. Because these matters are reported elsewhere, that part of this report has been omitted here.

However, the bulk of the report is devoted to another of those reflections on the Aboriginal people that one might wish he had not written. A significant point of interest is the criticism the mission is receiving from certain quarters over the lack of converts, and Kempe's response to that criticism.

1 October 1880, Hermannsburg[12] *(Kempe to Th Harms)*
Dear Pastor!

... One cannot expect great success in a short time with people that have sunken so deeply as the local heathen. The folk back home would like to receive wonderful reports of conversion. They imagine the heathen to be like the degenerate creatures at home who have thrown overboard all traces of Christianity that still abound in the old Christendom. But this view is wrong, because the heathen have sunken incomparably deeper than anyone in old Christendom. Why?

Quite apart from the fact that they[13] have all been baptised and that the Lord through his Spirit continues to work in their hearts, they are still carried and influenced by Christian customs since their youth, even if they do not know this or want to acknowledge it. That is totally missing with the local heathen. Back home the seed can be sown in soil that has, to a certain degree, been prepared. By comparison, the land here must first be made arable. That takes a lot of work and patience. All the views and feelings of the heathen have to be turned upside down, as it were. They have to be instructed to adopt completely different views and taught different customs, all of which is to serve what they see and hear from us. It is totally beyond their comprehension that we are here among them not to get rich but to speak to them the Word of God. Everything they see and hear with us is foreign: that we are always working, that we have a separate day for resting and hearing God's Word, that we sing and pray every morning and evening, that we build houses and live in them permanently, that we are always clothed, that we have only one wife, one who has a completely different status with us. All that, as small as it might seem to be, must serve to convince them that we have something better than they. They cannot escape this influence; it affects them without them knowing it, though we can see it well.

I give only one example. During the time when we were first here, we could seldom get any people to work for us, because they would be mocked by others. The situation has changed totally, with the opposite now being the case. Those who work here are envied by the others since they now see that an ordered life is much better than roaming about continuously. That is what is happening with everyone. Without them noticing it, their total view of things is changed.

All that belongs to the preparatory work, to preparing the soil, so that they more and more learn to grasp what it is about God's Word that it is not merely a way of speaking but truth and life.

How are these heathen in their natural state to understand anything about God's Word? That there is one God who created and maintains heaven and earth they do not comprehend but believe that everything has always existed. All of this first has to be taught them. How are they otherwise to understand that this God is a being who is more than a mere human and who thus has the power to punish and reward people according to how they form their attitudes to him? We are already telling them stories from the sacred scriptures, but they are a long way from understanding more than the mere words and getting to the real meaning. Our work can serve to teach them how to rightly understand God's Word. To prepare the way, long sermons are not needed, and we do not preach any, but simply tell Bible stories, discussing them and referring to them as often as opportunity arises.

Our whole way of life must also play a role in this preparatory work; they well understand that we are different people compared to the other Europeans living here.

For example, they well understand that they are not to use disgraceful swear words that they hear other Europeans using and, unfortunately, soon learn to imitate. The only trace of religion they show is the opinion that there is an evil being who causes sickness, death and all the evil that they fear.

We had the chance to note that several times in the last quarter when three persons suddenly died, one after the other. First was a small child with a burn wound on the knee, then a blind woman, and finally a man who had been a cripple for a long time and always had to be transported from one place to the other. In them we saw how bleak their situation is, and what it means to die like heathen who have no hope. When I asked them whether they fear death they all said, 'Yes.' At that I told them that we were not afraid since we knew we would go to heaven, because we believed in the Lord Jesus who said: 'Whoever believes in me will never die.'

At that one of them wanted to demonstrate his courage and replied that he, too, was not afraid. I said to him, 'Why then did you recently run away from Brother Schulze?' (He had taken him along on his travels.) 'Did you not say that the Blacks down South wanted to kill you? So you were scared to die.' At this he did not know how to reply and was ashamed, for he is otherwise a very timid man who can be frightened and terrified by the slightest thing.

So our work progresses well, even if slowly, and I am convinced that when some have made their way to being baptised, others will soon follow them.

As I said, that cannot happen quickly. Indeed, I believe none of the men will get so far because they are too rarely here. Thus we have to focus most of our attention on the next generation, especially on the children. It is what we have so far preferred to do, teaching the children to write and read, reading them Bible stories and having them learn Bible texts until they are able to recite them, especially those that deal with the essence and characteristics of God, to teach them some idea of God. Some children learn quickly and give us much joy. The worst of it is that when the parents go away, they take their children with them. Naturally, when they come back, they have forgotten much, and in many respects we have to begin all over again.

An old man was here on the station for nearly a year, together with his four very gifted children who made good progress and were the most advanced among the pupils. In the month of August he went away with his wife and children, possibly for a long time. That is a pity for the children. Had they remained here, something really good could have been achieved with them. The desire to go walkabout is too deeply ingrained in their flesh and blood to let them endure remaining stationary in one place. This will certainly not soon change. Once a few of them are baptised, there can perhaps be a chance of blessing. As things stand, the situation is bad…

H Kempe

* * *

More New Arrivals

Already anticipated in recent letters, the next lot of personnel for the mission have arrived. Their ship, the *Chimborazo*, docked in Adelaide on 11 August 1880. It had sailed from Plymouth on 26 June. Destined for the Centre were the fiancées of Schulze (Charlotte Gutmann) and H Jürgens (Dorothea Schiermann), as well as settler Heinrich Wolf.

As indicated, Schulze and Jürgens had left the mission station on 2 July, with a wagon, to pick up the new arrivals. Our letters and reports had no information about their trip down (another indication of missing material). But in *The silver miner's son*, Altmann says that 'the weather was so cold that Jürgens had taken his feather bed to be more comfortable at nights ... (and) that the drinking water was poor so the women [on the station] sent some dried cake with [Schulze] on account of his stomach trouble.' (55)

When the pair reached Farina, Schulze went ahead by himself. In his upcoming report of 18 January 1881, Schulze says that he travelled from Edeowie to Bethany by train, and Altmann says he was 'carrying the mail'. (55) Schulze arranged for Jürgens to wait for him at Edeowie until he came back on the return journey, presumably to care for the horses and wagons which would not have been able to travel by train with them (expense no doubt being the major factor in this).

In a letter to Harms of 15 October,[14] Heidenreich reports that he had picked up the travellers from Adelaide, and they stayed with him in Bethany. While there they attended the annual mission festival at Rosenthal. Heidenreich later provides a fuller report in the *Kirchenbote*.

1 December 1880, Bethany[15] *(Heidenreich to ELSA members)*
Dear Mission congregations.
... The brides of Missionary Schulze and the settler Jürgens were in attendance at the mission festival, as also the colonist Heinrich Wolf, sent with them from Hermannsburg. They were present to be edified with us in our most sacred faith, and to receive strength for the holy work of mission. They are three humble souls who will be a blessing to the mission.

The brother of Missionary Dierks, well known among us and now in New Zealand, brought them to Pastor Homann in Adelaide. From there they found refuge with me until Missionary Schulze came to Bethany on 1 October, while settler Jürgens drove to the last rail station at Edeowie to wait for them there. Everything had to happen in a great hurry, and there were so many questions, so much to say, to buy, to pack, and to send off.

When all this was reasonably put in order, there was Schulze's wedding on 7 October at my place. On the last day a large crate was packed with dried fruit, honey, jam, butter, eggs, bacon, sausages and ham that my dear people at Bethany and Schönborn generously supplied. It was packed up, loaded at night, and next morning they went to Adelaide with Brother Ahrens to make new purchases and to set many other things in order.

Loaded up with many goods from Germany and here, our travellers went to Port Augusta by ship, where they had to put most of it in storage until transportation became easier. From there they travelled with the rest of their things by train to Edeowie, where Jürgens' wedding was conducted by Schulze.

After everything was loaded and the horses rounded up in preparation for setting off, they discovered one of their horses in a waterhole. Despite all efforts, the poor animal was lost. Then a young horse fell sick, and they had to buy three horses. The blow was unexpected, so it was felt acutely by us in financial terms. This proves once again that the most expensive cartage to the North is with one's own wagon. I have experienced that enough when travelling there. We are not the only ones to do so, but also the government and cattle station owners prefer to pay £80 a ton for transportation than to drive their own wagon teams.

What were we to do in the present case? Schulze was already underway with the wagon, the brides were here. All our efforts to get them to Peake with the mail or by camel proved futile. Thus, we had to accept what we could not change and commend it to God. He rescued us from fear for the lives of people and animals by sending wonderful rain. It was all the more welcome since the news from all around us was depressing. Reviewing God's ways, I must say to his honour: He has directed everything for the best with his grace and mercy, for has not our gracious God spread his wings over us when we were in great fear and distress?

According to the latest news, our dear travellers are making rapid progress and send you all many greetings from Beltana. I also have oral reports about their journey up to Alice Creek. By now they will have passed the miserable Finniss at the southernmost point of Lake Eyre. They are eagerly awaited at the station where the brothers and sisters cannot manage all the work, especially the two wives of the Missionaries Kempe and Schwarz. With diligence and industry they take care of the feeding and needs of the pupils, but have an intolerable workload. May the Lord soon give them the help of the two young women and, furthermore, give them joy and blessing to influence the hearts of the poor heathen with quiet Christian behaviour...

Your Heidenreich

* * *

From the next letter, it is apparent that Schulze ruffled Heidenreich's feathers by some 'unauthorised' activity, putting himself offside with other Church officials in the process. Heidenreich's strong language about it all does not augur well for his and Schulze's relationship, especially considering that, according to Altmann, the two were supposed to be close friends.[16]

3 December 1880, Bethany[17] *(Heidenreich to Th Harms)*
Highly honoured, much-loved Father!
... Missionary Schulze has caused us a lot of trouble and unnecessary heavy expenses by his unauthorised departure. He has already purchased three horses on his way back and I shudder to think what might still come. God grant that I am able to spare you new distress, and that Schulze humbly pays homage to the truth. He was faithfully warned by Kempe and Schwarz against taking this step.

Here in the Mission Council he first wanted to push the blame onto them until I showed him Kempe's letter to me on the matter. Even then he still asserted that he was right, until I explained to him: I have no choice but to place the matter before our Father. Only on the morning of his departure did he give in, and he told councillor Ahrens, whom I sent him with him to make purchases and to provision the departure, that he would give it back again to the other missionaries.[18]

Had he not done this, out of love for you I would have reserved the right to take the first action, but now it would be a sin against our holy undertaking if I did not prepare you, as well as the brothers on the station, so that he can be met on all sides with love and seriousness. Again I say, God grant that I do not need to write a word more to you about this.

In private I am sorry for his quiet, gentle wife whom we have grown very fond of, together with the rest of the brothers and sisters on the trip under the domineering and tyrannical personality of Schulze which revealed itself in a noticeable way in the presence of Brother Ahrens on the way from Bethany to Port Adelaide. Because we know that God resists the proud, we have to be prepared for much, and fervently pray that God gives him a contrite heart.

Unfortunately, this trip has already cost us £300, and I ask you to send me a money order soon, especially since the harvest here has turned out poor and little [money] is coming in.
Heidenreich

* * *

Pastoral Interlude

Interspersed with these letters, Heidenreich recounts touching experiences with one of his colleagues, Dietrich Georg, pastor at Emmaus-Peters Hill parish, and a classmate of Kempe and Schwarz. These happenings provide us a glimpse of Heidenreich's pastoral heart.

15 October 1880, Bethany[19] *(Heidenreich to Th Harms)*
… I am a really unlucky person, for I always have to bring you bitterness with joy. This time it is my dear, precious brother, Pastor Georg, in Emmaus. He gave the main sermon at the mission festival in Rosenthal on 29 September this year. After that we had the conference and I drove home in the evening and left him with his dear wife. Next day I received a postcard from him saying he was coughing blood and was still in Rosenthal. I immediately sent my son on horseback to him and issued him an invitation to the wedding conducted by Schulze. He had just arrived and had to leave with the others as soon as possible. My son brought news that Pastor Georg was on the mend, and he came to the wedding with his wife and eldest daughter. The danger seemed to be over. He travelled home with his splendid wife, but the coughing up of blood returned and he lies prostrate without hope.

Unfortunately, I cannot get there for three weeks to serve his congregations. I soon have confirmation, my wife is expecting her confinement any day, I have to go to Hahndorf for a Church Council meeting, and I still have school exams in two congregations. But I long to see him so acutely since I have no one else who has the same mind as I. For me, his loss would be irreplaceable in the immediate future. O please pray with me for him and his poor Maria who, in addition to everything, is carrying a third child under her heart. If at all possible, write a few lines to the good Georg…
    G A Heidenreich

3 December 1880, Bethany[20] *(Heidenreich to Th Harms)*
… On the first Sunday of Advent I was with Pastor Georg to confirm his[21] children and to serve his congregation with preaching and sacrament. Thank God, he is recovering but, according to the testimony of his doctor with whom I spent a half an hour in private, it could be a very long time before he is allowed to preach again. We discussed back and forth what we should do to procure help in serving his parish. Since the doctor suggested

he take a holiday in New Zealand, I had a good mind to call the last-arrived Dierks to act as a locum. However, this suggestion ran into difficulties, since Georg could not undertake the journey because of his wife and, then, because you would first have to give Dierks orders, and we could not wait so long for help.

So, we moved on to another plan, to call a preacher in consultation with you to serve as a co-worker [with him] and, after this has been set up with Georg, to turn our two parishes into three, for at present I have five congregations, and Georg will soon be forming his fourth. My congregation at Neukirch has a manse that could serve as the pastoral hub, and it would be in the middle between us. We agreed on this and, since he had to apply to the President for further pastoral help for his parish, I let him suggest the following: He would now go to the peninsula and, if his condition did not soon improve, it would be better for his congregation to call from you a co-worker for him. This will be discussed at the next session, and I will be able to tell you more after that. All this must remain between us. What I am doing I do for you alone, that you can act at the appropriate time in both cases…

Heidenreich

* * *

Dedication of the Church and School

For some months now the mission staff has been busy erecting their church and school, long anticipating the joyous occasion of the dedication of this important part of their ministry. This occurred on 12 November. Both Kempe and Schwarz reported this event. However, in the interests of space, only Kempe's report is included here, as the more detailed of the two. Schwarz's is available in *The Translation*.

Even though the building is really quite small (considering it contains both the church and the school), and even though it would have been relatively crude and naive, the community celebrates this occasion as if they are dedicating a cathedral in Germany! This is so very impressive, for the seriousness of the service and the ceremony around it are a witness to the Ntaria community of the sense of the sacred within Christianity. There is something absolutely moving about the whole enterprise; i.e. both the building and its dedication.

November 1880, Hermannsburg[22] *(Kempe to ELSA members)*
The main thing I must report this month is the dedication of our church or chapel, called Bethlehem.

First, I must briefly describe it. The entire building is 30 feet long and 16 feet wide, built in half-timber. In plastering and whitewashing the walls and ceiling, the Aboriginal people gave us lots of help, though it was mainly built for them. It includes the school; in fact, the school takes up most of the space, being 18 by 16 feet, while the chapel is only 12 feet long.

A dividing wall separates the church and school. Since the whole building is constructed with half-timbered panelling, we had to add a verandah 6 feet deep all round it to protect the walls against wind and rain. The whole building is an ornament to the station, especially since it is carefully whitewashed on the exterior. As already mentioned, the church is 12 feet wide and 16 feet long.[23]

Facing east, there are windows on both sides of the altar, with a window also on the western side. Out of necessity we made the entrance from the school, otherwise we would have always had to walk right around the building. This is not usual for a church, but here we could do nothing else. The altar is built of bricks, and the text above it reads, 'Blessed are those who are invited to the marriage feast of the lamb.' Left of the altar stands the pulpit, made out of one piece of wood, a hollow tree, with the text on the front, 'The word of the Lord endures forever.' The harmonium stands alongside it to the west, and on the western wall are the pews for the listeners. We hope their number will increase in time with the heathen being incorporated into our congregation by baptism. The dedication took place on Friday, 12 November, in the evening, so that the shepherds could also participate.

We first assembled in our old house in which we had held our services until now. After we had sung the first two verses of the hymn, 'God has hitherto brought us', Brother Schwarz read Psalm 121, and together we all knelt down to thank the Lord for the blessing we had received from his Word and Sacrament. Then we proceeded to our new little church, singing the last verse of the hymn just named. Pastor (Brother Schwarz) and congregation first sung the *Te Deum Laudamus* responsively, or: 'Lord God, we praise you'. Then Brother Schwarz conducted the liturgy and, kneeling in prayer, asked for the blessing of the triune God on what was henceforth to be our house of God.

After we had sung the familiar hymn 'We all believe in one true God', I delivered the dedicatory address, consisting of the following main points:

Text: Genesis 28:16–19.

We have gathered here to dedicate this house as God's house. All of our houses ought to be God's houses, where we come together as community and where, as community, we offer our thanks and praise to the Lord and desire to receive his gracious gifts of Word and Sacrament. Is here, far from all Christians and in the middle of the heathen world, the right place? Yes, certainly. Look at our text. The patriarch Jacob was fleeing from his brother Esau, and while resting during the quiet night under God's open sky he saw the angels of God ascending and descending. The faithful God of the covenant renewed the promises already made to his forefathers. In holy wonder he cries out: 'How blessed is this place; it is nothing other than the house of God, here is the gate of heaven'. Therefore he named the place Bethel, i.e. House of God.

We can be just as certain that the Lord is in this place and that this house is truly God's house, even though it is situated in a spiritual and physical wilderness. May the Lord God grant that it becomes a real Bethel, particularly also for the poor heathen living here. May the living water that flows out of this house in the sacred Word of God and the holy sacraments turn the spiritual desert green so that it becomes a joyful garden of God.

Therefore, the subject of our meditation is

Bethel, i.e. the house of God.

We consider 1) the master of the house, 2) the house community, and 3) the house order.

1). The master of the house is none other than the Lord God, the same God who here appeared to the patriarch Jacob in a dream, the same God whom all the saints of the Old Testament honoured as their God and to whom they prayed.

But we know even more. What God promised in the Old Testament has now been fulfilled. Out of love for us poor sinners, Jesus Christ became a human being. He suffered, died, was buried, rose from the dead, and ascended into heaven. After returning to the Father, he now sends the Holy Spirit. Behold, this God, this true, triune God who has revealed himself in his Word, he is the Lord of the house. He is to be and always remain the Lord also of this house.

Is it not an honour for us poor, sinful human beings that God, the Lord of all lords, the King of all kings, should stoop so low as to dwell with us himself? Yes, he not only wants to be our Lord and King, but also our dear Father.

2). What is the community of this house?

St Paul says in 1 Timothy 3 what the community of the living God is. He first speaks of the household of God and then says that this is the community of the living God, so bringing the two things together into one. And that is how it is, for we confess in the Third Article: 'I believe in one holy Christian church, the community of saints'. We, too, are a small part of this large community of the living God. He is the head, we are the members. He is the light, we are the reflection. He is the master, we are the brothers and sisters. He is ours, we are his.

This community is called the community of saints not as though its members were holy in themselves, but because they have by faith taken hold of Christ's righteousness and holiness. Yet this community should grow both inwardly and outwardly, for the Lord God has placed us in this heathen world as leaven, so that we should by our speech and behaviour bear witness to the grace and truth of Jesus Christ. In this way the heathen will come in great numbers and turn from the power of Satan to the living God. This can happen only if we as a household faithfully and completely adhere to

3). the household order.

This is the gospel order of salvation that is in few words contained in the text, 'God so loved the world, etc.' That should be the main theme of every gospel sermon, also here with us: we are justified by faith alone without the works of the law. But how do we achieve such faith? Article V of the Augsburg Confession provides the answer: 'In order to receive such faith, God has instituted the preaching office, given the gospel and the sacraments through which means he gives the Holy Spirit who creates faith, etc.' We should not despise these God-ordained means, but make use of them often and diligently.

Now may the triune God grant grace that this house is always a true house of God, that we as his community always hold on firmly to his precious Word and the holy sacraments, and that the community continues to grow, also outwardly, so that many poor heathen are incorporated into his church through the washing of new birth and join us in praying to the triune God as their God and Lord, so that this small Bethel will soon be too small. Yes, may the dear Lord grant that, and make us faithful in everything, so that we in the future may pass through a blessed little hour of death into God's blessed heaven where we will have no further need of a house of God, for Almighty God himself and the Lamb will be the temple. Amen.

After that we again joined in kneeling to pray, thanking the Lord for the first fruits of his blessing, and asking for his continued rich blessing in this house. We then sang at the close: 'Remain with your grace'.[24] Indeed, the Lord be thanked for his blessing that is to be the guarantee for further blessings. May he graciously grant that this celebration may leave a lasting blessing in all our hearts.

Otherwise everything is proceeding normally, and nothing worth mentioning has happened. We are now hard at work teaching the children some Christian carols. They seem to like this but it takes a lot of effort to get their untrained and unpractised voices to the point where they can follow some simple melodies. We hope that when they have mastered one or two melodies, others can be learnt with less effort.

The language still provides lots of trouble and a barrier. We daily experience how much we still lack before we can use it to freely preach the gospel.

There is still much work to be done working at the language and with it. We have only recently learnt that they do have a name for God, and indeed ascribe to him the creation of heaven and earth. They say he is in heaven. We have previously helped ourselves out with the name *Goda*, that is, God; but if they have a name in their own language and imagine this being to be a good being, why should we not use this name? I think it much better, if they have a word in their own language, to use that in preference to a foreign name. They then understand much better what one is trying to say.

This month the Lord has granted us another shower of rain on the 19th. It was very welcome for our garden, but otherwise is not of much use because the heat soon dries everything up again. But we thank our faithful Lord for everything.

H Kempe

* * *

And, of course, there's the matter of a bell for the church!

10 December 1880, Bethany[25] (*Heidenreich to Th Harms*)
Highly respected, dear Father!

… You will recall that I wrote about a bell. My congregation has now finally decided on a bell of three hundredweight with the inscription on one side: Evangelical Lutheran Church of Bethany, South Australia, and on the other side: John 8:31–32. You will kindly have this taken care of, since I am not acquainted with any bell makers, and let me know the price, and when a bell of three hundredweight will be sent to me. However, I ask that this be attended to soon because my congregation wants to give our present bell to the mission, and the church on our station is soon to be dedicated.

* * *

Christmas in the new church

At the heart of the last report for 1880 is the oh-so-wonderful account of the first Christmas worship in their new church. As with the dedication service, it is as if they picture themselves in their congregations back home in Germany, and one can only imagine the homesickness they may have experienced at this time.

Yet, around that very special occasion, life goes on as usual.

30 December 1880, Hermannsburg[26] *(Schwarz to Th Harms)*
Dear Pastor!

... First of all, as far as our mission family is concerned, we are healthy and well, including Brother Tündemann, so that all are able to carry out the work assigned to them, though not without the discomfort of having to endure the current great heat, namely, 50° R. As a result, we lose almost all appetite for food. Thank God that we still always have enough water to quench our increased thirst.

It is a miracle of God that we seven brothers and sisters on the station are so far still healthy, despite such great heat, since in more recent times, even with less heat, we were not at all healthy. At the beginning of this month Brother Kempe was laid low in bed with a severe headache, together with an eye ailment. For 14 days at the beginning of October, and then again for some time in November, Brother Mirus had to stop his shepherding work due to a foot problem. Brother Holtermann was always able to carry out his duties, but he complained of great fatigue in all his limbs as well as giddiness in the head and pains in the lower body. My wife suffered especially from a cold fever, with coughing, hoarseness and a runny nose. Last month we were all to a greater or lesser degree afflicted with this latter ailment. Brother Tündemann, who is suffering at the moment from a slight head wound (on 27 December he was hit from behind on the right cheek bone by one of our horses), was also afflicted with an eye ailment. Sister Kempe and I remain the most spared from sickness for this quarter of the year.

All these sicknesses and indispositions have stemmed, for the greater part, from the changeable weather of the previous months. Sometimes it rained and was almost as cold as winter, while 24 hours earlier the temperature reached up to 40° and even more. Still, the Lord, in whose hand lies also the control of the forces of nature, best knows what is good for us. Our wish and prayer are that he might soon again visit us with gracious and saturating rain, so that humans, stock and all creatures of this land are revived. We firmly hope that you, O Lord, are so gracious!

As far as our work is concerned, under God's protection and help we were permitted and able to carry it out during these three months, so we must also say and confess: God be praised! It happily went well. We have been able to continue school lessons without interruption, praise God, even though there were not always many of the same students present. In mid-November, unfortunately, only six students attended. Currently there are 16. Also, as far as the school is concerned, it may be said: Endurance produces character. A year has now flown by since we began the school with the local heathen children; and from the success up to this point we can ascertain with certainty that our previous work has not been in vain, and that our future efforts will not remain without fruit.

Most of the students can read and write, but barely as well as a European child learns in the first year of school. Furthermore, they have mastered a number of Bible texts and stories, together with the holy Ten Commandments and the seven petitions of the Lord's Prayer. They already know the name of the continent on which they live and equally well know the names of the other continents. The names of the days and the months are not completely unknown to them. In addition, on the eve of holy Christmas, the happy black students sang two Christmas songs to the honour of the dear Christ-child.[27] This, then, in brief is what is worth reporting in respect to the school work with which, of course, the language studies go hand in hand...

On 14 November, the 25th Sunday after Trinity, we held the first regular service in Bethlehem Church (for Brother Kempe wants to call it that), and we heartily rejoiced in God for having come so far that the station now has its own special, designated space for this purpose, as well as a large, fine school room alongside it. In the latter, on Christmas day and in the evening of that day, we had an exceedingly lively and joyful celebration. Besides our missionary brothers and sisters and our beloved school youth, all the heathen present at the station, husbands and wives, old and young, from the youngest suckling baby to the oldest old man, everything that had breath, also the blind, dumb, and lame, gathered around the brightly-lit Christmas tree and listened with great attentiveness to the good news from Brother Kempe's mouth.

With faces beaming with joy, the dear school children sang in childlike simplicity the angels' song, translated by Brother Kempe into their language, 'In Bethlehem is born to us a child', and so (unwittingly preachers of the Lord)[28] they gave much joy to the old and young of their people, as well as to us, their teachers. Previously we had hardly any hope that the children would become so accomplished in their singing prior to the festival as to give joy to the Christ-child at his birth with their song.

After the children had brought the gift of their singing to the baby Jesus, the moment that had been so long-awaited by great and small arrived. For, now the gifts designated for the children and working heathen were handed out in return.

These had been laid out for this purpose in an orderly manner on the school tables, each with the name of the intended recipient. First came the six adult workers, one-by-one, each of whom received a new cotton shirt, and a white clay pipe, together with two sticks of tobacco and four sugar cakes. The children were summoned to decipher the attached written name and to hand over the gift. Since two of the workers had children among the students—one of them two and the other three—their great joy was multiplied by the joy of their dear children, who vied to find the name of their father among the six workers, and to triumphantly hand over the gift. In the blink of an eye the six had everything in their eyes, hands and mouths, for into the latter some small ginger nuts that had been hidden inside the sugar cakes immediately found their way.

Now it was the turn of those students who only needed to help themselves, because they had long since found their names. Each of these received a new shirt, as well as five smaller and larger sugar cakes, and just as many small ginger nuts. The boys received a shirt made of white calico with a belt, short sleeves and red stripes on the shoulders. The girls received from our ladies specially made colourful shifts sent to us from Europe. How happy these children were! —and not only they, but also the entire little group of needy heathen present there.

While the students now took off their everyday shirts and put on the new ones, having received permission to do so, all the heathen present (around 60 in number) also each received a small festive gift consisting of two sugar cakes and some ginger nuts. In addition, the men each received half a stick of tobacco. Brother Kempe and I distributed the gifts among the latter, while our wives were busily occupied with the women and small children. Now the joy was even more communal.

Meanwhile, however, the temperature in the room had become pretty humid, so that bright drops of perspiration stood out on the faces and bare bodies of the heathen, even though the door and window were wide open (at the present moment neither window pane nor actual door has been installed), and the room goes right up to the roof without a ceiling. But, regardless of the great heat and the crowd in the school room, not one soul left the place. Only when we brothers and sisters had sung some Christmas songs, had dressed the children with new clothes and, standing on the benches, had sung for the second time *Altjira alkiela*, and then gently encouraged them to go home, only then did they finally leave the room—the women leaving with the small children, after them the menfolk, and then the students. They were allowed to take the new shirts with them straightaway, and to wear them over the festival. They left the old ones behind in the school, to put them back on after the festival. Sadly, during the night between the first and second day of Christmas, two of the dear little ones (Natata, a boy, and Adilka, a quiet, gentle girl) had the misfortune to lose their shirts through fire. However, it was in no way their fault, and they consequently soon afterwards received another shirt, so that on the second festival morning all of the distress that afflicted their child-like hearts was suddenly banished.

We brothers and sisters ended the holy Eve with praise and thanks to the Lord, after we had first moved to the common dining room and taken a little physical refreshment. The Brothers Mirus, Holtermann and Tündemann on this occasion received a small Christmas gift as well. Then at the end of this holy and blessed evening I read sermon No 2 for Christmas Eve from the Hermannsburg festival booklet. Afterwards we bent our knees for the communal evening prayer, and after we had held our devotion went happily to rest. Under the protection and blessing of the Lord we were thus able to celebrate the precious festival in quietness and peace to its end.

On the first festival day, the Brothers Mirus and Holtermann went to the sacred Lord's Supper and rejoiced with the shepherds at Bethlehem that the Saviour was born and died also for them. Meanwhile, Brothers Kempe and Tündemann had gone out in their place to look after the flocks, while I carried out preaching duty for the day.

On the second festival day Brother Kempe preached, and I conducted a Bible study in the evening on Isaiah 57, while Brother Kempe did this on the previous evening on Isaiah 56...

So then, may you too, dear Pastor, together with the dear mission community, pray to the Lord for us, as well as for the local heathen, that they might have a receptive heart for the joyous good news, so that they will turn from the darkness to the light that shines a thousand times brighter, and with more joy and blessing than all the Christmas tree candles in the whole world.

How and where our dear brothers and sisters who are travelling celebrated the beloved Christmas festival, they will tell you themselves. We do not know how things are with them at the moment, for we have received no news of them for three months. However, we daily remember our brothers and sisters in prayer, and hope to God that they are safe and well and will soon arrive to be with us...

For you, dear Pastor, we cordially wish and pray all the best for the new year, 1881. Greetings to you, together with your dear family, and the whole mission community, also on behalf of all the brothers and sisters here.

Your unworthy, W F Schwarz

***

Meanwhile, in the rest of the world in 1880:

- Construction of the Panama Canal began (1 January), and after 632 years in the making, Cologne cathedral was completed, the building having commenced in 1248 (14 August).
- There was an assassination attempt on Tsar Alexander II of Russia (17 February).
- The First Boer War broke out between Britain and the South African Republic (Transvaal), 16 December.
- In the UK general election, Gladstone defeated Disraeli for the second time (April 18).
- In New Jersey, Thomas Edison conducted the first test of the electric railway (May 13).
- Future American general Douglas MacArthur was born (26 January). So was Helen Keller, future writer, born deaf and blind (27 June), and John Flynn, pioneer of the flying doctor service in Central Australia (25 November).
- Australian bushranger, Ned Kelly, was hanged in Melbourne (11 November).

17.

A Year in the Life of the Mission

1881

It was still an isolated, desolate and sparsely populated place in which to live, but by the beginning of 1881 the Centre was showing signs of upturn in activity and growth compared to when the missionaries arrived in Ntaria four years before. The Northern Territory population was around 9800 (3450 Whites and 6350 Aboriginal people),[1] with pockets of settlements in both Alice Springs and Darwin. Pastoral stations or runs had marginally developed and mining was shaping up as a promising investment. Transportation systems were still very basic (horse, wagon, camel), and, though expanding, road networks were mostly little more than dirt tracks. A railway line was under construction.

Consequently, more people were travelling more and further. The Hermannsburg mission station was part of that increasing busyness.

So, as 1881 begins, staff members are on their way back from Adelaide to the mission. Some of these will stay, others will leave. And every now and then a wandering traveller calls in, one to visit, another to work.

What, then, typically happened over the course of a year on the mission? This chapter provides an almost uninterrupted look at the wide and varied activities that occupy the time and energy of the expanding mission on the Finke over the course of 12 months.

18 January 1881[2] *(Schulze to Harms)*

The new arrivals on the way

Dear Pastor,

You may well be aware that I am on a journey again and, as directed by the Superintendent, I have to write a report to you about it. However, our trip is not proceeding as fast as I had expected or wished for, so I believe it might be quite acceptable to you to hear something of our earlier activity.

On 2 July last year, Jürgens and myself set out from our mission station with horses and wagon. Because of the drought everyone was longing for rain. The rain eventually came in September, to everyone's great joy. We had to take several days off because of the rain, but we did so gladly, with the expectation of then being able to travel all the faster.

I left Brother Jürgens with the horses and wagon at Edeowie, while I continued per train to Bethany,[3] where I arrived on 30 September 1880.

After the Superintendent conducted our marriage on 5 October and some purchases had been made on Thursday, 7 October, I set out on the return journey together with my wife and the new arrivals. Because of the pressing work up at the station, I wanted to return as soon as possible. Furthermore, I did not want to miss out on the result of the rains—the wonderful rain water and the green feed—so we left early. We arrived back at Edeowie on Thursday, 14 October 1880. This is a cattle station about 120 English miles north of Port Augusta.

The railway which is being built from Port Augusta to 'The Gums' (Farina), about 230 miles, is finished up to Edeowie. Only half of this section, from Port Augusta to Wonoka, has been opened for public traffic. There I asked the railway building inspector if he would take us up to Edeowie, which he did. Now we had a choice where to take our seats, either on a load of rails, or a load of sleepers. We chose the latter because the rails were rather rusty, but the choice was a bad one, since the sleepers started to slide about and gave us a lot of anxiety. At the first stop we changed over to the load of rails; at least they did not move about.

On the day of our arrival at Edeowie, I performed the marriage of Jürgens in a tent. The lush green and the beautiful flowering bushes did their best to enhance the celebration.

After we got all the boxes and crates in order, we left Edeowie the following week. What a joy it was to travel through the wonderful meadows of green grass and beautiful flowering bushes. No one would have been inwardly more cheerful than I was, as I had high hopes that our journey would have a blessed continuation and that we would reach our destination soon, with God's help.

At sandy Bagot, there was a beautiful rain water hole and ten miles beyond 'The Gums' (Farina) there was a delightful region. We stayed there for several days because of the good pasture.

When we left there, it was as if we had been taken to a different country, and so it remained up to here (Strangways Springs). On this stretch of 150 miles, nothing has come up after that September rain; desolate and empty, like a desert, that is what this region looks like.

People have different opinions about the ineffectiveness of the rain in this area. Some say, 'It gets too cold after the rains'. Further south and 50 miles west of here there is the most beautiful grass and it is just as cold. I agree with the opinion of others that the cause lies in the salty soil. The whole region is literally littered with sodium and other minerals. They must surely have an influence on the soil. It may well be that this soil needs more warmth to produce some growth, which was not the case after this last rain.

The rain enticed out many carters or drivers, but nearly all had bad experiences. One bullock driver, who was driving with us and helped us over the difficult sandhills, had lost 12 bullocks on such a short trip. Another lost four horses, and so on. You may well understand that one is in low spirits and anxious at heart. I lie down at night and get up in the morning in this state.

I was ever so glad when we reached Strangways Springs on the third day of Christmas. Three of our horses have become rather skinny. The following day after our arrival I sent Jürgens with the horses to pasture 14 miles away, and he was to stay with them until they recovered. All too soon I got the sad news that two of them had died. It is a bad blow for us, especially since we had barely enough horses anyway and, besides, I hear that 90 miles away around Charlotte Waters all the water is said to have dried up. Therefore, all passage is cut off until rain comes again. Oh, that the Lord would have pity on us and send beautiful rain soon; everything up here is languishing for it so very much. Pray about it earnestly, you and the mission congregation.

We have, praise God, no complaints about our well-being, not counting such trifles as the effects of the heat or the bad water. Around Christmas we had 112°F temperature in the shade, and one often does not know what to do in this intense heat. There is barely enough room for two to sit in the doorway on the wagon, and then the head pushes the canvas roof up. The coolest spot is under the wagon. Each one of us tries to get there to carry out their tasks, such as eating, writing, reading, sewing or knitting, etc. Most have to do this lying down or partly sitting up, as one can hardly sit up.

You see what gross inconveniences this life entails, especially for the women who are concerned with the daily washing and changing of clothes, and so on. It is fortunate that we have no strangers with us...

Louis Schulze

* * *

Inter-Church Relationships: Germany, Missourians

To our shame, we Lutherans have a frightening capacity for arguing with and dividing from each other. Not only is this aptitude painful to live with; it is also a poor witness to the world.

Those statements are not intended to discourage respectful disagreement and healthy, robust debate. However, Lutheran history all too often shows us stumbling over our ability to deal with differences; and, instead of these becoming healthy stepping stones to a more dynamic and vibrant Church, they become brick walls between people and stagnation and death to the Church.

Already in *Missionaries, Madness and Miracles* there have been instances of this kind of behaviour. Now, in this next letter Kempe refers to two other lots of similar division and potential for division. Each of these will recur in future chapters, and each has been the subject of articles and books of their own. Here we provide the briefest of summaries of the two thorny issues, and leave readers to follow up each for themselves.

The first disagreement takes place in Germany. We have previously noted the early divisions that led to the first Lutherans deciding to emigrate to Australia, and those were around pressure to combine Lutheran and Reformed into a 'united' State Church. Now, however, those forces are again being felt in Hermannsburg, Germany, where elements of a more liberal theology are raising their head. There are also whispers of a possible move back to a relationship with the State Church, which would bring financial and other benefits to the Hermannsburgers in Germany; and, while those debates are essentially matters for the Lutherans in Germany, they also are felt in Australia, both among the missionaries and other ELSA members, who still have ecclesiastical, personal and emotional bonds with the Church 'back home'.

The second disagreement is centred on the Missouri Synod in the United States. For some years the ELSA and Missouri Synod had developed an ecclesiastical friendship which, in 1881, resulted in the sending of the first Missouri Synod pastor to Australia, K Dorsch. More pastors followed, and their presence caused tension on two fronts. Firstly, the Missouri influence prompted movement away from the Hermannsburg Mission Society as the provider of pastoral supply to Australia. (Although, this particular tie was already being weakened by the possible Hermannsburg alignment with the State Church). And, secondly, there was tension over theological differences between certain parts of the ELSA and Missouri.

One of those main differences was around the issue Kempe names in the next letter: divine election. Without going into interminable detail on a topic that can be mystifying to many people at the best of times, the basic question was: On what basis does God elect people to salvation? The stated Missouri position, simply put, was that God's election to salvation is an act of God's grace, through which people are elected to faith, brought to faith. The opposing view was that only those who have already been brought to faith are those whom God elects to salvation.

There were other doctrinal differences (around chiliasm, lodges, for example). But the main one was the question of election.

20 January 1881[4] *(Kempe to Th Harms)*

Melon seeds and inter-church tensions

Dear Pastor!

With this letter I am sending you, dear Pastor, a small packet of melon seeds. They are very fine fruit, the best we have. I need only note, assuming that they arrive there safely, that they should be planted in a very sunny spot. They like warmth and soil that is not too wet. The fruit is ripe when the stems begin to wither. The flesh of the fruit inside is red and tastes very good. They can be eaten like or instead of cucumber salad.

I am happy that this gives me the chance to write a private letter to you since all official correspondence has to pass through the hands of the Superintendent. So one can better and on a more confidential manner say what is on one's heart than is the case with official letters.

We are now following with amazement and interest the church developments back home where the struggle is once again blazing in every corner and in every camp. It often turns out that just those whose reliability could not be counted on, do fall away in the decisive moment, thus fulfilling what the old father Simeon said when he prophesied over the infant Jesus.[5] The behaviour of Inspector von Lüpke[6] has offended us most of all. We cannot grasp, even now, that he has thereby gone back on everything he taught us in Dogmatics. Still more troubling are the arguments and strife in the Lutheran Free Churches themselves. Especially offensive is the attitude of the Missourians which almost means that if one is not with the Missouri Synod one cannot be saved. One can sense this blunt attitude also in our Synod. Then again, here on earth there never will be peace and concord. The strife is itself a sign that the church is still alive. We have never feared that the measures of the State Church would harm our Lutheran mission, but one is amazed that the wise have forgotten the advice of Gamaliel.[7]

H Kempe

20 January 1881[8] *(Kempe to Th Harms)*

The heat, plight of the Aboriginal people, their fear of death

Dear Pastor!

Just now our mission is certainly going through a severe testing, but it is just as certain that the Lord will not allow his people to go to ruin and leave them in the lurch. And so, forward we go, in humility and the strength of faith alone! Nor are we here spared trials, especially since it seems that the faithful Lord this year is treating us quite harshly in physical matters. There is such cruel heat here this summer, such as has never before been experienced, with the thermometer rising up to 55°R on several days. For the past two months a hot wind has been blowing every day so that it is barely tolerable; the sweat just streams down the body. We used to have various plants and trees that at first stood magnificently—even various kinds of cereals. But the hot, dry wind has totally dried up all of that. Our wish and daily prayer is now for rain so that the air might once again be cooled down a bit.

Nonetheless, we believe that the Lord has good intentions for us, even though we are not able to understand them. One often has to feel shame over the poor heathen here. We still have meat and bread, but we still often murmur our complaints, while the poor heathen have to make do with their roots and seeds and water, and are nevertheless always content with that. They also have many other things which should reasonably be expected of Christians, and yet are so rare, e.g. compassion and sympathy for the misfortune of others who are close to them. We have again been able to observe that these days. In order to tell you about that I have to digress somewhat.

Already in November 1880, there was completely unusual heat, hotter than it had ever been around this time. At the beginning of December there were some storms, accompanied by some rain. As a consequence, the atmosphere was cooled so suddenly that one could easily put up with wearing a thick coat. This sudden change from extreme heat to the greatest possible cold produced many ills, eye infections and encephalitis, fever, runny noses and the like. It was not only the heathen who succumbed to these illnesses, but also almost all Europeans. Nearly all of us here suffered. This sickness has greatly increased among the heathen living at Owens Springs where five alone died while our people were spared, except for a girl who has been blinded in one eye as a result of the sickness.

Now, the heathen believe that when one of their tribe dies, the people of another tribe are to blame for this. That was the case in this instance as well, and this time suspicion fell on our people. On the evening of the 2nd Sunday after Epiphany, the heathen came to us with the report that men from another tribe had come from the east to kill them, and for the whole night they [the Aboriginal people] did not leave the station, apart from a few men who wanted to see this for themselves.

Then, on Monday, two women and their children came here with considerable wounds. As it turned out, these did not result from spearing. They had received them on their flight over the hills and in the scrub. However, they brought the news that a man by the name of Kolkinja[9] had been murdered. This man usually stayed quite alone with his family at Gilbert Springs, 25 miles from here, and he was, so to speak, the middle-man or watchman between this tribe and the western tribe. The murderers knew this, and for this reason they had chosen him as a victim, because as an individual he was not able to offer resistance.

Immediately, a number of men set out to look for him, and on Tuesday they returned with the sad news that he was dead and they had buried him. He had several spear wounds in his shoulders, back, and chest. Then the wailing and weeping immediately began; and they howl and wail almost the whole night, and each evening begin all over again.

The dead man has often been here, sometimes for quite a while, and we are really sorry that he lost his life in this way.

If one thinks about it, one has to be a bit surprised that these poor heathen are still so compassionate and brotherly, so that the suffering of one is regarded as the suffering of the community. Many Christians could learn from that.

On the other hand, one also sees how they are still life-long slaves to their fear of death, so that they live in constant fear, with one unable to trust the other. Satan has so completely blinded them that they cannot understand that diseases are not caused by humans but by something else. When one sees this, one would very much like to be able to persuade them that it is not what they think. Indeed, one can become very impatient at not being able to talk better with them about the grace of God, as is the case. The extremely inadequate language still leaves us much to work on. We are indeed able to speak with them, but as soon as one comes to speak of spiritual and moral matters one bumps into all sorts of difficulties because they have no way of expressing these things in their language, so that one is forced to paraphrase and explain every single word.

Just one example: law. We want to tell them that God punishes evil and rewards goodness. So, one has first of all to explain to them what is meant by punishment, or use an expression that they understand, and then explain.

The same applies to the word 'reward' and the concepts of good and evil, for what they call good and evil is often the exact opposite of its correct meaning. That often takes too long for us, and we would much rather prefer to capture the fortress by storm than to deal with a drawn-out siege. But that does not work. And so it is a case of us continuing to work with patience. May God grant that our work is not in vain ...

H Kempe

2 February 1881[10] *(Heidenreich to Harms)*

The travellers, rations, Baron von Müller, the harvest, statutes

Highly honoured, much-loved Father!

... The travel party under the leadership of Missionary Schulze has barely covered half of the way, and is now quartered with Mr Hogarth at Strangway Springs. Since there is no water up on the track, and two draught horses have again fallen, I have today by a telegram given the instruction to Schulze to remain there until it rains so that we suffer no more losses of property and life. People and stock have food and water there until the Lord gives further help. We have to buy two more horses there and whatever else becomes necessary. Thank God that our dear brothers and sisters are safe and well despite the hardship on the difficult journey.

The Minister for Education has also this time received the annual report with approval. I showed him from the distribution list of our station that we each month need almost 1000 pounds of flour for the school children, old people and nursing mothers, and asked him to approve that amount of flour and rations annually from now on. He asked me whether this approval was to the benefit of the mission. I replied, 'Yes, for without the government support of provision for the heathen we could not successfully continue this costly work'. 'Good,' he said, 'then attach a letter to this report that I will support in the Council of Ministers.' At the same time I asked him where the rations sent last April were; our missionaries had no news of them. He immediately checked his papers and saw that they were at Peake in November, and said, 'I intend shortly to wire Alice Springs to make inquiries'. I said to him, 'It is better to contact Charlotte Waters', so he did that. Soon after the answer came: 'No water or people at the station'. The minister then said, 'I will send them in writing the reply that I have received'. But unfortunately the rations are still 60 miles below Charlotte Waters and without rain cannot reach our brothers'. I am glad that our own rations were on the station before Christmas.

Baron von Müller, who at great expense equipped an expedition to explore Central Australia and has written the book about Mr Giles, is one of the world's greatest botanists and has been honoured with orders by almost all living princes. He is also a warm friend of our mission. With great care he supplies the mission, free of charge, with seeds of fruit and grass from around the world. He is constantly in contact by letter with our missionaries, giving advice and directions, and has these days expressed praise for our missionaries and the mission's work to our treasurer, Carl Schmidt, and promised his further help with advice and action.[11]

We also have to thank God that he allows people with such knowledge and skills to consider our poor work worthy of using their gifts and goods for the betterment of the mission ...

Now something more about the necessary evil.[12] ... I ask you to let us have the cost of the bell as soon as you know it, and to indicate the total amount including transportation costs, so that I can immediately pay the amount here. It will be quite difficult for me to request that you send some money by cheque since I know that there are many claims on your finances. Yet I cannot help it. I intended to sell young geldings, but in the present circumstances we cannot bring them South without most of them being lost by death.

The harvest has turned out to be very sad ... Pastor Georg is still quite sick, which is also a setback for our finances.

Synod will soon take place and about £1000 will have to be found for the High School.[13] Homann and Bertram have attained their goal of having two pastors called from Missouri.

I still have no word from you about the statutes and the incorporation of the local mission. This is as necessary as one's daily bread. In the eyes of the state and the world we have no legal power ...

G A Heidenreich

* * *

In earlier correspondence to Harms Heidenreich has broached the topic of his (Heidenreich's) son, Georg, undertaking his education with the Hermannsburg Mission Society in Germany. Harms has been amenable to the proposal.

Estimating in today's currency the cost of young George's education (plus other related expenses such as books, travel and so on) is difficult to do. However, using the guidelines suggested earlier in the section on *Currency*, it is evidently a substantial amount. Yet Heidenreich never seems to have personal financial concerns. In fact, he is able to assist the mission out on more than one occasion with funds from his own pocket. One gets the impression he was a reasonably wealthy man.

11 February 1881[14] *(Th Harms to Heidenreich)*

School fees, church bell, and Schulze

My dear Heidenreich,

With regard to your son, Georg, I inform you that Inspector Schüren would very much like to take him into his house. If it does not seem too high to you, he is asking for 130 to 150 marks annually, everything included. If that is too high, he is satisfied with less for board. However, I think that the desired amount will not seem too great for you. Naturally, you will have to pay extra for books and clothing. He is in very good hands with Schüren, and his wife is an outstanding person, a real mother to her wards.

I have ordered the bell from the bellmaker Otto in H—lingen near …, the same man who so beautifully made our set of three bells. He delivers them at the very low price of 115 marks a hundredweight, which for three hundredweight is 345 marks … The bell will be ready in ten weeks and will come to you via Bremerhaven. Otto himself will eventually write to you. You will certainly receive an excellent bell. Bellcaster Otto deserves to be recommended over there by you.

It gives me great joy that your congregation wants to give its old bell to the mission. Pass on to it warm greetings from me and thanks in my name. May the Lord reward it…

What you wrote to me about Brother Schulze's wilfulness has deeply troubled me. Keep a sharp eye on him; when necessary, rebuke him lovingly and earnestly. If absolutely necessary, refer him to me so that I can do what is expected of me …

Th Harms

16 March 1881[15] *(Heidenreich to Th Harms)*

The travellers, Wolf pulling out, rations, finances

Highly honoured, sincerely loved Father!

... Brother Schulze and the travelling party are well, but they have to wait in Strangway until rain comes. Impatience plagues them there, and Wolf wants to come back. But I will seek to stop him, because we need a shepherd, and that is better for everyone.

This time, the Minister for Education has given five and a half tons of flour and 400 pounds of sugar for our heathen, with the freight and purchase price over £800 sterling in value... Our treasury has consumption,[16] and I am waiting for help from you for it in the near future. Because of the failed harvest, our mission sponsors also are not able to do as much as usual. We have paid off everything up until now, and also paid the £190 sterling for the freight, but we have an overdraft with the bank of £80. Admittedly, I have personally stood security for £300 with our bankers here, but we have to buy two more horses for the travellers, and we have to pay the incoming bills from the station, with the result that we have to limit ourselves very considerably...

G A Heidenreich

30 March 1881[17] *(Kempe to Th Harms)*

Drought, transport disruptions, school news, a murder, a birth

Dear Pastor!

... It is not without some degree of anxiety that I submit the report for this quarter. We would much rather always report only pleasant matters, but what I have to report this time is really not very pleasant at all—at least, it does not seem to be that way to us. We are in a really tight spot; and what now brings us yet again into a tight spot is the long-lasting drought, and everything else connected with it. This time it seems to have stretched across the whole Australian continent, for on all sides one reads complaints about it in the papers. However, the Centre has been visited especially hard by it, for we have received no satisfactory rain here since 1879. The rain that did fall came in winter and has produced little, very little, fodder. In addition, this summer, in the months from December to March, there was really severe heat and an unusually stronger and drier easterly wind. So, things now look terribly bleak. In many places the stock are already dying in great numbers from a lack of water and feed. Several human lives, too, have already fallen victim to the drought. They died on the road from thirst before they were able to reach water. However, that applies less to us, for we still have enough feed and water; and even if it is not very close, it is still within reaching distance. Consequently, together with our sheep, we have driven about 12 miles north-west from here.

Because of all this, we also have to put up with what goes together with such a drought, namely, that on the one hand all transport has been discontinued because no driver can travel under such circumstances, and so it is difficult to receive provisions and other things. On the other hand, because their food supply is continually becoming more scarce, the heathen increasingly move away from here, and the more so because we are unable to provide them with any provisions from the government. Although these provisions were sent up already a year ago, the driver is not able to take them any further but has to wait until the rain comes. Just this is what is most necessary at this time, because even the usual supplies for the heathen are now so very scarce.

In addition to that, Brother Schulze, together with Brother Jürgens, has driven down South with the wagon, but on account of the drought cannot travel back here again before the rain comes.

If we had a lot of work before, we have so much more now, since we have been forced by the drought to drove the sheep further away, so that our few resources are now also split up. We do not know how things will turn out; we freely admit that we are at our wits' end.

Under such circumstances it is natural that no gardening or agricultural work can be considered. Even the melons, which we usually had in abundance all year, failed us this year. How often the question arises in our hearts: Why does the Lord want to do this? For him it is just a small thing to provide help and counsel. Why does he not do that?

Now, certainly his ways are always the best, and so also here the Lord will have his wise purposes, though we are not quite able to understand them at all.

Nevertheless, our work with and for the heathen is constantly progressing, and the children in the school particularly bring us much joy. The only pity is that there are now so few here: on average we have had 10 to 12 in the school. Some of them are making good progress, and the memory work especially is much better than it used to be. Only, independent thinking about anything still does not seem to be working. It is just impossible to say how lazy they are in their thinking. They readily understand what they are told, but to think for themselves simply does not occur to them.

A really troubling case occurred at the beginning of this year that once again gives us a glimpse into the dark night of their superstitions. It happened on the 2nd Sunday after Epiphany, when in the evening the heathen came to the station extremely worked up, and reported to us that a number of men from the neighbouring tribe at Owen Springs had come and murdered one of their own. Initially, we thought this was just empty chatter. However, it proved to be true; for on the Tuesday several men came and told us that a man by the name of Kalkinya, who had very often been here on the station, had been murdered, and they had buried him.

The usual wailing for the dead immediately began.

But why was this man murdered? He was simply a victim of their superstition. In December he had brought an epidemic to the heathen in Owen Springs, and this had carried off a lot of people.

Now, the heathen believe that if a number of a tribe die in a short period, then of necessity the people of another tribe must have caused that. And so they go seeking revenge, even if it is only one person who falls into their hands. This shows how deeply they have sunken, how they no longer have anything at all of natural nobility; for it does not at all occur to them to have it out with their supposed enemies in an open, honourable fight, but they seek to sneak up on their victim with cunning and deceit. So, they chose a man who they knew usually resided with his family in a somewhat isolated place. And it is quite astounding what cunning they employed to achieve their purpose. For example, in order to get the local heathen to believe that only one man had come in, they all got in a row, and each of those following behind stepped exactly in the footprints of the one in front. Furthermore, to leave as few traces as possible, they also stepped on pieces of stick and stone that were lying on the track, in order to get their pursuers off their trail.

We now sought by every means to persuade the local heathen not to take revenge again in such a way. As far as we know up until now no more [revenge killings] have been carried out, even though that was their strong inclination. When will light shine in their pitch-black hearts? God have mercy on these poor, poor people, and bless our weak efforts to that end.

As I have already said above, the dear Lord has graciously kept us from serious illness, so that we have always been able to continue our work. The Lord has granted me a special measure of grace in that, on 28 January, my dear wife was happily delivered of a baby son.[18] May the Lord God grant that children will soon also be born to him from among the heathen, just like the dew at dawn...

H Kempe

26 April 1881[19] *(Heidenreich to Th Harms)*

This and that from Heidenreich

Highly honoured, much-loved Father!

... Sincere thanks for your welcome, valued letter of February this year and for sending the first and second money orders for £200 from Major von Rauschenbusch...I have straightaway written to our dear missionaries about altar vessels and clothing for the heathen...

We are certainly under pressure because of lack of rain, both for the station and for our travellers...

I am surprised that you make no mention of the statutes that I sent. Have they reached you? Or has your work not reached me?

Please greet Inspector Schüren; I accept his offer with thanks. I want to see how my Heinrich[20] goes in confirmation instruction; perhaps I will send both of them, if the Lord wills.

George is making his new teacher very happy in learning English and German. It is a pity that he is so timid about the long voyage...

We are all happy about the bell, and the bellmaker will, no doubt, receive more orders. How do you want to handle it? Shall I pay the money for the bell into the mission account here, or send it to you? If it is not yet packed up when you receive this, could my books by Dächsel, ordered from our printery, be packed in with it? ...

Pastor Georg is somewhat better. I spoke with him on Palm Sunday when I confirmed his children at Peters Hill. But he has become very weak mentally, which is the more painful for me since we are likely facing conflicts that I have always wanted to avoid for the sake of the mission. But the Missourians want war, so they will get it. They are starting on again about marriage... They will also gladly receive the announcement from the Buffalo Synod that 'the Hermannsburg people in America are to continue to study in America', for that is in tune with Homann's statement at the Dutton Synod that 'in Hermannsburg they do not learn enough'...

G A Heidenreich

22 May 1881[21] (Schulze to Th Harms)

The travellers, Mrs Jürgens pregnant, rain, Wolf leaves

... We are on our way again and are now, with the Lord's help, only 150 English miles from our place. We hope to get up there in the week of Pentecost, but not with our heavy wagon, but with a light one that Mr Hogarth did the favour of selling to me for £45.

On this we loaded the most necessary possessions, especially for the women, and drove off commending ourselves to God, leaving behind the heavy wagon, to be fetched after the rain. What drove me to leave Strangways, where we had been for three months, was the evermore approaching confinement of Mrs Jürgens. I was not in a very happy mood when thinking of the long, waterless stages ahead, although we had had a light rain and that allowed us to travel faster ...

It was Wednesday after Easter when we drove off from Strangways. On the stretch to Peake we received a few drops of rain as a down payment for what the dear Lord would further send us at the right time and hour, and that is what happened. The long, waterless stages begin after the Cadnowy Springs, 30 miles this side of Peake. We camped there for several days to let the horses recover; fortunately, there was good fodder there.

Just when we were harnessing up to travel on by night so that the horses would not get so thirsty on this long stretch, what should happen? The skies were covered in thick clouds, especially where we were headed, and it soon began to rain, so that we had to unharness the horses and stay there. But it was only a good shower with which we were not really satisfied.

[Then] during the night, solid rain fell so that next day water was lying everywhere in small holes and depressions. My heart leapt for joy over this really precious gift. We could now for the first time travel by day thus making our journey in short or long stages as we wished, and as our horses desired. We could also travel in a straight line, without needing to make many detours to visit wells.

The showers fell right up to Charlotte Waters, which was the last long, waterless stretch. As we got close to there, the precious rainwater again became very scarce. The last of it, where we camped for a night, was residual water on the ground, as thick as mud. The Lord had so graciously brought us through the waterless region. Had we left Strangways earlier or later, we would have been without the rainwater. So we have special reason to thank the Lord.

We have likewise not yet had such cold nights as we have otherwise had about this time, when one really froze with cold, despite fire and blankets. Here there are now wells in the creeks. We hope that we have the worst behind us. Please pray faithfully that the dear Lord sends a proper rain so that the large creeks run and all waterholes are filled, allowing heavy vehicles again to travel. Otherwise, all rations have to be sent up by camel, which is more expensive.

I have certainly reported to our Director about Brother Wolf. I have described everything in detail for him, so I have only to briefly note a few things. He went back home at Strangways. All my arguments and appeals for him to stay were in vain. He said it was too hot for him here, that his chest could not take it any longer, to which I replied that if that were the case, he could die in the service of the Lord and what harm was there with that? To which he replied: 'One does not have to ruin one's health.'

When he said this I said nothing and then let him have his own way. But I asked him, as I had already done several times, that he should first write to you and wait for an answer. He answered, as always, that he had paid his own travel costs and so was in a quite different position from us. I rebutted this without success. As he was leaving I again asked him to visit you since you would be happy to have an oral report from us; at this he remained silent.

As far as I have learned to understand him, it is chiefly the food and drink that have moved him to travel back South. Our food here is very basic; at mealtimes we do not have the potatoes and vegetables that he spoke about, though the latter are necessary for our physical well-being. That is why so many people up here suffer from scurvy. We, too, have it to a greater or lesser degree.

I do not know if anyone has written to you requesting settlers. We absolutely have to have a shepherd. It would be good if you were able to send us a really skilled man who knows how to handle horses or wants to do that. Naturally, he must be a person of special ability whom one can send out into the wilderness without being worried that he will get lost. Jürgens no longer has the desire to stay with the horses and would prefer to be a shepherd. It would be good if more settlers came, so that we could get to more actual mission work…

L Schulze

30 May 1881[22] *(Heidenreich ELSA members)*

Drought, hunger, the school, congregational donations

Dear Mission congregations,

… We have lived through a difficult period at the mission, and I do not have more favourable news in a telegram from Missionary Kempe. The lack of water and fodder was extreme in the North, and our stock had to be brought 12 miles from the station to the upper Finke where new yards and huts were built. Since Missionary Schulze and the Jürgens were still on the return trip, the missionaries had to get the help of labourers. The hunger crisis among the heathen is also said to have been boundless. About that Missionary Kempe wrote: 'In their hunger the heathen eat reeds and cane, everything imaginable and unimaginable. We need help as soon as possible.' …

Missionary Schwarz writes that the school at our station has made wonderful progress. The pupils have learnt some Lenten hymns and sung them lustily with their fine voices. The missionaries were forced to share our rations with the pupils, the sick and labourers to provide as much care as possible, and to alleviate the crisis and keep the school running.

I again express my sincere thanks to the sisters at Hahndorf; courtesy of Brother Wotzke they sent a large wheat bag full of excellent dried fruit for the mission. Likewise, thanks to the dear sister E Nitschke in Krondorf for 40 bottles of tomato sauce and three tins of jam, and to the dear sisters in Schönborn and Bethany for grapes, jam, honey, etc. May the faithful Lord richly reward them and all dear donors of our mission...

Heidenreich

15 June 1881[23] *(Schulze to Th Harms)*

The travellers arrive at the mission station

Dear Pastor,

With the Lord's help we finally finished our long, weary and difficult journey last Saturday.[24] ... We waited for over three months at Strangways for rain and got none; instead, it became drier all the time.

Circumstances concerning Mrs Jürgens forced us to get going on the road as fast as possible ... Because we did not have many horses and we really needed a lighter wagon on the station, I bought one at Strangways. We packed only the most necessary goods on it and departed Wednesday after Easter from there with our horses ...

We would have loved to celebrate the beloved festival of Pentecost at our place, Hermannsburg, but we were unable to reach the station. We had to be patient for another week. I had written to the brothers and sisters at the mission that we would arrive around Pentecost. From that time on no day went by without them looking for us and sending people out to look for us, but always in vain. Last Saturday they gave up all hope of seeing the day of our return come about. Then at long last, shortly before sundown, they saw my wife who had gone ahead with our heathen appear in the distance. But neither Brother Kempe nor Schwarz recognised her at first greeting,[25] until Mrs Kempe told them who it was. Soon after, we pulled up with the wagon.

The farmyard and our buildings were adorned with palm fronds and all sorts of decoration. Even the baker and the cooks had put on a display of their wares for the welcoming meal. Now, thanks be to the Lord, who has not only wondrously led us, but also splendidly brought everything to pass.

As soon as we get a good rain, we will get the heavy wagon up here, too. Pray on our behalf for rain...

Louis Schulze

4 July 1881[26] (*Heidenreich to Th Harms*)

Complaints, business deals, the Missourians again

Highly honoured, much-loved Father!

Brother Schulze and his party have caused us a lot of worry and cost us a ridiculous amount of money. At Strangway Springs alone they chewed up £70 sterling and, finally, against all advice to the contrary, they bought a buggy for £54, while leaving our best wagon with most of its load standing at Strangway. Before it now gets up North, everything will be rotten and, what is more, will cost a lot. Sometimes it has caused my head and heart to ache, and still does, that I cannot change anything.

The brothers on the station have bravely endured and worked in difficult times. On St John's Day ... a telegram arrived from Kempe saying he could sell 1000 mixed sheep at 12 shillings a head, and asking whether he should. Since I was not at home, Brother Schmidt gave the approval. That brings in £800. At the same time Kempe had also traded cattle with our neighbour. His manager had also written to Mr Gilbert who is my neighbour here, and who offered me young cows for sale. Then, through Brother Schmidt, I have asked him what he wants for young cows and mares. I do not yet have his reply. In any case we will soon finalise the sale with him even if we have to pay a few shillings more per head than they cost here. If we wanted to send some from here, they would be just as expensive because of having to take out a loan and the hiring of people, besides which half of the animals could die on the way.

Wolf has unfortunately returned, with the pretext that he cannot stand the climate, nor Schulze. He is at present with me and does not appear to want to go away. His work is not up to much. Tündemann also wants to leave because he cannot get on with the missionaries. We do not think it is good for such people to stay. Also, the missionaries will soon see reason and let the heathen help more with the external work instead of relying on inept people ...

Our people who have become Missourian boldly defend the Missourian false teaching on the election [to salvation] by grace, as well as other errors. That now brings us into open conflict. Unfortunately, not many take their stand with me, but waver to and fro. They even fear that they do not have enough evidence for an attack against the Missourian false teaching. I have tried to remove this fear from them. Pastor Holtermann has written to me from America about the imaginations of Homann. When I invited Homann to a person-to-person conversation, he made all kinds of excuses until his smart wife got involved and criticised me in front of the entire wedding assembly. In due course I put her in her place. Now they are complaining about me everywhere and think that I should, moreover, apologise. However, I am remaining silent. I have written to Holtermann that he himself should write to Homann about the whole fraud.

I am very pleased that, with your attack, you are coming to my help at just the right time, though the harm done is still very hurtful. Yet we can help in no other way than to defend ourselves against harm, with God's help. On 11 July I have parish conference where we will demand from the Church Council clear proof that Missouri does not hold this and many other errors, and we will submit a protest against the installation of the Missourians who have been appointed. More later, God willing, and if we are alive...

Heidenreich

12 July 1881[27] *(Schwarz to Th Harms)*

Hard work

Dear Pastor!

Moses sings in Psalm 90 [verse 10]: 'A human life lasts for a short time, and [even] if it is enjoyable, it is trouble and toil.' According to this yardstick from God's Word, we mission brothers and sisters here in the heart of Australia have also for the last three months, as previously, led a rich life and enjoyed much goodness, for we have certainly not lacked trouble and toil.[28] ...

At last, the Lord has brought our travelling brothers and sisters home. They arrived here at the station on 11 June at 6 o'clock in the evening. Thank God, all are healthy and well ...

Also, the Lord all the time gave us the gift of heathen present here on the station, and especially students, although we were not able to provide them with the necessary food and clothing, as we had initially done, since we had nothing to spare. Until now, the government rations for the poor heathen have not yet arrived. The daily number of students in the last three months averaged nine, and I would like to say that the children have more zest for learning than we have time to teach, which surely ought not be the case.

However, that was the reality, since the Brothers Schulze and Jürgens were away, fetching their brides and the expected colonists. And that is how it is now because, even with the brothers here with their wives, things have not become much better, for we are still far too few for the tasks that exist and for those expected of us. However, we certainly did not come here to have a good time, or to become rich, albeit through great deprivation and hard work. No, nothing like that! Rather, we were sent out of love for God and the heathen, and from our youth we have been used to work and were also prepared for work in our mission calling in this place. However, the work which is demanded of us exceeds many times more the strength of a handful of people like us. Six of us are required to turn the Australian bush into farming land and the desert into blooming garden, and to establish irrigation systems. In addition, we are meant to look after the sheep, to care for the horses and cattle, as well as to erect big hurdles or yards, to tame wild bulls, cows and horses, so that they become well-behaved domestic animals to be used and handled. Furthermore, we are to build houses and to extend and maintain those already built, and so on, apart from anything else. Above everything else there is the actual mission work in which nothing is to be accomplished by our own strength.

So, you see, we are not lacking work—but also not God's blessing. May the Lord continue graciously to help us.

And now, dear Pastor, there follows a brief appendix on the activity which has occupied us in the last three months, and partly still does.

1. In April, as always, three men were actively engaged with the flocks of sheep about 12 English miles from the station. Then, several young bullocks were fetched from the neighbouring station and trained for work. Also, all of our cattle were rounded up and branded. Tree felling was also commenced and presently continues, since we have to cut down the timber we will need for winter.

2. In May we ploughed and sowed, and also planted a new, large garden, and marked and branded lambs and horses. At the same time, Brother Kempe was travelling for eight days and likewise the same in June.

3. In June two more young, wild bullocks were broken in and, with a mighty effort, trees were felled, sawn up, and the trunks were dragged off and formed into a so-called stockyard which is in the process of being built (it is 55 square yards in area). Timber is also being felled for building that has begun and is partially finished. Finally, we are attacking a stretch of land, 150 feet long and 20 feet wide, and which will be dug six feet deep, in order to make it into a water basin. At the same time, we are making a 100-foot wide dam for the same purpose, for which we await water from future rain from the Lord. However, we commend everything to the Lord. Amen.

W F Schwarz

* * *

30 July 1881[29]

Cannibalism

The following report was made to the Mission Festival in Hermannsburg, Germany, and then published in *Missionsblatt*.

> In Australia with its islands, where the soil of the heart is even more desolate than the land itself, there still burn at this time hundreds of devil's altars with human sacrifice.
>
> While we here are so at peace and happily live together in God, there the inhabitants of one village probably fight against those of another in fratricide. The arms of those who are captured are broken by the victors at the elbows, and the legs at the knees.
>
> So, the poor victims are taken away to be roasted and devoured. Such cannibalism the heathen consider to be service to God. So that the love of the mission does not appear to be in vain also here, a converted Australian prince of these people, whose father was still a cannibal, will, God willing, be a witness during the year in person. He wants to come to Hermannsburg to be trained as a missionary to his own people. Oh, ought we not be that much more eager to bring to the heathen the gospel of God's love, the Word of Life, lest they die without themselves having experienced the love of God, and perish forever.

This is a confronting report. It raises the vexed question of whether Australian Aboriginal people practised cannibalism. The instinctive natural reaction is to say that they did not.

However, there are sufficient accounts from multiple sources that say otherwise. Those accounts are both anecdotal and eye-witness, and they are sourced from a variety of Aboriginal tribes, including the Arrarnta. Frieda Strehlow, for example, records stockmen telling 'tales of hardship about life in the drought-stricken West. "They said in the West it is very dry and that the blacks there were beginning to eat their children"... they claimed "they had seen the cannibals too."'[30]

In describing life in the Killalpaninna mission, Luise Homann recalls:

> But we had our problems even with [four talented young native lads who stayed with us]. One became very angry one day and said to me: "Your Elizabeth is getting pretty fat; when will you eat her?" The

remark struck terror in my heart. Already in our five years of work here, five Aboriginal children had died unnecessarily. One had been eaten, and two, not wanted, had been destroyed—one trampled to death and the other buried alive. "Too much trouble to look after" was the only unfeeling comment.[31]

There is also the very unusual story of William Buckley, a white man who lived for over 30 years among Aboriginal peoples in Victoria, cut off from all contact with Whites during that time. He was accepted into the Wathaurong tribe and became immersed in their customs, ways and language. On more than one occasion he witnessed cannibalism.

> They have a brutal aversion to children who happen to be deformed at their birth. I saw the brains of one dashed out at a blow, and a boy belonging to the same woman made to eat the mangled remains.[32]
>
> It is true they are cannibals—I have seen them eat small portions of the flesh of their adversaries slain in Battle ... They eat also of the flesh of their own children to whom they have been much attached should they die a natural death.[33]

Also, a Google search on this topic results in multiple references to this vexed subject. The endnotes contain examples of those.[34]

As uncomfortable as it may be to accept, it does appear that there were instances of cannibalistic practises among Australian Aboriginal people. Later in *Missionaries, Madness and Miracles* we also receive further personal evidence of this fact from our own missionaries (Chapter 31).

What is not always clear is the type of cannibalism, i.e. whether flesh was eaten simply because the person was dead, or whether a person was intentionally killed for the purposes of consumption. Also often unclear is the reason for any of these practices. Sometimes they were done out of hunger. Other times it was for ritualistic purposes. Yet again, it was because a person had simply died, and their body was treated like any other food would be.

On the White side of the Aboriginal-White relationship, the majority response to tales such as these is horror or disbelief and denial. There are Christian people who will point to those passages in Scripture that decry cannibalistic practices (e.g. Leviticus 26:29; Deuteronomy 28:53–57; Jeremiah 19:9; Lamentations 2:20; Ezekiel 5:10; 2 Kings 6:27–29) and join in the condemnation.

There surely needs to be a degree of nuancing in responding to this issue, both in relation to the practice itself and to the cited Scripture passages. The Bible verses quoted above are not as black and white in terms of condemnation as might first appear. Many of them are simply statements of sad fact. As for the Aboriginal people, cannibalism had been intertwined with their system of beliefs and practice for centuries. As the Aboriginal man, Waipuldanya, protests the principle in *I the Aboriginal*:

> What right did white men have to tell us that we should forsake a ritual act which had been practised by the tribes for more than ten thousand years? What right had they to force upon us a belief in their own God-in-the-Sky, the one who frowned upon us...?[35]

Thus, as much as anyone may deplore it, Cannibalistic practise is quite likely a fact of Aboriginal history. But, as the above-mentioned Waipuldanya points out in various places in *I, the Aboriginal*, to Aboriginal people many of the beliefs and practices of, say, Christianity are as offensive and bizarre in their eyes as is anything Aboriginal people might believe or do in ours. People in glass houses need put down their stones.

* * *

15 August 1881[36] (Heidenreich to Th Harms)

Mrs Homann, the Missourians, Schulze, and Harms

Highly honoured, much-loved Father!

What the heart is full of, flows out of one's mouth... You will forgive me if this time I begin with my unworthy person; for I carry a burden that does not allow me to approach the other person until I have laid out my anguish at your feet.

You will recall that I wrote to you that I had driven to Schmidt's wedding with Mrs Homann and that I was supposed to apologise to her. Once again I had been thoroughly mistaken in my good opinion of her, that she would upon quiet reflection reach the correct understanding. The dispute had flared up over Hermannsburg and Missouri, and the smart lady wanted to be referee. But since I did not allow her to put me down, she sent her son Bernhard to my wife whom I had an hour earlier driven home with our children. He reported her as saying that I had so badly offended her at the wedding that she could no longer enter our house, and she had him fetch her things.

Next day the wedding folk drove to my place. I was giving confirmation instruction, and my wife got to the wagon before I did. Mrs Homann declared before witnesses that she would hand over the matter to the judgement of God! We kept quiet, but Homann called together a number of the pastors, whom he misled, and who gave him the advice to write to me. That he did, but also adding 'according to God's Word'. He chastised me for my 'agitated state'; and I well know that, unfortunately, I do easily become fired up, as I admitted in a written response.

But now they are filling the whole world with the lie that I was drunk and that I had acknowledged this. Had that been true I would certainly not have denied it. However, I certainly could not align 'drunken state' with 'agitated state', as was interpreted behind my back at the Pastors Conference, so that also Pastor Hoopmann today expressed to me his deep sorrow, holding the same opinion. Wiese also seems to be of the same opinion, even if he, like Hoopmann, does not believe everything. He wrote to me that Homann is said to have written to America that I was drunk at mission festivals and weddings. Ahrens, my councillor and household friend was asked what was wrong with me that I was placed under a ban by the pastors because of drinking. He replied that that was a lie; I had given Homann a piece of my mind at the wedding, but there was no question of being drunk.

When I received these reports from all quarters I could not be indifferent to them, though I myself had a good conscience. I spoke with Brother Roth who sat beside us at the wedding feast and acted as our butler, saying that the Homanns were spreading abroad that I was drunk at the wedding. He said, 'Well that's the limit! Homann drank as much as you, if not more, and he wasn't even drunk.' Now that the rumour is spreading there are many wedding guests ready, if necessary, to swear that what the Homanns are spreading are infamous lies.

Hoopman writes to me that he is glad that the matter between me and Homann is settled. Well, I ask you. Contrary to Matthew 18, Homann consults other pastors, and in five weeks gives no reply to my letter of reply asking whether or not there should be peace. Now I hear, also behind my back, that peace has been declared without my involvement, and so I remain a drunkard in the opinion of all gentlemen. Only Missouri scholars can achieve something like that. I am neither consulted nor listened to, neither judged nor cleared. They have decided, and that is how it must firmly remain in heaven and on earth.

However, as unpleasant as this matter is for me—for it is in no way an honour even if witnesses vindicate me, and people can believe what they want to—I cannot accept that there is peace. I will get more information from Hoopman who was the only one of us at the conference—Georg is said to be worse again—and write to him with the facts of the matter. So far for now.

You will wonder how such things are possible; I want to provide the key for you to understand. Together with my parish I have given up responsibility for the High School[37] because it is not Lutheran and because religion is not on its curriculum. Then, from the Church Council we are demanding clear and unambiguous proof that Missouri has acknowledged and taken back its false doctrine, otherwise we will protest against the installation of pastors from there. Furthermore, we have attacked our infallible editors and, since that is the more bitter pill, they intend to kill me off with charges of immorality, so that no dog will take a piece of bread from me. So, now my heart is lighter, and I intend to carry out my official duties.

Our bell has, thank God, arrived safely. We like it very much ...

As Hoopmann has written to me, Pastors Strempel, Hensel, Appelt, and Oster (?)[38] are also opposed to the Missourian teaching on election. On the other hand, Homann, Bertram, Ey and others not only declared that they stand for the most correct teaching but have declared it to be the only true teaching. Things are said to have become heated. I could not and would not enter Homann's house to where they had transferred the conference, so as not to gripe. Now their turn has come and, still better, will come [for us].

In the mission things are so far taking their usual course. Schulze's report is not totally true and accurate. When you publish it, you will have to prune a lot out of it. He also shows no thankfulness for all the kindnesses they received here from the congregations and in my house. We do not demand it, but it is sad that there is not one mention in his report that my congregations donated a chest full of hams, metwurst, bacon, butter, honey, jam, etc. That will have results in the future. For a long time others have done nothing more, but every year my congregations deliver jam, honey, dried fruit, etc. But that amounts to nothing. They seem to see it as a graciousness that they can take for granted...

It is very tedious for us that we still do not have back the statutes in the version, or in the form, changed by you. The longer this goes on, the worse you will make the bad blood between the missionaries and the local Church. It is high time that you take this step, otherwise I will not be responsible for what follows ...

Your son, Heidenreich

They sound like a pack of squabbling children. But, indubitably, being accused of being drunk at a wedding was a rather serious matter. The bell, at least, has done the right thing.

12 September 1881[39] (Heidenreich to Missionsblatt)

Students, building, livestock, revenue

Dear, precious mission community!
... The administrative tasks and work with the souls of the heathen have been very demanding. It has been extremely difficult for our missionaries because the government rations for the heathen could not get through. A fortnight ago, as I heard from the Minister, they have after almost two years of wandering finally arrived at our station in good condition.[40]

Up to that point our missionaries had been unable to supply enough support for the parents of our pupils, so they went off looking for food and took a good portion of the students with them. As a consequence, the number of students averaged nine, but they demonstrated a great desire and stamina in their learning, especially in singing, writing and geography. We are not yet able to tell any stories of their awakening and conversion ...

The brothers have had a lot of building work to do on the main station and the new shepherd station with yards and pens over at the McDonnell Ranges. Also, the field and garden work has again been attacked in earnest ...

Our livestock numbers are constantly growing. This year we have 22 foals, but I have not yet received a report on the number of calves from our 20 to 30 cows. In respect to the lambs, we suffered great loss due to the heat, and they are said to have been small mouselike things, so that there are good lambs from only 40 percent of the 100 ewes, whereas in the previous year we had 85 percent. Since we have up to 4000 sheep that bring us nothing from their wool and, in addition, the missionaries are tired of the sheep in such big mobs, and our land is better suited for cattle and horses, we (i.e. my advisors and I) have sold 1000 head at 12 shillings each to the government for its telegraph station. As soon as rain comes the government is sending their people from Alice Springs to our station and we will let them select for themselves up to 1000 head of sheep suitable for slaughtering.

Since this is the first significant revenue from the station, we have last week bought from Mr Gilbert's station at Owen Springs 50 young breeding cows for between £5 to £10 sterling each, and two mares for £30 sterling. These were chosen by his manager and Missionary Kempe, and then brought by

Gilbert's people to our station about 45 miles away. We want to pay for these cattle with the proceeds from the sheep, so that as a result and with God's blessing, our best stock experiences substantial growth.

Thus, we have taken a further step towards the mission being self-supporting, and I will bless the day when my wish is completely fulfilled ...

Heidenreich

30 September 1881[41] *(Schulze to Th Harms)*

Misbehaving students, language, healing

In the last three months everything has quietly proceeded at our mission, despite the dry weather ...

As for our mission staff, we are all well, praise God, and our number has increased by one. On 18 July a son was born to Brother Jürgens. On the following Sunday he received the blessing of holy baptism. Oh, that we could carry out this holy sacrament on some of our black heathen. But here, too, the words of scripture are true: 'Be still before the Lord and wait for him'.

In recent times there has always been a good number of them present here due to the dry weather and the resulting lack of food supplies. We are happy about this because we can work on many of them, though our animal herds will feel their presence. Despite keeping careful guard, they sometimes succeed in stealing a sheep or goat only to disappear over the hills. After a while others try to discover if we are still angry at the thieves. If we say 'No', the same people are soon back on the place with the friendliest of faces and docile attitude. This lasts only a short time, unfortunately; stealing and lying seem to be innate with them.

Some time ago several children stole 15 pounds of sugar from the rations brought here. When we asked who had done it, one was as innocent as the other, though the criminals betrayed themselves with their guilty looks. As punishment, all went without supper. Next day at school we again took the children in hand. A little girl eventually identified all the thieves, whereupon she received from us her rightful portion of refined sugar. What an uproar and rush suddenly occurred following the shouting of those who were punished! At first all the other children joined the shouting, then the men came running from all directions, grumbling and scolding, the women howling and screaming, to help their children.

It took a lot of effort to convince the men that their misbehaving children had to be punished; because they did not do so, we had to do it. Discipline of children is, unfortunately, something totally foreign to them. We have often seen children hitting or throwing something at their parents; the latter have quietly let this happen. Since our scolding accomplished nothing, we ourselves had to start punishing the children.

As for the communal life of the heathen, quarrels and strife do arise among them, but these do not develop as bad as they might sound or seem to be. They inflict some wounds on the upper thigh of their opponent, but as soon as they see a flow of blood, their anger seems to abate, and their mind is put at rest.

The women here suffer the worst. When they do not do what their men want, they get such a belting that they later can barely walk. Yet many still behave contrary to their husband's will and get their treatment when they fall into his hands. Some almost every evening!

To prevent the people from stealing we have used them, where possible, to build yards and dig waterholes. That does cost a lot of meat and bread, and a necessary amount of effort to get them working and to keep them at it. One does not achieve anything with a whip; we would thereby only drive them away from the place. Only patience works, dear people.

They take their place quickly at mealtime and show the kind of attention that I have often told them they should show at work and in school. If one calls them to a lesson, they suddenly need to do all sorts of other things, and hardly are the last in school than the first want to go out again. When they have been made quiet, the hardest task begins for the teacher: to make the little folk attentive and keep them so. Nothing is more foreign and irksome for them than thinking. The subjects taught are: biblical history, reading, writing, geography, and singing. They like the last the best, which is the reason why we have to deal with that a lot.

Translating our spiritual songs into their language causes little difficulty, because rhyming is easy: almost all words end with '*a*'. The length of a verse is a problem, because they have almost no monosyllabic words, and only a few with two syllables; they instead have words of three or more syllables.

Study of the language is no easy task for us. We face many difficulties on all sides. There are different expressions for one and the same thing. For example, the one uses the word *cima* for 'go', another *coma*, a third *cuma*. That is the case with many words. We now use the word *cima*, which in the dual form is *cinoma* and *cirinoma* in the plural.

Another difficult thing is their dullness of mind. If one wants to pick out something that demands reflection, one is hard pressed.

Another difficulty is that they conceive of things quite differently than we do. The word 'family' does not seem to exist among them because they have no concept of family. Their system of class division seems to have suppressed the concept of family.

The words *kniritja, inajura* and *negua* are used not only for their natural father but also for other men. It is the same with the words *maia, magura*, and *megua* with which they designate their mother and other old women. The oldest brother is called *kalga*, the older sister is *onumba*, the youngest sibling *idia*. The same words are used for others belonging to their class.

They call God *alyra*, the devil *erinya*. Yet each person has his own view of and opinion about them, except that God is the source of all things good, the devil the source of all things evil. Some suggest that they have seen both; these seem to be their witch doctors whom they call *angangara*.

One of these wanted to cure the sore eyes of Brother Schwarz, who let him have a go. The heathen man placed his mouth over the eye and sucked a long time until he removed from his mouth a small piece of charcoal that he was supposed to have sucked out of the eye. The rest of the heathen were very amazed. Some time much later, the same heathen man contracted a bad eye, and Brother Schwarz said he could cure him. He had earlier put a small wood shaving in his mouth. After sucking for a short time, he showed it to the patient and the onlookers. The whole crowd, and especially the patient, were amazed. Thereupon we told them from where Brother Schwarz had got the wood shaving, likewise how their supposed doctor had fetched the charcoal. At this the whole crowd began to laugh, but their doctor was all the more upset, and had nothing to say in reply.

Since then they have wanted to hear nothing more of their art, but frequently come to us for medicine. Eye ailments are not uncommon here, and several heathen have become blind from them.

At the moment they are again holding their annual festival. No night passes without their monotonous dances being performed. That is all they talk about; they cannot get off work quickly enough to make their appearance at the festival site. May the Lord God grant that they soon hurry to his glorious festivals.

As for our comings and goings, we are all together at present. The shepherds have had to come here with their flocks for shearing. We are all happy, especially the shepherds, that we can now hold our wonderful divine services with all present. However, the joy will not last long; the sheep have to be taken away again after shearing, if no rain falls. So, we all the more want to enjoy this happy time when we will thank and praise God freely with each other...

With sincere greetings, Louis Schulze

24 October 1881[42] (Heidenreich to Th Harms)

Finances, sheep, Missouri

Highly honoured, much-loved Father!

I can send you the annual financial records with praise and thanks to God, for we have managed our affairs and still have funds left over. Schulze's trip has cost a lot of money, including the three horses and buggy, but I did not want to include that, for the sake of our mission friends. That was an expensive wedding trip and, hopefully, will not be repeated. And any wagon coming down South again will do so over my dead body. But complaining does not help at all, and the Lord has helped us through it all.

A thousand sheep have been sold at 12 marks a head, but I still have no news that the government has taken delivery of them. We are getting a nice amount of money, and I hope that you do not need to send any cheque next year. And something always comes through from the printery. The congregations are also contributing in a praiseworthy way, despite all the hostility and suspicion from various sides ...

The conflict with Missouri goes on and will really burst into flames at the next Pastors Conference. The new Missourian is a genuine follower of Walther[43] and is well trained in the prickly question of election. Since he is married to Pastor Strempel's daughter, he has changed his opinion, for which I am very sorry, since earlier he mostly attacked the Missourians.

Pastor Georg is better, praise God, but Pastor Wiese is said to be very ill, as a member of his told me yesterday...

Heidenreich

31 October 1881[44] (Th Harms to Heidenreich)

Official documents, Missourians, arrival of the bell

My dear Heidenreich.

Enclosed you are receiving the long-awaited document. As important as this may be for instructions for the Provost, I do not believe that it will give you what you are rightly aiming for, namely the incorporation of the mission property in Central Australia. May the Lord graciously grant that your efforts are crowned with success ...

The Mission Committee has resolved to send out three colonists, as you have requested ... We hope to get them on their way in the New Year at the latest...

Do not let the Missourians tire you out or make you bitter. People are all the more presumptuous the more superficial they are. They will not be able to force matters in the long run …Arrogant, unthankful people are an abomination to the Lord. But you, good Heidenreich, be confident and undaunted. The Lord is, and will be, with you.

I am glad that the bell has turned out to your satisfaction. Payment to the bellmaker has been made immediately from here.

Yours, Th Harms

30 November 1881[45] *(Heidenreich to ELSA members)*

Sheep sale

Dear mission congregations!

… I note that on 4 October the government had two men fetch 300 head of sheep; the others will be fetched as soon as rain comes. The dryness makes transport very difficult. Even the mail comes through irregularly. The faithful Lord can soon change this too. In him we happily put our trust and act only according to his heart's desire …

Heidenreich

* * *

Kempe and Schwarz are pushing the boundaries—again! We have no indication of the extent to which Schulze is involved in their ploy; the silence on that would indicate he was not part of it.

Whatever the dynamic between the three, Schwarz and Kempe have obviously gone to Heidenreich with the request that they be able to own and raise their own livestock, and to keep the proceeds from any sales of these. It seems, in fact, that they have already begun to put their plan into action. The reason for the request is their dissatisfaction with the salary they are—or are not—receiving. They see this arrangement as a way to relieve their financial need.

Heidenreich is not impressed, especially since they are critical of the Mission Council in the process.

28 December 1881[46] (*Heidenreich to Kempe and Schwarz*)

A proposed business deal

Dear Brothers Kempe and Schwarz,

Regarding the last letter that has arrived from both of you concerning your attitude to the Council and your submission (missionaries and colonists) to have your own animals with your own officials, this is our unanimous response to you after careful consideration of the circumstances and situation:

1. To send you the statutes from the Mission Director from which you can see clearly and unambiguously that my Council is not guilty of any overbearance but has only fulfilled its duty.
2. We cannot approve your request that you raise your own livestock, alongside those of the mission. That would be a death-blow for our mission, for how could we be accountable to the government for such a business?

    As well it would place you and us in a bad light, both in the mission community and also among others who are envious of our mission. The judgement has already been expressed several times by many members of the mission community that the mission people are striving to make themselves wealthy by means of cattle more than doing mission work. You know well enough, as do we, how many squatters up North, as well as the Parliament down here in the South, have shown themselves to be hostile and keen to swallow up our place. So far we have been able to decisively resist both the Government and the local congregations. Also, with you, we have to continue to be able to do that in the future, before God and people. Thus, we can only direct that, for a reasonable price, you either leave to the mission the cattle that each of you possesses, or that you sell them elsewhere, and then as soon as possible refund the money that each of you has withdrawn from the mission treasury.

    I must at the same time mention that in future money can no longer be drawn from the mission treasury for private use. (To provide you with some help, I am sending you forms with instructions for your bank account.)

As much as it pains me to have to maintain such regulations for the smooth continuation of our mission, we are gladly ready to extensively improve your salary as soon as the dear Lord blesses us with more means. We do that all the more gladly because we recognise your mission activity before God and people.

This decision, word for word, will be sent to the honourable directors with the suggestion that your salary be raised, since that does not lie in our power alone. It is also very good for you and us that we finally have collated formulated statutes; in many earlier writings they have appeared piecemeal. I am sending you a word for word copy of them and will in due course send you a copy of the trust deed of the incorporation of our mission. You will do well to enter both into your station chronicle so that they are doubly preserved with you and us for future times ...

G A Heidenreich

31 December 1881[47] (Kempe to Th Harms)

Kempe's report on the year

Dear Pastor!

Again we stand at the end of a year, and so have also come a big step closer to our grave and to eternity. As we look back on the year past we have cause, on the one hand, to praise and thank God for the countless physical and spiritual blessings that he has showered upon us. For everything we are and have is his gift. On the other hand, we must also cast our eyes down in shame because of our unthankfulness, our smallness of faith, our lukewarmness and lethargy in our office and calling.

Looked at from the outside, it was a very, very difficult year because of the great drought, a drought the likes of which we Whites have not experienced here in the Centre. It is now almost two years and six months since it has rained sufficiently for our needs, and we have experienced in full measure this year what is written in chapter 28 of the 5th book of Moses, which is the reading for the day of repentance before Christmas, namely in verses 23 and 24: 'Your heaven, which is over your head, will be bronze, and the earth beneath you iron. The Lord will rain down dust and ashes upon you from heaven.' This is what was threatened the people of Israel in case they forsook the Lord their God, and no longer obeyed his commandments.

Very often such questions as these arise in our hearts: On account of whose sins does this drought come over this land? Is it because of the sins of the Aboriginal people? Have they perhaps already earlier had the Word of God, or has it at least been offered to them and they have wilfully made light of grace? Finding natural causes for the long, oft-recurring drought here would certainly be very difficult. Does a curse perhaps lie over the land on account of the sins of its inhabitants? Or is it a punishment for the sins of the Whites who are living here, which are even worse than those of the heathen?

However, rightly viewed, such questions do not seem appropriate to us, for this is the language of the Pharisee. Rather, we ourselves must beat our breast and confess that it is also because of our sins that such a thing casts its shadow over us and the land. It is certainly possible that these things might happen because of the sins of those mentioned above; but we dare not exclude ourselves, for we are in no way any better.

I do not consider it necessary to report any further on this, for it is so vividly clear that those who stand far off in the distance could form a clear picture of the distress and misery that such a drought entails. One cannot describe it; it is something you have to have seen for yourself. It was and is, in truth, still so that the heaven above us is bronze; for so often black, dark clouds appear, and heavy storms roll up from all sides, but without rain falling. We have all the more reason to be thankful that the faithful, gracious God has so far kept us reasonably well, for it is enough of a miracle to remain healthy in such a hot climate and on such a heavy diet of meat.

Our wives feel it most of all. Recently they have become quite run-down, and I fear they will not hold out in the long run.

However, we hope for rain soon. The right hand of the Lord can change everything, and we are really looking forward to that, for then we will also once again have some greens to eat. We have enough seed; it just does not rain. We received a lot of seeds and other plants from Baron Ferdinand von Müller in Melbourne, to whom we owe a lot of thanks, because he is making every possible effort to introduce some edible and otherwise useful kinds of plants and make then grow here. Of course, in this long, dry period we have not yet had any success; however, I do not doubt that in response to our pleas he will again send something to us in more favourable times. We owe this man the greatest recognition for his great efforts.

If we now look at our work amongst and for the heathen, we are able to say that everything has quietly progressed forwards, even if the progress of the students this year has not kept pace with that of the previous year. This, too, was to be expected, for it is now becoming more and more familiar and is losing the attraction of novelty. Nevertheless, there are some students who have made significant progress. The average number of students in the last quarter of the year was ten. What still holds us back too much in the work in the school is the small number of workers. We are always being forced to do too much physical work, to the detriment of our mission work.

Hopefully we will soon receive help from Germany. We could well do with three industrious colonists. Even four would not be too many, since two of our current workers will soon be leaving. But they must be faithful, competent and reliable people, otherwise they are more of a hindrance to us than a help. To come here for the purpose of an easy life and for the sake of the pay is plainly wrong, for again I say: Here there is no paradise, but a desert...

We have also been given well-intentioned advice from various quarters, even from dear Hermannsburg, that we should, for example, set up a modest irrigation system like the old Egyptians and Indians did. It is just a pity that all these pieces of advice are not practicable here, for we lack the Egyptian Nile and the Indian Ganges—indeed, even running water. If only we had a small brook, like the Lutter brook at Hermannsburg, that would allow us to try something, provided there were enough people here to carry out such work, but that is not the case. The Aboriginal people here are not at all able to grasp the idea of doing something for the long term. They care nothing for the next morning, but live only from hand to mouth. At the moment, for example, there are a whole lot of seeds of various kinds of *acacia*, but it does not occur to them to gather a stockpile from these, which they could easily do. Instead, in the morning they gather only as much as they need for the day. In general, they do not like continuous, ongoing work. In addition, there is the fact that they do not see the need for all this work. So far, all of our efforts have been in vain.

For this reason one comes more and more to the conviction that the breeding of cattle is the only rewarding undertaking here. The only trouble is that in such an activity there is little work for the Aboriginal people, and their engagement in such activity is a main condition for the blessed progress of the mission work. So, the question often raised by us: 'How are we able to provide work for the heathen?' remains unsolved.

This year's drought was also fairly difficult for the Aboriginal people. That the great Indian famine was not replicated here on a small scale is due alone to their insatiable appetite which allows them to consume anything edible.[48] Who in Germany, for example, would gather the roots of reeds, rushes and other plants, and eat them? The heathen here have lived for almost the whole year on reed and rush roots. That, despite this, they have stayed so much on the station, as has happened, is surprising to us. It seems that they now trust us more than they did earlier. Whether this will continue will only become evident when a decent rain falls, and abundant greenery grows everywhere for them. By this I am not saying that it is the attraction of the Word of God that binds them to the station, but that it is above all the food and drink. That is their one and only topic of conversation by day and night—indeed, the basis and reason for all their squabbles. There is not even a trace of an understanding of the Word of God, or even a desire to understand that Word. 'Yes, yes,' they say, 'we have heard that', and that is how it remains. And if the conversation goes on too long for them, they interrupt us at times with *kala*, i.e. 'That's enough.' May God have mercy on them and make alive in their hearts a desire for something better.

By God's grace, we were permitted to celebrate the beloved Christmas festival even though the days were quite warm, with the thermometer reaching 32°R in the shade of our verandah. Nevertheless, on Christmas Eve all of the Aboriginal people still gathered around the candle-lit Christmas tree in the school, and one could see on their faces how full of expectation they were of all the things that were meant to follow, especially the gifts which would be given to them.

They first of all sang some Christmas carols in their language, e.g. 'Praise to you, Jesus Christ', 'Now sing we and rejoice', 'Glory to God in the highest', and others, and they were told a short version of the Christmas story by Brother Schulze. Then they each received some pastry, each of them a new shirt, and the men each received some tobacco and a clay pipe.

They dispersed only after our repeated reminders, and one could hear them long into the night, telling each other what they had heard and seen, what they had eaten and drunk. The singing this year was much better than last year, and they seemed to get the greatest joy from that. Above all, our wish and prayer in that regard is that they might also be able to join in singing from the heart, which is not yet the case ...

We here on the station all send hearty greetings to all dear brothers and sisters in the old homeland. I hope and wish, as we all here do, that we might soon be in a position to share happy news ...

H Kempe

* * *

Correspondence with Baron von Müller

The botanist Baron von Müller[49] was keenly interested in the flora of Central Australia, and he developed a fascinating relationship with the Hermannsburg missionaries, exchanging correspondence and plant samples with them.

21 April 1879[50] *(Kempe to von Müller)*
Right Honourable Sir will excuse that I was so long in sending you the plants. It could not be helped, though, because last year, when I received your esteemed letter, the so badly wanted rain did not come here, and with that we missed out on the flowering of some many grasses and plants, which I would have been pleased to send you. I hope, however, that I am still in time, so you can make some use of them. There is only one thing that worries me: that, with the poor postal facilities here, the parcels will be rather damaged by the time they reach you. I am posting four parcels to you.

Parcel No. 1 contains a leaf and seed of the palms discovered by E Giles in the Glen of Palms, so named by him. I have cut the petiole and the tips of the lobes to make the parcel a little smaller... Unfortunately, I was unable to obtain flowers for you, but I can tell you that the flower has the shape of a bunch of grapes, only much larger, about 8-10 feet long and 2-3 inches wide at the base, and the colour of the flower is also like that of the grapevine, a whitish-green. The fruit, too, has the appearance of a gigantic bunch of grapes when ripe. The pith of the trunk high up in the crown is edible and tastes similar to coconut. I have enclosed a piece of wood as well, cut from the middle of the trunk ...

Parcel No. 2 contains a leaf and some seed from palms growing in the gully of Ellery's Creek. I have cut about two feet off the leaf stalk. I am sorry I cannot send you a complete seed cone. I could not grow one ...

Parcel No. 3 contains a collection of all the grasses growing here, at least I could not find any others.

And, finally, parcel No. 4 contains all kinds of plants and shrubs ... [These] are not all the species growing here by any means, for if I were to send a sample of every species they would fill ten such parcels ...

H Kempe

There are other similar letters. And in a letter to von Müller of **7 August 1880**, Kempe includes the following little note concerning reciprocity:

With the last mail I received several packets with various grass and vegetable seeds. Also one from Sydney with sweet potatoes and yams. I thank you cordially for your kindness.

Schulze also corresponded with von Müller.

23 November 18?[date unclear] [51] *(Schulze to von Müller)*
With this mail I am sending you a parcel containing four palm kernels and two pieces of leaf stalk. The kernels or seeds are quite round and the size of small shot. The petioles are somewhat prickly when young, but lose most of the prickles in time ...

Of the 20 fig cuttings sent to me, two seem to come along nicely, they are beginning to shoot to my great joy, and thanks to the kind donor. Hopefully more would have taken, if only they had not taken eight weeks to get here ...

L Schulze

This correspondence provides helpful insight into the collaborative way in which the missionaries collated their information on the flora of Central Australia. It also helps to make sense, for example, of the introductory note by von Müller to Kempe's paper in 1880 to the Royal Society of South Australia:

> I had named the species of the following list of plants from Mr Kempe's successive collections.[52]

It is also worthy of note that von Müller named six apparent new species of *flora* after Kempe, and two after Schwarz. Sadly, Schulze appears to have missed out. Those species are as follows:[53]

Acacia kempeana (the witchetty grub bush)
Calotis kempei (a small perennial daisy)
Helichrysum kempei (an 'everlasting' daisy bush)
Millotia greevessii /kempei (an annual daisy)
Commersonia kempeana, a synonym of *Rulingia loxophyllia* (a small shrub common on the red, spinifex-covered dunes of Central Australia)
Sarajusticia kempeana (a subshrub, with blue, purple, pink or white tubular flowers, that commonly occurs around waterholes in Central Australia)
Actinotus schwarzii (a flannel flower found only in the MacDonnell Ranges)
Ptilotus schwarzii (a mulla mulla or pussy-tail)

* * *

And in the rest of the world in 1881:

- Tsar Alexander II, Emperor of Russia, was assassinated by bomb in St Petersburg (13 March), and US President James Garfield was shot in New Jersey (2 July).
- There were anti-Jewish riots in Jerusalem (1 April), and Kyiv, Ukraine (5 May), a petition by 250,000 Germans to bar Jews from entering Germany (25 April), and pogroms against Russian Jews began in Elisabethgrad (27 April).
- Significant births: Anna Pavlova, Russian ballerina (12 February); Scottish bacteriologist, Alexander Fleming (6 August); artist Pablo Picasso (25 October).
- Deaths: Russian novelist, Fyodor Dostoyevsky (9 February); Benjamin Disraeli, British Prime Minister (19 April); outlaw Billy the Kid, in a gunfight (14 July).
- Opening of the British Natural History Museum in London (18 April).
- Clara Barton founded the American Red Cross (21 May).
- World's first electric tram service inaugurated in Berlin (16 May).

18.

Friction, Fighting and Fred

1882

The new year of 1882 does not get off to the most propitious of beginnings as far as inter-personal relationships are concerned. Kempe and Schwarz pick up where they left off last year by requesting the autonomy to conduct their own side business with some of the animals. However, Kempe has upped the stakes somewhat by making autonomous business decisions, as well as criticising the quality of food and conditions on the station. Heidenreich is miffed by all this, and in another 'missing' letter has told Kempe so. But he does graciously promise them extra rations. It would be great to have a copy of all their correspondence on this matter. It would make for juicy reading.

In the background, Jürgens is not happy. Neither is Tündemann. At times, the mood around the station must have been quite tense. Some are talking of leaving.

But also in the background the missionaries manage to continue their work with the Aboriginal people, tackling sensitive pastoral and theological issues in the process.

30 January, Bethany 1882[1] *(Heidenreich to the Missionaries)*
Dear Brothers![2]

In recent times your demands and requests have been so extravagant that, in the last mail, we had to refuse both you missionaries and the colonists your request to have your own stock. We also gave you our reasons for that. Unfortunately, I must also reject the proposal that has come in today, 'that you place your orders with Tusil or other (merchants) and have the list of orders sent to us from there'. We have no right to allow you to do that for, as the statutes state, we are responsible for such things, particularly the directive that 'we should resolutely resist all excessive demands', as you know from previous communications. I must therefore urgently plead with you to keep this in mind in the future and spare us such new impertinences that we can neither defend ethically nor finance with our own funds.

Dear Brother Kempe, your remarks about your daily food and needs are very hurtful to me and my Council. We have a good conscience before God and people that it has never occurred to us, nor will it if we can help it, to allow you to suffer lack of food. You know as well as I that we have demonstrated that as much as possible with our actions. Schulze purchased all sorts of things with Ahrens,[3] and if these are not yet in your hands, that is not our fault; for who can go against God?[4] You also know that this deficiency can only be permanently removed from our place once the transport finds faster routes.

You write: 'We must have sent up all kinds of foods (plant foods, especially easily digested foods), or else we all will soon come down with sickness'. Now, if you are not able remain up there that is neither our desire nor wish. And so we have sent off all sorts of things and will do so in the future; and because, as it turns out, you cannot rely on your garden produce, we will send you more, for we are not unconcerned about your health.

What you write about having a cook for the station is also something that we here cannot understand. The fact is, there are three women on the station, and they cannot manage the mission kitchen? Why do you men not arrange for the women to be allotted times for work and for rest? It is not our wish that some work while others look on. You can regulate this only on the spot and we want you to decide this for the sake of peace.

I must also take issue with your remark in the report to Director Harms 'that Tündemann appealed to a letter from me in which I had given him permission to leave'. I wrote nothing at all to Tündemann, only to you, and with easily understood provisos to Drögemüller's communications. You have not responded to me about that, but I later heard that he is staying. How can you report in this way to the directors? At the same time you write to me, 'I am not responsible for Tündemann wanting to leave us; none of us are, for which we are glad'. If that means to say that I am responsible, you are wrong.

However, the matter becomes even stranger since Tündemann writes in the same mail, 'The missionaries told me, when I wanted to shepherd the sheep not on the Day of Repentance but on the First Day of Christmas, that "I should go as soon as possible; they could manage quite well without me"'. He continues, 'That was said to me not just once but, oh no, several times, but I have so far said nothing for I always thought I was doing them a favour by staying. But now I have found out that it is not so. That is why I want to hurry to get away and not waste time'.[5]

As a result of that Day of Repentance, Brother Jürgens has also applied to be released. Since he does not exactly specify his reasons for this, but also wants to wait for a year before being discharged from Hermannsburg, and we like and value him, I will try to get him to stay. To that end I have written him a letter that will arrive with this one to you.

Dear brothers, keep me fully informed about the Tündemann matter, so that I can from the outset address all inquiries truthfully.[6]

In addition to these matters, I have provisionally answered the question of the missionaries about the baptism of sick heathen children. I want to raise this as a matter for discussion with the pastors here and attach it here for your response. The missionaries ask:

'1. Whether we are ever allowed to baptise a heathen child who is dying, if the parents give their consent when asked'. I have said, "Yes, if you have been asked to do so and do not consider the initiative of the missionaries to be sin"'.

'2. Whether in the case of a child getting better again, the parents must before baptism give the specific assurance that the child will be raised on the station as a Christian'. My reply: "By all means, Yes"'.

I have explained to them my two answers but want you to give the decisive answer.

The missionaries touch on another point with reference to the liturgy. They have different views on this but have unfortunately not said how and what they are. I have directed them to the Lüneburg Church Order and said that it is binding for them as far as it can be used in a foreign language in the chief matters. I have asked them for a statement on the points of difference, and regret that I cannot immediately share these with you...

From the *Kirchenbote* you have probably gotten a deep sense of the tension between us and Missouri. This could not continue but had to come to a head. That took place on 11 and 12 January in Bethany, beyond our prayers and expectations. The conference was attended by all healthy pastors, and the proceedings were quiet and orderly, contrary to expectation. Each side worked with diligence and patience to understand the other and not to offend.

Nevertheless, with the best of intentions, it could not all go smoothly. The rift was too great, so that a split in our Synod stood before us. But God worked wonders among us, as the next issue of the *Kirchenbote* will demonstrate ...

Heidenreich

* * *

Announcement.
15 February 1882, Bethany

I, *Georg Adam Heidenreich of Bethany near Tanunda, one of the trustees of the Evangelical Lutheran Mission on the Finke River, hereby give notice that I wish* to incorporate this institution according to the regulations of the Incorporation of Associations Act of 1858.

G A Heidenreich

Following is a copy of the document I intend to submit in the Supreme Court as prescribed by the Incorporation of Associations Act.

Deed of the Evangelical Lutheran Mission on the Finke River submitted as prescribed by the Incorporation of Associations Act of 1858.

1. The name of the institution is the Evangelical Lutheran Mission on the Finke River.
2. The purpose and goal of the institution is the civilisation and conversion to Christianity of the Aboriginal people of Central Australia.
3. It is situated and established on the mission reserve of about 200 square miles on and between the Krichauff and MacDonnell Ranges.
4. The names of the trustees are Georg Adam Heidenreich, Adolf Hensel, Henry Gerhard Ahrens, Carl Friedrich Schmidt, and Henry Drögemüller.
5. The management of the institution rests in the hands of the trustees of which the said Georg Adam Heidenreich functions as business manager and superintendent. The trustees are appointed by the directors of the Evangelical Lutheran Mission at Hermannsburg in Germany by a document, dated 31 October 1881, signed by the pastor and director of missions, Th Harms, and bearing the church seal of Hermannsburg.

* * *

The Missourian thorn in the flesh continues to prickle. Sometimes it is difficult to ascertain what a particular tussle is about; nevertheless, one easily detects the in-fighting and subsequent disruption to the work.

2 March 1882, Bethany[7] *(Heidenreich to Th Harms)*
Highly honoured, much loved Father!
… The local Missourians have broken off the summit in our Pastors Conference. We are one with them 'that the teaching of Johann Gerhard on the election by grace is pure Lutheran doctrine', but they changed that in the *Kirchenbote* to 'his teaching contains Lutheran teaching'. It might also be contained in the Koran!?

So our joy has again turned to water, unfortunately. New pastors have submitted a counter-declaration from us that has no prospect of being accepted by the Missouri editor, but since the Synodical president, Pastor Oster, is on our side, it will be brought to a special synod. People are becoming ever more bold with their unbiblical and unconfessional teaching on election and regard all who, for reasons of conscience, cannot join them, as synergists, and berate them ... I was very glad that you sent them packing as you did, with their choice bundle of false teachings that one cannot count on two hands! ...

Things look sad on the station, but we have no rain here either, and dreadful heat as never before. My beautiful pear trees, planted on my arrival here and that have been bearing fruit for years, have partly dried up. And Bethany is considered a paradise with ample water! ...

Heidenreich

* * *

Kempe, Schwarz and Schulze submit to their superiors their suggestions for dealing with the recent problems. They also attempt to lay down a few principles which they hope will nullify the kind of squabbles they have been experiencing. Then, with typical German over-efficiency and torturous detail Heidenreich addresses the exceedingly serious matter of filling out forms!

18 March 1882, Hermannsburg[8] *(Kempe, Schwarz, Schulze to Heidenreich)*
Dear Brother Heidenreich!
We have received your letter of 30/1/82, and I am replying in the name of all, dealing with the points in order.

1. That we should send our order directly to A D Tassy[9] and each time send you a copy of the order was only a suggestion on our part to avoid complications. It makes no difference to us if it is not accepted. We merely want to avoid giving the impression of making extravagant demands and being wasteful, as any unbiased reader will deduce from your letter. It is sad for both sides, for us and for you, when we are no longer met with trust.
2. As for my remarks about our food and pressing needs, my intention was not to hurt anyone. I beg forgiveness if that has occurred. I only wanted to achieve one thing: that more would be sent to us. This is necessary if we are to stay here. We cannot understand why you refer

to what Schulze and Ahrens bought which, according to Schulze's own statement, is just a box of potatoes, and to the fact that much of what was sent from the South either spoiled along the way or did not arrive at all.[10] To our knowledge, everything consigned from down South arrived here and nothing was ruined apart from a box of seeds that stood at Beltana for a long time.

Your hopes with reference to gardening and agriculture suggested that they are no more than illusions. That is worse for you than for us since you once, without possessing the slightest knowledge of the facts, trumpeted to the wide world 'that we have become a wonderful heritage and that nothing stands in the way of establishing an extensive farm, etc.' This has misled people into believing that we here have a veritable paradise, only to be disappointed that our reports tell a different tale, completely contradicting your statements back then.

3. The matter referring to the work our wives do has been settled and does not need to be regulated by you. They have divided the workload. That you do not understand how much work there is here is easily explained: you do not nor cannot have any idea about this.

4. With reference to the settlers, note the following. Tündemann referred to a letter from you in which you gave him permission to leave. I was of the opinion that you had written to him especially, but later it turned out that Schwarz communicated to him what you had written to us, namely, that he could leave if he did not want to stay at all. That was an error on my part and I ask your pardon. Tündemann wrote to you: 'The missionaries say so and so'. Schwarz will himself write to you about that, since Schulze and I did not say that, and would not say anything of the sort.

Tündemann certainly wants to leave but has given no reason. However, I believe I can suggest, on the basis of many years of experience, that the main reason is his disinterest in the mission generally and working for nothing in particular. Jürgens will write to you himself so I will not say anything on his behalf.

We want to stipulate the following to avoid similar disagreements in the future.

a) If we are to work with the settlers in future, we must demand that they follow and obey our instructions. You cannot have everyone giving orders, for where would that lead to? Nor can we grant the settlers any decision making or advisory voice dealing with administration, for what we do not understand they do not either. Naturally, fraternal advice and suggestions are not thereby excluded.

b) We reject all the scribbling of letters behind our backs, both from the settlers to you and from you to them. Just as all matters directed to Harms should and must pass through your hands, so we demand that all letters to the settlers shall pass through our hands. If that does not happen, we are under fire from two directions and do not know if we are betrayed or sold out. We do not want that.

c) If we are not granted these conditions, only one way out is left. You have to appoint a man, either an outsider or a settler, as administrator to take on each and every external task, placing orders, attending to the business etc., and to be responsible for that. We then no longer want to have anything to do with all that but only to take care of spiritual work relating to our pastoral office and mission and to do such physical work as time and inclination allow. Naturally, we cannot allow any administrative meddling with our work.

5. With reference to the question of baptism, as we have already mentioned, we have reached clarity from what J Gerhard has said, with all dogmaticians of our church in agreement. What you have mentioned is not valid.

6. As for filling out the forms, I want to write out a verbatim copy of the relevant part of your report of 17 September 1881. There you write:

'I herewith send you three different forms that I have to submit to the government in the new year. We have to fill out two of them here, but I am sending you templates so that you can fill in for me the details from the station, so that I can submit them together with our details as faithfully as possible.

However, you have to fill out the one form with everything it asks for, but without filling out the date above and the two names below (N.B. no blank form was sent, which is why I had to write the detailed information in the margin of the one we filled out, with them more or less corresponding). Mr Flint can sign it as JP but I can also have it signed by a JP here, because he must see me sign in his presence. For this eventuality I have enclosed blank forms. At the end of the year you fill out all the details, to the best of your knowledge and certainty, and send the form to me anew every year with the December mail.

Buildings and wagons have to be listed anew with changes showing increase or decrease.'

Now, judge for yourself if I could have acted differently from what I did. If you think you are doing me a great favour by allowing me to do this, you are wrong. On the contrary, I would be delighted if I were to be relieved of this task and it were given to an administrator...

H Kempe, W F Schwarz, L Schulze

* * *

A terse Jürgens Interlude

Around this time (we cannot be sure exactly when, because the letters involved are undated) there is a terse exchange of communication between Kempe and Jürgens. From time to time Kempe shows he can be a feisty fellow, and it is easy to see how he might have got under someone else's skin.

The situation is that a mob of the sheep has been moved some distance from the station in order to find better feeding grounds. At least one shepherd went with the sheep, taking a cook with him, and they set up a camp out in the bush. There were also arrangements—occasionally fuzzy—for one or the other of the missionaries to take a service at the camp from time to time.

At the time of the following exchange of opinions, Jürgens had been sent out to the camp as cook, and also to look after the lambs, but without his wife. He is not happy about this, and after three days at the camp (and when he later tells Director Harms about this, Kempe really emphasises the 'after only three days') he sends Kempe the following letter.

Undated, Hermannsburg[11]

Send us some coffee and tobacco by Sunday.

There are now five lambs here. Everything is in good shape, but I am a bit worked up because you have needlessly separated me from my wife and child. I have to admit to you that I have reached the point where I do not know whether to submit to your 'wise' advice or to avoid it. It is contrary to God's Word and will. Husband and wife should live together where they work together... You should trust them when they both want to be heard on their need, and not listen to the whims of others. If a person is found who is ready to live in this 'paradise' with wife and child, then I am prepared to take on, with my wife, the kitchen duties, laying the table and milking for as long as you like. It seems that might comes before right.

H Jürgens

Kempe replies:

Dear brother Jürgens!

I do not understand why you are worked up. If it is contrary to God's Word and will not to always be with one's wife, then I am in trouble, for no-one has been separated more than I have.

You are not showing love for your wife and child in wanting to have your wife there. The flies would eat away at your child's eyes and your wife would be without any comforts there. But if you think that one of us should come up north with a wife and a child, while you want to fiddle around here with your wife all the time, then that is unbrotherly, to say the least.

I do not know how you have decided to attribute whims to us. We have truly not been ruled by whims ... That accusation could be turned around.

In general, much in your letter remains baffling and it seems that you yourself did not know what you wanted to say. The devil is again looking for an opportunity to sift you, so watch and pray!

H Kempe

Enclosed are coffee and tobacco for the men. Only the men received tobacco, half a stick on Sundays.

P.S.[12] We have decided that if Jürgens refuses to obey us, we will terminate his stay on the station at a certain date. If he has not left by that date, we will deny him upkeep and we cannot be responsible for the consequences. But we hope we do not have to act in this way.

If you are of a different opinion, tell us immediately and tell us what to do.

H Kempe

Shortly after this, a rather curt note is sent by Kempe to Jurgens: 'Reply to my letter.' Obviously, Jürgens had not done that. Consequent to that, Kempe then receives this letter from Jürgens:

To Kempe.

The answer to your arrogant letter has arrived. I demand that it be returned to me after you have carefully read it again and examined if I have written anything wrong. If you leave out syllables anyone can interpret the letter as saying what I did not write: that the husband should always be at his wife's side or it would not be God's will. I did not write that someone should come up with a wife and child. What I did write was that I wanted you to indicate what you would do, and show you how serious this matter is to me.

As for showing lovelessness for my wife and child, neither you nor I can judge this. This much I do know, that God's gift is very dear to me, and I also know that I would be showing no love to my wife if I went against her.

So, that is what I wrote.

Again, I have written that I would join my wife in taking on kitchen, table and milking duties as long as necessary to show you how small a thing it would be for you to help your wives instead of occasionally waiting to do that. But the most offensive thing you say is that you consider the work I would take on nothing but fiddling around with my wife.

I know that if I was doing the station work alone it would not be called fiddling about. Whoever ... works hard is not doing enough, but whoever is slack, is working well, well enough for 35 shillings.

I now no longer want my wife to be here; nothing is gained by me having to fight for happiness. I take back my 'Yes', that I would stay here (for eight days from Sunday), for it is also not God's will that one person should be the cause of annoyance to another.

And just one more thing: If it were so that the devil was tempting me, it would be all the more necessary to have my partner with me so that, on this score, he would have no power over me.

I will not reply to a refutation.

H Jürgens

That is where the correspondence ends. Not too long after that, Jürgens was due back at the mission station, anyway, and so the matter ended. A little later Kempe informed Heidenreich: 'I had a brotherly discussion with Jürgens on Sunday ... There was mutual forgiveness and Jürgens finally explained that he was happy to have spoken out and was now happy to stay on.'[13]

* * *

While Schulze may appear to be the quiet member of the missionary trio, he certainly knows how to wade into an issue if he feels so inclined. This next letter gives the Schulze version of the friction with Jürgens and Tündemann.

20 March 1882, Hermannsburg[14] *(Schulze to Th Harms)*
Dear Director!

Brothers Kempe and Schwarz have already written to you with reference to our settlers, Jürgens and Tündemann, so a letter from me is no longer necessary. Nevertheless, I do want to write to help you to perhaps gain more clarity, and also to give you my view and judgement on the matter.

With respect to Tündemann, it has long been known that he has served the mission reluctantly and has thus caused some trouble. His nature is changeable; today he wants to do this, tomorrow something else. At one moment he wants to work at the joiner's bench, the next at shepherding, etc. But that is not always the case. If we call on him to do what he does not want to do just then, he growls and snarls like a mad dog. This is why it has sometimes come to a serious exchange of words.

Furthermore, he cannot be used for every task because of his limited intelligence. What I have always liked about him until recently is that he was open to advice and correction, and this allowed me to relate successfully to him several times.

However, this time he has stubbornly insisted that he wants to leave. What is the reason for this? Certainly no one other than Jürgens. Before we left to go South, Jürgens and Tündemann were always at each other. But since our arrival back here they have become close friends. How did that happen? I have no idea; though I must confess that Jürgens has completely changed since his wedding. I previously got on with him quite well, but since then he has constantly tried to avoid me and, on the way up here, was several times very unruly, even crass.

Just one example. Because there was good fodder at Bednowie[15] Springs, we camped there for several days. When we broke camp and it was rather fresh in the morning after a good rain during the night, two horses had become a bit feisty and run off after their hobbles were removed. At that Jürgens became quite furious. I, on the other hand, was glad that they showed such spirit before the difficult stretch that lay before us. What did Jürgens say? 'They'll pay for that; I'll drive them back hobbled.' I said: 'No you won't. It can easily happen that one of them breaks a leg or catches a fever.' He insisted: 'I'm going to do it.' I said ... 'If you do that we must talk this out in front of other people. What are we to do if one or both horses have an accident? We have with us only as many horses as are necessary. If you drive them ... revenge, as far as I am concerned, thoroughly in the buggy.'[16]

But what happened? He saddled a horse and drove off with a whip. When he got to the horses, he dismounted, hobbled both, and drove them the whole one and a half miles back to the wagon. When they arrived there, they looked as though they had come out of the horse pond, such an amount of sweat was dripping from them. My blood boiled with anger, but what was I to do? If he had been an Englishman, I would have driven him off on the spot and taken on the driving myself.

I could give you more such anecdotes, but enough for now. The worst thing is that he does not seem to consider that he has done anything wrong in this and similar instances, even after Brothers Kempe and Schwarz also expressed their disapproval. He does not know how to handle horses. His opinion (on which he insists) is that they have to be treated roughly and hard. My experience has been that more can be accomplished with most horses by quietly treating them with kindness, rather than roughness. The latter is in no way fitting for a Christian. If one speaks against his opinion and of the way he handles horses, that is called being 'overbearing'. He seems no longer to want (or need) to submit to and follow our wishes and directions, but to do *as he* wishes, probably at the instigation of his wife. The reason is his *arrogance* that is not happy to submit to our directions but wants to stand over us.

If an undertaking is to endure, no one can do just what he wants to. I am very sorry that Jürgens has allowed himself to be led astray by the devil. What is to be done? Faithfully pray for him. As far as I am concerned, I think no other person is responsible for Tündemann being stubborn. This pains me. I should not at all be surprised if Holterman also leaves; he is only human, and we know the nature of our hearts from personal experience. So prayer, faithful intercession! The devil is now severely attacking our mission. Is he to be the victor? May the dear Lord graciously avert that! ...

L Schulze

* * *

Director Th Harms is, of course, being kept apprised of all the shenanigans and hardships in the Australian mission, and is disturbed by them.

20 April 1882, Hermannsburg, Germany[17] (*Th Harms to Heidenreich*)
My dear Heidenreich,

In recent days I have received your last letters and they have moved me deeply. What is happening to you dear people there is happening also to us: internal conflict, internal frustration, everywhere ... great hostility ... and yet we survive... Just remain upright and honest, firm in faith and resolute, and yet full of love for your enemies, and the Lord will be with you and graciously help you get through everything.

Hopefully, Tündemann can be placated so that he stays. If not, let him go. It seems to me better that the colonists be paid a little more salary than in the past, and the missionaries should be urged to treat the colonists with love and kindness so that no bitterness arises.

Immediately after the mission festival three settlers will be sent off to you, faithful people, it seems: Koch, Eggers and Baden, all from this area. Your people there will then gain new heart. Koch is presently with a carpenter, Eggers with a mason, and Baden with a shepherd and tanner. I hope they learn enough handiwork that they can make themselves really useful there.

May God now turn around the terrible drought so that the land produces its growth …

I am glad that you manfully defended yourselves against the Missourian false teaching. The Calvinism of Missouri is a fundamental error which must cause the downfall of the Lutheran Church. It is sad that so many brothers hold to the error, all the more since they have no correct understanding of the essence and danger of this false teaching. Yet the truth must always be victorious…

Th Harms

*   *   *

The tragic story of Fred

It is Schwarz's turn to write the next quarterly report. In it he again complains of his sore eyes, and the horrendous heat. Temperatures have been the hottest since Europeans arrived, up to 180°F = 66°R.[18] However, everyone else in the mission is well, with the Schulzes welcoming their first child (Maria Charlotte Dorothea) on 25 February. It is interesting that in this report Schwarz designates Schulze as 'School Teacher Schulze', an indication of the role particularly given to him in their work.

The animals are doing well, a cellar has been built, a new well dug for the station, and a cemetery established. He also reports that:

> school has begun again, and there are 12 students. Besides them there are a number of old men and women, as well as mothers with babes in arms. But there are no employable men except the cow and goat herders. It seems as if the heathen use our station as a refuge and hospital for their children, their sick, and their elderly.

Then he recounts the story of Fred.

17 April 1882, Hermannsburg[19] *(Schwarz to Th Harms)*
It took place on the last day of February this year, just after midday lunch, when the heathen disappeared from the station with almost lightning speed, and the heathen in the camp were all deathly quiet. All of a sudden, this eerie silence was broken by a cry of lament that pierced marrow and bone, and in which the voices of both men and women were to be heard. We had already often had occasion to hear a heathenish uproar and howling, but so far we had never experienced something like this. It sounded like nothing else than the desperate cries for help of those who find themselves at the mercy of the clubs and hands of their murderers.

Since this screaming was down towards the Finke, about a thousand paces away, my first thoughts were: How could it possibly be that the heathen of a distant tribe could be so brazen as to set upon the locals right before our eyes, as it were? Brother Schulze and I set off to investigate the matter. Meanwhile, we had heard a rumour of the death of a heathen but we wanted to ascertain for ourselves what had happened and what the cause of such wretched screaming was. It was obvious that if this really was only a keening over death, even this had to have been a violent incident, because otherwise such howling appeared to us to be completely impossible.

Suddenly, it became quiet again and we had difficulty in finding the relevant spot. However, we finally found it on the opposite bank of the Finke. In the shade of the gum trees there sat around about six men, sunk in deep silence. Alongside these we saw a tight ball of people, all adults, lying in the sand, while the children sat some distance away. Brother Schulze and I initially surveyed the scene in silence because we knew the custom of the heathen that in such situations they do not speak at all but only point and indicate; and if they do speak to us, it is only quietly and reluctantly.

But what is it with that bunch of people lying on top of each other in the sand, all with their faces turned downwards, so that one cannot know whether they are male or female, and with a few women sitting around about them? In addition, they do not even move or lift or turn their heads to satisfy their curiosity, which is still so great among our heathen that by now they normally would have been overcome by it.

But look, the blood of some of them is seeping through the hair on their heads. What is this? What does it mean? We broke the silence and asked them what it all meant. We also reached out our hands to lift up those who were lying on top of each other, and to inspect them. We found five women with wounded heads and blood flowing onto their faces. I knew all the women, and the one lying right on the bottom was Ilgalita, the eldest wife of our Fred. We now learned from the men that Fred had died the day before. And so the whole thing was a part of a mourning ritual.

However, as we looked at the bleeding women we became somewhat shocked with the men, and Brother Schulze gave them a dressing down because we know of the harshness of the heathen towards their wives. In the end we learned that the wives had done this to themselves; but we went home sad. Who was this Fred for whom this mourning ritual was held? The actual name of this poor heathen was Tnubauka.

He was one of the first four heathen who connected with us soon after our arrival here, two at a time. At that time he was just a young man, as was his companion. With his companion he loved staying with us for some time and performed the most diverse tasks quite well. At that time I gave him the name 'Fred' (which is the English abbreviation for the German 'Friedrich'). Oh that in death he might have found the right kind of peace. In his life he at least always sought to keep the peace, although it was often made very difficult for him to do so.[20]

After he had given us good service for a considerable time he left us and later returned here as a married man. After that he was with us very often and for some considerable time, whereas sometimes all the other heathen went walkabout. How wonderful it was that he and his wife became more dear to us than others.

Tnubauka was a really imposing and handsome man, equipped with really outstanding gifts and manly virtues, strong, able, courageous, more honest and humble than all the other heathen. And since he was also fairly clean, he became the station butcher and in this field achieved the expertise a European would seldom possess. In short, what he saw he quickly understood, and so he was of great use to us. He had done most of the work at the school and the church.

He was also the one whom Brother L Schulze wanted to take with him to Bethany when he and Jürgens brought back their brides. But his love for his wife and child was so powerful that he left Brother Schulze after a few days and returned back here. We teased him and called him faint-hearted. He was a little bit ashamed about this, but kept silent, and was happy to be with his wife and child again. For he loved his child with his whole heart. I was really happy about that, and I think all the brothers and sisters on the station felt the same when Fred sat in his camp in his free hours and played fondly with his little son or carried him around on his arm, which other heathen seldom do—or not at all.

However, the child only had a few healthy days during his one and a half years, and he died here in the camp on the station on the evening of 29 December 1881. After a long absence, Tnubauka was again present with wife and child on the station for three days. He had left the station last time, as well as several other times, because of peace—or the lack of peace. He was not born on the Finke, but 20 English miles north-east of here; so, strictly speaking, he belonged not to the tribe in whose area our station is situated, but was related to two tribes which are near each other. Tnubauka's second wife, Katabukoia, was from the local tribe. Notwithstanding that, the local heathen envied him so much that they were never at peace with him, and the two worst were Rengerika, his own father-in-law, and Ratara, his brother.

Now, since he had already had some bloody conflicts with these two, he would never have come here again unless his child had become terminally ill, and he hoped to get help for him here. We were all happy when we saw him again, but we were sorry that his child was so sick, and saddened to see him so emaciated. Brother Kempe gave the child some medicine, but we had little hope for the child's life. Fred and his wife were given something to eat, and they were again taken on as workers. But evening had hardly come when a noise and screaming arose in the camp. Children and women were coming to the station, and howling, while in the camp the men, armed with spears and knives, were running around each other and making a noise, so that one could not really work out what was actually going on.

We quickly intervened but the blood was already flowing. Tnubauka had a severe wound in his thigh, and Rengerika, together with another man, was also wounded. What was the cause of this strife? Nothing but the toxic heathen envy and resentment from which even the already deeply distressed father and son-in-law were not immune.[21] We took Fred with us so that there might be peace, and we bound up his wounds. This was a right royal heathenish evening. The following was also the same, but quite the opposite to the evening of 29 December. For on that evening, at the same time as before, there was an unusual stillness in the camp of the heathen, although a large number of them were here.

What is the reason for this?

Fred's son lies in his last throes, and all the heathen, small and large, have gathered in his camp in such harmony that it is hard to believe: not one word is spoken, and the old people are listening anxiously to the child's every breath.

The child died, and the whole crowd raised up a most mournful howling. Some of the men and women held the mother of the child tightly, while other men took hold of the child and immediately buried him.

Since I had just been present and had handled the child, I did not believe that he would die so soon.

On hearing the cry, I turned around again just at the moment when the men were hurrying out with the body. I asked them where the child might be, and several of the children silently pointed upwards with their hands.

However, Fred and his wife, Ilgalita, left the station the next day at around midday. Wounded in body and soul, he moved forward supporting himself on a spear, while his wife, with the few possessions she carried in a bowl, followed him at a distance.

We were so sorry to see both of them again leaving here so soon. Yet it is the custom of the heathen to remove themselves as soon as possible from the place where any member of their family has died.

Fred headed in the direction of his home, and we did not see him again. Eight weeks later, the father followed his child. How he died is not quite clear to us. On the day of the above-mentioned mourning, his brother and the doctor of the heathen[22] told me and Brother Schulze in the presence of the remaining heathen that a poisonous snake had bitten him. Some days later we specifically took one young man aside and asked him about Fred's death. He definitely confirmed for us that he had met a violent death in that five heathen from a tribe in the north had attacked and killed him. A spear had pierced Fred's chest.

Now which of the two statements contains the truth we have to leave unanswered, as also everything else that distresses us. And it will not become clear before the Last Day...

W F Schwarz

* * *

To conclude this chapter, it is sufficient to provide excerpts from the reports on miscellaneous happenings. These take us to the middle of 1882.

1 May 1882, Bethany[23] *(Heidenreich to Th Harms)*
Highly respected, much-loved Father!
... It would be very good for the young people [who come out to Australia] not to have fiancées and to find women here if office and calling demand it. Any prospect of marrying can take years before actually happening. A long engagement at such a distance is dangerous for both sides. I could sing you a long song about some who would rather have seen their fiancées not come out

and, when they here got to know their rivals, there was conflict and heartache. Certainly, there are also some very happy marriages among the brothers. But it is not important for me whether the men are engaged or not engaged, as long as they carry out their official duties and are loyal to Hermannsburg and the confession of our Church.

You see how wonderfully God rules, that he turns enemies into friends. Oster's letter to you and his loyal, upright attitude to me in the struggle against the Missourians is a miracle before my eyes. It has cost him a lot before he regained my trust and that of the brothers...

Pastor Georg is improving. I was with him again on Wednesday, held a Day of Repentance service and administered the Lord's Supper... From Georg I went to Adelaide to call on the Minister. He was very friendly and granted me £400 of rations for the heathen this year, and intends to do more when need arises.

The incorporation is complete... The bell for the mission has also arrived. Lacking still are the altar vessels, if they were sent off.

Our missionaries and settlers are well but, regretfully, still argue about who has the authority...

G A Heidenreich

19 June 1882, Bethany[24] *(Heidenreich to Th Harms)*
Highly honoured, much-loved Father!

[Your last letter] arrived just at the right moment, in the middle of the heated struggle against the Missourians who have wanted to suppress us completely with the *Kirchenbote*. Now that they see that the ground is shaking under their feet in their own congregations, they are taking a more tolerant position...

Pastor Hensel's death is expected any moment, and Pastor Georg is still experiencing relapses all the time. In addition, the Missourians have thrown themselves into attempts to break off fraternal relationships with us ten and to no longer join us in serving the two parishes as guest pastors...

I also record with thanks that I have received £200 from Major Rauschenbusch. We still had good reserves, but sending the colonists up north is again costing us a lot of money...

In Schwarz's report you can read how things are up there. The missionaries are not completely at one with the colonists, yet I hope for a peaceful solution...

G A Heidenreich

19 June 1882, Hermannsburg, Germany[25] *(Th Harms to Heidenreich)*
My very dear Heidenreich,

Next month on 5 July four settlers leave for Australia for the mission there: carpenters, masons and tanners who are also well acquainted with farm work. The strife there between missionaries and colonists is very distressing. Do what you can by way of negotiations so that there is peace and no separation results. The friends of the mission here are sad about what they have heard of the strife, as unreliable as news may be. I hope that the four young people turn out well...

Do not be fearful of the Missourians. These people have a big mouth and nothing much behind it. The unfortunate doctrine on election is the last straw.[26] ...

Th Harms

21 June 1882, Bethany, Hermannsburg[27] *(Heidenreich to ELSA members)*
... To the news from the station, I add the information taken from a letter of Director Harms of April this year that, after the mission festival of St John's birth[28], three colonists, Koch, Eggers and Baden, would be sent from Hermannsburg for our mission here. Koch is learning carpentry, Eggers building, and Baden is learning tanning and shoemaking, so these three will make themselves very useful at our Mission...

G A Heidenreich

19.

The Cold, Colonists, Rabbits and Railways

Anyone accustomed to imagining the Centre of Australia as permanently hot, dry, dusty and dead, will be awed the first time they discover that it can be anything but. The first time you experience a downpour at Uluru, or witness the flood waters of the Todd River sweeping through the middle of Alice Springs. The first time you get bogged outback. The first time you witness the amazing wildflowers in full bloom. And the first time you get so cold lying in your swag at night you can hardly find enough spare clothes in your pack to keep yourself warm. These are awesome, unexpected, yet not uncommon, experiences in the heart of this magnificent land.

In his next letter, Schulze muses about these kinds of things. He also continues the missionaries' lament.

9 July 1882, Hermannsburg[1] *(Schulze to Th Harms)*
Dear Pastor,

As you realise, we are now in the middle of winter here. It is not as severe as in the homeland. We have not had snow since our arrival and it is most unlikely we will get any in the future. We have had ice every winter. Last year we had frost every night for five weeks without a break. The ice does not get very thick and is not strong enough to skate on. It does not even last for 24 hours; before the sun reaches its highest point, it disappears, despite the cold south-east winds. The thermometer does not fall much below zero. Some of you in the old homeland probably think how good we have it in that respect, that is, that we do not have to freeze here. However, every one of us declares that we feel the cold here more than the severe cold in the homeland. Maybe it is because the summer heat makes the body too soft and susceptible to cold weather. Warm clothes are therefore still a necessity and one looks forward to 'rugging up', especially on our beloved Sundays. Even our heathen have learnt that, too, and they like a thick woollen shirt much better than a linen or cotton one.

If you, our mission friends, could take note of that fact, it would be a good thing. You would probably feel the same if you could see the tribe bent huddled, shivering and teeth chattering, with a fire stick in their hand, walking to the station. When they arrive they put the fire stick down, gather some wood quickly to put on the fire, and huddle as close as possible to the warmth with their hands held over it. Because not all of them can sit around one fire, they have quite a few going in a small area. The men sit around on one side of the kitchen building and the women huddle on the other side with the children here, there and everywhere. It is difficult to get them away from their fires to say grace near the kitchen door. You have to call them not just once, but several times. After the 'Amen' they sit at their fires, all ready. The children have to take the portions of meat and bread over to the fires. If we did not ration the food, some would get a lot, some a little and some nothing. As soon as it is practicable, they should be eating at the table as we do.

Because of their great liking for the fire, it happens quite a lot that the clothes they like to wear in winter catch alight. On our part there is always a lot for us to do to warn them and to chastise them. In summer we have to push them to put clothes on, and in winter we have to see that they do not burn them or wilfully rip them to shreds.

As I said before, we do feel the cold very much, but despite that we prefer winter to summer. Just as you look forward to spring in the homeland, so we look forward to winter here. It is a pity that it lasts only four months, from the beginning of May to the end of August. This is our time of recuperation, despite the heavy workload. If we did not have this time, we would not be able to endure it here. In winter even our vegetable garden looks lovely, especially when the Lord, as now, occasionally sends us some rain. To him be thanks for that. Our entire area is now ablaze in a beautiful green, even though it consists only of weeds. Grass does not grow here in winter, despite the rain. Please pray with us that the Lord might grant us sufficient rain next summer so that the grass might grow and the waterholes in the dry river beds fill again, which would save the carting of water by road. One waterhole after the other is drying up.

Due to the work, we prefer winter to summer. While it is a joy to toil now, it is more of a burden when it is hot. As I said before, it is a pity that winter is so short because we have no shortage of work. We have to use these few months profitably before the summer comes with its heat. Regretfully, the spiritual work has to suffer then.

This winter we have started some major projects which we hope to finish with God's help. There is the erection of a stone building, 36 feet long, 18 feet wide and 9 feet high, the largest room of which is to house the blacksmith shop, carpenter's shop, and also the iron worker. The smaller room is for storing the horse harness and the verandah for keeping the wagon under cover.

Besides that, we will continue to work on the dam which we started last winter. We will also dig a well close to the dam and fence off a piece of land to make a garden. For this work we will use our heathen as much as possible. This will cost us a lot of bread and meat. Besides the bread, two sheep a day is hardly enough, but what shall we do? We have to teach them to work, for how should they learn to do otherwise if we do not teach them? If we fail in that, then they are forced to find their food in the wilderness. Their vagabond life is our biggest obstacle. Whatever they learn here is all forgotten when they return after a few days, weeks or months, and one has to start with the children from the beginning all over again. If they would all return at the one time it would not be so bad, but there are some today, some tomorrow, etc. We try to keep them busy whenever they arrive and we do not tolerate anybody that does not want to work; maybe that way they will forget about their walkabout; but then the question arises, how shall we keep everybody busy? Farming would be the best way to employ them but it cannot be done here. We have spoken on this subject on previous occasions. We also considered processing our wool. It would be a constant occupation for them. What do you think about this? It would, of course, mean acquiring equipment.

There is not much to say about the life of this tribe. They have heard and learned so much but that is where it has stopped. A desire for the Word of God does not manifest itself. They would rather do some physical work instead of listening to the Word of God. After one has gathered them together with much effort, it is difficult to rouse their interest. With all that done, they say, 'Yes, yes' to what they have heard and that is where it stops. Observing their lifestyle superficially, one would assume that they are a happy race of people. You can see and hear them laugh, but on closer examination their physical and spiritual poverty becomes evident. Syphilis is quite prevalent. Some suffer more, some less.

The fear of death is very real to all of them. They do not like to hear about it or talk about it, nor do they talk about their dead. In the case of men, especially young men, they claim they have been killed by poisonous animals or other men but never from natural causes. Such was the case in the last three months when two old men departed from this world or, as our heathen say, they were 'slain by somebody'. If only they would receive life, the true life, so that they would not have to fear death. That of course can only happen if they realise their present woeful state. However, with them this is not the case. Please help by praying for them that this may soon happen. There is quite a large number of them here now. May God give them understanding that they may soon bend their knees and pray to him.

In the last three months nothing new has happened here except the appearance of a comet in the western sky, which is now beginning to fade...²

Louis Schulze

* * *

The Colonists – 1882

There was considerable movement with colonists on the station in 1882. A number of new settlers arrived, and Jürgens decided to stay.

In this next letter Jürgens reports on the arrival and non-arrival of his and his wife's possessions from Germany. If the goods Jürgens is talking about refer to what he brought when he arrived in Australia in October 1877, he has been waiting for almost four years for these. His wife arrived in August 1880; which means she has been waiting two years for hers.

11 July 1882, Hermannsburg³ (Jürgens to Th Harms)
Dear Superintendent:

You will forgive me for again bothering you with a letter. Above all, my wish is that this letter finds you and your entire family in good health.

I am enclosing a voucher for the treasurer. I hope you will be so kind as to receive the money and then send it to my parents-in-law with the next mail, if possible. If that is possible, I would like the money to be paid out in Hermannsburg by Major Rauschenbusch, and let you retain the money in the mission treasury here, since it is very expensive to send it from here. You can take the costs out of the money. The address of my parents-in-law is: Mr H Schiermann, Schweimke bei Hankensbüttel, PO, Hanover, Germany.

I must also inform you, dear Superintendent, that our load of possessions has arrived, but what my wife also packed into Wolf's chest in Adelaide has not arrived. Schulze had handed over to Wolf a letter addressed to Tassi and Co saying that they were to send the load up North with the things that Wolf would give them. My wife had enclosed her best woollen clothes and other valuable things, and Mrs Schulze also packed in some old clothes. We would now like to know whether Wolf has told you anything about this matter.

Finally, I must also inform you that I have now decided to stay here on the station until God orders otherwise. I told the missionaries about this long ago and I hope that they have written to you. I did not write to you because I did not want to put pressure on you, but thought that you would accept as God's will what you and Pastor Harms would conclude from the missionaries' letters and the one from myself. If you now find that I am a hindrance to the work and the missionaries, just send me my dismissal. If the other is true, I will sit still and take the bad with the good...

Our young son is just starting to walk.

This winter we are building a smithy and a harness room out of stone.

Loving greetings to you and your family,

H Jürgens D Jürgens

* * *

As anticipated in recent correspondence, the next lot of colonists from Germany have arrived at the mission station. These are Christian Eggers, Christoph Freiboth, Heinrich Baden and Heinrich Koch. They arrived in Adelaide on 25 September, having left from Hamburg on the *Wodan* on 5 July. They departed from Bethany on 13 October, their journey expected to take six weeks. That would have had them arriving at the Finke at the end of November. Instead, they actually arrived on 15 December. Those extra couple of weeks or so were brought about, not because of any hiccups in their transport arrangements themselves, but because they finished up walking most of the way. Their camels broke down somewhere near Finniss Springs, approximately 600 miles, or 960 kilometres, from the Centre.

Eggers wrote an account of the whole journey, beginning with the departure from Germany.

27 September 1882, Adelaide[4] (Eggers to Th Harms)

Dear Director and Father!

The God and Father of our Lord Jesus Christ be praised and thanked for finally bringing us poor sinners to this point, according to his counsel and will. He has now brought our journey on the water to an end, and we have been able to set foot on Australian soil. How glad we were to be able to leave the slow ship *Wodan*.

Yet, despite the long sea voyage, we are looking forward to the journey by land, which we can hopefully complete in six weeks. It begins on 12 October at the point where the railway finishes. The line already goes 500 miles inland, and from there we will be brought further by camel to the station. That is why the journey will not take so long.

On 5 August we sailed from Port Said through the Suez Canal. At about 6 o'clock in the evening our ship ran aground on a sand bar and so had to cast anchor in the evening. No ship is permitted to pass through the canal at night, because it is too narrow. We remained stuck until almost midnight when the tide rose and lifted our ship and they were able to right it again.

Next morning we sailed on, and at 2:30 in the afternoon our ship ran onto sand in the Great Bitter Lake. At first the ship was in 22 feet of water, but then the front of the ship rose so high that it was in only 17 feet of water, and everything had to be off-loaded. A tugboat had to come to pull us off the sand bar, and 61 Arabs came on board to unload everything. On the third day a large steam ship came sailing by under full power, and the wash of the water helped us to get away.

We lost four days over this event so that we arrived at the town of Suez only on 10 August. There we had to take on drinking water. With that done, we entered the Red Sea.

In the morning of 11 August we saw the Sinai and Horeb Ranges. It was nicely warm on the Red Sea. We perspired continuously since on 16 August we were directly under the sun's rays.

On the 17th we arrived in Aden and had to take on coal there. After travelling for one day out of Aden, we encountered rather bad weather for four days, so that we could sail only at half power; the captain was fearful for the horses we had on board. We had got them on deck in London, and they stood in stalls. If the ship rocked too severely, they and the stalls could topple overboard. We have to say we had good weather the whole time.

On 30 August at 1 o'clock in the afternoon we arrived at the coral island Degar Gary, and there had to take on coal again because of the wind that had been against us. There were many coconut palms on this island.

On the first of September we set off again and thought that the next stopping place would be Adelaide, but we were mistaken. We had to take on coal in the city of Albany which is situated in Western Australia. From there we had six days to Adelaide, so we arrived at 2 o'clock in the afternoon of 25 September and disembarked at 5 o'clock.

We went to Consul Mücke, since Mücke's father came on board and told me that Pastor Heidenreich had written to his son saying that we were to come there first. Young Mücke gave us the address of Pastor Homann and we made our way to the train station. When we had our ticket, Pastor Homann came and sought us out, so we were in good hands.

On the 26th, Pastor Heidenreich arrived; Georg had arrived on the previous evening. There was great joy that we were there, and we were told that our overland travel would not take longer than six weeks...

Christian Eggers

* * *

Heidenreich is happy with all the travelling arrangements for these newcomers, including the costs involved. Of course, he must make pointed reference to his intrepid initial incursion into the site of the mission (he is probably referring to the original trip North, including the reconnaissance trip), seeming to overlook the fact that he did not make that trip alone.

10 October 1882, Bethany[5] *(Heidenreich to Th Harms)*
On 13 October the new brothers will set out on their journey North under the leadership of Councillor Ahrens. So, from water to sandy desert. The first 400 miles are by train to Farina, formerly Government Gums, where Brother Ahrens hands them over to the camel contractor, Ross, and makes all the necessary arrangement for the further trip and then returns here. The brothers, however, continue their journey on the ships of the desert for another 600 miles and in six weeks will be on our station. We have never before been able to get people up there so cheaply and quickly. I had to struggle for ten months, enduring indescribable crises, hardship and misery among people and animals before God crowned my faith and allowed me to see our beautiful territory and to ride about it for 12 days. Now I am glad that the dear brothers will be able to celebrate Christmas at their new home.

As for the travel costs this time, they are not to be compared with those earlier. We pay £2/10 = 50 marks per person on the train, £7 = 140 marks per person by camel, including food. Earlier travellers have cost us more travelling by horse than these marks. Also, with the train, freight is now £20 a tonne cheaper.

* * *

Eggers later wrote a report on the journey, and this is included in *The Translation*. Twenty-five years after the event, Freiboth wrote a similar report, but it is more detailed and graphic than Eggers' account. For that reason Freiboth's version is the one chosen for inclusion here.

A Camel Journey through the Desert on Foot[6] *(G C Freiboth)*
At last the day dawned for the continuation of our journey into the Interior, that is, per camel—an animal well adapted to the desert. Here in Australia only the one-humped camel is to be found. I shall now describe as well as I can

this frightful journey by camel from the township of Farina to the place of our destination, namely, the Hermannsburg mission station on the Finke River.

I can no longer recall the date we left. The camel caravan was headed by two Englishmen. The senior driver was Jim Willers by name. That is the correct name, but his surname is no longer familiar to me. His partner was Frank Wallers, a youth of 16 or 17, at the most 18 years of age. This fellow reprimanded us every now and then for some reason or another, but since we could not understand each other, we simply let things be.

From Farina they took along a good supply of provisions for all of us, like tomato sauce and other kinds of sauce, all sorts of pickles, an assortment of jams and honey, and a sack full of bakers bread, so that the riding camel had a good and full load. In addition to foodstuffs, it had to carry two ten-gallon and two five-gallon leather waterbags, thus a total of 30 gallons of water. It also had a waterbag slung around its neck, from which we six people could drink when we were thirsty. Unfortunately, we were often thirsty. The first man to unleash the bag saw to it that the bag went the round to all six, and the last man to drink had the dubious pleasure of returning and fastening it to the camels. This proved an awkward and tedious task, as the camel string was never halted.

We were supposed to have ridden to the mission station on these camels but, unfortunately, the camel drivers on the down journey had lost three animals. Actually, these camels were the property of Undoolya station, which lies in the MacDonnell Rangers of Central Australia, 12 miles east of Alice Springs telegraph station.

And now we were even taking back a sick camel, without a load, except that it bore its own saddle. However, it died on Finniss Springs station, 75 miles out of Farina. This is the very camel that we four (Heinrich Baden, Christian Eggers, Heinrich Koch and I, Christoph Freiboth) were supposed to have ridden, if it got better. But now it was the fourth animal to be lost, so, for us, riding was now entirely out of the question.

By now we had tramped 75 miles on foot, but there still remained well over 600 miles ahead of us, for it was estimated to be about 800 miles to our destination at Hermannsburg. Daily we kept up the march, never going less than 12 miles. Only once in a while did we have a day of rest, or perhaps two in succession. So, day by day we grew more and more tired and exhausted.

We had to drink various kinds of water: greenish, yellowish, whitish, brackish, etc. In some waterholes the cattle had lain and died, so that the water gave off an awful stench. But that did not help the situation: there was no other water available. It had to be fetched and scooped up as far away as possible from the presence of dead cattle, and the nose and mouth held shut. When boiled, such water leaves a scum around the edge as thick as one's thumb. After this has been pulled off, the tea is added. We had to drink this in order not to suffer tormenting thirst in the dreadful heat, for very often waterholes were many miles apart.

Wagon horses or bullocks which are driven out in the morning can often not drink until the following day. After being unharnessed [at the end of the day], they may have to be driven forward another 6, 8, or even 10 miles to the next waterhole for a drink, or, if the distance is still too far, they may have to wait until the following day. Then, when water is reached, they are taken out of their harness except for collar and winkers. Finished with drinking, they are returned to the wagon and reharnessed. The weary journey then continues on that day as far as possible. And so it goes for hundreds of miles, until they reach the station for which the loading is destined. After a recovery period of several weeks, the wagon horses or bullocks then go back for a fresh load.

It should be mentioned in this connection that the teamster always carries sufficient water kegs for his own use, filling them from waterhole to waterhole, so that he never runs short. Here one learns to value water. Water that one would not look at in Germany has to be drunk in this Australian wilderness. This was the experience of us four newcomers: the heat was so intense, and we were so unaccustomed to the climate, that we drank all kinds of water and, in consequence, contracted dysentery; indeed, one of us even got acute diarrhoea. Another developed swollen feet from a sprained ankle. And yet we were forced to continue day after day. One waterhole to the next was as far as 100 miles apart.

When the day was over, we often lay down dead tired, without partaking of an evening meal, for we could not eat on account of the strain of the day's march. In fact, one would not expect a tired person to get to that stage that he did not care whether he remained dead or alive, or saw the light of another day. But that is quite feasible, for we ourselves experienced this state of affairs. At times we were so exhausted, that we could only utter a sigh: 'Into your hands, O faithful God, we commend ourselves', or 'Faithful Lord and Saviour, keep us in your grace and mercy', or 'Lord and faithful Saviour, be our support again throughout this night; you have helped us hitherto, graciously continue to help us.' In this way we entrusted ourselves to his grace and help for the following day, believing, if it were his will, he would give us renewed strength to carry on.

It so happened one day, after we had come a long way, that the track took a wide bend toward two long and low hills. While the telegraph line went over the hill to the left, I followed the camels. Brother H Baden and I had taken a short rest together, but since I did not like to stay too far behind, I hurried and arrived at the same time as the camels at the natural springs where we were to camp for the night. H Baden came into camp not long after me. We both wanted to help unload (which we did whenever possible), but this time were so exhausted that we desisted, our strength simply forsaking us. The senior camel driver did not want us to help either, so merely told us to rest ourselves.

Brother Christian Eggers had sat down on a telegraph pole to take a rest. Later he, too, came crawling into camp. After all the camels had been unloaded, he was about to take one of the riding camels to go and fetch H Koch who was still further in the rear, and probably the most tired of us all. Just as he was about to leave, a black dot became visible on top of the hill over which the telegraph line crossed. It was the head of Brother H Koch. It grew taller and taller, until the whole man appeared. With great pain and difficulty he, too, then arrived in camp.

Some time later that evening Brother Christian Eggers, in a few words of broken English, said to Jim Willers, the senior driver: 'Tomorrow stop here!' But Willers replied: 'No, tomorrow 18 miles.' Chris Eggers contradicted his orders; but that is where the matter ended. There was no rest for us the next day, yet, with God's help we survived the tally of miles.

It occurred to us one morning whether it would not be better and more convenient for us to have the way indicated to us each morning and that we start out on the road before the camels got going. We tried this, going on ahead, and found it to be much better. We could go at our own pace, and when we got well ahead we could sit down for a while until the camels drew nearer. Then we got up again to stay in the lead. That is how we proceeded from that day onward, and felt considerably relieved.

In due course we came to Strangway Springs station, and camped at one of the springs. Here a sheep was slaughtered and taken along for our use. Several hundreds of miles further on we reached Peake, the second telegraph station, where mound springs abounded. We camped near one of these. It was merely an elevation where we had set up our nocturnal quarters.

I noticed that Frank Willers walked along this mound for some distance armed with a dish, soap, and some clothing to be washed. After he was finished, I walked to the spot to have a look at the water, but could not find any. In the end it occurred to me that everything sounded so hollow under foot. I was right. Pushing aside a stone plate, I discovered the water below: beautiful, sweet spring water.[7]

It is quite extraordinary here in Australia that there are places full of springs. On the other hand, waterholes may exist 100 or more miles apart, in creeks or in watercourses and last for months. Indeed, if the waterhole is a large one, it may hold out for a whole year, until it rains again. In Australia's Interior the rain can even fail for months on end. This has been my personal experience. It is now 25 years since we left the Finke River mission at Hermannsburg, but this still stands out quite clearly in my memory.

From the Peake station we proceeded for several hundred miles into quite different country, where man and beast are dependent only on such stagnant static water holes. I will name a few cattle, horse or sheep stations through which we passed. But before we left the Peake station, Brother Eggers wrote a letter to the mission folk [at Hermannsburg], requesting them to come and meet us [with horses] and thus relieve us of our daily trials and difficulties.

Anyway, we left Peake station and camped next day alongside a beautiful spring in a shady creek, from whence lovely clear spring water flowed from a rock. During the days and weeks that followed we had to be satisfied with rainwater from static pools that resulted from rain and thunder storms. Cattle, horses and sheep drank from these pools, and the water had to suffice for humans as well, if they did not want to die of thirst. And many have perished from thirst in this Australian desert. As we continued on our way, we came across several such waterholes from which animals and humans had to drink.

At last we reached Charlotte Waters station. We could see the roof of this place from an elevation many miles away. They told us it was still a long way to go, 18 miles. We bypassed the station by a short mile and camped on the bank of the Charlotte Waters Creek. Next day we continued on our way and now had only 250 miles to get to Hermannsburg.

At length we came to Goyder's Creek, where we camped at a well, then to Crown Point station where we saw the Finke River for the first time. The next station was Horseshoe Bend which also lies on the Finke River. Here we bought a bottle of rum to add to our drinking water. We had not realised till now that our camel drivers carried two casks of rum, and we had been too dumb to observe them drawing their daily supply for drinking. But now he saw them walking over to the station with several bottles.[8]

We could not see the station from where we were, nor could we see the Finke River, for we were camped a considerable way off, behind the first large sandhill. From here we had nine of these extremely high sandhills to cross over between each of which was a hard plain about 1 or 2 miles in width. Between two of these giant sandhills we set up camp for the night.

Our kind Mr Jim Willers lent us his tarpaulin for the nights that followed. Our mission friends [in the South] should have made us aware of this need and should have supplied each of us with a calico groundsheet, for how were we to know what was required? Here we had to learn everything by personal experience. How could we even have bought our own tarpaulin? We were sent out on an 800-mile trek lasting several weeks before reaching our destination and were given only £2 between us, that is 10 shillings per person. But with this money we bought a bottle of rum, so that every time we had a drink of water we could add a small gulp to the stale water, and be able to tolerate it better. Our [mission] superiors had treated us very inconsiderately to have sent us out into the desert in such a lighthearted manner. With God's help, we survived the situation, and the faithful God brought us nearer to our goal each day.

The tarpaulin with which Mr Jim Willers provided us each night as a groundsheet for our blankets we were using again on this particular night. There were several fine trees nearby, coniferous trees known as 'desert oak', with a fine carpet of soft needles on which to spread our sleeping gear. We thought this would be more comfortable to sleep on than to lie on the hard ground. Jim Willers and Frank Wallers, on the other hand, had set up their camp in the middle of the track.

We were lying there on the soft needles under these trees, when at midnight or even earlier Mr Willers was astir, and with a firestick in hand was searching around on the ground. Next thing Brother Eggers and H Koch were up also, and since Baden and I were in the middle, we kept lying a little longer. However, before long we, too, had to retreat from a small army of troublesome ants that had declared war on us. Of course, they always gained the victory. So, we had to shift our camp to a new spot. After a few hours, without further incident, we were able to get to sleep again, for we sorely need sleep on account of our daily trials and marching on foot. In this camp a fresh damper was baked. Later on, in another place, I will describe how meat is cooked or grilled during bush travel, or how bread or damper is made, or johnny-cakes cooked on the hot open coals in order to have something quick to eat.

From this last camp we had to travel several days before reaching Mount Burrrell station. Here we were met by Mr Schleicher from the Hermannsburg mission station, who had brought packhorses and a riding horse for each of us four. At that time Mr Schleicher was working on our station, and was in charge of the wagon horses. So, if anything had to be carted, the job fell to him. We were due to ride off next day. At midday the horses on which we were to ride were brought in, hobbled. Kempe's mare, also hobbled, came in at a gallop. H Baden was to ride this animal, but when he saw it galloping, he said I should ride that wild horse. No wonder!—for all of us, with the exception of H Koch (who had been an artillery man) were no riders.

Next day Mr Schleicher saddled the horses for us. We farewelled the camels and when all was ready we proudly set out on our journey. I also had to take along my umbrella which I fastened to the side of my saddle. Our immediate destination was Henbury, a neighbouring station 80 miles from Hermannsburg and also situated on the Finke River. But we were such skilled new chums in riding, that we followed each other in Indian file. Every now and again our horses would dip their heads to stop and chomp at the nice green grass along the way. In their attempt to make up for lost time, they would then break into a trot, causing us to slide from one side of the saddle to the other, sometimes in fear of making contact with the ground. During such a trot they would at times stop quite suddenly at a nice bunch of grass, so that we were placed in a new danger of flying over their heads. However, we clung firmly to the pommel of our saddles, and even held onto the horses' manes.

But—oh dear!—when we made a midday lunch break or struck camp for the night, how our bones ached and our limbs had grown stiff—to such a degree, that we could scarcely walk or sit down. And when we lay down at night we could hardly get to sleep on account of our aching limbs. But with the passing of time our stiff joints grew more flexible, so that our riding improved from day to day.

At length we reached Henbury station owned by Mr E Parkes, our nearest neighbour, but who still lives 80 miles from the mission. The following day we journeyed further towards home, but had to make one more open-air camp and two midday halts before reaching it. At about 50 miles from Henbury we struck camp, just as we were about to leave the Finke to negotiate a pass through the range known as Parkes Pass. After rejoining the Finke, we set up our last camp at Running Waters. This waterhole is a vast spring that runs for about 7 or more miles and then disappears into the sand. Strange, indeed, very strange, but later we came across this phenomenon on several occasions. Here we had the misfortune next morning of finding our blankets full of prickles, which are very difficult to remove.

We continued our journey that day, and from now on had to follow the soft dry sandy riverbed, with high and steep mountains to right and left of us. Mr Schleicher shot a kangaroo (actually a 'whiptail') which he immediately skinned. We had midday lunch at Parkes' Old Station on the Ellery's Creek. That was the first kangaroo meat we got to eat during our long foot-slogging desert journey here in Australia, and we found it splendid, first-rate.

We were now only seven miles from home, so, after we had lunched and our horses had eaten their fill and had a rest, we moved on towards the mission where we arrived hale and hearty on the 15th of December 1882. The first to help welcome us were August Tündemann and H Jürgens. After a while came Missionaries L Schulze, F Schwarz and H Kempe. Towards evening these were joined by the two shepherds, H Holtermann and J G Mirus, who at that time were tending the station sheep.

Altogether we had been eight weeks on the road to accomplish our 800-mile journey through the desert. But on seven days we rested. So, it is easy to calculate how many miles we averaged each day. As long as God gives us life and health here on earth, none of us will ever forget that arduous journey.

* * *

Harms was full of praise for these people. He was a little concerned, however, about the relationship between them and the rest of the staff, and was eager to see that matters in that regard were well managed.

23 October 1882, Hermannsburg, Germany[9] (*Th Harms to Heidenreich*)
Hopefully, the four colonists will soon be in Hermannsburg. Make sure that the relationship of the colonists to the missionaries is strictly regulated. I consider it advisable that the colonists be placed under an administrator to whom the missionaries also are responsible. Give this some thought and write to me about it when you have the opportunity.[10]

24 December 1882, Hermannsburg[11] (*Th Harms*)
Our brothers, the colonists, have made such a journey in 51 days from Farina to Hermannsburg in Australia, through the desert sand and burning summer heat. They are brave young people, undaunted, and persevering. The Lord bless them for their faithfulness and grant that they be a rich blessing to the mission. They fortunately got through with their English gibberish and the Lord has not forsaken them. It is indeed a precious thing, this thing called faith.

* * *

Between now and the end of the year, Heidenreich sends off six letters, five of them to Harms, and two lots of them written on the same day. Much of their content is similar to previous reports. Therefore, to avoid an abundance of repetition, only extracts from those letters are produced here. In the midst of those letters, there is one from Director Harms to Heidenreich—an occasion that Heidenreich always eagerly anticipated, and which gave him much encouragement.

14 August 1882, Bethany[12] *(Heidenreich to Th Harms)*
Highly honoured, much-loved Father!
... I have again been seriously ill for ten days, so that I had already given up hope of a full recovery.

Meanwhile, the struggle with the local Missourians has intensified sharply. From the last day of July until 4 August there was a Pastors Conference and Church Council meeting where the opposing teachings were either to be resolved, or else brought to a general synod for decision. All the Missourians were present with the exception of one. On our side, Pastor Hensel had died,[13] five brothers were not present, old Pastor Appelt's memory was weak,[14] and Georg and I were still half sick. So, Pastor Oster had virtually to rely on God and himself.

The other side talked at length and prepped and urged on the young Missourian coming from the struggles in America in which he had personally participated and from which he had brought a good supply of catch-words written on paper. They chose him to be their spokesperson. Humanly speaking, there was little hope for us. But the truth set us free, and they did not overcome us.

The outcome was again a weak agreement, each side sticking to its position ... That the Missiourians are not honest, however, became quite clear after the much-lauded peace agreement, as it concerned the notification of the calling of pastors from Hermannsburg. Pastor Oster announced that he had called a pastor for Blumberg, as well as an assistant for Georg and you. Immediately, three members of the Church Council protested and disclaimed all responsibility. Oh, what renegades! They wanted to cancel the call and bring Dorsch from Missouri to Blumberg, where he could actively work on the Church Council and the *Kirchenbote*. And with that they have now revealed their cards. Pastor Oster, Drögemüller and Schmidt are to be removed from the Church Council, and Dorsch becomes the President to bring in the Missourian regime. They will not succeed, since the doctrinal struggle will be followed by a sad struggle for control, and it will tear the Synod apart...

Heidenreich

* * *

Even though Heidenreich does not in this next letter specify the exact nature of the conflict between the missionaries and the settlers, it most likely relates to the authority the one group has in relation to the other. There is a history of the colonists resenting any orders the missionaries gave them, and of the missionaries being annoyed by the lack of compliance on the part of the colonists. There could also be dissatisfaction between the two groups regarding different levels of pay and salary.

14 August 1882, Bethany[15] *(Heidenreich to Th Harms)*
Highly honoured, much-loved Father!

A thousand thanks for your precious, welcome letter of 19 June 1882 in which you first provide notification that four colonists are leaving for here on 5 July...

Regarding the strife between the missionaries and colonists, I can by God's grace report that it is coming to a peaceful end. Already in his previous report, Brother Schwarz brought you the first news [about this], and with this I am sending you letters from the missionaries and colonists that will attest for you that the desired peace is at the door... [and I am hopeful] that this will bring the conflict to an end. Thank God for that.

... Also, our sheep have lambed well, providing 939 lambs...

When Major Rauschenbusch sent me the £200 I imagined I was so rich that I thought they could have kept the money in Germany. Now I know that I had done my calculations without the heavenly proprietor. The account for freight for the previous year's rations arrived, requiring our treasurer to pay £250. We had paid the final debts of £100, and we made over six tonnes of purchases for a year, which will cost well over £300. We are now already stuck in the sand again, even before the new colonists have arrived. Their journey to the station will cost at least £150. With us it is a matter of being poor at one time, then wealthy at another, then having nothing at all; and yet the work goes on without gold and silver...

G A Heidenreich

10 October 1882, Bethany[16] *(Heidenreich to Th Harms)*
Highly honoured, much-loved Father!

... The Missourians continue their activity and have not joined us for the mission festival at (Pastor) Georg's. The Missourian Dorsch has divulged that he has been charged with founding an American mission here. Now, all those who in all countries are working against Hermannsburg ... disloyal missionaries, [are] withdrawing their donations and counteracting [Hermannsburg]...

Heidenreich

* * *

This next letter provides a quite detailed description of the various ways in which the mission is being funded and otherwise supported.

10 October 1882, Bethany[17] *(Heidenreich to Th Harms)*
Highly honoured, much-loved Father!
... Everything became pressing before the end of the financial year. On 25 September the dear brothers, the colonists Baden, Eggers, Freiboth, and Koch, arrived. On the 26th I went to meet them at Port Adelaide where there was much to do; on the 27th my councillor met with our treasurer to prepare the financial report for the year; on the 28th Drögemüller, treasurer Schmidt with his Bethany choir and I travelled to the mission festival at Pastor Georg's congregation at Emmaus. Unfortunately, Baden and Ahrens, who had just come back from Queensland, were still occupied with customs and unpacking, so that they could not be at the mission festival like the other brothers and councillors.

Despite storm and dust, the festival was truly wonderful. The folk at Emmaus had erected a fine festival site in the open, with great artistry and taste. The local brass band, the choir from Bethany, and the six festival speakers faithfully played their parts, and God blessed everything with peace and joy in our hearts. The collection, with later contributions, amounted to £20 = 400 marks, the greatest amount so far in the country for our mission.

Our respected Senior Pastor Hensel in Blumberg, had died, so with him the mission had lost its spiritual advisor. Consequently, I had the seven pastors present elect someone to fill the vacancy among the directors. The vote fell on our dear, longstanding president of our Synod's Church Council, Pastor Oster in Rosenthal. He willingly took on the added burden of mission, for which I heartily thank God...

When I went to meet the brothers at the ship. I went to Parliament House with Baden and Eggers and presented my card to the Minister for Education, and also to the Member of Parliament, F Basedow, the representative for my district. Both came, and I told the Minister that we had to have rations for the heathen. This year he had so far given me nothing and it was high time that he did something. As a man of the world, he was very gallant, and said, 'Give me your wishes in writing, and I will give you £300 = 6000 marks for the mission. With that you can buy what you want and take care of more besides'. I said that I thanked him for the trust he placed in me, but that it would be better for me if he stayed with the old arrangement where he allowed purchases to be made according to my order invoice and he paid the freight...

By the way, if the government annually budgeted £300 = 6000 marks, I would accept this with thanks. Then the government would be paying a third of the maintenance costs of the mission, without the land, and we would thus be able to regulate everything better. Now that the incorporation of the mission has been brought into being and into force, I will attempt to bring clarity to our position with respect to rations. Beyond this I have another plan, to found another station, if God so wills and gives us the means.

The Church here has again supported our mission in ways worthy of thanks. The local congregations have donated £369/5/1, about 7500 marks. May the Lord reward all the dear donors.

On behalf of us all, I particularly express our sincere thanks to our dear mother, the mission community in Germany, for so generously providing for our mission here with all things necessary and useful. To my joy I found at Port Adelaide six large crates full of clothes, shirts, skirts, hose, bed linen, rolls of linen, dolls, toys, shoes, writing materials, men's coats, vests, trousers, underpants, scarves and so on in great supply, beyond my expectation and to the amazement of custom officials. Our honoured treasurer, Major Rauschenbusch, previously wrote that, for some years, he has been collecting gifts especially intended for us and we should simply send him a wish list. That is what happened. So, we have now also received, beyond what we requested or thought of and in addition to the above abundance, wonderful ornaments for our chapel, consisting of altar vessels, paraments, a small bell, instruments and music for our brass band, and so on.

May our faithful God and Saviour richly reward all donors who have in this way lovingly thought of us. May he especially look with grace and faithfulness on our dear sister who has sacrificed her entire bridal finery for the sanctuary[18] of the poorest of our heathen, as have also the dear brothers and sisters and the dear state of Hanover, Holstein, Silesia, Hesse, Russia, and so on…

G A Heidenreich

23 October 1882, Hermannsburg, Germany[19] *(Th Harms to Heidenreich)*
My dear Heidenreich.

God willing, the young brothers will set sail on the *Katarina* for Adelaide from Hamburg on 5 November. There are eight brothers, not four, of which you are to receive four, namely Darsow, Christoph and Heinrich Harms, and Fulbohm. The other four, Prenzler, Joachim and Johann Koehnke and Heuer are to go to Queensland…[20]

Among the four brothers designated for your Synod, Darsow is probably the most scholarly. Fulbohm is a valuable man, deep and sincere. He will,

I hope, give you much joy. They have been examined and ordained, as their certificates prove.

As for the conflict with Missouri, do not allow yourself to be intimidated. Truth always wins, especially when attacked by such ... people as you have there...

Schulze's suggestion to set up weaving in Hermannsburg to process raw material and provide work for the heathen has appealed to us. I will present it to the Mission Council...

Th Harms

3 December 1882[21] *(Heidenreich to ELSA members)*
Dear congregations in mission!

The start of the new mission year was very exciting. Shortly before the end of the year, the four colonists, H Bader, Chr Eggers, Chr Freiboth and H Koch, arrived from Hermannsburg. They brought with them many large cases with all sorts of clothes, rolls of linen, stockings, skirts and shirts, shoes, etc., for our heathen. In addition, they brought coverings for the altar vessels and a whole set of wind instruments. All gifts, as well as a clock from the German friends of our mission, men and women, from Hanover, Holstein, Hesse, Silesia, and even from Russia were designated for our mission.

It is touching to see the zeal for mission developed by the large Hermannsburg Mission community. For example, a bride gave all of her bridal finery for the altar vessels in our chapel for the heathen. The faithful Lord will richly reward her and we all wish for her that the heavenly bridegroom will clothe her in his finery and robe of honour, and give her grace to clothe herself with the adornment of holy women...

Heidenreich

12 December 1882, Bethany[22] *(Heidenreich to Th Harms)*
Highly respected, much-loved Father!

... There will be a real shock here in the land over eight pastors coming from Hermannsburg. The Lord who is sending them will also provide us with the ways and means for placing them. The harvest on the land is poor, unfortunately, but I have two congregations in the bush where one of them would find work and upkeep. The four meant for us[23] we will soon accommodate, but there will be snags with Queensland. However, I will write there immediately. It would be best if I kept them all here, for who knows what our synod on 20 February will bring; perhaps a band of Missourians will leave for America, if the Lord graciously grants us victory over them. With some 40 congregations in our ten parishes, we have unanimously presented a motion to the synod in session: 'Protest against the Missourian doctrine of election to faith, the kind of doctrine previously unknown to our Synod and which we do not want to hold in the future'...

Everything is proceeding quietly in the mission...

G A Heidenreich

* * *

The missionaries have now been on the station for five years. This next report from Kempe provides another overview of the incredible amount of work they had to do, and the complex variety of that work. However, they never lose sight of the fact that their main purpose in establishing the mission is the conversion of the Aboriginal people to the Christian faith. Yet, after five years that is still not happening, and one senses the discouragement that is beginning to creep into the missionaries' hearts as a result.

What is also obvious is the immense gap between the Aboriginal and missional worlds. This does not seem to bother the Arrarnta people too much. But it puzzles the missionaries no end.

Allied with that is the gap between the White and Black worlds, generally. And for the first time in *Missionaries, Madness and Miracles* we encounter an episode of White and Black killings in the vicinity of the station.[24] These, too, are the consequence of the different understandings of the two groups, this time around stock ownership.

30 September 1882, Hermannsburg[25] *(Kempe to Th Harms)*

> 'In life, human beings are like grass. They blossom like flowers in the field. When the wind blows over it, they are no more, and their place no longer knows it.' PSALM 103:14–15

Dear Pastor!

This Bible passage, like many others, e.g. Psalm 90, portrays the transience of human life very clearly and vividly before one's mind. In these days I have been thinking how one first really learns to understand such references here in this land, because it is exactly here that the glory of the grass and flowers is extremely brief.

Three months ago, when Brother Schulze wrote his last report, everything was fresh and green. And now? Hardly has the warmth and dryness set in than all this glory is gone. Truly, barely a month ago everything looked so fresh, and now everything is again a desert. And human life is also over just as quickly. But well for us that we are able to say: 'Lord God, you are our refuge for ever and ever', and: 'Christ is my life and death is my gain.' How highly graced are we as Christians that we are able thus to speak in faith.

One especially learns to recognise that when one considers the condition of the heathen here. They are indeed as Paul says, slaves through fear of death throughout their lives. They sense danger to their lives everywhere and they actually never escape that fear at all. That every person must die on account of sin does not occur to them at all. They always think that when one dies, either the devil or some person from another tribe has murdered them. That is also why there is a continuous procession of murder back and forth. If someone from another tribe has died, then men come here and murder the best one they can get their hands on. The locals here do the same. We have tried everything to discourage them from doing this, to show them the uselessness, the stupidity, the damage, the despicable nature and sinfulness of such actions, but all in vain.

Earlier, I have often wondered about the small number of heathen living in Australia, but the more insight one gains into their views and foolish customs, the more it becomes clear to me that in actual fact it cannot be due to anything else at all than that they are mutually wiping each other out.

I said before that they are slaves through fear of death their whole lives. We experienced this recently also through the death of a woman near here on the station. This woman belonged to a southern tribe and along with several others had been shot by Whites. This happened because a number of Blacks had stolen some head of cattle and slaughtered them. Out of revenge the Whites rode out, shot some whom they first encountered among the Aboriginal people, but who were sleeping unsuspectingly. They wounded three of them, but two later died. As far as we later learned, all of these people were quite innocent of the matter. But this is the general tactic of the Whites here, and gives a better example, better than a long description, of the children to whose spirit they belong.

One of those wounded was the old lady I mentioned, and in addition there were two other men, all of whom came here. In the beginning we knew nothing at all about the old woman for the heathen had kept it quiet from us. Only when matters were really bad did Brother Schwarz by chance come into the camp and find her there, but unfortunately too late, for the lower body where the shot had entered was totally eaten away by maggots and she already lay quite unconscious.

One Sunday evening the heathen came here and asked for a shovel because, they said, the old lady had died. We hurried down, fearful that they might bury her alive, and we found her still alive, although already in the throes of death. They were all so full of fear that I believe if we had not gone down there, they would really have interred her alive, so fearful are they of death. Alongside the sick person a man was standing armed with two large spears in order, according to what they said, to drive away the devil, or at least to make him frightened. Indeed, even as some of them dug the grave, one of them had to stand by in readiness with the weapons.

We asked them how it came about that people had to die, to which they answered: 'Other people killed her'. That gave us the opportunity earnestly to explain to them the true cause of death, namely sin, and to point them to the one who alone is able to save us from sin and death, the Lord Jesus. I have never seen them all listen so quietly and attentively as they did on that evening.

During the night the old lady did indeed die, and also during the night they buried the body, so that they would as soon as possible be free of the offensive sight. As always in such cases, so also this time, next morning they all left their camp and went several hundred paces westwards. It is really difficult to convince them of their folly and their nonsense and wrong. Indeed, it almost seems as if they thought they knew much better and that we were much too stupid to understand ...

As far as the school is concerned, everything this quarter went very erratically. This was partly because some of them once again demonstrated their quick-silver nature, constantly coming and going; it was also partly because we were so overloaded with work that we were not able to take the necessary supervisory care, for we had to hurry to complete the work before the beginning of the hot season. Namely: we have built a larger stone smithy to replace the old one made of wood, and connected that with a harness room and two sheds for the wagons. In addition, there were several other things we had not at all counted on, so that we all had our hands full of things to do. Hopefully, the colonists who are coming are industrious people, so that once they are here we can be spared a little more of the physical work, which is also very necessary.

As for the rest, by God's grace everything has gone very well. This winter we have once again, through God's blessing, had so many green vegetables as never before; indeed, so many that we could not deal with them and have still pickled some for summer. Through experience we increasingly come ever more to the conviction that winter is the best time to work in the garden, for the sun does not have such a burning effect, and one can at least manage something with watering, which is not the case in summer.

The best and the most positive thing, for us as well as for the heathen, would be if we were able to continue farming. But that is not the case, and so we have to see how we are able to keep them occupied in some other way...

H Kempe

* * *

The final report for 1882 is from the *Missionsblatt* editor in Germany, and it makes references to three characteristics of the Centre at that time: the railways, the rabbits, and freedom. After the report there is an extended, but brief, introduction to the formation of the railway system in South Australia and the Northern Territory. First, though, it might be of interest to say a few words about the rabbits.

Rabbits were brought into Australia in 1788, with the first British fleet. At first, they were kept in cages, and bred for food. The first report of rabbits in the wild is in 1827, in Tasmania, where they had been let loose for hunting.[26] On the mainland of Australia, they were first let loose into the wild in 1859, by a certain Thomas Austin. He was a wealthy settler, who also used them mainly for hunting on his estate in Victoria.[27] The rabbits quickly spread, and by 1886 were found throughout Victoria and New South Wales, then, soon after, in South Australia and, by 1894, in Western Australia. They spread into the Northern Territory only in the early 1900s. Thus, at the time of our next report (below), rabbits would have been alien to the Finke mission station.

What is staggering in that report is the information on the amount of money being spent on the eradication in South Australia of what had become a pest. It is difficult accurately to ascertain what 600,000 German marks in 1880 would be worth today, but it would certainly equate to tens of millions of dollars—a huge amount to get rid of a bunch of rabbits!

***December 1882, Hermannsburg, Germany*[28]** (Missionsblatt *editor*)
In a few years a railway line has been built 400 miles into the desert as far as Farina. One has to say that the South Australians bestir themselves mightily to unlock the Centre of this remarkable part of the world, for without the means of transport all work is as good as useless. A desert railway of 400 miles is magnificent. It is said that the South Australians have money, and I believe that, for as I read, the South Australian parliament has set aside 600,000

marks for the eradication of the rabbits that have become a great plague in the colony.

However, it is not the money alone that matters. They have something else that is much more precious than money, namely freedom. What the world achieves with money and freedom must benefit the kingdom of God, as the report clearly demonstrates.

* * *

The Coming of the Railway to South Australia/Northern Territory

As the State of South Australia/Northern Territory developed and its structures and systems gradually became more sophisticated, the Hermannsburg Mission on the Finke found various aspects of its life easier to manage. So, the mission staff in both Adelaide and Ntaria were vitally interested in the construction of the railway network. Horses, wagons, bullocks and camels could be replaced by trains and carriages and goods wagons, resulting in less cost, faster delivery, greater efficiency and more comfort.

The first 'proper' road in the colony had been constructed in 1839, and it linked Port Adelaide with Adelaide. This road was used by many of the early Lutheran settlers as their ships moored at the port. South Australia's first railway line was between Goolwa and Port Elliott, laid in 1854, but it consisted only of horse-drawn carriages. The first 'proper' railway line, 12 kilometre in length, was also between Port Adelaide and Adelaide. It was constructed in 1856. This, too, is mentioned in our letters and reports from those early settlers.

A year after the Port Adelaide line, in 1857, the 40 kilometre track between Adelaide and Gawler, was completed. As the pastoral and mining industries flourished, the railway system played an increasing role in the transportation of goods and people. In the period between 1860 and 1875, ports were established in Port Augusta, Port Germein, Port Pirie, Wallaroo, Port Victoria, for example, and these were connected by rail to towns on and around York Peninsula to transport wheat, wool, copper, general freight and passengers. The Kapunda line was extended to Morgan on the River Murray to tap into the paddle steamer trade. In the south-east of the State, the Kingston-Naracoorte line began operating in 1876.

When the question arose as to how far north the railway ought to extend, opinions were divided. There was a point beyond which, because of poor rainfall and soil quality, crop and stock production became increasingly less viable, and therefore less profitable. In 1865 the Colony's Surveyor General, George Goyder, established a line of rainfall that became known as Goyder's Line. The line roughly ran east-west and marked the divide where the annual rainfull fell to approximately 250 millimetres and less. Most of the country north of Port Augusta came into that bracket, and the general consensus was that establishing an extensive rail network beyond that point was not advisable.

However, there were those who disagreed. One of those was James Boucat, South Australian lawyer and parliamentarian, who in 1874 began advocating for the 'pushing forward of railways into the interior, particularly north from Port Augusta'.[29] He and his like-minded supporters had visions of a line extending as far as Darwin, convinced that such a railway would open up South Australia and the Northern Territory to South-East Asia and the rest of the world, making Central Australia a critical cog in the Australian international transport system.

Over time, the Boucat philosophy gained traction, and subsequently the railway to the North began. In many places, the line followed the tracks that Aboriginal people had used for centuries, and the Aboriginal people often assisted construction workers, coming to their aid when stuck, and making use of their bush tracking and hunting skills.

The section of line from Port Augusta to Hawker was opened on 28 June 1880. The section from there to Hergott Springs/Maree was opened on 7 February 1884; and from there to Oodnadatta was completed in 1891. Which was as far as the line reached until 1929.

At the Darwin end of this idea to connect South and North by rail, a beginning was made with a line from Port Darwin to Pine Creek (approximately 250 kilometres), in 1887. That was as far as that part of the system got until 1911.

This, then, is a very brief introduction to the construction of what eventually became one of the world's great railways. And what is described in this introduction is, as it must be, a very brief overview of the state of play during the period covered in *Missionaries, Madness and Miracles*.

Constructing these lines created a demand for extra labour which, naturally, increased the population of those areas. However, many of the navvies, as such labourers were often called, did not always blend well with the locals, earning for themselves less-than-favourable reputations through their drunkenness, swearing, offensive language and fighting. Gibbs tells, for example, of an incident in a Naracoorte hotel that was filled with 'a crowd of men using disgraceful language in the bar and outside ... [In] one room two strong men, stripped to the skin and attended by seconds, fought savagely for round after round in front of fifty people. Attempts were made to provoke further fights, and much noise continued.'[30] Such stories are typical of those early railway towns everywhere.

Inevitably, every now and then one or the other of the characters in the mission story encountered this kind of behaviour. Not surprisingly, pietists that they were, they were usually shocked by it. Though, 'Australian' Lutherans that they were, one can imagine some of them sitting in the middle of the chaos, enjoying a beer.

Finke River Mission staff embraced the railway with great thankfulness. Not that the experience was the luxurious one we 21st century travellers enjoy. The average speed of trains on the line, for example, was around 25 kph. And, as Hines, tells it:

> ... the soot and cinders blowing into the windows (were) a problem, making (one's) eyes smart with grit, but it was necessary to have the windows open to allow the breeze to circulate through the otherwise airless carriage. On the downhill slopes at least sometimes the breeze kept the flies temporarily at bay.'[31]

* * *

Meantime, elsewhere in the world in 1882:

- The attempted assassination by shooting of Queen Victoria (2 March).
- The first stone was laid for Gaudi's *Sagrada Familia* in Barcelona (19 March). Slated for completion in 2026.
- Born: Winnie the Pooh author, A A Milne (18 January); Author Virginia Woolf, in London (25 January); US President, Franklin D Roosevelt, in New York (30 January); Russian composer, Igor Stravinsky (17 June); Rocket pioneer, Robert Goddard, in Worcester, Mass (5 October).
- Died: Charles Darwin, English naturalist (19 April); Italian general Guiseppe Garibaldi (2 June).
- In Wimbledon Men's Tennis final, William Renshaw defeated his twin brother, Ernest 6–1, 2–6, 4–6, 6–2, 6–2 (17 July).
- Britain's first electric trams commenced service in East London (4 March).

- Electric iron patented by Henry Seely, New York (6 June). It weighed about 7 kilograms and took a long time to heat.
- Richard E Wagner's *Parsifal* premiered in Bayreuth (26 July), and Pyotr Ilyich Tchakovsy's *1812 Overture* in Moscow (20 August).

20.

Death of Dmataka.
More on Language and Culture

1883

This chapter incorporates two extensive papers that again demonstrate the missionaries' proficiency as anthropologists and linguists. These presentations are woven around and within information on other daily happenings in the community.

The focus of the first report is death; and of all the experiences the missionaries have with the culture and customs of the Arrarnta people, those around dying and death hold a special fascination for them. The attention to detail around such happenings is almost obsessive. It may also be the mark of a skilled and faithful anthropologist.

The earlier story in Chapter 18 of, Fred/Tnubauka, for example, was a case in point. Now, in a very extensive account from Schwarz, we are drawn into the tragic drama around the dying, death and funeral of a young lad, Dmataka, a much-loved student of the mission.

For the missionaries, the interest is not only in the events *per se*, but also, and understandably, in the spiritual beliefs associated with these events—the spiritual beliefs of both the Aboriginal people and the missionaries. As much as there is a terrible fear about death on the part of the Aboriginal people, there is a horror on the part of the missionaries that anyone might die without knowing Jesus.

In the midst of this death, life goes on, this time taking in even the excitement around a comet.

* * *

18 January 1883, Hermannsburg[1] *(Schwarz to Th Harms)*
We Australians have reason to thank the Lord that he has again sustained us with great patience and forbearance, has blessed us in body and soul, and has graciously and paternally protected and preserved us so that we were all able to conclude the year healthy and happy, and indeed in an expanded community, because a little daughter was born to Brother Schulze, and a little son to me. Together with the other children they are, to the present hour, sound and well.

In addition, on 15 December the four colonists arrived in our midst safe and unharmed, so that the number of mission personnel has now risen to 21 souls. Since the sheep were also here on the station during the last three months, we were able to celebrate the Christmas festival really properly as a community.

Since in earlier reports I have several times already described the way we normally celebrate the precious festival, this time, to keep things brief, I can simply refer to the earlier descriptions, but with the additional information that the number of the heathen was greater than usual for the festival. The students, 24 in number, sang their Christmas carols very well, and all of the poor assembled heathen very attentively heard the good news more clearly than ever. In general, our heathen notice that the language of God (*Angatia Alxiraka*) grips them and gnaws at their hearts.

The school was well attended this quarter. There were only a few days when there were less than 20 pupils. The highest number for October was 23, 25 in November, 25 again in December.

Dmataka, our best pupil, a 10-year old boy, was taken from us at 12 midday on 11 November, right next to the school. By none of the nine cases of death which have occurred among the heathen this year has the Lord so gripped our hearts as through that of our dear Dmataka, because he died so unexpectedly from pneumonia. Five days before his death he was still teaching the youngest pupils their ABC. Since he had a special gift for teaching, I was quietly happy about this and promised him a sugar cake at Christmas for each of his pupils as a reward for all of his efforts. But the lad was sicker than we thought, and even though we saw that he was restless, sitting sometimes here, sometimes there, we did not pay much attention because we put it down to his infected leg; for as long as we had known him he had been afflicted with this. For years we endeavoured to free the lad of this affliction, but neither herb nor plaster helped, so that we finally simply put on a bandage as protection against flies and the like. However, one day when he did not turn up at the station either for school or food, and the children in response to the question, 'Where is Dmataka?', replied, 'He is in the camp, very sick', we went to him and found his camp surrounded by several women, with his father and mother right alongside him, even partly lying on top of him, so that the sick lad could scarcely breath. The boy had already become really quite weak but he was still conscious and answered our questions by pointing with his hand. He also asked for a drink, summoning all his strength to push out the word *kwaxa* (water).

After we examined his pulse and heartbeat and told his parents that they should make some shade over his camp, we went back to the station to collect medicine for the sick child. This was in the morning of 9 November, and the medicine was taken quite willingly by the boy in short intervals. But there was no improvement.

On 10 November he was already unconscious and the medicine had to be administered with force. However, the heathen were already bewailing him as dead, and they no longer wanted to be comforted. Rather, they wanted to dig his grave on the hill on the other side of the Finke.

In the evening they set up such a great death wail that it pierced bone and marrow, even though the boy was still alive and remained so for another day, until 12 o'clock midday. The death wailing of the heathen lasted the whole night, and at the dawning of the morning of 11 November, it started all over again.

I am unable to imagine what such lamentable howling must mean for a lamented sick person, if they still have some awareness. I wish that the dear mission supporters might once hear such wailing for the dead by our heathen and observe their misery which displays itself here most clearly.

Certainly, only a few of our dear brothers and sisters would be able to ward off the tears, but would ward off none of the prayers and pleading to God for this poor little group of people, nor the voice of thanks and praise to the Lord for the grace of God in Christ Jesus which has made us Christians. The beautiful festival hymns: 'Praise to you, Jesus Christ', 'How brightly shines the morning star, which we have in heaven', and many others would henceforth be sung with greater and more heartfelt recognition and deep joyfulness to the praise of our Lord Jesus Christ. Oh, how blessed are we Christians who are already in that place where we are able confidently to look death in the face, whereas the heathen take fright already at the mere thought of death and quake with fear. That is why they also carefully seek to avoid anything that in any way could remind them of death. None of them speaks the name of a dead person.

However, if the king of terror arrives among them and tears one of them away, then, despite all their precautionary measures and magic through which they believe they can drive away death and the devil (*Arinjakuna*), at that very moment a mood of real despair engulfs them.

We were permitted to see and hear such a thing with our own eyes and ears on 11 November at 12 o'clock midday with the death of Dmataka, because his camp was barely 50 paces distant from the school. The heathen had already sat there for the whole morning, old and young, large and small, so closely crowded around the sick one lying in the open air that we were able only with great effort to work our way through to him when we visited him from time to time. No-one wanted to budge, to make room, so firmly did the fear of death hold them on the sand on which they sat.

Only two men who were employed on the station were unable to be in the camp all the time, but even these also quite often left their work to be with the rest.

Shortly before 12 o'clock, when only a few of the labourers' tasks had been completed out of all the things that had to be done, one of them said to me: 'May I now go, for the sun is already high?' As he pointed with his hand straight above himself, he said: 'When it reaches there, Dmataka must be buried.' I was really shocked by this information, for I had already strongly suspected for over a year that our heathen were actually not burying people dead, but rather still alive. Such expression as: 'When the sun stands there, he should and must be buried', certainly did nothing to remove my mistrust of them, for I still had not heard that the child had died.

I let the heathen worker go, told the brothers and our wives what he had said, and went as quickly as possible into the camp, while Brother Schulze and all the station residents immediately followed. About 60 heathen were together, all sitting on the ground in the sand, most of the men in fearful silence, similar to the eery silence of nature before the eruption of a severe storm.

Some of the oldest began to wail over the dead lad, and the women followed. While we made our way there to see him, the [witch]doctor stood up and said, 'He has died', and some of the men confirmed the statement. Suddenly, it was deathly quiet again and all eyes were turned on us in great suspense, for we were now examining whether the sick person was alive or dead. The women, especially the lad's mother and father, wanted us to declare that he was still alive, but the men were very eager that we should declare him dead so that he might be buried as quickly as possible, and that they might be freed from their distressing situation; for to submit quietly to death is the most extreme torment for the heathen.

With veritable lynx eyes, the doctor carefully observed everything we said and did in the process. We found ourselves in a difficult situation. Why? We ourselves were not totally sure whether we had a completely dead corpse before us or not. We were unable to detect any pulse or heartbeat despite our efforts to do so, for the whole body was still warm and its limbs could be easily manipulated. We attributed this partly to the sickness, but mostly to exposure to the sun. I finally grasped both large toes and tugged them several times with all my might, but there was no perceptible movement. We did not want to use a knife or similar instrument for a further examination, so we stopped and looked questioningly at each other. The heathen [witch] doctor noted this straight away, came closer and said: 'He is dead. Should we bury him?'

Brother Schulze and I again looked at each other and, after we had weighed up all the circumstances and briefly discussed the whole situation with respect to the heathen, we finally said that we, too, considered the lad to be dead and that they could bury him.

What then followed can hardly be described. It was as if nothing less than a horde of demons suddenly came upon the people; men and women screamed and howled, gesticulating in despair. They threw themselves face down onto the ground and pressed their faces deep into the sand. Standing up again, they beat their heads, faces, shoulders, or chests and thighs with their fists. Some did service by doing this to each other. Men with knives and sharp stones in their hands embraced, struck, cut, sliced and stabbed each other. Others, especially women, knelt and struck the ground with their fists at one moment, and then in the next took up sand and stones to throw into their faces with all their might, likewise on their heads and backs. Other women, especially the younger ones, seized their *tnuma* (a heavy solid stick, sharpened at the end), and stabbed themselves in the scalp with the sharp end, so that blood streamed down their faces and necks. The boy's mother and two other women, however, had thrown themselves down across the corpse, to contest the men's right to remove it. Who are these men, and what do they want? There are six in all: the doctor with four strong, young men, chosen from the rest with a gentle tap on the head at the crucial moment to serve as his assistants at the burial. The sixth is a *knirixa* (elder).

It presented a strange scene as the doctor chose his assistants from the crowd; like the rest of the heathen, they crouched naked in the sand, having previously taken off their shirts and other clothing, laying them aside in order, it seems, to participate in the mourning in proper native style. As they felt the doctor's hand touch their head, they immediately stood up without any objection, but with faces etched with fear and deep displeasure. Nevertheless, their hands hastily went to their throat and head to remove all the adornment they were wearing and to throw it to the ground. They now tilted their head forward, then backwards, then down, while using their hands to free even more the long loose hair on their heads to bind it at the back so that it fell down over shoulders and neck. This all happened in the blink of an eye.

Now they step up to the doctor and with him at their head immediately approach the lifeless body, totally covered and held firm by the bodies of the women. What is to happen now? That is my thinking as the doctor wants to seize the body. Will the men and women actually struggle over the deceased? Both sides appear to be equally resolute.

But look, what happens? From behind, the doctor steps up to the head end of the corpse; quickly stooping, he suddenly grabs his long black beard from below with one hand and presses it between his teeth. While holding it firmly with his lips, he makes such a terrible face that the women immediately give up any resistance. Then from above he grabs the deceased under both arms so as to raise him slightly, so that the four men, with equally horrible gestures, can take a hold of him to hoist him onto their shoulders and carry him away.

At this moment the entire action described has reached its climax, and the thoroughly heathen bewailing of the dead is in full swing. We, however, now leave the camp and follow the corpse with no time to lose; the bearers carry it on their shoulders, head first and face upwards. They run quickly with almost anxious haste to the other side of the Finke. Suddenly they stand still, and the doctor who has up to this point helped to carry the deceased with the head on his shoulder steps away to supervise matters and no longer helps with the carrying.

Matters now proceed further. The corpse is carried by the four under its arms, head first and face upwards. But are there any other heathen beside the six men who follow the corpse? Yes, three fairly elderly women follow it, holding branches of gum tree with dry leaves. They proceed behind each other on the right side, the elder and the doctor on the left side. They go forward at a trot and in absolute silence.

This made a truly weird impression on me, especially when the doctor again touched the dead body, twisted the legs together and folded them back. He also bound the arms together and had the body carried in a sitting position with face forward. This way of carrying it appeared to be really cumbersome for the bearers, since there was no easy way to approach the task. Most of the load was left to the two who had the deceased sideways in front of them. After a few steps they changed places for a fourth and final time. The corpse, with the head to the right and face looking forward, was carried the whole way on the arms of the bearers who walked close to each other until they reached the right spot, thoroughly exhausted.

The path through the river bed was long and difficult. Water was no hindrance but the path was totally unbeaten and, besides, it was high noon. Despite this there was no pause for recovery, and the burial proceeded without delay as one of the bearers jumped into the grave, and the doctor again bound together the corpse which had been placed on the ground.

The bearers then handed it over to the man standing in the grave. The latter placed the dead one in a sitting position in the depression below which sloped sideways, and immediately began to pack the loose soil into the grave, and with such haste and gestures that it occurred to me: he must be very afraid that the dead body can do something bad to him. Meanwhile, this heathen man has now become tired and wants to be relieved. Immediately another man jumps into the hole; the first has long since made his way out and is now gasping for breath.

At the request of the man in the hole they hand him a *tnuma* with which he bores and picks away below at the side walls of the grave and stamps down the loose soil with his feet. This *tnuma* carried by the doctor is the only tool used at this burial; otherwise, no spear or anything similar was present. The man, however, has worked hard and used his *tnuma* skilfully, for he now begins to work on the heavily undermined earth from the surface of the ground above. He holds the *tnuma* with both hands about 9 to 12 inches back from the sharpened end, and digs into the ground with all his might. In this way, in a few moments, one clump after another is wedged loose, stamped down, and then used to fill the grave. Now all hands and feet set to work, for there are nine persons present: six men and three women.

What do they do next? Using their hands, they now carefully search for and remove every bit of grass, plants, bush, leaves, wood, stones and the like in the immediate vicinity of the grave site. Next, with their feet they stamp down every slightest rise in the area they have cleaned. With their heels they smash soil to dust, especially the ridges of earth that have arisen from wedging loose clumps of soil. They push this to the centre of the hole that had been filled in, since there is still a slight shallow depression and near it a small tapering mound about 3 feet wide and high.

How has this come about and what does it mean? It is the soil they have carefully pounded and heaped up; it came to the surface in the process of digging the round, perpendicular hole, 4 feet deep and 2 feet in diameter, and it represents the exact spot where the lifeless body rests. They then cast an assessing eye over the little mound and the area about 24 steps in circumference that has been cleared and levelled out, and the small depression at the base of the mound. Without any ceremony, they leave the grave in silence and return to the camp, immersed in gloomy brooding.

Here, too, it has become rather quiet. Men and women sit in separate groups facing each other. Only here and there can one hear a single woman utter a lament, while the men, with tears in their eyes, longingly look out for those who are returning, in a way that suggests that those who carried out the burial should bring them some comfort from the grave.

Next, one of the men suddenly stands up and approaches the doctor with a questioning look. The two embrace and move a few steps aside, whispering or murmuring a few words in each other's ears, as in question and answer. They then sit down and repeatedly nod their heads, deep in thought, and with secretive expressions directed to the others. After this, all the men take turns in speaking into each other's ears, nodding their heads.

For hours the heathen sat together like this without making a sound. When the sun went down and dusk set in, the lament again broke out and lasted nearly all night. Early next day, an hour before sunrise, they resumed the mournful dirge with all their might. By evening they had already shifted camp, for this happens whenever a death occurs in the camp.

After dawn, Arabinja, the father of the dead boy, left the station and its surrounds with his entire family of two wives and three children, and travelled far to the north. He returned with his family several days before Christmas, not to join our celebration of the festival, but to conduct rites at the grave of his son. Several days after the festival, when the heathen customs had been completed, he again went off with two direct siblings and the mother of the dead boy. He has never returned.

I did not observe the ceremony just mentioned, one that usually takes place three to four weeks after the burial that is immediately conducted on the day of death, so I can tell you nothing more about it. I did observe such a ceremony earlier and hope, in time, to describe it if my dear Brothers H Kempe or L Schulze do not do this before me with a similar version in the quarterly reports that will next follow.

To avoid error, I must note that, subsequent to the first terrible wailing at the decease of a dying person, when those present acted as if crazy and drew their own blood, the same people did not behave in that way at all in the following laments over those who had died. Rather, their mourning is something akin to a professional task that is mainly carried out by mourning women daubed with white paint. However, when news of the death of a particular heathen reaches tribal companions camping far away, the first horrible scene is immediately repeated there. We clearly observed this at the news of Fred's death. I note also with reference to that event, that it was only part of a mourning ceremony.

One could mention much more about the mourning rites of our heathen, how long they last and how they are of different grades. We know from experience that the vehemence of the wailing depends on the gender and social standing of the person. For example, mourning and lament are kept to a minimum at the death of an old woman, and there is hardly anyone to bury her. In the case of young women the men lend a hand with the burial but no one draws blood by cutting themselves, as we saw that done at the mourning for Dmataka, although he was still an uncircumcised boy. Furthermore, at the mourning for Fred, blood flowed more freely than at the one just mentioned.

In short, everything seems to rest on old, traditional orders that are still guarded by certain persons. Clearly, there is still much to be researched about our small group. We are earnestly striving, with God's help, to gain a more thorough understanding of their circumstances. In particular we want to be able to use No 412 from the hymn book, 'Singing and praying Zion', at future burials.

Dear Pastor, lest I hold you up too long I will now write more briefly, even though I had intended to write about quite a few other things. I already mentioned at the beginning that, by God's grace, we were able to celebrate a truly happy and blessed Christmas, and that our heathen clearly listened to the gospel message of the festival with great attention. But not merely at the festival, since day by day over the last three months all the heathen, grown ups and young, have heard the Word of God in the early morning hours, and still hear it. God grant that it leads to conversion rather than hardness of heart. This little group can no longer make excuses, since most know what is at issue.

The school has been well attended and is so at present. Pupils receive instruction in the morning and afternoon, but for no more than two and a half to three hours a day. The government looks after the food provisions and, partly, clothing for the pupils as well as for the old, sick, crippled and pregnant women among the heathen. However, the government supplies only 100 to 150 yards of woollen material for shirts and skirts every 12 to 18 months. This is far too little for our pupils and the women who need to be clothed, and much too warm for summer clothing. So, things like light cotton fabrics, even finished linen and cotton shirts, are really welcome. We offer our sincere thanks to our dear friends here and overseas for the loving kindnesses shown to us in this matter.

It was a really lovely sight at Christmas when the happy crowd of children came in wearing bright red coloured shirts, their brown faces twice as happy as usual. As for us, we also had every good reason to be happy. Firstly, there was no lack of God's precious Word and we were all well and had our daily bread as well as green garden vegetables (a great rarity at this time). Then we had some showers of rain each month, and especially heavy downpours in the days before Christmas. The river came up higher than previously so that our garden in the bed of the Finke was pretty well totally washed away. Finally, shortly before Christmas the brothers and sisters here supplied a whole load of refreshments, such as jam, honey, dried fruit, tomato sauce, and the like. What more could we want? Thanks to God for everything! Amen.

It is common knowledge that until now all the brothers and sisters, missionaries and colonists, together with hired labourers, have sat together at meal-time. Since 12 November, however, when we ate together for the last time, we missionaries now each have our own table. The colonists and hired hands usually eat at one table. Jürgens, with his wife, does the domestic duties, and naturally occupies the role of house father and priest at table. We all still come together for morning and evening devotions; we missionaries conduct them on a weekly roster.

Previously, we had a hired shepherd by the name of Mirus who had already served the mission here for more than seven years and was paid a wage of 25 marks a week. Last December he was let go and has already left the station, so our mission staff numbers 20 souls. We can soon release the last paid workers, and that is truly a blessing. The four young and strong settlers are good for the mission in more than one respect and are fully occupied. With the three older colonists, they are engaged in the following external work. Tündemann took on the flock of rams previously tended by Mirus, Eggers took over the ewes that had previously been looked after by Holtermann.

A fortnight ago both flocks were again driven away and are stationed about 22 to 23 English miles from here on Rudoles Creek, and Baden went along as cook. Freiboth remains on the station as carpenter and does not lack work. Koch who is soon to look after the wagon is here, too. Holtermann has taken on the goats and rams. Jürgens is also on the station, works at this and that and gives his wife a bit of help in the kitchen. He also has to help when the work with cattle and horses gets too much.

Finally, with reference to the outside work completed in this quarter, the heathen have served us well. For a long time we have daily given work to 10 to 15 adult heathen. It should also be mentioned that: a. the shearing of the sheep was completed in the first weeks of October, then b. the horses and cattle were mustered. This is work that can be quickly and easily spoken of here in this report, but when carried out it often occupies several weeks and is in fact something of a back-breaking job. I thought of describing this type of work in detail this time so that our dear mission friends really understand what it means that 'horses and cattle were mustered'; but I see that I have to postpone that for next time.

And finally, a piece of land has been laid out as a new garden, a well has been dug and lined, a large chimney has been dismantled and then built taller, and a verandah has been built. Apart from that, a lot has happened which cannot be dealt with in detail.

Lastly, I note that along with all this work the dear sun has faithfully done its duty; it has conscientiously allowed us to enjoy its light and warmth, especially the latter, with which it is not at all miserly! In October it was 21 degrees Rem in the shade; in November we had 29 degrees, but 30 to 33 degrees in December. In these days it has already reached 34 degrees and more in the shade. It is truly no wonder that one perspires when sitting still and that as I write this report I have to cover the unwritten sheets of paper in front of me with three leaves of blotting paper, together with a handkerchief folded double, so that my perspiration does not render the paper unusable.

As much as I am perspiring and would gladly put aside the writing, I must not overlook mentioning that an uncommonly large and majestic comet appeared in the sky this quarter. We observed it first on 12 September deep down on the eastern horizon; for some time we could only see the tail pointing straight to the west. Daily the comet rose higher and turned its head more to the south, while the tail got closer to the north; so we soon had the broad side right before our eyes and thus could properly observe the star's splendour, enjoy the sight, and be edified by it. Advent was already approaching, pointing us to the precious Christmas festival, and to the sweet baby child in the crib. So, it was impossible not to closely link our present comet with that marvellous star that once directed those first heathen to the Saviour of them all. I must at least admit that the thought often occurred to me as I observed the star when it stood in all its glory at dawn in the morning: the star of the wise men from the east cannot have been more beautiful.

What did our heathen say this star meant? They say it is a flaming spear and means many heathen will die. What do the Australian people out in the bush and cattle station owners say, or secular people in Australia? Two years ago a comet appeared in the west, though not as large and bright as this one. There was the usual talk that that comet meant a long drought. I heard this with my own ears from the mouth of an Englishman. In fact, the dry weather and great drought were clearly experienced last year, causing the cattle owners large losses; so that comet must be to blame!

What about the latest comet that can be hardly seen anymore with naked eyes? When the comet first appeared it was immediately prophesied that it was bringing rain and good times. Some secular people expressed the opinion in the newspaper: 'If this comet brings rain or indicates good times, the best thing would be that it takes to its heels so that the rain comes earlier.'

Now the rain has already arrived and it seems that more will soon follow, so this latest comet must be the benefactor. We, however, receive the rain as a gift from the Lord, and as a kind and gracious answer to our own prayers and petitions and those of our precious mission friends for such a gift. So then: honour and thanks for his grace belong alone to God in the heights! ...
W F Schwarz

* * *

Once again, down South in his Bethany parish, Heidenreich is caught up in the Missouri conflict. He is somewhat ambivalent about recent outcomes on this matter. It is also obvious that ecclesiastical politics play a considerable role in sorting out the Missouri conundrum: it is as much a matter of who is on whose side and who can exercise the most power as it is about anything theological.

Heidenreich also faces the perennial challenge of the mission finances. In his opinion, the missionaries do not always help the situation, either. So, they need to be called to account. They might also appreciate a little pastoral care.

27 March 1883, Bethany[2] *(Heidenreich to Th Harms)*
Highly respected and much-loved Father!
I should have written a few words to you a long time ago, but work, festivals, illness and strife did not let me get to it...

The Lord's wonderful grace and goodness prevailed at our synod. It threatened to unfold badly, but the Lord turned hearts in such a way that it is still a miracle in my sight, one that the synod report will better explain in detail. I want briefly to say only this: The synod unanimously adopted the last minutes from the Pastors' Conference (in which the so-called Missourian 'election to faith' and our position of 'election in view of faith' were declared mutually acceptable for us to hold). The Missourians openly declared that, with this doctrine, what counted was not what Missouri taught, but what God's Word and our Confessions teach. Nonetheless, the synod decided that 'election by faith' was to be used neither in our church papers nor in sermons, nor in public lectures. When it was pointed out to us that we no longer therefore needed to use the expression 'election in view of faith', we were able all the more easily to consent since the simple expression has never been used in our congregations. Thus was peace established. May God grant that doctrinal peace prevails in our Synod, as before.

The synod also showed its thinking in the election of the new Church Council (the three protesters, Bertram, Homann and Sudholz stood down) and the older pastors from each side were elected, Strempel and Ey [from the other side], Oster and I from our side. Also in the Mission Council we have three out of the four, since Ahrens was elected to replace Sudholz. Thus, the whole mission leadership and Church Council have been changed. Oster is again President and we are thus five against three in the Church Council.

I find more grounds for peace in our Synod, humanly speaking, in the election of the Church Council than in the decisions on doctrine. According to all I read, hear and see, the papistic Missourian spirit cannot subordinate itself but always has to be hovering on top. That is why I am happy, with trembling, at the outcomes of the last synod. However, I firmly believe that the Lord will lead his kingdom of truth to complete victory among us.

In the mission, I am shocked and horrified by our debts. In a short time the missionaries have spent over £380 on the station. On two occasions drivers arrived with freight where we had to pay nearly £400. Added to that, the shepherd Mirus who had worked for us for seven years and 20 weeks, arrived here, and he is to receive 25 shillings more a week. So, he is now to receive £364.

In addition, we had to buy five tons of new rations that cost £100 in the shops, with the freight at £45/12/5, without mentioning small expenses for daily needs. Thus, our bank debts have risen to about £1000. Even if I receive the ordered £300 in three days, that is like a drop in a bucket. I could do nothing except forbid the missionaries to write cheques for buildings, purchase of cattle, and pay for workers. Mirus told us that they still have one labourer whom they pay 85 shillings a week = £4/15/0. They are not selling horses and have bought a second stallion.

I am standing helpless and powerless before a great mountain, and do not know how to get over it. Whatever I grasp at costs money, otherwise I would send up a commission to sort out and regulate matters on the spot. I would prefer to go myself, but without a *locum tenens* that is impossible…All that remains are patience and the comfort that my Jesus lives and that I, too, together with the mission, will live. Pray that I receive wisdom, faithfulness and constancy…

G A Heidenreich

* * *

After almost six years of association with the Arrarnta people, the missionaries are obviously growing in their familiarity and proficiency with the Arrarnta culture and language. Whether they are becoming equally adept in the development of their sensitivity to that culture remains a matter for debate. However, there can be no doubting their commitment to the task and their awareness of the challenges still before them.

As a follow-up to the information provided in the last chapter on the construction of the railway, Schulze's observations on that project to date are helpful in following its progress.

2 April 1883, Hermannsburg[3] *(Schulze to Th Harms)*
Dear Pastor!

Our Hermannsburg Mission has its messengers also in Australia.[4] They have already shared much about this unfamiliar land and its inhabitants and, in recent years, about the little clan[5] on the Finke in the heart of Australia. Yet there is still much to be told. Firstly, something new happens all the time and then, because of longer acquaintance with these people, one gets a better knowledge of their language, customs, and practices.

The latest and biggest event in the whole country is the planned and partly finished construction of a railway through the whole country from south to north, or from Adelaide to Port Darwin. It is already completed up to Farina, which is 400 English miles inland. When the whole long stretch will be finished is nowhere in sight. If the parliament were agreed on this point it would perhaps happen soon. But one party wants the government to build it, the other wants an English company to build it so that the government does not get too deeply into debt.

The building of the rail line would be a great benefit to our mission. Earlier we had to pay more than £60 sterling per ton (20 hundredweight) of freight to our place. Last time we needed to pay only £47. The closer the railway comes, the cheaper the freight will be. From here to the first train station, Farina, is still more than 600 English miles.

This building of the railway will certainly not profit the heathen. They will have all the more contact with the Whites, which only accelerates their ruin. They learn nothing good from the Whites to begin with; and then one now hears quite often that one was shot by the Whites here and there. How terrible! Yet they do not become smart, but time and again kill the cattle of the Whites. It really shows their blindness from which only God's Word can liberate them. Oh, if only they would listen to it!

Learning their language has given us many a headache and still does. How much easier it is to learn a language already written down than one where not one word has been written. One difficulty with the language of this tribe is that one object has so many names or, better, that each little clan names the same object differently. So, e.g. some of our local heathen call water *kwotja*, others *kopi*. Some say *rula* for wood, others call it *ina*, etc.

This gave us some trouble before we understood that this had to be connected to the many tribes. We thought they were saying something different from what we wanted, which is unfortunately all too often the case with them. They are definitely not friends of accurate listening and sharp thinking. If pressed to get something out of them, they say any word or sentence, be it ever so wrong.

Pronunciation is another difficulty. They never say a word clearly. For example, one says *lima* 'to go', the other says *loma*, yet another *luma*, etc. We now put less weight on their pronunciation but this has its negative side. Sometimes one hears a word thinking one knows it, but it does not make sense in the context, no matter how much one struggles to make it fit with what is being said. On closer questioning, one often learns that it is a completely different word which they simply pronounce very similarly to the word we thought we heard, as e.g. the word *kuma* (bad) and *gunna* (not). Finally, some of them, especially women, speak so unclearly that we can hardly understand a word, while almost understanding others.

Abstract concepts create the biggest difficulty. They do not have many and the few they do have are hard to get out of them, much as one tries.

From time to time much has already been written in our reports about their marriages. We learn more and more from our growing familiarity with them and from penetrating deeper into their language. As far as I have ascertained, the whole language group far and wide, extending 200 English miles to the north and to the south, is divided into four classes: 1) *Beltara*, 2) *Bunanka*, 3) *Burula* and 4) *Gomara*. As far as we have learned, this division is of importance only with reference to marriage. This is a laudable arrangement and protects against marriage with blood relatives. 1) A *Beltara* may only marry a *Gomara*; the children from this marriage are *Bunanka*. 2) A *Bunanka* may only marry a *Burula*; the children of this marriage are *Beltara*. 3) A *Burula* may only marry a *Bunanka*; the children of this marriage are *Gomara*. 4) A *Gomara* may only marry a *Beltara*; the children of this marriage are *Burula*.

As is known, the local groups are small in size. One cannot say with certainty how far a clan extends. It seems as if they have no concept of belonging together as a nation or tribe. We have often enquired after their tribe's name, but have yet to gain clarity on this matter. Those who were born here or along the Finke call themselves *Mbonderinga*, i.e. river-dwellers. Those who were born in the hills some distance from here call themselves *Puteringa*,[6] i.e.

hills-dwellers. But they live all mixed up together like a tribe. All the heathen living further away call themselves after the relevant section in the sky. Those living in the West are called *Aldolinga*, etc.

Since nearly all the small clans are mutually hostile so that none can easily step across anyone's borders, each tribe has to look to itself to set up a marriage. It seldom happens that they marry into a friendly tribe. This system of four classes is thus good. The parents and elders of the tribe arrange the marriage of children. They actually determine very early, when a girl has just been born, whom she is to have as her husband. Sometimes her future husband is also at the time a youth but he is often a man who already has a wife and children, indeed occasionally already an old man. Some already have two wives when a third is promised them

The actual wedding or being given in marriage is, like everything else with them, very simple. If the girl has reached puberty her promised husband goes out and fetches her as his wife. Sometimes son-in-law and father-in-law are not of the same mind. Whereas the former considers his bride ready for marriage, the latter does not. Sometimes arguments and strife arise, in which case the bridegroom gets the worst of it, receiving a spear stab wound in the thigh instead of a wife.

As for marital life, that differs greatly. Some couples live very cordially and peacefully together. The husband does his own thing, going off hunting for *gara* (meat). If he comes home laden with spoils, he shares his *gara* with his people. He does not need to go hungry if he comes home empty handed. His wife has meanwhile fetched *mana* (roots, plants or seeds) with the children, and steamed or roasted it in hot sand. This they all eat together. I note in passing that almost all their food is prepared with fire. They do not eat the meat if it is still a bit red, but place it in glowing hot sand.

They actually have only one meal a day, when they get into camp with their *mana* or *gara*. The meal lasts for a short or long time depending on the number gathered. If the man has hunted down lots of game, he shares it with others. Nothing is kept for the next day; they eat until everything is consumed. Sometimes this lasts late into the night, even until morning, with them setting up a heathenish racket by singing, clapping their hands, or striking the ground. By day they then sleep.

Some married couples cannot stand each other. Why is that? It is caused by marriage being forced. The wives have no love for their husbands and as a result disobey them. At this the husband tries to kindle love with a club. Sometimes he uses it so heftily that one must wonder how the wife endures it. A husband recently so mistreated his wife that she could no longer stand upright. What caused this? The husband had several times summoned his wife into his hut in the evening but she did not obey. Subsequently, he went to her and beat her very severely. We rebuked the husband for his merciless beating and the wife for her disobedience. She is, like his other wife, generally unfaithful. Previously they were always sleeping with the Whites on the neighbouring station. When he wanted to fetch them, the Whites threatened him with a revolver, which he complained about to us. Scandalous behaviour from such Whites!

Something similar happened to another man whose wife was always running away. Naturally, he hauled her back with a proper thrashing. These women must have a pretty thick skin and little feeling. When a male person dies, the related women strike themselves so severely on top of their heads with a sharp club that the blood spurts out and runs down on all sides.

Their marriages are not richly blessed with children. A mother has two, three at the most. If twins or triplets are born, the strongest remains alive, the other or others are killed. If a boy and girl are born, the life of the second is snuffed out, letting the first live, even if he is weaker than the girl. They kill all children fathered by a White. I have seen half-caste girls in some places, but no boys. I do not know how to explain that. Our local heathen want to have nothing to do with half caste girls.

The birth event shows how their life is like that of an animal in many respects. When her time comes, the mother goes a little way from the camp, and there bears her child naked on nothing but the sand and under the open sky. Sometimes a woman or child attends her. When the child is born it is washed with sand and laid in a bowl, irrespective of whether there is shade or hot sunshine.

Yet one must say that parents are attached to the children with deep love. To punish them for their naughtiness they seem to consider gross cruelty. At least that was the case when we arrived here. If we went to hit a child, all who could run usually rushed to its aid. Now they are happy to look on, and sometimes even approve of it. Yet it is still a rare event when they themselves hit a child, even though children shove, hit and throw stones in their bad behaviour.

There are few widowers here. If a man's wife dies he has another or several others, or has one intended. On the other hand, there are many widows; they remain that as long as they live.

As already noted above, the institution or practice of a four-class system with reference to marriage is a laudable thing. It is only a pity that they do not stay within these boundaries but give way to their evil lust with anyone, be it a widow or a child of 7 to 8 years. It is not only girls or maidens but also married women who chase after Whites to sleep with them. Their parents and husbands dislike this but do not know what to do about it, at most tanning their hides when they have them in their power, which does not bother the women much...

Their greetings are odd. Here, too, the proud heathen is evident. There is a greeting only for men. No woman is greeted. Nor do they do this amongst themselves. The greeting consists of slapping the upper thigh with an open hand. The one who is giving the greeting and the one being greeted do that. It is especially interesting to observe a greeting with someone of a different tribe or a number of them. Some time ago we had the chance to observe this scene close-up. One fine day two men suddenly asked for permission to leave their work and enter the camp. When we asked why, they answered quite excitedly: *atue ntjaraknira buxirinima*, i.e. a lot of men are coming. Since they first had some things to put in place, one of them quickly untied his hair into disarray and then tied it up in a—at least to them—better shape. They then hurried off to the camp. Hardly a minute later we also went there.

All the men were running around in great expectation, holding their spears and woomeras, looking around to spot the *atuas*.[7] Among them there was also a stranger who had announced that others were coming. At the beginning I did not know why they were so excited, whether it was friends or enemies who were coming. But I soon found out from someone.

It was not at all long before a troop of men became visible among the trees in the distance, all with throwing spears in their hands and a tuft of colourful feathers made into a pyramid on their heads. They trotted forward in rank and file, following after each other two by two. One of our heathen immediately hurried out, accompanied by the messenger who had announced their coming. They trotted forward to meet them, also with spears raised, ready for throwing. The strangers had advanced a considerable distance closer when one of their men turned aside to trot at the side of the troop, while one of our heathen hurriedly trotted around from the back to the other side. Then both of them, to the right and left of the troop in the middle, came to meet us.

Hardly had the two men with the troop arrived when an old woman hurried out of her hut, her whole body covered with bright paint. Holding a cudgel 6 feet long and 2 inches thick, she trotted back and forth on the track on which the troop had come, one moment swinging her cudgel up to the sky, then thrusting it into the earth.

When they all drew close to her, she swung away and trotted around one side to the rear and remained standing at a distance. At the same moment our chief—if one can call him that—called out, 'Halt!' They immediately all stopped and laid down their spears. Next, three of our heathen quickly trotted out to them with spears at the ready, not in a straight line but bending right and left and strangely throwing their legs sideways. They trotted around the troop in this way three times and then trotted back. Three others did the same thing, then two more. Thereupon all put down their spears and approached each other. After embracing, they all then conversed with each other.

At this we also approached them and talked with them. The strangers were a bit shy with us, but not for long. When we asked a woman how she would show hospitality to her guests, she laughed with surprise and said that they had already eaten. However, she quickly changed her mind and said we should give them something. That is what we did, and on the following morning they were all fed with heavenly bread.[8] The Lord grant that it was not given to them in vain.

Up to the beginning of March we were able to hold school regularly on all days, but no more since then. Almost all of them got the wanderlust. We hope to get the school children back soon. What we have learned is that even food cannot hold them back when they want to go walkabout.

Mission personnel have increased by one during the last quarter, the Lord presenting a healthy baby to Brother and Sister Jürgens on 21 February. The child received holy baptism on the following Sunday.

We had a very long period of hot weather this summer, from the new year until mid-February. During this time we had between 30° and 35°R. in the shade. How one longed for some cool weather. That then arrived, very sudden and severe. One morning shortly after this, the thermometer was showing 7°R. Little wonder that this caused many colds. Most got inflamed eyes. Some children suffered rather badly with this, and still do.

As may be imagined, our work proceeds only slowly in this heat. In two places we have built sheep yards and huts for the shepherds. The sheep are lambing at present; this will go on for six weeks.

This keeps the two shepherds, with their cook plus two men and several heathen, busy. Apart from some small jobs, the time is spent in the gardens and pump house. We found out that things grow better when one waters more. The soil is allowed to go dry only on top. This requires quite a lot of water for a little area. It cannot be done the usual way, watering with buckets. For this reason we have long ago asked for an iron pump. But we have still not got one. So Brother Jürgens set about and built one. It is really quite good and useful. The worst of it is that he has to be on hand to repair it, and so it becomes a very expensive pump. Brother Kempe is at work now, building a more simple one to see what is best for the local conditions. The weather has a very marked affect on timber here. Either it swells up a lot during wet weather, or it shrinks greatly in the heat and splits so much that one can stick a finger into the gaps. Furthermore, our corrosive water quickly eats away the leather. Therefore, an iron pump is best.

The heavy rains last Christmas were not as useful as the lesser ones in the year 1879. At that time the country was resplendent in the most beautiful green, 14 days after the rain. The whole region was like an open parkland. The grass was thick and high everywhere. This time no grass grew. How this comes about is a riddle to us. On the other hand, melons are doing very well this year. We have more of them than ever before, watermelons as well as pie melons. The former are a substitute for fruit which we do not have. They taste agreeably sweet and are very juicy. So they are just right for this hot land. The pie melons substitute for potatoes, so we make vegetables with them. But as they keep for only half a year, and we have such a lot this time, we just cannot eat them all. We cook them for the heathen too, which helps to save bread and meat. May the Lord give us thankful hearts for this gift, something we are always lacking in, too...

Louis Schulze

21.

Finances, Synods, and Routine

The Hermannsburg missionaries were an enterprising lot, ever seeking new ways to make money, and thus to contribute to the goal of making the mission self-sufficient. Of course, this mind-set was an integral part of their mission training and thinking; and so, in this chapter, too, we find them hard at work on those kind of endeavours. But, despite the best efforts of everyone involved in the mission, Heidenreich continues to be exasperated by both financial and administrative headaches. He and the missionaries are, however, meticulous in their financial accounting—a quality of the highest value to them and also instilled as part of their training.

* * *

15 May 1883, Hermannsburg[1] *(Schulze to Th Harms)*
Dear Pastor,
    How often have we wished we had a weaver's loom. We have on several occasions expressed this wish in our reports. However, we have never seriously requested one for the reason that, until now, we did not have the time. Now that we have had reinforcements[2] and will receive more, I think we can also try weaving. We have enough wool and we and the heathen need a good deal of cloth. If we could therefore weave some for ourselves, that would certainly be very good. The return from the sale of wool is too little because of the distance it has to be transported. We therefore hope that you will send the necessary components for a loom with the fiancées of the colonists, that is, those parts we are unable to make here ourselves. Brother Eggers told me he has written about this to his fiancée. In any case, it is preferable that such an article is station property rather than private property. This was Brother Eggers' wish, too, and he asked me to convey it to you.
    On the first Pentecost morning we had the first frost for the winter. Melons and several other vegetables died in the frost. Nevertheless, we have every cause to thank the Lord this year. We have harvested more melons than ever. Our vegetable garden looks quite good, too. The only thing which threatens

to discourage us somewhat at times is the apathy, the indifference of our heathen. There is not the least sign of an inner restlessness or anguish of mind amongst any of them. Only when reminded of death do they become somewhat agitated. Unfortunately, they avoid such conversations whenever possible. Also, they never admit they have to die, although they experience it so often in their midst. At present not many of them are here. The last good rain was of great benefit to them. In the large waterholes there are especially many large fish, weighing up to one pound. Before the flood not one of these fish was to be seen and now there are so many. We cannot explain where they suddenly appear from…

L Schulze

P.S. The enclosed letter is from Brother Eggers. Would you please hand it on to his fiancée.

1 June 1883, Bethany[3] *(Heidenreich to Th Harms)*
Highly respected and much-loved Father!

First of all, my sincere thanks for the £200 that I received from our dear Major Rauschenbusch on 26 May this year. Unfortunately, a large part of our debt remains since the missionaries have reached too deeply into our funds for buildings and to pay hired labourers. I must therefore make a heartfelt plea to send me £20 more for this year, if possible. I have directed the missionaries to sell young geldings but have still received no reply from them. Bank interests are too high: 10 percent. We also have to pay £145 for freight on 5 July.

Our local treasurer, Carl Schmidt, is visiting his father in Pomerania and will call on you on his return journey, God willing. With him you can learn and discuss in detail the situation of our mission and Church. He is not a deep believer but earnestly strives to build the kingdom of God internally and externally. He spares no sacrifice for that. He belongs to the few who, with me, have taken on the mission anew and promoted it with equal faithfulness. Also, in the Church he has served with great merit as a member of the Church Council. His legacy of £1000 safeguards the Hermannsburg mission as long as Hermannsburg Lutheran mission is pursued here in Hermannsburg or in any part of the world by giving a third of the interest, £20 annually. When the fiancées of Harms and Darsow are ready to travel, he intends to bring them with him back to Australia. This is a very good opportunity, and the brothers need them…

30 June 1883, Hermannsburg/Bethany[4] *(Kempe, Heidenreich to Th Harms)*
[Extracts]
Expenditure from June 1882 to June 1883:

Wages (Schleicher); wages; mail bag; wages; wages; 12 shirts and wages; items which Schleicher needed; wages; one bullock and wages; beef for Schleicher's trip; 10 bars soap; stores for Schleicher's trip; Schleicher shirts, shoes, etc.; wages; 6 belts; beef; tobacco; tea; stores for Schleicher's trip; stores for Schleicher's trip; cartage; rams; cartage for colonists' clothes and tobacco; wages; wages; a horse; payment for bringing up the people; telegrams and stamps; wages; tobacco, etc.;

Total expenses are £406/3/4.

Income [includes]:

Things from the store; things from the store, wool; things from the store; 1 sheep, 33 pounds flour.

Income totals £107/8/5.

There is a separate itemised list for Schleicher's wages totalling £127/8/3.

I must note that the total expenditure is actually higher than shown, because the income from the store has, for the most part, been subtracted from the wages, so that the income can actually not be declared, apart from the few sales to outsiders.

As for our livestock, we can say that our cattle numbers have really increased with God's blessing so that in the next few years we will have enough animals to slaughter, provided nothing changes in the meantime. In the first six months of the year we already had 64 calves, and the total number of branded cattle is 230. We have 100 horses, possibly more, since we intend to brand only in September. In addition there are 2800 sheep and 200 goats.

That is all there is to report; everything else is contained in the quarterly report.

H Kempe

Dear Father!

These terrible expenses provide me with lots of headaches and deep concern. I myself have repeatedly written and pointed out that the mission treasury cannot bear such expenditure, but despite that it still increases. What should I do? This mission field is difficult. I want to make things reasonably comfortable for the brothers, so that they do not have to eat their bread with sorrow. But they push this to the point where our mission will fail.

I have another request. Please have Major Ruschenbusch immediately send £3 for the sister of Missionary Kempe to this address: Mrs Auguste Pietzsch, nee Kempe, Upper Gittersee Peterhappel (?), Kingdom of Saxony. Kempe has paid the £3 at this end...

G A Heidenreich

* * *

Synods – and the Missionaries. A personal reflection.

In the second part of his letter of 1 June 1883, Heidenreich discusses the possibility of the formation of a Lutheran Synod in Queensland. By now, readers will be accustomed to the constant references in the Heidenreich correspondence to pastoral placements all over South Australia, other parts of the country and New Zealand. They will also be familiar with the way he agonises over the suitability of people for various positions, and over the formation of ecclesiastical alliances on both a personal and regional level. Rightly or wrongly, Heidenreich involved himself very much in such issues.

They were important matters. By 1883 the Lutheran communities throughout Australia and New Zealand had grown to the extent that, for the sake of good order, efficiency and the unity of the Church, there was an increasing need for functional structure within those communities.

One familiar way in which the Church framed that structure was through Synodical alliances. Unfortunately, however, the creation and maintenance of these alliances was often fraught and complex for those Lutherans. When one seeks to make a diagram, say, of that process, the result is something like a badly-drawn map of Paris!

A full and faithful account of the Synodical story of Lutherans in Australia would require a book or two of its own, and such an account is best left for another author at another time. However, insofar as the Synodical manoeuvrings do connect, albeit tangentially, with the mission on the Finke, a brief foray into the various Synods is a part of the story of *Missionaries, Madness and Miracles*.

The first Australian Lutheran Synod comprised one pastor (Kavel) and three congregations (Klemzig, Hahndorf and Glen Osmond). It was formed in March 1839 (five months after the arrival of the first Lutherans) and was simply known as the Australian Lutheran Synod. The Synod doubled in size with Fritzsche's arrival in 1841, and with the addition of other congregations, most notably Langmeil/Tanunda, Bethany and Lobethal. The point to note here is that we are not talking huge numbers and big organisation. This was a small Church and, relative to the larger Christian denominations in Australia, always has been.

The big split between the two pastors in 1846 saw the number of Synods double, with the formation of Fritzsche's Evangelical Lutheran Synod of South Australia (ELSSA). Later, as the ELSSA established bonds with congregations that formed in Victoria and New South Wales, this became the Evangelical Synod of Australia (ELSA), in 1863. Kavel's group became known as the Immanuel Synod.

Of these two Synods, Immanuel has the more colourful history. As time passed, Lutheran pastors and groups came to Australia from disparate parts of the world and established their own congregations or groups of congregations. Thus, for example, there were the various undertakings by the Gossner missionaries in Queensland, the arrival of people like Goethe in Victoria in 1856, and Staudenmayer in Light Pass and Tanunda in 1860, to mention a few. Pastors and groups like these were largely independent at first, but over time aligned themselves or merged into what eventually became the United Evangelical Church of Australia (UELCA).

The ELSA, on the other hand, was more staid and homogenous in its development and complexion. At first, most of its pastors came from Hermannsburg or were 'home grown', with the exception in the early days of the Dresden missionaries. But now, in the 1880s, the Missourians from the USA are beginning to make their presence felt and, as has already become evident in the reports, are causing a stir in various quarters. Meantime, though, ELSA Lutherans have moved from South Australia to Victoria and New South Wales, and formed congregations there. In time, these have become Districts of the ELSA. But, as we have also already seen, these comings and goings were often accompanied by arguments about correct doctrine, faithfulness or not to the Lutheran Confessions and an almost pathological fear of 'sinful unionism'.

The missionaries at Hermannsburg on the Finke belonged to the ELSSA/ELSA, but at the same time maintained bonds with the Hermannsburg Lutherans in Germany. In the main, the various Synodical happenings in Australia had no real impact on them. For them, what was synodically relevant were the financial and other supports they received for the mission from congregations, especially in South Australia, and the administration of the mission by the South Australian District. They were kept informed of Synodical happenings via the *Kirchenbote*, *Missionsblatt*, and various correspondence, but were not directly involved in most of those happenings.

All of which speaks to the isolation those first missionaries experienced in the Centre. Locally and personally, they had no fraternal or pastoral inter-action with the wider Synod. During the entire 17 years they served the mission, one could count on the fingers of one hand the number of times that, between them, they travelled South and were thus able to meet up with their Synodical brothers and sisters. And, apart from official investigations into the mission, Heidenreich, as the Superintendent of the mission, never once visited the mission itself. Nor did any members of the District Church or Mission Council.

There is a personal element in all this, in that for many years of my own ministry I served in small, isolated congregations in Tasmania and New Zealand—in times when cheap phone calls, cheap air fares, computers, i-phones and the internet were not even on the horizon. Thus, I have a heart for any pastors, missionaries, or congregations that continue to experience that same sense of Synodical isolation today. I particularly resonate with, though nevertheless cannot fully imagine, how detrimental to their own well-being that Synodical isolation must have been for that small community on the Finke, especially on top of the physical isolation

There is also a lesson in all this for any Church that has pastors and other personnel serving in isolated and remote setting. Synodical inclusion, as a reality as well as a notion, is crucial to the well-being of such communities. Those within such communities know this well. Unfortunately, those in larger towns and cities often have no real sense at all of what it feels like to minister in isolation, and the Church is the poorer for such ignorance.

1 June 1883, Bethany[5] *(Heidenreich to Th Harms)*
Highly respected and much-loved Father!
... Yesterday Brother Gössling wrote to me that all four brothers in Queensland have been installed as pastors, and that they are capable men for the difficult field of work there. He also said it was a pity that they had not received five men at the same time. But you will once again open your generous hands when the next group of graduates is ready.

Finally, Brother Gössling and the young brothers, all of whom except Heuer have written, have expressed the hope that a Lutheran Synod will be formed in Queensland. The young brothers are very glad that they first were in South Australia for some months, learning about the country and its people. Where possible, you should keep in mind that new people sent out could stop here for four to six weeks. That can easily be arranged with the shipping companies if the ticket is bought for Sydney, so that they stay in Adelaide for one or two months and then sail for Sydney with the same company. This is of the greatest importance for united working of Hermannsburg people in the Church and mission. We have enough experience of how things went in New Zealand; had the elder Dierks not been here, the situation would have been worse than when he left here.

I repeat that a mission in Queensland has little prospect of success. I am pleased with the zeal for mission there, but let things happen as they will and demand from the outset detailed reports on everything necessary.[6] See what brilliant reports have come to us from New Zealand, and look at how in our mission there they are now fighting for its existence…

G A Heidenreich

* * *

The last reports for 1883 come from the pens of Kempe, Schwarz and Heidenreich. Here and there parts of the original reports have been omitted, either because they are repetitious of material elsewhere, or because they do not add significantly to the narrative.

The work of the mission goes on, much of it fairly routine by now. However, as demonstrated in Kempe's report below for the second quarter of the year, their knowledge and understanding of the Aboriginal people is expanding. So also does their relationship with the people, and here and there Kempe gives us delightful peeks into that inter-action. Despite any aversion to the term 'heathen', there is a detectable note of affection in Kempe's reference to the Aboriginal people as 'our heathen'. Their response to a totally different kind of people, the Muslims, is intriguing.

There are still no converts, nor any sign of any. One cannot help admiring the patience on the part of the missionaries. It is also noteworthy in this next letter that Kempe stresses the importance of not in any way imposing Christianity upon the people. The missionaries regard faith as gift from God, freely offered, freely received.

At the same time, there are hints that the strain of their situation and isolation is beginning to tell on their little party.

31 July 1883, Hermannsburg[7] *(Kempe to Th Harms)*
Dear Pastor!

This last quarter was a really quiet one, not as if we had no work. On the contrary, we had too much. In that regard we will also not get much rest next year, for after the new brothers have arrived we will have to be busy building homes also for them, and that requires some years even without anything else going on. Consequently, we actually always have to take into account what needs to be done for the whole year. But that does not matter, for the Scripture says that life is full of trouble and work is difficult. Our heathen, of course, are of a completely different opinion.

I have called it a quiet quarter because neither among us nor amongst the heathen has anything worth mentioning happened, though one would have to designate as worthy of mention that recently again one of the heathen here was murdered by the heathen of another tribe. This has to be seen as an act of revenge for some alleged injustice against that person.

An event that does not occur every day was a trader recently coming here with all sorts of wares he had loaded on 11 camels, far more than I had seen here before. This trader was an Afghan and he was a Muslim in terms of religion, as were his two companions. Our heathen were naturally very curious to see what it was all about and whether there was something in it for them as well. And so it was that they saw that these people earnestly prayed evening and morning and always with the face turned to the sun, and that they fell down on their face to the ground, stood up again and knelt down again.

As we spoke about this amongst ourselves, and the heathen noticed what they were doing, one of them was immediately ready to show us how to do it. He had picked it up from them really well. We asked him what and why people had done that. He answered: 'They were speaking to the sun'. That was the impression they had gotten, and that must indeed be the impression anyone would get who does not understand what was going on. When we then asked the heathen with whom they were actually speaking, they had to be a little ashamed, for they had to say that they do nothing like that.[8]

One thing Christians can learn from the Mohammedans is the open, free confession of their faith. They are never and under no circumstances ashamed of that, and yet their religion is nothing better than heathendom. How much less do we have cause to be ashamed of our faith, and yet how cowardly and faithless are most Christians in this regard.

After the rain at the end of last year almost all of the heathen left us. There was enough to eat away from the station, and they prefer that to our food, especially since they are able to get it without much effort, while here on the station they always have to do at least some work for it.

For a few weeks now a small number have again returned; and since we are just at the point of developing several gardens and digging wells, and also ought in the near future to begin some building, we are now able to employ a lot of them, and without it costing us too much, for this year we could harvest many melons and could feed the heathen with these.

We have now begun to irrigate our garden properly and hope that we will have more success with this than earlier. So far this year everything is thriving very well. Whether in the future and in the still drier years things will grow so well, experience will tell.

No effort and work are spared for this, and everywhere around the station there is now hammering, carpentry, sawing, as if there were a factory here. Pumps and windmills have to be built, channels dug out and laid, fences made, and so on.

All of this appears highly comical to the heathen. When something is finished, they stand in front of it in amazement and say: '*Indota*' – 'How clever!' They thereby learn to recognise their own ignorance, and that is something good and can only help to suppress their arrogance, for although they are generally foolish and poor, they nevertheless consider themselves, in true heathen fashion, to be wonderful and great.

I said earlier that when they have plenty to eat elsewhere, which is the case only after rain, the heathen much prefer that to our food. Admittedly, when one sees it for the first time, e.g. when a number of them are sitting in the camp and are occupied with the preparation of food, one probably feels little desire to eat with them. However, the more one becomes familiar with them and their way of life, the more one learns to accept that they know best how to prepare their food, and also what is the most tasty. Who would think, e.g. that the rock-hard kernel of the *acacia* could be eaten? And yet the Aboriginal people know how to make it edible. They first of all roast the kernels in hot ashes, then grate them between two stones with water, making a thin paste which, during the process of rubbing, is wiped off with the hand and licked.

They employ a similar process with almost all seeds. Early in the year a kind of cress very frequently grows here (*Lepidium ruderale*). From it they make a kind of vegetable in the following way. After they have been collected, the plants are placed on a hot plate which they make from stones heated on the fire, so that the plants lie in a hollow and in this way are only steamed.

After this the plant is shaped into clumps by hand, and eaten. This is a really tasty and healthy meal.

Less appetising, at least for us, is when one sees how they prepare their meat. They never skin an animal, but only rub off a little of the hair or feathers, and lay the animal like that in the hot ashes, covering it completely. When it is roasted tender, they then first make a hole in the stomach and carefully suck out the juice, which seems to be the most important thing. Nothing is thrown away, not even the intestines, and even in the case of small birds they just remove the crop and eat everything, including head and legs. It does not really matter if as a result they sometimes swallow a few feathers. When we go to roast a bird and first of all remove all the feathers, that to them seems laughable.

Noteworthy is the sign language which they engage in amongst themselves. It is performed in such a way that, if one really wanted to learn it, one would have to acquire a proper degree. This sign language is found not only in this area but also among all Aboriginal people in Australia. For each animal, for each person, whether a man or a woman, a boy or a girl, for everything, they have a specific sign. Also for every command, e.g.: 'Come here! Go! Stay! etc. '

All these signs are produced by various movements of the arms and positions of the fingers. When, e.g. someone sees several people coming and wants to communicate with his companions who are sitting some distance away, he points upwards with the index finger of his right hand and makes several horizontal rings or circles with his hand. His companions immediately understand and ask: 'Is it a friend or a foe?' by several times turning the hollow part of their hand towards their face. The other man several times turns the hollow of his hand away from his face and in that way gives the answer: 'No, it is a friend!' In this way they are able to speak with each other even when they are so far away from one another that they can hardly see each other. It is amazing how well they make themselves understood that way. Naturally, their sharp eyes help them a lot in the process.

Their superstitions have already been mentioned in the reports now and then. This time I want to add only one thing, namely, how they view sickness and deal with it. They have something similar to doctors whom they call *nungara* and who pretend to be able to heal sicknesses by doing all kinds of silly, foolish stuff with the sick. However, even though they are still not able to heal the sickness they know how to save face. They simply say: 'The sickness has been caused by some person and they were not able to cure it, and probably it is something which the devil has caused'. Or they say: 'The illness is *ekilta*', i.e. strong or firm.

They also claim they are able to drive away the rain by throwing a stick into the air with all their strength in the direction in which they want the rain to go. Whether at the same time they utter any magic formulas I do not know, but I doubt it.

When we once asked them who had told them all this, e.g. about the place where they go after death and so on, they answered that their oldest man had told them, and he had heard it from an old man who formerly lived north of here, and who had heard it from another old man who had been there, but had come back.

They imagine the earth as a great plain. In their thinking the sun is a woman who, after going down in the west, at night returns again unseen in order to rise next morning in the east. They say that she gathers firewood along the way and burns it, and depending on whether she burns more or less wood, the day will be more or less hot.

On the other hand the moon is a man who returns across the earth from the west to the east.

The ebbing and waning of the moon they explain thus: After new moon the man is at first quite small, so he eats a lot and as a result his stomach grows every day until at the full moon he has the fattest stomach. However, afterwards the belly shrinks from lack of meat until it completely disappears.

The starry sky is *Altjira's* (God's) campsite. The stars are the campfires. And when a shooting star falls, that is a spark falling from one of the fires. The great comet that was visible in the east at the beginning of last year they believed to be a huge spear that some enemy showed them and with which he threatened to kill them.

Absolutely everything that in any way rarely occurs and is therefore strange strikes them with fear and terror.[9] They are totally subject to fear. Oh, if only they would grasp the salvation offered to them in Christ Jesus, for by that alone can they be freed from their fear of death and be brought to peace. Meanwhile, they seem still to be far from that and, at least as far as we can see, that time is still far in the future. May God give us patience and love not to doubt their redemption and at all times persist in holding out to them as precious their salvation in Christ.

As far as our physical situation is concerned we are, thank the Lord, all safe and well; a slight discomfort now and then, or an eye ailment and so on, is not worth mentioning further. We all have cause to be thankful that the Lord has graciously protected us from serious illness until now. Admittedly, the climate very quickly erodes our strength. The longer we are here the more we feel that. Earlier, e.g. I have felled trees all day without it particularly exhausting me; but now I can hardly chop a few or, if it is a reasonably big tree, without first having to rest several times.

The English people here travel back down to Adelaide after four, at the most five, years in order to recuperate, and I am inclined to believe that this is very advisable. Whether this will also be granted to us, we do not know. In any case it would be no great disadvantage to the mission...

H Kempe

* * *

Schwarz's next letter highlights the multiplicity of practical tasks that occupy their lives. As with Kempe's letter above it is noteworthy to see how much the lives of Black and White entwine. There is, for example, the case of the young man who falls into the fire while he is sleeping. This was a not-uncommon nor unexpected occurrence, given that people slept so closely to their fires at night.

Also in this report is an account of another violent inter-action between the Arrarnta and some other tribe. The role the missionaries play in resolving this situation is a further example of the trust they have obviously earned among the people.

2 October 1883, Hermannsburg[10] *(Schwarz to Hermannsburg, Germany)*
... All we brothers and sisters have been able to finish this quarter healthy and safe. In the course of this quarter no sickness, and especially no serious sickness, has befallen us and we are fairly familiar with the evils that make their home among us, such as stomach and eye problems.

This whole quarter all of the brothers and sisters were here on the station, since the shepherds came back here with their flocks at the end of June. Since all of our human resources were here together, something worthwhile could again be accomplished this winter. The tasks we accomplished are the following: We have smashed and carted rocks and dug and carted clay. In addition, we have felled, carted, and cut timber, and also have established a big new garden with a well, around 22 feet deep, which is lined with stones and covered.

Similarly, a lot of brush has been cut for a garden fence and has been carted. A brush fence like this is here the cheapest and the best because, if it is properly built, it protects just as well against the sharp east wind as it does against the rats.

With God's help, we are making constant progress in building the garden, so that in the future, also in the dry years, God willing, we will never lack green vegetables. Four wells have already been dug for this purpose and are in use; in addition two more are in progress. For nine months we have such rich, fresh garden vegetables that we are not only able to serve our neighbours with them (and they accept these with hearty thanks), but also our pupils and nearly the whole little clan of heathens receive a meal from our garden almost every day.

One of the most important tasks was the erection of the stone walls of a new building about 80 feet long and 20 feet wide, as well as the sheep shed which was begun on 17 September and will be completed tomorrow. In addition, reeds were cut, the garden was established, watered and newly laid out, all of which took a lot of work.

The three of us, and occasionally four workmen and three heathen, were occupied with the protection of the sheep and the goats. Furthermore, there was a lot of smithing to do, as well as carpentry work and building, also tailoring and shoe-making, as well as carting a lot of firewood, because not since 1876 have we had such a cold and long winter. Up to mid-September we froze, with ice almost each morning. Several times we had 5° R. The weather was very constant this winter: cold nights and a lot of wind and dust during the day, with clear skies. We have received as good as no rain. At the beginning of August it looked like rain, but we did not receive even enough to settle the dust down for a day.

Last week we had some thunder storms, but hardly anything worth mentioning, though a decent rain is very much desired and necessary, because the fodder for the cattle is in short supply, as is also the water in the river beds.

By the way, I must make mention of a natural phenomenon which our heathen in their belief or better, their superstition, know how to explain in their own peculiar way. In the days from 24 to 27 August, several among us at different times heard a din, partly above us in the air, partly at some distance away at ground level, like the thunder of a canon fired twice in short intervals, like a double-barrelled shotgun being fired. A weaker noise followed these shots, like real thunder in the distance. But there was no storm, because if one listened carefully, the noise was already over.

We connect all of this with meteorites.[11] But what about our heathen? They say: The hungry devil, who snaps at them with drawn fangs, sometimes on the earth and sometimes in the air, makes the noise by the opening and closing of his jaws. When the devil does not succeed in catching an *atua* (man), he incites their enemies against them so that they come and kill several men.

That is how our poor heathen explain for themselves an inauspicious sign, such as when a comet appears in the sky or a lot of shooting stars appear. In short, anything that is unclear to them and is feared by them, as well as all evil and sickness that befall them, have to be attributed to the devil or to their enemies who continually seek their death.

Now, our heathen are not totally wrong in this, and occasionally unexplained things happen among them, as we experienced this winter in the case of a young man. His name is Kuatimbulka and he is well known to us all because earlier he was with us for a long time. Last year he also helped with the sheep shearing, then left the station, returned here after approximately three months with other young people and stayed in the heathens' camp. At that time I often saw and spoke to him and his companions, and know that he was well.

One morning after breakfast we suddenly heard the familiar howling of the women. To our question, 'Who has died?' we were told, 'The devil has thrown Kuatimbulka into the fire.' His young friend Eregerika said this to me. He had straightaway come from the camp, where he had just snatched Kuatimbulka from the glowing coals. He himself seemed quite surprised about this event and was barely able to speak a word.

Since I had gotten to know Eregerika as an unreliable young lad, I thought: 'You rascal. Either the whole thing is a lie, or you yourself have thrown Kuatimbulka into the fire.' However, I asked him to show me the unfortunate spot. But since he was pointing quite far away, I went back and did some work in the garden.

What really happened was that when Kuatimbulka went to get up from his sleeping site that same morning, he had fallen into his own camp fire and, not capable of moving on his own, lay there until Eregerika found him and saved him. However, Kuatimbulka was so badly burnt that one side of his body was quite roasted.

We then tried to lay the blame on this or that heathen person, but all the heathen—and the person himself—are united in saying: 'The devil has done this.' ...

We, particularly Brother Schulze, took Kuatimbulka into our care; but after barely eight weeks of lying sick in his bed he was again on his feet and left the station. He has not been here since.

Although our heathen appear to be very frightened of the devil, they are nevertheless so proud—especially the doctors—that they maintain that they are stronger than the devil, for what he does to them they are able to undo. However, what the evil people do to them, that they are not able to cure.

Yet again they are so blinded that when one speaks with them about death they simply say that they do not die.

So then, it is very good for them to be truly humbled, as was the case on 24 September. Just after midday, 28 men from several hostile tribes came right up to our station with the intention of killing three of our heathen. There was great distress among the otherwise immortals. They all trembled with fear of death and asked us if we might drive the enemies back with our weapons. However, we said they should call out to the strangers that we would like to see them, for we did not at first believe that they had come with such malicious intent. But ours cried out with one voice: 'No, no. They will kill us.' The women were also already beginning their death wailing, and all were greatly agitated.

Meanwhile, we had taken our weapons in hand in order possibly to prevent the shedding of blood and to settle the matter as well and as soon as possible, for we ourselves had a lot to do and no time to lose. With my weapon on my shoulder I went out to look at those people seeking blood revenge and to dissuade them from their evil plans. This was completely successful. Half an hour later friend and enemy were on the station and made peace with sugar water that we served up to them, peace sealed with blood and tears. Some of the strangers struck themselves on the forehead with stones at the end of their woomeras, so that the blood streamed out. Thereupon they bowed to some of our people who sat in a circle on the ground. They embraced, spoke some words to them and finally wept with each other. These and other ceremonies we observed on this occasion. Finally, both friend and enemy grasped their weapons which during the negotiations had been lying on the ground or propped up here and there, and then returned to the camp in the nicest order, holding their spears perfectly upright, accompanied on the right and left by a woman carrying a proper cudgel.

The rest of the afternoon passed quietly, but after we had enjoyed the evening meal and it had become quite dark, and still before evening devotion, some of our heathen came to us at the station in great haste and fear of death and asked us whether we might allow them to stay on the station overnight. They said that their enemies had only appeared to make peace with them because they had been frightened of us, and they would this night carry out their intention and set to fire to our thatched roofs.

Now what were we to do? We were not worried about ourselves and the station, but for the poor heathen who were totally possessed by the fear of death. We allowed them all to come to the station and to stay within the newly-built walls, which they gladly did; and since it was cold we also gave them some firewood. That night the men had no sleep, but the feared attack did not take place.

In the middle of the night the main enemies, who had come from the far west, went away. The others, a tribe more closely related to our heathen and who lived more southerly and south-westerly, stayed until it was day and said goodbye in a proper way before they left. In the end, our heathen were happy that at least this time they had come away with their skin intact, and they went off to hunt, to settle their hungry stomachs...

At present there are 60 heathen here, 20 students. In employment we have eight adults, five men and three women. The older students also all have to work. There are 11 old, fragile people here, among them three blind men and one blind woman. All these are more or less the people for whom we daily provide food, but we together with them are daily provided for by the Lord...

W F Schwarz

* * *

As Heidenreich tidies up the mission finances for the financial year, he is again not happy at what he regards as the mismanagement of money by the missionaries, especially Kempe. Yet, there is obviously discussion going on about the possibility of one of the staff on the Finke actually taking over the administration of the mission on site. Heidenreich has his reservations about such a move.

The administrative disjoint between the mission in the Centre and its oversight down South has often been a bone of contention. The workers at the coal-face are obviously the ones who best know the work and its needs, both over-all and, especially, on a day-to-day basis. However, there is a reluctance to take the natural, obvious step of relocating the administration.

26 October 1883, Bethany[12] *(Heidenreich to Th Harms)*
Highly honoured, much-loved Father!

First of all, I am sending you as an attachment the mission's financial statement for the past year. In it you will see an entry for a large debt that has increased, in part from the sending up of the colonists and in part from expenses on the station for workers' salaries and building costs. Brother Kempe alone has spent £400 by cheques, despite me having written to him about the state of affairs and also my councillors writing to him. For, if the financial management continues like this, we must end up in bankruptcy. What is to be done? I cannot close the bank account to the missionaries because we cannot send them cash for necessary running expenses, and also because they will then not learn proper economic management. Please give me direction on this matter.

All three missionaries have finally declared their opposition to the matter of administration. In these days I will, after the confirmation of my children on the Festival of Reformation, summon my advisory council, so that we can again discuss the topic in detail and present the outcome to you for approval. Schwarz is suggesting that Koch be appointed administrator, Schulze is proposing Kempe, and Kempe is willing to take on the administration only if he is given complete freedom of his actions so that no one orders him around anymore.

In that case, the role of superintendent down here is only a check or a spoilsport and, should that happen, it is better to entrust Kempe with the superintendency. A hybrid rule has achieved little in both Church and mission. Whether (or not) I and my Council are happy that Kempe is granted his desired complete power, we are convinced that this path will lead to the burial of our mission here, not only in the external financial management, but also internally through the lack of peace among our people themselves. But I am here giving just a few details; the full picture will come only later when you receive as much clarity as possible...

The missionaries write that, unfortunately, they are unable to sell any horses, and so I must urgently ask you soon to send a generous subsidy...

G A Heidenreich

* * *

Kempe's and Schwarz's final two reports for 1883 round off the year with a few paintbrush strokes of various aspects of the mission, especially the physical state of things.

30 November 1883, Hermannsburg[13] *(Kempe to ELSA members)*
The (European) personnel on the station at present consists of 21 persons, 10 men, 4 women and 7 children. New buildings have not been added this year; the large house (80 by 20 feet) will not be completed before winter. We have the same number of appliances as in the previous year (wagon, buggy, carts). Our inventory of livestock comprises: 110 horses, 250 cattle, 2500 sheep, 300 goats.

During the year there were always heathen on the station. The children are making good progress in school. They are given instruction in the Christian religion, reading, writing, arithmetic and geography. They likewise are taught various handicrafts like sewing, gardening, etc.

We believe that we can already perceive a change for the better with them. The heathen staying on our station have totally given up stealing and slaughtering our animals, whereas all of our neighbours are right now complaining of that a lot. Furthermore, they increasingly understand that an ordered life is much better than roaming about and being idle. Once they grasp that fully and become accustomed to an ordered, settled life, a major barrier will be overcome.

It certainly costs the mission a lot to maintain a number of people with bread, meat and clothing. Thus, in this year we have used no less than 11 bullocks and about 500 sheep for ourselves and for the heathen. We would have needed more had we not had so many melons in our garden this year and been able to give them some.

This year we had more success than before with gardening. We have begun to irrigate the gardens regularly. For this we have sunk a number of wells, installed pumps, and a windmill drives the water to the gardens. The reason for digging so many wells is that we soon strike red sandstone everywhere and the wells can thus hold only a small amount of water. We do not have the tools to dig through the sandstone, nor do we know how deep it goes and if we will find water under it... The success of this irrigating surpassed our expectation. With its use we found the following plants flourishing: various kinds of cabbage, cauliflower, various beets, melons, carrots, parsnips, spinach, maze, millet, radishes, potatoes, onions, also beans and other vegetables.

We had a little success planting trees. This is because slips and cuttings take six to nine weeks to get here and mostly arrive ruined. Those that do grow from cuttings and vines sent to us flourish quite well. In this respect we owe a lot to Baron von Müller who has not ceased to encourage us to plant things and has sent us many seeds, cuttings, and vines...

Although high costs and lots of effort are involved, one can see that it is rewarding and that this land only lacks a proper amount of water to transform it from a desert into a fruitful land.

H Kempe

30 November 1883[14] *(Schwarz to ELSA members)*
Herewith the annual report on the government rations for our heathen. This year it has been no better than previously, since fresh rations for them have still not arrived. We hope that the driver will still arrive here before the Christmas festival. Fortunately for us, you sent a good supply of flour for our own stores the previous time, otherwise we and our heathen would have been badly off, as far as bread is concerned. Our heathen suffer no lack of nourishment,

though we have had to restrict the distribution of bread somewhat. Instead, we have given them more vegetables and milk. If they have fresh vegetables, meat, milk and some bread they can get by very well.

Thank God for the blessings of our gardens where greenery and flowers flourish after the faithful Lord several times this month gave us good rains.

The heathen show a real interest and skill in gardening. They are no less happy than we when everything grows and flourishes so well. They are making progress in all areas, even if it is slow; they progress in physical as well as in spiritual matters. Patience only! We will still thank God for everything.

Heathen presently here number 60, pupils 20, adult men 5, women 3. The older pupils have to work with us. There are 11 elderly and fragile people here, including 3 blind men and a blind woman. Our heathen have had 6 new-born, 2 boys and 4 girls. 4 people died, 3 males and 1 female.

The school is well attended on average, but during the entire year there were fewer pupils attending than in the previous year.

All these daily eat at our table but we, with them, eat at the table of the Lord our God. May he graciously grant that we all some day sit at the table of the great marriage feast.

Last week I was extremely sick after experiencing a so-called heatstroke (or sunstroke). God be praised that I am again fairly active but, like all those living on the station, Whites and Blacks, I am suffering with the flu or a feverish cold…

W Schwarz

* * *

Elsewhere in the world in 1883

- In Cricket: although the term 'the Ashes' had been coined the year before, the actual Ashes were first presented to the winning English team after the Sydney Test on 30 January. The ashes were made from a bail used in the match.
- 24 May: New York's Brooklyn Bridge was opened. A week later a stampede occurred on the bridge after rumours that it was about to collapse. Twelve people were killed.
- 27 May: Alexander III was crowned as Tsar of Russia in Moscow.
- On 1 August, Great Britain inaugurated its inland postal service.
- The Orient Express departed on its first journey from Paris to Istanbul, 4 October.

- New York's Metropolitan Opera House was opened (22 October), with a performance of Gounod's *Faust*.
- Robert Louis Stevenson's *Treasure Island* was published, 14 November.
- Born: Author Franz Kafka (3 July), Italian dictator, Benito Mussolini (29 July).
- Died: Karl Marx (14 March).

Image credits

Schwarz, Schulze, Kempe / Lutheran Archives PO2601 05001
Heidenreich / Lutheran Archives MO1507 00594
Th Harms / Lutheran Archives PO9526 18625
First Australian Lutheran Seminary, Lobethal / Australian Lutheran Archives P02230 04289
Engagement of AH Kempe & Dorothea Queckenstedt, 1865 / Author's personal collection
Hermannsburg Mission Institute / From the HMI website
L Schulze & wife, Charlotte Gutmann / Lutheran Archives PO2028 03936
G Heidenrech, wife, Anna Meyer, and child / Lutheran Archives M00302 00071
Engagement of WF Schwarz & Dorothea Schulz, 1865 (?) / Author's personal collection
Departure to Killalpaninna from Bethany, 1865 / Australian Lutheran Archives PO2740 05315
Killalpaninna Mission Station (sketch) Date unknown / Australian Lutheran Archives PO3807 07879
AH Kempe / Lutheran Archives M00313 00140
WF Schwarz / Lutheran Archives PO2601 05002
LG Schulze / Lutheran Archives P020 03940
Original Kempe letter to Th Harms, from Pricerla Watercourse, 7 February 1876. / Australian Lutheran Archives, Microfiche files, AU3, K1+, 31b
Baron von Müller / Various sources [Wikipedia]
Hermannsburg cattle / Australian Lutheran Archives P02611 05025
Acacia Kempeana (witchetty grub bush), with author / Personal photo
Drought / Australian Lutheran Archives P03750 07789
Finke in flood / Australian Lutheran Archives P02634 05085
The Swan Taplin Inquiry, 1890 [Stipendiary magistrate Henry C.Swan seated on camel in foreground, probably Mr Charles Eaton Taplin (centre) and Police Inspector Bryan Charles Beasley (extreme right)] / Australian Lutheran Archives P02603 0500
Palm Valley / Australian Lutheran Archives P02632 050813
Peake Telegraph Station / State Library of SA B6131
Alice Springs (Stuart), 1891 / Source not known

Bibliography

(A selection of related materials. All referenced, but not all cited within the book.)

Books
—*Koonibba jubilee booklet, 1901-1926*, Lutheran Publishing House, Adelaide, 1926.
—*The personal touch: a look at South Australia's postal history* Australia Post publication, undated.
Albrecht, Paul. *From mission to church: 1877-2002 Finke River Mission*, Openbook Publishers, Adelaide, 2002.
Albrecht, Paul. *Relhilperra: about Aborigines*, Quadrant Online, 2012.
Altmann, Max (compiler). *The silver miner's son: the history of Louis Gustav Schulze, missionary*, Fox Publishing, Hahndorf, SA, 1980.
Brauer, A. *Under the southern cross: history of Evangelical Lutheran Church of Australia*, Lutheran Publishing House, Adelaide, 1956.
Broome, Richard. *Aboriginal Australians: a history since 1788, 4th edition*, Allen and Unwin, Crows Nest NSW, 2010.
Butler, Reg. *A college in the wattles: Hahndorf and its academy*, Lutheran Publishing House, Adelaide, 1989.
Chatwin, Bruce. *The songlines*, Picador, London, 1987.
Cross, Jack. *Great central state. The foundation of the Northern Territory*, Wakefield Press, Kent Town, SA, 2011.
Flannery, Tim (ed), William Buckley, *The life and adventures of William Buckley*, Text Publishing, Melbourne, 2017.
Dodd, Reg and Malcolm McKinnon. *Talking sideways: stories and conversations from Finniss Springs*, University of Queensland Press, St Lucia, Qld, 2019.
Dowling, Peter. *Fatal contact: how epidemics nearly wiped out Australia's first peoples*, Monash University Publishing, Clayton, Vic, 2021.
Eckermann, CV. *Koonibba: the mission and the Nunga people*, Openbook Howden Design & Print, Adelaide, 2010.
Folds, Ralph. *Crossed purposes: the Pintupi and Australia's indigenous policy*, UNSW Press, 2001.
Gammage, Bill. *The biggest estate on earth: how Aborigines made Australia*, Allen and Unwin, Crows Nest, NSW, 2012.
Gibbs, R M. *Under the burning sun: a history of colonial South Australia, 1836-1900*, Southern Heritage, Adelaide, 2013.
Gill, Sam D. *Storytracking: texts, stories, and histories in Central Australia*, Oxford University Press, New York, 1998.
Graetz, Joyce. *An open book*, Lutheran Publishing House, Adelaide, 1988.

Grant, Stan. *The Queen is dead: the time has come for a reckoning,* Harper Collins, Sydney, 2023.

Groom, Arthur. *I saw a stranghe land,* Angus and Robertson, Sydney, NSW, 1950. Also Text Publishing, Melbourne, Vic, 2015.

Hamilton, Reg. *Colony: strange origins of one of the earliest modern democracies,* Wakefield Press, Adelaide, 2010.

Hardy, Olga. *Like a bird on the wing.* Lutheran Publishing House, Adelaide, 1984.

Harms, Hartwig F. *Träume und Tränen: Hermannsburger missionare und die wirkungen ihrer arbeit in Australien und Neuseeland.* Verlag Ludwig-Harms-Haus, 2004.

Harris, John. *One blood. 200 years of Aboriginal encounter with Christianity: a story of hope,* Albatross Books, Sutherland, NSW, 1990.

Hauser, R J. *The patriarchs: a history of Australian Lutheran schooling 1839–1919,* Lutheran Education Australia, 2009.

Hebart, Theodor. *The United Evangelical Lutheran Church in Australia (UELCA): its history, activities and characteristics, 1838–1938,* Lutheran Book Depot, Adelaide, 1938.

Henson, Barbara. *A straight-out man. F W Albrecht and Central Australian Aborigines,* Melbourne University Press, 1994.

Hill, Barry. *Broken song: T G H Strehlow and Aboriginal possession,* Random House, Milsons Point, NSW, 2002.

Hill, Ernestine. *The territory: a sprawling saga of Australia's tropic north,* Angus and Robertson, North Ryde, NSW, 1951, 1985 reprint

Hines, Colleen. *Jim and Annie on the overland telegraph,* self-published, Wallendbeen, NSW, 1997.

Hooper, Kenneth Francis. *The mining sector and its role within the Northern Territory economy.* A thesis for the Faculty of Business, Northern Territory University, 1997.

Iwan W (ed David Schubert. *Because of their beliefs: emigration from Prussia to Australia,* H Schubert, Magill, SA, 1995.

Judd, Barry and Katherine Ellinghaus. *Enlightened Aboriginal futures,* Routledge, Oxford, 2024.

Kempe, A H (tr P A Scherer). *From joiner's bench to pulpit,* Lutheran Publishing House, Adelaide, 1973.

Kettle, Ellen. *Health services in the Northern Territory—a history 1824–1970,* Australian National University North Australia Research Unit, Darwin (2 Vols), 1991.

Koch, John. *When the Murray meets the Mississippi: Australian-American Lutheran contacts,* Lutheran Publishing House, Adelaide, 1975.

Latz, Peter. *Blind Moses,* Self-published, 2014.

Leske, Everard. *For faith and freedom: the story of Lutherans and Lutheranism in Australia 1838–1996,* Friends of Lutheran Archives, Bowden, SA, 1996.

Leske, Everard (ed). *Hermannsburg: a vision and a mission,* Lutheran Publishing House, Adelaide, 1977.

Linnell, Garry, *Buckley's chance,* Penguin Books, 2020.

Lockwood, Douglas, *I, the Aboriginal,* New Holland Publishers, Sydney, 2004. (First published by Rigby Press, 1962.)

McNally, Ward. *Aborigines, artefacts and anguish.* Lutheran Publishing House, Adelaide, 1981.

Mahood, Kim. *Wandering with intent,* Scribe Publications, Melbourne, 2022.

Marcus, Julie. *Sex and savagery: South Australia 1836–1901*, Wakefield Press, Mile End, SA, 2025.

Marks, Greg, Paul Albrecht and Garry Stoll. *Aboriginal land rights and self-determination at Hermannsburg 1972–1982*, Friends of Lutheran Archives, Bowden, SA, 2022.

Monteath, Peter (ed). *Germans: travellers, settlers and their descendants in South Australia*, Wakefield Press, Mile End, South Australia, 2015.

Monteath, Peter & Matthew P Fitzpatrick (eds), *An indigenous South: German writers on colonial South Australia*, Wakefield Press, Mile End, SA, 2024.

Mühlhäusler, Peter (ed). *Hermann Koeler's Adelaide: observations on the language and culture of South Australia by the first German visitor*, Australian Humanities Press, Unley, SA, 2006.

Nettlebeck Amanda and Robert Foster. *In the name of the law: William Willshire and the policing of the Australian frontier*, Wakefield Press, Mile End, SA, 2018.

Peterson, Nicolas & Anna Kenny (eds), *German ethnography in Australia*, Australian National University Press, ACT, 2017.

Proeve, HFW. *A dwelling-place at Bethany*, Lutheran Publishing House, Adelaide, 1983.

Reller, Jobst. *Ausbildung für mission: das Missionsseminar Hermannsburg von 1849 bis 2012*, Lit Verlag, Berlin, 2015.

Reynolds, Henry. *Truth-telling. History, Sovereignty and the Uluru Statement*, NewSouth Publishing, Sydney, 2021.

Roennfeldt, David. *Iaakinha rraatja: Western Arrarnta literacy 1877–2017*, Hermannsburg, NT, undated.

Scherer, Philipp. *Venture of faith*, Auricht Printing Office, Tanunda, SA, 1963.

Scherer, Philipp. *Camel treks in the outback*, Self-published, 1994.

Schild, Maurice E and Hughes, Philip J. *The Lutherans in Australia*, Australian Government Publishing Service, Canberra, 1996.

Schubert, David. *Kavel's people: from Prussia to South Australia*, Lutheran Publishing House, Adelaide, 1985.

Stegemann, Luke. *Amnesia road: landscape, violence and memory*, NewSouth Publishing, Sydney, 2021.

Stevens Christine. *White man's dreaming: Killalpaninna mission*, Oxford University Press, South Melbourne, 1994.

Strehlow, John. *The tale of Frieda Keysser, Vol I:1875–1910*, Wild Cat Press, London, 2011.

Strehlow, T G H. *Journey to Horseshoe Bend*, Rigby Press, Sydney, 1969.

Tampke, Jurgen and Colin Doxford. *Australia, willkommen: a history of the Germans in Australia*, NSW University Press, Kensington NSW, 1990.

Traynor, Stuart. *Alice Springs. From singing wire to iconic outback town*, Wakefield Press, Mile End, SA, 2017.

Trudgen, Richard. *Why warriors lie down and die*, Openbook Publishers, Adelaide, SA, 2001.

Vallee, Peter, *God, guns and government on the Central Australian frontier*, Restoration Books, Canberra, 2007.

Articles, and Papers

Albrecht, Paul. *Aboriginal Australians*. Paper published by Lutheran Publishing House, Adelaide, undated.

Albrecht, Paul. *Relhiperra: about aborigines.* [paper 231 pages]. In personal files.
Albrecht, Paul. *Learning from past missionary work in central Australia for ministry to Aboriginal people today.* Lutheran Theological Journal, 47/2, August 2013, 122–9.
Albrecht, Paul. *The journey broken at Horseshoe Bend.* Friends of Lutheran Archives, Bowden, SA, 2006.
Centralian Advocate article, 1955. Personal files.
— Balaclava Church History [Filing cabinet, Balaclava]
John, Lloyd. *On collision course: Sir Baldwin Spencer and the Finke River Mission,* Journal of Friends of Lutheran Archives, 20/October 2010, 5–16.
Moore, David, *The reformation, Lutheran tradition and missionary linguistics.* Lutheran Theological Journal. 49/1, May 2015, 36–47
Nettelbeck, Amanda, *Writing and remembering frontier conflict: the rule of law in 1880s central Australia,* Aboriginal History, Vol 28, 2004, ANU Press, 190–206.
Paterson, AG. *Confronting the sources: the archaeology of culture-contact in the south-western Lake Eyre basin, Central Australia,* a thesis for the degree of Doctor of Philosophy, University of Sydney, May 1999.
Schoknecht, Alan Carl, Colin Paul, Carl Heinrich Martin (compilers). *Missionary Carl Schoknecht, Killalpaninna mission 1871–1873: selected correspondence,* South Oakleigh, Vic. A & C Schoknecht, 1997.
Schwarz, W. *The theory of translation.* [Personal file.]
Strehlow, T G H. *Assimilation problems: the Aboriginal viewpoint.* Aborigines Advancement League Inc. of South Australia, Adelaide, 1964.
Worthing, Mark. *Theological adventurism among early Australian Lutherans: the strange case of Pastor August Kavel's protestations against the Lutheran Confessions.* Lutheran Theological Journal, 47/2, August 2013, 102–9.
Zweck, Lois. *Kavel and the missionaries.* Lutheran Theological Journal, 47/2, August 2013, 91–101.

Websites & Online

Aboriginal History Journal https://press.anu.edu.au/publications/journals/Aboriginal-history-journal
Ganter, Regina of Griffith University. *German missionaries in Australia.* http://missionaries.griffith.edu.au
Harms, Louis. *Devoted Pastor and Mission Pioneer* at Prevailing Intercessory Prayer : Louis Harms: Devoted Pastor and Mission Pioneer (path2prayer.com)

New Zealand References

Briars Jenny and Jenny Leith. *The road to Sarau: from Germany to Upper Moutere.* Published by Jenny Briars and Jenny Leith, RD2 Upper Moutere, Nelson, New Zealand, 1993
King, Jean A. *The Lutheran story: a brief history of the Lutheran Church in New Zealand 1843–1993.* Lutheran Church of New Zealand, Palmerston North, 1994.
Natusch, Sheila. *Brother Wohlers,* Pegasus Press, Christchurch, 1969.
Olsen, Steen. *Papers on the history of the Lutheran Church in New Zealand.* (From the files of Steen Olsen).
The history of the Lutheran Church in New Zealand, Lance Steicke
Pioneers of Lutheranism in New Zealand, Clem Koch

Lutheranism in Taranaki, FJH Blaess
German immigration and settlement in New Zealand 1842–1914, I H Burnley
Some aspects of the establishment of a Lutheran Maori mission at Maxwelltown, Dorothy M Jurgens
The Lutheran Church of New Zealand: past, present and future, Lance Steicke
Mission work in the vicinity of Maxwelltown, FKG Blaess (?)
The work in and around Parihaka, FKG Blaess (?)
The mission and its beginning in New Zealand generally, FKG Blaess

Endnotes

Preface
1. *The Concise Oxford Dictionary*, 9th edition (1979), H W Fowler and F G Fowler (eds). Oxford University Press, Oxford. *The Macquarie Encyclopedic Dictionary*, 1991, Arthur Delbridge (editor in chief). Macquarie University, NSW. Google search.

About this book
1. op cit 166.

What this book is about
1. Gill, viii.
2. Kempe, 3.
3. Kempe autobiographical statement. Private file.
4. Kempe, 6.
5. Kempe autobiographical statement. Private file.
6. Kempe, 8.
7. Kempe, 9.
8. ibid
9. Finding information on Schwarz has been difficult, both because there is very little available published material on him, and because of difficulties in ascertaining and contacting his descendants. The material in this section is almost wholly taken from his obituary, published in *The Australian Lutheran*, 26 May 1920, 83–6. That obituary is largely based on an outline of Schwarz's life written by him shortly before he died.
10. Valle, 12. Vallee does not detail his source for this claim.
11. Obituary, 83.
12. *Lutheran Hymnal*, 409. Modernised version, LCA Worship Resources. Tr cento based on Arthur Tozer Russell (1851).
13. Obituary, 83.
14. ibid
15. Altmann, 18.
16. Altmann, 19.
17. Altmann, 20.
18. ibid
19. Altmann, 20–21.
20. Altmann, 21
21. Personal correspondence, 1 March 2024.
22. ibid
23. op cit, 93.

24 Variations on the spelling include *Arrernte, Aranda, Arunda*. At best, the introductory material here provided on the Arrarnta people is the bare minimum. See the Bibliography for publications and other materials that provide extensive resources for a more in-depth investigation into their history and life.
25 Estimates vary as to when the Aboriginal people actually arrived in this land. The 60,000 years cited here is based on the claim in the *Uluru Statement from the Heart* that 'our Aboriginal and Torres Strait Islander tribes were the first sovereign Nations of the Australian continent and its adjacent islands, and possessed it under our own laws and customs ... according to the reckoning of our culture, from the Creation, according to the common law from "time immemorial", and according to science more than 60,000 years ago.'
26 https://www.abs.gov.au/statistics/people/Aboriginal-and-torres-strait-islander-peoples/estimates-Aboriginal-and-torres-strait-islander-australians/latest-release
27 https://www.Aboriginalart.com.au/culture/arrernte2.html
28 In a letter dated 8 July 1878, Schulze estimates the number of Aboriginal people within the locale of the mission site as 'about 100'.
29 See, for example, Marks, Albrecht and Stoll, op cit
30 In actual fact, a small group from Pomerania had landed on Kangaroo Island in October 1837, a year before Kavel. Also, the two Dresden missionaries, Schürmann and Teichelmann, arrived in Adelaide just weeks before Kavel. But they came as a pair of missionaries sent out almost as independents chiefly to convert the Aboriginal people, whereas Kavel's people came out as a community with the intention of integrating into the new colony. The Gossner missionaries in Moreton Bay, Queensland, also arrived in Australia a short time before Kavel but, again, their focus was more on mission work than on congregational settlement.
31 'Unionism' and 'sinful unionism' are phrases that occur throughout the book. In brief, they refer to what was common belief and practice among various Lutherans that different Lutheran communities/Synods could only be in fellowship/union with each other (i.e. worship and work together) if they shared and agreed upon a common doctrine on central faith tenets. To come together for worship or work where such agreement did not exist was considered 'sinful', hence 'sinful unionism'. This belief still exists in a variety of forms among a number of Lutheran Synods still today. Discussions among Lutherans on this convoluted subject are lengthy, involved and mystifying to most people, including many Lutherans themselves. But those discussions have occupied an important place in the history of Lutheranism around the world.
32 At this point it is well to note the distinction that exists between 'missionary' and 'pastor', 'mission' and 'Church', at least as far as the Hermannsburg Mission Society is concerned. The chief task of HMS was to train people for work in mission fields around the world ('mission'). However, it also undertook to train people for pastoral ministry in regular congregation and parish ministry ('Church'). The groups were different in terms of (a) their training, with the pastoral/'Church' students more intensively focussed on the theological content of their course work, and not as focussed on the practical, hands-on aspects of the study required for the missionaries; and (b) their status, with those designated for 'mission' almost jealously guarded by Harms for that work, for life. To move into parish work/'Church' was not a step he favoured.

33 This later becomes known as the 'old' Hermannsburg to which reference is made in the reports that follow.
34 Slide 58 in his presentation.
35 Two books listed in the Bibliography especially helpful in gaining an appreciation of the work of the Hermannsburg Mission Society are those by Hartwig Harms and Jobst Reller. Both are written in German. A helpful website on the same topic, but including information on the much broader area of German mission work in Australia, has been produced by the Griffith University at http://missionaries.griffith.edu.au
36 However, most of them did not continue through to ordination.
37 After the split, the ELSA retained the College, and the Immanuel Synod relied upon other sources in Germany for pastoral supply.
38 op cit, 193.
39 Griffith University website.
40 From Wikipedia article on Louis Harms at https://en.wikipedia.org/wiki/Louis_Harms (Accessed 12/1/24)
41 Thus Greenwald in the online material in *Prevailing Intercessory Prayer* at https://www.path2prayer.com/famous-christians-their-lives-and-writings-including-free-books/louis-harms-devoted-pastor-and-mission-pioneer/david-greenwald-the-life-and-ministry-of-louis-harms
42 Regina Ganter, op cit.
43 As one would expect, at that time the ordained ministry was the prerogative of men only, also in Germany. However, there is anecdotal evidence that the Harms brothers did invite women into the Seminary, but mainly as service staff, and as potential partners for the male students. Moreover, some—like both Dorothea Queckenstedt and Dorothea Schulz, Kempe's and Schwarz's fiancées—were provided with midwifery instruction through HMS as part of their preparation for the Australian experience. This was done not only for their own possible personal need, but also as a way of serving other women in and around the mission field.
44 op cit, 160, 161.
45 See Reller, *passim*.
46 Scherer, 7.
47 *Adelaide Advertiser*, 25/4/1864.
48 op cit, 1.
49 A guesstimate, based on the population of 1881 according to the 1891 census being 3,450.
50 See Gibbs, 47–56.
51 A helpful statistical website on SA/NT population is the 1891 Census report at https://hccda.ada.edu.au/Collated_Census_Tables/SA-1891-census.html
52 This map is from Gibbs' excellent, detailed and comprehensive history of colonial South Australia, 1836–1900, 166 (see Bibliography).
53 On the Goyder Line, see Goyder in the section on *People*.
54 The final actual cost was almost £500,000.
55 These figures tally with some random examples taken from our reports. For example, Kempe in his major report states that £60=1200 marks; Heidenreich on 10 October 1882 says that £7=140 marks, and £300=6000 marks.

Source Material and Abbreviations
1. Pages 90–98.

1. Arrivals and Commissionings
1. Previously unpublished. LCA Archives Microfiche, AU 3,0 K 1+, 18–21. Transc DAP. Tr VCP/RJK.
2. Original hard to read and unable to identify this person.
3. Uncertain what these are.
4. Lit: 'islands of the ships/sailor/skipper' or 'captain's island'. The name for Samoa.
5. By this time Homann was the pastor at the Bethlehem congregation in Adelaide, and he and his wife regularly became hosts for Hermannsburg people.
6. That would be the Arrarnta language, not English.
7. Original unclear here.
8. Also prior to Heidenreich's appointment as Superintendent.
9. Proeve, 49,50.
10. Kempe, 10.
11. ibid
12. *Missionsblatt*, December 1875, 250–4. Tr VCP/RJK.
13. *Missionsblatt*, October 1880, 191. Tr CJP. Rev VCP.
14. Hundredweight or 112 pounds, with 20 hundredweight to a ton = 2240 pounds.
15. A merry jester, wag, a local wise person who gives advice. In German literature, Till Eulenspiegel is a peasant trickster who plays pranks on people.
16. He actually uses the word 'damper', the English word taken into the German.
17. There is only vague reference to assistance from Aboriginal people on the original trek to the Centre, and there is no concrete evidence that they were an integral or permanent part of that journey. Kempe is likely referring to later, similar trips, once connections had been made with Aboriginal people.
18. *Kirchenbote*, 24 November 1875, 91–2. Tr VCP/RJK.
19. Addressing the *Kirchenbote* as a person. *Kirchenbote* lit = 'church messenger'.
20. Wiese.
21. As distinct from missionaries.
22. 1 Chronicles 28:20 in English Bible.

2. The Journey: Bethany to Hergott Springs
1. Previously unpublished. LCA Archives Microfiche, AU 3,0 H2, 3+, 2321–6. Transc DAP. Tr VCP/RJK.
2. A hymn verse.
3. Probably von Lüpke.
4. i.e. Murtoa, Victoria.
5. This information gives the impression it was only at this point that Heidenreich decides to join the trek north. His wife's reaction to the news supports that conclusion. If this is so, it makes confusing the earlier reports that Heidenreich's inclusion in the party had been decided upon earlier than this.
6. Rechner was president of the Immanuel Synod, and a member of the joint Mission Committee tasked with finalising arrangements for winding up the partnership at Killalpaninna.

7   These additions to the travelling party had obviously been pre-arranged.
8   Killalpaninna.
9   Unknown.
10 i.e. Heidenreich himself.
11 He had made the trip to Killalpaninna on those three previous occasions. But the Finke is 600 miles further than that, that is from the junction at Hergott Springs/Maree.
12 German unclear.
13 Where is Schwarz?
14 Accessible in the Translation.
15 Can be accessed in the Translation.
16 *Missionsblatt*, February 1876, 18–26. Tr VCP/RJK.
17 *Jesu, geh voran auf der Lebensbahn.*
18 Once again, this is confusing in relation to the Heidenreich plans for the trip. It could be an indefinite 'Goodbye'. Or it could be a 'Goodbye' until we meet as planned along the way.
19 The money from the fee paid to stay there.
20 Saddleworth and Burra.
21 German: *Stonhut*. Near Appila.
22 Scherer translates this as Kempe preferring to go up the mountain on the horse that Schwarz had hitherto been riding. The understanding is that Kempe achieved on a horse what Schwarz had undertaken on foot.
23 i.e. from his mountain climb.
24 Horrocks Pass.
25 Reller lists a Claus Böhmke as a classmate of Kempe and Schwarz, op cit 359. On graduation he was assigned to South Africa.
26 Afghans.
27 Ludwig Harms, who died in 1865.
28 Continuation of above report, *Missionsblatt*, March 1876, 34–6. Tr VCP/RJK.
29 In his report of 6 December (below) Schwarz puns on the name, and locates the place at 25 miles south of Mundowdna.
30 Killalpaninna.
31 His calculation is out by about a hundred miles!
32 i.e. two months earlier in the year than when Kempe and Schwarz arrived, in order to avoid the summer heat.
33 *Kirchenbote*, 22 December 1875, 95. Tr VCP/RJK. This is the report Kempe refers to in the travel diary above, on Sunday 14 November.
34 *Kirchenbote*, 7 January 1876, 5–6. Tr VCP/RJK.
35 Accessed from *Together in Song*, No 554. Georg Neumark (1621–81). Translation by David Schubert.
36 'The holy setting' probably refers to their commissioning at St Michael's, Hahndorf, on 20 October.
37 Even though Aboriginal people did not accompany the missionaries for any great length of time, they did on occasion travel with and assist the party for short spells, usually for specific tasks.
38 Previously unpublished. LCA Archives Microfiche, AU 3,0 H2 4+, 2329a-31. Transc DAP. Tr VCP/RJK.

39 In Victoria.

3. Around the 'Old' Station

1. *Kirchenbote*, 7 January 1876, 6. Tr VCP/RJK.
2. Kempe, 11.
3. ibid
4. Previously unpublished. LCA Archives Microfiche, AU 3,0, H2 4+, 2331a-6. Transc DAP. Tr VCP/RJK.
5. At Peake.
6. German = sponge.
7. A continuation of the above letter of 27 December.
8. A proverb = that the property will not be handed on.
9. *Missionsblatt*, January 1876, 7–9. Tr VCP/RJK.
10. *Kirchenbote*, 4 February 1876, 14. Tr VCP/RJK.
11. The report of 6 December 1875 (above).
12. Manager of Mundowdna station.
13. The Frome River runs past Mundowdna station on the south, then turns north towards Hergott Springs/Maree.
14. Associated with Colana station (manager?).
15. At Coolong Springs, Kempe, Schwarz and Bähr.
16. He receives an unexpected financial windfall from the past, probably something other than the funds from the settlement of the Killalpaninna property.
17. Bethany.
18. Previously unpublished. LCA Archives Microfiche AU 3,0 H2 4+, 2336a-39. Transc DAP. Tr VCP/RJK. Written just before he begins his journey back to the missionaries at Mundowdna. Church business.
19. Difficult to know what this is all about. It may well be a reference to the fact that he is being attacked for his protests over the closure of Killalpaninna.
20. Meaning his home Church.
21. Diagram from https://commons.wikimedia.org/w/index.php?curid=26822532

4. The Journey: To Dalhousie Springs

1. *Kirchenbote*, 7 April 1876, 32. Tr VCP/RJK.
2. Approximately mid-way between Beltana and Farina.
3. He takes for granted all his readers will know who Mr Coulthard is. Scherer simply says he was someone 'from a neighbouring homestead'. op cit, 27.
4. LCA Archives Microfiche, AU 3,0 h2 4+, 2342-6. Transc DAP. Tr VCP/RJK.
5. In Peake. They have presumably headed up there with supplies for the shepherds.
6. Unspecified. The wagons had been left at Mundowdna as Heidenreich left for his Christmas break, but since there was water at Mundowdna, that cannot be the reference here.
7. Mr Coulthard is feeling not quite as hospitable, second time around!
8. In that way, rather than walking, he would get a ride.
9. *Kirchenbote*, 5 May 1876, 40–41. Tr VCP/RJK. This is Part IV of Heidenreich's travel report.
10. Shortly after they left on the journey from Killalpaninna.

11 lit = the butter fell from my bread.
12 Other parties who are also droving stock to various pastoral runs.
13 *Missionsblatt*, May 1876, 69. Tr VCP/RJK.
14 Previously unpublished. LCA Archives. Microfiche AU 3,0 H2 4+, 2346a-8. Transcr DAP. Tr VCP/RJK.
15 *Missionsblatt*, August 1876,168–70. Tr. VCP/RJK.
16 Hübbe.
17 i.e. the Neales River.
18 i.e. in Bethany.
19 *Kirchenbote*, 9 June 1876, 48–9. Tr VCP/RJK.
20 There are those who are envious of the perceived favouritism shown towards the Lutherans by the government.
21 Kempe says Wadlu. (Detailed comment is made on this in Kempe's account, below.)
22 *Kirchenbote*, 4 August 1876, 64–5. Tr VCP/RJK.
23 German: *eigenwillig*. Also can be translated 'headstrong'. There are critical overtones in this comment.
24 German; *auf dem letzten Zuge*. Uncertain what he is referring to, but could be 'on the last stretch'.
25 That is, the rainwater stored in (a) barrel(s) on the wagons.
26 i.e. in sections – not the whole route.
27 4 June in 1876.
28 Previously unpublished. LCA Archives Microfiche, AU 3,0 H2 5+, 2352–6. Transcr DAP. Tr VCP/RJK.
29 Probably a reference to Isaiah 53.
30 Referring to the area on the Finke proposed for the new mission station. Obviously, someone has already visited there.
31 Previously unpublished. LCA Archives Microfiche AU 3,0 H2 5+, 2357–9. Transc DAP. Tr VCP/RJK.
32 op cit, 27.
33 *Missionsblatt*, May 1876, 66–9. Tr VCP/RJK.
34 First part previously unpublished. LCA Archives Microfiche, AU 3,0 K 1+, 33–4a. Transc DAP. Tr VCP/RJK. Then *Missionsblatt*, August 1876, 162–8. Tr VCP/RJK.
35 German: *Stearinlichte*. Crude candles made from a mixture of stearic and palmitic acids. Tallow candles.
36 There is obviously some kind of postal system along the way already at this stage in the Centre's history, and it sounds like it was a quite efficient one, given the ease with which they get messages to one another. Note the reference to the Strangways Springs post-station a little further into the report.
37 i.e. at Priscilla Waters?
38 That they only discovered this information at this point in the journey speaks to the lack of information (and preparation?) prior to the commencement of the trip.
39 *Rindvieh* = cattle. The sheep are already near Peake, or on the way.
40 Other reports say 700.
41 *Kirchenbote*, 11 July 1876, 55–6. Tr VCP/RJK.
42 i.e. Dalhousie.
43 *Missionsblatt*, January 1877, 13–16. Tr VCP/RJK.

44 There is also an Eringa further north, west of Dalhousie.
45 i.e. in search of water.
46 *Missionsblatt*, June 1876, 101–4. Tr VCP/RJK.
47 The Réaumur is a French temperature scale, also known as the 'octogesimal division' in which freezing and boiling points of water are designated at 0 and 80 degrees respectively. The scale is named after René Antoine Ferchault de Réaumur, who first proposed a similar scale in 1730.
48 Kempe says five.
49 *Kirchenbote*, 4 August 1876, 64. Tr VCP/RJK.

5. Reconnaissance Trip

1 *Kirchenbote*, 6 October 1876, 79–80. Tr VCP/RJK. Written after the reconnaissance party has arrived back at Dalhousie. A noticeable difference between the Kempe and Heidenreich version of events is the place names mentioned by each of them.
2 A waterhole in the Hugh River.
3 Lack of water restricts extent of hospitality.
4 The German text literally has 'native well'.
5 The only record of the missionaries encountering Warburton. See his reference in the *People* section.
6 They are on the verge of entering Owen Springs station, and do not want to do so while its manager is not on site.
7 Obtained, apparently, from Conway.
8 *Missionsblatt*, January 1877, 13–16 and February 1877, 18–22. Tr VCP/RJK. These are written a month after the return from the reconnaissance trip.
9 i.e. after the earlier-mentioned trip back to Peake.
10 *Missionsblatt*, December 1876, 226–32. Tr VCP/RJK.
11 German: *Ich hatte zu predigen*. Probably simply mean, 'It was my turn to preach'—to a congregation of two!
12 The Cross.
13 Lit = 'hill of waiting'. Here and below, Heidenreich is playing on the word Wartburg, which he has here changed to Warteberg. He has to wait until he has consulted with Goyder before he can establish the exact boundaries of the mission lease.
14 Have not been able to ascertain the significance of Drommelberg, nor of Amathal.
15 The play on the word Wartburg continues, with Heidenreich's focus at this point now being on the Wartburg Castle. Heidenreich later discovered that the spot on which he was standing ('the hill of waiting') was not a part of the mission lease, and this reminds him of the story of Louis the Springer and the building of the Wartburg Castle.
16 Louis the Springer (1042 – 1123) was a German nobleman, the ruling count of the state of Thuringia from 1056 until his death. According to legend, he received his nickname 'the Springer (or Jumper)' when he leapt into a river from a castle in which he was a prisoner. Louis had earlier failed in an attempt to take possession of part of Saxony, stabbing the ruling count at the time in the process. Louis was arrested, incarcerated for three years in a castle on the banks of the River Saale in Halle, the capital of Saxony, and was likely to be executed. However, he escaped by leaping from the castle tower into the River Saale, where a servant was waiting for him with a boat. Another legend relates how he came to build the Wartburg. He found the location in

17 1067, while he was hunting in the area. He saw the mountain and exclaimed: "Wait, mountain, thou shalt bear me a castle!". However, this mountain was outside his territory. To circumvent this problem, he had his men carry dirt from his own territory and dump it on the mountain. He then had 12 of his most loyal knights stand on that spot, stick their swords in the ground and swear that the soil they were standing on, rightfully belonged to Louis. https://en.wikipedia.org/wiki/Louis the Springer
17 Martin Luther. God will provide what this new mission requires: there is no need to resort to the kind of trickery employed by Louis the Springer.
18 i.e. as their day of worship and rest.
19 L Harms.
20 …to the throne.
21 Mt Carmel?
22 He makes these small plans of preparation for the anticipated, later arrival of the whole party.
23 *Missionsblatt*, November 1876, 217-9. Tr VCP/RJK.
24 The *Missionsblatt* editor has misunderstood the situation, mistakenly believing that the whole party has already arrived at the site.
25 i.e. the border of the mission field.
26 There is a play on words here: '*Herr*' and '*herrlicher*'. The 'Lord' will become more 'lordly'. Heidenreich claims the land as the Lord's, the place where God will rule. A reflection of the mission philosophy of the time.
27 German: *die Wilde*.
28 *Kirchenbote*, 6 October 1876, 80. Tr VCP/RJK.
29 i.e. to the mission site.
30 Difficult to know precisely what Heidenreich is concerned about here. A major part of his thinking has been that the mission station would utilise Aboriginal people for the running of the station. So, is he concerned that, if the station is built close to the Aboriginal camps, the people will move from the camps onto the station, and he does not want that situation to occur? Or is part of his concern about the need to be protected from the Aboriginal people: i.e. if these live on the station they are more likely to attack it than if they remain in their camps? Or is he concerned that, if the mission establishes its station close to the Aboriginal camps, people will leave the camps and go elsewhere, thus depriving the station of important and necessary contact with the Aboriginal people, and of potential workers for the station?
31 From here = *Kirchenbote*, 3 November 1876, 89-90. Tr VCP/RJK.
32 Possibly a reference to the mound springs, of which it seems he had a rudimentary understanding.
33 A pun: 'Wartberg' = hill of waiting. The two spellings, Wartberg and Wartburg, are intentional.
34 An emu.
35 From here = *Kirchenbote*, 1 December 1876, 96. Tr VCP/RJK.
36 Previously unpublished. LCA Archives Microfiche, 3,0 H2 5+, 2360-2. Transc DAP. Tr VCP/RJK.
37 Unclear as to the story behind this sentence.
38 Serving in Bethany.
39 op cit, 74.

40 id, 104. Tr VCP.
41 Previously unpublished. LCA Archives Microfiche, AU 3,0 H2 5+, 2363-2364. Transc DAP. Tr VCP/RJK.

6. Waiting at Dalhousie

1   *Kirchenbote*, 6 October 1876, 80. Tr VCP/RJK.
2   i.e. the reconnaissance trip.
3   *Missionsblatt*, January 1877, 13-16 and February 1877, 18-22. Tr VCP/RJK.
4   i.e. South Australia.
5   i.e. at Dalhousie Springs.
6   Reaumur scale = 25°C
7   i.e. after the reconnaissance trip.
8   Little bit optimistic!
9   Previously unpublished. LCA Archives Microfiche, AU 3,0 H2 5+, 2372a-4a. Transc DAP. Tr VCP/RJK.
10 German: rC.
11 i.e. the original building in Hermannsburg, Germany.
12 Dierks has taken over from Bode as locum tenens in Bethany congregation.
13 This report is contained in Heidenreich's report of 4 December 1876, included below, and from *Kirchenbote* of January 1877, 7. Tr VCP/RJK.
14 Elsewhere Carline.
15 *Kirchenbote*, 1 December 1876, 96-7. Tr VCP/RJK.
16 i.e. Heidenreich and Carline.
17 i.e. to Dalhousie.
18 Once it rains and the Dalhousie station is able to replenish its own stock, there will not be sufficient fodder for the station to host the mission party as well. Therefore, until that happens, the Hermannsburgers are able to remain at Dalhousie.
19 German: *vermeintlich*. He is not happy. Even God, it seems, thinks differently from him.
20 to Finniss.
21 i.e. from Dalhousie, on this present journey. And it is Kempe's fault that the white ants were not discovered earlier, as they ought to have been.
22 German: *an dem schlechtesten Rade* = on the worst wheel. Others were dodgy, too.
23 Unclear as to what he is referring. Possibly that, before he left Dalhousie on the present stressful trip, he was able at the last moment to use the wagon to bring in a load of supplies. The 'double joy' is that these supplies came on top of the supplies that are due, as ordered, in three weeks' time.
24 Also unclear just where this incident fits into the present narrative.
25 This is a literal translation of the German. What he means is that other parties along the way have not been as well provisioned because of poor timing of the arrival of goods and laziness or slackness on the part of those responsible for the necessary provisions and arrangements.
26 God is a generous provider.
27 … with the emphasis on the 'two'.
28 i.e. regarding plans for the journey from here.
29 Previously unpublished, although similar to the report in *Kirchenbote*, 1 December

1876, 96–7. LCA Archives Microfiche, AU 3,0 H2 5+, 2375a-9. Transc DAP. Tr VCP/RJK.
30. This report is contained in Heidenreich's report of 4 December 1876 (below), from *Kirchenbote* of January 1877, 7–8. Tr VCP/RJK.
31. *Kirchenbote*, January 1877, 7–8. Tr VCP/RJK.
32. Previously unpublished. LCA Archives Microfiche, AU 3,0 Sch 4 1+, 283–4. Transc DAP. Tr VCP/RJK.
33. Probably a reference to Matthew 23:9: 'And call no one your father on earth, for you have one Father—the one in heaven.' Harms insisted that the students referred to him as Father.
34. Previously unpublished. LCA Archives. Microfiche, AU 3,0 H2 5+, 2380a-3a. Transc DAP. Tr VCP/RJK.
35. This is the only place this name appears. Unknown.
36. Previously unpublished. LCA Archives Microfiche, AU 3,0 H2 5+, 2385–6. Transc DAP. Tr VCP/RJK.
37. King's Mountain/Range.
38. Wolf Range.
39. Th Harms himself.
40. Previously unpublished. LCA Archives Microfiche, AU 3,0 K 1+, 45-7a. Transc DAP. Tr VCP/RJK.
41. Previously unpublished. LCA Archives Microfiche, AU 3,0 K 1+, 48–52. Transc DAP. Tr VCP/RJK.
42. Throughout the reports 'English' refers to Australian people, i.e. those Whites who have been in the country for some time.
43. The question of who is in charge of decision-making and the daily administration of the mission is a vexed one, not just in this instance, but also later. Kempe and Schwarz do not want that responsibility. At the same time, they do not believe that any of the colonists are qualified for it, either.
44. As a former missionary at Killalpannina he is, in Kempe's opinion, qualified to manage this new mission.
45. Previously unpublished. LCA Archives Microfiche, AU 3,0 K 1+, 53–5. Transc DAP. Tr VCP/RJK. Again note all the running around being done!
46. This is another of the 'missing' letters from our collection.
47. That is, the mission station on the Finke River site.
48. From joiners' bench to pulpit

7. The Journey: Arriving at the Mission Site

1. *Kirchenbote*, March 1877, 54–5. Tr VCP/RJK
2. The first mention of the new wagon to replace the one that had broken down on this last trip South. As matters eventuate, this wagon does not immediately head up the Centre, but is stored with farmers along the way, set aside for the anticipated arrival of Kempe's and Schwarz's fiancées.
3. Previously unpublished. LCA Archives Microfiche, AU 3,0 H2 5+, 2387–9. Transc DAP. Tr VCP/RJK.
4. In New Zealand.
5. *Kirchenbote*, April 1877, 70–1. Tr VCP/RJK.

6   *Kirchenbote*, May 1877, 77. Tr VCP/RJK.
7   Probably the Thomas Mills mentioned in the next sentence.
8   *Kirchenbote*, May 1877, 77. Tr VCP/RJK.
9   On the reconnaissance trip.
10 Generous Church members who are prepared to help out along the way by storing vehicles and caring for the horses.
11 Previously unpublished. LCA Archives Microfiche, AU 3,0 H2 6+, 2389a-2392. Transc DAP. Tr VCP/RJK.
12 *Kirchenbote*, June 1877, 90-1. Tr VCP/RJK.
13 Crown Point, encountered on the reconnaissance trip, 31 August 1876 report. Kempe calls it 'tip of the crown'.
14 *Kirchenbote*, July 1877, 117-8. Tr VCP/RJK.
15 Kempe alludes to this mishap in the report of 24 May below. No details are given.
16 *Kirchenbote*, June 1877, 90-1. Tr VCP/RJK.
17 *Kirchenbote*, July 1877, 117-8. Tr VCP/RJK.
18 *Kirchenbote*, July 1877, 117-8. Tr VCP/RJK.
19 *Missionsblatt*, November 1877, 215-8. Tr VCP/RJK. Also published in *Kirchenbote*, June 1877, 140-1.
20 1 June.
21 *Missionsblatt*, November 1877, 215. Tr VCP/RJK.
22 Previously unpublished. LCA Archives Microfiche, AU 3,0 H2 6+, 2392b. Transc DAP. Tr VCP/RJK.
23 op cit, 9.

8. Setting Up

1   For a detailed account of the Kuprilya Springs story, see Jose Petrick's book listed in the Bibliography.
2   *Missionsblatt*, November 1877, 218. Tr VCP/RJK. Also published in *Kirchenbote*, June 1877, 141.
3   7 June.
4   *Missionsblatt*, February 1878, 27-32. Tr VCP/RJK.
5   A reference to a German fairy tale from the Brothers Grimm about a group of seven Swabians who become involved in various pranks. In this instance, Schwarz reckons that the joke has been played on God. The incident also gives a glimpse into Schwarz's sense of humour.
6   Readers will recall that a previous report had suggested the missionaries had arrived at the mission site much earlier than they actually did.
7   Literally. Could also be 'under God's clear sky'. Or 'Under the stars'.
8   Dingoes. According to the National Geographic magazine, 'the dingo is legendary as Australia's wild dog, though it also occurs in Southeast Asia. The Australian animals may be descendents of Asian dingoes that were introduced to the continent some 3,000 to 4,000 years ago.' https://www.nationalgeographic.com/animals/mammals/d/dingo/#close
9   Already they had learnt to be wary of the Whites, no doubt from experience.
10 Note – English. Not German!
11 The report continues in *Missionsblatt*, March 1878, 41-4. Tr VCP/RJK

12 From Owen Springs.
13 *Journal of the Cross*. Magazine/journal from the Church of the Cross in Hermannsburg, Germany.
14 *Kirchenbote*, August 1877, 147–8. Tr VCP/RJK.
15 Yet, the report presented above does indicate contact with the Aboriginal folk. Given that report was written in October, this would indicate that the first contacts occurred some time between August and October.
16 *Kirchenbote*, August 1877, 158–9. Tr VCP/RJK.
17 *Kirchenbote*, 4 December 1877, 189–90. Tr VCP/RJK.
18 This is written in English in the original report, and it reveals a little of the communication methods being employed at this early stage in the life of the mission.
19 Animal pleurisy.
20 He is probably referring to the house cows. The mission had far more than three cattle in total.
21 *Kirchenbote*, January 1878, 13–14. Tr VCP/RJK.
22 This reference raises the question of what languages the missionaries used in their various inter-actions. Obviously, they spoke German with each other. But they also spoke some English, as here, with the Aboriginal people. English was one of the subjects in the Hermannsburg curriculum, so they had some knowledge of it before they arrived. As they became more integrated into their new Australia culture, their proficiency in the English language would have naturally improved. Of course, though, their goal was to be able to speak with the Aboriginal people in their own Arrarnta language.
23 *Kirchenbote*, January 1878, 13. Tr VCP/RJK.
24 Apart from the people who travelled up with the missionaries from the South, other labour help was readily available, apparently. As previously mentioned, many of those who worked on the Overland Telegraph Line stayed on in the Centre once the Line was completed. Increasingly, too, more people were moving into the Centre, providing a supply of itinerant workers for the settlement and the stations.
25 His first trip into Palm Valley.
26 Previously unpublished. LCA Archives Microfiche, AU 3,0 H2 6+, 2396b-9. Transc DAP. Tr VCP/RJK.
27 These are the next lot of arrivals to Australia, among whom are Kempe's and Schwarz's fiancées, as well as Schulze and Jürgens.
28 Treasurer for Hermannsburg Mission in Germany.
29 Yet he also complains that he has not heard from Harms for months.
30 A great deal of the luggage that came out with the first mission party (or soon after) has not yet been transported to the Centre and is in storage somewhere in Adelaide or nearby. Here and there in the letters one or the other of the mission staff make brief mention of these possessions of theirs that they would dearly love to have with them.
31 Previously unpublished. LCA Archives Microfiche, AU 3,0 H2 6+, 2413–16. Transc DAP. Tr VCP/RJK.

9. The Arrival of Schulze, the Fiancées, and Others

1 Previously unpublished. LCA Archives Microfiche, AU 3,0 H2 6+, 2418b. Transc DAP. Tr VCP/RJK.

2   Previously unpublished (although a similar report was published in *Kirchenbote*, 4 December 1877), LCA Archives Microfiche, AU 3,0 H2 6+, 2420b-2. Transc DAP. Tr VCP/RJK. Sections of the original handwritten report are illegible, making it necessary either to omit them or guess their meaning.
3   *Kirchenbote*, December 1877, 188–90. Tr VCP/RJK.
4   That is, to travel to the Centre with the fiancées and as a missionary.
5   The next section is from his letter of 26 November to Harms.
6   The remainder of this letter if from *Kirchenbote* report of December 1877.
7   This is the newly-procured wagon mentioned previously, to replace the broken-down vehicle from the Centre.
8   They were glad to be rid of these drivers, partly because of the cost, partly because they are 'outsiders'.
9   This was a difficult paragraph to translate mainly because of the way Heidenreich has written it. His dilemma concerns the safest way to escort the party on their trip to the Centre, with special concern for the women. He considers three options, and it is not altogether clear when evaluating those options whether he is thinking of what did happen on the first trip, or of what would happen on this next trip. Option 1 creates concerning relational issues within the party. Option 2 creates extra expense in having to pay for return costs to Port Augusta of the wagoner and horses from however far north the party gets. Also unclear is the problem with the horses being spoiled or pampered. Somehow it seems that this option allows for more horses to be taken along than is necessary, and that the horses are therefore under-worked, hence pampered. In addition, the cost of getting them back home is greater than if they had taken fewer horses and worked them harder. Option 3 leaves the party to themselves, and that opens them to danger.
10 They resolve the dilemma by hiring Brown as their driver for the trip North.
11 The convoy has become a substantial and impressive caravan of wagons, horses and bullocks.
12 LCA Archives Microfiche, AU 3,0 H2 6+, 2417b-8. Transc DAP. Tr VCP/RJK.
13 *Kirchenbote*, March 1878, 45–6. Tr VCP/RJK
14 Already the missionaries are seeking to have the Aboriginal people work for them, also as shepherds. However, their 'coming and going' renders their services unreliable, so that at times there were not enough shepherds to look after the flocks.
15 The missionaries had left these at Owen Springs on the way to the mission station for the first time.
16 Previously unpublished. LCA Archives Microfiche, AU 3,0 H2 6+, 2393b-5b. Transc DAP. Tr VCP/RJK.
17 The original hand-written text in this letter is so corrupt that it is difficult, and at times impossible, to read. We have had to guess at certain parts of it.
18 One of the new arrivals, probably sent out as a shepherd.
19 The comparison is in relation to the first trip to Killalpaninna in 1865.
20 Wilhelm Peters was one of the pastors among this last lot of arrivals, freshly graduated from Hermannsburg. He has certainly wasted no time in making a worrying mark, and over the years to come he and Heidenreich have a rocky relationship. Yet, Peters becomes quite influential in the ELSA. (See further details in the *People* section.)

21 German: *stinkend*. Making you smelly, stinky, on the nose.
22 Bobby Boy.
23 *Missionsblatt*, April 1878, 56–60. Translated by Max Altmann, and accessed from the *Schulze Family History Supplement*, Letter No 2. Revised VCP.
24 The ratios are correct, with a German mile approximately equivalent to 4.6 English miles, or 7.5 kilometres.
25 i.e. English miles = 16–19 kilometres.
26 Killalpaninna.
27 German: *Alles durcheinander*. A little unclear. Could be 'all mixed up' (and translated as we have). Or 'in a poor state'.
28 Previously unpublished. LCA Archives Microfiche, AU 3,0 H2 6+, 2417b-8. Transc DAP. Tr VCP/RJK.
29 German (lit) = put the chair in front of the door.
30 Previously unpublished. LCA Archives Microfiche, AU3,0 H2 6+, 2426b-28. Transc DAP. Tr VCP/RJK. Large parts of this report are illegible in the original handwritten form.
31 The handwriting in the rest of the original report becomes too blurry for accurate transcription.
32 op cit, 254
33 Previously unpublished. LCA Archives Microfiche, AU 3,0 H2 6+, 2428b-30. Transc DAP. Tr VCP/RJK. Much of the original handwritten material is indecipherable.
34 i.e. the last lot of new arrivals.
35 *Kirchenbote*, April 1878, 67. Tr VCP/RJK
36 Previously unpublished. LCA Archives, Microfiche AU 3,0 K 2+, 68–9. Transc DAP. Tr VCP/RJK.
37 Original handwritten copy illegible here, but the distance from Hermannsburg to Charlotte Waters following this route is in the vicinity of 400 kilometres = 250 miles.
38 In the original, the letter becomes unreadable from here.
39 *Kirchenbote*, April 1878, pp 66–7. Tr VCP/RJK
40 Previously unpublished. LCA Archives, Microfiche, AU 3,0, K, 2+, 70. Transc DAP. Tr VCP/RJK.
41 Previously unpublished. LCA Archives Microfiche, AU 3,0 H2 7+, 2434b-5. Transc DAP. Tr VCP/RJK.
42 Again, he has actually written 'Natives'.
43 *Kirchenbote*, May 1878, 92–3. Tr Max Altmann, *Schulze Family History Supplement*, Letter No 3. Rev VCP.
44 Unknown.
45 Previously unpublished. LCA Archives Microfiche, AU 3,0 H2 7+, 2430b-33b. Trans DAP. Tr VCP/RJK. Sections of the original handwritten report are corrupted, illegible.
46 This is what he says. It is not clear what he means.
47 DAP: The rest of the page seems to deal with Peters and the failed China Mission, but is too blurry to read confidently.
48 *Kirchenbote*, May 1878, 93. Tr VCP/RJK.
49 Wagons with rations, or possibly still goods and chattels belonging to the new arrivals.

10. Settling In

1. *Kirchenbote*, July 1878, 110. Tr VCP/RJK.
2. Because the report he has to write will be short, his poor fingers get a bit of a rest.
3. i.e. the Easter weekend.
4. *Kirchenbote*, July 1878, 110. Tr VCP/RJK.
5. A local, only appears once, here, probably worked for their regular driver, Brown.
6. Previously unpublished. LCA Archives Microfiche, AU 3,0 H2 7+, 2437b-9b. Transc DAP. Tr VCP/RJK.
7. *Kirchenbote*, July 1878, 110-11. Tr VCP/RJK.
8. *Missionsblatt*, October 1878, 173-6. Tr Max Altmann in the *Schulze Family History Supplement*, Letter No 4. Rev VCP.
9. *Kirchenbote*, August 1878, 173. Tr VCP/RJK.
10. Previously unpublished. LCA Archives Microfiche, AU3,0 Sch3 1+, 180. Transc DAP. Tr VCP/RJK.
11. *Missionsblatt*, January 1879, 13-15. Tr VCP/RJK.
12. Mission St Hermannsburg.
13. German = *Naturvölker*.
14. Mirus.
15. *Kirchenbote*, November 1878., 222. Tr VCP/RJK. From Heidenreich's report of 25 November 1878.)
16. Previously unpublished. LCA Archives Microfiche AU 4,2 1-, 4330. Transc DAP. Tr VCP/RJK.
17. *Missionsblatt*, April 1879, 59-65. Tr VCP/RJK.
18. Corrugated iron?
19. Assumes that this is the Schwarz residence for now?
20. R, not C.
21. 'little hour'. A favorite expression of the Pietist, the last hour, death.
22. Previously unpublished. LCA Archives Microfiche, AU 3,0 H2 7+, 2440b-2b. Transc DAP. Tr VCP/RJK.
23. Previously unpublished. LCA Archives Microfiche, AU 3,0 H2 7+, 2443b-6b. Trans DAP. Tr VCP/RJK.
24. *Kirchenbote*, November 1878, 221-2. Tr VCP/RJK.
25. Previously unpublished. LCA Archives Microfiche AU 3,0 K 2+, 71-2. Transc DAP. Tr VCP/RJK.
26. Heidenreich.
27. i.e. the staff and Aboriginal people at the mission station.

11. The Removal of Theodor Harms

1. *Missionsblatt*, January 1878, 14-16. Tr VCP/RJK.
2. Bergen was the administrative centre for Hermannsburg and the surrounding district.
3. German: *fröhlich*. An unusual word to use, given the circumstances.
4. But, as such, they are not properly married.

(Note: item 50 at top — "This is a huge sum, but an indication of how expensive freight to the Centre was at that time.")

5   *Missionsblatt*, February 1878, 18–22. Tr VCP/RJK.
6   *Missionsblatt*, March 1878, 33–41. Tr VCP/RJK.
7   Also known as Quinquagesima Sunday.
8   Previously unpublished. LCA Archives Microfiche, AU 3,0 H2 7+, 2435b-6b. Transc DAP. Tr VCP/RJK.

12. Language, Weather and Mumblings

1   *Beiblatt zum Lutherischen Kirchenboten fur Australien*, 14 March 1879, 57–58. Also published in *Kirchenbote*, April, 1879. Tr. VCP/RJK.
2   The *Kirchenbote* editor adds the footnote: 'Those are concepts not perceived through the physical senses.'
3   *Beiblatt zum Lutherischen Kirchenboten fur Australien*, 14 March 1879, 57–58. Also published in *Kirchenbote*, April, 1879. Tr. VCP/RJK.
4   *Kirchenbote*, May 1879, 102. Tr VCP/RJK.
5   *Kirchenbote*, May 1879, 102. Tr VCP/RJK.
6   Previously unpublished. LCA Archives Microfiche, AU 3,0 H2 7+, 2450b-52b. Transc DAP. Tr VCP/RJK.
7   Previously unpublished, LCA Archives Microfiche, AU 3,0 Sch3 1+, 188–9. Transc DAP. Tr VCP/RJK.
8   Previously unpublished. LCA Archives Microfiche, AU 3,0 H2 7+, 2453b-56. Transc DAP. Tr VCP/RJK.
9   This appears to contradict what he just wrote, that he was not in favour of a second station. He has either changed his mind, or else is not being totally up-front with the missionaries. That is, he was always actually in favour of a second station (which is what the missionaries were suggesting), but would only proceed with that second station if Harms would provide the funds for it.
10 Previously unpublished. LCA Archives Microfiche, AU 3,0 K 2+, 80–2. Transcr DAP. Tr RJK/VCP.
11 i.e. when he goes to collect his fiancée.
12 As will be elaborated upon in the next chapter, this was work for the Aboriginal people!
13 Parish pastor would be a much easier position.
14 Not published. LCA Archives Microfiche, AU 3,0 SCH3 1+, 183–4. Tr Max Altmann, *Schulze Family History Supplement*. Letter No 5. Rev VCP.
15 *Kirchenbote*, May 1879, 101–2. Tr VCP/RJK. In places, Heidenreich writes as if these are his own personal experiences and observations. However, he is obviously reproducing information he has received from the missionaries.
16 The *Kirchenbote* editor adds the following footnote: 'Readers who attended our synodical convention in Blumberg in 1877 will be able to remember this well-built black chap.'
17 *Kirchenbote*, August 1879, 174. Part of Heidenreich's report of 29 July 1879. Tr VCP/RJK.
18 There is a misspelling in this title. It ought to be *Allolinga anghax*, a pointer to the likelihood that the originally submitted manuscript was handwritten.
19 Roennfeldt, op cit, 43.
20 op cit, 129–37.

21 ibid, 137.
22 op cit, 135.
23 This is the only reference to Tepper in *Missionaries, Madness and Miracles*. For more information on him, see Leske in the *Bibliography*, 118–9.
24 *Kirchenbote*, August 1879, 174. Part of Heidenreich's report of 29 July 1879. Tr VCP/RJK.

13. Mixed Blessings

1 Previously unpublished, LCA Archives Microfiche, AU 3,0 Sch3 1+, 185. Transc DAP. Tr VCP/RJK.
2 For example, https://territorystories.nt.gov.au/10070/596840/0/73
3 Previously unpublished. LCA Archives Microfiche. AU 3,0 K1 Korrektur, 0381–4. Transc DAP. Tr VCP/RJK.
4 *Kirchenbote*, December 1879, 268–9. Tr VCP/RJK.
5 Also used for the Arrarnta language.
6 The primer mentioned in the previous chapter.
7 *Missionsblatt*, March 1880, 39–43. Tr Max Altmann, *Supplement to Schulze family history*, Letter No 6. Modified VCP.
8 The Reamur scale of measuring temperature, where 1°R = 1.25°C. Hence, 53°R =66°C. This is an incredibly high reading. Note, though, it is probably 'in the sun', direct heat, as distinct from the usual 'in the shade'.
9 *Kirchenbote*, December 1879, 268–9. Tr VCP/RJK

14. The Flint Report and Afterwards

1 *Missionsblatt*, March 1880, 43.
2 op cit, 366.
3 See, e.g., the *Northern Territory Times and Gazette*, Friday 27 February 1874, 3. Access via *Trove*.
4 Reported numbers vary between 150 and 200.
5 Though over the next few days there were several newspaper reports with details on the incident, it is Flint's own account seven years later that provides one of the most detailed accounts. See *Northern Argus*, 16 August 1881, 2. Accessed via *Trove*.
6 Nettlebeck & Foster, 7.
7 *Kirchenbote*, March 1880, 35–7. Tr VCP/RJK.
8 ...to the mission staff, that is. They had not been informed of his impending visit, and so were not able to 'pretty' up the station. Flint finds it in its natural state.
9 *Missionsblatt*, March 1880, 45. Tr VCP/RJK.
10 *Kirchenbote*, May 1880, 79–80, Tr VCP/RJK.
11 Previously unpublished. LCA Archives Microfiche, AU 3,0 Sch3 1+, 196–7. Transc DAP. Tr VCP/RJK.
12 Previously unpublished. LCA Archives Microfiche, AU 3,0 Sch3 1+, 197a–8. Transc DAP. Tr VCP/RJK.
13 i.e. Owen Springs.
14 Previously unpublished. LCA Archives Microfiche, AU 3,0 K 2+, 92–3. Transcr DAP. Tr VCP/RJK.
15 i.e. anything beyond the physical.
16 A skin infection.

15. Kempe Major Report

1 *Missionsblatt*, August 1880, 153–9. Tr CJP. Rev VCP/RJK. Also published in *Kirchenbote*, August 1880.
2 Unfortunately, this diagram did not arrive in Germany with the rest of the document and is lost.
3 German: *Welfenhohen*.
4 In Germany.
5 The German royals.
6 These are peppercorn rates. Compare the cost of land with the cost of freight.
7 *Missionsblatt*, September 1880, 171–7. Tr CJP. Rev VCP/RJK. Also published in *Kirchenbote*, September 1880,
8 This plan is not included in the report. Perhaps it got lost, or the publishers were unable to reproduce it, or it was deliberately omitted.
9 Spinifex.
10 *Missionsblatt*, October 1880, 186–92. Tr CJP. Rev VCP/RJK. Also published in *Kirchenbote*, October 1880.
11 Marsupials.
12 German = *Schakale*. Jackal.
13 German: *Schildpapageien*. Budgerigars?
14 German: *Geier*. Possibly also a type of hawk, but difficult to ascertain what he means. German lit = vulture, but we do not have vultures in Australia. They are found on every continent except Australia. The German can also translate as cormorant.
15 German: *Braten* = a roast.
16 In this next section he diverts from his stated subject matter in the heading above, from the 'animal world' to 'taking a trip in the bush'. It is a little side-trip.
17 Note: For purposes of interest and continuity, this part of the report was extrapolated to Chapter 1 [rf p]
18 *Missionsblatt*, November 1880, 202–8. Tr CJP. Rev VCP/RJK. Also published in *Kirchenbote*, November 1880.
19 Can only surmise to whom or what he is referring. Probably people of bias, for example, like Spencer and Gillen.
20 German = *Beutelratten*. Pouch rats or marsupial rats?
21 German: *Schakal*.
22 Could be witchetty grubs.
23 …except witchetty grubs are found in *acacia* trees – the *acacia Kempeana*, in fact.
24 Totemic?
25 To give something inferior in the hope of getting something better. Or like 'salting the mine'. The important thing is the fact of giving, not what actually is given, thus making the other beholden to the giver.
26 *Missionsblatt*, February 1881, 21–32. Tr CJP. Rev VCP/RJK. Also published in *Kirchenbote*, December 1880.
27 German: *Feuerstein*. Fire-stone.
28 A woomera?
29 German: *Krummstock*. Lit = 'crooked stick'. CJP says: 'The reference is, of course, to their boomerang; the butcher uses a similarly shaped piece of wood, or steel nowadays, for hoisting a sheep or beast onto a gallows for dressing.'

30 *Missionsblatt*, March 1881, 45–8. Tr CJP. Rev VCP/RJK. Also published in *Kirchenbote*, January 1881.
31 German: *Hilfsmittel* = lit. aids, suggesting books in particular. However, there was at least Schürmanns' and Teichelmann's work amongst the Kuarna, and Schoknecht's amongst the Dieri. Elsewhere in Our Place writers have made reference to their knowledge of the Dieri work.
32 *Missionsblatt*, April 1881, 54–62. Tr CJP. Rev VCP/RJK. Also published in *Kirchenbote*, May 1881.
33 Or *Altjira*.
34 Kempe incorrectly has cassowary.
35 Unclear which report this is.

16. Business Matters, More Arrivals, New Church and School, Christmas

1 *Missionsblatt*, May 1880, 66–7. Tr VCP/RJK.
2 *Kirchenbote*, May 1880, 79–80. VCP/RJK.
3 *Missionsblatt*, May 1880, 67–8. Tr VCP/RJK.
4 *Kirchenbote*, 16 July 1880, 146. Tr VCP/RJK.
5 Previously unpublished. LCA Archives Microfiche, AU 3,0 H2 8+, 2470–72b. Transc DAP. Tr VCP/RJK.
6 The major report of Chapter 15.
7 For the record, he died in August 1910, 30 years after he wrote this letter.
8 *Kirchenbote* Beiblatt, 16 July 1880, 145–6. Tr VCP/RJK.
9 Previously unpublished. LCA Archives Microfiche, AU 3,0 Sch4, 1+, 310–12. Transc DAP. Tr VCP/RJK. There is no date on this report, but it is written when Schulze and Jürgens are on the trip to bring their fiancées back to Hermannsburg.
10 2 July 1880.
11 What was fourthly? Maybe he lost count, although it is more likely that fourthly merged with thirdly!
12 Previously unpublished. LCA Archives Microfiche, AU 3,0 K 2+, 94–7. Transc DAP. Tr VCP/RJK.
13 i.e. those in the 'old Christendom'.
14 LCA Archives Microfiche, AU 3,0 H2 8+, 2481b-4. Transc DAP. Tr VCP/RJK.
15 *Kirchenbote*, December 1880, 282–3. Tr VCP/RJK.
16 op cit, 57.
17 Previously unpublished. LCA Archives Microfiche, AU 3,0 H2 8+, 2484b-7. Transc DAP. Tr VCP/RJK.
18 Meaning unclear.
19 Previously unpublished. LCA Archives Microfiche, AU 3,0 H2 8+, 2481b-4. Transc DAP. Tr VCP/RJK.
20 Previously unpublished. LCA Archives Microfiche, AU 3,0 H2 8+, 2484b-7. Transc DAP. Tr VCP/RJK.
21 He means he confirmed the children of Georg's congregation, and not Georg's own children.
22 *Kirchenbote*, February 1881, 18–19. Tr VCP/RJK. *Kirchenbote*, March 1881, 31–2. Tr VCP/RJK.
23 An interesting little change in specifications here from that just given above. It seems

24 Abide, O dear Redeemer.
25 Previously unpublished. LCA Archives Microfiche, AU 3,0 H2 8+, 2487b-89. Transc DAP. Tr VCP/RJK.
26 *Missionsblatt*, May 1881, 71–7. Tr VCP/RJK.
27 Lit = Jesus child.
28 A touching image: the children as preachers, proclaimers of the Gospel.

17. A Year in the Life of the Mission

1 The population of South Australia was approximately 285,000, and of Australia, 2,250,000. (Statistics accessed via Google search.)
2 Schulze is writing to Harms from Strangway Springs. 18 January, 1881, *Schulze Family History Supplement*, Letter No 7. Emended VCP. This letter picks up and continues the story begun in the previous chapter.
3 This is still a distance of almost 400 kilometres. With the railway line now in service from Edeowie this arrangement was the quickest and most convenient way for Schulze to travel from here to Adelaide/Bethany, and at the same time take care of the rest of the travelling party.
4 Previously unpublished. LCA Archives Microfiche, AU 3,0 K 3+, 98–9. Transc DAP. Tr VCP/RJK.
5 A reference to Luke 2:34–35a.
6 Teacher at Hermannsburg Mission Society.
7 Based on Acts 5, the Gamaliel principle states that if an idea or action is only of human origin, and not from God, it will fail. But if it does come from God, nothing will be able to overthrow it: God will ensure that it works. Therefore, do nothing, and trust God to work what is right. This attitude is different from fatalism, which renders humans powerless pawns to a predetermined and unchangeable fate, as distinct from living in a loving relationship with a gracious God who desires and partners what is best for creation and its people.
8 *Missionsblatt*, May 1881, 77–80. Tr VCP/RJK.
9 Kempe provides a fuller account of this murder in his report of 30 March, where the victim is named Kalkinya.
10 Previously unpublished. LCA Archives Microfiche, AU 3,0 H2 8+, 2489b-92b. Transc DAP. Tr VCP/RJK.
11 Baron von Müller enjoyed a unique relationship with the Hermannsburg missionaries, and appears at regular intervals in our story. See a fuller reference to him under *People*.
12 He is referring to finances, money.
13 Probably the Hahndorf College.
14 Th Harms to Heidenreich. Previously unpublished. LCA Archives Microfiche, AU 3,0 H2 8+, 2493b. Transc DAP. Tr VCP/RJK.
15 *Missionsblatt*, October 1881, 214–15. Tr VCP/RJK.
16 lit = 'disappearing disease'.
17 *Missionsblatt*, September 1881, 197–200. Tr VCP/RJK.
18 This was Johannes Friedrich Georg.
19 Previously unpublished. LCA Archives Microfiche, AU 3,0 H2 8+, 2495b-7b. Transc DAP. Tr VCP/RJK.

20 His second son.
21 Written from the Finke Crossing. Previously unpublished. LCA Archives Microfiche, AU 3,0 Sch3 1+, 202–4. Transc DAP. Tr VCP/RJK.
22 *Kirchenbote*, 8 June 1881, 127. Tr VCP/RJK.
23 Not published. Tr Max Altmann, *Schulze Family History Supplement*, Letter No. 8. Emended VCP.
24 If the date at the head of the letter is correct, Schulze and party arrived back at the station on 11 June.
25 They had never met before.
26 Previously unpublished. LCA Archives Microfiche, AU 3,0 H2 8+, 2498b-500. Transc DAP. Tr VCP/RJK.
27 *Missionsblatt*, December 1881, 245–8. Tr VCP/RJK.
28 Schwarz is referencing Psalm 90, Luther Bible, and he sees the irony in this passage and their situation. Their lives have been rich and full because they have been miserable.
29 *Missionsblatt*, July 1881, 135–6. Tr VCP/RJK.
30 Strehlow, op cit, 785.
31 Hardy, op cit, 78.
32 Buckley, op cit, Loc 1183.
33 id, Loc2157.
34 https://quadrant.org.au/magazine/2021/09/the-incidence-of-cannibalism-in-Aboriginal-society/
https://trove.nla.gov.au/newspaper/article/57041911#
http://www.hesperianpress.com/index.php/dollypot-articles/34-dollypot-articles/486-australian-Aboriginal-cannibalism-an-eyewitness-account
35 op cit, 100
36 Previously unpublished. LCA Archives Microfiche, AU 3,0 H2 8+, 2500b-04b. Transc DAP. Tr VCP/RJK.
37 Probably the Hahndorf College which was going through tumultuous times. rf Brauer, 242; Butler, op cit.
38 He is not sure where Oster stands on this.
39 *Missionsblatt*, November 1881, 222–5. Tr VCP/RJK. Also published in *Kirchenbote*, November 1881, 207–9.
40 It is hard to believe that goods took so long to get to the mission station. The protracted process must have been frustrating for all staff concerned.
41 *Kirchenbote*, December 1881, 275–7. Tr VCP/RJK.
42 Previously unpublished. LCA Archives Microfiche, 3,0 H2 8+, 2507–9. Transc DAP. Tr VCP/RJK.
43 C F W Walther, an eminent Missouri Synod theologian of the time.
44 Previously unpublished. LCA Archives Microfiche, AU 3,0 H2 8+, 2505b-6b. Transc DAP. Tr VCP/RJK.
45 December 1881, 275, 7. Tr VCP/RJK.
46 Previously unpublished. LCA Archives Microfiche, AU 3,0 H2 8+, 2509b-11. Transc DAP. Tr RJK/VCP.
47 *Missionsblatt*, May 1882, 67–71. Tr VCP/RJK.
48 i.e. the drought in India is not repeated in Australia because the Aboriginal people will eat anything.

49 For information on von Müller, see his entry under *People*.
50 This letter, and some of the information on von Müller, are from an article by botanist Philip Short in the *Northern Territory Trust News*, Vol 6/3, September 1989. The translation of the letter is reproduced as it appeared in that publication.
51 ibid
52 The *Royal Society Report*, Vol III, for 1879–80, 129.
53 These descriptions are taken from the article in the *Northern Territory Trust News* mentioned above.

18. Friction, Fighting and Fred

1 Previously unpublished. LCA Archives Microfiche, AU 3,0 H2 9+, 2511–15b. Transc DAP. Tr VCP/RJK.
2 Assume he is writing to Kempe, Schwarz and Schulze, though Kempe is the only one named in the letter.
3 That would have been on Schulze's trip in 1880–81. Readers will recall that Schulze was sharply criticised for purchases made at that time, too.
4 All things are done 'as God wills', including when supplies arrive at the station.
5 The issue is when Tündemann will finish his stint of sheep care. He is prepared to stay on longer (until after Christmas), but the missionaries want him gone several weeks earlier (the Day of Repentance).
6 At this point there is a change in the persons Heidenreich addresses. The following is written to Harms, though there is no evident break in the letter. So, the previous pages must be a copy of letters he wrote to the missionaries and inserted in his letter to Harms. DAP
7 Previously unpublished. LCA Archives Microfiche, AU 3,0 H2 9+, 2516b-18b. Transc DAP. Tr VCP/RJK.
8 Previously unpublished. LCA Archives Microfiche, AU 3.0 K 3+, 106–9. Transc DAP. Tr VCP/RJK.
9 Port Augusta merchant.
10 It was a little more than a few potatoes! If memory serves aright, a horse and wagon were also involved in the expenditure to which Heidenrech is referring.
11 Previously unpublished. LCA Archives Microfiche files, AU 3,0 K 4-, 162–3b. Transc DAP. Tr VCP/RJK. The quality of the original letter is poor and therefore difficult to read at times.
12 The PS is likely addressed to Heidenreich who, presumably, would also have been appraised of the correspondence between the two men.
13 LCA Archives Microfiche, AU 3.0 K 3+, 109. Transc DAP. Tr VCP/RJK.
14 Previously unpublished. LCA Archives Microfiche, AU 3,0 Sch 3 2+, 211–13. Transc DAP. Tr VCP/RJK.
15 Original text unclear.
16 Because of the corrupt text at this point, it is difficult to know how this sentence is to be translated.
17 Previously unpublished. LCA Archives Microfiche, AU 3,0 H2 9+, 2519b. Transc DAP. Tr VCP/RJK. Portions of the original text are impossible to read.
18 This seems overly excessive, but is probably, as before, the temperature in the direct, unshaded sun.

19 *Missionsblatt*, September 1882, 170–8. Tr VCP/RJK. This report is also published in an abbreviated version in *Kirchenbote*, 5 July 1882.
20 A play here on the name 'Friedrich' : *Friede* = peace.
21 He had been speared because his marriage to Katabukoia was considered by the local people to be wrong.
22 i.e. witchdoctor.
23 Previously unpublished. LCA Archives Microfiche AU 3,0 H2 9+, 2520b-2. Transc DAP. Tr VCP/RJK.
24 Previously unpublished. LCA Archives Microfiche, AU 3,0 H2 9+, 2523b-5. Transc DAP. Tr VCP/RJK.
25 Previously unpublished. LCA Archives Microfiche, AU 3,0 H2 9+, 2522b. Transc DAP. Tr VCP/RJK.
26 German lit = 'has knocked the bottom out of the barrel'.
27 *Kirchenbote*, 5 July 1882, 157–9. Tr VCP/RJK.
28 Johannistag celebrated the birth of John the Baptist, 24 June.

19. The Cold, Colonists, Rabbits and Railways

1 *Missionsblatt*, October 1882, 196–200. Tr Max Altmann, *Schulze Family History Supplement*, Letter No 9. Emended VCP.
2 Possibly what became known as the Great Comet of 1882, except that reports describe this as being at its peak in September.
3 Previously unpublished. LCA Archives Microfiche AU 4,2 1-, pp 4331a-2a. Transc DAP. Tr VCP/RJK.
4 Previously unpublished. LCA Archives Microfiche, AU 4,0, 1-, 4293–5. Transc DAP. Tr VCP/RJK.
5 *Missionsblatt*, December 1882, 230–3. Also, LCA Archives Microfiche, AU 3,0 H2 9+, 2531b-35. Transc DAP. Tr VCP/RJK.
6 The Freiboth saga was translated by Philipp Scherer from Freiboth's autobiography, and is included in Scherer's paper, *Camel treks in the outback* (self-published in 1994).
7 Why did their guide not inform them of this water so they could make use of it themselves? An exceedingly ungracious act on his part.
8 Hospitality in the Centre does not seem to have been a priority at that time.
9 Previously unpublished. LCA Archives Microfiche, AU 3,0 H2 9+, 2535b. Transc DAP. Tr VCP/RJK.
10 LCA Archives Microfiche, AU 3,0 H2 9+, 2535b. Transc DAP. Tr VCP/RJK.
11 *Missionsblatt*, March 1883, 47. Tr. VCP/RJK.
12 Previously unpublished. LCA Archives Microfiche AU 3,0 H2 9+, 2526b-8. Transc DAP. Tr VCP/RJK.
13 He died on 1 July that year at Blumberg and was buried there on 4 July. He was in his 66th year. Oster, Strempel, Ey, Heidenreich, Appelt, Homann and Meischel took part in the funeral service.
14 He was almost 72 years of age at this time, but still had another nine years of life left to him.
15 Previously unpublished. LCA Archives Microfiche, AU 3,0 H2 9+, 2528b-30. Transc DAP. Tr VCP/RJK.

16 Previously unpublished. LCA Archives Microfiche, AU 3,0 H2 9+, 2530b-31. Transc DAP. Tr VCP/RJK.
17 *Missionsblatt*, December 1882, 230-3. Even though published, we have selected for inclusion here the translation of the original report from the LCA Archives Microfiche, AU 3,0 H2 9+, 2531b-35. Transc DAP. Tr VCP/RJK. This is also another instance of two reports on the same day.
18 i.e. the church in Hermannsburg on the Finke.
19 Previously unpublished. LCA Archives Microfiche, AU 3,0 H2 9+, 2535b. Transc DAP. Tr VCP/RJK.
20 Another group of Hermannsburgers, but none of these is designated for the Centre.
21 *Kirchenbote*, 10 January 1883, 3-4. Tr. VCP/RJK.
22 Previously unpublished. LCA Archives microfiche. AU 3,0 H2 9+, 2536b-38. Transc DAP. Tr VCP/RJK.
23 i.e. for ELSA/South Australia.
24 There have previously been accounts of killings between the Aboriginal people, and of White and Black killings in other places. But this is the first White and Black killings so close to home.
25 *Missionsblatt*, February 1883, 18-21. Tr VCP/RJK.
26 https://nre.tas.gov.au/invasive-species/invasive-animals/invasive-mammals/european-rabbits
27 https://education.nationalgeographic.org/resource/how-european-rabbits-took-over-australia/
28 *Missionsblatt*, December 1882, 233-4. Tr VCP/RJK.
29 Giles, 266
30 op cit, 265.
31 op cit, 27.

20. Death of Dmataka. More on Language and Culture
1 *Missionsblatt*, September 1883, 179-92. Tr VCP/RJK.
2 Previously unpublished. LCA Archives Microfiche, AU 3,0 H2 9+, 2540b-2b. Transc DAP. Tr VCP/RJK.
3 *Missionsblatt*, October 1883, 201-8. Letter No 10 in the *Schulze Family History Supplement*, Tr Max Altmann. However, that translation is somewhat incomplete and inadequate in places. This translation has been done by VCP, using the Altmann translation as a base. Also published in *Kirchenbote*, September 1883, but with significant variations.
4 A play on *Kirchenbote*, i.e. Church messenger.
5 German = *Völklein*.
6 Tuberinga in *Kirchenbote*.
7 rf *atue ntjaraknira buxirinima* above -? = the men who are coming...
8 Probably the community devotional time, where the 'heavenly bread' is the Bible, the Word.

21. Finances, Synods, and Routine
1 Not published in either *Kirchenbote* or *Missionsblatt*. Tr Max Altmann, *Schulze Family History Supplement*, Letter No 11. Rev VCP.

2   A reference to the arrival of the latest batch of settlers to the mission station.
3   Previously unpublished. LCA Archives Microfiche, AU 3,0 H2 9+, 2545b-7. Transc DAP. Tr VCP/RJK.
4   Previously unpublished. LCA Archives Microfiche, AU 3,0 H2 9+, 2543b-4b. Transc DAP. Tr VCP/RJK.
5   Previously unpublished. LCA Archives Microfiche, AU 3,0 H2 9+, 2545b-7. Transc DAP. Tr VCP/RJK.
6   The Lutheran Synod of Queensland was officially formed at a synod on 16 September 1885.
7   *Missionsblatt*, December 1883, 234–9. Tr VCP/RJK. An abbreviated version also published in *Kirchenbote*, November 1883. It is not published here, but is available in *The Translation*.
8   i.e. the Aboriginal people admitted that they had no prayer god(s).
9   Literally translates as 'hunts fear and terror into them'.
10 *Missionsblatt*, April 1884, 54–9. Tr VCP/RJK.
11 These explosions were probably the eruption of Krakatoa, in Indonesia. The mountain had been erupting since May that year, with the peak eruption occurring on 27 August. Although over 3000 kilometres from Alice Springs, there were reports of the eruption being heard there. The eruption killed approximately 40,000 people.
12 Previously unpublished. LCA Archives Microfiche, AU 3,0 H2 9+, 2547b-51b. Transc DAP. Tr VCP/RJK.
13 This report has been extracted from Heidenreich's report of March 1884, published in *Kirchenbote*, March 1884, 38–9, and relocated here in its proper chronological order, Tr VCP/RJK.
14 This report has been extracted from Heidenreich's report of March 1884, published in *Kirchenbote*, March 1884, 399, and relocated here in its proper chronological order, Tr VCP/RJK.

Wakefield Press is an independent publishing and
distribution company based in Adelaide, South Australia.
We love good stories and publish beautiful books.
To see our full range of books, please visit our website at
www.wakefieldpress.com.au
where all titles are available for purchase.
To keep up with our latest releases and news,
subscribe to the Wakefield Weekly at
https://mailchi.mp/wakefieldpress/subscribe

Find us!

Facebook: www.facebook.com/wakefield.press
Instagram: www.instagram.com/wakefieldpress

www.ingramcontent.com/pod-product-compliance
Lightning Source LLC
Chambersburg PA
CBHW011141290426
44108CB00022B/2706